# The Age of Agade

MW00831702

*The Age of Agade* is the first book-length study of the Akkadian period of Mesopotamian history, which saw the rise and fall of the world's first empire during more than a century of extraordinary political, social, and cultural innovation. It draws together over 40 years of research by one of the world's leading experts in Assyriology to offer an exhaustive survey of the Akkadian empire.

Addressing all aspects of the empire, including its statecraft and military, territory and cities, arts, religion, economy, and production, *The Age of Agade* considers what can be said of Akkadian political and social history, material culture, and daily life. A final chapter also explores how the empire has been presented in modern historiography, from the decipherment of cuneiform to the present, including the extensive research of Soviet historians, summarized here in English for the first time. Drawing on contemporaneous written and artifactual sources, as well as relevant materials from succeeding generations, Foster introduces the reader to the wealth of evidence available. Accessibly written by a specialist in the field, this book is an engaging examination of a critical era in the history of early Mesopotamia.

**Benjamin R. Foster** is Professor of Assyriology at Yale University, USA.

# The Age of Agade

Inventing empire in ancient Mesopotamia

**Benjamin R. Foster**

 Routledge
Taylor & Francis Group

LONDON AND NEW YORK

First published 2016
by Routledge
2 Park Square, Milton Park, Abingdon, Oxon OX14 4RN

and by Routledge
711 Third Avenue, New York, NY 10017

*Routledge is an imprint of the Taylor & Francis Group,
an informa business*

*British Library Cataloguing-in-Publication Data*
A catalogue record for this book is available from the British Library

*Library of Congress Cataloging-in-Publication Data*
Foster, Benjamin R. (Benjamin Read), author.
   The age of Agade : inventing empire in ancient Mesopotamia /
Benjamin R. Foster.
      pages cm
   Includes bibliographical references.
   1. Akkadians.   2. Iraq—History—To 634.   I. Title.
   DS72.3.F67  2015
   935'.01—dc23
   2015011530

ISBN: 978-1-138-90971-7 (hbk)
ISBN: 978-1-138-90975-5 (pbk)
ISBN: 978-1-315-68656-1 (ebk)


Typeset in Baskerville
by Apex CoVantage, LLC

Printed and bound in Great Britain by
TJ International Ltd, Padstow, Cornwall

# Contents

*Fat*

*Statway*

*Realism*

# Figures

# Maps

# Acknowledgments

In the course of my work on the Akkadian period, I have benefited from the research of everyone who has written on this fascinating phase of Mesopotamian history. More particularly, two invitations helped in the evolution of this study: from Mario Liverani and the University of Rome "La Sapienza" to participate in "Akkad. Il primo impero universale: strutture, ideologia, tradizioni" in 1990, and from Jean-Marie Durand and the Collège de France to present four general lectures on "L'Age d'Agadé" (2010), from which portions of this book are derived. It is a great pleasure for me to thank them and to acknowledge the host institutions for their interest and support.

I am grateful to those colleagues who have shared ideas, information, and manuscripts with me for use in advance of their publication, notably Karen Polinger Foster, Abather Saadoon, Emanuelle Salgues, Ingo Schrakamp, and Aage Westenholz. Many others gave me references, answered queries, sent me their publications, or directed my attention to important issues and evidence; I hope that they will accept this book as my appreciative acknowledgment of my debt to them all. Studies that reached me after the end of 2014, except for the occasional preprint, could not be included here.

For advice and assistance with the illustrations and permission to use certain images, my particular thanks go to Sidney Babcock, Erika Bleibtreu, Giorgio Buccellati, Dominique Charpin, Sophie Cluzan, McGuire Gibson, Ulla Kasten, Lutz Martin, Augusta McMahon, Joan Oates, Julian Reade, Abather Saadoon, Jonathan Taylor, Michaela Weszeli, Irene Winter, and Richard Zettler. The maps were drawn by Alberto Urcia, using drafts by Thomas Eby.

Eckart Frahm and Daniel Potts read portions of the manuscript and saved me from various mistakes and omissions. Aage Westenholz read the whole amid other more pressing tasks and honored me with a searching and sometimes scathing criticism of what I had done. This led me to rethink many a statement and claim and allowed me to correct some blunders. I thank all three for their generosity with their time and knowledge, without intending to suggest that they are in any way responsible for the outcome.

My greatest personal and intellectual debt is to Karen Polinger Foster, who drew various of the plates, read the entire work repeatedly, and made innumerable improvements in its content, style, accuracy, logic, and organization, leaving it much better than when she started.

Benjamin R. Foster

# Abbreviations, citation conventions, and symbols

| | |
|---|---|
| BdI Adab | Pomponio, Visicato, and Westenholz 2006 |
| BIN 8 | Hackman and Stephens 1958 |
| CT 1 | King 1896 |
| CT 19 | Campbell Thompson 1904 |
| CUSAS 13 | Maiocchi 2009 |
| CUSAS 17 | George 2011 |
| CUSAS 19 | Maiocchi and Visicato 2012 |
| CUSAS 23 | Bartash 2013 |
| CUSAS 26 | A. Westenholz 2014 |
| ECTJ | A. Westenholz 1975b |
| ECTSL | Electronic Text Corpus of Sumerian Literature |
| FM | Gelb 1955 |
| ITT I | Thureau-Dangin 1910 |
| MAD 1 | Gelb 1952a |
| MAD 3 | Gelb 1957 |
| MAD 4 | Gelb 1970a |
| MAD 5 | Gelb 1970b |
| MCS 9 | Cripps 2010 |
| MDP 14 | Legrain 1913 |
| *Muses* | Foster 2005a |
| MVN 3 | Owen 1975 |
| OSP 1 | A. Westenholz 1975a |
| OSP 2 | A. Westenholz 1987 |
| PBS 12 | Langdon 1917 |
| PBS 15 | Legrain 1926 |
| PUL | Limet 1973 |
| I R | Norris 1861 |
| II R | Norris 1866 |
| IV R | Pinches 1891 |
| RTC | Thureau-Dangin 1903 |
| SCTRAH | Molina 2014 |
| STTI | Foster and Donbaz 1982 |
| TS | Rasheed 1981 |

UET 8    Sollberger 1965
UTI      Yıldız and Gomi 2001

## Citation conventions

Citations using abbreviations are to primary sources. Of these, BIN, CT, ITT, MAD, RTC, STTI, and UET reproduce the original text only, in transliteration or copy, so are of interest only to Assyriologists, whereas BdI Adab, CUSAS, ECTJ, FM, MDP, OSP, SCTRAH, and TS may have translations and comments on the texts and so can be consulted by non-Assyriologists. Unpublished tablets are cited by museum number: L. (Istanbul Archaeological Museums, Lagash Collection) and NBC (Nies Babylonian Collection in the Yale Babylonian Collection).

## Special symbols

| | |
|---|---|
| [ ] | Restoration of broken passage in ancient text. |
| ( ) | Explanatory addition to translation of ancient text. |
| < > | Presumed unintentional omission by scribe of ancient text. |
| ? | Particularly doubtful translation or restoration of ancient text or guess. |
| * | Philological note below, in bibliography. |
| ... | Unclear words or signs in ancient text. |

# Introduction

The present work surveys the Akkadian period in Mesopotamian history, a century and a half of extraordinary political, social, and cultural innovation as well as of unexampled cruelty, violence, and exploitation on an international scale, which witnessed the founding and collapse of the world's first empire. In later Mesopotamian historical memory, it was both glorified and held up as a moral lesson in pride before a fall. However it was viewed, this brief age never ceased to fascinate educated Mesopotamians over the next two millennia. Any account of it must seek to explain why this was so: what set the Akkadian dynasty and its achievements apart?

The contemporaneous written and artifactual evidence is rich but fragmented, sometimes rewritten and smashed by succeeding generations. Earlier sources may assist with understanding the origins and development of the Akkadian achievement, later ones with tracing its outcomes and afterlife. I have preferred to work with the scattered materials dating to the period itself, but not enough remains from Akkadian times to consider many subjects using that evidence alone. If two or three Akkadian records can be compared to hundreds from a century later dealing with the same topic, then it seems a reasonable strategy to interpret the few on the basis of the many, while avoiding the temptation to cite masses of parallels and relevant studies. Instead, in addition to significant primary sources, I note a choice of general or well-documented publications that will introduce the reader to the wealth of evidence available in the literature of Assyriology.

Historians unfamiliar with cuneiform documents and Mesopotamian archaeology may not be aware that wide differences of opinion are possible among well-informed researchers using precisely the same evidence. Hardly any conclusion advanced here would stand uncontested by others who study and reflect on the relics of this age. I have considered contrasting views carefully, even if I do not refer to them systematically. The notes and bibliography will lead to other opinions.

There are equally good arguments for and against attempting a work like this. The textual record is large and varied, but it is smaller than for many other periods of Mesopotamian history and so can be studied as a whole. The archaeological record is extensive though fraught with major issues of dating and disagreement over what belongs to the Akkadian period and what does not. The more I delved into such matters as surface surveys, floor plans, burials, pottery, and collections of implements, the more I came to appreciate their importance for a sound interpretation of this phase of Mesopotamian history. Thus I make no apology for introducing them into my narrative, though I am well aware that most historians of Mesopotamia prefer not to use such data.[1] As for Akkadian art, this is the "classical" art of Mesopotamia, a brilliant chapter in the development of iconography and technique. I treat it here as a phenomenon in its historical context; the interested reader may seek appreciations of its wider aesthetic significance in the numerous excellent presentations to which reference is made.

This work is intended to be documentary and descriptive, rather than analytic or constructivist. To me it seemed challenge enough to marshal a coherent choice of facts and interpretations, rather than to propose broad explanations of causes and effects or to probe deep structures.[2] Four questions have guided me: (1) What were some major traits of the Age of Agade? (2) What can reasonably be said about its political and social history, its material culture and daily life, its spirituality, arts, and letters? (3) How and why was it remembered so vividly in later ages, even in those with comparable achievements? (4) How has this memory influenced modern views of the period?

I bear in mind the skepticism voiced by colleagues who believe that present understanding of the Akkadian era is based on little but the bombast of royal inscriptions and the period's long afterlife in Mesopotamian literature, revived with the decipherment of cuneiform.[3] I find these views at once salutary and sterile, the one because a dose of skepticism is always useful in keeping the fervent imagination in check, the other because there is no gain without venture. Recent history, with its ample sources, is laden with its own mythologies, so one need not hold the fragmentary sources for the ancient world to a higher standard than our own. Furthermore, today's mind is cloyed with imperial ideologies, making it a special challenge to go back to a time when imperialism was new and dramatic. The Akkadian rulers who swore before the gods that their written statements were true may well be credible, for the facts and figures at our disposal from everyday records seem to bear out their veracity.

With respect to terminology, by "Akkadian" I generally mean anything pertaining to the period in question, without nuance as to language or ethnicity. Hence, "Akkadian pottery" means pottery made during this period, not necessarily by speakers of the Akkadian language. I also use "Akkadians," as they did themselves, to refer to the ruling elite, bound to the royal house, regardless of their language or ethnic origin; hence an "Akkadian governor" or "notable" could well have spoken Sumerian or some other tongue as his native language.[4]

In antiquity, the city and region that are the focus of this book were both known as "Akkade." However, I use the term "Akkad" to refer to the region and "Agade" to refer to the city. This distinction, like Assur versus Assyria and Babylon versus Babylonia, is purely a modern convenience. "Agade" is derived from a sign-for-sign transliteration of the name as it was usually spelled in Akkadian times, whereas "Akkade" is a phonetic rendering of how the name was actually pronounced.[5] Certain other place names found in this book, such as Syria, Anatolia, and Iran, are likewise used only for convenience and do not correspond to geographical concepts of the third millennium BCE. Units of measure are converted into the metric system using the approximate equivalents of Kienast and Volk 1995: v–vi.

As for chronology, various beginnings, endings, and subdivisions of the Akkadian period have been proposed.[6] The following terms, which derive more from epigraphy than from other aspects of Akkadian culture, are in current use: Pre-Akkadian, for the late Early Dynastic period, especially Early Dynastic IIIb; Early Akkadian, for the reigns of Sargon and Rimush; Middle Akkadian, for the reign of Manishtusu and the first decades of Naram-Sin; Classical Akkadian, for the later reign of Naram-Sin and the reign of Sharkalisharri; and Post-Akkadian, for the poorly defined span of time between Sharkalisharri and the accession of Ur-Namma of Ur.

Culturally, Pre- and Early Akkadian are two phases of the same period, divided today for political and historical reasons. In many respects, this is also true for the Post-Akkadian and early Ur III periods. It is the cultural and political quickening after the beginning of the Akkadian period, its climax in the middle, and the abrupt disintegration of its political order towards the end that have come to define the Age of Agade and to set it apart from what came before and after.

## Notes

1  For archaeology and the writing of history in Mesopotamia, Liverani 1999; focus on this problem for the Akkadian period in McMahon 2012.
2  For comments on methodology in writing Mesopotamian history, Van de Mieroop 1997, 1999a, 2013.
3  Liverani, ed. 1993b is a collection of papers balancing positivist and skeptical approaches to the historiography of the Akkadian Empire; further Chapter 12 part 5 and for an analytic study, Buccellati 2013.
4  B. Foster 2000.
5  For transcription versus phonetic rendering, Civil 1973: 33. There is no agreement on this matter. In their comprehensive treatments of the royal inscriptions of this period, Frayne 1993 uses "Agade," whereas Gelb and Kienast 1990 use "Akkade."
6  Nissen 1966: 36–37; 1993; Gibson 2011: 83; for a complex subdivision of the period combining art history with later Mesopotamian historical memory, Boehmer 1965.

# 1   The rise and fall of the Akkadian Empire

## 1.   The king's feast

About 2260 BCE, 964 men in the land of Akkad sat down to a royal feast, but
they had little to celebrate. True, some had been given new clothes and jewelry.
Some boasted new teams of mules and a wagon to go with them, as well as implements and other gifts. A few had sufficient cash to buy and furnish good-sized
houses. The food, no doubt, was excellent, probably pork roasted over an open
fire and assorted delicacies more typical of the royal table than of private life.
Yet these men had just sold their ancestral lands to the king, Manishtusu, son of
Sargon. Since portions of these lands bordered on royal domains, their owners
could scarcely have refused the king's offer. Using a productivity ratio from irrigated lands farther south, we find that the price paid in grain was only two years'
estimated harvest. What farmer would willingly sell his land for that amount?[1]

Forty-nine men, called "Akkadians" in the sale document, were witnesses to the
sale. They included scribes, administrators, military officers, governors, and temple staff, all dependent upon the king's patronage. There can be little doubt that
the purchase was to provide them with productive land in return for their service
to the crown. The beneficiaries of such largesse were, like Manishtusu himself,
only the second generation of a new elite, some of them the sons of governors
and senior administrators from important cities, who had now assumed a new,
Akkadian, identity. They had forsaken their own communities to serve the king,
awaiting his command and assignment anywhere in the realm, "from the Upper
Sea to the Lower Sea."[2]

The years of recent memory had been eventful ones, filled with repression and
bloodshed. Manishtusu's younger brother, Rimush, who had succeeded to their
father Sargon's throne ahead of his sibling, had been assassinated in a court conspiracy.[3] The new king needed loyal followers, men he could rely on, in the military and in his administration. This purchase of 3430 hectares of arable land, if
evenly divided among the forty-nine Akkadian witnesses, would yield individual
parcels of seventy hectares, more than ten times larger than the six-hectare lots
typically given to administrators barely a day's journey south, but comparable
to the average parcel of sixty-two hectares given to privileged administrators at
Girsu, the Akkadian provincial capital of Sumer.[4] So important was this transaction to the king that he had it carved in hard, black diorite, a stone brought by

boat from the land of Magan in the Gulf and hauled upstream, along with ship-
loads of other exotic goods now pouring into the capital city, Agade. The resulting
monument, an impressive obelisk (Figure 1.1), a shape previously unknown in
Mesopotamia, was set up in a temple, perhaps at Agade itself or at nearby Marad,
where Manishtusu's grandson, Lipit-ili, would one day rebuild the temple of the
local god. On it are recorded the prices paid, the gifts the king bestowed, the parcels sold and their locations, the names of the sellers, and the names of the forty-
nine Akkadian witnesses and beneficiaries. By this major outlay, Sargon's elder son
sought to enlarge his royal domains, to reward his followers, and to "make firm the
foundations" of his kingdom, as the Akkadians expressed it.[5]

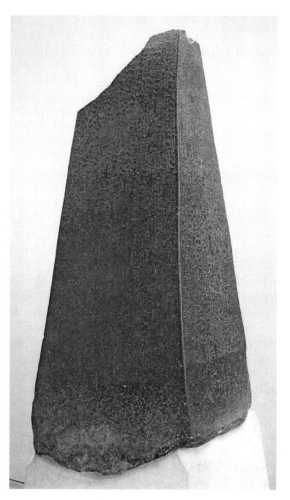

*Figure 1.1* Diorite monument of Manishtusu, recording the king's
    purchase of lands in Akkad.

## 2. Sargon the victorious

In his commemorative inscriptions, Sargon proclaims that he was victorious in thirty-four military campaigns. Whatever the reverses of his early career may have been, his triumphs began in Sumer, where he defeated and captured Lugalzagesi, king of Uruk, who had extended his hegemony over many of the Sumerian city-states and marched as far as the Mediterranean seacoast and the "Cedar Forest" of Lebanon. Besides Uruk, Sargon defeated Umma, Lagash, and Ur, and Uruk, enabling him to rule all of Sumer to the headwaters of the Gulf.[6] Sargon also invaded Elam and Susa. Few future Mesopotamian dynasties would rule in this region, protected as it was by the desert, which wore down even the most formidable fighting forces. Sargon's Elamite campaign may be commemorated in a massive diorite victory stele found there, showing Sargon himself and his retinue (Figure 1.2; compare Figure 9.5). At a later date, someone made a determined effort to destroy the stele, battering it with hammers and attempting to break or saw it into smaller pieces (Chapter 9 part 2; Chapter 11 part 2). Sargon's conquests reached to the neighboring territories of Sabum and Awan. He even routed forces from Marhashi, perhaps the region around Kerman, known in Mesopotamia as a source of precious stones, alabaster vessels, and other luxury goods.[7]

*Figure 1.2* Detail of a victory stele of Sargon, showing the king holding a battle net, a gash from later vandalism, a label reading "King Sargon," and an attendant carrying a sunshade.

To the north and west, Sargon enjoyed the submission of Mari, which controlled the mid-Euphrates, and Ebla, south of Aleppo, one of Mari's major rivals. By Sargon's own account, Dagan, the god of clouds, bestowed upon him the "Upper Lands," the territories and cities of the Upper Euphrates region and beyond.[8] His armies may have pushed into central Anatolia as well, known to the Akkadians as a land of cedar trees and "silver" or snow-covered mountains.[9] All this we read in his own records of his achievements.

In addition, Sargon wished to be remembered for three other accomplishments: placing Akkadians in governorships in the conquered lands; bringing international trade to his capital city, Agade; and having sufficient resources at his disposal to feed daily 5400 able-bodied men in his service.[10]

No previous ruler had ever made such claims of conquest and kingship. For ambitious conquerors of the future, Sargon posed a challenge to emulate, having changed forever the concept of what one warrior-king could achieve. The name and memory of Sargon remained in Mesopotamian consciousness, just as Alexander's lived on in the Mediterranean; his story was told in new ways to meet the expectations of different generations. Indeed, for a Mesopotamian historian of Alexander's own time, Sargon stood at the beginning of empirical human history, whereas the kings who lived before him were mythological figures whose exploits were performed in a world in which gods and human beings were characters in the same narratives. Sargon, though favored by the goddess Inanna/Ishtar, lived very much in the real world.[11]

Generations of Mesopotamian historians in times to come would wish that they knew more about him. His parentage is obscure, for Sargon's inscriptions, like those of his successors, do not name the father of the ruling king, as was customary in later periods.[12] A list of Mesopotamian kings, compiled a half-century or more after Sargon's death, included him among eight remarkable past rulers who were not of royal birth, but this may not be based on fact.[13] Imagination sought to fill in early incidents of his life.

According to one Sumerian tale, Sargon, charmed at birth, was cupbearer to Ur-Zababa, king of Kish. The cupbearer was a high official responsible for procuring and serving food and drink to the king and his court. As the young Sargon carries out his duties, he becomes aware that the goddess Inanna herself is close at hand, but he keeps his counsel. Inanna then forces the issue, appearing to Sargon in a terrifying dream, in which she covers him with blood. When he tells the king his dream, the king interprets the blood to be his own, so understands that his cupbearer will murder him. He sends a message to his chief smith, ordering him to kill Sargon when he arrives at a temple workshop with certain bronze drinking vessels the king will entrust to him, apparently for melting down. The plan seems to be to throw Sargon into the mold or crucible with the vessels. But Inanna stops Sargon just before he enters the building where the smith waits in ambush:

> Holy Inanna confronted him, she blocked his path.
> "Is the pure house not a holy temple? No man with blood on him may go
>     therein!"

He met the king's master smith outside the door of the house where
    his doom had been decided,
When he delivered the king's drinking vessels to the master smith,
Belish-tikal, the master smith, secured? them from him, cast them in the
    mold.
Sargon, after five days had passed, maybe ten,
Came in before Ur-Zababa, his king,
Came right in before him in his own palace, built solid as a mountain,
King Ur-Zababa was afraid, shook with fear in his own dwelling.[14]

The true significance of the dream becomes apparent: Inanna had covered
Sargon with blood to save him. The smith is awestruck by the goddess's intervention, as is the king, when Sargon returns to the royal palace alive and well.
Ur-Zababa realizes, as Sargon already knew, that his cupbearer has divine
protection.

The theme that Sargon was charmed at birth and favored by the goddess
Inanna was taken up more than a thousand years later, in an Akkadian composition that purports to be Sargon's narrative of his own infancy. In it, we
read that he was exposed as a newborn by his mother, a high priestess, making
Sargon the first instance of the story, told also of Moses and Cyrus, of the
foundling who later returns to claim his rightful inheritance. Sargon's mother,
as a high priestess, could have borne for the king an heir to the throne, but she
might have given up the child to hide him from rival claimants, if his father
had died.[15]

Although no literary works explicitly about Sargon or his exploits survive from
the time of his dynasty (for the poetry by his daughter Enheduanna, whom he
appointed high priestess at Ur, see Chapter 9 part 5 and Appendix II), heroic legends of his deeds were composed in Akkadian during the first half of the second
millennium (Chapter 11 part 6).[16] Some scholars consider these based on older
epic poems, whereas others suggest that they were original compositions of their
own time. In favor of the latter is their choice of setting, the north and west, that
is, Assyria, north Syria, and the Anatolian plateau, rather than Sumer or Iran,
the two areas stressed in authentic third-millennium texts. One of these legends
praises combat and ends with a challenge:

Yes, this is the encounter of valiant men,
Tomorrow Akkad will go to battle,
The celebration of the manly will be held,
The writhing ranks will writhe back and forth,
Two women in labor, bathed in their own blood!
Where are true comrades who just look on at the celebration?
Only the [coward] will stand aside. . .
Sargon informed the army,
"So there, any king who would rival me,
Let him go where I have gone!"[17]

In sum, Sargon played a vivid role in Mesopotamian literature and historical memory down to the Hellenistic period, as the type of the great conqueror. In the mid-second millennium, with the spread of Akkadian as an international language from Iran to the Mediterranean, Sargon's fame even reached the land of the Hittites, and from there Akhenaten's Egypt, where Egyptian scribes studied a simplified, abbreviated version of a legend about Sargon's attack on an Anatolian city famed for its wealth.[18]

## 3.   Sons of Sargon

Sargon died in the fifty-sixth year of his reign. When Rimush acceded to the throne of his father, he faced a rebellion in Sumer, which had clearly resented Sargon's rule. In a series of brutal campaigns, Rimush re-established his father's dominion there, boasting that he killed in battle more than 23,000 men and took twice that number captive, presumably killing them too.[19] He also expelled thousands of men of fighting age from the defeated cities and subjected them to cruel punishment, mass execution, or forced labor (Figures 1.3, 1.4). A group of records

*Figure 1.3*  "They rounded up their finest fighting men for captives" (poem of Enheduanna). Victory stele of an early Akkadian king.

*Figure 1.4* Stele attributed to Rimush, depicting (top to bottom) campaign against Sumer, victory in battle and massacre of unarmed prisoners, and destruction of city walls'. Two other fragments record redistribution of fourteen square kilometers of land in the region of Lagash.

from Umma, one of the rebellious cities, documents citizens and slaves working and dying in some labor-intensive activity in Iran, possibly cutting stone (Figure 1.8a).[20] Rimush faced opposition in Babylonia too, but quickly suppressed it, carrying out the same bloody policies as in Sumer.

Among his other punitive measures, Rimush expropriated some 134,000 hectares of prime agricultural land near Lagash and Umma to create a royal domain to distribute to his retainers, thereby endowing a new landed class in Sumer, which had, in principle, no ties to the old city-states nor to the great temples of the region. This is the largest single land transaction recorded in a Mesopotamian formal document (Figure 1.4).[21] For the two cities involved, which had fought bitterly for generations over a strip of land between them, this was humiliation and catastrophe.[22] They had no choice but to look on helplessly as Akkadian officials organized their manors in the surrounding countryside.

By this time a seasoned campaigner, Rimush next followed up on Sargon's invasion of Elam. A coalition led by the ruler of Marhashi, who had extended his authority west into Elam, formed a strategic alliance intended to counterbalance any Akkadian influence in Iran or the Gulf. Rimush's forces routed the coalition and captured its commanding officers, bringing Elam and Susiana once again under Akkadian influence or direct rule. The booty from this campaign was substantial. At the sanctuary of Nippur alone, Rimush dedicated 30 pounds of gold, 3600 pounds of copper, and 300 slaves (Chapter 6 part 5). Stone bowls, vases, seashells, mace heads, and other objects were inscribed with his name and dedicated at sanctuaries throughout the land, examples of which have turned up at Assur, Kish, Nippur, Sippar, Ur, Shuruppak, and Tutub, even as far away as the Khabur region.[23]

Rimush proudly recorded that his craftsmen produced a statue of himself made of tin, the rarest industrial metal in the Mesopotamian world.[24] This puts Rimush at the head of a line of Mesopotamian despots who vaunted their technological achievements. The statue was set up before the god Enlil in Nippur. In its dedication, Rimush says that he "accounted himself among the gods." Perhaps this extraordinary expression was tantamount to the self-deification that his nephew Naram-Sin would later proclaim. A generation or two after his reign, an ambitious courtier, eager to please the ruling family and grateful for his memory, took the name Ili-Rimush, "Rimush-is-My-God."[25]

Rimush's immediate successors, Manishtusu and Naram-Sin, followed his example of boasting about battle casualties in their campaigns by giving precise counts of the dead, a practice unknown in Mesopotamia before or after. Rimush even swore to the accuracy of his numbers before Enlil at Nippur, the central shrine of Sumer. In the later legends about Naram-Sin, these grim statistics were reversed to become fantastic losses of Akkadian troops (Chapter 11 part 6).

According to Mesopotamian historical tradition (Chapter 11 part 4), Rimush was assassinated by courtiers using cylinder seals. When people in authority carried cylinder seals, they suspended them around their necks on lanyards or pinned them to their cloaks. This may have suggested to some murderous mind that courtiers close to the king could kill him by strangling him with the cords or stabbing him with the long, sharp pins.[26]

Small wonder, then, having come to power after such a tumultuous reign and in violent circumstances, Manishtusu was eager to shore up his position. His brother had ruled at least nine years, though his inscriptions at Nippur stop earlier than that, leaving us to wonder what was happening in the years immediately preceding Rimush's assassination. Was there a civil war? Accounting for his own accession, Manishtusu stated simply that the god Enlil had called him to power.[27]

The new king continued where his brother had left off. His standard military inscription tells us that he conquered the lands of Anshan and Shirihum, in Iran east of Susa, and that he vanquished thirty-two cities "beyond the sea," that is, along the Gulf coast.[28] This gave him access to diorite, which was rarely seen in Mesopotamian sculpture until the Akkadian period, when it was used for royal figures during and after Manishtusu's reign, especially for funerary images of deceased kings. There are no private dedications in diorite, so the stone was perhaps reserved for royalty.[29] Because only a standard inscription of Manishtusu's campaigns is known, and because statues of the king were evidently widely distributed in the realm (Figure 1.5; Chapter 9 part 1), one may propose that most

*Figure 1.5* Manishtusu, wearing a tasseled garment, upon an unusual chair, perhaps for feasting or receiving obeisance.

of Manishtusu's reign was peaceful and devoted to consolidation of the monarchy and its claims.

In the absence of pertinent inscriptions, indirect evidence suggests that Manishtusu was active in Assyria and the Khabur region. A later king of Upper Mesopotamia, Shamshi-Adad, credits Manishtusu with construction of the temple of Ishtar at Nineveh and refers to inscriptions his Akkadian predecessor had set up there.[30] At Assur, a spear point dedicated by a servant of his was found, as well as a decapitated statue plausibly dated to his time (Chapter 9 part 1; Figure 5.5). Manishtusu's reign may correspond to an early phase of Akkadian domination at Nagar (Chapter 3 part 5). A post-Akkadian forgery made at Sippar, conceivably based on a genuine Manishtusu commemoration, was composed to justify benefactions to the temple of Shamash there.[31] It seems likely, therefore, that Manishtusu's reign was considerably more important than the surviving commemorative evidence and Mesopotamian historical tradition suggest. After ruling for fifteen years, Manishtusu was, according to later Mesopotamian memory, murdered in a palace conspiracy, leaving the throne to his eldest son, Naram-Sin, whom he had already entrusted with military commands.[32]

## 4.   Naram-Sin, campaigner

Naram-Sin's long reign of at least thirty-seven years was the apogee of the Akkadian Empire. No other ruler of the third millennium, save Sargon himself, made such an impression on Mesopotamian historical tradition. The shattered remnants of the elaborate commemorative prose of this reign give us only a glimpse of the extraordinary military achievements of this archetype warrior-king.

In a summary account of his conquests, Naram-Sin states that they stretched from Marhashi in the east as far as the Cedar Forest, presumably the slopes of the Amanus or Lebanon; from the Mediterranean to the "lands beyond the sea," perhaps as far as Oman, a claim fully justified by administrative documents from his reign (Chapter 3 part 6). The few extant records of individual campaigns include references to a march against the Lullubi, peoples of the northern Zagros (Figure 1.6), and against the land called Simurrum, somewhere in the Trans-Tigris or beyond the mountains on the Iranian plateau. In what is now Armenia, Naram-Sin traced the Tigris River to its source. He advanced up the Khabur River and through the passes into the uplands, reaching the source of the Euphrates as well. Naram-Sin also claimed to be the first king to have conquered Ebla, south of Aleppo, of which Sargon had said only it "served" him. He was the first Mesopotamian king to boast of his hunting exploits.[33] Unlike Sargon, Naram-Sin makes no reference in his inscriptions as to how he governed such a diverse territory, but the plentiful administrative records of the time suggest military colonization in Susa and also in Syria, where Akkadian buildings and mass-produced, standardized clay bowls that may date to his reign have been discovered (Chapter 3 parts 2, 4, 5).[34]

*Figure 1.6* Victory stele of Naram-Sin, commemorating his defeat of Lullubum. Shutruk-nahhunte, an Elamite King, carved his own inscription on the mountain when he took the monument to an Elamite King Susa nearly 1000 years later.

Whereas the cities of Sumer had sent out armies to fight the Akkadians in the open, those of Syria relied on their massive fortification walls and payment of tribute to keep the invaders at bay. A later epic poem about Naram-Sin expresses this difference by comparing him to a lion, seeking his prey in the plain, whereas a Syrian king was like the cowardly fox, hiding and boasting in his burrow.[35] It was thus a particular pride of Naram-Sin that he mastered the art of siege craft, penetrating the triple walls of the great fortress at Armanum, where the ruler made a valiant but futile stand in the doorway of his own palace. According to a later, defective student copy of Naram-Sin's inscription describing this siege, in which captions to images of the fortress were preserved, the wall near the waterfront stood twenty cubits high, the inner wall thirty cubits, the citadel wall forty-four cubits, and the distance from the waterfront to the citadel was 404 cubits.[36]

The most dramatic event of Naram-Sin's reign was a revolt that began in Mesopotamia itself, at Kish and Uruk, where pretenders chosen by the citizenry rebelled against the descendant of the divinely chosen Sargon, "[In Kish], they raised up [Iphur]-Kish to kingship, and in Uruk, they raised up Amar-girid to kingship as well."[37] Of the two, Kish was the greater threat. Not only was it closer to the capital, but Iphur-Kish had allied with other major cities nearby, including Borsippa, Cutha, Dilbat, Eresh, Sippar, and Kazallu, as well as with the Amorite tribesmen, perhaps from the Jebel Bishri region. Akkadian rule in northern Babylonia was profoundly unpopular.

According to Naram-Sin's account, he closed the gates of Agade and made a passionate speech to Shamash, god of justice and treaties. In it, one may surmise that he reminded the god of the great benefits the rule of his family had brought to Kish, lifting it from dishonorable servitude (to whom is unclear, perhaps Lugalzagesi) and making the title "King of Kish" resound once more. Now the ungrateful Kishites had turned against him. After appealing to Shamash, Naram-Sin rallied the men of Agade and marched out to battle, where he routed the Kishite army and its allies, taking many distinguished captives, whom his inscription lists by name. Iphur-Kish retreated to Kish, where Naram-Sin pursued him, and they fought a second battle, in which Naram-Sin was again victorious. The Euphrates River was choked with the bodies of defeated soldiers. Another 2500 Kishites fell in desperate street fighting in the city. Resolved to obliterate Kish, Naram-Sin dismantled its walls and diverted the river to flood it.

In the meantime, Amar-girid of Uruk had rallied to his cause many of the most important cities of Sumer, including Adab, Isin, Lagash. Nippur, Shuruppak, and Umma, together with various cities in the Gulf region. From this one can gauge the deep unpopularity of Akkadian rule in the south as well. He also sent messages to the rulers of the cities of the Upper Euphrates region and Assyria, begging them to join him, but most hesitated to do so. Fresh from his triumph at Kish, Naram-Sin marched north up the Tigris, then westward to the Euphrates, to punish the Amorite tribesmen whom Amar-girid had succeeded in bringing over to his side after the defeat of Kish. Naram-Sin met Amar-girid and his main force, defeated them, and took Amar-girid himself captive. Turning next to Sumer, he carried out harsh reprisals against Uruk, including flooding the city, as he had Kish. He followed up his victory over the Sumerian coalition with an invasion of the cities along the Gulf, booty from which he dedicated at various sanctuaries in the land.[38]

From the perspective of Agade, the capital had been surrounded by enemies in all directions, but Naram-Sin had delivered his city at every turn. Indeed, nine times in a single year the king had been forced to call up the troops of Agade to fight battles throughout Mesopotamia. In an inscription written on the base of a statue of a protective spirit, perhaps originally guarding a temple for his worship, at some point forcibly mutilated (Chapter 11 part 2; Figure 9.4), Naram-Sin tells what happened next:

> Naram-Sin the mighty, king of Agade, when the four quarters of the earth attacked him together, through the love Ishtar bore him was victorious in nine battles in a single year and captured the kings whom they had raised up against him. Because he defended his city in crisis, the people of his city asked of him that he be god of their city Agade, with Ishtar in Eanna, with Enlil in Nippur, with Dagan in Tuttul, with Ninhursag in Kesh, with Enki in Eridu, with Sin in Ur, with Shamash in Sippar, with Nergal in Cutha, and they built his temple in Agade.[39]

Thus the warrior-king Naram-Sin joined the ranks of the great gods.

Later Mesopotamian literary tradition took an altogether different view of these events (Chapter 11 part 6). Why this was so is a fascinating literary, rather than historical, problem.[40] Already in the early second millennium, an imaginary inscription of Naram-Sin was composed, which mixed phrases from genuine monuments of that king with outlandish names of enemies and figures of casualties. Successive versions of this composition added ever more dramatic and fantastic episodes. Naram-Sin, uncharacteristically, suffers massive defeats. The number nine recurs, taken from the authentic texts vaunting nine victories in a single year, but now they are setbacks: "Nine times they rebelled against me, nine times I let them go free!"[41] As the story grows increasingly improbable, 360,000 of Naram-Sin's soldiers die in a series of battles, leaving the king "at a loss, exhausted, anxious, and reduced to naught," while his land is decimated.[42] The enemy armies gradually become uncanny, "neither flesh nor blood."[43] In a version of the story from Hattusha, the capital of the Hittite Empire, Ea, the god of wisdom, pronounces a destiny for the enemy horde:

> Let it eat no food to sustain it,
> Let it smell no aroma of beer,
> Let it drink water.
> Let it wander all day,
> At night, let it lie down but find [no sleep].[44]

By the first millennium, the putative inscription had become an imaginary stele set up for the admonition of future generations. According to this, Naram-Sin's enemies were monsters, like those Tiamat, mother of all the gods, fashioned in the *Babylonian Epic of Creation*. Here she suckles the host, who are humans with the faces of ravens. Led by seven kings, 360,000 of these troops and their allies devastate all the lands around Mesopotamia, from Anatolia to the Gulf. Naram-Sin sends out a soldier to prick one of the enemy soldiers with a pin to see if it bleeds, then takes omens to learn what to do. The omens say that he should not oppose the horde, but he does so anyway, dispatching first 90,000 troops, not one of whom returns alive, then 60,700, with the same result. Naram-Sin concludes by recommending that rulers should withdraw behind ditches and walls (the very tactic the real king disdained), and he counsels prudence:

> Wrap up your weapons and [lean] them in a corner,
> Restrain your valor, take care of your person.
> Though he raids your land, go not out against him,
> Though he drives off your livestock, go not nigh him . . .
> Be moderate, control yourself,
> Answer them, "Yes, my lord!"
> To their wickedness, repay kindness,
> To kindness (add) gifts and gratification.[15]

This strays so far from its historical subject as to anticipate the tortuous fantasies of the medieval *Alexander Romance*. Naram-Sin, a brilliantly successful, supremely self-confident sovereign, had been wholly transformed into a chastened failure, parodying his own inscriptions. Among the many explanations that have been offered for this development, the most convincing is a later desire for historical symmetry, pairing a great empire builder (Sargon) with a hapless empire loser (Naram-Sin), thereby teaching that no dynasty can last forever, no city can rule the land forever. Perhaps too there was an element of wishful thinking or envy.[16]

## 5.   Naram-Sin, builder

As befit the patron goddess of his dynasty, Naram-Sin paid particular attention to the temples to Ishtar throughout Mesopotamia. He ordered construction on her temples at Nineveh in Assyria, where his father had done work before him, at Zabala in Sumer, using logs of cedar brought from the Amanus range, at Adab, and possibly at Babylon, not to mention at the capital, Agade. He also began projects on the temple of Sin at Ur, where he was to install his daughter, Enmenanna, as high priestess and successor to his aunt, Enheduanna (Chapter 9 part 5).[17]

The king further claimed special favor from the god Enlil. Crowned at Nippur, Naram-Sin attributed his accession to the throne and continued victories to Enlil's will, at least so he says in his inscriptions published in Sumer. At Nippur he presented in neck stocks the defeated and captured leaders of the coalitions against him, among them Amar-girid of Uruk, as Sargon had long ago treated Lugalzagesi. Rimush's benefactions to Ekur, Enlil's temple in Nippur, were surpassed by Naram-Sin's decision to rebuild Ekur entirely in a splendid imperial style, no doubt as a showpiece for his rule.

A fortunate chance has preserved a group of administrative records dealing with his reconstruction of Ekur, the only such corpus of its kind from the period. The documents give us an extraordinary glimpse of the day-to-day activities of Naram-Sin's workmen, under the direction of his son, the crown prince Sharkalisharri. The texts record expenditures of hundreds of kilograms of bronze, silver, and gold, as well as tons of copper. Large numbers of workmen were conscripted for the task. One tablet lists seventy-seven woodworkers under seven foremen, eighty-six goldsmiths with six foremen, ten sculptors with one foreman, fifty-four carpenters under three foremen, as well as engravers and other workers in fine materials, many of these workers drawn from various places in Mesopotamia and quartered on the local population.[18]

Some of the ornate fittings of the new Ekur temple may be visualized thanks to these documents. Flanking the main entrance, two great protective spirits of copper with gold-plated faces held standards. There were also four gold-plated bison figures set up on either side of the portal along the enclosure wall. The gateway itself was guarded by two large copper figures of winged dragons with gold plating in their open, snarling mouths. The doors were studded with copper nails with gold-plated heads and could be locked with heavy door-bolts fashioned as dragons or water buffaloes. The doorways of the inner shrines were flanked by smaller protective deities holding standards. These, too, had gold-plated faces.

Inside the temple buildings, the cultic implements included 100 large sun-disks and 100 large moon-crescents, containing in all about twenty-nine kilograms of gold. The various implements of silver belonging to a single shrine totaled about 200 kilograms. There were also votive statues of noble Akkadians, plated with gold. Ekur must have been a dazzling sight.[19] At Naram-Sin's death, the project was unfinished, but his son and successor, Sharkalisharri, took up the work and probably brought it to completion.

Yet a later Sumerian poem, *The Curse of Agade*, views the rebuilding of Ekur in quite a different light. The poet tells us that Naram-Sin had a dream of Agade's loss of glory. Hoping to win back the favor of Enlil, he therefore razed the old sanctuary to build a new one:

Like a sieger storming a city,
He laid tall ladders against the temple.
To stave in Ekur like a mighty ship,
To open its fabric, like mining a silver mountain,
To quarry it, like a mountain of lapis,                                  (110)
To make it collapse, like a city before a hurricane . . .
People (of Sumer) saw the inner chamber, a room that
    never sees the light,
Akkad saw the sacred vessels of the gods.                                (130)
Its guardian figures that stood by the ceremonial entryway,
Though they had done no forbidden thing,
Naram-Sin threw them into the fire.
Cedar, cypress, juniper, boxwood,
The woodwork of the god's dwelling he made
    ooze out in the flames.                                (135)
He put its gold in coffers,
He put its silver in sacks,
He heaped up its copper at the harborside, like a massive yield of grain.
The metal worker was to rework its precious metal,
The jeweler was to rework its precious stone,                            (140)
The smith was to rehammer its copper.[50]

Clearly the preservationist poet saw the demolition of the old temple and the salvage of its materials in preparation for construction of a new one as rash and sacrilegious acts (Figure 1.7).

*Figure 1.7* "Like a sieger storming a city, he laid tall ladders against the temple" (*The Curse of Agade*).

## 6.   Naram-Sin, administrative reformer

Naram-Sin confronted complex problems in administering his far-flung realm. The Akkadian kings portrayed themselves as warriors and hunters, whose wealth came from tribute and booty. But, as we see in Rimush's land appropriation and Manishtusu's land purchase, they had a definite agrarian policy, so were well aware of the twin pillars of the Mesopotamian economy – agriculture and animal husbandry. Sargon's installation of Akkadians as governors throughout the territories he had conquered points to the creation of a class of people fully dependent upon royal patronage for their maintenance and advancement. We find, therefore, a parallel military and civil structure, both headed by the king. Next after the king in the military hierarchy came generals and subordinate ranks. The chief civil administrator was the *shaperum*, "majordomo" or "steward of the royal household." No comparable office existed in Sumer, so the Akkadian word and concept were borrowed into Sumerian at this time.[51]

A key civil figure after the steward of the royal household was the land registrar, the man accountable for the extensive arable districts controlled by the royal household and used to maintain its officialdom. Important local officials, such as governors, received land by virtue of their office, and could also purchase use rights to more land, if they could afford it, by giving the royal household a "present" in cash. The record keeping for accountable land and the surveying of subdivisions and plots fell to the land registrar and his staff of scribes and surveyors. Each season, the scribes calculated the areas of arable land, depending on how far the irrigation water had flowed out into the long, narrow fields, then calculated the return due the patron or owner of this land from its users and their subordinates.[52]

Sumer and Akkad had quite different approaches to agricultural administration: the Akkadian based on extensive cultivation of large areas and the Sumerian on intensive cultivation of small ones. The Akkadian approach began with a broad vision of the total resources to hand and the systematic mathematical schemes for apportioning them. The details were then fitted into the scheme. Sumerian administration, on the other hand, began with the details, adding them up and carrying them forward. Like many agrarian cultures, Sumer knew a patchwork of local standards for measuring land and harvest. Sumerian management depended on dense concentrations of workers at the disposal of temples and other large institutions, minutely graded into teams and sets of entitlements. There were no such labor teams in Akkad, which depended instead on the use of patronage and the availability of lucrative opportunities to attract people willing to work the land.[53]

Akkadian administrators, therefore, brought to Sumer and other conquered territories, such as Susiana, their own ideas about effective management. They implemented a new, universal standard of measure for the accountable portion of the harvest, using the measure of Agade. If the grain was measured by a local standard as it was brought in from the field, when it was processed, stored, or delivered to royal officials, the figures had to be converted into the Akkadian standard. This was, so far as we know, the first time that anyone attempted to impose a unified standard on Sumer once a certain level of accountability was reached.

They also attempted to impose a unified system of weights and liquid measures throughout the empire.[54] In addition, Akkadian administrators were accustomed to mathematical models for agricultural management and production, for example, a standard ratio of how much land could be plowed by one team.[55] They used these in Sumer and in their own domains, but local institutions were permitted to keep their internal records in their traditional ways.[56]

There was a record-keeping and script reform as well. Sumerian administrative tablets had generally been round or rounded at the corners, with a flat obverse, a convex reverse, and varying degrees of thickness in proportion to their size. There were regional handwritings, tablet shapes, and record-keeping techniques. During the reign of Naram-Sin, a new type of tablet came into use. It was square or rectangular for composite records or ledgers, though more rounded shapes could be used for single transactions, or vouchers, so they were easily distinguishable. The new rectilinear tablets were thinner than most earlier records in proportion to their size (Figure 1.8d). Furthermore, a new style of handwriting became standard

(a)

*Figure 1.8* Evolution of Akkadian administrative documents: (a) account of death of citizens and slaves doing forced labor, attributed to reign of Rimush; (b) account of oils and aromatics, Middle Akkadian; (c) autograph list of expenses of the notable Mesag for a journey to Agade, Classical Akkadian; (d) record of dedication of children to a temple in Eshnunna, some to become singers, dated to the reign of Naram-Sin.

(b)

(c)

*Figure 1.8* (Continued)

(d)

*Figure 1.8* (Continued)

throughout the realm for official documents. This tended to be broadly spaced, written with finesse and attention to detail. A very formal, elegant version was used for documents at a high level of authority, and a more informal hand was used for everyday records. This Akkadian hand had to be learned by anyone who wished to advance in the administration, and there is evidence that older scribes retooled their skills so they could write in the new style.[57]

For reasons unknown, these innovations apparently led to an even more radical change: the angle of orientation of the cuneiform signs. These were now rotated 90° counterclockwise, with the earlier orientation retained only for glyptic and monuments.[58] Spelling was reformed to make Akkadian easier to read, and the old inventory of Sumerian word signs used to write Akkadian words was updated.[59] Overall, one has the impression of a major effort at standardization at the middle and upper levels of accounting and reporting.

Akkadian administrators expected beautifully written, summary ledgers, with easy to read and understand broad schemes of accounting, to be filed in every locality, ready for examination by the royal inspector (Figure 1.9). One may suppose that this person was an independent auditor who went from place to

*Figure 1.9* Seal of Kalaki (second from right), scribe to Ubil-Ishtar the "king's brother" (center), shown inspecting troops, symbolized by three soldiers, and attended by a chair-bearer.

place to ensure that the king's interests and rights were being maintained. There was no requirement that records be kept in a specific language; in Sumer they tended to be in Sumerian, though written in the new Akkadian script, whereas in Akkad, they tended to be in Akkadian. Sometimes both languages appeared in the same record, suggesting that the administration considered itself bilingual (Chapter 9 part 7).[60]

There were also changes in sealing practices. Previously in Sumer, sealing and writing were complementary actions, with seal use restricted to surfaces that had not been written on. In the Akkadian period, in both Sumer and Akkad a seal was rolled over the back of a letter of introduction, on formal contracts, or on other important records, adding another dimension of authority and identification.[61] During Naram-Sin's reign, a distinctive type of flat, sealed bulla came into general use, in response, perhaps, to the growing practice of senior Akkadian administrators to use personal cylinder seals, especially with combat scenes on them (Chapter 9 part 3; Figure 9.9).[62]

In summary, Naram-Sin's reign was a watershed in the development of Mesopotamian accounting and record-keeping techniques, setting the standard for the rest of the third millennium.

## 7.  The royal family and matrimonial alliances

Naram-Sin had at least ten children, to whom he gave major roles in his realm. The crown prince, Sharkalisharri, campaigned with him, as Naram-Sin had with his father, and was entrusted with supervision of the reconstruction of the Ekur

Temple at Nippur. Another son, Nabi-Ulmash, was governor of Tutub in Akkad. Seals or sealings of other sons and their servants point to important duties for them as well.[63]

Naram-Sin placed three of his daughters in key cultic positions. One of them, Tutanabshum, became high priestess of Enlil at Nippur; so important was this event that a year was named after it, which states that she was chosen by divination.[64] A second, Enmenanna, became high priestess of the moon-god at Ur, successor to her great-aunt, Enheduanna. A third, Shumshani, became high priestess of the sun-god at Sippar. Since these three sanctuaries are among the eight listed in Naram-Sin's inscription recording his deification, it is tempting to speculate that progeny or close relatives of Naram-Sin may have served in the other five, creating a network of family alliances linking Naram-Sin with the gods. Because of the language and imagery of intimacy between Naram-Sin and Ishtar, he himself may well have assumed some comparable role at the Eulmash, her temple in Agade, after which two of his sons and one of his daughters were named.

Naram-Sin evidently followed the practice, attested first at pre-Akkadian Ebla,[65] of arranging dynastic marriages. Sealings in the name of a daughter, Taram-Agade, have been found at Urkesh, strongly suggesting that she was married to a member of the royal family there.[66] It is noteworthy that her seal (Figure 9.9a) gives only her name and her father's name, but makes no reference to her new status as presumed queen or princess at Urkesh. Her name, "She-Loves-Agade," whether given at birth or assumed at marriage, was a constant reminder of her Akkadian loyalty. By contrast, a Mari-born wife of Shulgi, king of Ur, took the name Taram-Uram, "She-Loves-Ur," at marriage, thereby focusing on her new loyalty rather than on her birth allegiance.

Like her sister Taram-Agade, another of Naram-Sin's daughters, Simat-Ulmash "Pride-of-Ulmash," may have kept or assumed her name when she was married to a prince or ruler of Mari, because an inscribed copper platter with just her name and parentage was found there, along with a similarly inscribed bowl of her sister, Shumshani. Since the latter was high priestess of the sun-god at Sippar, there may have been a sanctuary of Shamash at Mari among the complex of Akkadian-period structures there called "les temples anonymes."[67] One may further speculate that possible matrimonial alliances of Naram-Sin with the "lords of the Upper Land" may have been a factor in their decision not to participate in the "Great Revolt," despite the pleas of the rebel king of Uruk, according to Naram-Sin's own account of that event. Naram-Sin may also have taken a Susian princess as wife to cement an alliance there (Chapter 7 part 5). One of his sons may have married a princess from Marhashi.[68]

## 8.   Sharkalisharri and the fall of the empire

Naram-Sin's son and successor, Sharkalisharri, inherited the empire built by the three generations of his forebears. His own reign began auspiciously enough with coronation at Nippur and a royal progress through Sumer, where he and his court were lavishly entertained at each stage of the journey. The new king appointed a general, Puzur-Ishtar, to supervise the continuation of the Ekur project at Nippur. He also carried out work at Babylon on the temples of Ishtar and Ilaba, tutelary deities of the dynasty. Babylon, first referred to in the reign of Sharkalisharri, may have begun to develop as a major urban center at this time, perhaps taking advantage of Naram-Sin's harsh treatment of neighboring Kish. Like Manisthusu, he purchased arable land, perhaps to reward his followers.[69]

Enemies pressed, however, on every front. Sharkalisharri campaigned successfully against the Amorites in the Jebel Bishri region, marched to the sources of the Euphrates and Tigris, and brought back cedar logs from the Amanus, just as his father had done. Perhaps some of these were in fact joint expeditions with his father, which he then claimed for himself. Closer to home, Sharkalisharri confronted an attack by the Elamites in Babylonia. New, persistent enemies were the Gutians, a people of the central Zagros region, whom the Akkadians despised as barbarians and cattle thieves, but who in fact could muster a redoubtable army under royal command.[70]

Unlike Sargon and Naram-Sin, Sharkalisharri was not remembered in later Mesopotamian historical tradition (Chapter 11 part 4), and the commemorative inscriptions of his own time are very sparse. Thus we do not know whether he held the empire together until his death, after which there was a period of anarchy, or if his twenty-five-year reign ended in disaster and collapse. The abrupt downfall of the Akkadian Empire was, in any case, cause for rejoicing in Sumer and in other lands that had experienced its brutal treatment and exploitation.[71]

This opened the way for the opportunistic and ambitious. One such was Puzur-Mama, a high-ranking military officer. He cannily took over the Akkadian administrative center and domains in the Lagash region and proclaimed himself "King of Lagash," though this was not the historic title of the rulers of Lagash. Another was Ili-ishmani at Susa, who seized power there.[72] The Gutians entered the Diyala region and Sumer, ruling at Umma and posing a threat to Adab, Uruk, and other cities; they too declared themselves kings.[73] At Agade itself, various short-lived rulers prevailed in a period of anarchy, which the Sumerian King List sums up as "Who was king? Who was not king?"[74] One of these ephemeral rulers, Irgigi, sent a letter to Lagash insisting that he was king in Agade and so had the right to decide capital cases concerning Akkadians.[75]

For the Sumerian poet who deplored Naram-Sin's rebuilding of the temple of Enlil at Nippur, the matter was simple yet far more dramatic: the Gutians were instruments of Enlil's divine wrath, sent to destroy the Akkadian Empire and Agade itself:

> Gutium, a race who know no order,
> Made like humans but with the brains of dogs, the shapes of apes,
> These Enlil brought down from the mountains!
> Like a plague of locusts they scoured the land,
> He let them stretch out their arms over it, as if corralling livestock.[76]

The poet paints a grim picture of famine, criminality, and disorder in Agade, ending his work with maledictions:

> People fought among themselves for hunger . . .
> The blood of the scoundrels running over the blood of the honest man . . .
> May the man who knew that city peer down into the clay pit where it was,
> May the man who knew a man there find no trace of him at all . . .
> May that city die of hunger,
> May your citizens who dined on finest foods lie down in the grass (like beasts),
> May your man who rose from a meal of first fruits
> Eat the binding from his roof,
> As for the grand door of his family home,
> May he gnaw its leather hinges.[77]

The reasons for the collapse of the Akkadian Empire are debatable. Weiss has argued that a decline in rainfall forced an abrupt evacuation of the Akkadian presence in much of the Khabur and the dislocation of the population to areas where water was available. This drought may also have been a consequence of a cataclysm in the late third millennium (about 4000 BCE) that was originally thought to be volcanic but is now identified as an "air blast" event, such as could have been caused by a major meteorite fall. This event burned off vegetation, resulting in wind erosion and dust bowl conditions.[78]

While the archaeological evidence presented in support of this thesis is strong and, according to Weiss, largely consistent throughout the Khabur region, it is not clear that the Akkadian Empire depended upon that area, rather than on Sumer, for its grain (Chapter 4 part 4). Therefore a retraction of Akkadian presence in the Khabur could have been a shock, rather than a decisive blow. In addition, certain major centers, such as Nagar and Urkesh, as well as their supporting hinterlands, seem not to have been affected by the alleged cataclysm, the traces of which are hard to date.

Nevertheless, any reduction in the Euphrates flow would have reduced the amount of arable land in Sumer that could be irrigated, causing a decline in production there at the same time as desertification in the north, especially in the large rural tracts reclaimed by Akkadian agrarian policy and redistributed to dependents of the Akkadian elite. If so, the Akkadian ruling class in Sumer might have felt the consequences of a drought sooner than the longer established population.[79] If, furthermore, the Akkadian Empire had weakened local forms of self-government, then marginal peoples could have forced their way into the settled areas more readily in time of drought and famine, causing social stress and disturbances directed against the ruling elite.[80] To summarize: drought and dislocation of population may have been significant, if indirect, factors in its collapse.

In Yoffee's discussions, he suggests that, because the Akkadian state promoted unprecedented social and economic mobility, it undermined the traditional city-states, draining their resources and fanning resistance among their ruling elites. In his view, the Akkadian ruling family failed to integrate traditional leadership into the new order of a territorial state and its expansionist programs, largely because they were too preoccupied with costly foreign ventures. Ironically, it is precisely these foreign ventures and the dramatic imperial downfall that have captured the minds of Mesopotamian and modern writers about the period.[81]

After the period of anarchy at Agade, a certain Dudu came to the throne and ruled for 21 years. Whether or not he was descended from Sargon is unknown. Agade became the center of a small but aggressive state that shared the horizon with several others, including Gutium, Lagash, Umma, and Uruk to the south. Dudu, who at his accession ruled as far south as Adab, attacked Umma and Lagash and may have invaded Elam, but otherwise nothing is known of his reign. He may have lost control of Sumer to a resurgent Uruk.[82] His son, Shu-Durul, ruled for fifteen years in northern Babylonia and the Diyala region, but seems in his turn to have lost territory to Puzur-Inshushinak of Elam, who was actively building his own kingdom.[83] With Shu-Durul, the political history of the Akkadian Empire comes to an end.

## Notes

1 Text: Gelb, Steinkeller, and Whiting 1991: 116–40; study of the prices paid: Milano 2003: 28. For early Mesopotamian land tenure in general: Bottéro 1970/71, 1971/72; Glassner 1985a, 1995; Renger 1995a; Steinkeller 1988c, 1999b, 1999c; Cripps 2007; Milano 2008; Pomponio 2013: 28, who remarks of the Akkadian period, "We can infer that a substantial part of communal or private land of Northern Babylonia and of the neighbouring region beyond the Tigris changed into a network of allotment fields of property of the king." For land tenure as a source of social conflict in the Akkadian period, Selz 2002: 185–87.

2 King 1910: 208–9; Gadd 1971: 449–50; Glassner 1986: 12; Liverani 1988b: 247–48; B. Foster 2000; for Upper and Lower Sea, Chapter 11 part 7 and note 164; in general, Yamada 2005.

3 Glassner 2004: 122–23; for the essential information about Manishtusu, Steinkeller 1987/90; A. Westenholz 1999: 44–46; for the name type "Who-Is-With-Him?" (meaning he has no rival), compare Sumerian Aba-indasa "Who-Is-Equal-to-Him?" and Aba-indane "Who-Came/Comes-Forth-with-Him?" (to be his comrade in arms(?), with Limet 1968: 90–91) versus the proposal that this could be the name of a twin and refer to coming out of the womb, Jacobsen 1939: 112 note 249; Liverani 2001/2: 180–81.

4 B. Foster 1982a: 110; B. Foster 2011a: 127–31.

5 For Marad, Appendix Ia 23; Frayne 1993: 112; Stol 1987/90a. For further discussion of royal acquisition of land, Chapter 4 part 1. The "Sippar Stone" (Gelb, Steinkeller, and Whiting 1991 no. 41) may also record a purchase by Manishtusu since it evidently mentions a style of garment that came into fashion during his reign and disappeared thereafter, B. Foster 2010a: 130–31.

6 Appendix Ib 1–8; Frayne 1993: 9–22; A. Westenholz 1987/90. For various proposed reconstructions of events in Sumer just prior to Sargon's rise to power, Liverani 1966a: 11 (Lugalzagesi destroys Kish, Sargon becomes king of Akkad, defeats Lugalzagesi, and restores Kish); Michalowski 1998b; Sallaberger 2004a; in general, Sallaberger and Schrakamp 2010. An important issue in any reconstruction is the meaning of "Kish" in the Ebla texts (Archi 1981, 1987a), including whether or not it means "totality" or "the world" rather than "Kish" and whether or not in some instances it could refer to the Akkadian kings, since Sargon called himself "king of Kish/the world"; further,

both for and against this understanding, Thureau-Dangin 1912: 34; Seux 1965; Maeda 1981; Durand 2012: 130; Steinkeller 2013c: 146 note 51. For the essential information about Sargon, Sommerfeld 2009/11. For his taking of Lugalzagesi's title, Chapter 6 note 83. The defection of Meskigal, ruler of Adab, from the hegemony of Uruk brought Sargon major support and guaranteed that strategic city an important place in the new order, as suggested by Schrakamp forthcoming: 199; further on Adab, chapter 3 part 3; further on Meskigal, Edzard 1993/97; Visicato 2010.

7   Appendix Ib 6; Frayne 1993: 24–27; Steinkeller 1982a, 2006, 2014; Glassner 2005b; for the problem of whether or not Marhashum was the same place as Parahshe, A. Westenholz 1999: 91–93 (skeptical, but not followed here).

8   Appendix Ib 2, 7; Frayne 1993: 15, 28.

9   Frayne 1993: 28–29. Liverani 1966a: 8 and Maeda 2005, studying Sargon's titles, conclude that they show the same geographical concepts as those of Lugalzagesi and that only with the reign of Naram-Sin do royal titles change from a southern Mesopotamian city-state tradition to a universal claim; further, Glassner 1984b; Liverani 1988b: 253, 2011: 146. For the Mesopotamian perspectives on (snow-covered) mountain ranges, Rollinger 2010: 13–15; Durand 2012: 127 with note 31. In favor of "snow-covered" for KÙ is their dramatic appearance when seen from the Mesopotamian or Syrian plain. In favor of "silver," as generally understood, is that the poet of the *Curse of Agade* evidently knew the expression and understood it to refer to mountains as places silver was mined (Appendix 3b, line 109). Manishtusu refers to "silver mines" in Iran, Appendix Ia 8, Ib 19.

10   Appendix Ib 7; Frayne 1993: 28–29.

11   J. Westenholz 1983a. Few administrative records certainly from the time of Sargon are known. One, BdI Adab 63, refers to a journey he made; others cite offerings in his name (ECTJ 85) and his military campaign against Simurrum (ECTJ 151). Among the many modern studies of Sargon and interpretations of his career are Diakonoff 1959: 201–27; Liverani 1966a, 1988b: 232–36, 2011: 133–35; Gadd 1971; A. Westenholz 1999: 34–40; Tricoli 2005; Heinz 2007; further, Chapter 12. One historian writes that Sargon was "peut-être le personnage central de l'histoire mésopotamienne," Garelli 1982: 85; further Chapter 12 part 4.

12   According to the *Sumerian Sargon Legend* (Chapter 1 part 2), his father was named La'ipum, Cooper and Heimpel 1983; Appendix IIIa.

13   Jacobsen 1939: 142–43.

14   Cooper and Heimpel 1983, with discussion of the major difficulties of this passage; ECTSL 2.1.4, for an integral translation, Appendix IIIa. For documentary evidence for the importance of the cupbearer, Chapter 4 part 7; further Chapter 6 note 83.

15   Lewis 1980; *Muses*, 911–13.

16   J. Westenholz 1997.

17   *Muses*, 109, 111.

18   *Muses*, 338–42; Beckman 2001.

19   Appendix Ib 1–17; Frayne 1993: 41–50; for the essential information about Rimush, Sommerfeld 2006/8.

20   B. Foster 1982b: 46–50; this interpretation is disputed, A. Westenholz 1999: 41 note 126 vs. Neumann 1989: 88 and Selz 2014: 270–71.

21   B. Foster 1985, 2011a. There is no unequivocal evidence that Rimush expropriated the land but it seems most unlikely that he acquired it any other way (further Chapter 4 note 8). Thureau-Dangin 1897c: 170 commented, "Les conséquences de la conquête furent considérables: le partage des terres détermina un afflux de population nouvelle; en même temps se créa un mouvement très actif d'échanges entre Shirpourla [= Lagash] et Agadé." Thureau-Dangin also noted that the recipients of these parcels, so far as preserved, had Akkadian names. He dated the monument earlier than Naram-Sin and later than Eannatum II and believed that the inscribed portion "probably" belonged with the relief (Figure 1.4). The two fragments were found in the same

season and the excavator himself believed that they were parts of the same monument, Heuzey 1893. The two Louvre fragments were accessioned together with consecutive museum numbers. It would be a remarkable coincidence if fragments of two early Akkadian stelae were found in close proximity at the same time, which did not belong to the same monument, but no traces of any other Akkadian monuments. The second inscribed fragment (B. Foster 1985) matches the Louvre inscribed fragment in chemical analysis, the width of its columns, and the size of the cases of writing.
22  Cooper 1983b.
23  Porada 1992; Appendix Ia 4–6; Frayne 1993: 60–67.
24  Appendix Ib 18; differently Frayne 1993: 68 ("meteoritic iron"); further J. Westenholz 1998: 46.
25  ITT I 1096.
26  Goetze 1947: 256; further Chapter 11 part 4.
27  Appendix Ib 21; Frayne 1993: 77; for a possible reference to civil war extracted from a genuine inscription of Manishtusu, Al-Rawi and George 1994: 148.
28  Appendix Ia 8; Ib 19; Frayne 1993: 76.
29  Using "diorite" broadly to refer to Moorey's "category 4" (Moorey 1994: 22); Eppihimer 2010.
30  Grayson 1972: 22–23; Reade 2011.
31  Gelb 1949; Sollberger 1967/8. Powell 1991 noted that the expression of metrological units in this text was characteristic of the late seventh century BCE or later.
32  According to an early second-millennium omen (Chapter 11 part 4), Manishtusu was killed by his "palace," but Goetze suggests a slight emendation to "his officers" (Goetze 1947: 257 note 27); further Chapter 11 part 4. A fragment of a praise poem, evidently in honor of Manishtusu (Chapter 9 part 5), suggests that Naram-Sin campaigned already as crown prince, CUSAS 26 270; Naram-Sin may likewise have included his son and successor, Sharkalisharri, on expeditions, part 8, this chapter.
33  Appendix Ib 24; Frayne 1993: 163; for the essential information about Naram-Sin, Frayne 1998/2001; A. Westenholz 1999: 46–55; for general accounts of his reign, Liverani 1988b: 236–41, 2011: 135–37; for a more skeptical approach, Michalowski 1980: 233. Frayne's chronology is based on his assumption that the presence or absence of the divine determinative in writing the king's name is decisive, whereas there appear to be regional factors at work in the choice of whether or not to use it (more regularly in Sumer than in Akkad); differently Farber 1983: 69 (trying to explain its absence in the Bassetki inscription commemorating Naram-Sin's deification) and below, note 39. For Naram-Sin as hunter of wild beasts and the possible influence of that on his depiction in art, Chapter 4 note 56 and Chapter 9 notes 47 and 48.
34  Oates, Oates, and McDonald 2001: 172; Senior and Weiss 1992.
35  *Muses*, 116.
36  Appendix Ib 26; Frayne 1993: 132–35; Otto 2006 (identifies with Tell Bazi); Archi 2011a (identifies with Simsat).
37  Appendix Ib 28; Frayne 1993: 104; Jacobsen 1978; in general Sommerfeld 2000.
38  Appendix Ib 28.
39  Appendix Ia 18; after that, Naram-Sin was referred to as "the god of Agade," e.g., CUSAS 23 122; further B. Foster 1979a; Chapter 2 note 66; Chapter 6 note 28; Beaulieu 2002/36. "House" and "temple" are the same word in Akkadian. Some scholars translate the inscription differently, understanding *ište*, rendered "with" here, as "from." This would mean that the citizens asked "from" the gods that Naram-Sin be their god, rather than, as here, that the citizens asked Naram-Sin that he a god "with" the other gods; for example Farber 1983; Frayne 1993: 104, versus Gelb and Kienast 1990: 83 and Kienast and Sommerfeld 1994: 220. Against Farber and Frayne, the Akkadian verb "to ask somebody for something" normally takes the accusative case of the person asked and the thing asked for, not a preposition "from." The passage is, however, difficult.
40  J. Westenholz 1997; Liverani 2011: 148–53.

41  *Muses*, 121.
42  *Muses*, 345.
43  *Muses*, 120.
44  *Muses*, 347.
45  *Muses*, 355.
46  Güterbock 1934/8: 18–21, 74. For Naram-Sin's proverbial wealth, Chapter 10 note 12.
47  Frayne 1993: 176–77.
48  A. Westenholz 1987: 35–36, 40–41.
49  Paraphrasing A. Westenholz 1987: 24–25; for an example of a protective figure, further Chapter 9 note 33 and Figure 9.4.
50  Cooper 1983a: 54–57; ECTSL 2.1.15; for an integral translation, Appendix IIIb.
51  B. Foster 1982a: 36.
52  B. Foster 1982a: 113–14; Liverani 1990.
53  B. Foster 1993a: 31.
54  Powell 1994: 102 . . . "the metrological system was already [in late Pre-Akkadian Girsu] moving towards rationalization by merging liquid and dry systems . . . and this incipient movement crystallized in the Akkad period, probably under Naram-Sin, which resulted in a unified system of interrelated weights and measures that became the standard for subsequent periods."
55  Chapter 4 note 3.
56  B. Foster 1982a: 69; 1982h.
57  Biggs 1973; B. Foster 1986b; Sommerfeld 1999: 7–9; further Alberti 1987. Parallel to rectilinear tablets, the rectilinear prism for scholarly texts appears about this time as well, Veldhuis 2014b: 139.
58  Studevent-Hickman 2007.
59  Gelb 1957: 5, 13.
60  B. Foster 1986b; Keetman 2014; further Chapter 9 note 108.
61  Zettler 1977: 37.
62  Oates and Oates 1995; J. Oates in Oates, Oates, and McDonald 2001: 130–38.
63  For the children of Naram-Sin, Frayne 1993: 87; for Naram-Sin and Manishtusu, above, note 32; for Enheduanna, Chapter 9 note 70.
64  Michalowski 1981; J. Westenholz 1983b. For the importance of Shamash as patron deity of truth, Chapter 6 part 1.
65  Archi 1987c; Biga 1987; Catagnoti 2003a: 232–33.
66  Buccellati and Kelly-Buccellati 2002.
67  Parrot 1954: 153; Gelb 1992: 151.
68  A. Westenholz 1987: 97; Steinkeller 2014: 692.
69  Frayne 1993: 183; Steinkeller 1999b; A. Westenholz 1999: 55–59. For the king's journey to Sumer, Thureau-Dangin 1897c: 170; B. Foster 1980.
70  Appendix Ib 34; Frayne 1993: 182–83, 192–93; for more on Gutians, below, note 73 and Chapter 2 note 18. An Akkadian school text mentions Agade and Guti but says nothing further about them, L. 5819.
71  Glassner 1986: 39–54.
72  Volk 1992; Frayne 1993: 269; for Ili-ishmani, M. Lambert 1979; D. Potts 1999: 109–10.
73  Hallo 1957/71, 2005; Glassner 1994a; Pomponio 2011.
74  Glassner 2004: 122–23.
75  Kienast and Volk 1995: 135, understanding, however, "There is a king in Agade!" (with Civil 1993:78 despite doubts of Wilcke 2007: 165). The name occurs, apparently as that of a military officer, in two Umma documents recording disbursements of bread and beer; it is tempting to suggest that this was the same man, B. Foster 1982i: 333.
76  Cooper 1983a: 56–59 (Appendix IIIb) lines 155–59.
77  Cooper 1983a: 62–63 (Appendix IIIb) lines 190, 192, 248–53.
78  Speiser 1952; Yoffee 1995: 292–94; McMahon 2012: 664–67; Weiss et al. 2012; dissent on the extent or impact of northern Mesopotamian desiccation at this time by

Wilkinson 1994; further Glassner 1994b; Zettler 2003: 17–29; Kolinski 2007; Ur 2010; Buccellati 2013: 172–73; for possible Mesopotamian historical memory of this alleged event as early as the Akkadian period, Chapter 11 part 4.

79 Adams 1978.

80 Nissen 1980.

81 Yoffee and Cowgill 1988: 46–49; 1995: 292–94; 2004: 142–44; Buccellati 2013: 172–73 (further, Chapter 3 part 6). For further comment on the relationship between the older city-states and the Akkadian Empire, M. Lambert 1974 (who suggested that they were reorganized into provinces); Stone 1997: 21 (who called them the "building blocks" of the Empire); in general A. Westenholz 2002; Garfinkle 2013.

82 Appendix Ia 30; Ib 36; Frayne 1993: 210–13; Pomponio 2011: 228–30.

83 Frayne 1993: 214–17; a delivery of an arrears of wool from Adab (BdI Adab 235) is dated to his accession year: "The year Shu-Durul took kingship"; Pomponio 2011: 230; Marchesi 2015: 426 (inscribed weight from Tuttul). For Puzur-Inshushinak, Boehmer 1966; Steve and Gasche 1971 plate 8 no. 2 (*ensi* of Susa and *shakkanakku* of Elam); André-Salvini 1989; Steinkeller 2013a.

# 2   The land and people of Akkad

## 1.   Akkad, Agade, and their neighbors

The land of Akkad, the city of the same name, and the people called Akkadians are at once a historical mystery and a certainty. Just as no one passing through the sultry marshes of Latium or the breezy shores of the Greek colony at Byzantion could have predicted that they would become the centers of vast human enterprises, so too, a traveler crossing the featureless, torrid plain of Akkad would have seen no presage of that region's destiny. Today, we are not even sure precisely where most ancient Akkad was – perhaps the area east of the Tigris around its confluence with the Diyala River. As the Akkadians and their empire expanded, Akkad came to include the entire alluvial plain, along the Euphrates from a point north of Nippur to Sippar, where the alluvium begins, and along the Tigris at least as far as the Adheim River and perhaps further north.[1]

Akkad knows two main seasons. A hot, cloudless summer lasts from May to October, when the soil is parched, the air dusty, and a stifling wind blows from the south. It is a season to stay indoors or go somewhere else. The harsh winter brings penetrating cold, clouds, rain, and frost, with the slushy, muddy ground susceptible to flooding. A brief sunny spring soon gives way to another hot season. This was not an attractive place and even during the Akkadian period it was not densely settled, compared to the territory between Nippur and Uruk.[2]

The inhabitants of this region called themselves and their language Akkadian and products, styles, and usages elsewhere associated with it were also called Akkadian (*Akkadu*). Under Sargon and his successors, "Akkadian" acquired a new meaning that referred to people who had adopted the values, culture, loyalty, and way of life characteristic of the ruling elite of their time. This development resembles that of "Ottoman," as it evolved from a tribal designation to signify a specific education, set of beliefs, and code of behavior without regard to a person's birth or ethnicity. Moreover, Akkadian was ever after used to mean the languages of Babylonia and Assyria, rather than the more accurate "Babylonian" or "Assyrian." The linguistic derivation of the name "Akkad" is unclear; in cuneiform writing it was spelled various ways, such as *Akkadu*, *Aggede*, or *Agati*.[3]

Nothing definite is known of Agade, the city Sargon chose as his capital. It may be one of several cities located near or north of the confluence of the Diyala and Tigris, or, further north, near Samarra, or, near the confluence of the Adheim and Tigris. Because the city name was not written with a pre-Akkadian word sign, as the names of very ancient cities like Uruk and Kish were, but was spelled out, it was probably founded not long before the Akkadian period, and, in fact, Agade is first mentioned only several generations before Sargon. Today, as a matter of convenience, Agade refers to the city and Akkad to the land, but in antiquity the same word was used for both.[1]

As for the origins of the Akkadian people, no tradition is preserved, in contrast to the later Assyrians, for instance, who honored ancestors who, they said, had once dwelt in tents.[5] To judge from the evidence of language, the Akkadians were the easternmost group of Semitic-speaking peoples who lived in a broad arc across northern Mesopotamia and Syria, from the Zagros to the Mediterranean. The term Semitic refers to a family of languages with distinctive phonology, morphology, and grammar.[6] A romantic belief that the early Semites were nomads hostile to agriculture and urban life helped define modern historical perceptions of the Akkadians and their history (Chapter 12 part 2).[7] This is misguided on two counts: first, there is no evidence that the early Akkadians were more nomadic than any other peoples of Mesopotamia; and second, far from being hostile to each other, nomadic, agricultural, and urban lifestyles coexisted and were mutually dependent in Akkad, for they occupied interlocking terrains in the same landscape. In fact, this interaction was characteristic of Akkad, distinguishing it from the south, where there was less scope for nomadism in the heavily cultivated areas around the cities and towns of Sumer.[8]

Semitic-speaking peoples may well have been present in Akkad long prior to the Akkadian period, their settlement an outcome of a productive relationship between pastoral nomadism and mixed farming, perhaps as far back as the seventh millennium. Their earliest known center of political power was at Kish, beginning sometime in the early third millennium. Historical memory in the north therefore focused on Kish, rather than on Akkad, and the Kishites may not have considered themselves Akkadians.[9]

Across the territory inhabited by the Semitic-speaking peoples in the mid-third millennium, Kish, Mari, Aleppo, and other cities were linked by water and overland routes, as well as by a common culture. There were zones of agriculture, especially along the Euphrates and its tributaries, the Balikh and Khabur, dotted with manors, villages, and towns, and there was open steppe, where pastoral nomads herded sheep and goats. Travel between Akkad and Syria was easy: one went across the plain, then up the Euphrates, or skirted the foothills of the mountains, or followed tracks directly across the steppe or desert. Getting to Iran was more difficult: up the Diyala or Zab valleys onto the plateau, or south along the foothills and then east across the desert into Elam. Sumer was reached by river or land.[10]

The environmental cohesiveness of the plains, the relative ease of communication across them, and the availability of food and water along the Euphrates favored the rapid formation of large political entities that tended to expand westward from northern Mesopotamia once their eastern and northern frontiers were secure. Agade thus shared with the future cities of Babylon, Ctesiphon, Seleucia, Baghdad, and Samarra, all imperial capitals founded in the roughly the same region, a strategic situation affording access to greater Mesopotamia and Syria, Anatolia, Iran, and the Gulf.

Five hundred years after Sargon's dynasty, Hammurabi's scribes still thought of Agade as a capital or crossroads city.[11] Largely abandoned by the end of the third millennium, its cult maintained at Sippar and probably at Babylon, Agade was reoccupied in the mid-seventh century, when the Assyrian king Esarhaddon rebuilt Ishtar's temple, and continued to be inhabited into the Persian period. The Babylonian king Nabonidus (555–539 BCE) claimed that he discovered the remains of the Akkadian-period temple of Ishtar there (Chapter 11 part 7).[12] Akkadian sources mention a neighborhood or sanctuary in it named Eulmash, "the house called Ulmash," a name of unknown language and meaning, which was sacred to the goddess Ishtar. Naram-Sin, who boasted that he enjoyed a close personal relationship with Ishtar, favored Ulmash, using it in names for a son and daughter (Chapter 1 part 8; Chapter 9 part 5).[13]

The Sumerian poem *The Curse of Agade*, composed a century or more after Naram-Sin, waxes lyrical about the city, setting the stage for its humiliation and downfall (Chapter 1 part 8; Chapter 11 part 6):

That its populace dine on the best of food,
That its populace draw the best of drinks,                                    (15)
That a person fresh washed make merry in the courtyard,
That people throng the festival grounds,
That people who knew each other feast together,
That outsiders circle like outlandish birds of prey aloft,
That even farthest Marhashi be writ once more on tribute lists,              (20)
That monkey, monstrous elephant, buffalo, beasts of exotic climes,
Rub shoulders in the broad streets with dogs and lions,
Mountain ibex, and shaggy sheep,
Holy Inanna never stopped to rest.
Then did she pack Agade's very granaries with gold,                          (25)
Its gleaming granaries did she pack with silver,
She delivered copper, tin, and blocks of lapis even to its barns,
Sealed them up in silos like heaps of grain. . . .
Its king, the shepherd, Naram-Sin,                                           (40)
Shone forth like the sun on the holy throne of Agade.
Its walls, like a mountain range, reached up to graze the sky.
Holy Inanna opened in them spacious gates,
Big enough to let the Tigris flow out through them to the sea.
She made Sumer haul boats upstream with its own goods,                       (45)

The upland Amorites, men who know not grain,
Brought before her gamboling bulls and prancing goats,
Meluhha, people of the black-stone mountains,
Brought up to her strange things they made,
Elam and Subir bore goods to her, like laden donkeys,                    (50)
The governors of cities, the managers of temples,
The scribes who parceled out the farmland in the steppe,
Brought in steadily their monthly and New Year offerings of food.[14]

Akkadians were by no means the only people inhabiting the land of Akkad. Speakers of Sumerian had long lived to the south, with the result that Akkadian language and literature were heavily influenced by Sumerian and vice versa. The Akkadians had adopted Sumerian writing to spell their language. They also wrote it using Sumerian words that the reader was supposed to translate into Akkadian as he went. With this writing system came much esoteric lore of a traditional Sumerian character. Little was of any practical use, yet it had to be mastered nonetheless by Akkadian scribes.[15] Sumerian culture, society, and economy were no doubt the most important influence on Akkad. Perhaps, beyond human memory, Sumerian colonists had once settled there, but in this period most speakers of Sumerian living in Akkad were clients of the king.[16]

Some names, such as Buzuzu or Ititi, have no indisputable meaning in either Sumerian or Akkadian, but were given in families that spoke one or the other, apparently more of them east of the Tigris than west of it. Some may have been descendants of pre-Akkadian Mesopotamian peoples. They were, in any case, as much part of Akkadian society as anyone with an Akkadian name and lineage. Indeed, one of Sargon's ablest generals, Ititi, bore a name of this type, as did an early ruler of Assur (perhaps the same man), and many of the Akkadians who came to Manishtusu's feast claimed descent from an ancestor with another such name.[17]

An eastern people more readily identifiable on the basis of their language, among other characteristics, were the Gutians, mountaineers whom the lowland population at times professed to despise. After the fall of the Akkadian Empire, the Gutians took over some Akkadian territories and called themselves kings in imitation of the Akkadians, even commissioning Akkadian royal inscriptions for themselves. Their land was known in Mesopotamia only for its cattle and slaves; their name was to become a by-word in later Mesopotamia for barbarian hordes from the east, and was scholastically applied, nearly 2000 years later, to the Persians.[18] Another eastern group were the Lullubi, a pastoral people at home in what is now Iraqi Kurdistan, near Suleimaniyya. The Victory Stele of Naram-Sin (Chapter 9 part 2; Figure 1.6) commemorates his invasion of this region.[19]

The Akkadians were also in contact with other peoples, including those of Simurrum, Awan, and Hamazi to the north and east; those of Elam, Marhashum, Dilmun, Magan, and Meluhha to the southeast and south; and Amorites to the west.[20] Immediately to the north and northeast of Akkad were the principalities of the Hurrians, a durable, warlike people whose origins have sometimes been sought in the mountains of Armenia or the Caucasus. They spoke a language unrelated to either Akkadian or Sumerian, but they adopted the cuneiform writing system from the Akkadians. The Hurrians had a large future role to play in the history of western Asia after the Akkadian period.[21]

The Akkadians knew two groups of Hurrians. One branch lived east of the Tigris, on the plains north of the Diyala or the Adheim, mainly above the Lower Zab, and across into the Iranian plateau, a region that the Mesopotamian states might invade but not subdue or occupy. The other branch was centered in the area of the mid-Euphrates, Khabur, and southeastern Anatolia. These Hurrians began to set up powerful kingdoms there, spreading thence across the plains toward the Mediterranean and north into Anatolia. Perhaps both branches of the Hurrians moved south independently from their original homeland, or the western Hurrians separated from the eastern branch once they were in greater Mesopotamia. Naram-Sin gave a daughter in marriage to the lord of one of the western Hurrian kingdoms.[22]

North of Akkad, west and especially east of the Tigris, lay the land of Subir or Subartu, perhaps including much of the region later known as Assyria. The later Assyrians recognized that Subartu could be used in Babylonian scholarship to refer to them, but they themselves located Subartu to the north and east in Iran, and considered it a foreign land, a source of slaves prized for their good looks. Although the Subarians might have been a more ancient population group in the region than the eastern or western Hurrians, in second-millennium Mari the Hurrian language was called "Subarian." Subartu was therefore an old, broad, historical, concept of the north, seen from Sumer, but a real place and people to those who lived near it, including the Akkadians, Kishites, Amorites, and Assyrians.[23]

In sum, the land of Akkad was a region with no clear boundaries and multiple ethnic, linguistic, and cultural traditions. The Akkadian language was perhaps most widely spoken among the elite, who nonetheless deemed Sumerian culture and language integral to their civilization. *The Curse of Agade*, like the modern historian, stresses the capital's economic and strategic advantages, built as it was near the crossroads of the rich cultivated lands of Sumer, the pastoral lands of the middle and upper Euphrates, and the highlands of Iran, with their exotic livestock, materials, and industries. The poetic description says nothing of diverse peoples, but paints instead a rosy picture of an urban population happy, prosperous, numerous, and well nourished, favored of the goddess Ishtar, who made her home among the citizens and partook of their plenty.[24]

## 2. Akkadian society

The countryside of Akkad was extensively irrigated so that barley and wheat were grown as winter crops, with a second, smaller, summer crop. Date orchards flourished in the moister areas. Herds of sheep and goats fed on both the sparse natural vegetation of the plains and on the first shoots of the field crops. This technique produced a lusher crop from the second growth and also allowed natural fertilization of the fields. Although no data are available, land sales suggest that large-scale holdings of notables, rich men, and extended families may have shared the landscape with small family farms, at least around the cities. To judge from modern times, yields were high in proportion to the seed sown. Irrigation and flooding meant that salinity was a problem since salts rise to the surface when the ground is moist, but this could be compensated for with crop and fallow rotation.[25]

Passing through the region from city to city during the Akkadian period, one might have seen villages, towns, and manors surrounded by gardens, orchards, and fields, as well as considerable expanses of uninhabited territory where nomadic people could move about freely and peaceably. In the time of the Akkadian Empire, the population of the region seems to have been less than it was two centuries before, but small rural settlements are hard to detect in surface surveys, and the limited evidence is difficult to interpret.[26] The only public waterworks that the Akkadian kings boasted of were in Sumer, not Akkad, suggesting that the Akkadian Empire depended upon Sumer as its main agricultural base, just as *The Curse of Agade* saw it and administrative records confirm.[27]

The men who sat down to Manishtusu's feast (Chapter 1 part 1) belonged to sixty-four families in thirty groupings, the largest number of related people known from third-millennium sources. Some have Akkadian names, a few Sumerian names, and others names neither Akkadian nor Sumerian. If the language of name-giving is significant, the banqueters well represented the diversity of Akkad and northern Babylonia. Yet one may question the extent to which these really were families in any meaningful sense. Perhaps the groupings were self-serving for the men concerned, or worked up by the king's agents in order to incorporate certain individuals into the Akkadian system of patronage. In modern times, defining tribes and creating notables was a standard technique of colonial administration in many parts of the world. The Manishtusu obelisk could be the first attestation of this practice. However, since later Mesopotamian historical tradition vaguely remembered the Akkadian kings as having displaced land owners and stationed their own clients throughout the realm, it seems best to assume that, even if these people did develop a dependent relationship with the royal house, they had been deprived of their ancestral lands in the process.[28]

There is, moreover, no clear indication that the Akkadian elite had a particular sense of nobility or lineage, even if some families could reckon back six or seven generations. Naram-Sin, for example, did not boast of his lineage in his inscriptions as later Assyrian kings were wont to do, nor, as among the Assyrians, can we document a sense of "old families" identified with a particular place. In fact, the most important Akkadians, such as the leading dignitaries in Sumer, identified themselves only by name, with no mention of their parentage nor formal title, as if their names were sufficient. Prominent officials sometimes bore flamboyant Akkadian names, such as Kashid-Ilaba ("Ilaba [a patron deity of Agade]-is-Victorious"), evidence, perhaps, for an Akkadian court style of self-identification and promotion. By contrast, people in more modest walks of life were identified by name, father's name, and profession.

With the growth of the Empire, Akkadian society developed a land-holding elite in Sumer, a land-owning elite in Akkad, and administrative and military elites throughout the realm. In Sumer, land-holding magnates, such as Mesag or the governor of Lagash, lived in rural, park-like enclaves, whereas in Akkad, as at Eshnunna, the governor's palace (Figure 3.1) gradually encroached on an urban neighborhood.[29]

Akkadian society comprised at least two legal estates: citizens with legal rights and chattel slaves. Since the word for chattel slave is apparently Semitic in derivation, one wonders if this status was originally more at home in the north than in Sumer. Economic classes were of course more differentiated than legal estates. Clients, dependents, workers, and menials may have had only limited mobility and legal rights but could not, so far as we know, be sold as slaves, so were subjects, rather than objects, of law. Some were probably little better than slaves in their way of life, and, in fact, chattel slaves in wealthy households may have enjoyed a better standard of living than many workers. Some workers may have been as tightly bound to their positions in society as chattel slaves, if not more so, because chattel slaves could be manumitted, but not workers. In any case, such workers were not referred to legally as slaves. Chattel slaves were expensive and probably not numerous even in proportion to the elite population; they were more likely used in service capacities than in production. Parents had the power to sell their children into slavery, a practice normally resorted to only in times of severe economic distress. Rather than chattel slavery, this was debt slavery, in which children worked for creditors to pay the interest on their parents' debt and could be redeemed if the loan was paid off. Apparently they could not be sold by the creditor, as chattel slaves were, but otherwise had few legal protections.[30]

The social and economic status of women in Akkadian society, outside of the royal family, must largely be a matter of conjecture. No women were invited to Manishtusu's feast, for example, so the model of land tenure in the male line applied in that transaction. But women occasionally appear in other land sale documents and could possess property of their own. Marriage was overwhelmingly monogamous, though men occasionally had more than one wife and concubinage was known among the elite and ruling class, among whom large families are documented. People of lower status, who appear most often in administrative lists of workers, did not usually have more than two or three children.[31]

Little is known of the ceremonies or rights of marriage. The Akkadian prospective groom gave gifts of clothing, household goods, and money to the bride herself, or to her father or other male representative, in advance of the wedding, which presumably became her private property after marriage.[32] Several lists of such gifts show that bridewealth could vary widely in its make-up and value. One fairly substantial gift comprised six pieces of jewelry, thirty containers of beer, thirty jars of beer mix, and fifty-four bushels of barley, some of which may have been intended for the wedding feast.[33] A more lavish bride gift included sheep, silver, five pigs, wool, dried fish, clothes and bedding.[34] Perhaps the most opulent of all, although the document is too broken to tell if it really concerns bride gifts, lists a gold ring, a wagon and draught animals, sheep, fine clothing, household utensils, and many other items, written out in four columns of text on a good-sized tablet – a trousseau, if that is what it was, fit for a princess.[35]

Land and houses are not mentioned in these bride gifts, but some of the earliest records of land transactions may be concerned with husband-wife settlements of important real estate assets. Women could own or sell houses and cases are known in which women, probably widows, sold to government officials their husband's rights of possession of certain arable lands that the government wished to reclaim.[36]

An elaborate legal document from Isin in the time of Naram-Sin records the breaking of an engagement. The prospective groom swore on the king's name that he would make no claim on the prospective bride, Nin-gula, perhaps meaning that she was not obliged to return her bride gift: "Let a groom after her own heart take Nin-gula, I will do absolutely nothing to prevent it." He was liable for not inconsiderable court costs.[37]

## 3.   Law and justice

Long before the dynasty of Sargon, Mesopotamia had both concepts and practices of law, governing certain relations between and among individuals, families, the community, and the government. Although no formal collection of legal decisions, promulgations, or pronouncements about law has come down to us from the Akkadian period, we can reconstruct aspects of its law from a rich inventory of documents recording instances of its practice, from both Sumer and Akkad, as well as the earliest known records of litigation.[38]

Historians of law suggest that some Mesopotamian legal practices arose from long-standing family and community patterns, such as inheritance and the powers of the head of a family, whereas some were imposed by rulers in the interest of control, consistency, and taxation, as well as to take certain powers out of the hands of community leaders, such as the execution of condemned criminals. The ruling elite sometimes described law as given by the gods, reflecting divinely sanctioned order, enforced and regulated by the divinely chosen ruler, but it seems unlikely that for most people going about their daily lives such grand assertions mattered much.[39]

Recourse to the uncanny was common in Akkadian legal practice in the form of oaths and ordeals. One swore to facts or promises by invoking a choice of gods, usually the most prominent local deity, or, after the deification of Naram-Sin, on the name of the king, in one instance on the "wall of Agade" (Chapter 6 part 6). Oaths may have been formally administered on holy ground, or may sometimes have been taken before divine symbols brought out for the occasion or held in the hand. The water ordeal was resorted to when other means of ascertaining the truth had failed and conflicting testimony had to be resolved. One or both parties were submerged in a river; coming up safely was deemed a divine judgment in favor of the person who did so. If both parties performed equally well in the ordeal, it is not clear what happened next, so in practice probably only one party underwent the ordeal or the guilty party gave up before submersion.[40]

Ownership, from a legal point of view, was somewhat different for real estate than for moveable goods; at least, different legal phraseology was used. There is abundant evidence that arable land was often considered to be owned by family groups, as shown by the efforts of Manishtusu's scribes to work out genealogies of the sellers of parcels over three, four, or more generations. Buyers of such land, in contrast, were usually individuals, suggesting that private was replacing communal ownership.[11] Houses, urban lots, orchards, and gardens, however, were often sold by one person to another, so this type of real estate was not communal property.

The sale of real and moveable property sometimes involved symbolic acts or gestures, such as driving a peg into the ground or into a wall. One practice attested in Akkad was called "making (the seller or the thing sold) go past the pestle," an action in which leaving behind a common household object stood for the transfer of the property sold to the new owner.[12] The sale of real property sometimes involved an elaborated price structure, in which there was a purchase price and additional payments in cash, kind, or food. The last suggests that there may have been a traditional practice of serving the seller a meal, as Manishtusu did, but that in some instances this may have turned into a gift of pots of soup or jars of beer.[13]

Moveable goods, such as money, furniture, textiles, and slaves, were generally understood as individually owned, unless they had been declared common goods in some formal way, for instance, the creation of family capital for investment or purchases. Goods owned in common may have been symbolized by such acts as putting funds in a money bag or a basket.[14]

The spread of writing throughout Mesopotamia not long before the Akkadian period gave legal practice an important new tool, the potentials of which were soon realized. Documents were drawn up by professional scribes in the presence of witnesses, sometimes sealed, though normally the list of witnesses was sufficient authority. Sales, loans, and transfers of moveable property were written out and witnessed, as were sales of real estate and significant changes in social status. The witnesses were usually men who were identified by their father's name and their own title or profession.[15] The outcomes of trials, resolution of disputes, division of inheritances, and sworn statements were also written down. These records were retained by the individuals concerned as evidence for what had taken place and in some cases, such as at Isin and Nippur, copies were retained in a special office. Compilations of legal phrases, originating long before the Akkadian period, were no doubt available for scribes to learn during their training, as well as model documents to copy, study, and memorize.

Later evidence suggests that disputes over property or social status were adjudicated in the first instance at the local level, using neighborhood, temple, or community authorities or notables, the last called "elders" or "mayors" in Akkadian times (part 5, this chapter).[16] There was also a formal court procedure before judges, but this cost money, so was presumably resorted to only by people with means. Judges were important dignitaries, entitled to enjoy the income from good-sized estates given them by the king's officials; the act of judging was a divine attribute, associated with profound knowledge, probity, fairness, and wisdom, rather than with specific legal training.[17]

The court procedure entailed appearing before a judge or judges, who may have been paid for hearing the case, and hiring a bailiff, whose task it was to schedule the trial and assemble the parties and witnesses at the right time and place, for which he too received a fee. A scribe was needed to draw up a summary of the case and finding. No doubt he received a fee as well. During the hearing, the contending parties spoke before the judge or judges, the plaintiff first, and proof or evidence would be offered. This could be followed by interrogation of the parties and witnesses. The proceeding closed with the court's verdict.[48]

Certain offenses, including murder, assault, theft, failure to pay debts, and flight to avoid obligations or responsibilities, could involve arrest and imprisonment. No police force with investigative and arrest powers is attested as such. The bailiffs used in court cases may have played some role in apprehending fugitives, and there is a shadowy figure usually translated as "constable" who may have been concerned with public peace and propriety. There were also armed men, probably soldiers, who were used to enforce court orders and apprehend offenders.[49]

In common with court procedures, jail (the "big house" or "bondage house," as it was sometimes euphemistically or descriptively called) was the subject of magic spells in the hope of successful release or escape (Chapter 6 part 8). These say nothing about how people were sustained while in jail, or how long they could expect to remain there, pending a resolution of their case. Long-term punitive imprisonment for crimes is not attested; the usual punishments were fines, multiple restitution, mutilation, enslavement, or death.[50]

Although crimes such as theft, robbery, murder, assault and rape are amply attested in later Mesopotamian legal documents and law collections, there is little basis for reconstructing their investigation and punishment in the Akkadian period, nor the extent to which vengeance anticipated community, administrative, or royal sanctions against offenders.[51]

## 4.   Patronage and administration

Mesopotamian common wisdom held that mighty rulers had far less impact on people's daily lives than local administrators – the bailiff, the scribes who measured parcels of land and houses, the men in charge of apportioning irrigation water, the foremen of teams of working men and women, the commander of the local military unit, the recruiting officer for military service and public works, the mayor or headman of the town or village.[52] The weight of outside authority was perhaps most heavily felt in exactions of labor and service, in division of the harvest on the threshing floor, in resentment of one's landlord, and when the army recruiter came around, looking for able-bodied men to die nobly in the service of the king.

One of the most effective means the Akkadian authorities had at their disposal for managing their subjects was their power to distribute major resources of arable land among people linked by common economic interests and their dependency on the ruler and his notables. As in many societies, these patronage networks were no doubt well understood by their participants, but their relationships were not set down in writing, so the historian has little chance of tracing their web of allegiances and duties. This form of patronage was characteristic of northern Mesopotamia, in which the ruler not only controlled extensive arable land and wealth, but was expected to make some of that land and wealth, as well as lucrative opportunities, available to his followers.[53]

A distinctively Akkadian form of patronage was the notables' practice of surrounding themselves with an entourage of personal followers or retainers. One class, called "the select," were men, possibly armed. There may have been a second class, called "the boys," perhaps more akin to menials or servants. Presumably both groups did their patron's bidding and were rewarded with housing, food, clothing, and employment, as their patron deemed fit, and competed for his favor. We know of no similar groups in traditional Sumerian society. Since the words for both the "select" and the "boys" were Akkadian, one may suggest that the Akkadians brought sophisticated arts of patronage to the lands they conquered, which were new to their restive subjects. In addition to these specific terms, Akkadian documents often noted subordination in a more general way, such as "the man of" a certain person, that is, a family member, client, or subordinate economically and socially dependent upon someone's favor.[54]

We can see patronage most clearly in the administration of arable land, as this affected the lives of both ordinary and notable people in Sumer and Akkad alike. Here a tripartite structure was developed: first the king's governors, whom he appointed and who served at his pleasure, being dignitaries of political, military, and economic importance; second, the heads of the ancient cult centers, which, in Sumer particularly, controlled considerable arable land; and third the notables, who received from the king's land office fields for their own support and for distribution as patronage to others. The Sumerian poet who gloated over the fall of Agade saw this three-part structure as one of the salient features of Akkadian administration and prosperity:

> The governors of cities, the managers of temples,
> The scribes who parceled out the farmland in the steppe.[55]

The governor of a city or city-state was called *ensi* in Sumerian, a pre-Akkadian title of uncertain meaning. Sargon singled out his appointment of specifically "Akkadian" *ensi*'s throughout the regions he conquered as one of the important deeds he wished to commemorate. To judge from the "Akkadians" who were witnesses to Manishtusu's land sale, this term referred to a new class of royal dependents who need not have been born in Akkad at all. What made them Akkadians was their willingness to leave their own city and community, to enter the king's service, and to depend upon him for preferment.[56]

In Sumer, the Akkadian *ensi*'s performed the same functions as the previously independent rulers of city-states had done before the conquest, but now they were appointed by the king. Some of these independent rulers, such as Lugalzagesi, Sargon's old opponent, had called themselves kings, but this title was now reserved for the Akkadian sovereign. Uruk had traditionally been ruled by the *en*, which the Akkadians understood to mean "lord," although this personage probably had a more important role in religious ritual than his *ensi* counterparts elsewhere. Thus the Akkadians imposed their governance on cities with long traditions of independent rule and different modes of self-presentation and structures of leadership.[57]

The new Akkadian *ensi*s had at their disposal land, buildings, labor, personnel, livestock, and wealth in specie and goods, which it was their agreeable task to administer with the assistance of a large staff of supervisors, managers, and scribes. They may sometimes have served as military commanders as well, so might be expected to take the field at the head of local troops if the king called them to do so. In any case, they were responsible for upholding security and law and order in their cities. Maintenance of roads, canals, and major buildings was another of their duties.[58]

Some of these *ensi*s, like the governors of Umma and Lagash in the time of Naram-Sin, served for decades and were educated men. To secure and keep their important and lucrative posts, they must have availed themselves of many opportunities to demonstrate their fidelity to the king, including enthusiastically attending court functions in the capital, bestowing regular gifts and entertainment upon the sovereign and members of his family, ensuring that the royal revenues flowed freely from their cities and domains, supporting national and local cults and praying for the king and his family, reporting regularly on both routine matters and items of intelligence value, honoring the king in inscriptions and dedications, and keeping the territory they ruled loyal and at peace. A new reign may have occasioned applications to receive or retain governorships in the form of expressions of fealty and lavish presents to the new king.

On the local level, governors needed a good sense of tact and strategy to deal with the Akkadian notables whose lands lay nearby, some of whom may well have wished for the governorship for themselves. It helped, no doubt, if a governor belonged to a prominent family through birth or marriage, so could rely on family ties in the hierarchy of subordinates most likely to support his interests. If the king saw fit, however, governors could be transferred to other cities, so some may have been newcomers in their communities.[59]

Literate governors belonged to a small, proud elite of school graduates who could write the elegant Akkadian hand, quote lightly literature they had studied in class, read and write their own sometimes florid letters, and understand the technical details of measuring land, estimating crops, and apportioning taxes and income. One of Naram-Sin's sons was such a man, the governor of Marad; so too Lugal-ushumgal of Lagash and Mesag, an Akkadian notable in Sumer (Figure 1.8).[60]

Though the old Sumerian cities still maintained boundaries, some Akkadian notables, such as Mesag of Umma and Lugal-ra of Lagash, held estates and administered territories lying outside them, sometimes embracing lands that belonged to more than one of them. We may see in the special status of these notables both an emerging provincial structure of governance and an Akkadian identity that transcended specific offices they may have held.[61]

Religious office was likewise a calling worthy of a member of the royal family. Sargon and Naram-Sin appointed their daughters high priestesses of the moon-god Nanna-Suen at Ur, so family connections may well have been important for temple officials too. The upper echelons of the new temple hierarchy were educated people sharing interests and background, if not a family tree, with their counterparts among the Akkadians in the provincial administration.[62]

Temples were traditionally the largest buildings in Sumerian cities, organized as manors, with an enclosed central complex for religious rites, as well as ancillary buildings, including staff residences, barns, and storage buildings. The leading cultic figure was a high priest or priestess, and the leading administrator was the *sanga*. The *sanga* had previously overseen the temple lands, gardens, herds, flocks, and other resources, but now, in Sumer at least, he was subordinate to both the local governor and the representatives of the king's household.[63]

Temple personnel numbered in the hundreds. There were stewards, herdsmen, building attendants, weavers, cultivators, and boatmen, as well as laborers, some of whom were dedicated to temple service by their families. The needy, orphaned or abandoned, handicapped, and mentally deficient were put to work in temple gardens and orchards to be useful and earn their keep. Specialists worked in industries or activities associated with certain temples, such as producing fine cloth or healing the sick.[64] Temple women, neither married nor under male familial authority, comprised a separate class in a male-dominated society. In the conquered dominions, where temples held substantial vested interests, the Akkadian kings claimed that their divine householders had entrusted their subjects to them. In Akkad, it seems, temples generally had far less land and staff, so they were more directly dependent on the king's household than in Sumer.

Although the relationship between the king and the temples must at times have been delicate to work out, they had strong mutual interests and shared a hierarchical view of the world: gods were like rulers and rulers were like gods, exercising their powers in the same ways over the same countryside. Rulers paid homage to the gods and credited them with their successes, lavishing their households with gifts, endowments, and projects. A strong and effective ruler enjoyed divine favor and requited that by sharing the fruits of his success with the gods who had singled him out to rule.[65]

The personalities of individual kings must, of course, have set the tone for Akkadian dealings with the great temples of Sumer. Sargon confidently proclaimed at Nippur, in Enlil's own Ekur temple, that he prayed to the god Dagan, a cloud deity at home in the Upper Euphrates region, who had given him authority over that area. But Sargon also brought the defeated Lugalzagesi before Enlil at Nippur and ordered commemorative inscriptions in both Sumerian and Akkadian set up there. Rimush recounted his exploits before Enlil and swore that they were true, as well as showered sanctuaries throughout the land with objects made from interesting and exotic stones, fruits of his campaigns in Iran. Naram-Sin began to rebuild and refurbish Ekur and allowed his grateful subjects to build a temple in Agade to himself as god of the city. Sharkalisharri finished the grand project at Nippur (Chapter 1 part 5).[66]

Thus, on the local horizon, officiants, priests, and temple managers enjoyed and expected the king's favor and largesse, which brought needed resources of labor, tools, transport, and draught animals to work their extensive domains. There was every reason for the temples to coordinate the exploitation of their resources with the governor and the city notables, and for the royal authorities to include temple staff in their networks of patronage and support. At Lagash, for example, one finds in the governor's records that the high priestess of Ilaba, one of the patron deities of Agade, held more than 400 hectares of arable land administered by the local governor. Perhaps, like Enheduanna, she was a princess by birth. The *sanga*s of various temples held large allotments as well, along with such professionals as cult singers, dream interpreters, and performers of rituals. Some of this land was worked by the governor's cultivators.[67]

The royal household conceived of its hierarchy along domestic lines. At the top was the royal family, then the majordomo or *shaperum*, an exalted, trusted personage who held executive responsibility for the king's resources in land and buildings, specie, livestock, and personnel (Figure 5.4). Courtiers included those who gave personal services to the royal family. They prepared and served their food and drink, dressed and groomed them, readied and maintained their transport animals and wagons, entertained them, served as their messengers and couriers, and did their confidential divination and secretarial work. There are no signs of an advisory cabinet. Other officials, such as the registrar of land, chief, and subordinate scribes, supervised specific tasks or offices, perhaps under the aegis of the major domo.[68]

The king, royal family, and Akkadian notables had their own agents to look after their interests. The work of these men may be followed in detail through their lists of lands and cultivators, subdivisions, calculations of areas and expenses of cultivation, and balances of harvests due. The scribes who carried out these tasks were subject to an exalted personage called by the Sumerian title *shassukkum*, "the registrar." This royal official had thousands of hectares of good land at his disposal, divided into large, individually named agricultural districts and smaller parcels, to distribute among members of the administration, ruling elite, professionals and their followers, families, and lessees. Some of this land may have been created by developing the countryside through irrigation works or settling people in agricultural hamlets. The registrar reckoned with blocks of territory, systematically cut up into schematic subsections, from which actual parcels were measured off by survey to those privileged to receive them. One registrar controlled more than 6200 hectares of arable land in three large districts near Lagash, which had some of Sumer's most fertile fields, fifteen times the size of the parcel held locally by the high priestess of Ilaba.[69]

Akkadian notables controlled even larger areas than those typically held by administrators. For example, Yetib-Mer, the majordomo of Naram-Sin, held in the Umma and Lagash provinces alone close to a thousand hectares, duly surveyed by royal scribes and recorded by the registrar.[70]

In sum, the Akkadian governing elite enjoyed resources far in excess of what Sumerian notables before them had known. Their patronage created new social groups who looked to the royal household for their maintenance and advancement. The ancient city-states were reorganized into provinces, and the ancient temples were now dependent on the Akkadian king for support, renovation, dedications, and gifts. If the farming families of Akkad sold their lands to the king, albeit at a loss, the Sumerian cities saw their best lands taken without any recompense. Small wonder, then, that they seized every opportunity to rebel.

## 5.   Resistance to Akkadian power

In the self-presentation of their inscriptions, the Akkadian kings were emphatic that they had no rivals, a phraseology new with them, so perhaps an Akkadian invention.[71] Yet at the same time, they themselves commemorated the crushing of numerous widespread revolts and rival claims to power. Some of these appear to have gained substantial popular support, whereas others may have been leaderless disturbances.[72] Some were led by men whose names are recorded and who were capable of mounting large-scale military actions in direct threat to Akkadian hegemony. Continued suppression of internal uprisings in Sumer and Akkad was, therefore, a key element in Akkadian royal ideology, in contrast to their successors, the kings of Ur, who referred only to challenges beyond their frontiers, never in the heartland of their state. The longest and most detailed preserved Akkadian inscription is Naram-Sin's account of his suppression of a rebellion.[73]

The assassinations of Sargon's two sons attest to power struggles within the royal family in the early phase of the Empire. Naram-Sin and his son faced no such problems, so far as known. This suggests that Naram-Sin, aware of the fates of his two predecessors, may have taken steps to promote Sharkalisharri to an active role in ruling the kingdom, in preparation for succession. This could explain why some of Sharkalisharri's achievements duplicate those of his father.[74] No evidence for rivalries among Naram-Sin's progeny can be detected; the royal family may in fact have stood together in the face of such threats as the unsuccessful revolt led by Kish and Uruk.

Conflicts between the royal house and entrenched constituencies often form the basis for modern narratives of how the Akkadian kings consolidated their power. One influential thesis holds that community organs of self-government, notably an alleged assembly of free citizens, stood in the way of expanding Akkadian authority. Descriptions of this assembly vary. According to Diakonoff,[75] participation in the assembly, called *ukken* in Sumerian and *puhrum* in Akkadian, was limited to free citizens chosen or elected. In principle, all of them could voice opinions, but in practice key decisions, such as declaration of war, were made by a subgroup of elders who appointed a war leader in time of threat. The assembly had control over local land resources through approving major real estate transactions. It could also set prices, fines, taxes, undertake public works and other communal actions, and administer community property, which originally included the temple before it evolved as a separate great household. In addition, the assembly exercised general control over administrative and governmental activity on the local level.

Diakonoff argued that during the Akkadian period there was a gradual transition from large land holdings controlled by extensive family groups to smaller ones controlled by nuclear family groups, resulting in individual ownership. This deprived the assembly of an important source of authority, since land transactions were becoming matters of individual initiative. The Akkadian kings hastened this process by purchasing extensive areas of arable land at low prices to distribute as patronage, as Manishtusu did.[76] The assembly could still decide non-capital disputes between citizens, involving ownership, inheritance, and social status, mediate disputes between government officials and citizens, and regulate certain types of agricultural activity and local prices and hiring rates.

Assemblies of this type would naturally have competed with the new bureaucratic and military elites serving the king.[77] If assemblies chose the war leaders to challenge the ruling house, that might explain Naram-Sin's statement that rivals to his power "were raised up" (by the people) in Uruk and Kish, unlike himself, who was chosen by the gods.[78] The response of the royal house was either to co-opt local notables, by incorporating them within the new power structure, or to destroy them, as Rimush did in Sumer by the thousands.[79] The Akkadian professional army, Diakonoff suggested, gave individual citizens another path to personal advancement, further undermining local community self-government.[80]

A major problem is that no direct evidence for such an assembly exists in Akkadian sources, even among the many legal documents of the period, although several details of local government are known. Some records refer to a "mayor" (*rabianum*), perhaps a headman of a tribe or settlement, who mediated disputes, was responsible for dealing with crime, and recruited men for labor and military service.[81] Others mention multiple "elders," who carried out many of the same functions.[82] Still others refer to the "town" or "city," local notables who oversaw such matters as the conduct of business and commerce; this suggests the existence of a city corporation or government.[83] The presence of one or more of these entities may have varied by locality and size of a community. For a village or rural area, a mayor or elders might have sufficed, whereas a larger agglomeration with a market and several local institutions might have had a "town" or "city" board.

The argument for the importance of the putative assembly in the Akkadian period rests solely on later Sumerian literary works, which mention human and divine assemblies at Uruk and Nippur, and on second-millennium references to assemblies in various contexts. In the poem *Gilgamesh and Agga*, for instance, the elders hesitate to declare war, whereas the young men are eager to do so. This scarcely need indicate a bicameral assembly, but rather a wisdom motif of sage old age versus rash youth.[84] In the *Babylonian Epic of Creation*, to cite another example, the threatened gods meet to transfer power to another god by acclamation.[85] This affords a slender basis for reconstructing local government nearly a thousand years earlier. Likewise, the notion of conflict between the assembly and the king stems from interpreting episodes in later Sumerian and Akkadian literature as reflecting support or resistance to Akkadian authority.[86]

Certainly the Akkadian dynasty was a fascinating subject to educated readers of Sumerian in the late third and early second millennia, as exemplified by the popularity of *The Curse of Agade* and the works attributed to Sargon's daughter, Enheduanna (Chapter 9 part 6; Appendix II). But there is no compelling reason to consider that the narrative poems about Gilgamesh, or about Inanna, Enlil, and other deities refer metaphorically to the Akkadian period.[87]

Other scholars offer religious explanations for resistance to the Akkadian kings. They posit that the temple staffs chafed under the direct royal control that interfered with their long-standing alliances with local elites.[88] Again, the problem is lack of evidence. The Akkadian kings did assume from local rulers responsibility for maintaining temples, but they lavishly patronized their deities with splendid gifts and the priesthood with grants of arable land and other benefits that could scarcely have been cause for complaint.[89] On the level of theology, some read the princess-priestess Enheduanna's work as part of a heavy-handed effort to integrate the Akkadian with the Sumerian pantheons, thereby seeking to force religious unity on the realm. Some see resentment of an alleged promulgation of a comprehensive royal theology, or anger at the Akkadian ruler's assumption of the right to appoint high priestesses and other key cultic personnel.[90]

Whatever the causes, there was strong resistance to Akkadian hegemony in Sumer and Akkad, among the Amorite tribesmen in the Jebel Bishri region, in the urban centers of northern Syria, such as Ebla, Armanum, and Aleppo, and in southwestern Iran and the Gulf. If the Akkadian kings claimed that they ruled the four quarters of the earth, they faced resolute enemies in all four as well. From the perspective of the ruling elite, however, these challenges offered opportunities to prove their supremacy. Indeed, in their commemorative inscriptions, they boasted how frequent and widespread rebellions were, the better to emphasize their triumphs in suppressing them.

## Notes

1  B. Foster 1997a; Gelb 1981: 71 (between Assur and the Diyala); Garelli 1982: 86 (the region between Eshnunna and Babylon).
2  Adams 1965: 4, 1972; Ur 2013: 149; for mid-twentieth-century agricultural practice further south, Poyck 1962: 40–47. Iraqi agriculture in Late Antiquity is studied by El-Samarraie 1972 (Arabic sources) and Newman 1932 (Talmud).
3  Ungnad 1908; Kraus 1970: 23–33, 36–42; Jacobsen 1978; B. Foster 1997a; Ziegler 2007: 285 notes 172–73, 2014: 189; George 2007a. For the specific form of Akkadian spoken by the ruling elite and its relationship to other related languages or dialects in the region, Sommerfeld 2003b.
4  Van Dijk 1970; Kraus 1970: 22–23; Frayne 1991: 395–98; Sallaberger 2004a: 24–25; for "Agade" versus Akkade, above, Introduction. For proposals for the location of Agade, Chapter 3 note 56.
5  Kraus 1965.
6  Hetzron 1997; Sommerfeld 2010.
7  Levi della Vida 1938: 34–38; further Chapter 12 note 15.
8  Rowton 1967; Adams 1974; Gelb 1986, 1992; Zarins 1990; Liverani 1995; Steinkeller 2007; Szuchman, ed. 2009.
9  Gelb 1981; Zarins 1990; Sommerfeld 2010; Steinkeller 2013c.
10  Gelb 1981, 1986, 1992; Biggs 1981; Postgate 1992: 3–21.
11  For Agade as a capital or hub city with a monumental square or boulevard, Durand 1991b; Charpin 1991, 2007: 69; Ziegler 2007: 284–85 with notes 172–73, 2014. For the Old Babylonian personal name *Ina-Agade-rabat* "She-is-the-Great-One-in-Agade," presumably meaning Ishtar, Ungnad 1908: 62 note 4; other names cited by Ziegler 2014: 187. Further Chapter 3 note 56 and Chapter 11 note 153.
12  McEwan 1982; Durand and Joannès 1988; Beaulieu 1989b; Frame 1993; Zadok 1995: 446–47 (two documents dated to Cambyses years 7 and 8); Jursa 1996; A. Westenholz 1999: 31–34.

13  Frayne 1993: 158–59.

14  Cooper 1983a: 50–53 (Appendix IIIb) lines 14–28, 40–53.

15  Cooper 1995.

16  Jacobsen 1960; Gelb 1960b; Kraus 1970; Cooper 1973; Heimpel 1974; B. Foster 1982i; Steinkeller 1993a; survey of the linguistic situation in Mesopotamia by Rubio 2005; Sallaberger 2011; review of the problem of ethnicity by Emberling and Yoffee 1999 and below, note 17; further Limet 2008 and below, note 17.

17  Steinkeller 1984; Landsberger 1924: 220–21 (who considers them derived by redupli-cation from Semitic names, perhaps because they were common in the Old Assyrian onomasticon); in general Sommerfeld 2013a: 231–76, who considers many to be of Semitic, pre-Akkadian origin; for Ititi, Durand 2012 and below, Chapter 3 part 2. For criticism of the idea that names of this type indicate a specific ethnicity, Rasheed 1981: 29–32. For a definition of ethnicity, based on large numbers of people, not tied to a territory, with a sense of kinship, specific cultural traits, having a single name, and exist-ing independent of organizational mechanisms, Buccellati 2013: 148; such a definition would exclude these name-bearers.

18  Diakonoff 1956: 104–15; Hallo 1957/71, 2005; a Gutian interpreter was issued beer at Adab, OIP 14 80.

19  Klengel 1966, 1987/90.

20  A. Westenholz 1999: 90–98; for Amorites in the third millennium, Buccellati 1966, 1992; Archi 1985c; J. Klein 1997; Verderame 2009; for Magan, Heimpel 1987/90; Michalowski 1988; Glassner 1989; for Elam, Selz 1999; D. Potts 1999; De Graef and Tavernier, 2013; for Meluhha, Heimpel 1993/7; for Marhashum, Chapter 1 note 7.

21  Güterbock 1954; Edzard and Kammenhuber 1972/75; Wilhelm 1989.

22  Kammenhuber 1976; Barrelet 1977, 1984; Hallo 1978/80; Michalowski 1986; Wilhelm 1989; Durand 1996; Frayne 1997b; Steinkeller 1998; Buccellati 1999; Hawkins 2007.

23  Gelb 1944; Barrelet 1977, 1984; Michalowski 1999a; Steinkeller 2013a. An Akka-dian administrative text seems to localize Subareans in the upper Diyala, CUSAS 23 163.

24  Cooper 1983a; Appendix IIIb.

25  Adams 1978; Powell 1985; Adams 1982 gives both a survey of the importance of irri-gation in the construction of Mesopotamian culture and specific figures for the scale of canalization required for cultivation (131–32).

26  Adams 1965: 42–45.

27  B. Foster 1986a; Frayne 1993: 86 (canal serving Nippur); further Chapter 4 parts 1 and 4.

28  Grayson 1975: 236; Gelb 1979, 1982; Glassner 2004: 268–69.

29  Gelb 1979; Glassner 1996a; Diakonoff 1982: 32–59.

30  Gelb 1970c; 1976; 1982; Diakonoff 1976; Dandamayev 1984: 67–76; Steinkeller 1993a: 121; Westbrook 1995; Glassner 2000; Culbertson ed. 2011; retrospective in Adams 2011. For a proposed Sumerian etymology for the word for slave (*wardum*), Krecher 1987; further Selz 2011; A. Westenholz, private communication, suggests that *wardum* was originally an ethnic term, like English "slave."

31  B. Foster 1987a; A. Westenholz 1999: 70–72, who notes that women could participate in public life but seldom did (further Winter 1987); for age at marriage, Wilcke 1985; in general, Stol 2012.

32  Wilcke 2007: 61–66; Stol 2012: 39–94 (mostly post-Akkadian evidence); for ordinary and princely dowries in the early second millennium, Dalley 1980; Charpin 2004c, 2008.

33  Milano 1987.

34  MAD 1 169.

35  Sommerfeld 1999 no. 47.

36  Steinkeller 1982b; Steinkeller and Postgate 1992: 99–100.

37  Edzard 1968 no. 85 (BIN 8 164), following the interpretation of Yoshikawa 1989: 589.

38  Selz 2002; Neumann 2003; Wilcke 2007.

39  Speiser 1967: 560; in general, Selz 2000a; 2002: 159–64; Neumann 2003. For a member of the royal family presiding at what may have been a capital trial, CUSAS 26 123.

40 For oath-taking, Edzard 1976; Steinkeller 1989: 71–80. For an oath on the wall of
   Agade, FM 9 and B. Foster 1979a. For taking an oath holding a symbol of a god, below,
   note 82; further Chapter 6 note 101. For the ordeal, Bottéro 1981; Van Soldt 2003/5;
   ECTJ 36, 79–81; CUSAS 11 256; Owen 1989; B. Foster 1989b. For the deified river as
   a theophoric element in Akkadian names, e.g. TS 23.9.
41 Steinkeller 1999c; for Akkadian-language terminology of sale and transfer of goods,
   Lipinski 1982.
42 Edzard 1970: 14–15; Wilcke 2007: 91.
43 Wilcke 1976/80: 492–93; Chapter 8 note 14.
44 I follow A. Westenholz 1987: 60 rather than Wilcke 2007: 71, who sees the "basket" as
   a tax; Pomponio 2013: 29.
45 For the written document, Larsen 1987; Selz 1999; for witnesses, Edzard 1968: 11;
   Oh'e 1979, who suggests a change in the role of witnesses in the Akkadian period.
46 Stol 1976: 77–83; A. Westenholz 2004: 600–601; Taylor 2010 and below, note 81.
47 A. Westenholz 2004: 603–4; Démare-Lafont 2006/8; Sommerfeld 2006b.
48 B. Foster 1982e (witnesses, records of court cases, court costs); Démare-Lafont 2006/8:
   73–74; Wilcke 2007; A. Westenholz 2004: 602–3.
49 Wilcke 2007: 117–19.
50 Hallo 1985; Steinkeller 1991 (with Akkadian contexts, 229); Civil 1993; Charpin 2011:
   415–16; Neumann 2012. In CUSAS 26 156, an early Akkadian record from Umma,
   two servants of a certain Mugesi are jailed and Mugesi's mother gets them out on the
   authority of the chief cupbearer.
51 Wilcke 1992; Durand 2003b.
52 Gelb 1960a; Steinkeller 2007; Taylor 2010.
53 For patronage in the Akkadian period, Bottéro 1965: 104; Glassner 1986: 29–32; Steinkeller 1993a: 121; in general Westbrook 2005.
54 B. Foster 1981; *suharum* is most uncertain, being attested in Akkadian sources, so far as
   I am aware, solely in a student text mentioning *nu-banda*s (military captains?), Agade
   and Gutium (ITT II 5819), but more common in later periods; Gelb 1979. The term
   *muškenum*, which refers to some sort of subordination, though known in pre-and post-
   Akkadian sources, does not occur in Akkadian documents so was not then in general use.
55 Cooper 1983a: 52–53 (Appendix IIIb) lines 51–52.
56 Frayne 1993: 11–12; B. Foster 2000.
57 Edzard 1974; Steinkeller 1999a; in general Stone 1997; for officialdom at early Mari
   and Ebla, Pomponio 2002.
58 Jacobsen 1991; B. Foster 1993a; Visicato 2000. CUSAS 23 169 may list a governor's
   staff, including a chief scribe, the retired or former governor, a commander of work
   troops, a singer, and others; further below, note 68.
59 Hallo 1972; Foster 1980; Zettler 1984; Bauer 1987/90; Steinkeller and Postgate 1992:
   54–60; Dahl 2007; for similar practice at Pre-Akkadian Umma, Monaco 2013: 749.
60 Mesag of Umma and Lugal-ushumgal of Lagash both used the title dub-sar, in Mesag's case even on his cylinder seal: UTI 6 3768: [Me]-ság dub-sar ensí Umma^{ki} 7 mu 7 iti;
   Schileiko 1914; M. Lambert 1975; B. Foster 1979b; Catagnoti 2003b; Salgues 2011.
   For taxation, Chapter 3, notes 76 and 179; Chapter 7 note 3.
61 For Lugal-ra, mentioned in the Lagash region, Umma, and Nippur, Kienast and Volk
   1995: 88; B. Foster 1982b: 38; 2010a: 138 (= ECTJ 108); in general M. Lambert 1974.
62 For high priestesses and their responsibilities, J. Westenholz 1991, 1992a; Zgoll 1997:
   112–13.
63 For temples in general, Kraus 1953; Oppenheim 1961; for the *sanga*, Renger 1967/69:
   104–21 (second-millennium evidence).
64 Charpin 2011.
65 For temples and kings most studies focus on pre- and post-Akkadian periods, Struve
   1963 (pre-Akkadian Lagash); Lipinski, ed. 1979 (post-Akkadian periods); Diakonoff
   1982: 59–79; Nissen 1982; in general, Lipinski, ed. 1979. For alleged conflict between
   the ruling house and the priesthood of Sumerian temples, below, part 5 and note 88.

66 Rebuilding of Nippur temple: A. Westenholz 1987; Naram-Sin's inscription of deification, Appendix Ia 18; further above, Chapter 1 part 4 and note 39; deification of kings in late third millennium: Hallo 1999; Sazonov 2007; Michalowski 2008.

67 B. Foster 1982a: 18–26, 38.

68 For management of the king's wealth, the oath of office taken by the palace steward at early second-millennium Mari is revealing, Durand 1991a: 16–23; in general Sallaberger 2013 and Chapter 7 part 5. The organization of the Akkadian court is suggested by the records from Susa (Chapter 3 part 4). The word for courtiers, *tiru*, may imply eunuchs (George 1997) but for the Akkadian period this is quite uncertain.

69 B. Foster 1982a: 58, 63. Bottéro 1965: 109–10 suggests that distribution of land to royal retainers was an innovation of the Akkadian period, though the principle of apportioning institutional land among staff was known earlier in the temple households of Sumer.

70 B. Foster 1982a: 36; CUSAS 19 78 (receives animals, along with king's *shaperum*).

71 Appendix Ib 1, 2, 16; Frayne 1993: 11, 14–15, 55; Liverani 1988b: 253. The phrase "who had no rival" became a tag for Sargon and the hero-king Gilgamesh in later extispicy, Goetze 1947: 255 and further Chapter 11 part 4.

72 Rimush stated that the city Kazallu "was hostile" to him and that he afterwards captured its governor; perhaps this signifies a popular revolt (Frayne 1993: 48–49 lines 44–63); further below, part 5, Chapter 11 part 4, Chapter 12 part 2.

73 Brisch 2010.

74 A. Westenholz 2000.

75 Diakonoff 1959: 217–19; 144–46.

76 Diakonoff 1959: 131–32.

77 Diakonoff 1959: 217.

78 Glassner 2004: 4–5.

79 Diakonoff 1959: 228.

80 Diakonoff 1959: 223.

81 Seri 2006, who thinks that *rabianum* is originally an Amorite term (51–96); for mayors in general, Stol 1976: 77–83; Taylor 2010. Seri suggests that elders (*shibutu*) at Mari were royal officials but local community leaders in Mesopotamia (97–137); the evidence for the assembly is reviewed pp. 159–80. Charpin 2007: 181 suggests that in fact *puhrum* may often mean "meeting" rather than refer to a formal body (leaving out of account "meeting" as used by English-speaking Quakers), so a search for an "assembly" may be misguided. For the assembly in pre-Akkadian Syria, Durand 1989. For elders enforcing a royal order, Chapter 9 part 8 and note 129.

82 Bottéro 1971; Sollberger 1982; Seri 2006. Elders seem mostly to have acted as witnesses; a letter from an Akkadian notable refers to an elder as someone unimportant, as follows: "Let them produce the [ ] of the elder, have him take up his staff and weapon and swear by Shakkan [god of livestock] and Shamash [god of oaths]. I really do not want to concern myself with the stray sheep of an elder . . ." (Kienast and Volk 1995: 154–56). For a proposal that "all" or "some elders" may have rebelled against Sargon (rather than "in his old age"), Diakonoff 1959: 213 and Grayson 1975: 153 note to 11–13.

83 A. Westenholz 2004.

84 Katz 1993.

85 Jacobsen 1943; Wilcke 1973, 1993.

86 Wilcke 1973, who also cited metrology and the *Royal Correspondence of Ur.* The references in the *Royal Correspondence of Ur* are not conclusive and the early second-millennium evidence may be indicative of social conditions peculiar to the Amorite period. Local standards of metrology prove nothing; only matters for royal accountability were accounted for by the royal standard.

87 Cooper 2001; A. Westenholz 1999: 77.

88 Kienast 1973: 498–99, writing of priestly "orthodoxy," followed by Nissen 1982: 198, 1988: 173–75, 2012: 81, who considers priestly opposition "automatic."

89 B. Foster 1982a: 102.

90 Diakonoff 1959: 219–21; Van Dijk 1969a; A. Westenholz 1999: 76–77.

# 3 Akkadian centers and settlements

## 1. Identifying Akkadian centers and settlements

The dating of late third-millennium Mesopotamian sites and material culture to the Akkadian period depends on a combination of strategies, since few of the abundant Akkadian written documents and inscriptions have an archaeological context and few of the other artifacts found in Akkadian levels are associated with texts.[1] Nevertheless, thanks to the Akkadian practice of inscribing sculpture and seals, not to mention metalwork, seashells, and other objects, many Akkadian pieces may be associated with the reigns of specific kings and the uninscribed monuments compared stylistically to those with writing.[2] Besides textual evidence, cylinder seals, which evolved stylistically more rapidly than architecture or ceramics, have proved most useful for recognizing Akkadian-period levels in excavated sites.

The archaeology of the Akkadian period falls into two main phases: early and Classical. The early phase, from the reigns of Sargon, Rimush, and Manishtusu to the first decade or so of Naram-Sin, continues the pre-Akkadian (or Early Dynastic IIIb) period, so it is difficult to distinguish from it without epigraphic evidence. The Classical phase, from Naram-Sin through Sharkalisharri, is characterized by innovations in art, architecture, and writing that can be readily identified. A tendency to expect to find features of Classical Akkadian culture in the first two generations of Akkadian rule has led to debate about such important issues as the chronological relationship between the Northern Palace at Eshnunna and the Akkadian administrative documents found nearby and within it. The end of the Akkadian period is likewise difficult to define archaeologically in the absence of written evidence or cylinder seals. The problems are compounded by the practice of the early Akkadian elite of using pre-Akkadian administrative buildings and that of the Ur III kings of using Akkadian structures and record-keeping techniques.

Six classes of artifacts are especially significant for dating Akkadian sites: cuneiform tablets, cylinder seals, statuary and relief sculpture, pottery, metal work, and architecture. Akkadian-period tablets may in the first instance be treated as physical objects. Dated tablets are very rare, so their shape and writing style are important considerations. Early Akkadian tablets are thicker and have a more rounded shape

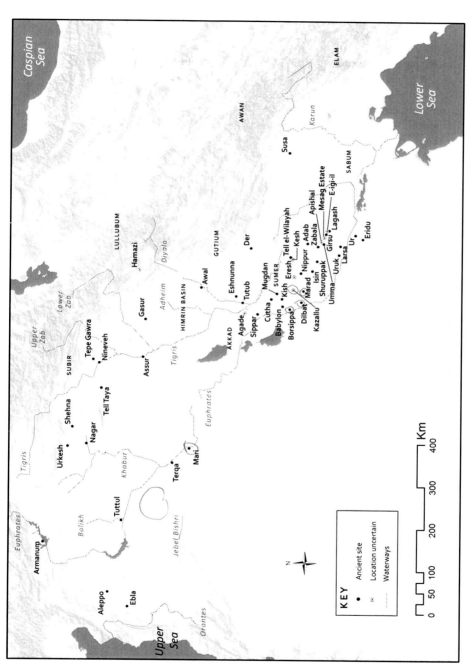

*Map 1* Sumer and Akkad in the Akkadian period.

than Classical ones, and they are written in the type of script taught in schools in the late pre-Akkadian period. Tablets of this phase are known from such Sumerian centers as Adab and Umma. Only in the time of Naram-Sin do administrative documents regularly acquire the characteristic rectilinear shape and the large, widely spaced, elegantly calligraphic "Akkadian writing," for which the period is noted (Chapter 1 part 6 and Figure 1.8). Private documents were less carefully made and written, so they often look older than contemporaneous administrative documents and can be more difficult to place chronologically. In the succeeding Ur III period, "Akkadian writing" was used for calligraphy, but a smaller, simplified script was preferred for routine matters. As late as the sixth century BCE, Akkadian spelling was affected in royal inscriptions for archaizing purposes.[3]

Glyptic of the Akkadian period has been divided into several phases (Chapter 9 part 3). In general, engraving technique, choice of stone, choice of subject, and inscriptions set Akkadian glyptic apart, even when the origins of some popular themes can be traced to the pre-Akkadian period. Subjects such as human or human/animal combats and wars among the gods were favored by Akkadian artists and are deemed cultural indicators of the period (Figure 9.9).[4]

Akkadian statuary and relief sculpture have likewise been divided into phases (Chapter 9 parts 1 and 2). When other works of art, notably ivory and metal figurines, exhibit the stylistic qualities of the inscribed stone pieces, they can be dated with some confidence.[5]

Although Akkadian pottery is the most abundant class of artifact found at Akkadian sites, its diagnostic typology is less well defined than that of glyptic (Figure 5.1). When certain shapes, decorations, and techniques of pottery manufacture cluster in stratigraphic contexts assignable to the Akkadian period, they can be used in two ways. First, their stylistic sequences may be calibrated with historical periods based on such other evidence as architecture, glyptic, or written sources. Second, they enable synchronisms to be made with comparable clusters at other sites so that a landscape or horizon of sites from the same period can be posited. Most Akkadian pottery, however, has not been correlated with glyptic or texts, but rather by association with stratigraphic transitions from pre-Akkadian to Akkadian, and from Akkadian to post-Akkadian.[6]

There were two regional traditions of Akkadian-period pottery, one in northern Mesopotamia, including Akkad and northeast Syria, the other in southern Mesopotamia. These are closely aligned with a preference for the Akkadian or Sumerian language in documents. At the same time, there was a relative uniformity of tablet shape, script, and glyptic imagery. This ceramic regionalism suggests that, within the larger cultural horizon of the Akkadian period, pottery had little ideological or aesthetic significance and was not a vehicle for artistic expression, but strictly utilitarian. In Mesopotamia, at least, there seems to be scant observable difference between palatial and domestic wares. Luxury vessels were probably made of materials such as metal, fine woods, and ivory, for which there is almost no evidence (Chapter 5 part 3).

Akkadian metalwork (Figure 5.2), better known from hordes and burials than from domestic contexts, is more difficult to date than ceramics, but as shown in

Chapter 5 part 3, analysis of its composition is helpful for distinguishing pre-Akkadian from Akkadian pieces. Very few finer specimens, in gold and silver, have survived. Moreover, the elaborate sets of bronze vessels known from Akkadian administrative texts have no clear counterparts in the modest grave goods that have been found (Chapter 5 part 3). The Mesopotamian climate has not preserved any Akkadian woodwork and only a few pieces of ivory (Chapter 5 parts 6 and 10).

Specifically Akkadian architectural styles are poorly known (Chapter 9 part 4; Figures 3.1–3.3, 6.1), especially in Sumer and Akkad, because the assignment of a building to the Akkadian period has normally been based on associated evidence such as writing, glyptic, or pottery, rather than on its plan, decoration, or construction technique. The use of rectangular bricks in preference to the plano-convex bricks typical of the pre-Akkadian period is a helpful dating criterion, but early Akkadian buildings were sometimes constructed in plano-convex bricks and Akkadian administrators sometimes continued to use earlier buildings. As a result, the transition from plano-convex to rectangular bricks is not a definitive marker for the onset of the Akkadian period, but only for new construction in the Classical phase, when plano-convex bricks were no longer used.[7]

Given the present knowledge of Akkadian material culture, any survey of Akkadian centers of authority, administration, production, and population must take an eclectic approach, favoring written evidence. The destruction of Akkadian centers in antiquity and by modern illicit diggers has meant that very few substantial buildings of indisputable Akkadian date, clearly associated with written documents, have been scientifically excavated and published.

Despite this imbalance, a pattern emerges of growing prosperity for the ruling class and increasing formality in the architectural expression of Akkadian authority, including fortified administrative structures designed to safeguard major accumulations of wealth (Figures 3.2, 3.3).[8] Changes also appear in the landscape of southern Mesopotamia during the Akkadian period. In certain areas, towns and urban centers were abandoned, but the number of small villages rose. It is impossible to determine if this was a long-term trend beginning in the preceding period or if Akkadian agrarian policy was a factor.[9]

Akkadian administrative centers and settlements have been identified in the Diyala region and Akkad, the Himrin Basin, Assyria, Sumer, southwestern Iran, and Syria. Some are known primarily from architectural remains, some only from documents, and some from both. The following sections survey the textual and archaeological data for these centers (Maps 1 and 2).

## 2.   The Diyala region and Akkad, the Himrin Basin, Assyria

### *Tutub/Khafaje*

Tutub and other Akkadian towns and cities have been identified along the lower course of the Diyala, after it cuts through the Jebel Himrin and flows toward the Tigris. Perhaps Agade itself was in this vicinity. At Tutub, an Akkadian administrative complex was located in the northwest portion of the main town. One large building, seventy-nine by eighty meters in extent and oriented to the cardinal points, was built over an area of various smaller buildings evidently demolished or cleared for the new structure.[10] Its four- to five-meter thick walls enclosed a series of subsidiary buildings consisting of irregularly shaped rooms surrounding large courtyards. An Akkadian cylinder seal and seven poorly preserved early Akkadian tablets were found inside, one of which mentions Agade. These record distributions of bread.[11] As at Nagar (part 5, this chapter), the building has an intrusive quality, but, unlike the later structure there, appears less systematically laid out. This suggests that during the reign of Naram-Sin there was a drive for uniformity and consistency in the planning of administrative structures, parallel to the reforms of metrology, record keeping, and self-presentation in prose and art.

About 300 meters to the northwest of this administrative center, traces were found of another, badly eroded Akkadian-period building, with the damaged remains of what was once a large group of high-level administrative records dating to the reign of Naram-Sin, exceptionally still in their original context. The sixty-five surviving documents deal with personnel, livestock, food, and industrial products. The establishment, presumably directed by the governor of the city, managed more than 1100 skilled artisans and able-bodied men, among them carpenters, smiths, weavers, workers in textile, reed, and leather, stone carvers and other craftsmen, plowmen, surveyors, and a land registrar, shepherds and fatteners; musicians, singers, barbers, messengers, cooks, and food servers, as well as staff for "The Chariot," "The Chair," and "The Chariot House," evidently equerries and attendants for the governor, as also attested at Susa.[12]

The governor, as befit an Akkadian notable, received a wardrobe appropriate to his exalted rank, including the toga and large gold medallion that came into fashion during the reign of Naram-Sin. He enjoyed the superior food of court life and the right to ride in a wheeled vehicle driven by a team. His responsibilities brought him into contact with the king and queen, lords and princes of the realm, as well as with the priestesses of the moon-god, whose sanctuary stood not far away. Perhaps he too was a member of the royal family.[13]

A yearly account from this establishment for barley, emmer, oils, fats, and other raw and finished goods itemized more than 23 hectoliters of barley, 100 kilograms of sheep's wool, 330 kilograms of goat hair, and an assortment of tools and utensils, presumably all positive balances and indicative of the wealth processed through Akkadian administrative headquarters of this kind.[14]

### Eshnunna/Tell Asmar

Although Eshnunna was one of the principal cities of northern Babylonia, little is known of its history in the pre-Akkadian period. A major Akkadian building, situated in the northwest corner of the city, essentially combined two large pre-existing dwellings and a smaller courtyard house into an irregularly shaped structure approximately seventy meters long and thirty meters wide (Figure 3.1). It

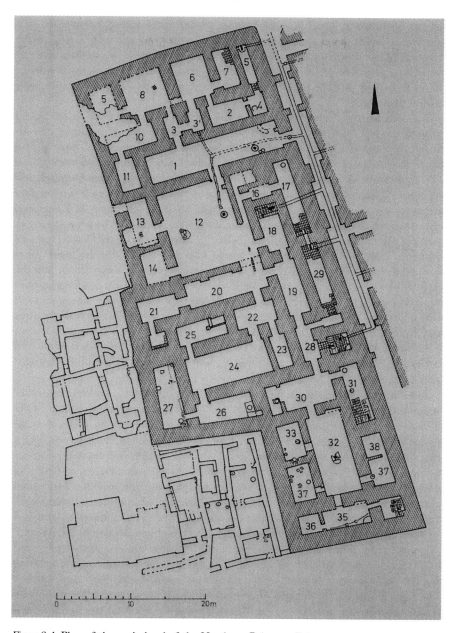

*Figure 3.1* Plan of the main level of the Northern Palace at Eshnunna.

thus has the somewhat haphazard quality that may have been typical of early Akkadian administrative structures. Its northwest location parallels that of other Akkadian buildings, such as the palaces at Tutub and Tell el-Wilayah and the temple of Ishtar at Assur. The excavators offered three interpretations for it: a residential palace for a prince; a center for industrial production, owing to the presence of six toilets and five bathrooms in the eastern side of the structure, far more than would be expected for strictly residential use; and third, the residence of an Akkadian notable family who built up wealth and urban real estate over several generations.[15]

The Akkadian tablets discovered in the northern courtyard of this building strongly suggest, however, that it was in fact an administrative center of considerable importance (Map 2), probably to be dated to the reigns of Sargon and Rimush, with a later phase in the reign of Naram-Sin.[16] The records correspond well to those of Akkadian administrative centers from other sites. Although few accounts of apportioning arable land survive in this group,[17] there is a letter that mentions several large parcels, including areas of 38.9, 19.5, and 32.4 hectares, one of which was held by the majordomo, then asks, "Why does he keep writing to me? We will not enter into a one-third lease."[18] This may refer to a lease type well known in later periods in which the tenant took two-thirds and the owner one-third of the yield. A group of records involving land payments may mean that the household was aggressively expanding its urban and agricultural holdings by buying land from private owners,[19] but because these purchases were not witnessed, as was normal for transactions in which transfer of ownership took place, they may instead involve leases of land for cash payments, which is a practice known from other Akkadian administrative centers. As at Mesag's Sumerian estate and at Gasur (see later discussion, this chapter), arable land was divided into standard plow units assigned to plow teams.[20]

Accounts of grain include distribution of grain rations to workers and other household personnel, not an activity to be expected in a private dwelling.[21] One of these is a monthly account of grain rations distributed to at least 105 male and 585 female workers. A few professional people appear in this list, including a joiner, server of food, textile worker, brewer, donkey herder, and the majordomo.[22] According to other records, barley was shipped to Agade and used to feed oxen and seed fields. Some grain was turned over to merchants, who collected substantial quantities from prominent men and women, perhaps for commercial purposes.[23] Barley was grown on household domains and delivered by cultivators, who had quotas to meet.[24] There was a tax on barley yields, perhaps payable to the crown.[25]

In contrast to other Akkadian archives, there are almost no records of prepared foods, such as flour and bread, or of brewing ingredients and beer, suggesting that the records for these were kept in a separate location and have disappeared.[26] The same is true for the records of personnel, which are often the largest portion of an Akkadian archive, but are strikingly rare among the tablets found here.[27] As at Umma and other centers (see part 3, this chapter), however, Eshnunna had a special bureau that maintained records for the acquisition and distribution of oils and aromatics, some distributed to women, some purchased, and others for miscellaneous purposes. A label was found for a basket of tablets accounting for a year's worth of oil rations.[28]

The center disposed of considerable livestock of sheep and goats; one account includes more than 2000 goats, another more than 1200 sheep.[29] As seen elsewhere, losses were accounted for by the presentation of hides, and some animals were culled to fatten for offerings and human consumption.[30] Records of wool show that some of it was bought and sold for silver.[31] Donkeys and oxen, often in large numbers, were used as beasts of burden and for plowing.[32] Their hides likewise had to be produced to prove natural loss,[33] or were sometimes purchased, presumably for leather working (Chapter 5 part 8).[34]

Silver was used for acquiring goods the center needed, but there are no accounts for precious objects, tools, furniture, and the like, so these tablets too must have been stored elsewhere.[35] In one record, silver was given to a man "for Subartu," but for what purpose is not clear, perhaps the purchase of slaves.[36]

In sum, the records from Eshnunna reveal a large and complex agricultural operation involving hundreds of hectares, teams of professional plowmen, hundreds of draught animals, and thousands of sheep and goats. Mention of the governor, the majordomo, shipment of grain to Agade, transactions involving Uruk and other distant places, the very large quantities accounted for, the presence of trading agents, and the records of juridical proceedings all point to an administrative center of importance, perhaps under the control of an Akkadian governor, who may have been a member of the royal family.[37]

There was a workforce of nearly 700 workers, in which women outnumbered men more than five to one. The number of workers may have been maintained or increased by occasional purchases of both male and female slaves for silver.[38] It was this disproportionate number of women, together with the unusual number of sanitary facilities in the building complex, which led to the proposal that it was an industrial center, perhaps for weaving, but no archaeological evidence for weaving was recovered. Furthermore, some of the rooms contained such items as fine combs and costly pieces of jewelry, which no doubt belonged to an Akkadian elite occupying part of the building, rather than to industrial workers.

A few tablets having to do with the administration of the temple of Tishpak, the major local deity, have turned up on the antiquities market; the location of the temple is unidentified. Two of them are witnessed records of boys and girls quitting their families to enter temple service or, in the case of some of the girls, to learn singing in the temple conservatory (Chapter 9 part 8; Figure 1.8).[39]

Akkadian, the language of record keeping, was the native language of this region, as shown by the names in the documents. Sumerian names are extremely rare; Hurrian names do not occur. Reduplicated names, such as Dababa, are common, much more so than in Sumer (Chapter 2 part 1).

## Kish/Ingharra/Uhaimir

Kish may have provided the model for Akkadian expansion and government, but Akkadian remains at the site are scanty. According to Mesopotamian historical tradition, Kish was the seat of a very ancient dynasty that ruled before the Flood, as well as of Etana, the first king to have ruled after the Flood, and the hero of a later Babylonian narrative poem. During the Early Dynastic period, Kish acquired hegemony over various Babylonian and Sumerian centers, at least as far south as Nippur and as far east as Assur. The king of Kish mediated a boundary dispute between Umma and Lagash in the pre-Akkadian period. Early Dynastic kings of Uruk and Ur were proud to claim the title "king of Kish," which could also be interpreted to mean "king of the world." Sargon, Rimush, and Manish-tusu used this as their royal title.[40]

According to a later Sumerian poem and *The Sumerian King List*, Sargon, before he became king, had served as cupbearer to the king of Kish (Chapter 1 part 1). In another later work of literature (Chapter 11 part 6), Naram-Sin claims that Sargon freed Kish from servitude. Sargon himself commemorated that he carried out a building project at Kish: "Sargon, king of the land, changed the two places of Kish, he made them occupied as one city."[41] The meaning of this is obscure, but since the site of Kish today consists of several mounds, Sargon may refer to enclosing two settlements into one city. In the post-Akkadian period, Kish had two ziggurats. A wall around them both may originally have been built in the Akkadian period, as suggested by the discovery of an Akkadian administrative document associated with it.[42] But the citizenry proved ungrateful for the benefits of Akkadian rule. Kish, along with Uruk, was a leader in the revolt against Naram-Sin. While he claims to have destroyed the city (Chapter 1 part 4), it was occupied till the end of Akkadian rule, as shown by a seal impression of a servant of Shu-Durul, last king of the dynasty, from an unknown context.[43]

Akkadian documents from Kish show that it was an administrative center disposing of major resources. A record of ten parcels of land totaling about 1127 hectares suggests a domain about one-third the size of the total parcels purchased by Manishtusu near Marad, about fifty kilometers south of Kish, thus in keeping with other extensive royal holdings in the region.[44] Perhaps this and a related document were likewise records of a royal purchase, which might explain a list of "lords" who "will receive barley" valued in silver, since "lords" was the term used in the Manishtusu purchase for certain of the original land owners who sold their interests.[45] A comparable purchase was concluded in Agade, rather than locally, it too suggesting absentee ownership.[46] At nearby Mugdan (see next section), the *shaperum* and a subordinate of the queen held parcels totaling 658 hectares. All this evidence shows that Akkadian notables acquired arable land in the region by purchase or grant, as they did at Eshnunna. The reason for purchasing or holding so much land was to lease it out profitably or to distribute it as patronage. Miscellaneous Kish records of grain and silver may be income to landlords from leased parcels.[47]

Records of workers in various locations also imply the existence of a large Akkadian establishment levying men from surrounding villages, as at Nagar, and disposing of teams of well over a hundred workers.[48] Letters and accounts refer to people who have fled, implying involuntary servitude or harsh living and working conditions for dependent personnel.[49] Accounts of prepared foods, sheep, goats, and oxen round out the dossier,[50] along with letters and learners' exercises (Chapter 10 part 2). Since the find spots of the Kish tablets are mostly unknown, it is not possible to regroup them in time or space.

### *Mugdan/Umm el-Jir*

This Akkadian town, located about twenty-seven kilometers northeast of Kish, was evidently the seat of a manor that dominated the local countryside. The excavated architectural remains of a substantial structure suggest that it was built in the pre-Akkadian period, occupied in the early Akkadian period, then rebuilt on a more regular plan in the later Akkadian period.[51] The levels were also datable through the presence of distinctive gray pottery, more typical of Akkad and further north than of Sumer, as well as cylinder seals. Cuneiform tablets include one dated with a year name of Naram-Sin, but they were found by illicit diggers so cannot be correlated with any of the excavated structures.

This manor belonged to members of the royal family or royal household, as shown by the mention of areas controlled by the king and of an official who served the queen, but it was evidently managed by a governor (*ensi*). Other local officials included the *shaperum* (majordomo) and a captain in command of a detachment of soldiers stationed there. Some high officials redistributed land they held to retainers or lessees in small, precisely measured plots. Unlike in Sumer, where land was distributed by a cadaster official, in Mugdan the governor was actively concerned in granting and taking back parcels of land. This regional difference might underlie the development of the word ensi/*iššiakkum* in second-millennium Akkadian, where it came to mean a tenant farmer holding royal land or a royal official concerned with land, rather than a governor.[52]

Of some fifty documents from the site, a summary report accounts for 396.9 hectares directly administered by the household, for the use of solders, craftsmen, and a local administrator. In another document, 645.6 hectares of land were assigned to various people, including high officials, presumably of regional importance. Some land was referred to as "the king's plow." Totaling the information in these records yields a manor of about 1042 hectares, a figure that may be compared to the putative 2200 hectares controlled by the very large, pre-Akkadian establishment at nearby Jamdat Nasr and the 3430 hectares purchased by Manishtusu in the same region.[53]

The manor derived its wealth either from direct exploitation of its land by the manor staff or from leasing out the rest. Cultivation of its own fields was done by plow teams who were responsible for standardized units of land called "plows." The main crops were barley, emmer, and legumes. From leasing, the manor received payments in grain, silver, and products of commercial value. The income was sufficiently great for the governor to be credited in one year with about 2856 hectoliters of barley and emmer from five fields, more than forty-seven times the price of a good-sized house of 70.5 square meters.[54]

Grain raised on the manor was also given as food rations to its inhabitants, including a "regular" ration measured by the royal standard. This reflects the dependence of the household on the crown, since other amounts were issued using a different standard, suggesting both a crown and a local accountability. Grain that belonged to the manor could also be loaned at interest and used to feed livestock.

The geographical horizon of the local administrative records embraced Kish and Cutha, and included seventeen smaller localities in the more immediate neighborhood, some of which, at least, were administratively dependent upon Mugdan.[55] The names of these places were generally neither Akkadian nor Semitic, allowing the supposition that this region had once been occupied by a non-Semitic people who had disappeared. The local language of record keeping and of name-giving was Akkadian. Sumerian names are very rare, and Hurrian names do not occur.

## Agade

The location of Agade is unknown.[56] In Chapter 2 part 1, it was suggested that the city lay near the confluence of the Diyala and Tigris rivers, or further north near Samarra or the Adheim River, that it was founded not long before the Akkadian period, and that Sargon made it his capital. Important monuments included the temple of Ishtar, called Eulmash (possibly depicted on a mold for gold work, Figure 9.8), and the royal palace complex. By the end of the third millennium, the city may have been abandoned. In the early nineteenth century BCE, Shamshi-Adad, ruler of the Kingdom of Upper Mesopotamia, visited the site and wrote letters "from Agade." In the same period, a group of musicians was kidnapped while passing through, implying a lawless place. Hammurabi still considered it a former capital or crossroads city.[57] Kings of the later second and first millennia explored the site and even carried out archaeological excavations hoping to find the foundations of the temple of Ishtar (Chapter 11 part 7). This was rebuilt in the reign of Esarhaddon of Assyria (mid-seventh century BCE) in connection with his restoration of ancient Babylonian religious centers and the return of cult statues that had been taken to Elam. The cult of Ishtar of Agade was maintained into the Persian period; there were people living at Agade as late as the reign of Darius the Great (early fifth century BCE).[58]

## The Himrin Basin

Continuing up the Diyala River, east of the Himrin, the traveler enters a basin referred to in Mesopotamian literature as the "latchkey of the land," for its strategic position as an entry point to and from the Iranian plateau.[59] In pre-modern times, the basin had a mixed economy of herding, cultivation, and fishing. One ancient route followed the left bank of the Diyala, went through the pass of the Himrin, then traversed the basin to modern Khaniqin and on to modern Kermanshah. A second major route went from Susa along the foothills, crossed the other road and the Diyala near modern Jalawla, and continued north toward Gasur, whence roads branched to Assur and Nineveh.[60] The interior of the basin was to some extent isolated by extensive marshes, especially east of the Narin River. Since the main roads tended to avoid the low-lying cultivated areas, local society and subsistence were generally unaffected by political developments outside the basin, except for the imposition of police posts. These were set up by powerful states to keep the routes secure from banditry and to gather intelligence about activity in the mountains, which usually lay beyond the control of any lowland authority.[61]

During the Akkadian period, this region became part of the Empire. Salvage excavations, undertaken ahead of the flooding of the area by a dam project, uncovered Akkadian remains at the north end of the basin, at Uch-tepe, and toward the south end of it, at Awalʾ/Suleimeh. At Uch-tepe, Akkadian burials were found, but no architecture or documents of the period.[62] A pre-Akkadian monumental building there suggests that the evident Akkadian effort to control and exploit this region may not have been the first of its kind. Several other sites, not fully explored, held the possibility of Akkadian material. One was Tepe al-Atiqeh, which may have been a large manor house. Near Awalʾ/Suleimeh was a place called "Fortress."[63] The ancient landscape may therefore have been dotted by the fortified manors of local notables. The Akkadians imposed outside control, bringing with them cuneiform writing, perhaps for the first time, as well as the use of Agade metrology and a small Akkadian elite of administrators and soldiers.[64] There is no evidence for the carving out of estates for Akkadian notables or the royal family, as in Babylonia or Sumer.

Awalʾ/Suleimeh[65] yielded Akkadian tablets, resembling those from Gasur, which could well date to the reign of Naram-Sin. They were found in one of a series of houses opening onto a narrow alleyway, not the thick-walled, courtyard-planned Akkadian administrative structure as known from other sites.[66] The tablets were lying on the floor of a room next to a substantial niched platform, which the excavators understood to be an altar.[67] Along with the tablets were at least two Classical Akkadian cylinder seals with combat scenes, of a type used by high-level Akkadian officials.[68] Although this is the only instance of Akkadian tablets found together with cylinder seals, it was probably a secondary context. This raises the possibility that some seals were kept with documents rather than worn pinned to garments (Chapter 9 part 3). As at Gasur and Eshnunna, the tablets appear to have been thrown out of their baskets onto the floor of the room. There is nothing to suggest deliberate sorting and retention from a larger group that was abandoned or discarded, as is sometimes the case with other tablet archives of later periods.

The records evidently pertain to the operations of an administrative center for animal husbandry and agriculture extending to some forty settlements in the surrounding area.[69] Awalʾ/Suleimeh was apparently the seat of an Akkadian governor, who, along with an untitled notable and a scribe, held, in one recorded village, for example, 13, 2.8, and 1.8 hectares of arable land, respectively, comparable to holdings in Sumer, where roughly half the attested accountable parcels ranged between 2 and 35 hectares.[70] Most of the Awalʾ/Suleimeh documents have to do with modest quantities of barley and workmen, some of whom were cultivators (sag-apin). The manor included seventy-two rationed personnel – twenty-three men, thirty-four women, eleven boys, and four girls, as well as fifty-eight draught animals, both oxen and donkeys. The larger number of women than men is paralleled in other Akkadian administrative centers, such as the Northern Palace at Eshnunna, where women outnumbered men more than five to one. This was not always the case; in the Mesag estate in Sumer, by contrast, men outnumbered women nearly four to one.[71]

As in more recent times, some Akkadian Himrin settlements were primarily pastoral in nature. Texts record the valuation or purchase of livestock for grain, for which few parallels can be found from Babylonia itself. At a place called Badali, for example, nineteen sheep, two goats, and nine pigs were recorded "for the value" of fifteen gur of grain, plus sixteen gur of grain, for a total of thirty-one gur reckoned.[72] This may mean that the assortment of animals was worth that much grain; if so, animals were cheap compared to grain.[73] This fits well the modern situation of the region, which lies outside the rainfall agricultural zone and where only limited irrigation is possible, so agriculture is challenging compared to husbandry.[74] Another Akkadian record lists small flocks of ewes, in thirteen localities, for a total of 192 ewes and 1 goat, called "sheep of the barley of the obligation," an obscure expression that occurs several times in the text group.[75] While this could refer to leasing of land parcels that entailed giving an animal as part of the rent, plus a portion of the harvest paid in kind, it is more likely that the texts show that villages had rendered animals from their herds as taxes, as at Nagar.[76] If so, this dossier of tablets consisted largely of receipts for grain and livestock payments due from parcel holders or as taxation, received at the manor itself or in the villages, with an unusual local custom of substituting livestock for grain amounts due.

As at other Akkadian centers such as Eshnunna, managers may have expanded their holdings by acquisitions. One document lists five such purchases, presumably all by the same person, of small parcels in exchange for silver and livestock.[77] Though there are only forty-seven tablets in the dossier, the variety of professional activity attested at Awal?/Suleimeh is impressive. Besides the governor, scribe, plowmen, and cultivators, there is mention of producers, such as the poultry man or bird catcher, fisherman, and gardener or orchardist; craftsmen, such as the carpenter, seal engraver, and brewer; people in service capacities, such as the launderer; specific social statuses, such as the elder and priest; military personnel, including the officer and foot soldier; and merchants. On the other hand, there are no officials suggestive of a court, for instance the courier, chair-bearer, or hairdresser.

Awal?/Suleimeh was therefore a low-level center dedicated to revenue-gathering from the local population, rather than a seat for extensive local direct exploitation, as seen on the lower Diyala, in Babylonia, and in Sumer. The language spoken in the Himrin Basin was Akkadian, to judge from the inventory of names, which resemble those of the lower Diyala basin. Sumerian names are extremely rare, and Hurrian names do not occur. There are also numerous reduplicated names (Chapter 2 part 1).[78] Akkadian was also the language of record keeping.

The Akkadian conquest of this region may be commemorated in a poem ascribed to Enheduanna, *Inanna and Ebih* (Appendix IIc). Ebih was evidently the Akkadian name for the Jebel Himrin, a mountain chain east of the Tigris and south of the Lower Zab, a prominent feature that the poem describes as forested and as a dwelling place of the gods. According to the poem, Enlil, rather than An, gave his consent to Inanna/Ishtar and an unnamed king to conquer the mountain when it refused to do homage to her, even after she had conquered Elam, Subir, and Lullubum, all of which were part of the Akkadian Empire by the reign of Naram-Sin.

## Assur

Located on a promontory on the west bank of the Tigris and surrounded by a small agricultural hinterland, Assur was an early cult center and a strategic intersection of north-south and east-west routes.[79] A mace head inscribed with the name of Rimush and a spear point found in the area of the Ishtar Temple, dedicated by a servant of Manishtusu, suggest that Assur was among Sargon's conquests and later ruled by his two sons. An uninscribed, beheaded statue found at Assur has generally been dated to the early Akkadian period, and could, on the basis of its costume and beard, represent Manishtusu or a notable of his time, such as Ititi (Figure 5.5).[80]

A monumental building, like the one at Nagar (part 5, this chapter), square in plan, but even larger (ca. 11,000 square meters), with a main courtyard and several subsidiary courtyards and halls, may have been constructed or renovated in the Akkadian period. A tablet, reputedly of Akkadian date, has sometimes been used as a dating criterion, but its association with the building is not clear and the tablet has not been published.[81] Various other Akkadian administrative documents and school texts have turned up at the site, but these too are incompletely published.[82]

Assur was not listed among the rebel cities in the inscriptions and later legends about the Great Revolt against Naram-Sin, so this region may have remained loyal to Akkadian rule. A governor of Assur, with the Akkadian name of Ilaba-andul, is mentioned in a fragmentary list found at Ur, and the title (*ensi*) was later used by Assyrian kings, perhaps parallel to the use of the Akkadian title *shakkanakku* at post-Akkadian Mari.[83] An inscription of Ititi, an early ruler in Assur, might be dated to the Akkadian period; it gives him the title "representative" or "overseer" (*waklum*), an office that may have had a priestly connotation. He may also have ruled at Mari with the title *shakkanakku*.[84]

The main importance of Assur at this time may have been as a religious and mercantile center.[85] Assur was well situated for receiving materials and commodities from Iran and further east, for which there was considerable demand in the Akkadian period. Indeed, Assur's rise to prominence as a commercial city could well have begun under the Akkadian kings, for their conquests opened new opportunities for Assyrian traders in Syria, northern Mesopotamia, and southern Anatolia. Naram-Sin mentions merchants in connection with his campaign to Subartu and Talmush, possibly located about forty kilometers north of present-day Mosul on the Khosr River, so Assyria may have developed its commercial network during his reign.[86]

According to a poem attributed to Enheduanna (Appendix IIc), Inanna/Ishtar conquered Ebih, the Jebel Himrin east of the Tigris, and built her temple there (above, Himrin Basin). If this refers to historical events of the Akkadian period, the cult of the Akkadian Ishtar may have been introduced to Assur and the Trans-Tigridian region at this time. This innovation would correspond well to the lowest levels (G, GF) of the temple of Ishtar at Assur, variously dated to the pre- or early Akkadian periods (Chapter 6 part 4). Like the Akkadian buildings at Eshnunna, Tutub, and Tell al-Wilayah, the Ishtar Temple was constructed at the northwest corner of the city, on the cleared remains of earlier buildings.[87]

### Nineveh

No architecture or inscriptions from the Akkadian period have been identified at Nineveh, nor is the city mentioned in any Akkadian administrative document or inscription. The copper head usually considered to represent an Akkadian ruler was brought there in the Neo-Assyrian period.[88] The city was the site of a temple dating back to remote antiquity, dedicated to the goddess called Ishtar of Nineveh, so it would be reasonable to expect Akkadian phases of construction there, but this remains unsubstantiated.[89] Traces of what might be an Akkadian burial were found under the southwestern court of the temple built in the early second millennium by Shamshi-Adad, king of Upper Mesopotamia.[90] In his building inscription, Shamshi-Adad refers to a previous project of Manishtusu, making the following claim, in the form of an oath reminiscent of the oaths typical of the inscriptions of Manishtusu himself and perhaps in response to the curses at the end of them: "(On my oath): The monuments and foundation deposits of Manishtusu, I did not remove them but I restored them to their places. I did indeed place [my own monuments and foundation deposits] alongside his monuments and foundation deposits."[91]

### Tepe Gawra

Akkadian Tepe Gawra (ancient name unknown, excavation Level VI) was a cluster of houses built on a hillside and grouped around a large central square, twenty-eight by seventeen meters in extent. The rear doors of these houses opened onto narrow paved streets on the hillside. Unlike Akkadian architecture further south, most of the houses have foundations of local stone. The town was surrounded by a fortification wall pierced by two gates to the south and east. North of the east gate apparently stood a stone tower on masonry walls eighty-five centimeters thick. There were no tablets or inscriptions and no signs of an Akkadian administrative presence. Seals and other finds suggest that this settlement dates to the transition into the early Akkadian period. Its numerous copper tools and implements were also of types typical of that time and, like most Akkadian tools and weapons, were made without tin (Chapter 5 part 3). Gawra gives the impression of a small but prosperous rural community. At some point during the early Akkadian period, an unknown dramatic event obliged the residents to quit their homes, leaving most of the contents behind.[92]

## *Gasur/Yorghan Tepe*

Located on a major road connecting Babylonia to Assyria, Gasur was the center of an Akkadian estate, managed by a land registrar named Zuzu, and perhaps held by a member of the royal family. More than 200 tablets and fragments were excavated, all in secondary context, as they had been discarded in antiquity. None of the tablets is dated by an Akkadian year name, but on the basis of their shape and style of writing, they may be assigned to the first half of the reign of Naram-Sin. Because they belong together as a single group of related documents, they invite quantitative and geographical analysis (Map 2). Some record distributions of parcels of land averaging 9.2 hectares, smaller than the average for Akkadian Sumer as a whole but comparable to the 9.8 hectare average for people without titles on Mesag's Sumerian estate.[93] Twenty-two percent of the parcels recorded were smaller than 2.11 hectares (6 iku), 3 percent larger than 35.28 hectares (100 iku), the rest in between.

Three principal groups of people appear in the records, listed here in descending order of status. First were administrators who received prepared foods and special rations from the estate, many of whom had titles, and some of whom had access to lucrative management opportunities. Surprisingly, when compared to their counterparts in Sumer with important areas of land, few of these upper-echelon people at Gasur were recorded as landholders. They were, however, often parties to grain transactions. Second were land users, responsible for fairly large tracts, for which seed grain was provided and from which threshed grain was delivered after certain deductions were made. Some of the land users may not have been personnel of the estate but local citizens who leased parcels from it. The records show how much land they held, how much seed and cultivation expenses they were entitled to, and how much grain they delivered to meet the terms of their contracts.[94] Third was the largest group attested in the surviving records. These people were recipients of raw rations, so had no direct access to the lands of the estate or its produce, but were hired or maintained by the estate in return for their labor.

Gasur had connections with other Akkadian centers both north and south (Map 2 and part 6, this chapter).

## 3. Sumer

### *Nippur*

Little architecture of the Akkadian period survives at Nippur. The Ekur, the temple of Enlil, was extensively rebuilt in post-Akkadian times, as was the temple of Inanna, obliterating their Akkadian phases. A deep sounding undertaken to clarify the transitions at the beginning and end of the Akkadian period has enhanced understanding of those ceramic sequences. A few documents were found as well.[95] The main groups of tablets from Akkadian Nippur, found elsewhere on the mound, are the records of the reconstruction of Ekur by Naram-Sin and Sharkalisharri; the records of an office concerned with regional management of onions from the time of Sharkalisharri; about 150 ration lists from the time of Naram-Sin; and the private records of the Enlile-maba family (Chapter 8 part 5).[96]

Like other Akkadian centers, Nippur had an Akkadian governor, under whose purview the regional onion office may have fallen and to whose administration the Akkadian ration lists might pertain. In one instance, a governor served simultaneously as chief administrator (*sanga*) of the temple of Enlil; in another, the temple administrator was separate, but in any case a royal appointee.[97]

None of this gives much indication of the extraordinary importance of this city as a religious center in the Akkadian period. Some, at least, of the Akkadian kings were crowned there. Sargon and his descendants set up their commemorative inscriptions in the Ekur stating that Enlil, chief god of the land, had favored their conquests. These were still present nearly 500 years later (Chapter 11 part 3) for historically minded scribes to study and copy as the earliest inscriptions known to them. Works of Sumerian literature stressed Nippur's moral and cultic supremacy, especially a long, flowery hymn praising Enlil, his city and his principal sanctuary (Chapter 7 part 1).[98] *The Curse of Agade* was likewise popular in the Sumerian schools of Nippur, showing that the Akkadian era was seen as a dramatic episode in the history of the city.

 The Gutian kings of post-Akkadian Nippur followed the Akkadian example of erecting elaborate monuments in Ekur. Their successors, the kings of Ur, accorded Nippur no less importance as a religious center. But they promoted Uruk, long a leader in resistance to Akkadian rule, as the font of their ancient Sumerian lineage and patronized Sumerian literature focusing on the legendary kings of Uruk and their deeds. Yet even as they made no overt reference to the Akkadians and despised the Gutians, the kings of Ur incorporated Naram-Sin's reforms into their administration, imitated his personality cult, and married princesses with Akkadian names (Chapter 11 part 8).[99] Throughout, Nippur occupied a unique position in both Akkadian and Sumerian religious thought.

### Adab/Tell Bismaya

Adab was an Akkadian administrative center of major importance throughout the Akkadian period, perhaps one of the largest cities in the region, with extensive connections elsewhere (Map 2). One of the principal sanctuaries was the Emah, a temple to the Sumerian birth goddess. The finds included an object made of thin gold foil, whose dedicatory inscription honored Naram-Sin.[100] The site has also yielded nearly 3000 Akkadian administrative documents through unscientific excavation and looting, but limited architectural evidence.[101] The principal administrative building was apparently located in the western portion of the city, on an elevation now referred to as Mound IV. This must have been the governor's palace, as a large group of Akkadian records was found there in early excavations, as well as a brick stamp of Naram-Sin. Many of these tablets are still unpublished.

Looters have turned up hundreds more belonging to the same period and, in some cases, to the same record groups; these have been scattered on the antiquities trade but published rapidly.[102]

The documents show the manifold concerns of the Akkadian governor's office. One of his tasks was the management of arable land. In this capacity, he received various letters and petitions, one of which addresses him in flowery terms as follows: "To the yoke of the land, beloved of the birth goddess, beloved of the god Ashgi, to the [servant? of] Sharkalisharri … I have no land with irrigation water, may (my lord) give me whatever land with irrigation water (he sees fit)."[103] As at Umma and Lagash, areas of land, often extending in long rectangles from an irrigation ditch, were measured off to men in the Akkadian patronage network, some of it for rental, some of it for subsistence. These ranged in size from about 880 square meters to more than 127 hectares, with 30 percent of the attested parcels smaller than 2.11 hectares (6 iku) and 16 percent larger than 35.28 hectares (100 iku), generally larger than the parcels at Gasur (above, part 2). To judge from the twelve-hectare tenant farms (Chapter 4 part 1) typical of the Diyala region in the early twentieth century, these grants ranged from subsistence size to areas many times that. Tenants delivered a portion of the harvest and, in some cases, a payment in cash.[104] One record shows that the canals were maintained by assigning sections of about 300 meters each, presumably to tenants of the adjoining fields.[105] There seem to have been various fees for using irrigation water, and also taxes on the crop, above and beyond the division of the harvest.[106]

The field and garden crops are noteworthy for their variety, including several kinds of barley and emmer, as well as sesame, radish, cassia, turnips, leeks, pulses, coriander, and dates.[107] Processed food production is well attested, especially different types and grades of flour, bread, and beer. These and other foods, such as fish, were distributed to sanctuaries and travelers, as well as to the governor himself and his staff.[108]

The records of sheep concern only those few given to individuals and offered to the gods.[109] Pigs were kept in considerable numbers and were slaughtered to provide meals for visiting dignitaries.[110] Both oxen and donkeys were used for field work.[111] As at Umma and Eshnunna, there was a special office for the management and distribution of oils and fats for personal use by soldiers, singers, prisoners, and others, as well as for industrial purposes, such as metal-working and treating textiles and leather.[112]

The records from the governor's archives show that his management responsibilities encompassed not only the lands, flocks, and materiel that came under his authority, but also obligations for supporting the city cult with regular deliveries of prepared food from the governor's kitchens and brewery. He was also expected to provide for travelers on official business, prisoners of war, diplomatic missions, and other transients.[113]

The records from nearby Mound III suggest that local notables maintained business relationships with the governor's establishment. Sometimes referred to, using Banks's term, as the "Semitic Quarter," this might have been a neighborhood of elite Akkadians, since the documents from this area contain a higher percentage of Akkadian names than seen elsewhere at Adab. One resident, Bizaza, provided fodder for oxen and rations for their herdsmen on a regional basis, so he may have been a herd master (Chapter 4 part 3). Another, Puzur-Ishtar, worked as the land agent for Ishkun-Dagan, an Akkadian notable who was perhaps the majordomo of the Akkadian queen. Based on his letters and a few other records, a certain Me-zi was also involved in the management of land and personnel.[114]

### Tell el-Wilayah (ancient name unknown)

Toward the northwest corner of this site, the remains of a large Akkadian building were found, the excavated part of which uncovered twenty-two rooms. The outer walls of this structure averaged a meter thick and were further protected by a fortification wall with towers (Figure 3.2). In one place, traces of a wooden column indicate a roofed hall or court. Since it was originally constructed of plano-convex

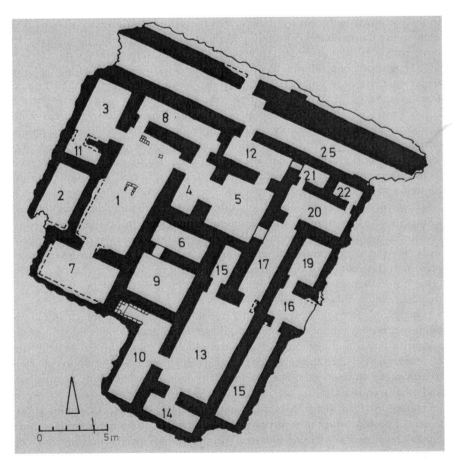

*Figure 3.2* Plan of the fortified palace at Tell el-Wilayah.

bricks, the excavator proposed a date in the late pre-Akkadian or early Akkadian period. The contents of the building indicate the latter, for they comprise Akkadian pottery, seals (a distinctive group of which, made of unidentified black stone, was found in one room), administrative documents, and an assortment of weights, tools, and weapons, as well as a female figurine the excavators thought was made of evergreen wood but is more likely ivory (Chapter 5 part 10). As at Nagar, two of the rooms contained burned grain.[115] Later salvage excavations at the site did not reopen this part of the mound, and most of the results were lost with the pillage of the Iraq Museum. Beginning in the 1990s and especially after 2003, the site was massively looted, and the finds, including Akkadian administrative documents, have been scattered through the antiquities trade.[116]

This site has sometimes been identified with Kesh, site of the principal sanctuary to the birth goddess in the Early Dynastic period. This identification remains uncertain. The priest of Kesh is known to have sold land to the governor of Adab, and one of the major sanctuaries at Adab, the Emah, was presumably a sanctuary of the birth goddess, so Adab may have gradually usurped the position of Kesh as the leading center for worship of this deity.[117]

## Umma (Tell Djokha)

All Akkadian-period tablets from Umma were found by looters, so nothing is known of their archaeological context. No Akkadian remains have been identified in the limited salvage operations carried out there, which focused on a monumental building of Ur III date. The major groups of documents from the site are those of the Akkadian governors during the reigns of Naram-Sin and Sharkalisharri.[118]

The accounts of distribution of parcels of land are comparable to those from Adab, though more numerous. Analysis of one closely dated group of thirty-one distributions shows that 32 percent of them were smaller than 2.11 hectares (6 iku) and only 3 percent larger than 35.28 hectares (100 iku), though much larger distributions are recorded in other Umma documents that do not belong to this group. The largest parcel recorded was held by Yetib-Mer, the majordomo (*šaperum*) of Naram-Sin, who had land near Umma totaling 444.5 hectares, more than 200 times larger than the plots typically found in these records. Cultic personnel held a lot of 31.8 hectares (one case); administrative, supervisory, and court personnel held lots averaging 5 hectares (seven cases); professional people 1.5 hectares (five cases), and people without titles held parcels averaging 3.3 hectares (fifty-one cases).

Some of these lots were assigned to retainers, administrators, and other members of the ruling establishment. Some of them were held by the governor by virtue of his office and gave him important patronage power. Still others were held by temples, but it appears that the governor provided land for leading members of the temple staff. Some land was leased for a percentage of the crop or for a combined cash payment and part of the crop. Surveyors were responsible for identifying the size and agricultural condition of the assigned parcels. In certain cases, the tenants on institutionally owned land worked the plots themselves. In the case of lands assigned to officials and managers, they were evidently worked by professional cultivators who kept records of their expenses for feed and seed and of the accountable portion of the harvest.[119]

The principal administrative building at Umma was called the "Scepter House" (Egidri). This was the seat of the governor, who took responsibility for the accuracy of the accounts, whose monthly summaries were drawn up from individual vouchers issued in his name and laid out in neat, four-column tablets, dated to his term of office, unusual for the Akkadian period. This building contained extensive documentation for the management of land, cereal crops, personnel and ration lists; for the preparation of bread and beer from cereal crops; for the herding of livestock (sheep, goats, donkeys, and oxen); and for manufacturing metal, wood, ceramic, and textile goods. As at Eshnunna and Adab, there was a separate oil office that kept accounts of various kinds of oils, aromatics, and fats. The Scepter House also contained a dossier of the governor's correspondence and some interesting records of the ceremonies, gifts, and entertainment in connection with a royal visit, perhaps when Sharkalisharri passed through on the way to or from Nippur for his coronation.[120]

A significant family archive from Umma documents the activities of a married couple, Ur-Shara and Ama-e, and their small group of associates. Ur-Shara worked as a herd master, overseeing livestock that perhaps belonged to different owners. Ama-e managed land, grain, wool, and metal. Their enterprises were complementary, as they do not appear in the same transactions. The twenty-five-year span of their activity suggests that they were successful and well connected on the local scene, though they seem to have had no direct interaction with Akkadian notables. One may therefore suggest that they were an established Ummaite family who prospered under Akkadian rule.[121]

Documents from Akkadian Susa show that families from Umma lived there and participated in long-distance trade using Susa as a base. From this and other evidence, it is plain that Umma was an important commercial center in the Akkadian and post-Akkadian periods.[122]

### Girsu/Telloh

Although no Akkadian architecture was recovered at Girsu, the principal city of the former city-state of Lagash, considerable finds of pottery, seals, seal impressions, metal work, and other artifacts have been dated to the Akkadian period by the excavators or subsequent researchers. The main Akkadian evidence consists of more than 3800 administrative documents, which were mostly dug up by illegal diggers and scattered among numerous museums and private collections. This was part of the largest find of third-millennium tablets ever made, many of which were still in their original magazines at the time of discovery, sorted into three sizes: small vouchers, medium records and accounts, and large combined ledgers. These tablets demonstrate that Girsu was one of the most important centers of Akkadian authority in Sumer, perhaps the capital of a newly created province embracing several former city-states (Map 2).[123]

The governor of Girsu was therefore an Akkadian notable of the highest rank. His palace may have lain slightly apart from the city, surrounded by gardens, and, to judge from Akkadian buildings elsewhere, a massive wall. An approximative typological analysis of the governor's archive shows that 4 percent of the records deal with land; 6 percent with grain; 29 percent with foods, including flour, bread and beer, fish and turtles, birds and eggs, spices and aromatics, fruit and nuts, and dairy products; 22 percent with management of personnel; 16 percent with live-stock, including sheep, goats, cattle, equids, pigs, and hides; 13 percent with indus-trial products, including wooden objects and logs, precious and semi-precious stones, reeds, textiles, thread, bricks, pottery, household goods, tools, bitumen, soap, alkali, and salt. Of the remainder, 2 percent of the documents were con-tracts and legal documents; 4 percent were bullae, letters, file labels, and blanks; and 4 percent were learner's and school texts.[124]

Comparing the land allotments to those of Umma and Adab, one finds that the land parcels distributed to privileged people at Girsu were significantly larger than elsewhere in Sumer. Fifty percent of them ranged between 2 and 35 hectares, 25 percent of them were larger, and 25 percent smaller.

Numerous officials held land at Girsu, among them couriers, equerries, the chief cupbearer, cultivators, military officers, scribes, and judges. The texts also mention members of the temple staff, including a high priestess, a chief temple administra-tor, a chief singer of laments, a dream interpreter, and a purifier.[125] Cultic personnel held very substantial areas; no titled secular official held parcels comparable to those of the high priestess of the Akkadian god Ilaba (409.9 hectares) or the chief admin-istrator of a smaller temple to a local Lagashite deity, Ninkimara (381 hectares).

The most important untitled Akkadian notable, Yetib-Mer, held 419.2 hectares near Girsu, in addition to 444.5 hectares in neighboring Umma. He was the major domo of Naram-Sin toward the end of his reign and served into the reign of Sharkalisharri, appearing in some lists of gifts directly after the king and queen. At Girsu alone he held three times as much land as the average for cultic personnel, nearly seven times as much the average for administrative personnel, more than fifteen times the average for professional people, and sixteen times the average for people without titles. With his Umma domains, he held thirty-three times the average at Girsu for people without titles, and he held 120 times the average for untitled people elsewhere in Sumer.[126]

The following figures of average land holdings, given in hectares, show just how privileged Akkadian officials at Girsu were in comparison to their counterparts elsewhere in Sumer:[127]

|  | *GIRSU* | *REST OF SUMER* |
| --- | --- | --- |
| Cultic officials | 139.75 | 13.06 |
| Courtiers and administrators | 62.1 | 6.45 |
| Professionals | 26.8 | 2.54 |
| Untitled people | 26.1 | 7.24 |

The disparity between land available to crown officials at Girsu and the rest of Sumer stems from the appropriation of nearly fourteen square kilometers of land in the former city-state of Lagash by an early Akkadian ruler, probably Rimush, as a punitive measure after he suppressed a rebellion there (Chapter 1 part 3; Figure 1.4). This placed unusually large tracts of prime arable land at the disposal of the Akkadian establishment. The area could have been further increased by the construction of irrigation canals, but there is no direct evidence for this. Portions, at least, of this great domain may have been taken over by the later kings of Ur, as suggested by the regional projections their clerks drew up for this same region.[128]

## The Mesag estate

Mesag was an Akkadian notable who held a very large estate in Sumer, in the former city-state Lagash, during the latter part of the reign of Naram-Sin and the early years of Sharkalisharri. The precise location of his domain is unknown, as the records from it were looted and sold on the antiquities market. Mesag was an educated man, writing a fine Akkadian hand, who drew up many of the records for his estate himself, and whose duties or obligations included occasional journeys to Agade, presumably to attend court functions (Figure 1.8c).[129]

Mesag's domain was assigned to him by an Akkadian cadaster official for a total area in the schematic amount of 360,000 surface units, about 1270 hectares of arable land. According to the cadaster record, one-third of this land he held as a grant for his subsistence; the remainder he held on the basis of a cash purchase of its use rights. From this estate, Mesag parceled out allotments to administrators, craftsmen, and other recipients of his patronage, in a combination of lease and grant. The land was cultivated by professional plow teams. Of the parcels distributed, 35 percent were 2.11 hectares or smaller, 12 percent were 35.28 hectares or larger, and the rest fell between. The Akkadian kings may have developed additional land in this region by digging canals.[130]

A list of personnel on this estate comprised 178 people, men outnumbering women 4 to 1, with 68 percent of the children male. There were 151 non-household people mentioned, only 4 percent of whom were women. Perhaps the records did not include the family and dependents of every accountable person. The documented women worked in the gardens and fields and fished; they may have had no familial protection and so appear in the list.[131] The estate owned large numbers of sheep, goats, donkeys, and cattle, placed with herd masters.[132]

The estate rendered substantial payments to Agade by boat, including grain, brewing ingredients, aromatics, and other valuables. Perhaps half the yield went to the crown, plus a tax on the actual annual harvest of about 10 percent, but the figures are difficult to interpret with certainty.[133]

At the accession of Sharkalisharri, Mesag may have assumed the governorship of Umma, but may still have maintained his estate. Perhaps it was he who offered the lavish assortment of gifts to the new king when he came to Sumer for his coronation at Nippur.[131]

## 4. Susiana

### Susa

Two levels of architectural remains, "early" and "late Agade," were excavated in 1964–5 on the acropolis at Susa; one Classical Akkadian document recording outgoing grain was associated with the later phase. Other Classical Akkadian tablets were discovered on the acropolis during the excavations of 1898–1910. They give a picture of a self-sustaining Akkadian enclave, under the direction of an Akkadian governor, which may have been called Dur-Agade, "Fort Akkad." The court maintained a cult of Ilaba, one of the patron deities of Agade, and honored a deified standard, perhaps a symbol of the royal house.[135]

The personnel lists of this settlement show that its population was divided into four groups: the ruling elite, courtiers and administrators, the skilled labor force, and unskilled laborers.[136] The ruling elite included the governor and a group of high dignitaries who, in accordance with Akkadian practice, were often referred to by their names only, without titles. They were not given standard rations as the other three groups were, so they presumably enjoyed a higher level of fare.

The administrators and courtiers included scribes, a diviner or physician (azu), attendants for the residential part of the palace, attendants in charge of crockery, a cupbearer, and a majordomo. Listed with them as recipients of food were supervisors of laborers, slaughterers, craftsmen, the officer in charge of the palace gate, a messenger and runner, a herald, soldiers, elders, and various foreigners (Marhashians, Lullubis, and Amorites). A special subgroup is called "those of the wagonry." Miscellaneous expenditures went for offerings to deities, feeding dogs, and other activities.[137]

The skilled laborers comprised sixty-nine artisans, five cooks, three barbers, one seal cutter, seven carpenters, three smiths, six leather workers, three fullers, twenty reed workers, and nineteen arrow makers. The workers of the household used in direct agricultural production are also reckoned here: seventeen cultivators, one shepherd, seven donkey herders, ten laborers, and ninety-two boys.

The unskilled labor force, listed separately from the preceding, consisted of 444 men and 27 boys, divided into the usual late third-millennium Mesopotamian categories of fitness for work, including blind men, and 392 women, 90 girls, and 81 babies, for a grand total of 836 adults, and 198 children. Girls outnumber boys three to one. Among other tasks, women worked at weaving and grinding flour. One-fifth of the women had nursing infants, and most of them may have had more than one child, judging from the numbers of boys and girls. There were numerous older men, but only a few old women.[138]

The size of the agricultural workforce and their families here appears exceptionally large, more than a thousand people. This raises the possibility that some of the men were military personnel, though the usual term for royal soldiery does not occur. Most of the male workforce had Sumerian or Akkadian names.[139] This again suggests an Akkadian enclave at or near Susa. A building the size of the northwest palace at Eshnunna (Figure 3.1) could have sustained them all.[140]

The agricultural basis of the governor's household was about 444 hectares, assuming fourteen standard plow units using fourteen pairs of donkeys, by coincidence perhaps corresponding to the number of able-bodied workers at one worker per hectare. Although this domain seems modest in comparison to other Akkadian estates, such as Mesag's, it is nonetheless sizeable for land presumably wrested from a hostile subject population.[141] It was cultivated by the plowmen who were accountable for certain quantities of grain to the household, much of which was delivered by boat, though the use of watercraft at Susa seems surprising today.[142] If the "standing place of one day" (about 14,400 square meters) refers to an area a workforce could cultivate, the entire estate could have been worked in three weeks.[143] This makes the Susa domain unique in the Akkadian period in that it need not have depended on land lease or levy to be cultivated, but was more or less self-sufficient on expatriate Mesopotamian labor.

The scattered household income and receipt documents are of the usual Akkadian types. A fragmentary letter order in Akkadian, copied as a justification to a land record, orders the "release" or the "holding" of certain lands, and the record goes on to show that this action was taken. This precise sense of this term, known elsewhere in Akkadian documents, is obscure.[144]

The leading Akkadian dignitary at Susa at the time of the records was Epir-mupi, who may have been a contemporary of Sharkalisharri, to judge from the style of his seals. Like Puzur-Mama of Lagash (Chapter 1 part 8), he may have begun his career as an Akkadian official, but, with the collapse of the Akkadian Empire, ruled for a time independently in his former province. Another important official of the period was Ili-ishmani, who may also have emerged as an independent ruler after the fall of the Empire.[145]

Records from Susa mention various Mesopotamian localities, including Der, Shuruppak, Sumer, Surgul, Uru'a, and Apishal, as well as places in Iran, such as Anshan. This and the presence of foreigners in the records shows that Susa was a crossroads or entrepot city under Akkadian rule (Chapter 8 part 3).[146]

In addition to the Akkadian governor and his entourage, there were Sumerian merchants at Susa. The records of their commercial activity are very fragmentary. One lists transactions with barley, wool, and copper purchased or valued in silver. The principals were a man and his three sons, all four of whom were merchants. Two of the sons held fields at Susa, so the family must have resided there, and it is clear that they were directly involved with the cultivation of this land. The father and one of his sons may also appear in a record from Girsu, in which bronze and tin for bronze are delivered. In that record, the father and son are said to be from a place in Lagash province, apparently to the south and east. Other records from Susa of wool, silver, and tin suggest close links with Umma.[147]

The presence of travelers from Dilmun, Magan, and Meluhha at Susa, far inland from the Gulf, raises the possibility that Susa was a base for the overland

caravan trade, both within Iran and farther afield. Commodities traded with Mesopotamia included copper, tin, silver, gold, lapis and other semi-precious stones,
fruit, spices, and stone vessels.[18]

## 5. Syria

### *Mari/Tell Hariri*

In the century prior to Sargon, Mari/Tell Hariri and Ebla/Tell Mardikh were the
main powers of the mid-Euphrates region and north-central Syria, while Nagar
dominated the northern Khabur region, and Kish northern Babylonia. Mari

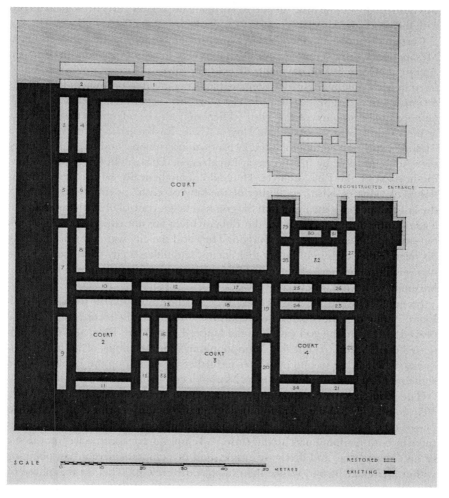

*Figure 3.3* Plan of Naram-Sin's fortified building at Nagar in Syria.

had developed into a large urban complex, with a palace and several temples. In a decisive showdown between Mari and her perennial rival, Ebla, Mari was defeated, after which Ebla was strong enough to forge an alliance with Nagar and Kish. A treaty of peace was drawn up, which left Ebla and her allies in a superior position.[149]

What happened next is not yet clear. There are two basic facts: (1) Ebla was totally destroyed, and (2) Naram-Sin claimed to be the first king to conquer Ebla. Although this is the only explicit synchronism of its kind between Syria and Mesopotamia, most Assyriologists do not credit Naram-Son's claim, but date the fall of Ebla earlier because they consider the palace archives found there to be pre-Akkadian.[150] Mari too suffered major or total destruction at the end of Ville 2, and a year name, usually attributed to Sargon, commemorates "the year Mari was destroyed."[151] The task, then, is to correlate the region's archaeological record with the onset of Akkadian power.

Certain documents in the Ebla archives provide tantalizing links with events in Mesopotamia, though they are not specific enough to be interpreted with certainty. Among these are lists of payments of gold and silver to foreign powers, some of them in Mesopotamia. Furthermore, textiles were given to prominent individuals on important occasions, for instance, to a man "who reported the defeat of Mari," perhaps Ebla's conquest of that city.[152] There may also be references to such events as the victories of a pre-Akkadian king of Uruk, Enshakushanna, over Kish and Akshak, which are commemorated in his own inscriptions, and to a later victory over Adab, possibly by his successor, Lugalzagesi. This would bring Sargon into the horizon of the Ebla archives. He could, hypothetically, be the person mentioned as "king of Kish" or "father of the king of Kish" or simply "the father," the last two perhaps meaning that Sargon had taken control of Kish and had put a son on the throne there. If so, the Ebla archives are not entirely pre-Akkadian but overlap the early career of Sargon. They and the city were destroyed during his reign, either by him or by another enemy, and unless a city of the same name was rebuilt somewhere else, Naram-Sin's claim appears impossible to bring into harmony with what is now known.[153]

Sargon, for his part, mentions Mari twice. In one inscription, he pairs Mari with Elam, stating that they "stood before him."[154] In another, he records that after he prayed to Dagan, the god gave him the Upper Land, Mari, Ebla, and Armanum (called there Yarmuti). The first inscription may mark the limits of his initial conquests, whereas the second may refer to further expansion up the Euphrates. No subsequent Akkadian ruler mentions Mari in a commemorative inscription.[155]

The Akkadian period apparently straddles two archaeological phases at Mari, Ville 2 and Ville 3. Ville 2 was founded about two centuries prior to the Akkadian period on the remains of an earlier city in the same location, but with new departures in both planning and architecture.[156] Temples were constructed on the site of an older palace, and there are ample signs of comprehensive urban planning within a circular layout, rather than haphazard growth. Whether this phase of the city was destroyed by Sargon, as commemorated in the year name mentioned above, or by someone else, remains uncertain.[157]

The third-millennium palace at Mari evidently had four building phases, two pre-Akkadian and two post-Akkadian. The oldest, $P_3$, was abandoned at the same time as the destruction and abandonment of the monumental city center of Ville 2. The proposed synchronism with Sargon is not supported thus far by the radio-carbon dates from the palace timbers, which have yielded dates earlier than those conventionally assigned to him.[158] Sealings found on the floor of this building bear the names of Mari kings who can be linked with the Ebla archives, so are presumably pre- or early Akkadian, though this is not certain.[159] In phase $P_2$, the palace was rebuilt then briefly abandoned, to be replaced by $P_1$, which followed more or less on the lines of the older structure, and was destroyed by fire, then partially replaced by $P_0$.[160]

At present, there is scant evidence for identifying buildings erected during the Akkadian period or under Akkadian rule. A large structure east of the zig-gurat, for example, evidently a temple or temple complex ("secteur des temples anonymes"), contained a Classical Akkadian cylinder seal[161] but was built in the same style as a nearby pre-Akkadian temple.[162] An unusual feature of this structure was a group of three altars, graduated in height, set in a paved, open-air courtyard, on each of which a statue had apparently stood, the feet of one remaining.[163] A comparable arrangement occurs in the courtyard of the Akkadian-period temple complex at Nagar, where a large and two smaller slabs of stone were laid. It seems possible that at both Mari and Nagar open-air ceremonies took place in the courtyards, which numerous people witnessed or participated in.[164] No inscribed material has revealed to what deity the Mari temple was dedicated. Are the Mari altars an instance of an early Akkadian renewal of a previous installation, or a new design, as was characteristic of the reign of Naram-Sin?

So too the Mari temple of Ninhursag may have had an Akkadian phase, to judge from an extensive remodeling, its unusually thick walls (4 m.), and com-manding position.[165] She was one of the major Mesopotamian deities recognized by Naram-Sin in the inscription recording his deification (Chapter 1 part 4), so it would be natural for the Akkadian kings to honor her cult at Mari by the renova-tion or new construction of her temple.[166]

By contrast, a substantial pre-Akkadian private dwelling, burned in a conflagra-tion, was replaced by an Akkadian-period administrative building. Buried under its floor were two important (but still unpublished) hordes of copper objects, includ-ing bowls, cups, a tray, a platter, knives, an axe, hoe, hook, and other implements. As with other Akkadian hordes (Chapter 5 part 3), these appear to be assortments rather than sets of related objects. Included were three inscribed vessels, two with the names of daughters of Naram-Sin. One of these, a platter, bears the name of Simat-Ulmash but no titles; the other, a bowl, bears the name of Shumshani, high priestess of Shamash at Sippar.[167] In Chapter 1 part 7, the proposal was offered that Simat-Ulmash may have come to Mari for a matrimonial alliance with one of the *shakkanakku*'s of Ville 3. This title was used by the eighteen military governors and independent rulers of Mari, beginning in the Akkadian and continuing into the post-Akkadian period.[168] Shumshani's bowl may be associated with a temple of Shamash at Mari, in which the alliance may have been drawn up. The third piece is a ring-base container inscribed and dedicated by Dabala the scribe.[169]

Leaving aside the problematic radiocarbon dates, the picture that emerges is that Sargon occupied the city, which may have been heavily damaged previously. The palace was rebuilt in the early Akkadian period, then briefly abandoned. It was reconstructed later in the Akkadian period, associated with the *shakkanakku's*, and remained in use until the post-Akkadian period, eventually replaced by the great Amorite palace.[170] This is similar to the architectural history of some of the buildings at Nagar, discussed in the following section, which were abandoned and rebuilt during the Akkadian period.

Mari was among the cities that rebelled against Naram-Sin, according to a later literary text called *The Great Revolt*, one of the few works of literature found there (Chapter 11 part 6). This names an otherwise unknown Migir-Dagan as the "king" of Mari.[171] If there was such a person, his defeat by Naram-Sin may mark the termination of kingship at Mari and the installation there of a new line of *shakkanakku's*, or military governors, which continued for a century or more. In the early second millennium, both the *shakkanakku's* and the Akkadian kings were honored in the funerary cult at Mari (Chapter 11 part 1).[172] Mari never seems to have become a significant Akkadian administrative site, however important it may have been commercially.

### Nagar/Tell Brak

In the period just before the Akkadian conquest, Nagar was one of the major cities in northeastern Syria, as well as the center of the cult of the goddess Belet-Nagar, a deity of regional stature.[173] Ruling over an area radiating at least fifty kilometers from its gates, Nagar enjoyed close diplomatic relations with Ebla; its chief rivals were Kish and Mari.[174] The city bred and exported a valuable type of mule, apparently the offspring of a male onager and a female donkey.[175]

The stratigraphy at Nagar suggests earlier and later phases of Akkadian presence, followed by an interlude in which the Akkadian-period religious complexes there were ritually dismantled, burned, and buried. The most likely correlations with the Akkadian dynasty are an initial conquest by Sargon, with rebuilding and Akkadian presence under Rimush and Manishtusu, possibly a hiatus, then a more substantial Akkadian presence under Naram-Sin, followed by the ritual dismantling of the temple, perhaps under one of Naram-Sin's successors (Chapter 6 part 4).[176]

The most impressive structure securely dated to the Akkadian period, on the basis of its inscribed bricks of Naram-Sin, tablets, and other objects, is an enormous fortress-like building, carefully planned and built specifically for the purpose of Akkadian domination, administration, and possibly as a base for operations further north and west (Figure 3.3). Its outer walls were ten meters thick, stood about fifteen meters high, and enclosed a space of more than 10,000 square meters (111 × 93, Figure 3.3). Inside were four courtyards flanked by numerous

storage magazines, three of which contained wheat and barley. The largest courtyard measured forty-one by forty-one meters. This building, built in an urban
area cleared for the purpose, must have towered over the city and surrounding
countryside and was evidently a place for the receipt and storage of great quantities of goods.[177]

The building was looted and burned in antiquity, then rebuilt, leaving only
scant vestiges of its rich contents. These included worked and unworked lapis, cylinder seals and beads of various materials, copper pins, gold jewelry, clay figurines,
pottery, and fragments of administrative documents. One of these is a list of 178
men, some in groups of 60, 30, and 20, presumably levied from towns and villages
in the Khabur region as workers or soldiers. Nagar supplied the most men; other
contingents came from Urkesh/Mozan, Shehna/Leilan, and Tadum/Hamidi.[178]
Another is a list of animals perhaps collected as herd taxes.[179]

Elsewhere at the site, there was extensive Akkadian adaptation of existing
structures (Chapter 9 part 4). Wealthy Akkadian private houses were also built
(ER, FS, SS).[180] A tablet found in one of these, of a type known from Awal?/
Suleimeh, is an account of sheep and goats levied from various small villages,
mostly one apiece, perhaps as herd taxes.[181]

All of this points to Nagar being an Akkadian administrative center, the gateway for Akkadian penetration of the Khabur region, drawing on the production
and labor of the villages scattered over the fertile plains surrounding the city, as
well as from other urban centers in the vicinity.[182] Nagar was also perhaps the capital of an Akkadian province in northeastern Syria, with a population of Akkadian
notables and administrators lavishly sustaining a local cult and maintaining good
trade connections with northern Mesopotamia and, presumably, Anatolia and
eastern Syria. In addition to a bulla of the governor of Gasur, a group of three
Akkadian-period tablets, probably from Sippar, provides evidence for relations
with Mesopotamia. These deal with substantial amounts of barley and emmer
belonging to various people in Sippar, Lugal-Suen, and a place written with the
Sumerian word sign NAGAR, which could well be a Sumerian writing for Nagar/
Tell Brak, otherwise spelled syllabically as Na-gàr in Akkadian sources. The sub-
scriptions of two of the tablets are broken, so the nature of the transactions is not
clear, but they might be commercial records.[183]

### Urkesh/Tell Mozan

A palace of basalt blocks and mud brick was constructed here in the early Akkadian period and rebuilt during the reign of Naram-Sin or Sharkalisharri. The date
of its second phase is established by clay door sealings, on which the royal cylinder
seal of Taram-Agade, a daughter of Naram-Sin, had been rolled.[184] This building
was probably the creation of the local Hurrian dynasty, rather than an Akkadian
imperial intrusion. Naram-Sin commemorated his victory over Tishatal, ruler of
a land called Azuhinnum; it is tempting to identify him with the Tishatal who commissioned the earliest known Hurrian inscription, in honor of his construction of
a temple. To judge from the script and from the style of the copper lion holding

the tablet, this Tishatal, if not the same person, was a contemporary of Naram-Sin or Sharkalisharri.[185]

### Shehna²/Tell Leilan

An administrative building here incorporated the remains of an earlier structure allegedly destroyed by Akkadian invaders. This large installation may have been a center for collecting, processing, and redistributing grain. Along with other structures on the acropolis and lower town which the excavator dated to the Akkadian period, it was abruptly abandoned after only a few decades of use. A survey of the surrounding area suggested that 87 percent of it was also abandoned at this time, leaving only small remnant populations living in reduced circumstances.[186]

## 6.   Was there an Akkadian Empire?

"Empire" is used here in its conventional sense of supreme and extensive political dominion, presided over by dynastic rulers, who claimed extraordinary, even superhuman or divine powers. It was an entity put together and maintained by force, with provinces administered by officials sent out from the capital in the heartland. This is precisely what we see in the Akkadian period.

Administrative measures, such as metrological reform and the imposition of uniform royal standards, and cultural measures, such as reform of writing and script, diffusion of images of the ruler from a central workshop, and the spread of the Akkadian language and record keeping to Sumer, Iran, and northern Syria, prove that there was much more to the Akkadian Empire than heroic marches, enhanced commerce, and accumulation of booty. The records of the garrison at Susa and the remains of the Naram-Sin building at Nagar show that regions far from Agade were under direct Akkadian rule. Although some scholars see the royal inscriptions as empty vaunt and explain away Naram-Sin's structure at Nagar as a purely local or ephemeral phenomenon, this ignores the ample administrative records and other evidence for full-fledged Akkadian imperialism.[187]

One aspect of the Akkadian Empire that sets it apart from its successors in Western Asia is its focus on Iran, in recognition of that region's importance in imperial strategy. The Akkadian Empire's occupation of Susiana and Elam and its thrusts further east and into the Gulf were crucial for its success, self-presentation, and ideology. The later Assyrian and Babylonian Empires, in contrast, tended, at the zenith of their powers, to concentrate on Syria-Palestine; neither was able to establish a long-term presence in Iran and both fell to invaders from there. Still later, Iran played a key role in the ultimate failure of Alexander's empire and the ultimate triumph and permanence of the Muslim conquests.[188]

The extent and duration of the Akkadian conquests are reflected in the broad geographical horizons of the major groups of Akkadian administrative and business documents, which show considerable expansion over those of their pre-Akkadian counterparts, as seen in the following four examples, two from Sumer and two from northern Mesopotamia (Map 2).

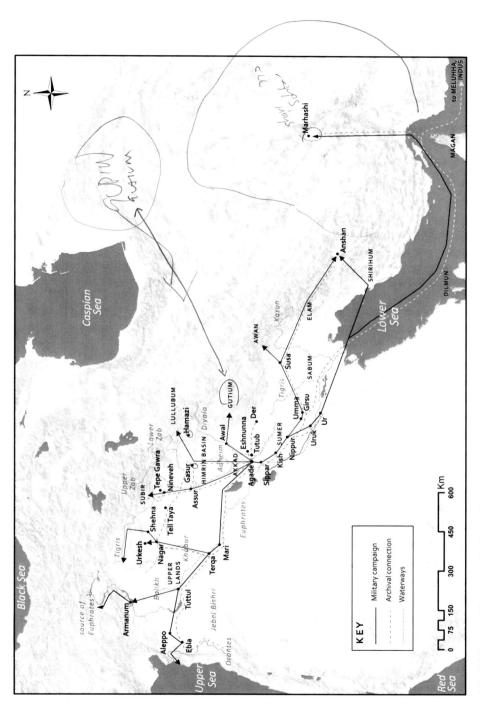

*Map 2* Western Asia under Akkadian rule.

Documents from pre-Akkadian Lagash, show a horizon largely restricted to Sumer, with commercial and diplomatic connections with Elam and the Gulf, whereas the geographical horizon of the Akkadian-period records from Girsu reaches to Ebla and Tutul in the northeast, Gasur in the north; to Elam as far as Anshan and Marhashi in the east, and to Dilmun, Magan, and the Indus Valley to the south.[189] Pre-Akkadian documents from Adab show a horizon limited to its immediate area and to Uruk, on which it was politically dependent. This saw an abrupt change in the time of Meskigal, a ruler contemporaneous with Lugalzagesi and Sargon, with connections throughout Sumer, as far north as Agade and Gasur. Meskigal even claims an expedition to the Cedar Forest (Lebanon or the Amanus), perhaps in conjunction with Sargon (Chapter 1 part 1). Under later Akkadian rule, the horizon expanded to Ebla and beyond to the northwest, to Elam and Marhashi in the east, and, to the south, the Gulf as far as Magan and the Indus Valley.[190]

Pre-Akkadian administrative documents from northern Mesopotamia are very rare, but those from the Akkadian period show the same wide horizons as do those from Sumer. Records from Eshnunna attest to interconnections throughout northern Babylonia, northwest to Syria, Assyria, the Trans-Tigris, and the Himrin Basin; up the Euphrates to Terqa and Mari, and south to Sumer and Elam.[191] The documents from Gasur show connections with Assur, the Trans-Tigris and Diyala regions, and northern Babylonia. The governor of Gasur is mentioned at Adab, Girsu, the Mesag estate, and Nagar.[192]

This network of political, economic, and diplomatic interconnections, stretching from northern Syria to eastern Iran and the Indus Valley and Oman, not only corresponds well to the territorial claims of Naram-Sin (Chapter 1 part 4), but also demonstrates that the Akkadian Empire was indeed a historical reality and the world's first documented empire.

From a more analytic perspective, Buccellati offered the most systematic evaluation of the Akkadian achievement as the invention of empire.[193] For him, it was a qualitative leap from homogeneous city-states to a heterogeneous, hegemonic, and expansionist entity with a capital city and provinces, totalitarian rule, and new possibilities for individual identity. The essence of the new state was institutionalization of conflict through a standing army and a shift of emphasis from internal public affairs to external aggression, based on a strong military, maintained by widely placed garrisons, managed by an administrative apparatus articulated in parallel to the military, enhanced by placement of members of the ruling family in key positions throughout the realm, and upheld in outlying regions by dynastic marriage alliances. The systematic destruction of city walls shows Akkadian determination to subjugate territory by removing a key symbol of social and political identity, not just to break resistance but to achieve imperial integration. Writing was redirected toward propagandistic inscriptions emphasizing warfare, both further away and more frequent than before, as well as harsh reprisals for rebellions. This was marked by an abrupt change in language, with the introduction of Akkadian already in the reign of Sargon, and the development of imperial calligraphy. To give the royal messages greater impact, they were carved onto impressive statues, which were themselves products of a brilliant artistic initiative. Distributed throughout the realm, the inscribed monuments focused on the king and his court, proclaiming a new vision of the world.

Key elements of the Akkadian program, according to Buccellati, can be seen in royal titulary and epithets, already in the reign of Sargon. These emphasized a new city, Agade, which is the first instance of a new capital created by a political act, from which the state took its name; a new deity, Ishtar, who, unlike other deities, was patron of a dynasty more than a specific city; incorporation of an old hegemony, Kish. They further invoked An as supreme deity, Enlil as king of the land, and Nippur as the center of the Sumerian league of cities. A new title taken by Naram-Sin, "king of the four world regions," was based on a new geographical concept whereby the Tigris and Euphrates formed a unified land, the four regions referring to the four banks (Akkadian *kibrum*) of these two great rivers. The steppe beyond was thereafter viewed as a kind of "counter-state." Thus the reign of Naram-Sin saw the invention of the concept now known as "Mesopotamia."

Brief as this astounding achievement was, Buccellati saw it as bringing permanent change to Western Asia, from city-state to a multi-ethnic state with universal claims. He argued that it showed all the characteristics of a coherent project rather than a haphazard development, but created the conditions for its own collapse. Its program of conquest often broke up local supply networks and disrupted local production, although trade flourished and became, for the first time, a matter of royal ideology commemorated in inscriptions. No imperial alternative was put in place after destruction of walls and killing of men of military age; it was easier to conquer than to administer. The Sumerian city-states were alienated, the steppe peoples had no share in the imperial ideal, and the Empire was vulnerable at its mountainous fringes, so the new *oikumene* was ultimately illusory, a premature but crucial undertaking in Syro-Mesopotamian state formation.

## Notes

1 For surveys of the archaeology of greater Mesopotamia in the Akkadian period, Ur 2010; Weiss 2012; McMahon 2012 and 2013.
2 Strommenger 1959; Nagel and Strommenger 1968; Asher-Greve 1989: 180; B. Foster 2010a: 121–23.
3 Gadd 1971: 450; B. Foster 1982b: 4–5; 1982h: 3–4; Sommerfeld 1999: 7–15.
4 Boehmer 1964, 1965; Collon 1982; Dittmann 1994; Rohn 2011.
5 Strommenger 1959; Spycket 1981.
6 Christian 1940; Delougaz 1952; Gibson 1982, 2011; Porada, Hasen, Dunham, and Babcock 1992; McMahon 2006.
7 Salonen 1972: 25–31.
8 Mallowan 1947; Heinrich 1984: 37.
9 Adams 1981: 138–43; Nissen 1993; Ur 2013: 142–43, 149–50.
10 Heinrich 1984: 32–35.
11 MAD 1 260–64; Sommerfeld 1999: 29–30; 2011a: 92–94.
12 Sommerfeld 1999: 63 (Tutub 10); Sommerfeld 2011a: 93–94; Schrakamp 2015: 256.
13 Sommerfeld 1999: 104 (Tutub 47).
14 Sommerfeld 1999: 102 (Tutub 46).
15 Frankfort 1934a: 29–33; Delougaz, Hill, and Lloyd 1967: 196–98; Heinrich 1984: 31–32; Gibson 2011. Curiously, the northwest corner of burials may have had some ritual significance, Winter 1999b: 235; in general Schott 1934: 305–6; Martiny 1932:

6–7, who suggests that the generally northwest orientation of northern temples, as opposed to the generally southwest orientation of Babylonian ones, was intended to point to the original homelands of the inhabitants, but he thought the Akkadians had come from the southwest, "bestimmt nicht von O und N."

16  Gibson ed. 1981: 94; Sommerfeld 2011a: 89; Gibson 2011: 66–67; Schrakamp 2014: 224–27.

17  MAD 1 90, 126; Martos 1991 nos. 6–7.

18  Kienast and Volk 1995: 178–79.

19  MAD 1 45, 48, 50–52, 58, 67, 74, 111, 119–20, 128, 158, 161.

20  MAD 1 47, 136.

21  MAD 1 3, 9, 12, 42, 46, 53, 61, 73, 81, 87, 96, 100, 153–54, 163.

22  MAD 1 163.

23  MAD 1 173; 138; 69; 18.

24  MAD 1 86.

25  MAD 1 2.

26  MAD 1 56; 41.

27  MAD 1 1, 79, 146, 182.

28  MAD 1 7, 11; 37; 77, 89, 104, 108, 139, 149; 49 (basket label).

29  MAD 1 27 and 29. Others include MAD 1 14 (over 300); 19 (over 200); 31, 84.

30  MAD 1 142 (380 hides); 159 (sent for fattening).

31  MAD 1 71, 115, 157, 162 (purchase).

32  MAD 1 8, 60, 82, 112–13, 131, 136, 138; 6, 47, 136.

33  MAD 1 98.

34  MAD 1 43.

35  MAD 1 32, 34, 125.

36  MAD 1 166; further Sommerfeld 2011a: 87.

37  MAD 1 4; 166; 173; 32; 135.

38  MAD 1 43, 140.

39  Martos 1991 no. 5; M. Cohen 1976a; further Visicato 1997.

40  Edzard 1976/80c; Maeda 1981; further Chapter 1 note 6 and Steinkeller 2013c: 145–51. He suggests that Kish was originally a Sumerian settlement, the population of which blended with "Proto-Akkadians" to produce a powerful, expansionist state in the early third millennium; further Chapter 12 part 5.

41  Frayne 1993: 12, 15; Appendix IIb 2; Edzard 1991.

42  MAD 5 1. For the excavations at Kish, Gibson 1972a; 1976/80, and Moorey 1970, 1978; for the documents, Schrakamp 2015: 232–33.

43  Frayne 1993: 215.

44  MAD 5 12.

45  MAD 5 3, 17, 102.

46  MAD 5 65.

47  MAD 5 6, 52.

48  MAD 5 18, 45, 57.

49  MAD 5 54 = Kienast and Volk 1995: 145; MAD 5 19, 45.

50  MAD 5 10, 23, 25, 26, 39, 41–43, 55, 61, 63.

51  Gibson 1972b: 246–63.

52  Kraus 1984: 349; Charpin 1990b: 15; Stol 2004: 762.

53  B. Foster 2011a: 129; in general Schrakamp 2015: 243–44.

54  B. Foster 1982c: 36–37. For house prices, Gelb, Steinkeller, and Whiting 1991, 1: 269–71.

55  For a study of the tablets from this site, B. Foster 1982c.

56  Weiss 1975 (identifies with the mound Ishhan-mizyad); McEwan 1982 (confluence of Diyala and Tigris); Wall-Romana 1990 (confluence of Diyala and Tigris); Frayne 1991: 396–402, 2004; A. Westenholz 1999: 32 (confluence of Adheim and Tigris); Reade 2002a (Samarra); Sommerfeld 2004: 289–90, 2014: 174 (Samarra, with arguments

against Frayne 2004); Buccellati 2013: 140 (a suburb of Kish?); Ziegler 2014: 190 (about 20 km north of Baghdad); Paulus 2014 (east of the old course of the Tigris); Marti 2014; Pethe 2014; Pirngruber 2014 (near confluence of Diyala and Tigris).

57 Chapter 2 note 11; Chapter 11 note 153.
58 Frame 1993; Chapter 2 note 11.
59 Literally "doorbolt", Reiner 1963: 173 note 4; for Ebih as a theophoric element, Edzard 1957: 35 note 152; Steinkeller 1981b (Ur III evidence).
60 Postgate 1979; Gibson 1981a: 11–14; Rasheed 1981: 5–8, who argues that in the Akkadian period the Himrin was economically self-sufficient but had good trade connections outside the valley.
61 Gibson 1981a: 21.
62 Gibson 1981a.
63 TS 35 ii 9.
64 Rasheed 1981: 12.
65 Rasheed 1981: 9–15; Al-Rawi 1992: 180–81 argues for identifying Tell Suleimeh with a place called Batir; Schrakamp 2014: 253–56.
66 For English summaries, Muhamed 1992: 19–20; Rumeidh 1981: 57–60; Philip 1995: 120–22, with map.
67 Rumeidh 1981: Plate 2 figure 2. The room that the tablets were found in is not apparent on the published plan.
68 Rumeidh 1981: Plate 4 figures 2 and 3.
69 For a general study of the tablets from this site, Visicato 1999.
70 TS 46.
71 TS 1.
72 TS 34; compare 12.
73 For analysis of prices or values at Awal, Rasheed 1981: 16–28.
74 Gibson 1981a: 15.
75 TS 10 iii 8, 21 i 11; 23:12, 24:7 (*a-na* HAR-kam, also 11:19, 13:15, 17:11, 28:5). In 23, še-HAR is issued to feed donkeys.
76 TS 25; for rental payments involving livestock, Steinkeller 1981a; for Nagar below, note 179; for taxation in general, Chapter 7 note 3.
77 TS 44.
78 Rasheed 1981: 29–32, who concludes that reduplicated names give no indication of belonging to an otherwise unidentified ethnic group (Chapter 2 part 2).
79 Oates 1968: 19; Mühl 2013: 128–30.
80 Mace head: Braun-Holzinger 1991: 47 K 24; spear point: Braun-Holzinger 1991: 88 (MW 4); for the statue, Chapter 9 note 19. For Ititi, below, note 84.
81 Heinrich 1984: 37–43; Pedde and Lundstrom 2008.
82 Neumann 1997.
83 UET 8 14 (date uncertain, possibly post-Akkadian); for an Akkadian king at Assur, Visicato 2001.
84 Grayson 1972: 2, 1987: 7; Durand 2012.
85 Charpin 2004b.
86 Frayne 1993: 88–89; Appendix IIb 23; for the later literary association of merchants in Anatolia with Akkadian rule, Chapter 11 part 6.
87 Bär 2003a, 2003b; for the northwest orientation of the building plan, Martiny 1932: 6–7 and above, note 15.
88 J. Westenholz 2004.
89 Reade 2011.
90 Reade 2011: 246–47.
91 Grayson 1987: 51–55. Further Gut, Reade, and Boehmer 2001; Zettler 2006.
92 Speiser 1935: 18–21.
93 B. Foster 1982f; further on the tablets Markina 2011; Schrakamp 2015: 227–30; for Gasur as a royal stronghold, Sommerfeld 2014: 165–66, 174–75.

94　B. Foster 1987b.
95　McMahon 2006.
96　B. Foster 1982h: 5; for Enlilemaba, Chapter 8 part 5; in general Schrakamp 2015: 247–48.
97　CUSAS 13 163; A. Westenholz 1987: 26, 28; Gelb and Kienast 1990: 107–9; further Chapter 7 note 6.
98　Sallaberger 1997.
99　Sallaberger 1999b: 140–63.
100　Banks 1912: 145; Wilson 2012, Plate 40a.
101　Wilson 2012; Zhi 1989; Adams 1981: 160: "The Adab region thus became particularly densely occupied, and it is arguably the largest urban concentration yet known within the Old Akkadian realm."
102　For a survey of the written sources, Maiocchi 2009: 1–16; Maiocchi and Visicato 2012: 1–8; in general Schrakamp 2015: 220–24; for the governors of Adab, e.g., Biga 2005 (duplicate of this inscription = CUSAS 17 No. 13); Maiocchi 2009: 3; BdI 65; CUSAS 17 10; Frayne 1993: 253–58.
103　Kienast and Volk 1995: 58–60.
104　Zhi 1989: 148–69.
105　Zhi 1989: 162–63.
106　Zhi 1989: 226–38.
107　Zhi 1989: 164–71.
108　Zhi 1989: 171–89; CUSAS 13 116; CUSAS 19 117–42.
109　Zhi 1989: 190–96; CUSAS 19 78; note, however, the record of 3000 sheepskins in CUSAS 13 34.
110　Zhi 1989: 197–98.
111　Zhi 1989: 198–201.
112　Zhi 1989: 208–12.
113　Zhi 1989: 259–68.
114　Zhi 1989: 270.
115　Madhloom 1960.
116　Postgate 1976; Hussein, Altaweel, and Rejeb 2009; Studevent-Hickman 2009; Saadoon 2014. A record of subsistence land plots, evidently the combined holdings of an Akkadian notable, kindly communicated by Abather Saadoon, shows five large parcels totaling over 80 hectares.
117　Saadoon 2014: 55 note 3; Zhi 1989: 87–8.
118　M. Lambert 1965, 1975; B. Foster 1982b; for governors of Umma, Cripps 2010: 10; in general Schrakamp 2015: 259–61. Umma (Djokha) may have replaced a larger settlement nearby (Umm al-Aqarib) in the early Akkadian period, owing to a change in the Euphrates channel, Monaco 2013; Almamori 2014; further W. Lambert 1990b. Numerous administrative documents from the Umma region shed light on conditions there just prior to the rise of Sargon, Powell 1978d; Milone 2005; Brumanti 2012.
119　B. Foster 1982b: 69–84.
120　B. Foster 1982b: 79–148; for "scepter," Van Buren 1956.
121　B. Foster 1982b: 52–78.
122　B. Foster 1993b.
123　B. Foster 1982a: 109–11; for governors of Lagash, Cripps 2010: 10.
124　B. Foster 1982a: 11.
125　B. Foster 1982a: 18–45.
126　B. Foster 1982a: 109–10.
127　B. Foster 1982a: 19–23.
128　B. Foster 1985.
129　Salgues 2011: 253–54 note 3; Schrakamp 2015: 249–50 (locates at Sagub but this is hypothetical).

130  B. Foster 1982a: 53–56; rural development in the area is suggested by BIN 8 117, a document from this archive, which mentions a canal built in "the steppe."

131  B. Foster 1987a: 54–55.

132  B. Foster 1986a. A comparable record of delivery is known from Adab, CUSAS 13 29; this includes two wagons and other goods sent to Agade, probably as a gift to an Akkadian notable or a member of the royal family.

133  B. Foster 2010a: 139.

134  Stève and Gasche 1971: 59–85.

135  MDP 14 71 ix 7–8. Jacobsen 1957: 137 note 103 called this an "Akkadian garrison." There is no good reason to suppose that the local population adopted Akkadian and Sumerian names under Akkadian hegemony (differently Zadok 1994; D. Potts 1999: 111). An unnamed Akkadian governor of Susa and another of Elam are listed as landholders in the area of Girsu, perhaps as refugees after the collapse of Akkadian power there, though cases of governors' holding land in cities besides the ones they governed are known, B. Foster 1982a: 36–37 note 31.

136  "Palace" staff: MDP 14 24, 59, 71. For Akkadian relations with Susiana, T. Potts 1994: 97–119; for Akkadian Susa in general, D. Potts 1999: 100–122; for the documents, Schrakamp 2015: 251–53, although there is no good reason to date some of the texts cited here to the Ur III period, as proposed there.

137  MDP 14 6, 9, 18; additional data in MDP 14 5, 14, 15, 23, 67, 81.

138  MDP 14 24, 61, 71, 72.

139  MDP 14 6 (post-Akkadian?), 10, 20 (boatmen, overwhelmingly with Sumerian names), 66; soldiers MDP 14 85, 86; further above, note 135.

140  Fieldwork: MDP 14 73; other records of unskilled labor include MDP 14 10, 11, 36, 47, 58?, 61, 72.

141  MDP 14 71: 9000 sar per team (31.75 hectares) times 14 = 126,000 sar (444.5 hectares); for comparative data, B. Foster 2011: 129. Mesag's domain was 2.8 times as large. One Akkadian resident bought real estate at Susa, MDP 14 4. One may compare the efforts of Greek settlers to develop Susa as an agricultural center, Wiesehöfer 2001: 142.

142  MDP 14 17, 45; 26, 32 (grain and boatmen); MDP 14 20 (list of Sumerian boatmen).

143  MDP 14 84.

144  MDP 14 33.

145  Boehmer 1967, who notes his adoption of the title "mighty," first used by Naram-Sin, perhaps after his conquest of Elam (Hallo 1980); T. Potts 1994: 109. The tablets mentioning Epirmupi tend to be beautifully written, and sometimes, rarely for Susa, written entirely in Sumerian, for example, MDP 14 58 and 60; perhaps, like Mesag, he wrote some administrative tablets himself. MDP 14 73, on the other hand, in which his name is also mentioned, is roughly made and written, though there is no reason to think it a school text (all tablets collated). For Ili-ishmani, M. Lambert 1979; D. Potts 1999: 109–10.

146  MDP 14 22.

147  B. Foster 1993b (previously noted by Gadd 1979: 445); for documentation of pre-Akkadian contacts between Elam and Sumer, Selz 1991: 37–42; T. Potts 1994: 87–96; Steinkeller 2013b.

148  T. Potts 1993, 1994: 144–275.

149  Michalowski 1985; Archi and Biga 2003; for Ebla and Nagar, Biga 1998; further, Archi 2014b; in general Matthiae 2010: 48–63.

150  Astour 2002: 58–76; Archi and Biga 2003: 30–31; Matthiae 2007, who dates the first major destruction at Ebla, which entombed the early Ebla archives, to Sargon.

151  Appendix Ib 2; Frayne 1993: 8.

152  Archi and Biga 2003: 14.

153  Sallaberger 2004a. For Ebla and Kish, Archi 1981, 1987a, 1987b, 2014b.

154  Appendix Ib 2; Frayne 1993: 14–15.

155 Archi 1985b: 49–50; Archi and Biga 2003: 30.
156 Margueron 2004: 49–314; 2013: 54–63 (dating the foundation of Ville 2 to about 2500 BCE); summary by Lecompte 2014, who suggests that Ebla attacked Mari, next Mari destroyed Ebla, finally Sargon destroyed Mari.
157 For various proposed correlations of the destruction levels with historical data, Margueron 2004: 304–12; Durand 2012; Lecompte 2014.
158 Margueron 1982: 103; Lebeau 1985: 127; Archi and Biga 2003: 30. Radiocarbon dates from regions with high volcanic activity may be subject to distorting phenomena as yet poorly understood, Wiener 2009a, b.
159 Archi and Biga 2003: 30–31; Margueron 2004: 307–8.
160 Tunca 1984: 65–73.
161 Parrot 1974; Boehmer 1965: 96–97.
162 Parrot 1954: 153.
163 Parrot 1940: 8–14.
164 Chapter 6 part 4 and note 56.
165 Parrot 1955: 210–11; Tunca 1984: 73–74.
166 Parrot 1955: 194–99; for centers of worship of Ninhursag in Akkadian Mesopotamia, Steinkeller 1995b.
167 Parrot 1955 pl. XVI; Frayne 1993: 113–14; Gelb and Kienast 1990: 104–5.
168 Durand 2006/8.
169 Gelb and Kienast 1990: 378–79; Margueron 2006: 305–6.
170 Margueron 1982: 86–106; 2006: 459–500; Durand 2012 suggests an occupation by Sargon, who destroyed Ebla, perhaps towards the end of his reign, and a destruction of Mari by Naram-Sin in connection with the "Great Revolt."
171 *Muses*, 119.
172 Durand 1985: 152, 158; in general Margueron 2006: 317–430. The placement of the *shakkanakku*'s in relation to the Ur III kings is debated, Boese and Sallaberger 1996; Michalowski 1999; Sharlach 2001; Durand 2006/8, 2012.
173 Archi 1998; Sallaberger 1999a; for interconnections in the region, Charpin 1992.
174 Astour 1992, 2002; Archi 1981, 1985a, 1985b, 1987a, 1987b, 1998.
175 Clutton-Brock and Davies 1993; Archi 1998; Sallaberger 1999a; Pruß and Sallaberger 2003/4; further Michalowski 2013: 303–5.
176 Oates, Oates, and McDonald 2001: 386; in general Steele, McDonald, Matthews, and Black 2003.
177 Mallowan 1947: 63–67.
178 Administrative documents published by Gadd 1940 plate V; republished by Eidem, Irving, and Bonechi in Oates, Oates, and McDonald 2001: 106–9 nos. 14–30; for the list of men, 106–7 no. 14; additional Akkadian administrative documents published by Michalowski in Emberling and McDonald 2003: 56–60; in general Schrakamp 2015: 244–47.
179 Eidem, Irving, and Bonechi in Oates, Oates, and McDonald 2001: 110 no. 31, TS 25; further above, note 76 and Chapter 7 note 3.
180 ER = Oates, Oates, and McDonald 2001: 34–36; FS = 41–73; SS = 73–98.
181 Eidem, Irving, and Bonecchi in Oates, Oates, and McDonald 2001: 106 no. 14.
182 Oates and Oates in Oates, Oates, and McDonald 2001: 379–96.
183 Eidem, Finkel, and Bonechi in Oates, Oates, and McDonald 2001: 106; CT 1 plate 1.
184 Buccellati and Kelly-Buccellati 2000.
185 Aruz and Wallenfels 2003: 222–23. For Naram-Sin and lion imagery, Chapter 1 note 35, Chapter 4 note 63, Chapter 9 notes 47 and 52.
186 Weiss 1986, 2012; Ristvet, Guilderson, and Weiss 2004; for the Khabur region in general in the post-Akkadian period, Sallaberger 2007.
187 For discussion of this issue, Michalowski 1985, 1993; Mann 1994; Doyle 1996; further bibliography in McMahon 2012: 659–64. Ur 2010: 407–8; McMahon 2012: 659–64;

further B. Foster 1986b and 2011a; theory and comparisons of empire in Gehler and Rollinger 2014. McMahon expects better ceramic evidence for an Akkadian Empire, but ceramics were not a significant element in Akkadian culture and ceramics are not generally used in connection with the definition of other, better-documented Mesopotamian empires, such as the Neo-Assyrian or Persian, so it seems gratuitous to posit a ceramic criterion for the Akkadian Empire. So too she expects changes in settlement patterns, though without explaining why (nor is this a criterion for defining the Assyrian and Babylonian empires); the most likely effect of Akkadian agrarian policy was creation of rural manors for the elite and these would not show up in surface surveys. She dismisses the rich archival evidence as "pockets," ignoring the important fact that the Akkadian period is the first and only instance in the third millennium, and, indeed, for most of Mesopotamian history, for which there is consistent administrative material from Syria, Northern and Southern Mesopotamia, and Susiana, so consistent that on the basis of script and tablet shape the local records are indistinguishable from each other, unlike late pre-Akkadian Mesopotamia, where there were pronounced local traditions of scripts and tablet shape even in neighboring cities (Biggs 1973). She expects evidence for transfer of goods from north to south, ignoring the model provided by Assyrian reliance on local enclaves in the same region (Liverani 1988) and the documentary proof that Agade was sustained by shipments of food and other goods from Sumer, not from the north (Chapter 4 part 4); further, influence from or through Syria on Akkadian art, as argued, e.g., by Porada, Hanson, Dunham and Babcock 1992 and Börker-Klähn 1982a is difficult to ascribe to mere seasonal raids. In short, McMahon's criteria for empire seem arbitrary and her study, its many merits notwithstanding, does not take adequate account of the contemporaneous written evidence.

188 Shaheed 1979. As noted in note 141, Akkadian inclusion of southwestern Iran in a Mesopotamian polity may foreshadow Achaemenid, Hellenistic, and Sassanian policies in the Gulf and Susiana.
189 Schrakamp 2015: 202–9; 233–42; 197–201.
190 Schrakamp 2015: 199.
191 Schrakamp 2015: 224–27.
192 Schrakamp 2015: 227–30.
193 Buccellati 2013: 137–73.

# 4 Works and days

## 1. Agricultural production

In the pre-modern Diyala region, the heart of Akkad, the median size of a privately owned farmstead was about six hectares, of a tenant farm about twelve. Despite rendering half or two-thirds of his crop to his landlord and in taxes, the tenant farmer could still support a family of six on such a plot. A full-time worker could cultivate productively about two hectares. Applying these figures to the richer Sumerian fields of ancient Lagash during the Akkadian period, one may propose that more than 500 tenant farmers and their families could have made their living from the 6000 hectares controlled by the royal land registrar there, even if they were obliged to give up half or more of their harvest to a landlord or patron.[1]

The elaborate rules for administering and distributing the vast agricultural land managed by the Akkadian government in Sumer can be reconstructed in outline from hundreds of detailed cases. The main purpose of the administrative records was to maintain accountability, ultimately on behalf of the king, for income, assets, and expenses in which the king and the elite who served at his pleasure had an interest or obligation. Important local servants of the king were given large areas for cultivation, lease, and redistribution to their own followers. There were two categories of this land, "sustenance," from which they were supposed to draw their income, and "paid for," which they could lease as a perquisite of office, for a cash payment or for a percentage of the harvest. If they had the means and the will to lease more, a "present" to the king or the local governor could get them additional land. The registrar's scribes measured off these parcels and were held accountable for their cultivation expenses (seed and feed for the draught animals), normally deducted from the landowner's share of the harvest, and the amount of harvest to be delivered to the landlord. The king's portion of the harvest could be stored locally or hauled upstream by boat to the capital. Royal inspectors were expected to verify the figures and to check the piles of grain.[2] The draft animals, plows, and skilled plow teams were also accountable, their work assignments and estimated returns and expenses projected according to mathematical models. On Mesag's estate, for example, the standard work assignment of one plow team (Figure 4.1a) was one bur (6.35 hectares).[3] The records were simple and

(a)

(b)

(c)

*Figure 4.1* Scenes of plowing, husbandry, and drinking. (a) A divine plow team of plowman, helper filling seed-hopper, and driver, whose body blends with that of the ox to become a "bull-man." (b) Sheep and goat, paddock with perching bird, seated person churning, storage and serving jars, tray of cheeses, shepherd god Dumuzi looking on. (c) Gods celebrating killing a monster, whose severed head, lances still stuck in it, rests on a table nearby.

straightforward, often using round numbers and relying on mathematical models rather than actual figures. There is no direct evidence for administrative interests in long-term trends until a later period.[1]

The strength of the Akkadian system in Sumer was that it involved very few fully dependent workers, who had to be fed and maintained by the land-holder. Rather, numerous tenant farmers and other lessees assumed both labor and risk, so the landholders and the king received important income (half or more of the crops raised), without significant investment in labor, which was perennially in short supply compared to the tasks at hand. As the poet of *The Curse of Agade* recognized, Sumerian agricultural production was crucial to the prosperity of the empire. Not even Ishtar herself, he says, could keep track of the grain surpluses pouring into her capital.[5] From the perspective of the defeated and depopulated Sumerian cities, some of their best lands had been carved up into manors for Akkadian dignitaries, the bulk of their produce harvested and taken away before their eyes.

When the Akkadian armies moved into the rolling farmlands along the Upper Euphrates and its tributaries, the Khabur and Balikh, their agricultural potential would have been obvious, not only from the fields themselves but also from the prosperity of the cities and their hinterlands of towns and villages. No Akkadian administrative documents have yet been discovered to give details of the management of this region or if, for example, manors were created there for Akkadian notables, as in Sumer. The poet of *The Curse of Agade* makes no mention of agricultural development in the north; for him, the Upper Euphrates was only a land of nomads. This was a persistent trope in Sumerian literature, which obstinately acknowledged no cities north or west of Mari, even as the Akkadian armies were laying siege to many of them.[6]

The abundant harvests of north Syria could have been shipped by boat to Agade, a much longer distance than from the fields of Lagash, Umma, or Gasur, but with less effort, as the boats would be going downstream. On the other hand, laborious wagon transport would have been required to bring the grain to the quays along the river. No contemporaneous document gives clear evidence for this, however, and, to judge from Assyrian policies later in the same region, keeping local stockpiles of agricultural surplus at strategic points might well have been more useful for the Akkadian military.[7] There was, after all, no need to send grain down the Euphrates if a single manor in the irrigated zone could produce enough food to sustain Sargon's entire army (further part 4, this chapter). Although there is limited unambiguous evidence for Akkadian agrarian development in Sumer or Akkad, expansion of arable land could account for the evident prosperity of centers like Adab, Girsu, and the Umma region (Chapter 3 part 3).

Since most of the best arable land in Sumer was owned by temples, the royal family was obliged to enlarge its domains there through confiscation, rural development, and gradual incorporation of the temples and their holdings into the royal household. They made use of all three strategies, the last by co-opting the priesthood through appointment of relatives and crown officials to high cultic office, by co-opting temple management through patronage, and by purchasing individual entitlements.[8]

The cycle of the agricultural year in Sumer began with field preparation (months 3–5), followed by sowing (months 6–7) and harvesting (months 12–1), when the barley was reaped, threshed, and brought to the granary.[9] Because Sumerian administrators worked out quantitative norms for all aspects of agricultural production, for which they kept detailed records, especially in the post-Akkadian Ur III period, and because they studied in school *The Farmer's Instructions*, a work of literature setting forth in detail procedures for the cultivator, the techniques of Sumerian irrigation agriculture are better known than those of agriculture in the northern rainfall zone, but the basic cycle and processes were often the same.[10]

From Sumer, then, with its highly productive, intensive, irrigation agriculture, came grain enough for an empire's prosperity and growth. The king's agents were there at the wharves, as the great barges were loaded with grain and other goods. They rolled their splendid seals over the manifests when they were satisfied that the count was correct, then the barges moved slowly out into the channel, bound for Agade.[11]

## 2. Labor

The success of Akkadian agricultural production and industrialization depended upon the acquisition and management of labor.[12] Prior to the Akkadian period, records from Lagash, for example, show minute gradations of workers by category and type of ration issued to them and suggest that granting access to agricultural land was an important means of acquiring manpower.[13] After the fall of the Akkadian Empire, records from the Ur III period reveal a more standardized ration system, no regular access to agricultural land, and a much larger labor pool, sometimes running to many thousands of able-bodied men. The Ur III texts also attest to a sophisticated accounting system for work time.[14] The Akkadian period provides a transition between these two strategies, the earlier one locally oriented, the later district-wide, even regional, in scale. The increase in the size of the Akkadian military (Chapter 7 part 3) no doubt provided new models for management and provisioning of large numbers of men, possibly providing the precedent for the labor policies of the kings of Ur. ~

The main sources of labor were levied citizenry and dependent personnel, who worked in return for rations for themselves and their families. Hired help and slaves were much less significant in terms of total output. Most Akkadian records show simply that people were produced for service, without reasons being given or explanations of their status. Only occasionally do texts note why people had been entered on the rolls, such as "having fled the steppe, they reside in Lagash" or "having left the army." Some laborers may have been levied by elders or recruiting officers, who produced a fixed number of workers at certain times, whereas others were presumably workers dependent on institutions for their maintenance.[15] Citizens were also sometimes added to rosters of rationed laborers, perhaps as a result of loss of social status. In addition, refugees and immigrants, called "settlers," could enter institutional service. Men newly added to the rolls were assigned to a foreman (*ugula*) and a captain (*nu-banda*). The *ugula* was in charge of laborers on the basis of where they reported for work, whereas the *nu-banda* was in charge of them on the basis of where they lived, which sometimes appears in the records.[16]

Sometimes laborers slept in the governor's palace or other major buildings of the city, or at the city wall, perhaps for guard duty.[17]

When laborers married, they were likely to marry other laborers or slaves. More rarely, they married women of higher social status than their own and moved into the father-in-law's household, especially if he had no sons. In laboring families two, three, or four sons were by no means exceptional. Children normally became laborers like their parents. They were listed in the records first as nursing infants, then as children, then as adults capable of a full day's work, and finally as old people. Some laborers were noted as "blind" or "mentally deficient."[18]

Regular institutional laborers were entitled to daily, monthly, and periodic rations of food, drink, oil, wool, or textiles over ten months of the year. They probably did not work for the other two months, when they were expected to sustain themselves. These workers usually received unprocessed materials, such as barley or wool, whereas personnel on temporary, levied duty or on military service were issued prepared foods and manufactured products, especially bread and beer, but occasionally meat, fish, dates, salt, and garments. Regular workers and household staff normally got bread and beer only on special occasions or as supplementary issues. These two types of rations, unprocessed and prepared, can also be distinguished in the records by the way they were distributed. Regular personnel received their rations individually or, less often, through their foremen, but levied and military personnel were often given bulk issues of prepared foods through a single individual, who might in his own name draw rations for platoons of men.[19]

Many regular laborers no doubt had families that helped provide them with food and clothing made from their unprocessed rations. This distribution continued in sickness and into old age, with an allowance added for each member of the family, whether of working capacity or not. On the other hand, temporary personnel, called away from their homes, needed to be fully supported by the institution during their term of service.[20]

Three types of work were given to unskilled dependent personnel. One involved jobs with definable quotas, such as a specified length of canal to be cleared, volume of ditch to be dug, number of bricks to be made or laid, amount of fish to be processed, or area to be sown or weeded. Record was kept of the work performed or not yet performed, deliveries made or not yet made. The second was day labor, usually such agricultural tasks as soil preparation, cultivation, and harvesting, carried out by numerous personnel on institutional land. No special record of this type of work was kept for regular workers, other than lists of men and their supervisors, and sometimes work days, but for levied personnel with a limited obligation, certain records were subscribed "work done." The third type assigned complements of unskilled labor, in established numbers, to work sites, teams, or to professionals, including cooks, blacksmiths, weavers, clerks, temple officers, and various other people. A leather worker, for example, might receive three men, a blacksmith two, a cook twenty-seven, a man in charge of the courtyard or public portion of a large building, three; a physician, one. Many of the skilled personnel were themselves of the ten-month rationed class. The highest number of laborers attested in an Akkadian document is just more than 600, far smaller than the teams of thousands of mobile workers characteristic of the Ur III period.[21]

Laborers went off the rolls for several reasons: natural attrition (illness, old age, death); flight; deployment to other places; and end of prescribed term of labor or military service. Absences were sometimes marked as illness or "not on duty." Death was indicated with a simple checkmark next to the name. When people disappeared without being accounted for, the record was marked "fled." Flight, a perennial problem, was the subject of treaties and laws and was frequently mentioned in correspondence.[22]

As noted in Chapter 2, limited chattel slavery existed in the Akkadian period. Slaves were expensive luxuries used in household service, rather than in agricultural or industrial production. While slaves, like laborers, could and did have families, many of them seem to have been single, captive women.[23] Most slaves or servants had Sumerian or Akkadian names, so there is no reason to suppose they were of foreign origin. Slaves were released from service by death and only rarely manumitted. They seem to have fled often and could be marked or branded. Slaves were seldom given patronymics or professional designations, but were identified with the person they served, as in "the governor's slaves" or "the king's slaves." Not all people so-called need have been chattel slaves, however, because the word for "servant" or "subject" was the same as the word for "slave."[24] Many laborers may have been little better than slaves in social and economic status but were nonetheless not chattels.

Given Sargon's statement that he fed 5400 men per day (Appendix Ib 7), one may suggest that the main thrust of royal Akkadian recruiting efforts was for the military. Sargon and his successors sought dependent labor for their armies rather than for fieldwork, thereby raising a military force that no other rulers of the time could match or withstand.

Local notables, on the other hand, such as the governor of Eshnunna, might have more than a thousand people in their service, many of them skilled, who were supported by regular rations from the governor's household. The labor needed for agriculture and animal husbandry was provided contractually by people who were not members of the great household, but who sought remunerative opportunities or access to means of production.[25] Such arrangements brought the royal house and its notables significant income without significant outlay beyond providing access to lands and herds. Public works, such as roads, canals, and the construction of major buildings, were undertaken with labor levied from the citizenry.[26]

Akkadian labor practice, therefore, resembled more closely age-old communal techniques of management and shared risk than it did those of the later kings of Ur, who tried to centralize production in the royal establishment by maintaining a large pool of dependent labor.

## 3. Flocks, herds, and land transport

Animal husbandry was vital to both food production and industry. The pastures of Sumer and Akkad were dotted with sheep and goats, as well as smaller numbers of cattle and donkeys.[27] There was also a powerful, valuable hybrid of the wild ass and the domestic donkey, a beast the Sumerians called the "kunga." The complex genealogy of this creature was ridiculed in a Sumerian proverb: "Kunga, do you know your family tree, do you even know your mother?"[28] As with the surrounding fields, the ownership of these flocks and herds was often mixed. Some belonged to local families, others to Akkadian dignitaries, whose agents kept track of them. The animals were counted regularly and the shepherds had to produce evidence of loss, such as the horns or skins of animals that had died naturally or been killed by predators. Herd masters compiled records of their animals, including their yield of young, where they were located, and how many animals were culled for such purposes as banquets, travel provisions, or sacrifices.

The special importance of sheep and goats was that they yielded the renewable resources of wool or hair, milk, and cheese, and they could also be consumed as food or offerings (Figure 4.1b). Wool in particular was a reliable source of money: one mina (one kilogram) of wool, the typical annual yield of a sheep, was worth one-quarter shekel of silver, so the 6000 plucked sheep known from a document at Adab would be worth about 1500 shekels of silver, enough to buy 270 hectares of arable land in rural Akkad or 3100 square meters of urban living space, vastly larger than a good-sized Akkadian-period house in Eshnunna (169 square meters) or even the Northern Palace there (2100 square meters).[29] Sheep were counted at plucking time and the herd masters expected to receive or be shown certain quantities of wool and young in proportion to the herds. The shepherds probably sustained themselves by retaining a percentage of the yield and wool, once the official quota had been met, as well as by periodic food rations. If the official quota for the season had not been met, the records noted how much the shepherds were in arrears on their obligation.[30] Compared to the tens of thousands of sheep and goats known from pre-Akkadian Ebla and post-Akkadian Ur, Akkadian records mention relatively small numbers of animals, such as 3000 sheep plucked for the governor of Adab; this may be a consequence of Akkadian preference for decentralized management.[31]

Donkeys and cattle were used as draught animals and were individually more valuable than sheep or goats. Strict records were kept of their number, age, and sex. Some wealthy people owned a prestigious transport vehicle called a "hand wagon," pulled by one or a pair of donkeys. Hand wagons were distributed by Manishtusu to some of the men who sold him land and are mentioned in lists of valuable domestic possessions and in a shipment of expensive goods sent to the capital.[32] The vehicle in question may have been a two-wheeled light cart, as opposed to the two- or four-wheeled "hauling" or "long" wagon, as the Sumerians called it. One type had the axle under the front shield and was a two-wheeled smaller version of the four-wheeled wagon. Another type, a straddle car in which the driver stood above the axle, was more maneuverable.[33]

A letter addressed to an unnamed Akkadian notable asks him, as an act of patronage, to authorize the appropriation of a two-wheeled cart from its present custodian or owner:

> I said to (my lord) "Issue me a two-wheeled cart," but he did not issue me one. There is a two-wheeled cart in Kibabbara, in the household of Bazizi, ready

to go, my man saw it there. As soon as (my lord's) messenger has returned, let him give it to me. I am his valued servant, so now let him make me happy. May my lord's written word about this reach (Bazizi), so my lord can be the one to inform him. Then I will be even happier![34]

There were of course roads in Sumer and Akkad, as well as the towpaths along the canals and rivers, but Akkadian sources make no reference to maintaining routes or post houses, as attested later in the third millennium.[35] The Sumerian poet of *The Curse of Agade*, resentful of Akkad's glory, evokes overgrown towpaths and roadways as signs of Akkadian decline, allowing himself some elaborate word plays:

> May rank grass grow tall where boats used to haul,
> May sad weeds curl where cartwheels would whirl.[36]

## 4.  Water transport

Akkad and especially Sumer were crisscrossed by natural and artificial water-courses that served dual purposes of irrigation and transportation. Modern surveys have revealed the outlines of many of these ancient water systems and Akkadian maps and an itinerary use them as landmarks (Chapter 9 part 9, Figure 9.11). The Euphrates linked Nippur to Shuruppak and Uruk, where it was joined by a major channel from the Tigris, branching off between Umma and Zabala. The main channel of the Tigris linked Adab with Umma via one branch, and with Girsu and Lagash via another, so, from the perspective of Agade, Adab was at the water gateway to two of Sumer's richest provinces, as well as the entrepot for goods being shipped to the capital and the royal family.[37]

Water transport was complicated by the paucity of useful wood in Mesopotamia, meaning that boats were expensive to build; by unstable watercourses, meaning that shipping routes could change abruptly; and by the use of watercourses for irrigation, which meant that ditches bringing water to fields could hamper boat hauling. Boats, nevertheless, had the great advantage of being able to move massive amounts of cargo. A typical Akkadian barge might be 5–7 meters wide and 12–15 long, with a capacity of 30 to 40 tons.[38]

Although *The Curse of Agade* does not specify what was the most important product shipped from Sumer to Akkad, it was undoubtedly grain. Of the 885,000 liters of barley in an account from Adab, for example, large quantities were shipped to Agade by boat. A scribe oversaw the loading of 120,000 liters, under the supervision of the "captain of hauled boats."[39] This shipment alone would have sustained Sargon's army of 5400 men for some time. Other people who appear in this record include merchants, a general, and royal soldiers, who perhaps guarded the grain and watched over the numerous boat haulers needed for the voyage upstream.

A shipping manifest for a "great boat" loaded from the estate of Mesag lists containers of oil and lard, skins, leather water bags and buckets, baskets of brewing materials, vegetables, containers of spices, baskets of fish, flour, fattened livestock

– enough to prepare a sumptuous meal worthy of the royal family, who may have been passing through the region.[10]

Despite the ubiquity of boats, Akkadian sources provide little information about their construction or maintenance, beyond what may be occasional repairs.[11] If *magula* "great boat," was a princely barge, more common vessels were referred to as *magur*.[12] These were classified by their capacity in dry measures: 120 gur (36,000 liters), 90 (27,000 liters), and 60 (18,000 liters). If boats of this type were used for sending grain to Agade, the 120,000 liters noted above would have filled a small flotilla of barges.

Shipping may have been a niche for private enterprise, in which boat owners offered their barges and crews for hauling goods, especially the huge quantities going to Akkad. A record from Adab gives the hire, slightly less than twenty shekels of silver, for two flotillas, one of five boats (four of 36,000 liters and one of 27,000 liters, for a total capacity of 171,000 liters), and the other of four boats (one of 36,000 liters, one of 27,000 liters, and two of 18,000 liters, for a total of 99,000 liters).[13]

Boatmen were valued for their skills. At the Akkadian court, the "chief boatman" was an honored dignitary, while the price of a slave who was a professional boatman was fifteen shekels of silver, considerably higher than average.[14]

In the words of *The Curse of Agade*, once boats reached Agade, laden with the fruits of Akkadian imperial expansion, "its harbor, where ships tied up, hummed cheerfully."[15]

## 5.   Fish, fowl, and swine

After grain and sheep, a third pillar of Akkadian food production, particularly in Sumer, was river and sea fishing. Yet this was a low prestige industry carried out by those who could tolerate the notorious stench associated with their work, as in this apostrophe to a fish:

> Your reek is offensive, you make people gag, they wrinkle up their noses at you.
> No trough would do for the slops you take in,
> Whoever has held you in his hand dares not touch his body anywhere else![16]

The fisherman could, however, comfort himself that he was a mainstay of the population, recalling the Sumerian proverb: "Be there commerce in a city, a fisherman caught the food!" and a later Babylonian epic even told of a time the human race had been saved from starvation by an abundance of fish.[17]

Akkadian administrative documents, especially from the Lagash. region, record enormous quantities of fish, as many as 60,000 in a delivery, not to mention other creatures of the marshes caught for food, such as turtles and birds. It seems that in years when plentiful irrigation water was available, fish appeared in great numbers in the pools in the fields. The great carp of the Euphrates was no doubt served as the main dish at gastronomic events. At Nagar, catfish was also favored.[18]

Although there is abundant evidence for raising poultry in subsequent periods of Mesopotamian history, there are few Akkadian sources, beyond records of delivery (up to 5400 in one case) and fattening of geese, ducks, and other domestic fowl.[49] Feathers and eggs occur in administrative documents, sometimes in large quantities, suggesting the existence of official poultry operations. The chicken (or francolin?) may not have been regularly present in Mesopotamia until the post-Akkadian period, probably introduced from the Indus Valley (part 6, this chapter). When exalted dignitaries, such as the majordomo of Naram-Sin's domains, received gifts of eggs, along with gold and other wealth, these may have been the eggs of the ostrich, a bird once indigenous to Mesopotamia. Akkadian artisans may well have seen decorative possibilities in these eggs, smooth and white as ivory, although no certain examples from this period are known.[50]

There is no Akkadian evidence for large-scale pig husbandry; swine were raised in small numbers by private individuals. Since an Akkadian bride gift (Chapter 2 part 2) includes several pigs, they may have been an appurtenance of a well-provided household. Kept near human settlements in sties, pigs were probably also allowed to range freely, as they improved urban sanitation by devouring offal and sewage in the streets.[51] Roast pork was an esteemed delicacy served to visiting dignitaries and, in post-Akkadian times, a treat for the gods and for members of the royal family. Pigs, especially young ones, were the preferred diet at Nagar and accounted for nearly half the bones found.[52] The first evidence for a taboo on pork consumption in Mesopotamia comes much later, from the ninth century BCE. Lard was an important item of diet and was issued to singers in particular, perhaps because it helped their voices.

The peculiar destiny of the pig, that it was productive only when killed, not to mention its voracious eating habits and fondness for wallowing, gave it a larger role in later Mesopotamian literature and folk sayings than the more numerous, but less colorful, sheep, donkeys, and cattle.[53] On the other hand, pigs were not so often modeled as toys as sheep, so were probably held in low esteem (Chapter 10 part 2). Ritual use is suggested by two Akkadian interments of heads or skulls of pigs at Nagar.[54]

## 6.  Wild and exotic animals

Wild animals were hunted and occasionally kept for food, sacrifices, display, and entertainment. At Adab, for example, there was a small herd of deer, and at Eshnunna deer were consumed. The bones of roe, red, and fallow deer were identified at Nagar, along with those of lion and gazelle, the latter being an important game item at Taya as well.[55] Hunting wild bulls was a kingly sport, explicitly commemorated by Naram-Sin, who declared that when he went to a place called Tibar, perhaps the Jebel Abd al-Aziz in Syria, "he himself slew a wild bull."[56]

Many species of exotic land and marine animals from as far as the Indus made their initial appearance in Mesopotamia during the Akkadian period, as gifts, tribute, or emblems of conquest, indicative of the international horizon of the age, just as other goods from distant regions, such as diorite and serpentine, appeared for the first time in significant quantities (Chapter 2 part 1). In art, the elephant, along with the rhinoceros and crocodile, may first be depicted in a seal engraving found at Akkadian-period Eshnunna (Figure 4.2).[57] The water buffalo, likely introduced from the Indus Valley (Meluhha) at this time, is also represented in Akkadian cylinder seals, perhaps as a symbol of the Gulf or regions further east (Chapter 9 part 3).[58] In texts, Meluhha-birds may refer to chickens or francolins; a spotted or particolored feline might be the cheetah or tiger.[59]

Monkeys, mentioned in *The Curse of Agade*, were probably brought to Mesopotamia in the Akkadian period; depictions of monkeys are known earlier. A small

(a)

(b)

*Figure 4.2* Scenes of wild and exotic beasts. (a) Seal of Isinnum the scribe, servant of Binka-lisharri, son of Naram-Sin, showing a bull-man subduing a lion, a hero mastering a water buffalo, and an oryx. (b) Indus Valley seal from Akkadian Eshnunna, with an elephant, rhinoceros, and crocodile.

stone monkey turned up at Akkadian Taya, a remote rural settlement, so simian imagery is attested among people who had probably never seen a living specimen.[60] A letter purportedly written by one named Monkey appeared in the post-Akkadian Sumerian curriculum:

> O passerby, tell my mother Monkey's message: If Ur is the city of the moon-god's glory, Eridu is the city of Enki's abundance. I, for my part, sit behind the door in the chief musician's house, consumed by longing. Don't leave me to die! Since my food is by no means fresh and my drink is by no means fresh, send me some by courier. This is urgent![61]

The passage in *The Curse of Agade* about exotic and wild animals jostling each other in the square of the Akkadian capital (Chapter 2 part 1; Appendix IIIb) may well reflect the fact that the Akkadian kings were the first in Mesopotamia to collect unusual animals as a sign of their far-flung dominions.[62]

The lion had special status in Akkadian art, in which its fur, mane, and snarling maw were depicted in new ways that were regularly imitated thereafter. Naram-Sin was compared to a lion in a later Babylonian poem praising his valor; the king and Ishtar herself sat on lion thrones and rode lions to battle.[63]

## 7.   Food and drink

Akkadian records provide much information about food production and consumption, brewing, and the diet of the elite. The main crops were grains, especially barley and wheat. These were supplemented by such cultivated foods as onions, chick peas, lentils, cress, coriander, cumin, and other vegetables and spices. Locally grown fruits included dates, figs, pomegranates, apples, and grapes.[64] Sheep, goats, cattle, and pigs were sources of protein, as were deer, gazelles, antelope, hares and rabbits, wild boars, field mice, jerboas, and hedgehogs. A rich variety of birds and fish was also available and consumed. In some cases, such delicacies as rare fish were transported considerable distances, for example from the Gulf to northern Syria, perhaps by salting them.[65] Dairy products included milk and cream, cheese, and butter, as well as related products, such as ghee and *kishik* (dried yogurt cakes).[66] Salt was a staple and regularly issued to soldiers and construction workers.[67]

Cooking techniques are seldom referred to in the documents. Meat and fish were consumed roasted or dried. Whole grains were parched or roasted over fire, or boiled in a small amount of water until soft, then spread in the sun to dry. This last, known today as *burghul*, can be prepared in large quantities and kept a year or more. It may be reheated by steaming or boiling, and eaten with oil, meat, or vegetables, or added to soup. Other cereal dishes included groats and semolina, made from emmer wheat or barley, mixed with water, milk, or oil, and served with additives, such as dates.[68]

The production of bread and beer, the twin mainstays of the Mesopotamian diet, was a major government-sponsored activity in the Akkadian period. The records focus mainly on the management of the raw and end products, so the tedious, repetitive labor and discipline that made these industries possible are left to the imagination of the historian. When barley, the ingredient needed in both, was harvested and threshed, the grain piles on the threshing floor were separated and measured by the workers under the supervision of scribes. After the administrative reforms of Naram-Sin, the quantities destined for the government storehouses and mills were converted into the new government standard of measure, and these figures checked against the harvest anticipated from the fields accounted for by the land registrar and his staff. Any deficiencies were noted, expenses were deducted, and payments due recorded. Then the grain was sent to the mills for grinding, to storehouses, or to breweries.[69]

At the family level, grinding was traditionally done by women. Every home probably had a grinding set for food preparation, consisting of a flat stone tray and a stone roller. For this, the preferred stone was basalt brought from the Jebel Bishri region of Syria. At the industrial level, grinding was done by women as well. The various grades of flour were mainly functions of the fineness of the grinding and the quality of the grain supplied to the mills.[70]

Industrial baking was regulated by standards that rated bread according to the amount of flour used to make an individual loaf. Ten measures of flour, for example, yielded twenty or thirty loaves of flat bread or small buns. For simplicity of record keeping, scribes reckoned the expenses of baking in terms of the unprocessed grain that was used to prepare the baked goods, deducting only raw grain from their inventories. To keep the withdrawals in accordance with the records, they regularly factored in the small amount of raw grain lost in grinding and preparation.[71]

The mass production and distribution of food were key elements in the expansion and maintenance of Akkadian power, ever farther afield as the empire expanded.[72] No figures are available for the size or output of government bakeries, but to judge from a series of records from Umma, in which bread was issued to large groups of men, perhaps soldiers, the local bakery supporting them had to make daily a thousand or more loaves. The teams of workers rebuilding the temple at Nippur for Naram-Sin would have required much more than that. Sargon boasted of feeding his army, a statement without parallel in commemorative inscriptions and so noteworthy as to be satirized in a later spoof (Chapter 11 part 6); perhaps his pride in this achievement derived from his alleged past as a cupbearer to a king. The labor project of Rimush at Sabum sustained some 500 workers at least a year and half. There, fifty women ground flour and a team of slave women prepared and served food. Manishtusu's two-day banquet for nearly 1000 men, in celebration of his land purchase, must have needed substantial quantities of bread, beer, meat, and other delicacies.

The two basic types of bread were unleavened and leavened. Unleavened bread was made by mixing flour and water into dough, then baking it, whereas leavened bread required yeast, naturally occurring or a sour mixture from the previous dough. For flat bread of either type, the dough was rolled or patted, then placed on the pre-heated wall of a *tannour*-oven. When the bread was ready, it dropped off the wall. Dough was also shaped into balls, crescents, rolls, and pockets, which were used to serve and eat hot foods such as meat or fish. Sweetened cakes were made by adding honey, syrup, nuts, dates, and spices to flour and oil.[73] Cakes were turned out of decorative pottery and metal molds.

Brewing, like bread-baking, was an activity that could be carried on in the home or in industrial installations. Unlike baking, however, many of the terms for brewing and brewing equipment were neither Sumerian nor Akkadian, so one may wonder what unnamed, gifted people first worked out the intricacies of this art. The most common beverage was beer brewed from fermented barley. Drinking it through a straw, as often shown in representations of feasts, brought on the heightened, relaxed mood celebrated in Mesopotamian literature, but with a relatively low intake and thus less of a hangover.[74]

For beer or malts, the brewer combined bruised grains with leaven to form a fermented substance that was crumbled and mixed with water to make a mash, to which was added malt, also made from barley. The mixture of mash and malt, or wort, could be dried and stored until needed. Once the wort was moistened and heated in a clay vessel with a pierced bottom, it produced beer.[75] Beverages deemed finer and in less common use included kvass, wines, lagers, or ales, some made from grapes, dates, and other fruit. Nothing is known of their production in the Akkadian period.[76]

As with bread, the scribes who kept the records for beer converted the liquid quantities of beer into their dry equivalents in barley, and then deducted them from their stock records. They rated beer according to four main grades, depending on how much brewing barley was used to make a standard liquid measure. This ranged from 1 to 2 1/3 dry measures to 1 liquid measure. To meet demand, government breweries had the capacity to produce and store thousands of liters of beer a day of various types, ready for distribution and consumption.[77]

In later periods, beer was readily available for purchase in taverns run by independent women. Wisdom literature advised against lingering in such places, not saying why but presumably to avoid low company and the dangers of disputes arising from *le vin mélancolique*. Some taverns had facilities for prostitution. No evidence is available for Akkadian attitudes toward prostitution or any of the other behaviors and vices often associated with excessive consumption of alcohol.[78] A Sumerian drinking song (Figure 4.1c), evidently sung by Ninkasi, the goddess of brewing, goes:

> I'll have the cupbearers, the waiters, the brewers stand by,
> While I make my rounds with a round of beer,
> While I feel cheerful, more and more cheerful,
> Drinking my beer, in a carefree mood,
> Quaffing with pleasure the fruit of the field,
> Happy in heart, merry of mind,
> As the happiness grows in my heart,
> I'll tie one on, that glad-suit fit for a queen![79]

As for feasts and elite menus, roast pork was likely the main dish served to honor country people, such as Manishtusu's guests, and foreigners, such as a visiting delegation of Gutians at Adab. On state occasions, as when the king came to Sumer, the meals included beef, mutton, goose, and venison and other game, accompanied by dishes made from chick peas, lentils, nuts and grains, cheese, honey, juniper berries, apples and figs, dates, and white wine – a richness foreshadowing the "royal repast" or "king's table" of later periods.[80] In private consumption, pork, especially from young pigs, was a preferred diet item at Nagar and in the Diyala region, and plentiful evidence was found at Eshnunna for meals of beef, lamb, pork, and various kinds of fowl.[81]

The chief provisioner in the Akkadian administrative hierarchy was the *sagi* or "cupbearer," like *šaperum* an Akkadian title imported into Sumer.[82] The records of Mesag, the cupbearer at Adab, show that he was concerned with the acquisition and preparation of food for daily meals, for offerings to the gods, and for serving official visitors. He also had charge of the table wares needed for banquets and was responsible for the purity of the repast served. In these capacities, he was the liaison between the slaughterhouse and the governor's kitchen, between the grain office and the bakery and brewery, and saw to the distribution of their finished products. The surviving records do not mention the spices, vegetables, fish, poultry, and other foods one would expect at the governor's table, so the cupbearer at Adab may have been involved primarily with basic commodities in bulk, whereas the more specialized cuisine of the governor's kitchen may have been the concern of another palace official, perhaps the head cook.[83]

The chief cupbearer at Girsu was also named Mesag, so it is tempting to speculate that these were the same man, who may have followed the governor to a new post. In any case, at Girsu he worked with a more diverse menu of foods, including bread and beer, fresh fish, ducks and ducklings, the *izi*, a domesticated bird, and the *ashe*, a game bird, perhaps a type of crane.[84] The governor's household at Girsu enjoyed varied, interesting, and no doubt carefully prepared meals, as befit an important regional center in the Akkadian Empire.

Did this same Mesag go on to become governor of Umma? If so, his rise through the hierarchy paralleled, albeit modestly, the legendary career of Sargon himself.

## Notes

1  Adams 1965: 13–29; B. Foster 1982a: 63; 1986a; for the Akkadian period, Liverani 1988b: 244–47; in general, Heermann and Sellnow 1982; D. Potts 1997: 56–90. For private or communal ownership of arable land, especially in northern Babylonia, and the steady acquisition of large areas of it by the crown, Chapter 1 note 1.

2  B. Foster 1985, 1982c: 15–18; in general Glassner 1985a; Renger 1995a; Cripps 2007; Milano 2008.

3  B. Foster 1982a, 1986b: 49. The plow unit (*charrue* in pre-Napoleonic France) is known in many cultures. In pre-modern Iran, the *juft*, or plow unit, was normally about seven hectares, though could vary from four to fourteen even in the same region. This was the area of land plowable in either a year or two years, depending on whether or not alternating year fallow was observed, C. Kramer 1982: 65.

4  Maekawa 1981.

5 B. Foster 1986a; Cooper 1983a: 52–53 (Appendix IIIb) lines 45–54. For different inter-pretations of this passage, Alster 1985: 162 and Attinger 1984: 100.

6 B. Foster 1986a; Liverani 1988; differently Weiss and Courty 1993: 139–41; for Sume-rian literary topoi about the Amorites and life on the mid- and upper Euphrates, J. Klein 1997; Jahn 2007.

7 B. Foster 1993a; in general, Wilkinson 1994, 2000; Jas ed., 2000; Zettler 2003: 20; for comparable Assyrian policies, Liverani 1988. B. Foster 2011a: 128–31 rashly discussed possible productivity figures and land areas in Sumer; in general D. Potts 2011.

8 For royal confiscation of land in Sumer, B. Foster 1985, 2011a: 127–31; further on confiscation Chapter 1 note 21; for the Akkadian royal family in priestly office, Chapter 6 part 3; for priesthood holding crown land parcels, B. Foster 1982a: 21; for a royal governor managing the temple of Enlil at Nippur, Chapter 3 note 97; for crown and royal governors' purchase of entitlements on land in Sumer, B. Foster 1982a: 29–31 (improved edition in Steinkeller 1999b) and MDP 14 19 (Steinkeller and Postgate 1992: 99); in general Pomponio 2013: 27–28 and for earlier discussions of this issue by Dia-konoff and others, Chapter 12 part 4; the different view of Kienast 1973, followed by Nissen 2012: 81, is unsupported by evidence, Chapter 2 note 88.

9 Seux 1965; Maeda 1979; Hruška 1990.

10 Maekawa 1984, 1990; Steinkeller 1988a; Civil 1994; Hruška 1995; Liverani 1997; D. Potts 1997: 70–86; for a bibliographical survey, B. Foster 1999; in general Poyck 1982; Van Driel 2000.

11 BIN 8 267, 276, 280 (M. Lambert 1965: 123; Bridges 1981).

12 For general discussions of labor in the third millennium, though without consideration of the Akkadian period, Powell 1987.

13 For a brief comparison of Pre-Akkadian and Ur III labor conditions, Maekawa 1987.

14 Discussions of Ur III labor include Englund 1990, 1991; for quantification, Robson 1999: 138–66, with evidence for pre-Ur III roots of the techniques.

15 B. Foster 2010b: 145–46.

16 B. Foster 2010b: 144–45; further below, Chapter 10 note 4.

17 B. Foster 2010b: 147.

18 B. Foster 2010b: 146; MAD 1 253 (igi nu-tuk, LUL).

19 Gelb 1965; B. Foster 2010b: 146; for the difference between rations and wages, Maekawa 1989.

20 Gelb 1965; B. Foster 2010b: 146.

21 B. Foster 2010b: 147; above, note 8.

22 B. Foster 2010b: 147–48.

23 B. Foster 2010b: 148.

24 B. Foster 2010b: 148.

25 B. Foster 1986a.

26 For a possible record of canal work, Robson 1999: 139; differently B. Foster 1982b: 26–27 (stone quarrying).

27 Postgate and Powell 1993, 1995; Kraus 1966; Heimpel and Liverani 1995; Hallo 1996b; Adams 2006.

28 Alster 1997 1: 307; for the kunga in northern Syria, Chapter 3 note 175. For equids in general, Zarins 2014.

29 Ryder 1993; B. Foster 2014b; for the buying power of wool, B. Foster 2014b; for exam-ples of records of sheep consumption, CUSAS 19: 28–30.

30 Kraus 1966; M. Lambert and Kientz 1967; Heimpel and Liverani 1995.

31 CUSAS 19 74; D. Potts 1997: 92–93, who estimates over half a million head for accountable herds in Ur III sources; Steinkeller 1995a.

32 B. Foster 2010a: 140–41; CUSAS 13 29; Chapter 3 note 132.

33 Salonen 1951: 28–35; Littauer and Crouwel 1979; Jans, Breetschneider, and Salla-berger 1998. For model wagons of the Akkadian period, J. Oates in Oates, Oates, and McDonald 2001: 280–85.

34  Kienast and Volk 1995: 48–50.
35  Frayne 1997a: 49 lines 155–60: "I [built] road houses in [the steppe], I planted gardens around them, I, the king, put gardeners in charge of them."
36  Cooper 1983a: 62–63 (Appendix IIIb) lines 264–65.
37  Adams and Nissen 1972: 36 figure 17; Steinkeller 2001; Stone 2003; Hritz 2010; Ur 2013: 153.
38  Adams 2006: 139–42; in general D. Potts 1997: 122–37.
39  CUSAS 13 78.
40  BIN 8 267; compare CUSAS 13 29.
41  BdI Adab 183, supply of bitumen for boats; CUSAS 26 252 records delivery of fir logs for boat building.
42  Salonen 1939: 12–16; perhaps the same kind of boat as the má-gur gu-la of ITT V 9311.
43  BdI Adab 90. For a letter requiring 6 boats of 30 gur (9000 liters), Kienast and Volk 1995: 133–34; for boats at Susa, Chapter 3 note 142; for ferries, Selz 1995a.
44  CUSAS 13 86; B. Foster 1983a: 149 no. 3.
45  Cooper 1983a: 52–53 (Appendix IIIb) line 37.
46  Vanstiphout in Hallo 1997: 582 lines 63–65.
47  Alster 1997 1: 74; for fish saving the human race from starvation, *Muses*, 267.
48  The fishing industry at Lagash is particularly well documented, including delivery, preparation and consumption, and management of fishermen. More than a dozen varieties of fish are attested, the identifications of which for the most part are unknown. Sample documentation: fish in forty-three installments: ITT II 4412; large numbers of fish: BdI Adab 260: 1500 fish in second installment; ITT V 9254, 9334, RTC 129 (59,280); rare types of fish: ITT I 1408; sea fish: ITT II 5750; CT 50 134, 173; fish quotas for fishermen: ITT II 5722; fish distributed in administrative headquarters ("scepter house"): ITT II 5759; in cult: ITT II 2941 (also CUSAS 23 167); salted: ITT I 1454; sent to Agade: ITT I 1083; issued to workers: CUSAS 23 166 (Adab?). The fishing industry in Ur III times has been studied by Englund 1990 and for Mesopotamia in general by Salonen 1970. For records of turtles, Farber 1974. For fish bones at Nagar, Dobney, Jaques, and Van Neer in Matthews 2003: 425–28.
49  The best evidence is from the south, especially Girsu: ITT II 5711 records delivery of 5400 birds called dar-ra "colored," for which there are various possibilities of identification, in any case indicative of a large poultry operation. Eggs are delivered or presented in ITT I 1312, 1396, 1472; ITT II 2897, 3073, 4561, 4566 (to the king himself); ITT V 6741; RTC 114. Delivery of Birds: ITT I 1157, 1225; ITT II 4444, 4699, specifically baby birds: ITT II 4561, 5708. Delivery of feathers: CUSAS 19 19 (9600 feathers or wings, probably to make arrows, Von der Osten-Sacker 2014); discussion by Scheil 1925 (2640 feathers or wings); B. Foster 1980: 35 (feathers for headdresses? Calmeyer 1970, mostly Neo-Assyrian evidence). Consumption is attested in CUSAS 19 196, a record of fattening 22 geese, and 89 ducks for a month, similarly ITT II 4374; further below, note 55. Geese were also used in offerings, as in an offering of fatted geese, sheep, goats, cheese, and other delicacies made by the governor of Lagash to the goddess Ba'u, ITT I 1225.
50  Laufer 1926; Finet 1982; Caubet 1983; Civil 2013: 32–33.
51  Zeder 1998; Lion and Michel 2006.
52  Dobney, Jaques, and Van Neer in Matthews 2003: 421–29.
53  Foster and Salgues 2006.
54  Weber in Matthews 2003; Dobney, Jaques, and Van Neer in Matthews 2003.
55  CUSAS 19 196 records systematic feeding of a horned animal (shegbar, a ram or deer, sometimes a mythological monster, Van Dijk 1969b: 544), presumably for slaughter; Weber 2001: 348–49; for later records of deer, Steinkeller 1995a: 50; Heimpel 1972/5. For archaeological and glyptic evidence of various periods for hunting wild boar, D.

Potts 1997: 86–88. Fattening of a "foreign" or "mountain" goat is recorded in ITT II 3108, while two such fattened creatures were included in a boatload of luxury foods, perhaps to feed the royal entourage (BIN 8 267 iv 1). For gazelle at Taya, Reade 1971: 90; 1973: 185. Trained bears are well known in the later third millennium, Gelb 1975; Michalowski 2013. For fragments of statuettes of the Asiatic red deer, possibly Akkadian in date, Harper, Klengel-Brandt, Aruz, and Benzel 1995: 41 no. 20.

56  Appendix Ib 24; Frayne 1993: 127; this is presumably *bos primigenius*, or wild aurochs, bones of which have only rarely been identified in Mesopotamia (Reade 1971: 90; 1973: 185 [only in Akkadian levels]; D. Potts 1997: 254–55); further below, Chapter 9 note 48.

57  Lion 1992: 357–58; D. Potts 1997: 260–62; for elephants, Brentjes 1961; Collon 1977 (for the seal, 219 note 4; During Caspers 1973: 261 [Iran]; A. Parpola 1994: 314 ["native Harappan"], references courtesy Eric Olijdam). For elephant bones and tusks in Mesopotamia, mostly from later periods, Collon 1977: 222 note 25.

58  Boehmer 1974 and Heimpel 1987: 59 with note 135.

59  For the Meluhha-bird and feline, Heimpel 1993/97: 55.

60  For the monkey, Dunham 1985; for the monkey figure from Tell Taya, Reade 1973: pl. 68a; in general, Spycket 1998; Hamoto 1995, Akkadian evidence discussed 23–28.

61  M. Cohen 1976b; Powell 1978b. In line 7, igi-tùm-lá refers to wanting something that one can or should not have, so might mean here "homesickness." The proposal of Wilcke 1978: 220–21 that the monkey is eating garbage is not convincing because the monkey's complaint is that in a city of abundance, he is not being given food as fresh as he wishes, not that he is dining on offal. In line 10, Powell (p. 165) objects to the previous translations of šu-tak$_t$ as "send" but then translates it himself as "send by diplomatic pouch" on p. 194.

62  Lion 1992; D. Potts 1997: 254–65.

63  Braun-Holzinger 1987/90: 92–93; K. Foster (forthcoming); further Chapter 1 note 35, Chapter 9 note 52; Appendix IIb line 23.

64  This and the following paragraphs are based on Ellison 1984, a summary of evidence for Mesopotamian diet and food preparation; further Bottéro 1980/83; D. Potts 1997: 56–70; Powell 2003/5; Brunke 2011a, 2011b. For dates, CUSAS 19 199 (given to two men traveling from Adab to Isin).

65  Izquierdo and Muniz in Oates, Oates and McDonald 2001.

66  Stol 1993/7.

67  D. Potts 1984; 1997: 103–6; Streck 2006/8 and BdI Adab 184. Salt was a ration item for workers away from home performing heavy labor, Cripps 2010 no. 45 (MCS 9 240); for soldiers, Chapter 7 part 3.

68  For basic food preparation, gastronomy, and the sociology of food consumption, Bottéro 1980/83; Milano 1994b; 2012.

69  B. Foster 1982b: 89–107; Postgate 1984.

70  For milling, Milano 1993/97a, 1993/97b; the Akkadian installation at Susa, for example, had 54 women for milling flour, including 34 able-bodied women with 10 babies among them, 16 girls, and 4 old women (MDP 14 71 iii 12–16). For millstones, Stol 1979: 83–98.

71  B. Foster 1982b: 15, 102; Brunke 2011a: 98–104.

72  B. Foster 1982b: 21–25; A. Westenholz 1987: 39–41; Frayne 1993: 29; Cripps 2010: 20–21.

73  W. Lambert 1972/5.

74  Milano 1994b.

75  Stol 1971, 1987/90; Sallaberger 2012.

76  Civil 1964; Stol 1971, 1987/90; Powell 1994; Milano 1994a; Worthington 2009/11.

77  B. Foster 1982b: 14.

78  Worthington 2009/11.
79  Text in Civil 1964; Sallaberger 2012; although drinking scenes occur in Akkadian glyptic, they are usually interpreted as cultic (De Graeve 1982); in general Milano 1994a; Bottéro 1994.
80  B. Foster 1982b: 123–24; Steinkeller and Postgate 1992: 54–60; Cripps 2010: 113–15. For later third-millennium evidence for feasting, Brunke 2011b.
81  Pollock 1999: 134–37.
82  Glassner 1993/7.
83  Maiocchi 2010a; perhaps the special secure kitchen or larder supporting the governor's table was called *e-uzga*, a term of uncertain meaning (differently Cripps 2010: 103).
84  Texts documenting this man's activities include ITT I 1454, CT 50 165, and ITT I 1360, all having to do with fish; for birds: ITT II 4464, 5771 and ITT II 4561 (eggs and birds; for the *i-zi* bird, Veldhuis 2004: 239; for the *á-še* bird, Veldhuis 2004: 214–15, perhaps a variant writing of *a-zag*?), ITT II 5771; for beer: ITT II 4452; note also ITT II 5812 and ITT II 4457, where is he is given the title *sagi-mah*. For the "governor's table" and the "onion office" at Akkadian Nippur, A. Westenholz 1987: 94–96. For banquets at Ebla, Milano, and Tonietti 2012; for Ur III, Brunke 2011b; for the second millennium, Charpin 2013c. For the concept of the "king's table" in later sources, Tolini 2009; Brunke 2011a: 193–94; Grandjean, Hugoniot, and Lion 2013.

# 5 Industries and crafts

## 1. Akkadian industrialization

The Akkadian development of industrial production under institutional or government patronage gives a good indication of the profound changes that took place in this period. Most Mesopotamian industries had originated centuries before in the basic activities needed to sustain human life in the region, but were mainly limited to individual artisans or small workshops.[1] Five important features characterize Akkadian industrialization. One was the organization and concentration of workers in teams performing repetitive tasks in large workshops. A second was output, as in the mass production of thousands of standardized pots. A third aspect was the increased availability of imported raw materials thanks to the Akkadian conquests, including stones, woods, and metals. A fourth difference was the systematic rationing of workers while they were performing industrial labor. And the fifth was an expanded consumer base; the ruling elite provided a greater market for skills, craftsmanship, and products than existed previously.

## 2. Ceramics

Ceramic production was industrialized in the late fourth millennium, to the detriment of the decorative verve that had characterized much previous pottery in Mesopotamia. By the Akkadian period, painted vessels were extremely rare and mostly imported. The abundant ceramic remains in the archaeological record have been the fundamental criteria for dating Akkadian sites, in the absence of written remains (Chapter 3 part 1).[2] In Akkad, the most securely stratified Akkadian pottery comes from Eshnunna, where the ceramic data from the Northern Palace and at least two levels of a neighborhood of private houses nearby were scrupulously recorded.[3] In Sumer, securely dated Akkadian ceramics are best known from Nippur, where excavations were undertaken to clarify the pre-Akkadian to Akkadian transition, and from Uruk for the post-Akkadian transition.[4] Nagar has provided good evidence for Akkadian-period ceramics in northern Syria.[5]

Although pottery is the most prevalent class of artifact from Akkadian sites (Figure 5.1), it is difficult to assign ancient uses or names to most shapes, or to draw historical conclusions from their chronology or distribution. Furthermore,

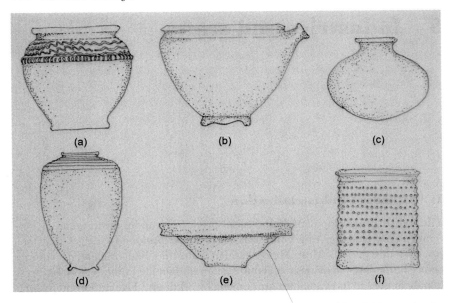

*Figure 5.1* Akkadian pottery types: (a) combed ware; (b) deep spouted bowl; (c) squat bottle; (d) ribbed storage jar; (e) conical bowl; (f) studded ware.

pottery is not often referred to in administrative documents, so there is little basis for matching words with artifacts. The vocabulary for ceramics in the Akkadian period includes names derived from contents, such as *dug-a-kum* "hot water jar"; from function, such as *nig-a-luh* "wash basin"; from shape, such as *dug-ka-dagal* "wide-mouthed jar"; and from size and volume, such as *sila*, a container of standard capacity.[6]

Archaeologists, for their part, record shape, decoration, and techniques of production, such as hand- or wheel-manufacture, type of temper, and the care taken in potting, but they do not address relative capacities beyond describing vessels as "large," "small," and "miniature," and hardly ever give modern capacities, even for fully preserved vessels. Furthermore, Akkadian documents sometimes record groups of different vessels kept in one place, such as a storeroom, but archaeologists generally publish pottery with emphasis on their diagnostic shapes rather than on their contextual interrelationships.

The following are the principal Akkadian vessel types referred to in archaeological publications, together with the words for these vessel types in Sumerian and Akkadian, though the words in the two languages may not always have the same meanings (Figure 4.1).

*Bowls and Plates*: Sumerian *utul*, Akkadian *diqarum*, used to heat and consume foods such as soups. Deep or footed bowls were called in Sumerian *bur*, Akkadian *purum*, especially if made of stone or metal. The standard bowl for grain rations was Sumerian *sila*.

*Cups*: Sumerian *shushala*, Akkadian *kasmu*, used to drink liquids. A cup with handles was written with the Sumerian sign GAL, but its pronunciation is uncertain.

*Beakers, Cooking Pots, and Storage Vessels*: Sumerian *dug*, Akkadian *diqarum* and *karpatum*, used to prepare, hold, and serve food and drink.

*Jars*: Sumerian *hal*, Akadian *hallum*, used to store and transport dry food and liquids; larger jar or basin, Sumerian *šab*, Akkadian *šappum*, also a large pitcher?

*Bottles or Flasks*: Sumerian *lahan*, Akkadian *lahannum*.

*Pitchers*: Sumerian *adagur* or *šab-gal* (used for libations); Akkadian *adagurrum*, vessels from which liquid was poured from over a lip on the rim.

*Cruses* or larger containers for valuable liquids: Sumerian *šakan*, Akkadian *šappatum*.

*Spouted Vessels*: Sumerian *ubur*, Akkadian *tulum*, for drinking or pouring liquids from a spout in the body of the vessel.

*Miscellaneous* clay vessels often had specific names, such as Sumerian *kir*, pithos or *lahtan*, a large jar used for brewing; Sumerian *bugin*, Akkadian *buginnum*, ladle or spoon; Sumerian *katab*, Akkadian *katappum* "stopper"; and the brazier, Akkadian *kinunum*.

Modern typologies do not necessarily correspond to ancient ones. An Akkadian record of nine deliveries of more than 6500 clay vessels classifies three types broadly as "pots": a cup (*kasum*), a large closed vessel to hold beer (*kurkurrum*), and another vessel, perhaps a pithos. This suggests that the Akkadian concept of a "pot" was above all that it held liquids, whatever its size or capacity.[7] Three other types, not classed as "pots" in the record, are a "combed" vessel (referring to its decoration), a *sila* (a bowl or measure of one sila capacity), and a cup.

One approach to understanding Akkadian pottery is to match depictions shown on Akkadian cylinder seals with examples known from archaeological contexts (Figure 4.1). There are pitfalls, however, in using such imagery. First is the possibility that some of the vessels shown were actually of metal or other materials. And second, they may not have been specifically Akkadian vessels, but stock imagery derived from earlier iconography.[8]

Small cups often appear in Akkadian seals. The vessels that seated deities hold, for instance, may be *shushala*-cups, whose name means "suspended in the hand," an apt description. In Akkadian burials (Chapter 10 part 7), the deceased sometimes hold similar small cups, as if raising them to the mouth for eternal sustenance. Comparable cups were found in Akkadian private houses in the Diyala region.[9]

Seals also frequently depict jars, perhaps as a sign of plenty, and other vessels, sometimes in sets of cups, pots, and jars. A group of seals with husbandry scenes (Figure 4.1b), for example, shows storage jars for dairy products that resemble those from Akkadian private houses.[10] Among them is a squat, round-bottom bottle and tall storage jars (Figure 4.1c, d).[11] A ribbed or studded beaker seen on seals is likewise Akkadian in style (Figure 5.1f), and other parallels between pottery in art and actual vessels are easily found.[12]

Decoration is usually absent. Some Akkadian bowls have narrow ridges of clay incised at regular intervals with a sharp tool. These form horizontal ribs or simple meanders (Figure 5.1d). Finer wares are occasionally combed (Figure 5.1a), referred to as such in the Akkadian delivery document noted above.[13] More elaborate decoration occurs in "mother goddess handled jars" with handles in the shape of animals or human beings, in jars with a row of hollow columns around the rim, and in a few pieces with relief in the form of scorpions, snakes, or lions.[14] There was also a ware fired to achieve a black sheen, perhaps in imitation of metal.[15] Only at Akkadian Mari is there evidence for a luxury class of pottery being used in the palace, but this may be local production and not typical of Akkadian sites as a rule.[16] Studded ware, decorated with small, conical protuberances of clay randomly distributed across the surface, was mostly restricted to small jars and bowls (Figure 5.1f).

The numerous examples of standard-sized, utilitarian bowls ("*sila* bowls") found at Shehna in the Khabur region suggest that they were mass-produced to hold rations, such as grain.[17] However, this type of ceramic is not so widely distributed as one might expect if it was normally used in rationing, so these pots may have had some special local purpose. In any case, large-scale pottery production is attested by the delivery records of large numbers of pots in installments.[18]

Most of the common ceramic forms in use during the Akkadian period originated earlier. A vase with a straight or upright handle, for example, was popular in the late pre-Akkadian period and appears sporadically in the early Akkadian. Ribbed and studded wares (Figure 5.1f), on the other hand, originated in the late pre-Akkadian but became more popular during the Akkadian period. This decoration was perhaps inspired by metal work, as was another Akkadian shape, a spouted vessel with a trumpet base and flaring mouth, likely used for libations. Tall, narrow cups, often crudely made with thick walls, and bowls with an inner rim were also types that persisted into the Akkadian period, then tended to disappear, as did a bowl with an inner rim. A distinctive squat bottle (Figure 5.1c) appeared first in the late pre-Akkadian period, was widely used during the Akkadian period, then died out in the early second millennium.[19]

A few shapes originated during the Akkadian period and remained in use for the rest of Mesopotamian history. These included a conical bowl with a rounded rim (Figure 5.1e) and a medium-sized jar with a ring base (Figure 5.1d). Deep spouted bowls (Figure 5.1b) are also typical of the period. Owing to the absence of data on the capacities of any excavated Akkadian vessel types besides the Shehna sila bowls, no correlation can be made between the metrological reforms of Naram-Sin and innovation or modification of existing forms during the Classical Akkadian period.[20]

The estate of the Akkadian notable Mesag had five potters among its personnel, more than reed workers and carpenters combined, a sign of the importance of ceramic production in the skilled labor output of such an establishment.[21] Later sources suggest that potters may have been organized into teams under a foreman and that potters in government service worked the year round for rations.[22] In any case, they were of low social status.

Potters may also have been responsible for maintaining a supply of good-quality clay for the manufacture of tablets. Suitable clay was evidently gathered at special places along watercourses and stored in large vats in the courtyards of administrative buildings. In addition to raw clay, this vat could contain cores or blanks of tablets, ready to be folded over and given a smooth coating for the writing surface.[23]

## 3. Metallurgy, faience, and glass

By the Akkadian period, metallurgy had already a long tradition in Mesopotamia.[24] The Akkadian conquests brought important quantities of metals into Sumer and Akkad, and new technologies were developed to work with them, under royal patronage. Despite the extraordinary technical skill shown in surviving Akkadian metalwork, the social status of metallurgists was not high. Neither those who produced bronze from copper and tin nor the masters who made gold and silver jewelry, implements, and ornaments received allotments of land, for example, as did administrators. Instead, they were among the echelons of people who were given food rations when they were working for an institutional patron; though artists sometimes received gifts when they delivered major works, Chapter 9 part 1.

Smiths are frequently mentioned in Akkadian administrative documents, often in teams. At Naram-Sin's reconstruction project of the Enlil temple at Nippur, for example, fifteen foremen supervised as many as ninety smiths. The men were given barley, fish, and salt, and presumably other food and drink, but were not otherwise paid for their work. The records of Akkadian manors occasionally list a smith among other people of subordinate status, like shepherds and mill hands.[25]

As was the case for other skilled workers, metallurgists in government workshops received orders from administrators, who weighed and distributed the raw materials.[26] Designs for major pieces were perhaps worked out with models and trial pieces.[27] The best surviving evidence for the production of metal sculpture comes from the records of Naram-Sin's building project at Nippur (Chapter 1 part 5).[28]

Copper was cheap in the pre-Akkadian period (1 shekel of silver to 195 shekels of copper), and it generally became even cheaper in the Akkadian period (as low as 1:240), when substantial hordes of copper implements are attested.[29] Copper was mined in Iraqi Kurdistan and in various localities in Iran, or brought by boat from Dilmun. Akkadian administrators thought copper came from Magan (Oman or the Gulf coast of Iran). In the century before Sargon, a single voyage to the international trading entrepot at Dilmun could purchase and bring back more than half a ton at a time.[30]

Copper was, therefore, available to the Akkadian authorities in large quantities. In one transaction, 8470 minas, well over four tons, were designated for the manufacture of hundreds of hammers for a project in distant Sabum, perhaps in the foothills of the Zagros Mountains. There, eleven smiths were needed to melt and rework the tools when they were worn out, probably from cutting stone (Chapter 1 part 3).[31]

As raw materials, copper and tin had been imported into Mesopotamia for centuries and alloyed there to make bronze, conventionally defined as containing at least 10 percent tin, though, for ancient Mesopotamia, some historians of metallurgy have used 5 percent and 2 percent, the lower percentages approaching the levels at which tin may occur naturally in copper ores. Mesopotamian metallurgy is one of the first instances in history of a sophisticated industry based entirely on imported raw materials, in which superior technology compensated for lack of resources.[32] The necessary heat for smelting was most easily obtained, in Sumer at least, by burning masses of dried reeds from the nearby marshes. As a result, those cities situated near marshes, such as Lagash, had extensive combustible materials readily to hand, so were centers for the fabrication of bronze.[33]

Administrators were sufficiently familiar with the details of the alloying process that they could record bronze objects according to the proportions of tin and copper used to manufacture them. They could also calculate the small percentages of material lost in smelting, so must have had mathematical norms for bronze production, as attested in administrative documents of other periods. Whereas modern analyses express the copper and tin as percentages of the whole, the ancient scribes expressed them as ratios to each other (copper:tin), without regard to other elements present in the metal.[34]

When the Akkadian establishment commissioned bronze pieces, the proportion of tin to copper could be specified, but in the records of this type, it appears that pre-made alloy was given to the metal worker, not the two separate components. One document, from early Akkadian Umma, specifies a tray in a proportion of 7 (copper) :1 (tin), corresponding well to a 7:1 Akkadian bowl from Burial 1374 at Ur.[35] In another such record, alloy in the proportion of 7:1 was turned over to a smith to make objects called "hand-ties," the precise nature of which is unknown, perhaps bracelets or manacles. This corresponds well to an Akkadian-period 7:1 toe ring from Ur. A bronze axe from an Akkadian burial at Uqair, near Ur, was also about 7:1.[36]

Yet such tin-rich bronze was not the general rule. Bronze was in fact in very limited distribution during the Akkadian period, whereas copper of a modern

| Ratio of Copper to Tin* | Number of Objects |
|---|---|
| 1:1 | 2 |
| 2:1 | 1 |
| 3:1 | 5 |
| 4:1 | 6 |
| 5:1 | 4 |
| 6:1 | 9 |
| 7:1 | 5 |
| 8:1 | 2 |
| 9:1 | 8 |
| 10:1 | 1 |
| 11:1 | 1 |
| 12:1 | 1 |
| 15:1 | 1 |
| 17:1 | 2 |

* Rounding up and down, so that 1.5 and 2.4 = 2.

metallurgical purity of 90 percent or better was the norm. The largest analyzed sample comes from Ur, mainly from burials. Of 173 objects securely dated to the Akkadian period, only 48, or about 27 percent, contained more than 5 percent tin, as seen in the table on the previous page.[37]

These figures show that while 6.1 and 9.1 were slightly preferred proportions, the composition of bronze was by no means standardized, even allowing for pre-Akkadian pieces with different proportions being melted down. The variability in tin content suggests that most metal work in private possession, such as in burials, was not mass-produced and that tin was not readily available outside of government workshops.

The limited presence of tin-rich bronze at Ur was by no means unique. At Nagar, for example, no bronze objects were found among the numerous tools, pins, and other copper utensils excavated.[38] Of the 334 metal objects recovered from the Akkadian-period level at Gawra, most were 95 percent or more copper; only one piece, a chisel, contained appreciable tin, in the proportion of 13:1.[39] The only certain Akkadian metal from Assur, a spearhead of Manishtusu, was 98 percent copper. The Akkadian lance point found at Tell Taya was nearly pure copper, as were two pins; two other pins contained tin in the proportions of 15:1 and 13:1. At Eshnunna about eighty objects were found together in a horde in the Abu Temple; some were bronze with up to 20 percent tin (5:1), but not all the pieces were analyzed, so the percentage of bronze objects in the horde cannot be determined. The only analyzed bowl from Girsu clearly datable to the Akkadian period was more than 96 percent copper, with no tin. Likewise, a kettle and other objects in the burials at Uruk were mostly copper. At Nippur, only four Akkadian bronze objects were found, with such tin contents as 10 percent.[40] Yet at Awal, in the Himrin Basin, by contrast, 14 percent of the fifty-five copper-based Akkadian-period objects had tin contents as high as 16 percent. The objects readily associated with the Akkadian military, such as spear points, axes, and daggers, hence produced in government workshops, were invariably copper; tin occurs mostly in small, personal bronze objects like garment pins, so they may have been made from older metal reworked by local artisans.[41]

Comparative pre-Akkadian data also show that the Akkadian period saw a decline in the use of bronze.[42] At Ur, for example, a random sample of forty-four metal objects of four types (bowls, axes, tools, and pins), securely dated to the pre-Akkadian period, found that 54 percent of them had tin content of 5 percent or more, as opposed to 27 percent of the Akkadian metal objects.[43]

If copper was cheaper, more readily available, and more widely distributed in the Akkadian period than before, even in rural areas such as Gawra, there may at the same time have been a decline in the availability of tin. Just prior to the time of Sargon, tin, like copper, was obtained in the Gulf. Ships brought copper and tin to Dilmun, where Sumerian merchants purchased them in ingot form, paying in wool and silver.[44] Akkadian expansion into Iran and the Gulf may have disrupted a long-standing mechanism of the tin trade, which could have caused a shortage of tin and a concentration of the existing supplies in the hands of the ruling establishment. Tin rarely occurs as such in Akkadian administrative documents, normally less than 250 grams at a time; occasional purchases of tin are noted.[45]

An inscription of Rimush commemorated the making of a tin statue of himself as an extraordinary achievement (Chapter 1 part 3). It is easy to see why Rimush boasted if, like many statues of Akkadian kings, it was nearly life size.[16]

Although Sargon claims that boats from Dilmun, Magan, and Meluhha came directly to Agade, it is not clear if these were Mesopotamian or foreign boats, or if they had bypassed their old entrepots in Sumer, or what their cargoes were. Men from Dilmun occasionally occur in administrative documents, but not in sufficient numbers to suggest they were boat crews. Perhaps Sargon is saying that he diverted international trade to his imperial capital, largely at the expense of Lagash, which previously had maintained regular connections with Dilmun and other centers further south.[17]

As for the uses of copper, a hardworking scholar at Kish, probably during the early Akkadian period or just before, drew up a seven-sided prism with a standardized encyclopedic list, inherited from pre-Akkadian times, of 128 words for utensils of copper, including pots, woodworking tools, daggers, and knives. Each entry is given twice, with the sign AN before the second entry, the meaning of which is unclear. One possibility is that he was indicating tin-bronze, abbreviating *annak* "tin," spelled AN.NA in the Rimush inscription commemorating his tin statue. Whatever the educational or speculative value of this list may have been, if even half of these objects were met with in daily life, the ideal kitchen, armory, workshop, and slaughterhouse would have had an impressive inventory of equipment. Metal pots, cups, bowls, and other vessels (Figure 5.2), rather than pottery, were the luxury ware of the Akkadian elite.[18]

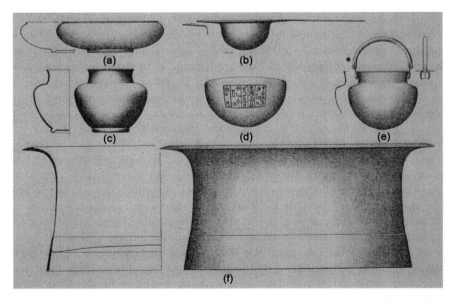

*Figure 5.2* Akkadian metal vessel types: (a) ring-base bowl; (b) strainer; (c) globular jar; (d) inscribed bowl; (e) kettle; (f) basin.

The Akkadian period produced the first known large-scale copper works using the lost-wax process, in which a wax figure is made, covered with clay, and fired so the wax melts out and a clay mold remains, into which molten copper is poured. Great care has to be taken to allow gases to escape so as not to leave blemishes on the copper (Figures 9.3, 9.4). Mesopotamia preserved no memory of who invented this sophisticated technique, which had been used to produce small objects long prior to the Akkadian period. The difference now, as with other industries, was scale: Akkadian craftsmen could cast statues weighing 400 kilograms or more.[49] The references to casting in Mesopotamian literature suggest that it was a prestigious technology that captured the poetic imagination. In the legend of Sargon's youth (Chapter 1 part 2; Appendix IIIa), for instance, the smith charged to murder him was to cast him into a mold of hot metal, like a statue, lifelike but lifeless.[50]

Akkadian smiths may also have experimented with other copper technology, including alloying it with silver, arsenic, and lead, with some combinations preferred for cast pieces and others for hammered pieces or finer work.[51]

Silver was used in Akkadian Mesopotamia as a standard of valuation, as a medium of exchange, and as a form of stored wealth, so can be considered both money and precious metal (Chapter 8 part 4). Akkadian inscriptions called the Taurus Mountains the "Silver Mountains," perhaps identifying them as a prime source of the silver in circulation, which appears to have increased in the Akkadian period, though "snow-capped" is another possible translation.[52] Basic commodities, such as wool or barley, had a silver value that fluctuated depending on conditions, in Akkadian terms, "a year of plenty" or a "year of dearth." In years of normal harvests, the silver to barley ratio was one shekel to one imperial measure of 300 dry liters.[53]

In addition, silver, measured by weight, circulated as currency in private and institutional contexts.[54] It was readily available to people of medium to high social status, as shown by its use in purchases of commodities and land, as well as by its appearance in lists of Akkadian bride gifts. Merchants used silver to make purchases on mercantile expeditions; lessees paid field rentals in silver.[55]

Silver was also used for luxury goods, such as table utensils, and jewelry. Silver diadems, for example, weighing twenty shekels each were distributed by Manishtusu to some of the men who had sold him their land (part 5, this chapter). A lavish gift to Sharkalisharri included what may be twenty silver cups (the text is damaged), wealth unlikely to be found in private possession, except among great notables.[56]

Gold was too rare to have a standard value; a 5:1 exchange rate of silver to gold is attested.[57] A few documents mention gold jewelry or presentations of gold to members of the royal family. A rich bride gift from Tutub, for example, includes a gold ring, while a four-strand gold necklace set with stones occurs with other jewelry in an inventory of wealth from Girsu (compare Figure 5.3). A notable of Umma gave Sharkalisharri, perhaps at the time of his coronation, a magnificent present of gold, perhaps thirty kilograms (the text is damaged). Another notable bought the income on extensive farmlands from Sargon himself, also for thirty kilograms of gold. Rimush, for his part, gave fifteen kilograms of gold to the temple of Enlil at Nippur after his successful campaign in Iran, no doubt derived from melting down art objects looted from Elam and Marhashi. The ten talents of gold (300 kilograms) appearing in one document, along with thirty talents of silver (900 kilograms), is no doubt a school-boy daydream of prodigious wealth.[58]

Akkadian metalwork is best known from vessels and implements found in burials and tools and weapons found in hordes. Metal vessels in gold, silver, bronze, and copper from the late pre-Akkadian period show a high degree of sophistication in workmanship, design, and purpose. Most pre-Akkadian types have Akkadian analogues.[59] During the Akkadian period, some new types developed, including a ring-based bowl, a footed goblet, a spouted pot with horizontal handle, and a circular lidded box (Figure 5.2).[60] The practice of inscribing vessels and other metal objects, including weapons and domestic utensils, expanded.[61] Foreign vessels were also esteemed and shown in art, such as the handled vessel, perhaps of Anatolian origin, one of Enheduanna's attendants holds in the relief depicting her performing a ritual (Figure 9.6), and the foreign vessel being carried as booty in the Nasiriyya stele of an early Akkadian king, perhaps Rimush.[62] The wide variation in composition of Akkadian metal objects, as noted above in connection with copper and bronze, may in part stem from an influx of foreign products that were melted down to make new pieces.

In common with the metallurgical industries, faience and glass production required high firing temperatures and considerable pyrotechnical skill. Manufacture of small faience beads and pendants was known at the local level in the Akkadian period, but evidence for more sophisticated objects is sparse both in texts and artifacts. A faience bowl from an elite house at Nagar shows that the ability to produce larger pieces existed.[63] There is tantalizing evidence to suggest that the Akkadian period could have seen the earliest glass-making in Mesopotamia. Scraps of glass have turned up at various sites, Akkadian in date or perhaps slightly later. No words for faience or glass have been identified in Akkadian-period documents; the "white clay" occasionally encountered may be gypsum.[64]

Although most of the mineral-based colorants for faience had to be imported, its essential components were readily available in the form of silicates (sand) and sodium carbonate binding agents (natron). In *Ninurta and the Stones*, a Sumerian poet, who probably lived a few generations after the collapse of Akkadian rule, disdains the raw ingredients of faience. Unlike more desirable stones, he says, they are so worthless that no one would want to buy them. Furthermore, their natural state has to be transformed by fire to be useful, and they lie everywhere in such quantities that they have to be cleared away as a nuisance:

> You, set aglow like fire,
> You, heaped up as if by a storm,
> You, pulled out like rushes,
> You, plucked up like weeds.
> Who ever reached out to get you?[65]

## 4. Stone

Along with gold, silver, and captives, stone was the most prestigious booty item specifically mentioned in inscriptions, brought back in the form of finished pieces or raw materials. In temples throughout the empire, the Akkadian kings, especially Rimush and Naram-Sin, dedicated both foreign stone objects, such as vases and bowls, and other works that had been newly fashioned from beautiful and interesting stones. The former were often inscribed with the royal name and a statement that they were booty "of Elam" or "of Magan."[66] Prized precisely because they had come from afar, these offered tangible proof of Akkadian triumph over distant lands (Chapter 11 part 6). Some stones, such as lapis, carnelian, and serpentine, were admired for their inherent properties as much as for their distant origin; flint arrowheads may also have been imported from the Zagros region.[67]

Northern Mesopotamia was rich in limestone, conglomerate, and sandstone, especially on the east bank of the Tigris, and there was basalt in the mountains. Stelae and other monuments in limestone, readily available and carved, were generally set up in Mesopotamian cities and temples to commemorate the king's military deeds.[68] With the growth of the Akkadian Empire, harder and more exotic stones, such as alabaster, were often chosen for this purpose. Diorite (or olivine gabbro) was mainly used to perpetuate the image of a ruler or high official, typically shown in ceremonial poses or in prayer. Such statues may have been intended to receive funerary offerings (Chapter 11 part 1).[69]

Although the Akkadian kings were not the first to be rendered in diorite, under the patronage of Manishtusu a brilliant school of sculptors began to turn out near life-size figures of the king in finely polished diorite, with highly naturalistic hands, feet, and musculature (Figure 1.5). The earliest statues in Mesopotamia to show folds in garments (Figure 5.4a), they convey a sense of strength in repose, markedly different from the stiffly formal attitudes seen previously.[70] Manishtusu even had his great land purchase recorded in diorite (Figure 1.1), whereas Rimush's land appropriation inscription (Figure 1.4) was done in limestone.[71]

In *Ninurta and the Stones*, the Sumerian poet who disdained sand had only praise for diorite:

> They shall bring you out from the Upper Lands,
> They shall bring you hither from the mountains of Magan,
> You shall wear out? hard copper like leather . . .
> The ruler who would establish his name for all time,
> Who has fashioned that statue for future days,
> Who shall place it in the mortuary chapel . . .,
> You shall be suited for that.[72]

Because Naram-Sin and other kings carved reliefs celebrating their victories on limestone cliffs in foreign lands, the poet considered this stone inherently loyal and obedient to Mesopotamian interests, destined to be kept in its natural state for commemorative stelae in the courtyards of important building. As the god Ninurta ordains:

> Your integrity shall in no way be diminished,
> It shall be wasteful to reduce your bulk to small pieces.
> My authority shall be fitly conveyed in your form,
> You shall be first of all suited for (showing) my defeat of slain heroes.
> You shall stand on a pedestal in my principal courtyard,
> This land shall look upon you with awe, it shall speak of you with
>    admiration.[73]

In the case of the Victory Stele of Naram-Sin (Figure 1.6), the limestone slab was shaped to look like a cliff relief, with the first landscape in Mesopotamian art carved upon it (Chapter 9 part 2).

Numerous other stones are blessed or cursed in *Ninurta and the Stones*. The ill-fated stones, such as flint, were destined to be broken up, ground, or pulverized, whereas the blessed stones, such as agate, chalcedony, carnelian, lapis lazuli, serpentine, jasper, and cat's eye gems, were to have their visual and tactile properties highlighted. A "stone of the land of Marhashi," the land in Iran that Manishtusu defeated and whose subjugation *The Curse of Agade* singles out as a sign of the dynasty's glory, was blessed as a container for fine oil and unguents and as an element in jewelry, so was probably chlorite or alabaster:

> May you become a cruse, may perfume be blended in you . . .
> May you be perfect for the head of a silver toggle pin.[74]

Serpentine, also from Iran, enjoyed a vogue in the Akkadian period as the new stone of choice for expensive Akkadian cylinder seals; cheaper ones and jewelry were made of more readily available stones and shell.[75] Imported carnelian, etched carnelian, and agate were particularly popular for luxury necklace beads. Lapis lazuli, the most prestigious exotic stone in the pre-Akkadian period, is not mentioned in *Ninurta and the Stones* at all and does not seem to have been so readily available as it had been previously.[76]

Evidence for an artisans' quarter that might date as early as the Akkadian period comes from a suburb of Ur, known by its modern name of Diqdiqqeh.[77] The finds of uncarved cylinders, beads, and an iris for the eye of a statue confirm the impression that Mesopotamian lapidaries produced different kinds of work in the same shop. A great atelier inaugurated by Naram-Sin, perhaps in connection with his Ekur project at Nippur (Chapter 1 part 5), was even commemorated in one of his year names. It may have housed sculptors, woodworkers, metal workers, and other craftsmen.[78] According to a very late source, the apprenticeship for an engraver of seals was four years.[79] The finest Akkadian seals were made by masters of the craft, who presumably specialized and took much longer than that to perfect their skill. Mentions of larger stone pieces are rare: one Akkadian document lists two daises delivered by a sculptor, one with an Anzu-bird image, weighing 173.8 kilograms, and the second perhaps with a decorative band of inlays running around it, weighing nearly 80 kilograms.[80]

## 5. Jewelry and personal adornment

The development of the jeweler's art in the Akkadian period reflects an expanded taste for personal adornment among the new, wealthy elite, as well as an influx of precious materials from conquest and trade. Jewelry adorned the head and hair, ears, neck and chest, arms, fingers, and occasionally toes.[81] Gold and silver were used for privately owned, expensive jewelry (Figure 5.3). In the approximately 1800 Akkadian-period burials at Ur, about 2 percent contained gold and 3 percent silver jewelry.

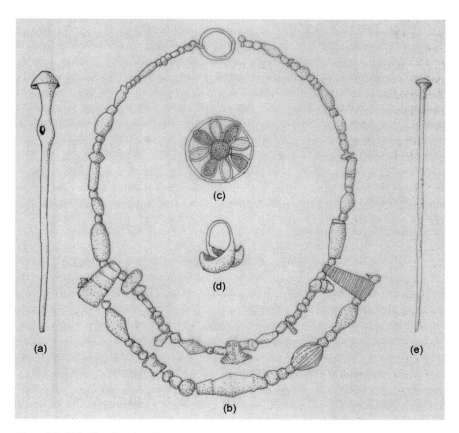

*Figure 5.3* Akkadian jewelry: (a) pierced garment pin; (b) double-strand necklace; (c) brooch centerpiece of gold, lapis, and carnelian; (d) gold lunate earring; (e) garment pin.

Diadems or frontlets of gold, secured with a ribbon, were worn across the forehead by the exceptionally wealthy. When Manishtusu purchased land, his agents distributed silver diadems to some of the leading sellers as part of the transaction. The elite also wore headbands made with roundels of silver, gold, and semi-precious stones, as well as plaited ribbons of silver and gold.[82] Hair spirals held formal coiffures in place, for both men and women.[83]

Men, except for priests and personal attendants to royalty, wore their hair long. On special occasions, men and women were fitted with wigs, whose beauty was extolled in later Sumerian poetry. Stone models of wigs, post-Akkadian in date, are known, apparently for statues to change their hair styles.[84] Barbers and hair-dressers, owing to their intimate access to the elite, enjoyed positions of some honor at court and appear in lists of dignitaries.[85] A sharp implement found in many male and female burials may be a tool for cutting hair.[86] Complicated coiffures were signs of high status (Figures 1.9, 9.3), whereas letting the hair flow loosely down the back was a sign of undress and deemed sensuous.[87] Slaves, on the other hand, wore a long lock of hair as a readily apparent mark of their servitude. Akkadian artists took particular interest in the exotic hairstyles of defeated foreigners, as seen for instance in the detailed renderings on one of Manishtusu's victory reliefs and the Victory Stele of Naram-Sin (Figure 1.6).

Elite women wore large, hollow, lunate earrings in gold and silver, for which the earliest textual reference dates to the Akkadian period (a pair in gold), while the earliest actual examples come from the pre-Akkadian Royal Tombs of Ur (Figure 5.3d).[88] Two jewelry collections, hidden for safekeeping near the end of the Akkadian period at Nagar, contained lunate earrings of several types and pendants of silver, gold, and electrum, as well as beads, spiralform and winged disks, and an assortment of pins (Figure 5.3a, e). These last, eight to eleven centimeters long, made of copper or precious metal, often with beaded heads, were worn on clothing and could be pierced or looped for cords to carry cylinder seals.[89] Men also wore earrings, especially single ones, to judge from the Akkadian-period interments at Ur. There, ten burials with single earrings also included an axe. That the earrings were intended to be singles is suggested by Graves 225 and 607, in each of which there were two single earrings in different metal combinations – silver and copper and silver and gold. Grave 622 had a single gold but a pair of silver earrings. Another five burials with axes had pairs of earrings. Grave 1386 contained a single earring with a dagger and arrow.[90] This evidence suggests that a single earring may have been the fashion for soldiers or other armed men.

Necklaces, strung on silver or gold, first came into fashion for men during the Akkadian period (Figure 5.3b). They were indicators of social status or rank, and were also associated with sexual attractiveness. Agate, carnelian and etched carnelian, cat's eye, crystal, and lapis beads have been found, sometimes capped with gold or worked into the shape of fruit or flowers, such as dates or nasturtiums. In Mesopotamian literature, fruit was commonly associated with male and female allure, so this may be the symbolism of the fruit-shaped beads. Other necklace elements included such animals as small dogs and frogs, as well as geometric pendants.[91]

Akkadian necklaces were also a sign of authority. The Sumerian warrior-king Eannatum wears no necklace in his triumphal relief, nor do the later kings of Ur, whereas Sargon and Naram-Sin both wear necklaces, as would later independent rulers in Elam. One Akkadian dignitary, when he was issued a magnificent suit of clothes, was also given a large, circular medallion of gold or silver, likely to be worn on a necklace chain.[92] The Akkadian king or notable (Ititi?) portrayed in a statue from Assur wears a heavy, single-strand necklace of large beads, with a counterpoise hanging down his back (Figure 5.5).

Bracelets and bangles adorned men and women. Naram-Sin wears a single, evidently jeweled, bracelet on each wrist on his Victory Stele. The majority of the bracelets and bangles found in the Akkadian period burials at Ur belonged to women. To judge from the ivory statuette from Tell el-Wilayah (part 10, this chapter), they could wear multiple large bracelets on their arms and wrists. A magnificent brooch in gold, lapis, and carnelian was buried with its wealthy owner at Adab (Figure 5.3c, Chapter 10 part 7).

## 6.  Wood

Woodworking and joinery of the Akkadian period are little known today because no wooden objects have survived and only a few types, such as chairs and stools, were represented in art. Moreover, accounts of lumber and wooden objects are not common, with the botanical identifications of the numerous words for wood in the sources often disputed, so this aspect of Akkadian industry is not well understood. A workshop at Adab included carpenters and joiners who made parts for wagons and boats and handles for weapons.[93]

In the Ur III period, administrative records of government forests, orchards, and plantations show that trees were tended by professionals, with the rights to cut them zealously guarded. The most common native trees mentioned were willow, tamarisk, pine, date palm, Euphrates poplar, black poplar, hackberry, juniper, fig, olive, and apple.[94] Presumably this was true in the preceding Akkadian period, but reconstruction of forestry and orchard work is not yet possible.[95]

The date palm was useful for timbers, whereas poplar, apple and other fruit woods made furniture, doors, and ladders. In a later work of literature, the date palm and the tamarisk debate their respective usefulness to the human race, the date palm stressing its importance as a source of food, timber, and matting material, the tamarisk, in its turn, boasting of its suitability for joinery and table or treen ware:

> What is there in the king's palace that is not mine? The king eats from my table, the queen drinks from my goblet, the warrior eats from my spoon, the cook kneads dough in my trough. I am the loom, I weave threads, I clothe common folk and I make the king splendid.[96]

Small quantities of exotic woods were known, including cypress, cedar, and fir, boxwood, cornel, pomegranate, Persian oak, and possibly bamboo, not to mention valuable rarities like ebony. It is not clear if these were acquired by exchange, looting, or purchase.[97]

The most prestigious wood was cedar, whose cutting on the slopes of faraway mountains was a project fit for a king. Naram-Sin claims that he did so on the Amanus.[98] This fragrant, strong, insect-proof, easily worked, and beautifully grained wood, which takes a high polish, was esteemed for roof beams in palaces and temples, the very logs, as they spanned halls and chambers, symbols of royal power and enterprise. The great number of carpenters and joiners employed on Naram-Sin's reconstruction of Ekur suggests that the inner walls or ceilings might have had wooden panels, screens, or coffering, but we have no texts describing the interior decoration. *The Curse of Agade* says with horror that the old woodwork of the Ekur temple was burned, perhaps as a way to make aromatics.[99]

Descriptions of private houses note only doors and ladders to the roof as standard, non-structural, wooden elements, so panels or screens seem unlikely to have been in ordinary dwellings. For decoration and privacy in the home, textile hangings were probable choices. Furniture included low-backed chairs with curved or flat seats, often with turned legs, as well as tables, stools, chests, and coffers.[100] Beds were apparently fashioned by stretching ropes across a wooden frame to support a mattress or sleeping pad.[101] The finest wooden furniture was inlaid or overlaid with panels and ornaments of metal, gemstones, ivory, and faience.[102] Luxury pieces might also have finials and animal feet and legs. Techniques of painting or other coloration, as well as caning or upholstery, are unknown. An inventory of furniture, either a dowry or the estate of an elite citizen of Adab, lists a Subarean-style wagon, a ladder (for reaching the roof of the house), a chair, possibly with a woven seat, a bed with ox-hoof feet, and a table-and-chair set.[103] An account of furniture for the king's use includes a "lion throne," daises, a stool, hard footstool, a hard chair inlaid with gold, an upholstered chair inlaid with gold, and a bed with bull's feet, made of exotic wood inlaid with gold. A more ordinary set consisted of a chair with back(?) and a footrest, both of poplar.[104]

The basic tools were the hammer, saw, drill, smoothing adze, chisel, and lathe, all readily obtained and repaired, and often found in hordes and burials. Carpentry and joinery were thus professions that could be pursued without important patronage, even at the village level, and in the specialized areas of boat-building and wagon-making. Nevertheless, the estate of the Akkadian notable Mesag had two carpenters among its personnel, the Akkadian colony at Susa seven.[105]

## 7.  Reed

The marshes of Sumer produced unlimited, durable reed. Workers in reed are mentioned in administrative documents of the Akkadian period, as are products of their work, such as fish baskets, but there is no evidence for government support and supervision, as was the case in the Ur III period. The estate of the Akkadian notable Mesag had two reed workers among its personnel, the Akkadian colony at Susa twelve.[106] The tools of the trade were simple: a stone implement for cutting, a flat stone to serve as a cutting surface, and a plaiting tool.[107]

Reed had many uses. It was of particular value as a fuel for cooking and for industrial kilns and furnaces, which required massive amounts to be cut, gathered, and dried.[108] Reed was also in demand for construction of roofs, shelters, and room partitions, fencing for livestock, storage trunks for food and household goods, protective covers for food, various types of baskets, boats, and even simple flutes.[109] Ur III documents show that there were established norms for certain classes of reed work.[110] In records of the industrial production of reed mats for transport barges at Umma, for example, a reed mat six by six meters in size was calculated to contain thirty-six bundles of reeds and take six man-days to produce, not counting the time spent cutting, bundling, and delivering the reeds to the workplace. Ur III administrators even knew how much reed was required to roast a pig.[111]

## 8.   Leather

After wool, leather and sinews were the most important non-consumables derived from animal husbandry. They were not commercial materials, as wool was, but rather accountable household goods turned over to professionals for making buckets, leather sacks for storing goods and holding water, purses, whips, sandals, belts, harness, thongs, protective battle gear, upholstery, and covers for the handles of tools.[112] The governors' archives of Girsu and Adab suggest that these officials had on hand large stocks of leather that could be issued to manufacture commissioned items, as well as stores of finished goods like sandals, ready to be given to functionaries.[113] Donkeys, cattle, pigs, sheep, and goats furnished the hides.[114] Although the various tasks of leatherworking are seldom referred to in Akkadian documents, one record states that the dehairing of certain skins has not yet been done.[115] Leather workers, *ashkapu* (the term survives in Iraqi Arabic today as *iskafi*, meaning "cobbler"), were routinely part of the staff of any large Akkadian establishment; Mesag's estate had two and the Akkadian colony at Susa had six of them.[116]

## 9.   Clothing and textiles

Weaving was an ancient household craft, aspects of which seem to have been industrialized by the Akkadian government. Although one might expect to identify mills where weavers, both men and women, toiled in the mass production of textiles, as in later periods, there is as yet no clear archaeological indication of them. The Northern Palace at Eshnunna/Tell Asmar (Chapter 3 part 2) is sometimes said to have included such an industrial weaving establishment, and one document from this building mentions 105 male and 585 female workers, some of whom may have worked with or produced textiles, but no firmer evidence (such as loom weights) for mass weaving there was found.[117]

A large textile workshop at Adab was supervised by a woman, Mama-ummi, who oversaw about 170 weaving women under eight female supervisors. These women wove textiles from wool purchased and supplied in large quantities, such as fifteen talents (30 kilograms). Another 130 workers were assigned to a separate establishment for cleaning and fulling.[118]

117.                                        118

A tablet of unknown origin, most likely from Adab or elsewhere in Sumer, records a delivery of more than 500 garments as the third installment, obviously the result of large-scale production. In another record, 3630 linen threads are turned over to linen workers. In a third, large quantities of clothing are shipped to Agade, along with two carts, perhaps as gifts or tribute to the royal family.[119]

The two major types of cloth were linen and wool. Linen, produced by specialized flax workers, was the more expensive and yielded finer garments; a class of priests was referred to as "men dressed in linen." Everyday garments were woven of wool. When laborers and their dependents were entitled to rations, they received raw wool, with the expectation that their families would make clothing and household items from it, another indication of local, rather than centralized, production.[120]

Although most wool-producing cultures distinguish lamb's wool from wool of older sheep, this was not noted in Akkadian administrative documents, and rarely was any distinction made among wools of different breeds of sheep. Wool was plucked regularly, and shepherds were required to deliver the fleeces of sheep that had died, as evidence of legitimate loss rather than theft. To judge from later sources, wool was graded by fineness: "best" or "royal," "next best," "below next best," and "ordinary." The best wool represented at most 3 percent of the wool taken from a herd. Wool was apparently not dyed; the natural colors were "shiny white," "white," "yellow," "black," and "red." After combing, the fibers were spun into different sizes of thread, depending on the fineness of the textile to be woven from it.[121]

Since no separate word for "loom" has been identified in either Sumerian or Akkadian of this period, it seems the loom was just called the "wood" or the "gear" and consisted only of a few simple pieces of wood. Bridal trousseaus included textiles, such as clothing and bedding, but no looms; household inventories and estates do not mention looms either. Therefore, they were not valuable, which is a supposition borne out by later magic and divination texts, in which demons or animals invading the home might cause significant damage by upsetting furniture or stoves and shattering crockery, but breakage of looms was not important enough to mention.[122] That every home had a loom is suggested by the fact that each family of workers received rations of raw wool (Chapter 4 part 2).

The basic garment was a heavy skirt or kilt, worn by both men and women over an undergarment, both tied around the waist. Different styles of the skirt or kilt were suitable for work or ceremony. The upper body was covered by a long light shirt, usually of linen, then a long outer wrap that left the right arm free (Figure 5.5).[123]

Fashions among the elite changed dramatically over the first three generations of the Akkadian kings, owing to an infusion of new styles from the conquests and experiences of strange lands and peoples. During the reign of Manishtusu, the shaggy, wrap-around garment worn by Sargon gave way to a smooth, elegant, body-hugging garment with elaborately tasseled borders, perhaps inspired by the fringed clothing encountered during his conquests in Iran (Figure 5.4a). A new type of shoe with a turned-up toe sporting a pom-pom appeared at about the same time (Figure 1.9). Later, during the reign of Naram-Sin, a quite different style of clothing was introduced. This was a kind of toga secured by tucking

(a)

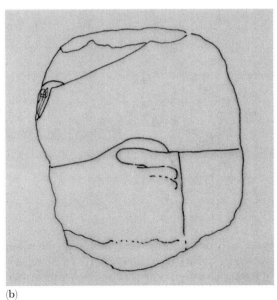

(b)

*Figure 5.4* Akkadian clothing: (a) tasseled wrap-around garment, statue of Manishtusu; (b) toga-garment, statue of Su'ash-takal, majordomo of Naram-Sin.

*Figure 5.5* Akkadian notable or king, wearing tasseled cloak and heavy necklace with counterpoise.

in a corner over the right breast, sometimes secured with a long garment pin (Figure 5.4b). The vogue spread among the elite, and the toga became the garment of choice in the depiction of Sumerian and Babylonian rulers for centuries to come, reflecting the prestige of the Akkadian dynasty. Many different styles of belts, sashes, garment pins, and headgear attest to the role of clothing as an important statement of status and wealth among the ruling elite. The high value attached to the finest clothing is suggested by a marble tablet that lists garments or textiles dedicated to a deity.[124]

## 10. Ivory

Ivory is a material to be expected in Akkadian luxury and palatial products, among them pins, combs, jewelry boxes, inlaid work, and small figurines. The ivory was probably imported from the Indus Valley, which had close trade connections with Mesopotamia at this time.[125] Little Mesopotamian ivory has survived, but an idea of the quality of Akkadian work may be gained from a group of figurines found at Assur on the floor of level G of the temple of Ishtar, and especially from a female statuette found in the Akkadian building at Tell al-Wilayah, which shows that Akkadian artists were adept at using this medium to convey sensuous contours and gleaming flesh. An ivory figure of a woman from an Akkadian building at Nagar shows some Egyptianizing influence, so Akkadian ivory carving may have been influenced by pieces brought back as booty, though pre-Akkadian examples, such as a figure from Mari, point to an indigenous Mesopotamian tradition as well.[126]

## 11. Oils and aromatics

Vegetable and animal oils and fats were basic ingredients in cooking and in unguents and salves for lubricating the skin, washing the hair, or treating illness. Oils were rubbed on animals and objects for cultic and other purposes.[127] Aromatic substances were part of religious rituals, typically burned as incense on stands that allowed the smoke to diffuse in the sacred space to attract and please the gods.[128] Perfumers were sometimes people of high social status, as witnessed by group of them mentioned as recipients of a large parcel of land in Rimush's Victory Stele from Lagash (Chapter 1 part 3, Figure 1.4).[129]

Oils were extracted from sesame and other plants, fish, sheep, donkeys, and pigs. Such oils, as well as dairy products, often formed the inactive basis for salves, to which other ingredients were added. Several types of resins routinely occur in post-Akkadian merchants' accounts, though usually their precise identification is unknown.[130] These, mixed with liquids, could also be used as aromatics and perfumes.

At Umma, a group of records shows an oil office at work, disbursing lard for a journey to Agade and for work troops constructing the temple of Inanna at Zabala (Chapter 1 part 5); butter or ghee for personal use and for treating a wagon, a gate, and a table covering; and sesame oil to various people, including the armed guard of a boat from Meluhha, as well as soldiers and workmen. Cedar and "white" oil were also disbursed in the project at Zabala and in the governor's palace for anointing. *Murranum*, perhaps an extract of ash, served many of the same purposes, and extract of almond was used during the celebration of a festival. Salves were kept in small, wide-mouth pots for ease of application, and perfumes in small closed jars or bottles. Some aromatics were purchased and delivered by merchants.[131] Valuable aromatics were included in shipments that the estate of Mesag sent to Agade.[132]

**Notes**

1 Neumann 1987; Stein and Blackman 1993; Renger 1996.
2 Frankfort 1927; Christian 1940. For a study of the historical background against which Akkadian ceramics of the north were a different tradition from those of the south, Milano and Rova 2000. For historical uses of third-millennium pottery, Eiland in Matthews 2003: 336–38.
3 Delougaz 1952; Gibson 1982, 2011. Delougaz dated the Northern Palace to the "Proto-imperial," that is, the late Pre-Akkadian period (now generally called Early Dynastic IIIb), but it is certainly Akkadian (Chapter 3 part 2). With respect to specific find spots and dating of this pottery, I have benefited from extensive manuscript annotations of Suzanne Kay Howe, a former student of McGuire Gibson, in my copy of Delougaz 1952.
4 Van Ess 1988, 1991; Gibson and McMahon 1995, 1997; McMahon 2006.
5 Oates, Oates, and McDonald 2001.
6 The most systematic definition of the modern terms is Christian 1940 1: x–xiii. For discussion of uses of these vessel types, Salonen 1966; Faivre 2009. Basic information on the ancient vocabulary can be gleaned from Salonen 1966 and Sallaberger 1996. Sallaberger 1996: 77–78 shows that some words for ceramics were based on content, function, form, size, and volume, whereas others were simply names.
7 Steinkeller and Postgate 1992: 52–53 no. 26, discussed by Sallaberger 1996: 28.
8 Collon 1982: 33. Note, however, that more and different pottery is shown on Akkadian seals than on those of other periods, Porada 1984. A commemorative relief includes an accurate depiction of a vessel, probably metal, from northern Mesopotamia or more likely from Anatolia; Mellink 1963, differently Liverani 2001/2: 181; Müller-Karpe 1993/97: 143.
9 Collon 1983 figs. 181, 193, 214, 216, 217; Delougaz 1952 plate 150.
10 Collon 1983 153; Delougaz 1952 plate 164, B.664.540a; plate 113, B.666.540a.
11 Collon 1983 153; Delougaz 1952 plate 111, C.757.540, C.777.340.
12 Collon 1983 153; Delougaz 1952 plate 189, C.805.210. Collon 1983 155 likewise shows storage jars and Collon 1983 223 a biconical vessel, for which no Akkadian ceramic parallel is known, so it may have been of metal. Collon 1983 145 shows a set of five cups, pots, and jars, presumably for food storage and consumption. Another spouted vessel appears in Collon 1983 32, a large brewing vessel in Collon 1983 149 (compare Figure 4.1c).
13 Adams 1965: 128; Adams and Nissen 1971: 103. For "combed ware," Adams 1981: 71; Oates, Oates, and McDonald 2001: 164–65; Steinkeller and Postgate 1992: 52–53 no. 26 i 3.
14 For mother-goddess handled jars, Moorey 1970: 97–98, 1978: 67–68 (associates with cult of Ishtar); for animal and human-handled jars, Delougaz 1952: 89–90; for the column decoration, Delougaz 1952: 121; for vessels with relief, R. Starr 1939, 1: 373–74 (Gasur); Lloyd 1940: 21 (Tell Khoshi, a small site in the Sinjar region), and Mallowan 1937: 144 (Tell Chagar Bazar in the Khabur region). I thank Karen Polinger Foster for some of these references.
15 Oates, Oates, and McDonald 2001: 151–59.
16 Lebeau 1985: 134–35.
17 Senior and Weiss 1992.
18 ITT I 1401; STTI 58; Sallaberger 1996: 28.
19 Delougaz 1952: 145–48; Gibson 1982, 2011; McMahon 2006.
20 Delougaz 1952: 147.
21 Sallaberger 1996: 27–28.
22 Waetzoldt 1971; Steinkeller 1996; Dahl 2010.
23 B. Foster 2011c.
24 For a survey of the history of metallurgy in Mesopotamia, Muhly 1993/7; for the Akkadian period, Limet 1972.
25 A. Westenholz 1987: 35–36 no. 11.

26 B. Foster 1982b: 33–35; SCTRAH 224–37 (for weapons); in general, Neumann 1987: 49–52, 97–106, 113–24 (Ur III).

27 Asher-Greve 1995; Winter 1996b; Reade 2002b.

28 A. Westenholz 1987; B. Foster 1997a.

29 B. Foster 1997a: 57.

30 For mining in Iran, Lafont 1996. Although copper was available in Anatolia, it was probably easier to import from Iran overland or by water. For copper sources in Iraqi Kurdistan in the Tiyari Mountains, north of Lizan, D. Potts 2010. This might lie in the ancient land called Kimash, differently Frayne 1999. For Magan as a source of copper, STTI 2864. For what may be a purchase of a talent of copper at Susa, MDP 14 16+46+55 iii 1–7: 1 gú urudu Ur-$^{d}$En-ki 30 še gur kù-bi 3 ma-na Lú-dingir-ra 3 dumu LUL.GU-ak dam-gàr-me "1 talent of copper (from?) Ur-Enki (and?) 30 gur of barley for 3 minas of silver (from?) Ludingirra, three sons of L., merchants." In NBC 9955 (unpublished, from Umma), a merchant delivers 7 minas 65 shekels of copper; further Chapter 8 note 36.

31 B. Foster 1982b: 35–37.

32 Hallo 1963; B. Foster 1983a: 154 no. 9.

33 Limet 1960: 116–17, 122–23; Salonen 1964; B. Foster 1982b: 39; BdI I Adab 93 (axes returned by smith); in general Steinkeller 2003b: 39–40; ITT V 9400; further Lafont 1991 and above, note 26.

34 Limet 1960: 66–73; Waetzoldt and Bachmann 1984.

35 B. Foster 1982b: 34; Hauptmann and Pernicka 2004 no. 1910.

36 B. Foster 2011a: 132 no. 1; Hauptmann and Pernicka 2004 no. 897.

37 All figures based on the analyses in Hauptmann and Pernicka 2004. A lower figure of 5 percent tin is used by some analysts, for example McKerrell 1978; further Moorey and Schweizer 1972; Müller-Karpe 1993: 269 note 35 defines bronze as containing only 2 percent tin on the basis of the fact that tin almost never occurs naturally in copper in a percentage of more than 2 percent, so any amount above that should be an additive. In any case, Müller-Karpe 1993: 300 figure 9 shows a higher proportion of bronze to copper vessels in the samples analyzed from the late pre-Akkadian in comparison to those of the Akkadian period, anticipating the results of the much larger sample in Hauptmann and Pernicka 2004, as argued here.

38 McDonald, Curtis, and Maxwell-Hyslop in Oates, Oates, and McDonald 2001: 233–42.

39 Hauptmann and Pernicka 2004 no. 228.

40 Hauptmann and Pernicka 2004, nos. 685, 686, 700, 703. For the horde of implements from Assur, which may well be Akkadian, Wartke 1995.

41 Hauptmann and Pernicka 2004, ranging from nos. 746 to 811.

42 Speiser 1935: 102–4; Gadd 1971: 452.

43 Hauptmann and Pernicka 2004, ranging from nos. 913 to 2077. Of eleven Early Dynastic bowls, nine (81 percent) had significant tin content, no two of them in the same proportions (2:1, 3:1, 4:1, 5:1, 7:1, 8:1, 10:1, 11:1, 16:1). Of eleven axes, four (36 percent) had significant tin content, no two with the same proportions (4:1, 5:1, 8:1, 10:1). Of eleven files and other tools, six (54 percent) had significant tin content, but in more consistent proportions (three at 4:1, two at 10:1, and one at 3:1). Of eleven garment pins, five (45 percent) had significant tin content, no two with the same proportions (4:1, 5:1, 9:1, 13:1).

44 Moorey 1994: 297–301.

45 For a purchase of tin, B. Foster 1983a: 160 (=STTI 54). An exceptionally large quantity is 1500 grams (ITT I 1154); 5 minas in MDP 14 35, along with lead (in the proportion of 8:1).

46 Chapter 1 note 24; further below, note 48.

47 Limet 1971; B. Foster 1997; Frayne 1993: 28

48 Gurney 1969; Civil 2008. The meaning of the sign AN with each object is unclear. If AN is an abbreviated writing for KÙ.AN, then the tools might be made of a very

precious metal worth, in the early second millennium, up to forty times the value of silver. For this, meteoritic iron, which in some cases can be polished to a silvery brightness, has been suggested, among several other interpretations (Bjorkman 1973: 110–13). On the other hand, Ge. Selz 1997: 170–71 with note 45 argues that these were "divine" implements rather than ones made of a specific kind of metal, but this seems unlikely in view of their being accounted for as luxury objects in an administrative text (B. Foster 1980: 33). This also rules out a suggestion that AN stands for the verb "to be," Cavigneaux 1980/3: 613. For serving implements, Steinkeller 1987b; J. Westenholz 2010.

49  Moorey 1994: 271.

50  Cooper and Heimpel 1983: 75 line 34 "Pour them out in the mold like a statue" (the set of bronze vessels and Sargon, who is carrying them); Appendix IIIa.

51  Percentages in Hauptmann and Pernicka 2004, but difficult for a non-metallurgist to tell whether or not arsenic, nickel, silver, or lead occurred naturally with the copper or were deliberate additives; Muhly 1993/7: 124–30.

52  Frayne 1993: 28–29; Moorey 1994: 234; for the increased availability of silver in the Akkadian period, Monaco and Pomponio 2009: 44; for "snow-capped," Chapter 1 note 9.

53  B. Foster 1983a: 154 no. 9; for prices, Limet 1971: 31–34; Monaco and Pomponio 2009. For a record of a weather event that would affect grain prices and was perhaps kept for that purpose, Zhi 1989: 136.

54  For the uses and circulation of silver in early Mesopotamia, with textual citations, Limet 1971; Moorey 1994: 232–39; Muhly 993/7: 130–1; Renger 1995b: 290–94; Van Driel 2002; Monaco and Pomponio 2009; Peyronel 2010. For silver as money, Chapter 8 notes 28 and 56.

55  For a bride gift with silver, Milano 1987; for payments of rental on land in silver, BdI Adab 212 and 213 are typical examples.

56  For the silver diadems, Gelb, Steinkeller, and Whiting 1991:1: 296 s.v. *ki-li-lum*; for the silver cups, B. Foster 1982b: 133–34 (CT 50 52); for distributions of valuable objects as a form of circulation of specie among the elite, Maiocchi 2010b; Sallaberger 2013.

57  CUSAS 13 72. Transactions with gold were not common, e.g., BdI Adab 84, in which two shekels go to two different buildings (the editors suggest that one is a personal name) and 8 are still on hand (gub-ba); CUSAS 23 128 ("gold of the governor"); in general, Ross 2001. For possible sources of gold in Anatolia and Iran, Maxwell-Hyslop 1977.

58  In general Limet 1971: 4–6; for the bride gift, Sommerfeld 1999 no. 49 and Chapter 2 part 2; for the notable's gift, B. Foster 1982b: 133–34 (CT 50 52); for the purchase from Sargon, Kienast and Volk 1995: 102–3; for the ten talents, ITT II 4598 (B. Foster 1982d: 239–40).

59  Müller-Karpe 1993, 1993/7.

60  Müller-Karpe 1993, nos. 714, 1131, 1310, 1493.

61  Müller-Karpe 1993, no. 275; J. Westenholz 2010; Chapter 3 note 80.

62  Müller-Karpe 1993/7: 143.

63  Oates in Oates, Oates, and McDonald 2001: 218; further Gibson 2011: 78.

64  Firth 2011; Moorey 1994: 173–75; 190–91; Oates in Oates, Oates, and McDonald 2001: 217; Gibson 2011: 78.

65  Van Dijk 1983: 1, 124–25 lines 562–66. The material addressed here, im-an-na, was a key element used in making faience, but its precise identification is unknown; "sand with high silicate content" seems a reasonable possibility and fits this passage well.

66  D. Potts 1986; T. Potts 1989.

67  Herrmann and Moorey 1980/83; Porada 1992; Tallon 1995; for flint arrowheads, Gibson 2011: 78.

68  Moorey 1994: 24–27.

69  Moorey 1994: 26–27.

70  Amiet 1972; Eppihimer 2010; Chapter 9 part 1.

71  Manishtusu Obelisk S[b] 20; Victory Stele AO 2678; Amiet 1976 and Chapter 9 part 1.

72 Van Dijk 1983: 1, 112–13 lines 471–84; B. Foster 2014a.
73 Van Dijk 1983: 1, 114–15 lines 491–96; B. Foster 2014a; on limestone in general, D. Potts 1997: 100–102.
74 Van Dijk 1983: 1, 130 lines 599–602.
75 Collon 1982: 26; Sax 1993; Chapter 9 part 3.
76 McDonald in Oates, Oates, and McDonald 2001: 227; Musche 1992: 103. B. Foster 1983a: 161 is an administrative text that records delivery of carnelians and other gemstones. For discussion of the origins and use of carnelian and other gemstones, Sax 1993; Tallon 1995. For a suggestion that lapis declined in popularity in the Akkadian period, Gadd 1971: 452; this was presumably based on the rich finds of the Royal Tombs of Ur, for which there is no Akkadian equivalent. For lapis as palace wealth, Pinnock 2006; in general Herrmann and Moorey 1980/83.
77 Asher-Greve 1995.
78 A. Westenholz 1987: 26–27; for workshops and craft production in general, Neumann 1987 (Ur III); NBC 8104, 8958 (unpublished).
79 W. Lambert 1979.
80 CUSAS 13 40. Perhaps the sculptor made the decorations rather than the object itself, and the weight of the object was recorded to guard against purloining of the stone.
81 For a catalogue of Akkadian jewelry, Musche 1992: 101–5.
82 Maxwell-Hyslop 1971: 22–23; Heinrich 1974: 34–45; Gelb, Steinkeller, and Whiting 1991: 1, 133 lines ix 16–21 (to a leading seller: team and wagon, silver diadem (*kililu*) weighing 20 shekels, a bronze axe, and a type of festival garment). The weight of the diadems distributed by Manishtusu, ca. 100 grams each, seems heavy in proportion to the objects studied by Maxwell-Hyslop, but no weights for the archaeologically attested examples have been provided by the excavators. Musche 1992: 101 stresses the focus of Akkadian jewelry on the head.
83 Maxwell-Hyslop 1971: 23.
84 Suter 2008: 8.
85 The Akkadian establishment at Susa, for example, had three barbers on staff (MDP 14 71 i 4'); in general Kleinerman 2013: 303–8.
86 Woolley 1934: 310.
87 Köcher and Oppenheim 1957/58: 63; Börker-Klähn 1972/75.
88 Maxwell-Hyslop 1971: 23–24.
89 Collon 2001.
90 Data from Woolley 1934, using dating of Nissen 1966.
91 Mallowan 1947: 177–78; Maxwell-Hyslop 1971: 26–27; Musche 1992: 102–3; textual references to gold and silver necklaces in Limet 1972: 5, 7. The goddess Inanna puts on a carnelian necklace when she wants to look her best, Appendix IIc line 56.
92 B. Foster 2010a: 137. The "necklace of Naram-Sin," along with the necklaces of other famous Mesopotamian kings such as Hammurabi, was invoked in later Mesopotamian magic for curative or protective purposes, Schuster-Brandis 2008: 163–67.
93 Powell 1992; Heimpel 2011.
94 Powell 1992: 102–3; D. Potts 1997: 106–15.
95 BdI Adab 59, for example, is a list of woods turned over to woodworkers for specific projects; for other examples, SCTRAH 239–43. For Ur III forestry, Steinkeller 1987c and Heimpel 2011; for Ur III organization of woodworkers, Neumann 1987: 135–42.
96 *Muses*, 928; further Streck 2004.
97 Moorey 1994: 347–61; for ebony, Stol 1979: 34–49. For the variety of evergreens available in the Amanus and Lebanon, different species of which may have been subsumed under one or two Akkadian words, Elayi 2013: 45, 55.
98 Frayne 1993: 86.
99 Cooper 1983a: 56–57 (Appendix IIIb) lines 134–35: "Cedar, cypress, juniper, and boxwood, wood for its temple chamber, he made ooze out in flames".
100 Salonen 1963.

101   Salonen 1963: 107–10.
102   B. Foster 1980: 33–34.
103   Zhi 1989: 217.
104   B. Foster 1980: 33; Sommerfeld, Markina, and Roudik 2005: 207 no. 14.
105   B. Foster 1987a: 57; MDP 14 71 i 6'-7'.
106   B. Foster 1987a: 57; MDP 14 71 i 14'-15'.
107   Ochsenschlager 1992; in general D. Potts 1997: 115–17. The reed worker's stone tool is referred to obscurely in the Sumerian poem in which stones are blessed and cursed, line 587: "May the reed worker make you leap from the reed, may he let you drop in your bed," Van Dijk 1983: 1,128 line 587.
108   BdI Adab 182, for example, accounts for 74 talents of woven reed, about 2220 kilograms; for burning of reed to melt down and rework copper tools at a work site, B. Foster 1982b: 39.
109   Ochsenschlager 1992.
110   Waetzoldt 1991/92.
111   Goetze 1948; Sallaberger 1989; Steinkeller 2008.
112   For the Mesopotamian leather industry in general, Stol 1980/3; for the leather-working shops of the Ur III period, Neumann 1987: 82–89; Scurlock 2008; Kleinerman 2011b. Various leather items occur throughout Akkadian records, though they are insufficient to reconstruct the industry of the time, for example ITT V 9283, 9296, 9308; MAD 4 64; MAD 5 61; OAIC 278, 282. For leather coverings for spears, B. Foster 1982b: 38 (USP 15ʲ; for the "white leather" accounted for there, Foxvog 1994: 14).
113   CUSAS 13 34 notes delivery in Adab of 3000 sheepskins by an agent of the *šaperum*. Distributions of leather and leather objects include CUSAS 13 33; ITT I 1130, 1210; ITT II 4450; RTC 105; SCTRAH 146–48. For sandals, CUSAS 19 171.
114   CT 50 185; CUSAS 13 32, 186; ITT II 5721.
115   CT 50 185.
116   B. Foster 1987a: 57; MDP 14 71 i 9.
117   Breniquet 2008: 64–65; B. Foster 2010a: 119; for the structure, operation, and output of an Ur III textile workshop on a large estate in Sumer, Kleinerman 2011b, Waetzoldt 2011.
118   Molina 2014: 35–36.
119   BdI Adab 163; CUSAS 13 147; SCTRAH 108–18; B. Foster 2010a: 141.
120   Gelb 1965; Waetzoldt 1971a: 77–84.
121   Waetzoldt 1971a: 45–60; Firth and Nosch 2012.; B. Foster 2014b.
122   Evidence for looms discussed by Waetzoldt 1971a: 130–32.
123   B. Foster 2010a: 129; 134–36.
124   Strommenger 1971, 1980/ 83; B. Foster 2010a; H. Klein 1992; for the marble tablet, perhaps a piece of booty brought to Nippur from Naram-Sin's campaigns against the Hurrian principalities in Syria, Gelb 1959.
125   Collon 1977.
126   Moortgat and Moortgat-Correns 1974: 157, who date the Assur and Tell el-Wilayah pieces to the late Early Dynastic period by comparison with the Early Dynastic "treasure of Ur." Since the archaeological context of the Tell el-Wilayah piece is clearly Akkadian, if his dating is correct, the statuette may have been an heirloom. For the figure from Nagar and its style, J. Oates in Oates, Oates, and McDonald, 2001: 295–96. For parallels in clay, Porada, Hansen, Dunham, and Babcock 1992, 1: 116, who prefer an Akkadian dating for the Assur and Nagar pieces; further Wicke 2010.
127   Jursa 2003/5; Pappi 2006/8; Worthington 2006/8.
128   Jursa 2006/8.
129   B. Foster 1985: 19.
130   Snell 1982: 150–68; BIN 8 300, 319.
131   Examples drawn from B. Foster 1982b: 116–22; delivery by merchant CUSAS 26 112.
132   Bridges 1981: 255–56, 390.

# 6 Religion

## 1. The gods of the Akkadians

The Akkadians and other Semitic-speaking peoples who lived in the band of territory across northern Mesopotamia and Syria had a common fund of religious tradition, from which local variations and innovations were constructed. Personal names, which often consisted of a one- or two-word prayer or praise of a divinity, tell us most of what we know about early Akkadian religion before the creation of an imperial pantheon. The gods were often described in familial terms, such as father, brother, father's kinsman, clan, extended family, community, or progenitor. One sees also that the gods and goddesses invoked in names were associated with attributes of empirical human leadership, rather than with their transcendent powers: they were kings and queens, guardians, brave defenders, or possessors of special knowledge.[1]

The Semitic-speaking peoples in northern Mesopotamia worshipped a deity Ilu(m) or Il, "God," who dwelt in *shama'u*, heaven, the great covering above the earth, which held back the rain. But to the Sumerians, heaven itself was a supreme being, distant, omnipotent, all-encompassing, whom they called An. The Akkadians adopted this name into their own language as Anum and, by the reign of Naram-Sin, wrote both Anu and Ilu with the same cuneiform sign, a radiant star. Ilu(m) meant to the Akkadians God as a specific being, god in general, the god of the local community, and an individual personal god who watched over each human being. When the Semitic gods were organized into a pantheon, Anum was made the head of it. In later times, Semitic speakers gave Anum a consort, Antum, whereas the Sumerians considered earth the female counterpart of the sky, calling her with a Sumerian name, ki, which implied irrigated soil, or with a Semitic name, Urash, which implied cultivated ground.[2]

Just as the Akkadians knew that there were many peoples and ways of life, so too they believed that gods and goddesses were as numerous as the stars in heaven, who dwelt in specific places and had individual temperaments, domains, activities, households, subordinates, and adherents. Yet unlike human beings, gods were transcendent and immortal. As with the happenstance of family, language, and society, individual human beings often owed particular devotion to one or a small number of deities, but nothing stood in the way of changing their preferred deity or adopting an additional one. This openness to new allegiances meant that when the Akkadians settled in different landscapes, they could introduce the gods who lived there into their spiritual horizon, and when other people came among them, new deities could set up dwellings in their heaven.[3]

The three denizens of the sky, when it was viewed as a dwelling, or children of the sky, when it was viewed as a father, were the sun, moon, and the morning and evening star. Among the northern Semitic peoples, the sun and moon were generally thought of as male beings with wives, whereas the morning and evening star was generally feminine, but not so easily placed in a conventional family structure, contradiction and conflict being inherent in her nature. Brighter than any other star, she dominated the evening sky after sunset and the morning sky before sunrise. The moon and the sun, by contrast, were thought to divide that same period evenly between them.[4]

The sun, whom the Akkadians called Shamash, had to run the entire breadth of heaven during the day, and an equal distance under the earth at night, so he could begin the next morning on the same side of the sky. Only a hero among the gods could have the stamina and speed to make such a journey, unwavering, day after day. He might run the course on foot or have some noble means of conveyance – a wagon, like an Akkadian dignitary; a barge, like a king on a journey; a strange and powerful beast, such as only a hero could master and ride.[5] The bright golden sheen of the sun, impossible to look upon, reached farther than anyone could see, across the plains to the mountains, and beyond to the shores of the world and ocean, where no Mesopotamian sovereign could pretend to rule. No secret was hidden from him in his daily journey; no mode of life, however remote, was beyond his ken. The sun as a radiant, all-seeing lord, high above the human race, was also the judge of the universe, whom no subterfuge could deceive. With his brother, the moon, he was the master of oracles, to whom one prayed to know the truth.[6]

Human occupations most like the way of the sun were those of the soldier, who marched to distant climes and saw sights most people never did; the sailor, who knew what lands lay beyond the ocean; the courier or herald, who proclaimed the king's words far and wide; and the merchant, who traveled to foreign lands and knew where to find exotic goods that people at home wanted. The sun's special relation to all these professions is hailed in one of the earliest known religious documents of the Semitic-speaking peoples, composed, perhaps, not long before Sargon's birth:

> Most exalted of the gods,
> Shamash, the sun, who holds in his hand the life of the land . . .
> Daylight, chief herald on the mountain ranges,
> Herald of the brightening sky . . .
> He sustains campaigners and traveling merchants in foreign lands,
> Foreign lands render up lapis and silver to the traveling merchants,
> Cedar forests yield virgin timber, boxwood, cypress, standing tall,
>     like splendid standards,

Fit for a prince to adorn his house.
He loads up his barge with aromatics, oils, honey,
   the goods that merchants bring . . .[7]

A major Akkadian sanctuary of the sun-god was at Sippar, where the Euphrates flowed out of the Syrian uplands into the Mesopotamian alluvium, an important transition point for any traveler between Mesopotamia and Syria. Indeed, some of the earliest documents of Akkadian commerce are the records of a certain Quradum of Sippar, whose name recalls a popular epithet of the sun, *qarradum*, the warrior whose valor never falters.[8]

Sin, the moon, was a less vivid, more mysterious figure than Shamash, in any case, not such a warrior.[9] He is represented in anthropomorphic form for the first time in Akkadian seals, where he is depicted as a slender youth, sometimes wearing a crescent on his head, sometimes armed and carrying a crescent standard, and sometimes standing near a standard with a flying ribbon or pennant on it. The moon's progress across the sky was less dramatic than that of the sun, his rising less fiery and insistent, and his disappearance brought less change to the nighttime heavens than the coming and going of the sun. The most wondrous behavior of the moon-god was his waning to a crescent, then waxing to fullness, only to wane again. This suggested a secret power of self-renewal beyond that of other beings, on a different order from the martial valor, fertility, or transcendence that characterized other members of his family. The crescent was envisioned as a boat, a tiara, or the horn of a great bull in the heavens.[10]

Like the sun, the moon was a god of oracles and decisions. The northern Semitic peoples believed that he etched replies to queries on the organs of sacrificial animals, which diviners cut open and interpreted. The Akkadian kings made this bloody and arcane procedure an instrument of state policy, and it remained so until the end of Mesopotamian civilization.[11]

In the Akkadian period, the principal sanctuary of the moon-god in Sumer was at Ur, in Akkad at Tutub. There was a special relationship between the Akkadian royal family and the moon-god, which remains unexplained, but might be related to the Akkadian interest in divination. Sargon appointed his daughter, Enheduanna, high priestess of the moon-god at Ur (Chapter 9 part 5); his example was followed for centuries thereafter. In one of her poems, the moon-god proves unresponsive to Enheduanna's pleas when a usurper threatens her, so she turns for rescue to Inanna-Ishtar, patron deity of her father's dynasty. The only member of the dynasty whose name included a god was Naram-Sin, "Beloved of the Moon-God." Names invoking Sin occur twenty-three times in records from Tutub, but not even once in those from nearby Eshnunna and only rarely in the Himrin. This suggests that the cult of the moon was restricted to only one city in the region.[12]

Sun and moon had in common the eclipse, a frightening moment when the heavenly orbs were dimmed by a mysterious shadow that portended evil for authority and the ruling house (Chapter 11 part 4). Unlike for rising and setting, waxing or waning, no algorithm was yet in place to predict eclipse, nor was it always visible in all parts of the realm, so for this, Akkadian students of the sky had no choice but to watch and wait.[13]

The morning and evening star, whom the Akkadians called Ishtar, was both a goddess of combat (Figure 9.8) and a goddess of protective, familial love. The poetry of Enheduanna (Appendix II) celebrates her warlike character, especially *Inanna and Ebih* (Appendix IIc). She was also a goddess of contrasts: violence and tenderness, happiness and grief, concord and strife, as celebrated in *Passionate Inanna* (Appendix IIb). One may also see her attributes in personal names: Ishtar-is-a-Lion, Ishtar-is-a-Valorous-Warrior, Ishtar-is-a-Slaughterer, Ishtar-is-Mighty; alongside Ishtar-is-My-Mother, Ishtar-is-My-Household, Ishtar-is-My-Clan, Ishtar-is-My-Ally, and, in response to the agony of childbirth, This-is-Too-Much-for-Me, O Ishtar. She was noble and queenly, giving and protective, awe-inspiring, firm like a mountain, but responsive to prayer. The warlike and nurturing aspects of Ishtar were not, perhaps, so far apart as they would seem in later Mesopotamian tradition, since they celebrated the sometimes fierce passion of motherly love, as a lioness defending her whelps. Yet even with this universal goddess, there were striking local variations in how frequently she appears in personal names. She occurs only twice in the documents from Tutub, where Sin is so favored, but twenty-five times at nearby Eshnunna, where Sin is absent, and regularly in the Himrin Basin, where the moon-god is rare in names.[14]

If Ishtar was popularly associated with the family, the mother goddess, often called Mama in both Sumerian and Akkadian, had childbirth and midwifery as her domain. Akkadian name-giving sometimes expressed the parents' joy and gratitude for a healthy child, referring to safe birth as a gift of the gods or as an answer to prayer. Like Ishtar, Mama was a queen, a mother, firm as a mountain, trustworthy, a healer of illness.[15]

Superior knowledge and insight were important aspects of both the gods and human leaders. No deity personified these traits so well as Ea, the life-giving power of water, who was strong, wise, and great (Figure 6.2). He determined destiny; what he said always came true. He solved problems and surmounted crises, as Naram-Sin would say of himself, and Hammurabi would later echo.[16] In later times, Ea had a special epithet that might mean "chieftain" or "sheikh," the personification of those attributes of wiliness and perception that were the qualifications for leadership in a community of equals (Chapter 7 part 2).[17] Although his name is presumably derived from a Semitic word, and has sometimes been compared to one that means "life" or "being," its meaning is unknown and even later Mesopotamian scholars did not speculate about it.[18] Ea does not occur in early Semitic names prior to the Akkadian period but occurs often among the names of the men who sold Manishtusu their family land. Perhaps there was a sanctuary to Ea in the region these people had at some point called their home, though the major god locally, so far as we can tell, was "the Lord of Marad," in later periods equated with Ninurta.[19]

## 2. Pantheon and mythology

As we have noted, theophoric personal names can be helpful for understanding a deity's attributes and for showing where deities were worshipped or popular. We can also use personal names to chart important developments in religion during the Akkadian period. The earliest Semitic-speaking peoples of greater Mesopotamia invoked Ilu and Ishtar in their names ten times as often as they did other gods. Akkadian names, by contrast, invoked many other gods and goddesses, so that, by the reign of Naram-Sin, these other deities occur in nearly half the instances, a sign of considerable diversification of religious belief on the local level or of substantially increased social mobility.[20] Gods who began to appear more frequently in personal names include Addu and Dagan, lords of storm, clouds, thunder, and rainfall. Dagan was considered at home in the Upper Euphrates region, where he had his major sanctuary at Tuttul. Another Syrian weather god, Mer or Wer, ~~Erh-mev~~ occasionally figures in Akkadian names as well. Two local warrior deities, Zababa of Kish and Ilaba of Agade, are found in Akkadian male names from those cities; Ilaba disappears from names after the Akkadian period. An otherwise unknown deity, Barish, occurs in the Himrin.[21]

No Akkadian mythology has survived in written form, nor can scenes in Akkadian art be securely correlated with mythological texts known from later periods, despite intensive studies of the imagery.[22] Since wars and combats among the gods were favorite themes in art, and since theophoric names often stressed the martial valor of the gods, the Akkadian cosmos appears to have been a violent place. In some seal images, a god leads a captive bird-monster before fellow gods, while in many others, a muscular, heroic figure with long, curly hair grapples with human enemies or fierce wild animals (Figure 9.9).[23] Long, curly hair, later deemed a sign of male beauty, became part of Akkadian sculpture's *beau idéal* of the well-fleshed, strong, physically attractive ruler worthy of the love of Ishtar herself.[24] On some seal images, a man riding an eagle has often been associated with Etana, known in later tradition as the legendary first king of Kish. According to a Babylonian poem, Etana was not content with his crown and throne, the divinely bestowed trappings of kingship, but wanted to establish the dynastic principle. He begged an eagle to carry him up to heaven so he could ask Ishtar for a son to be his successor. Important discrepancies, however, between the iconography and the story of Etana make it possible that the man riding an eagle is a certain Shena-Inanna-mi, who "went up to heaven in the presence of his son."[25]

In Akkadian glyptic, the sun-god is shown shining through mountain ranges or passing through the gates of heaven. He sometimes carries a tool that may be a saw, serrated knife, or key, as if, at his rising, he had to cut his way through the mountains or unlock the gates of heaven (Figure 6.2a). This emphasis on the rising sun is unique to Akkadian glyptic, so evidently had some special meaning, perhaps signifying triumph over obstacles.[26] Ea, god of fresh waters, is shown in the watery depths with his attendants (Figure 6.2). Other imagery involves vegetation-, snake-, and weather-gods, as well as a martial female deity perhaps to be identified with Ishtar.[27] In short, the vivid scenes on Akkadian cylinder seals suggest a rich and complex religious iconography and mythological tradition, but beyond the identification of a few important deities, such as Shamash, Ishtar, Sin, and Ea, little can be made of them, nor can one say whether these mythological scenes had special resonance with the owner of the seal, or whether they were generic templates.

## 3.    Developments in Akkadian religion

The vast changes in Mesopotamian society, culture, industry, and economy wrought by the creation of the Akkadian Empire included major shifts in religious belief and practice. Several of these are easy to detect, for instance, the elevation of the king to divinity. According to Naram-Sin, his deification was the positive response of the chief gods of Mesopotamia to the prayers of the citizens of Agade, grateful that he had saved their city in a time of crisis.[28] But already Rimush had hinted at a special relationship with the gods, Sargon and Rimush were invoked as gods in personal names; and the word "king" in personal names acquired many of the attributes previously accorded to gods.[29] Moreover, the Akkadian kings regularly claimed direct support for their exploits from the great deities of Mesopotamia: Dagan gave Sargon and Naram-Sin the Upper Lands; Enlil "revealed" his will through Rimush's conquest of Elam; Ishtar "loved" Naram-Sin. The gods, for their part, were perhaps conceived more and more like human royalty in a hierarchical universe; their rites increasingly resembled court ceremonial, their temple cellas throne rooms. The Akkadian king, as a god, acquired a cosmic role as creator, nurturer, and guardian of his subjects, as well as replacing the sun-god as guardian of oaths.[30] Whereas Sumerian conquerors had tended to attribute their victories to their local city gods, now royal triumphs were on a cosmic scale, "for all time, since the establishment of the human race."[31]

A second readily identified development was the practice of naming members of the royal family to high priesthood. Sargon's appointment of his daughter, Enheduanna, as high priestess to the moon-god at Ur, as well as the highly individual works of literature associated with her authorship (Appendix II), raise many questions: Why a priestess at Ur, but not one at Kish or Uruk, the other rival cities to Akkadian kingship? Was there something special about the cult of the moon-god, but not of other cults, which called or allowed for such an appointment? And what, if any, wider interpretations emerge from the difficult, allusive poetry attributed to Enheduana, centuries after her death? It is striking that women of high social status, some of them perhaps priestesses like Enheduanna, are depicted more frequently in Akkadian art than in any other period of Mesopotamian history. Naram-Sin appointed at least two of his daughters to be high priestesses, Shumshani for the sun-god at Sippar and Enmenanna for the moon-god at Ur as successor to Enheduanna.[32] One Akkadian governor of Nippur, perhaps also a member of the royal family, served simultaneously as chief administrator of the temple of Enlil.[33]

Third, the Akkadian period may have seen the first steps toward creating a systematic, national pantheon of the increasing number of deities worshipped in the new empire. Naram-Sin names eight leading gods in his deification account, listing them in hierarchical order: Ishtar in Eanna (at Uruk), Enlil in Nippur, Dagan in Tuttul, Ninhursag in Kesh, Enki in Eridu, Sin in Ur, Shamash in Sippar, and Nergal in Cutha. Anum is not mentioned in this list, nor are the cities of Uruk and Kish. Ninhursag was a Sumerian mother goddess of birth and Nergal was a god of death. Expounding a pantheon as a way of asserting political unity may have been built on earlier Mesopotamian beliefs that, on the one hand, deities were identified with specific cult centers, usually located in cities, but, on the other, they had a hierarchy or family relationships among themselves, an earthly consequence of which was that there was a "land" of which cities formed a part. Including the Akkadian king in the pantheon as god of his city, Agade, was a powerful innovation, as was promoting formerly local gods to universal dominion.[34]

Finally, the Akkadian period is unique for the special status accorded the goddess Ishtar. In the inscription commemorating his deification (Chapter 1 part 4), Naram-Sin placed Ishtar first among the deities. She was also his lover. On a stone mold, Naram-Sin is seated, bare-chested, while the goddess, enthroned by his side, hands him the lead ropes of defeated peoples, among them perhaps Elam and Marhashum (Figure 9.8).[35] His aunt, Enheduanna (Figure 9.6), considered Ishtar the divine force behind the original Akkadian conquest of Sumer. When a rival to her father's dynasty arose at Ur, Enheduanna poured out her venomous hatred of her enemies and her confidence in their demise through Ishtar's intervention, all in the strange, difficult style that characterizes her poetry (Appendix II):

> You brought havoc on the country, it was you who gave the storm its
>     strength,
> With Enlil's approval, you taught this land respect,
> Heaven itself assigned you this mission.
> My lady! The country will bow down again at your battle cry!
> When the trembling human race has found its place before you,
> Midst your awe-inspiring, overwhelming splendor,
> For of all cosmic powers you hold those most terrible,
> And at your behest the storage house of tears is opened wide,
> They walk the pathway to the house of deepest mourning,
> Defeated, ere the battle had begun.[36]

In later Mesopotamian historical thinking, the Akkadian period was, in fact, called "the reign of Ishtar."[37]

Some scholars have suggested that it was Enheduanna herself who undertook to integrate the Akkadian and Sumerian pantheons into one comprehensive system by equating Akkadian with Sumerian deities, most notably Ishtar with Inanna. This proposal proceeds from their metaphorical reading of several Sumerian literary works, some ascribed to her authorship, taking them to refer to the Akkadian Empire in the guise of poetic narratives about Ishtar. But there is little basis for imagining that official synthesis of Akkadian and Sumerian deities was ever envisaged, much less deemed necessary, and nothing in the texts themselves compels or even renders likely such an interpretation.[38] Therefore Akkadian religious innovation remains best attested and understood in the realm of royal ideology, in which the king had a special relationship with the great gods or was even reckoned among their number.

The divine status of the Akkadian king may also have been inspired by traditions of the Semitic-speaking peoples of the Upper Euphrates, who worshipped deceased kings as "Malku." This mysterious figure was at once a royal counselor to the living and a god of the dead, the essence of his leadership based on wisdom, experience, and regular communion with the uncanny, through which the ruler linked the living with those who had gone before.[39] In claiming to be gods, the Akkadian kings invoked the divinity that already hedged a king in their world, at the same time offering extraordinary personal achievement, supposedly resulting in universal popular support, as a criterion for their elevation to divine status.

## 4.   Temples, images, cult, prayer, and priesthood

Numerous temples are mentioned in inscriptions, literature, and administrative documents. For centuries before the Akkadian period, the most widely distributed, basic plan of the Mesopotamian temple was of the "bent-axis" type, in which one entered a rectangular cella from one of the long sides then turned to face the altar on the short side furthest from the entrance. There was an outer courtyard, perhaps for ceremonies involving more people than could be held in the cella. As buildings grew more elaborate, the courtyard was often enclosed as part of a larger architectural complex, and the cella approached through an anteroom or vestibule. Service rooms, for the preparation of offerings for example, opened directly onto the cella. Some of the staff may have lived in or near the complex; in later periods a special house was constructed for the high priest or priestess close by the sanctuary.[40]

The gods dwelt in their temples as images in human form, which were thought to localize the transcendent deity in the sanctuary as a householder.[41] In later periods, rituals and theology were elaborated to account for how a man-made object could partake of divinity.[42] To judge from later periods, the images of gods were offered food, drink, incense, and music. Although no cult statues from the Akkadian period have survived, they are depicted on Akkadian cylinder seals in scenes showing Ea, Shamash, or other deities seated in a structure (Figure 6.2).[43] Statues of their more distinguished human subjects do exist; they stood before them prayerfully, often with inscriptions identifying them (Chapter 9 part 1).

The most imposing remains of Akkadian-period temples are at Nagar, where two massive complexes (FS and SS) were constructed.[44] Since the architectural layout has no parallel in Mesopotamia, it may have been a local plan rebuilt in grand style by Naram-Sin. If so, this would recall his lavish transformation of the temple of Enlil at Nippur into a royal showpiece of consummate craftsmanship (Chapter 1 part 5). The temple buildings were abandoned and ritually filled in, perhaps in the late Akkadian period, after first a withdrawal and then a reassertion of Akkadian authority. These temples, as well as the palace there (Chapter 3 part 5), represented an enormous investment of labor and materials, suggestive of the empire at its height.

The FS temple complex was located at the northeast corner of the city and was built over substantial, perhaps residential, structures of the pre-Akkadian Kingdom of Nagar.[15] It was approached from a gate on the south, which opened into a large room supplied with bins, whence one continued through a double gateway into a vast courtyard, with administrative buildings on the left and the temple directly in front. This structure would have soared over the courtyard and was no doubt visible from a considerable distance across the plain. It was of the bent-access type, with the cella about 5 meters in length. Donkeys entered the courtyard through the large gate, perhaps to be tethered there, having carried goods in trade caravans, drawn conveyances for traveling notables (for whom wagon transport was a perquisite of their status), or pulled vehicles for some type of religious procession.[16]

This complex was abandoned briefly for unknown reasons. A thin layer of green ash resulting from intense heat (600–800°C) does not appear to come from burning on the spot, but was brought from somewhere else and spread over the floors. Its precise nature and origin remain undetermined. Above this was a thin layer of water-laid reddish clay, as if the area had lain open to rainfall for a short period. Next, teams of workmen came in to empty the structures of whatever remained, trampling down the layer of rubbish that had accumulated on the floors and lighting fires around the walls of the courtyard, the antecella of the temple, and the gateway to the courtyard. Fill was carried in and spread over the rooms and courtyards to a depth of about 35 cm.[17]

As this was being done, ceremonies took place that entailed burying a saluki dog and eight or more donkeys, including two aged females, one aged male, and a male and two females in the prime of life. The preserved teeth of the donkeys give evidence for cribbing, so they had been kept in stalls. They were in good health and had been well cared for. They were not harnessed and may not have been killed where they were carefully laid out. The aged male was positioned so that his head lay at the threshold of the main gate to the complex, facing out from the courtyard. An aged female was in the courtyard itself, just north of the main gate, opposite the portal that was not blocked by the other donkey. Three others were deposited, no doubt with considerable effort, in a small storage room in a building that evidently had a second story, even a tower that must have given a commanding view of the courtyard and the roadway approaching the complex. Two of these donkeys, an older and a younger female, were laid together as a pair and were perhaps mother and daughter. The third, a young male, faced the opposite direction. A sounding in a courtyard to the east of the main gate turned up yet another donkey set on the fill layer, this one a well-cared-for female in the prime of life. Two more donkeys were interred next to the temple outside its north and west walls, the one on the west with reed matting laid over it. All these animals were covered with more fill immediately after their killing and deposition.[18]

As the filling of the building continued, deposits of metal objects and jewelry were made. A box set in the courtyard contained copper tools and a bag of silver, gold, electrum, and copper jewelry and ingots. Nearby were two other deposits of tools and weapons, some in a basket, and a dagger and axe wrapped in fine cloth. Tools were left in the temple area as well. Three braziers and two clay tripods were set up on the fill level above the anteroom of the cella. The braziers showed signs of frequent use, perhaps in connection with the burial rituals. A small pile of gazelle horns was also left above the floor of the anteroom, together with a pig skull along the west wall, a two-pronged implement, and some pots.[49]

Dismembered human remains, including limbs and skulls, were scattered in the main courtyard inside the gate, not far from the first two donkeys. Three dismembered human skeletons were set on the first fill layer in a large room in a building abutting the gate structure, but entered from another courtyard to the west. One of these was a young man, perhaps beheaded, whose bone structure suggests that he frequently rode a donkey or drove a cart. A second adult male lay beside him, with a third mature or old man nearby, whose bone structure is consistent with habitual control of the reins of a cart team. He too may have been beheaded. A scatter of pots, broken at the time of deposit, surrounded this group. Since the men were not interred in the manner of an Akkadian burial, but were dumped on the fill and then covered, their remains were clearly part of the burial rite for the building. The filling of the complex continued, then the walls were toppled over the fill, after which more loads of debris were brought in and thrown on top.[50]

A second, even larger complex (SS) was in the southwest corner of the city, facing the Akkadian palace and opposite what may have been the principal southern gateway to the city.[51] It comprised a massive building 21.5 by 6.8 meters in size, with its long axis aligned approximately north-south, overlooking a large courtyard and enclosing a second. Its outer walls were 2 meters thick on the long sides and 2.8 meters thick on the short sides. The short sides were extended by pairs of projecting towers, decorated on the outside by a dado 1.8 meters high supporting shallow engaged columns. Between the southern towers, looking out onto a ceremonial courtyard, was a shelf a meter high, above which was a rectangular niche in the wall. At the foot of the shelf was a large slab of calcite, nearly 3 meters wide. The temple was of the bent-axis type, with an anteroom and was lined with benches, presumably to hold dedicatory objects. Its brickwork resembled that of the Akkadian palace, so the complex may have been built during the reign of Naram-Sin. An imposing administrative room, 10 by 9 meters in size, and probably roofed by a sophisticated system of framing, was accessible via a vestibule leading off the ceremonial court.

This complex too was ritually closed and interred after a brief abandonment, probably at the same time as the one on the northeast corner of the city. As seen there, workmen trampled back and forth on the debris left on the floor, before they began to fill the entire structure. The walls of the building and courtyard were toppled in, then a hard red surface was laid over the rubble. Ritual deposits were left both on the floors of the building and above the fill.

A statue of a human-faced bull rising from a recumbent position was found on top of the first layer of fill in the ceremonial courtyard. It may originally have been placed nearby, perhaps in the recessed niche west of the doorway connecting the ceremonial courtyard with the temple courtyard, above the large calcite slab. A plausible identification of this animal is the mythological creature called *kusarikkum* in Akkadian, which is sometimes represented in Akkadian glyptic.[52] In fact, eight images of *kusarikku*'s were made for Naram-Sin's reconstruction of the Ekur Temple at Nippur, plated with gold and studded with gems (Chapter 1 part 5). This piece might well be a more modest realization of the same animal.[53]

In addition, a large heap of valuables was left on the floor of the ceremonial courtyard, near the doorway to the temple. This contained about 5.5 kilograms of copper or bronze (analysis not available), together with beads and other objects of shell, faience, lapis, rock crystal, carnelian, and jet stone, the latter two probably imported from the Indus Valley. There were more than 100 nails, some with traces of gold leaf, perhaps the remains of the cult image and splendid door to the temple, as well as a silver animal pendant, cylinder seals, sealings, bullae, and a stone bowl broken before it had been deposited. The spine of a marine stingray more than a meter long and vertebrae of other stingrays were also present. Presumably these dangerous creatures were caught in the Gulf, rather than the Mediterranean, as seems the case with other marine life at Nagar, so had been transported 2000 kilometers overland without spoilage.[54] This pile of goods was set on fire.

A group of unusual bottles was left on the floor of the large room 15, which faced the ceremonial courtyard, suggestive of the "oil office" known from records at Eshnunna and Umma.[55] Behind it in room 17, a drinking set consisting of a beaker and five goblets was set in a niche. A considerable amount of pottery was left on the floor of room 35 and other service rooms, apparently as offerings, since some of the cups contained the remains of food. These small rooms included equipment for food preparation, such as a grinding platform, basalt grinding stone, and jars and pots of various kinds. Another drinking set consisting of a small red flask and a pair of footed goblets was placed on the floor of room 36, along with a larger vessel too damaged for reconstruction. When the filling was done, two ritual food deposits in covered bowls were set out above the buried façade.

In addition to their remarkable interment, the structures at Nagar provide the most substantial evidence for religious ritual in the Akkadian period. The monumental courtyard with a dais or altar at one side, facing the temple, and the *kusarik-kum* in a niche in the wall above it, was no doubt the locus for outdoor ceremonies involving far more people than could be admitted to the temple, who were carrying out an act in which religious awe was paramount. A tempting explanation is that these were occasions for local or tribal leaders to swear allegiance to the Akkadian king. The swearing of oaths (Chapter 6 part 6) was a well-known practice in Akkadian law (Chapter 2 part 3), which second-millennium sources indicate could take place at the gate of a temple. Because the oaths known from legal documents involved only a few people, for whom such a large space would scarcely be necessary, however awe-inspiring the setting, large-scale pledging ceremonies seem more likely.[56] Since oaths taken in the time of Naram-Sin or Sharkalisharri were normally done on the name of the king instead of the gods, a standard with the king's name on it or another emblem of the Akkadian royal house may have stood nearby.

A pre-Akkadian text from Ebla raises the possibility that springtime levies of soldiers may also have involved some sort of temple ceremony.[57] A comparable open space at Akkadian Mari, equipped with three outdoor altars of ascending height, on each of which stood either a figure or some large object, could have been used for the same purpose.[58] Whatever this event was or entailed, it was more characteristic of Syria than Mesopotamia, as no comparable spaces have been found at sites in Sumer and Akkad.

As for ritual burial, Akkadian royal inscriptions refer to monumental burial mounds heaped up over dead soldiers, so there may be an analogy in the way these Nagar temples were buried.[59] Like dead soldiers, they were stripped of their equipment. The temple furniture, precious items, and woodwork were burned, just as *The Curse of Agade* says happened in Nippur:

> Its guardian figures that stood by the ceremonial entryway,
> Though they had done no forbidden thing,
> Naram-Sin threw them into the fire,
> Cedar, cypress, juniper, and boxwood,
> The woodwork of its dwelling chamber, he made ooze out in flames.[60]

In addition, the mutilated corpses of human beings were laid out and covered with earth, as done in burial mounds over soldiers. The donkeys killed and arranged in various places could have belonged to two of the men, who could well have been donkey drivers by profession. Yet no evidence was found of any wagons buried with them, if the animals and men were meant to serve someone in another life. Instead, the burial of a prominent man with two equids at Tell Razuk[61] suggests that draught animals could be sacrificed at the time of the death of their owners.

Other aspects of the ritual remain unique and unexplainable. In the southern complex, for instance, on the east side of the ceremonial court, stood a large room opening onto the court, in front of which was an elaborate ladder-patterned brick pavement unlike any other there. Conceivably in connection with the ritual interment, its main door was blocked, a staircase was cut in the wall of this structure, north of its main entrance, and a human head or skull was placed on the ground nearby.[62]

At Assur, an extensive temple to Ishtar was located in the northwest corner of the city. The history of this building is problematic, but its first Akkadian phase (level G) seems to have been built at the end of the pre-Akkadian period and remained in use during early Akkadian times.[63] As at Nagar, there may have been a destruction during the Akkadian period, followed by a reconstruction. Most of the statuary found in the cella of this sanctuary is pre-Akkadian, after which the custom of placing limestone statues of individuals apparently declined, perhaps in favor of placing statues of royalty and notables made of more expensive materials. Also in this trove were the smashed remains of a statue possibly representing Manishtusu; a spear point dedicated by a servant of Manishtusu was found near the temple. Dating the heyday of this phase of the Ishtar Temple to the reign of Manishtusu thus seems a reasonable supposition.[64] The massive fire set in one end of the sanctuary, though possibly paralleled by burnings elsewhere in the city, could in fact be a deliberate bonfire as in the sanctuaries at Nagar, hence part of an intentional interment of the building during the Akkadian period.[65]

The Ishtar Temple was planned on a grand scale and could have housed a considerable number of people. It comprised many rooms and several courtyards, more like the northeast temple at Nagar than the smaller complexes further south in Mesopotamia. The main cella was approached through a courtyard about 10 meters wide and of undetermined length, opening into a suite of rooms, one of which gave access to the long side of the cella, so the worshipper turned to his left to face the deity. The cella itself was about six by eleven meters in size, with a platform at the end where the altar stood. Prior to its destruction, it had been adorned with statuary, three clay altars, three incense stands, a brazier, and other installations, consistent with rituals of burning and libation.[66] How the rest of the complex was used is unknown.

A temple at Eshnunna, often associated with the god Abu on the basis of an inscribed copper bowl found in a horde in the Northern Palace nearby, gives an idea of what a mid-size temple might have been like (Figure 6.1). Known as the Single-Shrine Temple, it may have been first built in the Akkadian period or slightly earlier, in a neighborhood of private houses, some of which abutted. It was rebuilt several times.[67] In the first and second phases, a cella 3.25 × 12.30 meters

*Figure 6.1* Reconstruction of the Single-Shrine Temple at Eshnunna.

in size was entered from the north long side. The worshipper then turned to his right to face the altar, on the west end. A small room adjoining contained an oven, perhaps for baking bread for the cult, as it was larger than the standard *tannur*-oven.[68] Comparable ovens are found in connection with other sanctuaries of the pre- and early Akkadian periods.[69]

In the third phase, perhaps during the time of Naram-Sin, the building was substantially overhauled, giving the impression of greater splendor and more carefully regulated access to the inner sanctum. The entrance was made more monumental, with a staircase and pilasters. To judge from the administrative records of Naram-Sin's reconstruction of the temple of Enlil at Nippur, the entrances to a major temple were guarded by statues of protective deities; provision for such statues was made on either side of the staircase (Figure 6.1).[70] In addition, the original cella was divided by a massive partition with a graduated doorway in the middle, narrowing as one entered the inner cella. This was perhaps closed by a door, or was meant to dramatize the approach to the divinity. The altar was enlarged to extend further out into the inner cella, with what seemed to be bases for at least two statues. The oven was removed from the adjoining room, as if at this point cult provisions were delivered to the temple by the local governor, rather than prepared there (Chapter 4 part 7).[71] Varied offerings were made, including a large bird, ostrich eggs, and possibly an antelope. Amulets, seals, beads, bowls, plaques, and mace heads attest to the richness of the sanctuary's gifts.[72]

In the first or second phase of the Eshnunna temple, pre-Akkadian statues of various sizes, including one kneeling and eleven standing males and two standing females, were carefully buried in a deposit, as if all had been cleared from the sanctuary at one time, perhaps for an Akkadian-period renovation. Some scholars consider the two largest to be images of the god Abu and his consort, and the remaining figurines to be worshippers, but others, more plausibly, view all of them as worshippers.[73] In the Akkadian period, it is by no means certain that the gods were represented in temples by anthropomorphic images, but they certainly were in glyptic, where they are shown seated (Figure 6.2b), with worshippers coming before them in attitudes of prayer.[74]

A small shrine at Tell Taya, a town at the northeastern corner of the Sinjar-Tell Afar plain, affords an example of a rural Akkadian-period temple. This stood at least 4 meters high, facing south, and comprised a single large cella with a finely plastered dais in the center of the west end. The floor in front of the dais was paved in white gypsum. To the left of the dais was a bell-shaped hole 1.3 meters deep, with part of a large bowl placed over the aperture, apparently to receive the run-off from libations. There was also a mud brick hearth in the middle of the room.[75]

A shift in the relationship between worshippers and gods in the Akkadian period is suggested by the development of glyptic imagery showing an individual led before a deity (Figure 6.2b).[76] This may respond to an increased emphasis on subordination and hierarchy in religious thought, parallel to the regular identification of people in administrative records in terms of their subordination to someone else (Chapter 2 part 2). Presentation scenes tended to replace the feasting

(a)

(b)

*Figure 6.2* Cult scenes: (a) two solar deities approach Enki/Ea enshrined; one climbs a mountain, mace in hand, while the other raises a saw or key and steps on a defeated god; (b) in his sanctuary guarded by *lahmu*-monsters, Enki/Ea receives Isimu, his advisor-god, who presents a worshipper.

tableaus of the preceding period. If, as some argue, gods were shown banqueting with humans, this implied a more communal relationship between the gods and their subjects in pre-Akkadian times. Others consider the change to presentation scenes indicative of a new artistic focus on the gods as divine rulers, moving away from the traditional depiction of religious festivals.[77] Architectural reflection of this concept may be seen in the partitioning of cellas into two rooms, as in the Single-Shrine Temple at Eshnunna, which served to make the deities more remote, accessible only to the privileged few.

The furnishings of these sanctuaries suggest that libations and burned offerings may have been major complementary elements in Akkadian temple rituals.

Libations were meant for the gods and also provided liquids to the human dead in the netherworld, while the fragrant smoke rising from burned offerings was intended to attract or please the gods in the heavens.[78] In cylinder seals, both gods and worshippers hold small cups, perhaps the "hand cup" (*šusala*) of administrative documents (Chapter 5 part 2). The disk of Enheduanna (Chapter 9 part 2) shows an attendant libating from a tall vessel (Chapter 5 part 3 and Figure 9.6); she is accompanied by priestesses or votaries. It would seem that an ancient rite of hospitality had developed into a way of seeking divine patronage: the suppliant offered food, drink, and other gifts in the hope that a deity would accept his petition or feel under obligation to him.

Preparation for such rituals may have included washing, shaving, massaging and anointing the body with oil, and donning special clothing. After performing entry rites, an officiant probably led a person making a prayer or offering before the deity. The petitioner could be represented in perpetuity by a statue posed in prayer (Chapter 9 part 1) or, in later periods, by a written prayer in the form of a letter. Liquids could be poured from a special vessel or an incense burner might be prepared with twigs and aromatics, then ignited. Spoken prayers were delivered in a specific stance and with prescribed gestures. In some cases, as when Sargon went before Dagan, god of clouds, the petitioner might prostrate himself.[79]

In Akkadian personal names, references occur to praying, such as "Pray to your god!" (Kurub-Ilak), as well as to prayers answered, for example, "Ea-blessed" (Ikrub-Ea), "My blessing" (Karabi), and "Blessing" (Kirbanum). No extended Akkadian prayers survive except for the heartfelt pleas of Enheduanna to Inanna:

> I am Enheduanna, let me speak to you my prayer,
> My tears flowing like some sweet intoxicant:
> "Holy Inanna, may I let you have your way?
>    I would have you judge my case.
> "I cannot make him, the silver nighttime orb, exert himself for me.
> "That man has defiled the rites decreed by holy heaven,
> "He has robbed An of his very temple!
> "He honors not the greatest god of all,
> "The abode that An himself could not exhaust its charms,
>    its beauty infinite,
> "He has turned that temple into a house of ill repute,
> "Forcing his way in as if he were an equal, he dared approach me in his
>    lust!
> "O wild bison, steadfast to me, do you be the one to hunt him down,
>    do you be the one to catch him!
> "What is to become of me in this place I had my living,
> "This unruly place that spurns your night-sky father? May heaven bring it
>    to heel!
> "May An slash it, through and through!
> "May Enlil cut short its destiny!
> "May no mother comfort any baby crying there.

"O Queen, any mourning for this place,
"Your cargo-ship of sorrow should jettison it off some foreign shore!"[80]

The staff of a temple included cultic and administrative personnel, as well as laborers and dependents. The hierarchy varied in different temples, and the priesthood sometimes had titles unique to their office. The leading cult officiant in a major temple was a high priest or priestess (the Sumerian *en* meant either one), who resided in a special house in the temple complex. High priestesses, such as Enheduanna, daughter of Sargon, or Shumshani, daughter of Naram-Sin, did not marry and in some cases may have been understood to have had a conjugal relationship with the deity they served. These women were evidently well educated, but how they learned their cultic duties is unknown.[81]

Another important officiant, whose precise duties are unclear, was the *lumahhum*, well known in Sumerian literature but not in Akkadian administrative documents.[82] In some temples, a person called the *pashishum* waited on a divinity by preparing and serving food and maintaining the purity of the food, vessels, and utensils used in the god's repast. In his inscriptions, Sargon calls himself "the *pashishum* of An." Since this was a title unique to Uruk, he may have adopted it after his defeat of Lugalzagesi, who had been proud to use it, as had his father before him.[83] At Girsu, the highest cultic official was the *nin-dingir*, or high priestess (presumably of Ningirsu), followed by the *sanga*, the chief administrator of temple resources, who may also have had cultic responsibilities.[84] According to the poems *Passionate Inanna* and *Inanna and Ebih*, attributed to Enheduanna (Appendix IIb, c), Ishtar's cultic staff included performers of rites who were men dressed as women, transvestites, and transsexual or altered people, who in some cases cut themselves or other performers as part of the rite (Appendix IIc lines 173–75; Appendix IIb line 88).

Music was an important part of temple rituals, notably in the performance of Sumerian ritual laments (Chapter 9 part 8). These were sung to appease the anger of deities, to mourn people who had died, and to bewail the destruction of cities and temples. No examples of laments survive from the Akkadian period, although the singer of laments (*kalûm*) is mentioned in administrative documents and poetry and was a personage of some standing in the temple hierarchy.[85]

People could also honor their gods with gifts for their temples; the deity might reciprocate by granting good health and long life. Royal gifts included captured weapons and vessels, precious metals, and slaves. Naram-Sin, for example, gave a magnificent jar, and the majordomo of Sargon's wife dedicated a limestone vessel to a god in her honor. Some gifts or offerings were prepared foods or their ingredients, such as flour. The seal of a governor of Lagash shows him carrying a lamb, presumably an offering or a greeting gift to a deity or the king.[86] One of the most impressive gifts from a private individual to a deity was the construction and staffing of an entire temple, evidently by a magnate who hoped that he and his family would be granted in return good destinies and long lives:

When the goddess Damgalnunna chose Ur-imma in her pure heart, and said to him, 'Build my temple for me!' and when Ur-imma told the goddess

Damgalnunna the matter in his heart and went to her, then did Ur-imma raise its structure? 6 ½ cubits (= approx. 3 m 30 high). He provided a priest, a cupbearer, slaves, and slave women in the temple. On account of this, the goddess Damgalnunna decreed a good destiny for Ur-imma, for his sake, she pronounced long life for his mother, long life for his wife and children, and long life for his brothers. The goddess Damgalnunna stood forward (among the gods) on Ur- imma's behalf.[87]

Regular meals were served to the gods, no doubt finer versions of what the human elite consumed. Little evidence for this is available from Akkadian sources because records of food deliveries to temples mostly refer to flour, seldom to other foodstuffs. In the Akkadian remodeling of the Single-Shrine Temple at Eshnunna, a baking facility near the cella was removed. This suggests that in some temples, meals were prepared from raw ingredients, whereas later in the Akkadian period the practice of delivering prepared foods from outside the temple may have begun.[88] Early second-millennium records from the temple of Ningal, spouse of the moon-god, at Ur show a steady diet of dairy products, dates, and oil, with occasional supplements of nuts, cassia, honey, and peas.[89]

## 5.   Standards, sacred objects, and dedications

In all periods, Mesopotamian religion accorded divine honors to objects belonging to the gods, such as musical instruments, thrones, chariots, weapons, and standards. To judge from later texts, standards were used to signify the gods in rituals and ceremonies, including the administration of oaths. They were made of wood, copper, gold, silver, bronze, or lapis and mounted on a pole.[90] Linking the numerous standards and symbols depicted in Akkadian art with specific gods is not often possible. Nevertheless, the moon-god was clearly associated in glyptic with a standard topped by a crescent moon, which he sometimes holds like a staff, as well as with another standard with a ribbon or cloth wrapped around it at the top. Why he had two symbols is unknown.[91]

Standards could also be carried in parades or marches, as a later epic poem relates:

Naram-Sin went on his way,
The god of the land indeed was going before him,
Ilaba, the vanguard, before him,
Zababa, splendid of horns, behind,
The emblems of Annunitum and Shi-laba, two by two,
Right and left, horn by horn . . .[92]

The Victory Stele of Naram-Sin shows two soldiers marching behind the king and carrying standards (Figure 1.6), so the poetic description may be based on Akkadian reality.

A standard at Susa was given offerings of flour, as was Ilaba, one of the patron deities of the dynasty and of Agade.[93] A document from Umma lists a substantial amount of flour offered to the "king's standard," as well as to the king's messenger, the king's boatman, eight soldiers, and a royal sheep and donkey. This suggests a traveling party that escorted the king's emblem from place to place. One imagines the standard set up in a precinct and used there for rites of oath-taking on "the king's name" (*mu lugal*, Chapter 2 part 3, Chapter 6 part 6).[94]

Temples and their divine indwellers were the recipients of objects, sometimes inscribed, dedicated for the well-being of the donor. Whereas in pre-Akkadian periods, private donors seem to account for many of the dedications, some of which are in honor of their families, in the Akkadian period private donations dwindled and royal ones increased, often with lengthy curses against anyone who would remove or appropriate them.[95] Inscriptions in honor of the ruler replaced inscriptions in honor of individuals and their families.[96] So too, life-size statues of the king and royal stelae and reliefs made of diorite, limestone, gold, wood, and other materials crowded out the more modest dedications of private individuals and notables. At Nippur and other cities, these royal monuments stood for centuries and were no doubt esteemed as treasures of the past (Chapter 9 part 3).

One of the Akkadian objects most frequently offered were mace heads of metal or a great variety of stones, some brought back as booty from expeditions abroad. To judge from Akkadian commemorative art, the mace was not part of the standard armament of the day, so was either a reference to tradition or a weapon preferred by the gods. Thus when Sargon(?) is shown smiting the head of Lugalzagesi(?) with a mace (Figure 9.5), he uses a weapon that is a divine attribute, rather than one his soldiers carried into battle.[97]

Stone and metal bowls, jars, plates, and other containers were also frequently presented, as were figurines of animals (lions, cattle, dogs, sheep, and goats, sometimes given their own names), carved and inscribed wall plaques, cylinder seals, beads, and statues often representing people in prayer (Chapter 9 part 1).[98] Cultic furniture, such as beds and chairs for the gods (Chapter 10 part 6), has not survived, though model beds, usually in clay, are known from various sites, perhaps toys or offered in the hope of successful conception and childbirth.[99] In later periods, clay plaques and other objects were mass-produced and evidently sold in emporia near temples for those who wished to make a gift to the gods.[100]

## 6. Oaths and curses

In Akkadian Mesopotamia, parties swore oaths to facts or promises, in the context of juridical or contractual procedures (Chapter 2 part 3).[101] Although these seldom specify where or how the oaths were administered, sacred spaces or in the presence of a symbol, such as a standard, were the most likely venues. The surviving examples of juridical oaths were sworn on the names of Naram-Sin and Sharkalisharri, in one case on the wall of Agade.[102] The absence of oaths on the names of earlier Akkadian kings may mean that the practice began with the deification of Naram-Sin and that before that oaths were typically taken on the names of deities.

Failing symbols, oaths could be taken in the presence of community elders, as attested in a letter from the Diyala region: "Let them bring . . . elders there, he should take up his staff and his weapon and let him be sworn by Shakkan [god of livestock] and Shamash [god of oaths]. I really do not want to concern myself with the stray sheep of an elder!"[103]

Rimush and Manishtusu recited before a deity their deeds and the number of people they had killed or captured and swore to their veracity. This may be a forerunner to the later Assyrian practice of the king's reporting to the god and to his community on the course and outcome of a royal expedition.[104]

Unlike during most periods of Mesopotamian history, people also resorted to oaths in non-juridical contexts for enhanced emphasis, as in this letter: "See here, I swear by the life of Sharkalisharri, if Gutians make off with the livestock, you yourself will pay!"[105] The writer was an Akkadian notable, so one may wonder whether or not rhetoric heightened by oaths was discourse characteristic of the ruling class. What may be humorous exaggeration of the usage is found in another Akkadian letter, sent by the same man: "By Ishtar and Ilaba, Ashgi and Ninhursag, by the king's life and by the queen's life you must swear it! So long as you have not seen my eyes, may you swallow neither food nor drink. Furthermore, so long as you do not come to me, do not sit on a chair."[106]

Curses in the name of gods were regularly appended to commemorative inscriptions, directed against anyone who would erase the words or appropriate the dedicated object. Although some of the curses that appear in the later Akkadian period do have parallels in pre-Akkadian inscriptions, they tend to be lengthier and more literary than those of preceding periods.[107] The elaboration of this practice may thus be seen as an Akkadian innovation related to the development of oath-taking and cursing in official and private life.

A short, typical curse from an inscription of Sargon reads, "The one who makes away with this inscription, may Enlil and Shamash tear up his foundations and take away his seed."[108] By the reign of Naram-Sin, the deities invoked had become more numerous, some with curses appropriate to their special powers. Here Ninhursag and Nintu, birth goddesses, render the malefactor childless:

> Whoever shall remove the name of Naram-Sin, king of the four quarters of the earth and shall set his own name on the statue of Naram-Sin the mighty and shall say "This is my statue," or shall show it to a stranger and shall say, "Erase his name and set my name on it," may Sin, owner of this statue, Ishtar-Annunitum, Anu, Enlil, Ilaba, Sin, Shamash, Nergal, Umu, Ninkarrak, all the great gods, curse him with a terrible curse. May he hold no scepter for Enlil nor kingship for Ishtar. May he not stand before his god. May Ninhursag and Nintu grant him no male heir nor offspring. May Adad and Nisaba not let his furrow give yield. May Enki measure out only mud(?) in his watercourses, may he not increase his understanding.[109]

The curses in this text fall into four main types, two personal and two public. As to the offender's person, disease ("terrible curse") is to befall his body and he will be unable to produce children to carry on his lineage and dynasty. In the sphere of public life, he will fail as a ruler because his power will be weakened or undermined. Agricultural prosperity, needed to generate revenue and patronage opportunities to keep his subjects loyal, will decline, to the extent that the canals of his realm will be silted up. He will lack the mental capacity to deal with these crises. Since curses of this type are not attested in private life, one may detect in these afflictions the fundamental anxieties of an Akkadian king.

*The Curse of Agade* develops the late Akkadian curse into a literary form, but turns it, ironically, against the very culture that had raised it to an art. In this passage, the poet wishes ill for everyone in Agade:

> Agade, may your strong man lose his strength,
> May he be unable to lift his sack of provisions to the saddle,
> May your riding donkey no longer rejoice in his strength
>     but lie motionless till nightfall.
> May that city die of hunger,
> May its citizens who dined on the finest foods lie down in
>     grass (like cattle),
> May the man who arose from a meal of first fruits
> Eat the binding from his roof,
> As for the grand door of his family home,
> May he gnaw its leather hinges.[110]

## 7.   Festivals and the calendar

The Akkadian Empire did not have a unified calendar, as was attempted by a successor state, the Kingdom of Ur. Each city and region had its own calendar and feast days, and, though the names of various months from different localities in the Akkadian period are preserved, little is known of their order or of any festivals associated with them. The scant evidence suggests that the Semitic-speaking peoples of the north may have had a more widespread uniformity in the names of the months, and perhaps the overall calendar, than the Sumerian south, where every city had its own month names and order of months.

Although the moon governed the Akkadian-period calendar, religious festivals depended on the solar year, in which the seasons and festivals remained fixed. The New Year began at the vernal equinox, in rhythm with start of the agricultural year and the warm, dry season. The discrepancy between the solar and lunar years, which the Mesopotamians were well aware of, had to be adjusted periodically, normally by the insertion of extra days or a month in the calendar. The months were generally named after local religious festivals and moments in the agricultural year.[111]

Among the important Mesopotamian festivals was the *akitum*. In later periods, the *akitum* entailed the city god leaving the city and then returning in a triumphal parade like a victorious king. At Adab, this was during the third or fourth month, whereas at later Ur it fell in the sixth month.[112] Nothing is known of the festival in the Akkadian period. A second major festival centered on the remembrance of deceased relatives, when their spirits were thought to come up from the netherworld to receive offerings of food and drink (Chapter 11 part 1). At Akkadian Adab, this fell in the second month of the year, whereas at Akkadian Nippur it fell in the fifth.[113] Other festivals better known from later sources included observances in honor of the gods who went down to the netherworld, such as Dumuzi/Tammuz, as well as the lighting of a brazier (*kinunum*) to observe the beginning of the cold season.[114] In the Akkadian period, there were also months named for the festivals of local deities, such as the celebration for Ninmug at Adab, but the majority of the month names known from Akkadian sources seem to refer to moments in the agricultural year and the earliest Semitic month names are largely of unknown meaning.[115]

Pre-Akkadian Sumerian month names, by contrast, abound in names for festivals: "the festival of the goddess Lisi," "the festival of the goddess Baba," "the festival of coming forth," and many others. This suggests that religious festivals may have been more important in the urban life of Sumer than among the Semitic peoples of the north. Sumerian sayings, literature, and records of expenditures show that such festivals were often public celebrations, involving watching religious processions, feasting on special foods, dancing, and listening to music.[116] They were times for the populace to circulate in the streets in holiday clothing as an affirmation of responsible citizenship, particularly during festivals honoring the principal city deity. In addition, throughout the agricultural year, offering ceremonies were carried out at sowing time, just before reaping, and at the threshing floor. One of the year's most important traditional feasts in Sumer may have been a thanksgiving banquet in gratitude for a successful harvest, during which offerings of the first fruits of the harvest were made to the local deities.[117] No specifically royal festival is attested in the Akkadian period, such as the king's birthday or a jubilee.

## 8.   Magic and divination

Magic of the Akkadian period is known from a few spells. Their existence presupposes powers that the magician believes he can address and influence to do his will. As with prayer, it was important to recite traditional words believed to be effective. Some spells were deemed potent in and of themselves, to the extent that anyone could say them and hope to achieve the desired result. Among these were spells intended to influence a woman to submit to a man's sexual desire (Chapter 10 part 5).

Spells were often poetic in language and style, such as one to help a person escape from prison, which is known from a post-Akkadian manuscript. Beginning with a universal appeal for a welcome, in or out of doors, the speaker seeks to reverse the function of each aspect of the prison and its warden so they will help rather than prevent his walking free. He concludes by saying that the spell has divine sanction.

79  Hallo 1981; Sallaberger 2006/8.
80  Zgoll 1997: 254–65 lines 81–99.
81  Weadock 1975; J. Westenholz 1992a; Suter 2007; Sallaberger and Huber Vulliet 2003/5: 626–27.
82  Sallaberger and Huber Vulliet 2003/5: 628.
83  Archi 1996b; Steinkeller 2003a; Sallaberger and Huber Vulliet 2003/5: 630. The same title was used of the god Ninurta and other gods, Sjöberg1967: 216–17. Perhaps Sargon's use of this title could be the origin of the story that he was once a cupbearer, Chapter 1 part 2.
84  STTI 1072, 1246; ITT II 2923; Sallaberger and Huber Vulliet 2003/5: 627–28.
85  STTI 1072; Schretter 1990; Dobbs-Allsopp 1993: 31–96; Sallaberger and Huber Vulliet 2003/5: 634; Pruzsinszky 2010; Gadotti 2010; Gabbay in Owen 2011: 67–74. The singer is mentioned in Enheduanna's poetry (Appendix II), for example IIc line 174.
86  Rosengarten 1960: 13–23; ITT II 3046 (fish), 4620 (wool).
87  Biga 2005; Steinkeller in CUSAS 17 no. 13; foundation deposits of the Akkadian period are otherwise unknown, Ellis 1968: 57–58.
88  ITT I 1201,1262, RTC 123 (monthly); ITT I 1324, 1455, 1457 (compare 1385); ITT II 4393, 4394; CT 50 110 (peas and flour), 111–22; RTC 120; MVN 3 43, 44, 48, 50, 54; BIN 8 232; OIP 14 107 (oil).
89  Figulla 1953.
90  Sjöberg 1967: 205–7; Ge. Selz 1997.
91  Colbow 1997: 20.
92  *Muses*, 115. Anunitum (later Annunitum) was a warlike form of Ishtar, so also, perhaps, Shi-laba; in general, Godecken 1973; Frame 1993: 27.
93  Chapter 3 note 135.
94  B. Foster 1982b: 106 (interpretation contested by Steinkeller 1987a: 194, who thinks that mu lugal should mean "royal cook," but his idea is excluded by the fact that, unlike the royal boatman and messenger, the alleged cook's name is not given, nor is a "royal cook" otherwise attested).
95  Braun-Holzinger 1991: 15.
96  Braun-Holzinger 1991: 26–42.
97  Braun-Holzinger 1991; for the iconography of dead enemies and a proposal that it derives from Egypt, Börker-Klähn 1982a.
98  Braun-Holzinger 1991: 15. For proper names of dedicatory objects, Gelb 1955.
99  Braun-Holzinger 1991: 375.
100 In general, Barrelet 1968; clay figurines are often very difficult to date, but there seems to be a specifically Akkadian type, Gibson 2011: 77; further Maxwell-Hyslop 1971: 24–25.
101 Wilcke 2007: 45–46; for general studies of Mesopotamian oaths and curses, Pomponio 1990 and Kitz 2014 (who, however, omits most of the Akkadian-period evidence).
102 Edzard 1968: 127 no. 71 (BIN 8 62), 135–36 no. 81 (BIN 8 169), 152 no. 96 (ITT II 5758); further Chapter 2 notes 40 and 82.
103 Kienast and Volk 1995: 154–56.
104 Frayne 1993: 58; 76; Borger 1957/71; in general Pongratz-Leisten 2002.
105 Kienast and Volk 1995: 90; somewhat different rendering in *Muses*, 70.
106 *Muses*, 69.
107 Braun-Holzinger 1991: 15; Franke 1989: 211–43, with detailed analysis of the Akkadian curses; in general Pomponio 1990; Kitz 2014 (Akkadian period omitted).
108 Appendix Ia 3 and passim; Frayne 1993: 25.
109 Frayne 1993: 101–2, with readings from Kienast and Sommerfeld 1994; variant Appendix Ib 26; further, Chapter 9 part 1 and note 20.
110 Cooper 1983a: 62 (Appendix IIIb), lines 245–53.
111 Hunger 1976/80; M. Cohen 1993:3–8; Sallaberger 1993 1: 7–11; Such-Gutierrez 2013.

112  Falkenstein 1959a; M. Cohen 1993: 400–453; Such-Gutiérrez 2013: 327.

113  M. Cohen 1993: 78; 100–104.

114  M. Cohen 1993: 454–65.

115  M. Cohen 1993: 392–94.

116  Hunger 1976/80: 299–300; M. Cohen 1993: 23–36. For processions, Pettinato 1969: 212.

117  Maeda 1979: 31.

118  Hallo 1985. My suggestion "(fire) pit" in line 2 is based on *Lugalbanda in the Wilderness*, line 284: gú ne-mur-ra-ka ba-an-še$_{21}$ "He put (the foods) in the fire pit" (Vanstiphout 2003: 118); for fire pits, Barrelet 1974. A quite different interpretation of this spell is offered by Veldhuis 2003, who proposes it is intended for a person to gain entry to the netherworld.

119  MDP 14 91. For a quite different understanding of this spell and an edition of later spells in this group, Geller 1980: 24–25; the *kishkanum* was an unidentified, rare tree, foreign to Mesopotamia, the wood of which was occasionally used to make valuable furniture.

120  *Muses*, 65; for literature on the evil eye in Mesopotamia, *Muses*, 176. For a spell against digestive disease, CUSAS 23 199.

121  Bottéro 1974; Jeyes 1980; Catagnoti and Bonechi 1998; in general Maul 2013.

122  Cripps 2010 no. 29 (MCS 9 234); further Chapter 7 note 30.

123  STTI 1072; Asher-Greve 1987; Bonechi and Durand 1992; Waetzoldt 1998; A. Westenholz 1999: 72 (understands to depict childbirth, so also Parayre 2006); Fronzaroli 2003: 15.

124  Rutten 1938; Durand 1983; Gelb 1992: 169–71; further Chapter 11 part 4.

125  Maul 2013: 187–91 suggests that the political importance of divination emerged somewhat later, under the kings of Ur.

# 7    Statecraft and the military

## 1.    Chosen of the gods

The Akkadian Empire successfully fused two regional and cultural traditions of governance, one Sumerian, the other northern Mesopotamian. The city-states of the irrigated zone thought themselves part of a "land," linked by vital waterways whose disruption could soon bring a city to submission. According to *The Sumerian King List*, an important document of early Mesopotamian political theory, the gods ordained that kingship would move regularly from city to city in both Sumer and Akkad, and occasionally to places in Iran and Syria as well.[1] Thus the land was not defined by the domain of a particular king, who held office temporarily at the will of the gods, but existed independently for different kings to control at different times. As a Sumerian poem puts it:

> From time out of mind, from the foundation of this land and the multiply-
>     ing of its people,
> Who has ever seen a royal dynasty that lasted uppermost for long?[2]

Prior to the Akkadian period, some of the Sumerian cities had joined an alliance or league, which may have had cultural, religious, and political ramifications. Vestiges of this may have survived in later periods in the form of a rotating tax obligation, but no clear Akkadian evidence for such a system is known, so it may instead have been an innovation of the Third Dynasty of Ur.[3] Whatever the nature of this league, it allowed city rulers to assert claims of hegemony over others and it enhanced the prestige of certain religious centers as legitimating political change brought about by force.

By the time of the Akkadian kings, Nippur, the city of Enlil, the ruling god on earth, enjoyed such cultural and religious prestige that Sargon and his successors credited Enlil with their victories in Sumer, presented defeated kings there, placed commemorative inscriptions in his temple, and, in the case of Naram-Sin, rebuilt it on a lavish scale (Chapter 1 part 5). He also installed his daughter, Tutanab-shum, as high priestess of Enlil, an act not mentioned in *The Curse of Agade*, which otherwise has much to say about his relationship to the city.[1] Since Nippur's status was not based on economic, political, or military power, nor was the city ruled by an aggressive potentate or dynasty, its urban institutions are little understood. In the Akkadian period, the city was ruled by a governor, who could also serve as high priest of Enlil. There may also have been an assembly of temple officials convened by royal command, and, under the kings of Ur, a prominent family and the priesthood were important in the management of Nippur's temples and community affairs.[5] For centuries after the Akkadian period, control of Nippur remained the paramount ideological basis for regional hegemony in both Sumer and Babylonia.[6]

A Sumerian poem, one of the most widely studied works of literature of the early second millennium, lauds the importance of Nippur as Enlil's residence:

> The very gods of this world bow down before him,
> The universal gods direct their wills by his,
> They stand obediently before him to await his instructions.
> This omnipotent lord, whose powers transcend in the universe,
> Whose will is decisive, whose knowledge knows no limits,
> He it is who, in his wisdom, made this city his dwelling,
> The pivot point of earth and sky:
> His noble nature sets his greatest sanctuary aglow with radiant glory,
> He makes his residence in Nippur, the joining link of heaven with earth![7]

It seems that a king chosen by Enlil and crowned at Nippur had a special legitimacy:[8]

> O Enlil, the shepherd you have looked upon steadfastly,
> Whom you have raised up in the land with your steadfast call,
> The barbarian beside him, the barbarian beneath him,
> The remotest lands bow down to him.
> Like a bracing stream of water, goods from all the world,
> Greeting gifts, with massive tribute,
> He arranges in its treasury,
> He arranges in its main courtyard,
> He brings into the gemstone Ekur as a monument to his name.
> Enlil, faithful shepherd of everything that multiplies,
> Herdsman and leader of all that lives,
> Has shown forth brilliantly his right to rule,
> Has made him fair with the holy crown.[9]

Sargon well understood this. After he had subdued the cities of Sumer, he brought Lugalzagesi, the defeated king of Uruk, to Nippur, where Enlil recognized the victor as king. Akkadian seals show corresponding moments of divine triumph, in which a warrior god presents a captive god to a seated deity.[10] Sargon used Enlil's "main courtyard," just as the poem says, to proclaim his achievement for all time. His sons, Rimush and Manishtusu, and his grandson, Naram-Sin, did the same and showered the sanctuary with gifts of booty from their conquests. Manishtusu credited Enlil with his rise to power. Sharkalisharri, and perhaps other Akkadian kings, were probably crowned at Nippur. Enheduanna singles out Enlil, as opposed to An, for his support of Ishtar's invasion of Mount Ebih (Appendix IIc).[11]

## 2.  The best man wins

In the absence of sources from Akkad itself, northern Mesopotamian political theory may be reconstructed using evidence from Syria. The mid- and Upper Euphrates region was a land of quite different political traditions from those in Sumer. Here were rival polities in walled cities, each with a surrounding territory of smaller settlements, and, unlike Sumer, extensive, uncultivated lands between them peopled by pastoral nomads. There was no central sanctuary as at Nippur, no ideology of a single land, no legitimation of kingship save that won and kept by force of arms. No one could cut off or divert the Euphrates or its tributaries to bring a city to submission, so any would-be conqueror had to breach its massive walls. Alliances were forged regularly, by treaties with solemn oaths or by marriage and broken just as regularly. Although some scholars consider the notion of universal kingship a "Semitic" phenomenon, early Semitic names built on the word for "king" (Part 6) do not bear out this thesis and the association of universality of rule with Kish remains unexplained.[12]

The chancellery of Ebla contained several remarkable documents on early statecraft, which may have originated at Mari, the westernmost city included in *The Sumerian King List*. One of these relates how a wily king of Mari, whose name is not given, shows his general, Henna-Dagan, how to circumvent obstacles to accomplish what he wants. This is one of the longest continuous prose narratives from the third millennium and the first of its scale and complexity in any Semitic language.[13] Henna-Dagan, at a loss in this piece, appears in another Ebla text as a triumphant author of a campaign narrative, so he was evidently a well-known figure in his day.[14]

The time in the story about the clever king of Mari is early summer, when a ruler should be launching a glorious campaign, but it seems that he has no suitable amount of grain ready to offer the temple for a dream oracle to portend its success: "He had not even enough for a poplar food box, nor for a poplar firkin for beer, nor for an oil cruse, there was not even enough for a spouted pot!"[15] The king presents himself for the oracle anyway, with only his wits to serve him, proposing to pay for it with booty from the campaign if it is successful. The priest and priestess, however, insist on their due beforehand and forbid him to levy troops: "Assembling of men is not commanded, the lord of heaven, the lord of lords, has not commanded the king's heedless assembling of men . . ."[16]

How the king of Mari resolves this impasse by leaving a sealed deposit of silver is the core of the next part of the story, which we need not consider here. The main lesson is that a successful leader needs to be cunning when he cannot use force. A similar thought was in the mind of a second-millennium Amorite ruler, Shamshi-Adad, when he advised his son that a ruler must size up his opponent like a wrestler: if he wants to win, he needs superior strategy when strength alone is not enough.[17] What the Mari piece demonstrates is that already the pre-Akkadian, Semitic-speaking cultures of northern Mesopotamia had an independent prose tradition, more didactic than commemorative, focusing on the deeds and resourcefulness of kings.

The Akkadian kings, for their part, encouraged the development of prose narrative to memorialize their accomplishments. In the first two generations of the Akkadian state, Sumerian was the primary literary language, as seen in Enheduanna's poetry, whereas the prose inscriptions largely consisted of brief declarative sentences. The reforms of Naram-Sin made the Akkadian language simpler to write, and his own royal inscriptions reveal a marked preference for Akkadian. These use longer sentences and direct speech, and comment on the events narrated (Chapter 9 part 6). As in the Mari story, the characters in Akkadian commemorative prose show no emotional response, such as fear, anger, or happiness, as would become commonplace in later Assyrian inscriptions; the narratives have the straightforward authority of Akkadian triumphal reliefs.

By contrast, when royal deeds were the subject of Sumerian poetry, the finished products were elegant court entertainments based on battles of wits and wills, beginning with the poem about Sargon's youth (Chapter 1 part 2, Chapter 11 part 6) and developed further in post-Akkadian times in the form of epics about legendary rulers of Uruk.[18] Although no examples survive, literature of this kind may well have flourished under the Akkadian dynasty, inverted by the poet of *The Curse of Agade* into a cautionary tale of kingly pride, divine fickleness, and imperial disaster.

## 3.   The king's arm

If gods had transcendent powers, kings had armies, which they normally accompanied to the field in person. An important development in the Akkadian period was that Mesopotamian warfare was now waged much farther from the home base, whereas earlier hostilities were mostly between neighboring city-states. When Sargon listed his achievements in Enlil's courtyard at Nippur, he singled out four: conquest, reform of administration, promotion of international trade, and the maintenance of a large, standing army. He alone, of all Mesopotamian rulers before or after him, states that he sustained 5400 fighting men every day in his service, so there was something new and important about this and the logistical support that made it possible. In the surviving art and commemorative inscriptions of the dynasty, military subjects prevail, though administrative documents dealing with military matters are rare or difficult to identify.[19]

The armed forces consisted of several corps: archers, spearmen, and axe bearers, for distant, close, and hand-to-hand fighting respectively. Since spearmen could carry only one lance, to be thrown or thrust at close quarters, it seems likely that they also bore an axe or other hand weapon. They were backed up by soldiers bearing only axes. On his Victory Stele (Figure 1.6), Naram-Sin carries a bow, lance, and axe to symbolize the three main weapon types in his arsenal, but his men are armed more in keeping with reality. Immediately behind him march a spearman carrying an axe and two soldiers carrying a different type of axe and two standards. Next is an archer with an axe in one hand, then two men armed with what may be a throw-stick or a sling, carrying either short and long darts or a container of sling bullets.[20] The soldiers at the head of columns are bearded, as was characteristic of the Akkadian elite (Chapter 9 part 1); the men behind them appear to be clean-shaven.

The artist was at pains to differentiate the weapons. The Akkadian lances shown are of two types, one slightly longer than a man's height and sometimes fitted with a knob at the butt end, the other shorter.[21] The axes also vary: Naram-Sin's has a narrow blade, an indented socket, and a point at the opposite end from the blade; the leading soldiers' axes have blades more than twice as large as the king's, set into a curved handle; other soldiers carry straight-handled axes.[22] These distinctions perhaps represent specific contingents of the Akkadian army. The arms of the Lullubi foes are comparable, so the Akkadians were not shown as having superior weapons, unless the prominence of Naram-Sin's bow is meant to suggest that Akkadian archery was superior. A general of archers appears among the Akkadian worthies for whom Manishtusu purchased land, and an entire team of arrow makers was maintained at Susa.[23] The Akkadian soldiers have no body protection beyond their helmets, although in earlier depictions of soldiers they are shown wearing a heavy sash crossed over the chests. Their helmets are of two types, rounded and pointed. The former may be felt or leather, the latter copper.[24]

The basic assault tactic may have been a triple shock: an initial barrage of arrows, darts, or sling bullets shot from a distance, then a charge of spearmen, who, once they had used their lances, wielded axes at close quarters, and finally a wave of reinforcements bearing axes. There is no evidence for the cumbersome battle wagons depicted in Sumerian art, although two and four-wheeled vehicles are known from Akkadian texts and from clay models (Chapter 4 part 3). If in fact the Akkadian military did not rely on battle vehicles, this may account for the speed and mobility of the armed forces and their readiness to traverse rugged terrain, where no Sumerian army had ever gone. Enheduanna visualized an Akkadian assault in much the same terms:

> I will aim a quivered shaft,
> I will pour forth sling stones in a stream,
> I will put some polish to my spear,
> I will hold my shield and throw-stick ready.[25]

Provisioning a field force of thousands in arid or mountainous territory presented a logistical challenge that the Akkadians met in two ways. First, they prepared for a campaign by acquiring detailed knowledge of the objective and its sources of water, as evidenced by a fragmentary itinerary carved on a stone monument, giving the precise marching distances between watercourses in the Khabur region (Chapter 9 part 9). Second, they assembled adequate weaponry and food supplies, the latter in preference to foraging en route. Few records exist for this or tell where the arms were warehoused.[26] A group of documents from Umma may record the provisioning of an Akkadian military force with large quantities of bread and beer, so Mesopotamian cities near troops on campaign may have been obliged to sustain them. At Girsu, 60 royal soldiers and a detachment of the "select" were issued five liters of fish and one liter of salt a month for three months, no doubt in addition to a basic food ration.[27]

In the Umma records are a general (*shakkanakkum*), colonel or major (*nu-banda*), captain (*ugula*), booty officer(?), the son of a governor in Syria (in training?), equerry, royal commissioner, door attendant, recruiter, courier, cupbearer, minister, quartermaster(?), *šaperum* with his clerk, quartermaster of garments(?), physician, porters, constable, an officer in charge of putting identification marks on (captured?) goods(? *šaper* ZAG.ŠUŠ), an ass herder, and an assortment of foreigners.[28]

The Akkadian army was also accompanied by scribes, who kept the supply records ("scribe of the cupbearer"), counted the casualties, noted the names of high-ranking enemies, and perhaps sketched exotic landscapes, weaponry, military attire, and people for later commemorative purposes.[29] A diviner consulted the gods for ongoing prognoses of tactical success or failure.[30]

The king was supreme commander, the general the top field officer. Defeated kings and field commanders were recorded in victory inscriptions and depicted in reliefs. The Victory Stele of Naram-Sin (Figure 1.6), for instance, shows the enemy king in the top row, begging for mercy. Immediately below is probably his general of spearmen. Like the defeated king, he wears a special uniform, but carries a broken spear.[31] Below him, the general of axe bearers also pleads for mercy, here from an advancing bowman.

The next command rank was the *nu-banda*, Akkadian *laputtum*, the officer in command of a battalion, likely of 600 men. At the town of Mugdan, near Kish, 90 *iku* of land (about 30 hectares), were set aside for a military force of unspecified size, commanded by a *nu-banda*. The leader of a smaller unit, such as a 60-man company or platoon, was the *ugula*, Akkadian *waklum*.[32] The only reference to military organization is a comment by Sargon that he called up the nine "contingents" of Agade, implying that the military maintained muster lists of able-bodied men in the community who could be summoned to duty on short notice.[33]

In the aftermath of a battle, it appears that defeated troops were stripped and executed or mutilated and enslaved (Figure 1.3).[34] Beginning with the reign of Rimush, inscriptions specify how many enemies were killed in battle or captured. A relief, perhaps from the time of Rimush, shows the execution of unarmed, naked men begging for mercy (Figure 1.4).[35] The enemy slain in battle were interred under a burial mound as a victory monument and a warning to the future (Figure 9.7; Appendix Ia 21). The Akkadian dead may have been included as well, or buried separately.[36] Akkadian losses were never mentioned. A later poem about an Akkadian campaign refers to statues erected in honor of fallen warriors.[37]

## 4.  The king's eyes and ears

If the divine warrior Shamash saw everything in the world, and all-wise Ea heard everything that was said, Akkadian kings needed the eyes and ears of others. Throughout the far-flung empire, a cadre of people loyal to the king watched over his political, economic, and strategic interests and reported on them regularly. Trusted officials traveled the realm to be shown resources, records, and livestock. When boats bound for the capital were loaded, for example, their cargoes were sometimes checked and sealed by a royal official who was not part of the local administrative hierarchy but an Akkadian notable. On one occasion a substantial stockpile of grain, silver, flour, and oil on an estate near Kish was shown to a royal inspector named GAL.ZU-sharrusin, who was likely an Akkadian notable. A royal inspector was also posted at the Akkadian center in Susa.[38]

So important was inspection that it was sometimes carried out by a member of the royal family. Nabi-Ulmash, a son of Naram-Sin and governor of Tutub, made an inspection, as noted on a tablet from that city. An Akkadian seal (Figure 1.9) may show a review of troops by a male kinsman of Manishtusu, labeled the "king's brother," although many other interpretations of this image have been offered. He is presumably the bearded figure in the center, with his hair dressed in the royal manner. Behind him stands the scribe Kalaki, owner of the seal, wearing a tasseled garment, while troops march by, eyes right and left. A chair-bearer accompanies the dignitaries.[39]

There is no evidence for precisely how the king was kept informed, since no political or diplomatic archives exist from the Akkadian period comparable to the documents from Ebla. Naram-Sin states that he undertook a campaign after he heard of enemy activity, and he mentions that this enemy sent messages to "the lords of the Upper Lands," but there is no indication as to how he learned of these matters.[40] Letters were surely exchanged between courts, as known from the Ebla archives, but no Akkadian royal letter has survived or was copied into the later school curriculum. There are, however, later fabrications, some of humorous intent, such as a putative letter of Sargon, in which he summons an absurd array of court officials, but no soldiers, to accompany him on a campaign.[41]

The sole extant letter addressed to a person at the highest level of authority is administrative, rather than political, in nature. Written in Sumerian, it concerns control of two parcels of land. evidently in dispute between two governors. Since an unpublished text records that Naram-Sin himself mediated a boundary dispute between two cities, this letter may have been sent to Sharkalisharri.[42] The surviving manuscript is the file copy kept at Lagash, where the letter originated.

> [Say to my lord]: This is what Puzur-Mama, governor of Lagash said: Sulum and E-apin, since the time of Sargon, belonged to the territory of Lagash. Ur-Utu, when he served as governor of Ur for Naram-Sin, paid 2 minas of gold for them. Ur-e, governor of Lagash, took them back. The consequence is that Puzur-Mama should [   ].[43]

Of interest is the matter-of-fact tone. Like others of the Akkadian period, this letter offers none of the flowery salutations characteristic of later royal correspondence or even the blessings normative for private letters from the early second millennium on.[11] Akkadian official written communication was apparently supposed to be a concise, factual, third-person statement, with a respectful request for authority or action (like the letter quoted in Chapter 4 part 3). In rare instances, a letter of petition shifts to a more intimate second person, to add a note of urgency:

> Thus says Iddin-Erra to Mesag: He has a remainder of 32, 425 liters of barley, plus 100,800 liters of barley that Ishar-beli gave him, total: 133,225 liters of barley. My barley is that very remainder, it is my barley he has. See here, my people are dying of hunger while even Gutians are receiving grain rations! My lord knows this. May he quickly do what is right. [So], my lord, do take (this matter) in hand![15]

But it may be that in oral communication artistry was more valued and expected. To judge from later asides to the scribes who were to read correspondence aloud, a letter such as Puzur-Mama's may have served as an *aide-mémoire* for a fuller, more oratorical presentation of the message, the tablet itself proof that the speaker represented the petitioner.[16] Support for this view may be provided by later scribal exercises in writing letters or prayers of petition. These often open with elaborate, carefully written salutations appealing to the specific aspects of the addressee's powers that the writer wishes to call upon, and close with expressions of hope and blessing.[17] Therefore one may wonder if Puzur-Mama's letter was in fact presented more eloquently in oral form, with the speaker standing in a prayerful stance and embellishing the spare language of his brief in accordance with court etiquette.

In fact, the ideal spokesman for the king is described in the hymn about Nippur as a man who knows the royal will without a word being said:

> His sublime courier, . . ., who relays his commands,
> The command already spoken in his heart
> He knows from it directly, he heeds it well.
> He takes out with him his comprehensive will,
> He seeks his blessing in reverent prayer, in solemn duty.[48]

Transmission of commands was the task of a network of inter-city messengers, called riders or couriers, who could expect to receive food and lodging from local authorities along the way.[49] What credentials they offered besides the documents they carried is unknown. A tablet with a seal impression or just a name on it may have served as a kind of introduction or passport; such tablets have turned up in administrative archives.[50] On the community level criers or heralds were used.[51]

## 5.   Diplomacy and gift exchange

No collection of diplomatic correspondence is known for the Akkadian kings. Although there may not have been an established international etiquette, as would be observed among the royal courts of Western Asia a millennium later,[52] its principles of exchange of valuable goods and professions of friendship are frankly stated in a pre-Akkadian letter from a high official of Ebla to a high official of Hamazi, a city perhaps located somewhere on the lower Zab River. It too gives a sense of the personal yet businesslike style of the age, without flowery salutations or titles, as befit dialogue between equals, though it may have been delivered in a more fulsome manner:

> Thus says Ibubu, steward of the king's palace, to the envoy: I am your brother and you are my brother. Whatever wish my brother may express, I grant, whatever wish I express, you grant. You have delivered to me a fine mule. You are my brother and I am your brother. I, Ibubu, give you, the envoy, ten boxwood planks and two boxwood wheels. Yirkab-Damu, king of Ebla, is the brother of Zizi, king of Hamazi. Zizi, king of Hamazi, is the brother of Yirkab-Damu, king of Ebla. And thus says Tira-il, the scribe: I gave a tablet to the envoy of Zizi.[53]

The gifts were deliberately symmetrical, a vehicle, disassembled for shipment, in exchange for a dray animal. The royal scribe also notes that he entrusted the envoy of Hamazi with a tablet, either a letter or a treaty, to carry back to his lord.

Loyalty and patronage were initiated and built up by gift exchange. Normally a notable was expected to feed and clothe his followers, but those seeking patronage offered food and clothing to him in anticipation of such returns as high office.[54] Subordinates routinely presented "greeting gifts" to their superiors to show their gratitude for patronage and bearers of good news were rewarded with clothing, jewelry, sandals, and aromatic oil.[55]

Royal gifts are known abundantly from the Ebla archives, in which staggering quantities of specie were given to royal ministers as rewards for their diplomatic services. In some instances, these gifts took the form of massive jars of silver and gold. One such jar was fashioned from more than 400 kilograms of gold, about 2 percent of which was lost in the production process, for a final weight of 386.34 kilos, nor was this piece by any means unique.[56] The 7.5 kilograms of gold reported lost in the fabrication of a single Ebla jar is half the total gift of gold Rimush bestowed upon the temple of Enlil in Nippur after his successful campaign in Iran. To put these figures in perspective, 30 kilograms of gold were given to Sargon for the use of an entire agricultural district near Lagash.[57]

The Ebla figures are astounding by any standard, ancient or modern, to the extent that the historian does not know what to make of them. They are particularly baffling since no Mesopotamian administrative text mentions even a fraction of the amounts listed in the gift lists of Ebla, not to mention the textiles, copper, and implements of various kinds they record as well. The Ebla palace archives raise the possibility of an Early Bronze Age inter-palace gift exchange at least as substantial as that known from the Late Bronze Age Amarna correspondence among the great powers of the Near East, when gold was plentiful enough that Mesopotamia went briefly on a gold standard, and a figure as high as 600 kilograms of gold is recorded.[58] The occasions for gift exchange may have been comparable: marriage, accession to the throne, conclusion of a treaty of alliance, victory over an enemy, celebration of festivals, birth of an heir, and arrival of messengers.[59]

The only surviving treaty of an Akkadian king is the Elamite version found at Susa of an alliance between Naram-Sin and a ruler of Susa, drawn up in the style of a loyalty oath imposed by a lord upon a subordinate:

§ 1 O Pinnikir and ye gracious gods of heaven, Humban, Amba, Zit, Nahiti, Inshushinak, Simut, Sirnapir, Husa, Uggabna, Imitiki . . . Tullat, Hurbi, Hutran, Ninurta, Siashum, Maziat, Ninkarrak, Narunde, Gugumuktir, Humkat, Ruhuishna, Ruhusak, . . . , Niarzina, Lambani, Kirwasir, Hurbahir, Ishara, Nitutir, Titik, Simit-sararar, . . . grant that!

§ 2 Kings swear their oaths upon the gods. (As) a king is devoted to (the sun-god) Nahiti, (as) a king is obedient to Inshushinak, (as) a king is faithful[?] to Siashum, Napir, and Narunde . . .: I will not allow any disloyalty[?] to Agade. My general[?] shall protect[?] this treaty[?] against disloyalty[?]. Naram-Sin's enemy is my enemy, Naram-Sin's friend is my friend. His gifts were received. In recognition of these gifts, my subjects shall uphold[?] those bound by treaty with Naram-Sin. Naram-Sin's enemy [is my enemy. Naram-Sin's friend is my friend. His gifts were received. In recognition of his gifts, my subjects shall uphold those bound by treaty with Naram-Sin . . .] I will harbor no fugitive and my general[?] shall not breach[?] the treaty[?] of the envoy of Agade.

§ 3 Kings swear their oaths upon the gods. (As) a king is devoted to Nahiti, (as) a king is obedient to Inshushinak, (as) a king is faithful[?] to Siashum, Napir, and Narunde: My general[?] shall sustain no . . . by night or by day, he shall sustain your prosperity by night and by day. Out of loyalty[?], I will love no one who asks Naram-Sin for support but then is treacherous[?].

§ 4 Kings swear their oaths upon the gods. (As) a king is devoted to Nahiti, (as) a king is obedient to Inshushinak, (as) a king is faithful[?] to Siashum, Napir, and Narunde . . . : My general[?] shall protect[?] Agade from evil with the army. He shall not spare[?] any hostile people. I will allow no falsehood against Agade in Elam . . . I will love no one who asks Naram-Sin for support but then is treacherous[?].

§ 5 Kings swear their oaths upon the gods. (As) a king is devoted to Nahiti, (as) a king is obedient to Inshushinak (as) a king is faithful[?] to Siashum, Napir, and Narunde: In recognition of his gifts, my subjects [shall uphold those bound by treaty with Naram-Sin]. I will make a statue of you, it shall be dedicated[?] to [the gods of Susa[?]]. I will keep it from harm. No one here shall make away with it[?] . . . I will make a statue of you . . .

§ 6 Kings swear their oaths upon the gods. (As) a king is devoted to Nahiti, (as) a king is obedient to Inshushinak, (as) a king is faithful[?] to Siashum, Napir, and Narunde . . . Naram-Sin's envoy with gifts was received with honor[?] . . . he may stay here forever with no cause for complaint[?]. Your statue shall be kept here with honor and be well sustained. [the enemy land] shall be forced to submit³, its produce carried off³ and taken for booty. You shall overwhelm your ill-wisher with power. I will hold forces in readiness for this, they shall not . . . May your wife be fruitful³. May Simut bless her with her command³. No enemy of Naram-Sin shall . . . May love blossom for you. May your wife bear a son to succeed you³ . . .

§ 7 Kings swear their oaths upon the gods. Put an end to cries of woe! May all evil behavior³ come to an end! These statues shall be kept with honor. No disrespect for you shall be harbored here! Our subjects shall honor your triumph³. The depositing of this treaty³ before the standard³ shall be honored.

§ 8 Kings swear their oaths upon the gods. (As) a king is obedient to Nahiti, [(as) a king is subordinate to Inshushinak], (as) a king is faithful³ to Siashum, Napir, and Narunde: Everyone reveres the . . .of Naram-Sin, we have offered to Inshushinak. (This treaty) has been presented to the gods [          ] forever. May he (Inshushinak³) guard your statue forever. May there be offspring from your spouse! May your wife be fruitful! I will bless your children![60]

According to this document, Naram-Sin sent an envoy to Susa with gifts, perhaps as lavish as the Ebla jars. The grateful king of Elam made available to his new ally troops under an Elamite general, the modalities to be worked out. References to Naram-Sin's wife suggest that an Elamite princess may have been sent to marry him as part of the alliance; the Elamite ruler hoped that her son might succeed Naram-Sin. In conclusion, the Elamite ruler pledged the wholehearted loyalty of himself and his subjects to Naram-Sin, whose statue he swore to maintain faithfully in the temple of Inshushinak.

## 6.  The king as seen by his subjects

Popular attitudes toward the king can be gleaned from studies of Akkadian and Sumerian personal names in which the element "king" appears.[61] The Sumerian word for king, *lugal*, was far more common in names, even during the Akkadian period, than *šarrum*, its Akkadian counterpart. Sumerian names for which there are no Akkadian counterparts express lordship or ownership (Ur-lugal "Man³-of-the King"), or refer to insignia of authority (Lugal-gidri "The-King-[Holds³]-the-Scepter"). Names referring to the king as a kinsman occur in both languages (Lugal-ab-ba and šarrum-aba "The-King-is-a-Father").

Names referring to the king's effective, unchangeable, and truthful speech were popular in Sumerian, but had no Akkadian counterparts (Lugal-dugani-zi "What-the-King-Says-is-Reliable"). Likewise, the king's special role in the community of citizens and his unique power in the land were alluded to in Sumerian, but not Akkadian, names (Lugal-ab-ba-uru "The-King-is-a-City-Father," Lugal-amah "The-King-is-the-Supreme-Power").

Many names in both languages invoked to the king's protection of the individual, his city, and his land (Lugal-bad "The-King-is-a-Fortress," Lugal-palil "The-King-is-He-Who-Goes-Before," Lugal-alšin "The-King-is-Their (the people's)-City," šarriš-takal "Trust-in-the-King!"). The king was also supposed to care for his people, city, and land, and this nurturing aspect of rule was invoked in such names as Lugal-hamati "O-Lord-May-(the child)-Survive-for-My-Sake!," with Akkadian counterparts like šarrum-ili "The King-is-My-God." The king as progenitor and protector of children is found in such names such as Lugal-mudah "The-King-Added" (another child), with Akkadian counterparts such as Ibni-šarrum "The-King-Begot-(Me)," the last becoming a common name later, though still rare in the Akkadian period. The king was a faithful steward and farmer (Lugal-engar-zi),[62] Lugal-zi-kalam-ma "The-King-is-the-Life-of-the-Land"). These names have no Akkadian counterparts, nor does the inventory of Sumerian names referring to the king's relation to the cult. Names focusing on the king's personal qualities of wisdom, knowledge, perception, valor, fame, beauty, justice, and glory are common in both Sumerian and Akkadian (Lugal-ur-sag "The-King-is-a-Hero," šarru-dan "The-King-is-Strong").

The greater richness and linguistic productivity of Sumerian versus Akkadian names built on the word for king strongly suggest that Akkadian concepts of kingship owed much to well-established Sumerian political traditions.[63] In the pre-Akkadian Semitic-speaking world, as argued in part 2, a king ruled like a strong, resourceful, clever, and protective tribal leader, but had no special connection to the gods, as he did in Sumerian thought. Even with the robust development of royal ideology in the Akkadian period, name-giving in Akkadian was slow to reflect those aspects of royalty commonplace in Sumerian. One man, however, perhaps an army officer, bore the worshipful name of Naram-Sin-ili ("Naram-Sin-is-My-God").[64]

Royal journeys through the realm were an opportunity for subjects to see their king, his family, and retinue, as well as for the king to observe for himself the development and prosperity of different parts of his land. These journeys were occasions for exchanging gifts, feasting, and expressions of fealty.[65]

## Notes

1   Different perspectives on Mesopotamian kingship and polity of the third millennium include Jacobsen 1957; Kienast 1973; Ge. Selz 1998b; Steinkeller 1993a, 1999a; Andersson 2012; in general, Steinkeller 1992; Michalowski 1999b. For *The Sumerian King List*, Jacobsen 1939; Glassner 2004: 117–26, and Chapter 11 part 4. For the Mesopotamian city-state, Garfinkle 2013 and Chapter 1 note 81.

2   Michalowski 1989: 58–59 lines 367–68.

3   Jacobsen 1957; Hallo 1960; Steinkeller 2002b, 2002c; Sharlach 2004: 17–21; Pomponio and Visicato 2011: 173–76 (*bala* in Pre-Akkadian sales of real estate). Occasional references to a rotating obligation in Akkadian sources, e.g., CUSAS 19 167, are not conclusive. Instances of moving large numbers of livestock between cities could also be understood to refer to tax obligations, though they may be for commercial purposes as well: cattle and sheep through Agade (ITT II 5845); more than 3500 sheep and goats sent from Umma to Girsu (ITT V 6691, compare ITT II 4563); sheep and goats sent from Umma to Uruk (ITT I 1047). Since Umma bore the heaviest burden of the Ur III rotating tax obligations, it is tempting to see in these large herds going from Umma to Akkadian administrative centers a forerunner of the same procedures; further Glassner 1986: 10.

4  Michalowski 1981; J. Westenholz 1983b; for remarks on the invocation of Enlil by the Akkadian kings, Liverani 1988b: 253, in general, Liverani 2011: 137, 145.

5  Hallo 1972; Zettler 1984; J. Westenholz 1991; the governor of Nippur is mentioned in a legal document CUSAS 13: 163 and J. Westenholz 1997: 244–45 line 32.

6  W. Lambert 1992; Ge. Selz 1992; Lieberman 1992; Sallaberger 1997.

7  Falkenstein 1959: 11, lines 7–13; updated editions in Reisman 1969: 42–43; ETCSL 4.05.1.

8  Steiner 1992.

9  Falkenstein 1959: 15–16 lines 84–95; Reisman 1969: 51–52 lines 84–96.

10  Boehmer 1965 Nos. 509–19.

11  Note 6, this chapter; B. Foster 1980: 39–40.

12  Kienast 1973: 494–95; for "king of Kish," Chapter 1 note 6.

13  Fronzaroli 2003 No. 1.

14  Fronzaroli 2003 No. 4.

15  Fronzaroli 2003: 3 (1) and (2).

16  Fronzaroli 2003: 8 (39).

17  Durand 1998 2: 115; in general Durand 2010.

18  Vanstiphout 2003; for a fragment of Akkadian-period praise poetry, Chapter 9 part 6. For possible later echoes of Akkadian martial verse, Chapter 11 part 8.

19  For the theaters of war, Glassner 1986: 6–7; for the presence of the king, Archi 2014a. For weaponry, Scheil 1913 = MDP 14 85–86; ECTJ 151–52; Sommerfeld 2006; Schrakamp 2006; Collon 1983 (imagery); Civil 2003 (for further discussion of bows, arrows, quivers, and early lexical evidence for selected weapons, see note 20, this chapter); for issues of daggers to soldiers, BdI Adab 198, CUSAS 23 103; for the mace and net, weapons of divinity but used by Akkadian kings in art and poetry, Chapter 9 notes 37 and 74. For a general discussion of the Akkadian military, Abrahami 2008 and especially Schrakamp 2010, with reference to distinguishing troops of workmen from soldiers; for Ebla, Waetzoldt 1990a; Schrakamp 2010. The Ur III military may also be considered for comparison, Lafont 2008. The suggestion of McMahon 2012: 61 that the number 5400 "defies solid interpretation" and might include workers and administrators can safely be rejected. GURUŠ.GURUŠ means "fighting men" in Old Akkadian inscriptions (e.g., Frayne 1993: 94), and is not used to mean "workers" (GURUŠ.ME); furthermore, large numbers of workers, as known from Ur III labor records, do not occur in the Akkadian period, from which the numerous records of workers do not include groups of more than a few hundred at most (Foster 2010b); further and in more detail Schrakamp 2010: 84.

20  Oates, Oates, and McDonald 2001: 275; for the word for sling bullet (im-dug/tak$_4$), Civil 2003: 52 to 291; in Akkadian texts, e.g., Zhi 1989 220, 365; for other discoveries of sling bullets, A. Westenholz 1999: 66 note 294. More than 30,000 sling bullets were found in a single deposit at Nagar; Oates, Oates, and McDonald 2001: 275–76; further Schrakamp 2009/11.

21  Schrakamp 2010: 121–23; for the shafted points of Akkadian lances, de Maigret 1976: 48–69; 169–70. The Akkadian lance point was no significant innovation over Sumerian lance points, which were some of the most effective weapons of the second half of the third millennium and diffused widely both east and west.

22  De Morgan 1900: 150; Maxwell-Hyslop 1949 (axes); Schrakamp 2010: 121–23. The numerous surviving Akkadian weapons, such as axes, daggers, and arrowheads, have not been studied as a group (Maxwell-Hyslop 1946, for daggers), though chemically analyzed (Hauptmann and Pernicka 2004); for the possibilities, Philip 1995 and A. Westenholz 1999: 66–67.

23  Gelb, Steinkeller, and Whiting 1991, 1:123 (A xii 6); MDP 14 71 i 16': zadim? giš-ti; von der Osten-Sackler 2014: 621. There seems little basis for the belief that the Akkadian armies in Mesopotamia were the first to use archery, Diakonoff 1991: 85; Schrakamp

2010: 16 suggests that the Akkadian army's increased reliance on projectiles or "distance weapons" may have been a significant innovation in tactics.

24  De Morgan 1900: 151; Scheil 1913. De Morgan's suggestion is possibly supported by a Girsu(?) text that records production of a leather helmet by a leather worker, Sommerfeld, Markina, and Roudik 2005, no. 16; both copper and woolen helmets in SCTRAH 159.

25  For model wagons of the Akkadian period, J. Oates in Oates, Oates, and McDonald 2001: 280–85; for wagons in general, Littauer and Crouwel 1979; for military applications, Schrakamp 2010: 120–21; for the Enheduanna passage, Appendix IIc Inanna and Ebih, lines 41–44. The expression "in a stream" translates Sumerian "like a string," comparing the Levantine Arabic expression for a downpour, "raining ropes" (*hibal hibal*). "Polishing" the spear probably refers to the sheen or patina the point will acquire through frequent use.

26  Itinerary: Frayne 1993: 124–25; storage of weapons: SCTRAH 155–59.

27  B. Foster 1982b: 109–15. For a letter complaining that grain has not been given to soldiers, Kienast and Volk 1995: 162; for rations apparently distributed to troops on a campaign to Gutium, MAD 5 9; the Girsu record of troop rationing is L. 4631 (unpublished). For the "select," Chapter 2 part 4.

28  List in Foster 1982b: 111–13; for marking of goods, de Maaijer 2001. For the term tentatively given here as "quartermaster of garments," Cripps 2010: 69, who reads umuš (meaning unknown); for the general, Schrakamp 2010: 199–208; further Archi 2014a.

29  For evidence that scribes in later period had training in drawing, Finkel 2011.

30  B. Foster 1982b: 113, 111; for diviners traveling with armies in later periods, Jeyes 1989: 22–23.

31  For the spear pointing downwards in Mesopotamian art, Hallager 1985: 23–24 (reference courtesy Karen Foster).

32  BIN 8 144 iv 52–53 (5! bùr, collated); for the term aga-ús, Schrakamp 2010: 21–32, who argues that the conventional translation "soldier" may be too restrictive but that in some instances these were armed men with enforcement powers.

33  Appendix Ib 4; Frayne 1993: 16; for the term "contingent," Gelb and Kienast 1990: 170; Schrakamp 2010: 84. Naram-Sin mentions nine "commanders" of Agade, so it may be significant that there are at least nine Akkadian soldiers in the image, as opposed to eight enemy (for different counts, Chapter 9 note 49), although the number "nine" recurs in Naram-Sin's inscriptions as the number of battles he fought in a single year; further A. Westenholz 1999: 68.

34  Gelb 1973.

35  B. Foster 1985; Chapter 8 part 1 and Figure 1.3.

36  A. Westenholz 1970.

37  J. Westenholz 1997: 66 ii 38 and 88 iii 6'.

38  B. Foster 1982c: 17; B. Foster 1986b: 49–50; MDP 14 81.

39  Foster 1986b: 49–50; 2010: 131, with reference to other analyses of this image, to which many more can be added, most recently Steinkeller 2014.

40  Appendix Ib 28; Frayne 1993: 90; 108; for keeping the king informed, Charpin 2013b.

41  J. Westenholz 1997: 141–69.

42  To be published by B. Lafont.

43  Volk 1992.

44  Kleinerman 2011a.

45  Kienast and Volk 1995: 131–32, with a different understanding.

46  Oppenheim 1965.

47  Kleinerman 2011a.

48  Falkenstein 1959: 22 lines 103–7; Reisman 1969: 53 lines 104–8.

49  For references to messengers of various types and grades, CUSAS 19: 138; CUSAS 13 85; for messengers who may well be from another city, CUSAS 13 108, 109; further B. Foster 1982b: 16–17. A messenger (ragaba) from Magan receives beer at Umma in Cripps 2010 No. 18 (MCS 9 245).

50  BdI Adab 67.
51  A. Westenholz 2004: 603.
52  For an instance of what could be a document from the Ebla denouncing the conduct of the city of Mari, Sallaberger 2008; for the text type, Hirsch 1967. Lafont 2001 argues that there were ample communications among Amorite courts in the early second millennium but for varying reasons and often ad-hoc purposes, rather than the regular diplomatic contact that was characteristic of the Late Bronze Age.
53  Fronzaroli 2003: 30–34 No. 3. Although I have followed his interpretation in the main, I suggest that the tablet mentioned at the end is not this document, which would be of no interest to the king of Hamazi, but another one, the text of which is not preserved. For a proposed location of Hamazi, Wilcke 1989: 560–61. For exchange of gifts at Ebla, Waetzoldt 1984; more to follow in note 59.
54  Westbrook 2005.
55  Appendix Ib 16; Frayne 1993: 55; Glassner 1985a, 1986: 257; Charpin 1994: 186–88; Bartash in CUSAS 23: 116; Prentice 2010: 187–98. For a collection of Akkadian-period documents recording greeting gifts, B. Foster 1989a; for a gift for bringing good news (Arabic *bushra*), CUSAS 26 167, other instances SCTRAH 20–34; for delivering a statue Chapter 9 note 3.
56  Archi 1996c; 1999: 154; 2011b; the best known from the contemporaneous Levant were stone bowls and other small objects sent by the pharaohs of Egypt to trading partners, Elayi 2013: 50–51; for royal treasuries and distributions of gifts, Paoletti 2012 (Ur III); Sallaberger 2013.
57  Glassner 1985a: 19–20.
58  Zaccagnini 1973: 81; Edzard 1960b.
59  Zaccagnini 1973: 9–58; Archi 1987c, 1987c, 1996c, 1999, 2002; Maioccchi 2010b; Sallaberger 2013; for the early second millennium, Charpin 1994: 186–89; Lerouxel 2002. Royal gift-giving and feasting were developed into an elaborate ritual by the Achaemenid kings, uniting them with their subjects, great and small, Wiesehöfer 2001: 38–41.
60  Hinz 1967. Elamite is poorly understood, so any translation of this document contains much guesswork. The rendering given here depends fully on Hinz's work, as the writer has no competence to treat this text independently.
61  For collection and analysis of Sumerian and Akkadian names built on the element "king," Andersson 2012, from which this section is derived; in general A. Westenholz 1979.
62  For the evolution of "farmer" in personal names, B. Foster 1999: 5–6.
63  Jacobsen 1957; Steinkeller 1999a.
64  B. Foster 1982i: 342.
65  B. Foster 1980; Volk 1992; Visicato 2001; for a suggestive parallels in Achaemenid Iran, Wiesehöfer 2001: 41.

# 8    Trade, business, and the economy

## 1.   The circulation of goods

Mesopotamia was poor in prestige commodities for elite and ruling groups to accumulate, display, and deploy as wealth and symbols of status. This meant that from the time of the earliest cities onward, mechanisms were found to acquire such goods as semi-precious stones, fragrant conifers, spices, fine hardwoods, and industrial and luxury metals through exploration, plundering expeditions, overland caravans, and sea trade. During the centuries immediately prior to the Akkadian period, the cities of southern Mesopotamia largely depended on sea trade with the entrepots of Bahrein (Dilmun), Qatar, Oman and the coast of Iran (Magan), as well as the Indus Valley (Meluhha).[1] The principal commodities referred to in pre-Akkadian commercial documents were copper, tin, and tin-bronze, as well as conifer woods and the aromatics made from them, which were purchased with wool, textiles, and silver.[2]

In the Akkadian period, while northern overland routes to Iran, Anatolia, and Syria are to be expected, through Mari and Assur, there is scant evidence for them; in fact, internal trade on the Iranian plateau shows little direct contact with Mesopotamia. On the other hand, records of maritime activity in the Gulf suggest that the sea trade, at least as far as the Indus Valley, was the vital link to the east for Akkadian Mesopotamia.[3] Sargon boasted of the foreign boats coming to Agade.[4] Fish were even sent from the Gulf to Nagar in Syria.[5]

Although the Akkadian military campaigns in the Gulf and Iran disrupted traditional trade patterns (Chapter 5 part 3), they must have created opportunities for Mesopotamian merchants to seek new markets, as shown by the colony at Susa.[6] At the same time, the centers of Akkadian authority and cult were flooded with booty brought back from campaigns in Syria, Iran, and the Gulf. Inscriptions record gold, copper, and human beings as plunder, but best-known archaeologically are the stone vases and mace heads made abroad and secondarily engraved with the names of Akkadian kings, notably Rimush and Naram-Sin.[7]

After his successful Gulf campaign, Manishtusu commemorated an expedition to quarry black stone there.[8] This coincides with a great increase in the use of hard, dark stone (modern identifications include diorite, dolerite, or olivine gabbro) for portrait statues of the king (Chapter 9 part 1; Figure 1.5).[9]

Despite Manishtusu's campaigns in Iran, it is striking how few booty vessels are known from his reign, as opposed to those of his predecessor and successor. For this Akkadian king, the stone quarried in the Gulf may have been more important than the stone bowls and vases gotten from the east.

The Akkadian disruption of trade patterns in Syria may have been no less drastic. Ebla had built up a substantial commercial network, with its main focus to the east rather than the Mediterranean, though there were some contacts with coastal cities and perhaps even relations with Egypt. Mari may have been the main entrepot for Eblaite goods headed to Mesopotamia. The destruction of Ebla and occupation of Mari put an end to this situation, perhaps opening the way into Anatolia for merchants from Assur, and into northern Syria for traders from Mari.[10]

Since Akkadian military successes meant that many luxury and industrial goods became available to the ruling elite, there was less impetus to acquire them commercially than there had been for the pre-Akkadian rulers of Lagash, for whom long-distance campaigns in Iran or the Gulf were unthinkable.[11] Yet precisely this influx of prestige wares and foreign materials may have stimulated demand for them among people on the fringes of the ruling elite. Venture trade may have served a prosperous sector of the population that had no direct access to booty, but which had the means and the motivation to obtain foreign goods.[12]

## 2.   The profit motive

In the Akkadian period, most of the surviving trade and business documents are records of transactions intended to be profitable to one of the parties. Many individuals, sometimes on their own, sometimes as agents for others, participated in for-profit enterprises.[13] There are several ways to distinguish private from governmental business records. Some businessmen kept personal accounts and memoranda that they wrote themselves. These are characterized by their vernacular language, absence of formal administrative terminology, scripts and tablet forms often less refined than those of administrative records, and use of the first person rather than the third person favored in official documents.

Quradum, an entrepreneur at home in Sippar, for example, mentions in a letter that he went into partnership with a man who put up money for a slave whom Quradum agreed to support for six years. In another of his records, he notes that he had paid the money for a certain slave whom he had not yet received at the time he drew up his accounts. An idea of the extent of his affairs can be gleaned from his summary account of copper, silver, livestock, oils, garments, and fruits in Tuttul, Mari, and Al-Sharraki, as well as from a record of his dealings with more than a dozen people.[14]

At Akkadian Umma, Ama-e, the wife of a herd master, received extensive land parcels from a government agent requiring accountability, presumably on a rental or contractual basis, and dealt in real estate, metal, and grain. She invested her wealth with various agents. To one man, she entrusted foods, aromatics, and wood; to another silver; through a third man, she bought and sold wool.[15]

Some holders of official posts took advantage of their positions to engage in commercial activities on their own behalf. Some did not themselves trade, but consigned commodities to agents who traded for them. One way to do this was to invest in a fund managed by a trading agent, who would return interest to his clients. A trading agent at Umma, for instance, held investments from a granary officer, a cook, and a royal carpenter.[16] Other officials were active in business for themselves and kept their records in their offices rather than at home. Zuzu, for example, a cadaster official at Gasur, loaned fats, barley, livestock, and silver, and filed the debt notes with his official records. Somewhere in the Diyala region, a certain Ginunu was involved in a range of official and business matters and kept all the documents together.[17]

## 3.  Merchants and their clients

The professional merchant or agent was called *tamkarum*, from a root meaning "to do business." Merchants seldom appear in accounts of food distributed to courtiers nor did they receive parcels of land, so they were not members of the royal household, local administration, or temple staff. On occasion they did receive assistance in the form of government labor or prepared foods.[18] Some were wealthy and educated, others were unsuccessful and their children laborers.[19] An organization of merchants, headed by a "chief merchant," resembled a chamber of commerce and may have had some role in maintaining standards and adjudicating disputes.[20] Another kind of merchant, the *gaeshshum*, may have served as a purchasing agent for temples or other institutions that needed specific goods.[21] As in later periods of Mesopotamian history, some commerce was also carried on by families.

When the Akkadian Empire expanded to include Susiana, an Akkadian garrison and administrative center were set up there, apparently called Dur-Akkad ("Fort Akkad," Chapter 3 part 4). In addition, merchants from Umma founded a colony and dealt in grain, wool, copper, silver, and tin, with several traders belonging to a single family.[22]

Akkadian-period documents from Susa mention Sumerian cities, such as Shuruppak and Umma; cities near or in Iran, such as Der, Awal, and Anshan; and more distant lands, such as Marhashum, Dilmun, Magan, and Meluhha. All this suggests that Susa was a hub in an international trade network linking southern Mesopotamia with the Iranian plateau, the Gulf, and the Indus Valley, likely connecting by sea rather than overland (Chapter 3 parts 4 and 6).

The procedures whereby merchants carried out their business for a temple, the governor's palace, or other large establishments probably resembled those known from later periods.[23] The majordomo or head of the royal household (*šaperum*, Figure 5.4b) maintained an account including on the one hand animals, wool, or grain for marketing and silver for purchasing or investing, and on the other, a list of commodities desired. The grain, wool, and livestock came from the assets of the household, the silver from land rentals.[24] Privileged merchants were granted access to the fund or were provided with capital from it. At Umma, this fund was called "the fund of the balanced account," meaning that its income, balance on hand, and outgo were accountable.

Merchants may have been the key agents in converting commodities from one medium of exchange to another, for example, agricultural products to silver. Large institutions may have had more need for silver than for great quantities of grain or wool, so could turn to merchants to market their surpluses on favorable terms. Merchants thereby played an intermediary role between producers and those who sought wealth in the form of specie, typically the Akkadian elite. They were also of service to anyone seeking to raise silver from other goods in order, for instance, to pay a rent, a legal settlement, or the purchase price of a piece of property.[25] The mercantile class was therefore among the private citizenry who benefited most from the new Akkadian order.[26]

## 4. Buying and selling

The two basic commodities of Mesopotamian commerce were silver and barley. When an official household needed to buy goods, either silver or grain was used, as when a temple official at Adab gave a merchant 300 gur (900 hectoliters) of grain "for a journey."[27] Silver, which may be considered money in the modern sense of the word, was bought and sold like any other commodity and appears in inventories of goods that were probably commercial in nature. Widely used in personal loans, to purchase real estate or slaves, or to pay rent, silver was often to be found in the possession of both private citizens and officials.[28] A businessman might have it on deposit at various places; for example, a man at Eshnunna had silver at Uruk. Silver was sometimes offered to the king or high officials as a gift, perhaps a way of securing or acknowledging their patronage.[29] Grain, like silver, was used for buying, selling, and paying rent. It could be loaned at interest or interest free and could be exchanged for other commodities.[30]

Many city dwellers, if they did not own, rent, or hold parcels of agricultural land, presumably had to purchase some of their food on the open market. Oils and fats were important items of commerce, as well as dates, flour, aromatics, spices, extracts of various kinds of trees, different kinds of wood, garments, and textiles.[31] Livestock was frequently bought and sold, especially donkeys, cattle, oxen, and swine.[32] The slave trade may have been a particularly profitable undertaking. Although chattel slaves were not important in production, they were prestigious and expensive possessions, normally paid for in silver. Therefore slaves appear in various merchants' accounts along with other commodities, or in separate transactions, with or without witnesses.[33]

Whereas some business agents may have specialized in one or another commodity, inventories of merchants' stocks usually list a variety of goods. For example, the goods registered in a balanced account at the disposal of a certain Sikkur, which were maintained by the majordomo of the governor's household at Umma, included silver, garments, wool, and oil, the whole worth nearly twelve minas (about six kilograms) of silver.[34]

It is instructive to consider what commodities are not found in commercial records. Strikingly absent are the very products one might most expect to find there if an important role of trading agents was to acquire goods not available locally in Mesopotamia. One searches in vain for accounts of steatite, lapis, or other precious and semi-precious stones and their imitations.[35] Nor are there records of bulk acquisition of copper or silver, but only records of transactions and stocks on hand, sometimes very large amounts and often in the possession of private people.[36] While shipments of small quantities of wood do occur in the records, these seem to reflect private enterprise on a modest scale.

In short, there is little evidence that Akkadian merchants played any significant part in the bulk purchase and sale of products foreign to Mesopotamia, or were anyone other than profit-minded businessmen who carried out various transactions for clients, including the government, in Mesopotamian markets with mostly Mesopotamian goods or foreign commodities on a small scale. This contrasts with the depiction of merchants in literature, such as in the early hymn to Shamash (Chapter 6 part 1), in which they purchase exotic goods in faraway lands. If this was based on a pre-Akkadian reality, borne out by the records of the copper trade in the Gulf, then some shift in the main locus of mercantile activities may have occurred under Akkadian rule. For merchants, the burgeoning Akkadian ruling establishment offered plentiful, lucrative opportunities from converting in-kind goods to silver, to meeting clients' needs by purchasing and delivering in-kind goods, to loaning money or grain at interest. These and other transactions requiring acumen, knowledge of market conditions, and a good network of personal connections made merchants the natural recourse for those who needed to cross the boundaries of their own sphere of official or private activity.

## 5. Accumulating a competency

For later periods of Mesopotamian history, abundant private archives over several generations of the same family show in detail how enterprising individuals built personal fortunes by loaning money and staples at high interest, buying fields, orchards, and urban house lots, leasing land and subleasing it to others, or acting as intermediaries for landlords by advancing cash for crops and then marketing the harvest. The private archives of later merchants show that selling such commodities as tin or textiles were profitable pursuits as well.[37] For the Akkadian period, however, large groups of comparable private business documents have not yet been found, though there is ample evidence for buying, selling, lending, and leasing.

The fullest dossier of private records from the Akkadian period concerns a lengthy inheritance dispute among a family of merchants at Nippur over at least three generations. It is, however, impossible to reconstruct their genealogy or to glean even a vague idea of the issues involved and their resolution. Some of the disputed property belonged to women who had apparently married into the

family and who sought to recover their interests after their assets had been com-
mingled with others.[38]

## 6. Wages, prices, and taxes

Hiring of workers is rarely attested in Akkadian sources. A document from Mugdan (Chapter 3 part 2) shows that the labor of a field worker was valued there
at one shekel of silver per month in the Classical period, low compared to silver amounts given to surveyors and plowmen managing irrigated land at Adab,
but higher than in the Ur III period, when plentiful state-supported labor was
available.[39] Other forms of hire and rental well known in later periods, such as
for houses, draft animals, and boats, are sparsely or never attested in Akkadian
sources.[40]

Prices for arable land were low because they often seem pegged to not more
than a few years' production from the parcel in question. Manishtusu's scribes
calculated the basic sale price of the arable land the king purchased at 3 1/3
shekels per iku (3600 square meters), equivalent to about 800 liters of barley, with additional payments of valuables to certain family members.[41] The
parcels on the contemporaneous Sippar stone generally range from 2/3 to 2
shekels per iku, and later sales are in the same range as these.[42] House lots were
much more expensive, as much as 60 shekels for 35 square meters.[43] Gardens
and orchards often cost only a few grains of silver per square meter.[44] Slave
prices varied widely, from only a few shekels to as much as 27; 10–15 shekels
was the normal range for an able-bodied adult.[45] Donkeys ranged from 5 to
14 shekels.[46]

Commodity prices varied according to "years of plenty" and "years of dearth,"
necessitating complicated calculation of interest on long-term loans figured in
silver but paid in grain.[47] Manishtusu's scribes set the rate of one shekel of silver equal to one gur of barley (about 240 liters) and wool at 1/4 shekel for 1
mina (about 500 grams),[48] although higher rates for barley are attested.[49] In *The
Curse of Agade*, as elsewhere in Mesopotamian literature, very inflated commodity
prices, soaring to twenty times the norm, are quoted to show the supposed des-
peration of the starving populace; barley soared to twenty times the normal rate,
for example.[50]

Comparing Akkadian wages and prices to those of earlier and later periods is
difficult because of changes in metrology and the scattered nature of the data.[51]
Yet it seems that the price of wool dropped considerably under the kings of Ur,
likely because the royal administration greatly expanded government-sponsored
sheep herding.[52]

There is little evidence for taxation in the form of a pecuniary levy on persons
or property. Taxes are difficult to distinguish from rents and from fees collected for
certain activities. Taxes may have been levied on urban landed property (at least
on the death of the owner), on field crops as a percentage of the harvest, on the
use of water for irrigation, for grazing rights on sown fields, and for boat transport.[53] The tax assessor (*makisum*) is occasionally attested in Akkadian documents,

in one case in connection with sale or transfer of arable land, but without any indication as to precisely what he did.[54]

## 7.   Akkadian economics

There are two principal models proposed for third-millennium Mesopotamian economics. One holds that its determining mechanism was the redistribution of subsistence from the ruling and managerial classes to the rest of the population and that there was a barter system, with no open market.[55] According to the other, however, most of the population did not receive food distributions or rations, but depended on other means to subsist and to accumulate wealth. Since in the Akkadian period money was in the form of silver, used as a medium of exchange, as a basis for wealth, and as a standard of valuation, to buy real estate, moveable property, livestock, and food, it follows that there must have been a market for commodities and a market place.[56] The commercial transactions discussed in this chapter demonstrate that money regularly changed hands in the Akkadian economy. Furthermore, only a small percentage of the population received rations (Chapter 4 part 2). Accordingly, the model of redistribution and barter cannot be sustained for the Akkadian period.

The Akkadian state also had characteristics of a classic tributary economy, in which the king acquired exotic and prestige goods by force or tribute, using them to pay for a large military establishment and to reward his followers.[57] Pre-Akkadian Sumer, on the other hand, had an economy based on the production of staples (grain and livestock) in sufficient surplus that they could be redeployed to ration sizeable work forces or to buy foreign materials.[58] The traditional Sumerian pattern was profoundly disturbed by Akkadian occupation and exploitation, which were ferociously resisted by the local elites. Yet at the same time, Akkadian rule brought with it development of rural areas, greatly expanded cultural, political, and commercial horizons, and, perhaps, a sense among the ambitious that the old ways had yielded to new opportunities.

Administrative records show that the Akkadian kings implemented a well-defined agricultural policy, in which arable land was the basis for royal patronage, and that the agricultural surplus of Sumer was more than enough to sustain the Akkadian military, through direct taxation and through leasing and sharecropping networks on appropriated, newly developed, or purchased land. Ultimately, Akkadian wealth and power derived more from these agrarian policies than from the acquisition of prestige goods by force or tribute.

The Akkadian Empire was, therefore, a tributary economy for both luxuries and staples, the first of its kind that can be documented. The Sumerian poet of *The Curse of Agade* likewise considered this mix of prestige goods, livestock, and grain the basis of the city's wealth (Chapter 2 part 1). The modern historian can only hope to emulate his panoramic view and comprehensive understanding of this period.

# Notes

1 Pettinato 1972 offers a survey that needs updating but is still worth consulting for its breadth of view; Crawford 2013; for Iran, T. Potts 1993, 1994; for the Gulf and Indus Valley, During Caspers 1973; Maekawa and Mori 2011; Thornton 2013; Steinkeller 2013b; focus on the Akkadian period, Liverani 1988b: 249–51, 2011: 141–43. For Ebla, Pinnock 1985.

2 M. Lambert 1953; Leemans 1972/5; Foster 1997a; Dercksen 1999; Prentice 2010.

3 T. Potts 1993; a tablet from Adab (BdI Adab 102) recording an issue of lard to someone for a voyage to Meluhha suggests a direct link between Sumer and the Indus Valley, as does an Akkadian seal of an interpreter of the language of Meluhha (Edzard 1968/9: 15). For Magan (Makkan), Heimpel 1987/90; for a commercial voyage to Magan, see note 21, this chapter. For Meluhha, Heimpel 1987; 1993/7. For contact between Sumer and Anshan, MDP 14 22. For the spice trade between Susa and Sumer, MDP 14 8.

4 Appendix Ib 7; Frayne 1993: 28.

5 Izquierdo and Muñiz in Oates, Oates, and McDonald 2001: 340–43.

6 Maekawa and Mori 2011.

7 T. Potts 1989; 1993: 387–89.

8 T. Potts 1993: 386–87.

9 Amiet 1972.

10 Pinnock 1985.

11 Leemans 1972/5: 78–79.

12 T. Potts 1993: 395–96; A. Westenholz 1984: 27. A different interpretation of Akkadian intervention in the Gulf has been offered by Steinkeller 2013b: 415, who suggests that "Sargon and his followers created a commercial empire, which extended from the Mediterranean coast to the borders of Kerman ... Rather than a real territorial empire, the creation of Sargon and his successors was largely a commercial enterprise, whose primary objective was to control – and thereby to exploit economically – the main trade routes of the region ...," without noting that this idea was advanced already by Bottéro in 1965 (Chapter 12 part 4). Generally in Mesopotamian history, political control was not necessary to promote or to profit from foreign trade, as Steinkeller himself argued elsewhere (Steinkeller 1993a: 109: "the procurement of foreign resources, though unquestionably one of the aims of imperial policy, was not the primary reason why the [Uruk] expansion took place"), and the clear decline in availability of a crucial commodity of foreign trade of all periods, tin, during the Akkadian period, supports the contrary thesis advanced here.

13 B. Foster 1977, 1983a; differently A. Westenholz 1984: 29. For discussion of profit, Powell 1977, 1978a; Steinkeller 2002a; for private or individual activity, Steinkeller 2004a.

14 B. Foster 1977: 32; Sollberger 1988 no. 6 (290 talents = 8700 kilograms of bitumen sold and distributed to various people); he also provided 60 sheep to a merchant and bought twenty sheep for five silver rings (Powell 1978c); in Sollberger 1988 no. 7 he buys a house, and, like Manishtusu [Chapter 1 part 1] gives a banquet for the sellers. For other transactions with bitumen, CUSAS 26 113 (turned over to a man for a commercial venture) and CUSAS 26 116 (delivered).

15 B. Foster 1977: 32–33.

16 B. Foster 1977: 33.

17 B. Foster 1977: 32; for Ginunu, A. Westenholz 1984: 25 note 31.

18 OIP 14 150 and Nik II 41: food to a trading agent; MDP 14 73 and RTC 91 ii 3, workers assigned to trading agents and merchants. Steinkeller 2004a argues that in the post-Akkadian period, under the kings of Ur, merchants who did government business tended to be drawn into the crown sector as dependents or office holders, even if they kept up private dealings on their own behalf. The evidence for the Akkadian period is insufficient to judge if this was the case then as well.

19  B. Foster 1977: 34 note 33; for literacy among merchants, Wilcke 2000: 47.
20  A "chief merchant" is mentioned in BdI Adab 196.
21  ITT I 1422 notes a quantity of copper delivered to the palace "for a commercial voyage to Magan" (nam ga-raš-ak [x?] Má-gan).
22  B. Foster 1993b; for the development of Susiana as a maritime province in the early Achaemenid period, Wiesehöfer 2001: 78.
23  Sallaberger 1999b: 341–42; Garfinkle 2010 (with earlier literature).
24  B. Foster 1977: 34 and note 37.
25  Van Driel 2002: 10–11; B. Foster 1977 35 note 52.
26  Diakonoff 1959: 221–22; Liverani 1966a: 12; a possible example of a "letter of introduction" for a merchant is L. 3015, which reads, "Lugal-gu the merchant, Mesag is supervisor of this transaction."
27  BdI Adab 47.
28  A. Westenholz 1984: 26–27; Monaco and Pomponio 2009: 42–43. For instances of silver in private hands, B. Foster 1977: 35–37; silver payments were routine for field rentals (BdI Adab 212, 213); to rent two draught oxen for a year, three households pooled goods worth one, a half, and a third shekels of silver (BdI Adab 97). For land rental payment and a merchant, Cripps 2010: 55–56 (MCS 9 244). Further Chapter 5 note 54; for silver as money, see note 56, this chapter.
29  OIP 14 111, 159; B. Foster 1989a No. 18. For this type of gift or offering, Zhi 1989: 239–40; Sallaberger 1993 1: 161 (gift to a temporal ruler); Ge. Selz 1995b: 251–74.
30  B. Foster 1977: 36.
31  MAD 1 279, 300, 328 (oils and fats); 291 and 304?; 37 and 300 (sales of aromatics); MAD 1 318, OAIC 4 (sale of a log), OAIC 33, shipment of logs valued in gold.
32  MVN 3 100: sale of donkey; ITT I 1452 donkeys to a merchant. Purchases of cattle include BIN 8 180, 181; MVN 3 77. In MAD 1 269, barley and silver are used to buy cattle in Gutium. Unsold oxen: ITT I 2926. Sales of pigs: HSS 10 105–7. Sales of sheep: MVN 3 93; MVN 3 57 (sold in Agade); MDP 14 16; a merchant delivers a sheep in ITT I 1413; for more on buying and selling sheep, see note 14, this chapter. For movements of large numbers of sheep and goats between cities, B. Foster 1977: 36 and Chapter 7 note 3.
33  B. Foster 1977: 37.
34  BIN 8 286.
35  For carnelian and related stones, available on the Iranian side of the Gulf at Rishire, Tosi 1976/80. For a rare instance of a merchant delivering carnelian, B. Foster 1983a: 161.
36  NBC 9955 (unpublished); SCTRAH 153 (merchant delivers 5 minas [2.5 kilograms] of copper with 9 1/6 shekels of silver); further Chapter 5 note 30.
37  For a survey, Leemans 1972/5; for references, Chapter 5 note 30.
38  Wilcke 2007: 70–71; Pomponio 2013: 29.
39  Maekawa 1989; differently Krecher 1993/7: 157, with an incorrect conversion into barley.
40  For the hiring of boatmen or assessment of fees on cargoes, Zhi 1989: 232–39; in general Selz 1995a.
41  Gelb, Steinkeller, and Whiting 1991: 261–62.
42  Gelb, Steinkeller, and Whiting 1991: 262–63.
43  Gelb, Steinkeller, and Whiting 1991: 270–73.
44  Gelb, Steinkeller, and Whiting 1991: 273–74.
45  Gelb, Steinkeller, and Whiting 1991: 275–76; Notizia and Schrakamp 2010: 243.
46  Gelb, Steinkeller, and Whiting 1991: 278, 290.
47  Gelb, Steinkeller, and Whiting 1991: 288; further Chapter 5 note 53.
48  Gelb, Steinkeller, and Whiting 1991: 289.
49  Gelb, Steinkeller, and Whiting 1991: 288.
50  J. Klein 2014.

51 Maekawa 1989; B. Foster 1997b: 57–58.
52 B. Foster 2014b.
53 Zhi 1989: 226–38.
54 CUSAS 13 2; MAD 5 45; Cripps 2010 13 (= MCS 9 244).
55 Renger 1994, 1995b, 2002. For example, Renger 2007: 190 writes, "The *oikos* economy was the dominant economic organization in Mesopotamia during the later part of the fourth and the third millennia.... . the patrimonial household (*oikos*) of the ruler is identical in institutional as well as in spatial terms with the 'state'. Integrated into it is more or less the entire population which provides the necessary labour needed for the reproduction of the state and its institutions ... Characteristic of the *oikos* economy is the redistributive mode of production by which the results of collective labour ... are appropriated by the central authority ... and subsequently redistributed among the producers, i.e., the entire population of the state ...".
56 Hallo 1959; Powell 1977, 1978a, 1996, 1999 (omitting reference to Hallo's study); Renger 1995b; Glassner 2001; Neumann 2002; in general Jursa 2010: 563–64.
57 For the third-millennium palace as a center for accumulation and distribution of wealth in specie, Sallaberger 2013 and Chapter 7 part 5; for Naram-Sin's proverbial wealth, Chapter 10 note 12.
58 For the tributary versus the surplus economy, Frangipane 1996: 143–46. These concepts have not, however, been extensively or systematically tested or applied to late third-millennium Mesopotamia. Portions of this part were used in B. Foster 2015.

# 9  Arts, letters, and numeracy

## 1.  Sculpture in the round

Today, Akkadian sculpture is considered the "classical" sculpture of ancient Mesopotamia, its masterpieces among the most frequently reproduced and most intensively studied works from the entire ancient Near East.[1] Its origins may be seen in the development of freestanding sculpture during the millennium prior to the Akkadian period, when it seems that there were parallel traditions in stone, wood, and metal, as well as cross-craft transferences, not always successful.[2] Composite statues of stone, metal, wood, bitumen, and gemstones were also made.[3]

The surviving works of third-millennium sculpture depict the elite – high officials, priests and priestesses, military officers, distinguished musicians, notables, and the ruler and his family – some of which were inscribed with their names and titles.[4] Divinities, demons, and spirits are rare; indeed, no indisputably divine figure in stone is known from third-millennium Mesopotamia.[5] Rather, it is striking that clothed humans are the subjects of nearly all the extant stone statuary, whereas protective spirits and hero figures are generally made of metal and wear only a kilt or are entirely naked.[6] Male dress was often of a type shown already in the late fourth millennium, raising the question as to whether this evidently ceremonial garment continued to be worn by the elite, or was a sculptural convention.[7]

Although individual pieces come from throughout Mesopotamia, the main groups of pre-Akkadian limestone statuary are from Mari and stratified contexts in the temples of the Diyala region. The prayerful attitude of many of these figures, the fact that they were found in temples, sometimes in hoards, some repaired, some intentionally destroyed, shows that they were intended to represent important people in perpetual prayer before the gods, and were placed in temples for that purpose.[8] Frequenting sanctuaries and praying regularly were activities of the virtuous and successful ruler, who sought guidance, support, long life, stability of reign, and victory over his enemies. More generally, prayer reminded the gods of the needs, fears, accomplishments, and deserts of their human subjects (Chapter 6 part 4).[9]

The poses for men and women are standing or seated, often with the hands in a gesture of prayer or sometimes holding a vessel, as if for offering or libation. The majority are considerably smaller than life size, though there is scattered evidence for life-size or even larger figures.[10] Stylistically, some scholars see the earlier statues as more abstract and geometric in their presentation and the later ones as more naturalistic. Toward the end of the pre-Akkadian period, there was also a tendency to depart from inherited sculptural norms to concentrate on the face and arms, at the expense of other features, in an apparent effort to depict specific people.[11] With a growing sense of self-importance, members of the elite seem to have expected sculptors to individuate and emphasize the arms to suggest strength and competence; the eyes and ears to suggest piety and wisdom; and the mouth to suggest effectiveness in speech. In some pieces, especially of women, the modern viewer sees a smile or even a laugh (Figure 9.2a). While this may hint at the personality of the subject, it more likely reflected benevolence or favor, to judge from an early second-millennium personal name "She-Smiles-At-Her-City."[12] Later vandals regularly decapitated these statues and carried the heads away, perhaps as trophies.[13]

Although there is no stratified group of Akkadian worshipper-statues comparable to those from the Diyala, the few pieces found in their presumed original context, such as the fragmentary Akkadian statue from the temple of Ishtar at Assur (discussed later in this section), suggest that they were conceived for the same purposes. Moreover, Akkadian inscriptions contain abundant references to royal statues being set up in the principal sanctuaries of the land, of which the best known was the temple of Enlil at Nippur. Most of the surviving Akkadian sculpture was carried off from Mesopotamian sites to Susa as booty, so could well have been in the temples looted by the Elamites.[14]

Whereas the statues of early Akkadian rulers and notables initially continued pre-Akkadian traditions, Akkadian art soon developed the increasing naturalism and individuation of the previous period into an idealization of the well-fleshed, well-proportioned body, with an added element of sexual attractiveness and vitality. Akkadian sculpture also faithfully reflected the changing fashions in elite clothing, which reflected imperial expansion.[15] The differences between Classical Akkadian statues and their forerunners are so great as to justify considering them a new departure for freestanding sculpture.

Akkadian statuary mostly focuses on the figure of the ruler, often with a commemorative inscription rather than just his name.[16] The earliest works are attributed to Manishtusu and are made in hard black stone (diorite, dolerite, or olivine gabbro), which he boasts that he brought by ship from the mountains of Magan, along the Gulf coast of Oman or Iran. These nearly life-size statues, brilliantly carved and polished, suggest his royal patronage of a school of highly skilled sculptors, who strove to represent hands, feet, musculature, and the body under garments in a naturalistic, if idealized, form. Some figures are seated, in the manner of a king feasting or receiving obeisance (Figure 1.5), others standing, as if praying in the presence of a deity (Figure 5.4a). They were evidently distributed from one or two specialized workshops throughout the realm to unite the various cities under his rule by manifesting a consistent presence in their principal sanctuaries.[17]

In addition, they bore an overt political message. The statue bases were inscribed with a standard text announcing Manishtusu's name and titles and stressing his achievement of successfully invading Anshan and Shirihum on the Iranian plateau and "the cities beyond the sea," whose tangible attestations were the statues' very stone and, in some cases, the depiction of defeated enemies under Manishtusu's feet (Appendix Ia 8). Manishtusu's artistic program may have been the first of its kind, in which the king of the land proclaimed both his deeds and his respectful relationship to the local deity in the same splendid self-image.[18] These dark, gleaming statues must have stood out dramatically among the temples' modest, pre-Akkadian limestone figures ranged nearby. Even if these had already been cleared away by order of the new regime, the Akkadian works would have made an impressive and innovative display.

A massive diorite statue from Assur may depict Manishtusu or the Akkadian notable Ititi, who served as governor there during his reign (Figure 5.5, body only).[19] The figure wears a necklace of large beads, a thin garment, through which his shoulder blades and spine show, and a plain cap, with his side curls hanging below. He has a heavy beard and long moustache. His prominent ears imply wisdom; a fragment of an inscription of an unknown Akkadian ruler in fact claims that Shamash and another god "gave him superior understanding."[20]

Male Akkadian notables, including perhaps military officers, likewise had standing or seated statues, but only the heads survive (Figure 9.1). Their careful

(a)

*Figure 9.1* Akkadian notable men, from (a) Girsu and (b) Adab.

(b)

*Figure 9.1* (Continued)

treatment of the hair and beard strongly suggests an Akkadian date, as does the resemblance between their hair style and that of soldiers on Akkadian stelae and reliefs (Figures 1.4, 1.6).[21] Such figures are referred to in a later epic poem about the Akkadian period, in which an officer, exhorting his troops, says, "May the king himself proclaim you 'my brave warrior,' he shall set up your statue in the presence of his own!"[22]

Two statues of female notables from Umma and Assur (Figure 9.2), may also date to the first two or three reigns of the Akkadian dynasty. The former, of limestone, has round cheeks, finely cut lips, and a sturdy body. Her elaborate double chignon and old-fashioned pleated garment indicate that she was a priestess.[23] The latter, an accomplished piece in yellow alabaster, has high, round cheeks; her carefully modeled lips hold the ghost of a smile. She probably once wore gold earrings.[24] A later hymn to the goddess Ishtar invokes some of the qualities of this

(a)

(b)

*Figure 9.2* Akkadian notable women, from (a) Assur and (b) Umma.

face: "In her lips she is sweetness, vitality her mouth, while on her features laughter bursts into bloom . . ."[25] Two heads of women from Ur, one in alabaster, the other in diorite, have also been dated to the early Akkadian period on the basis of their headdress, exceptionally delicate modeling, and expressive features.[26]

Other stone statues are too fragmentary for discussion. Only the finely carved feet remain, for example, of a life-size standing diorite statue of Naram-Sin, which was carried off as booty to Susa.[27]

The two most important works of Classical Akkadian sculpture are both of copper. The first is a head found at Nineveh, originally part of a composite statue (Figure 9.3).[28] This hollow-cast and chiseled masterpiece is the finest metal

*Figure 9.3* Copper head of an Akkadian king, perhaps Naram-Sin. *yes because*

*no Sophs: Casting before*
*= late*
*post - reform NS*

object to survive from Mesopotamia. It was evidently displayed in a seventh-century building in the Neo-Assyrian capital, but when and how it made its way to Nineveh are unknown.[29]

The head provides detailed evidence for Akkadian elite coiffure and facial hair. According to a London barber consulted by Mallowan, the downy hair shown along the upper and lower lip was characteristic of a mature man who had never shaved there. The upper rows of the beard and the side curls may represent additions made of real hair. The rest of the coiffure was achieved with great skill: the long hair was pulled back into a bun, supported on a pad and held in place by three contiguous rings.[30] It is tempting to see the face of Naram-Sin in the regal, powerful nobility and manly *beau idéal* of this extraordinary work. The nose, ears, beard and left eye were deliberately mutilated in antiquity.[31] A diorite stone head from Girsu, smashed and separated from its body, may also depict Naram-Sin, for it has the same elaborate coiffure as the Nineveh head.[32]

The second copper piece (Figure 9.4) is the lower half of a nude male figure, evidently intended to be a heroic guardian spirit, seated on a low, round pedestal

*Figure 9.4* Copper guardian hero, with an inscription recording the deification of Naram-Sin.

with a socket to hold a standard. The lithe, slender body and muscular legs, bent so that the right foot nearly touches the left knee, are rendered with superb craftsmanship, the feet flexed and the toes curling as one would expect in such an awkward sitting position. The sculptor surely used a live model at some point in the process. This piece, like the Nineveh head, is a work of consummate skill and sophistication, attesting to the Akkadian kings' patronage of workshops with an unexampled array of talent, encouragement of new ideas, and vast resources. The inscription on the pedestal records the deification of the victorious Naram-Sin (Chapter 1 part 4; Appendix Ia 18). Found in a rural area about seventy kilometers northeast of Mosul, it was perhaps being hauled away as booty and abandoned because of its still considerable weight (400 kg), despite having been cut down.[33]

Akkadian statues of deities are known only from glyptic (Figure 6.2), from which it appears likely that they were depicted anthropomorphically, most commonly seated but occasionally standing, the latter perhaps a more archaic form (Chapter 6 part 4).[34]

## 2.   Reliefs and stelae

Mesopotamian historical memory (Chapter 11 part 5) recalled, even parodied, that Sargon had set up stelae in the lands he had conquered; indeed, triumphal stelae of Sargon and his descendants could be seen in major sanctuaries for centuries after their deaths. Only scant remains have survived of what was clearly an increasingly innovative and effective program to commemorate in image and text the military victories of the Akkadian kings and their ritualized aftermaths of slaughter and offerings to the gods.[35]

The earliest of these, much in the style, spirit, and artistic vocabulary of pre-Akkadian triumphal imagery, shows Sargon, wearing a shaggy wrap-around garment, sash, and necklet, with his right shoulder exposed, followed by an attendant holding a sunshade, then soldiers (Figure 1.2).[36] He grasps a battle net in his right hand, in which foes have been gathered up, iconography known from the pre-Akkadian Stele of the Vultures, though not referred to in Akkadian commemorative prose.[37] The important difference is that now it is the king holding the net, rather than a god, as on the Stele of the Vultures. With his left arm, he perhaps carries a now-missing weapon, such as a mace. In the register above, captives are being led in procession; other possible fragments of the monument show more captives and soldiers. This stele was systematically mutilated by being sawn into pieces, smashed, and apparently burned.

Fragments of other stelae from the early Akkadian period likewise emphasize dead foes and the parading of male prisoners (Figure 1.3); precise head-counts of killed and captured are given in the commemorative inscriptions of Rimush. A diorite ogival stele probably showed Ishtar enthroned on one side and Sargon' standing on the other, wielding a mace in his muscular arm. Here too he holds a net full of defeated prisoners, prime among them a figure who may be Lugalzagesi. Unlike the captives on the Stele of the Vultures, who are tumbled together in the net, Sargon's are arranged in neat rows, making gestures of submission, suggesting that his victory brought about a new order (Figure 9.5).[38]

(a)

*Figure 9.5* Early Akkadian victory monument: (a) Sargon' holds battle net before seated deity; (b) Sargon' smites Lugalzagesi' in net.

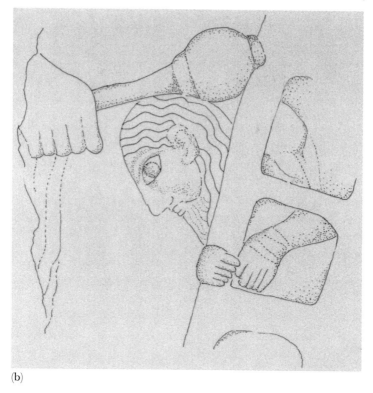

(b)

*Figure 9.5* (Continued)

A limestone disk from Ur (Figure 9.6) depicts Enheduanna, dressed in a tiered garment and roll-brim cap, performing a ritual. A nude male priest pours a libation from an imported spouted vessel, while she looks on. Two other attendants stand behind her, one with a small object in his hand, perhaps a musical instrument, the other holding a loop-handled metal vessel.[39] The disk was defaced and discarded in antiquity, though it may have long been preserved as an important relic. The damaged inscription on the reverse is often restored from a tablet found at Ur with a copy of an inscription of Enheduanna. Although the disk's text refers to Enheduanna as the "wife" of Nanna, the moon-god, the copy refers to her serving Inanna, who is called by a name known otherwise only at Mari.[40]

A relief from Girsu was smashed in antiquity and the name of the king defaced, but probably dates to the reign of Rimush (Figure 1.4). To it may belong two

*Figure 9.6* Disk of Enheduanna (wearing fluted garment) presiding over a ceremony, temple
tower to left.

inscribed fragments, unique of their kind, which begin with an account of the
king's coming to power, then enumerate large parcels of land distributed to individuals (Chapter I part 3). The top register shows the Akkadian army on the
march, the bottom two the massacre of unarmed and naked prisoners, some
begging for mercy, among them perhaps the governor of Lagash and his son, as
recounted in Rimush's inscription commemorating his campaign against that city-
state. The relief's expanded use of negative space and its attention to detail set it
apart from the earlier, denser triumphal stelae attributed to the reign of Sargon.[11]
A fragmentary, uninscribed relief, which may be slightly later than the Rimush
stele, shows prisoners paraded in neck stocks.[12]

Two inscribed reliefs of Naram-Sin are known: a basalt monument (Figure 9.7)
and the red limestone Victory Stele (Figure 1.6). The former, broken in antiquity,

*Figure 9.7* Stele of Naram-Sin, commemorating a victory in Anatolia.

was found at Pir Huseyin, near Diyarbekir in Anatolia, presumably not far from where it was originally set up, since a large Akkadian site is said to be in the area.[13] The nearly intact Victory Stele was erected somewhere in Mesopotamia and carried off to Susa as booty.[14] A third relief, an uninscribed cliff carving at Darband-i-Gaur in Kurdistan, about fifty kilometers south of Suleimaniyya, is plausibly dated to the reign of Naram-Sin and may, like the Victory Stele, commemorate his campaign against the Lullubi.[45]

The Pir Huseyin relief (Figure 9.7) shows Naram-Sin in a fluted garment, with his right shoulder bare. Not normally worn during military activity, this apparel may signify that the king is acting in a cultic capacity or that he has divine status, for this is standard dress for deities. Yet he does not wear the horned headdress associated in Mesopotamia with divinity, but a helmet-like cap, perhaps a northern attribute of kingship. Much of his face is covered by the full and elaborately treated beard characteristic of the Akkadian kings. The muscles of his body bulge beneath his clothing. He holds a staff in each hand, possibly the handles of maces or other weapons.[46] The inscription (Appendix Ia 21) commemorates a victory and heaping-up of a burial mound over the dead.

The Victory Stele of Naram-Sin (Figure 1.6), about two meters high by a meter wide, commemorates in text and image his triumph over the Lullubi, a people of the Zagros range. The relief shows a paraboloid mountain, similar in shape to that of the stele itself, with native trees on its lower flanks, through which the Akkadian soldiers, looking up at their king, march over a crushed, dying, and retreating foe. Some of the Lullubi have just died, so their bodies are not yet stiff. Naram-Sin, higher and almost twice the size of the other figures, ascends through a pass and pauses, his upper foot on a cluster of dead enemies. Naram-Sin's epithet "the mighty" is effectively conveyed by his magnificent body, hierarchical expression of leadership, and complete armament of bow, short lance, and axe (Chapter 7 part 3). His light, shawl-like garment is knotted at his upper thigh.[47] More likely worn in parade and triumph than in combat, the royal costume may further signify his victory. Here, he wears the horned cap of the gods. Nothing stands between him and the radiant celestial bodies in the sky above, whether they represent his divine allies or the rapid passage of time.[48] The stele unambiguously proclaims Naram-Sin's kingly divinity.

There may originally have been nine Akkadian soldiers, their number and varied armament representing nine tactical units of the army of Naram-Sin (Chapter 7 part 3). The officers are bearded and may include members of the royal family. As for the enemy, who also appear to be nine in number, their dress, hairstyle, and facial hair have been carefully recorded and differentiated from the Akkadians'. The enemy king, wearing a distinctive tasseled garment, barely reaches to Naram-Sin's elbow. He turns toward him, begging for mercy, while one of his men dies in agony at his feet, a lance through his throat.[49]

This brilliantly conceived and executed monument, even in its present damaged condition, is rightly deemed one of the masterworks of ancient Near Eastern art. It stands as the first pictorial statement of an art of empire, with its idealized king dominating the enemy in a landscape whose vegetation and topography demonstrate the full sweep of Akkadian power.[50]

In the same spirit, a stele now lost may have depicted the successful siege of Armanum, since the later scribe who copied its text included the captions giving the height of the defensive walls and the distances the Akkadians had to traverse from the river to the outer wall and then to the citadel (Appendix Ib 26).[51] One may speculate that one or more truly distinguished artists worked in the service of Naram-Sin to design grand images of the king's triumphs, with precisely observed local details. Their vision went far beyond their predecessors' orderly marching and individual combat scenes in registers on monuments, or the crowded but dramatic struggles on cylinder seals, to create something wholly new that would have had a stunning effect on the viewer. Some artists must have traveled with the Akkadian army, or at least had access to sketches and notes from the campaigns. Perhaps the royal family that produced the creative talent of Enheduanna gave rise to gifted artists as well.

A fragmentary stone mold (Figure 9.8), finely carved, presumably to make a work of art in sheet gold, shows Ishtar seated on a lion throne (as attested in texts

*Figure 9.8* Impression of mold for sheet gold depicting Ishtar handing Naram-Sin the lead ropes of defeated peoples, possibly Elam and Marhashi.

for the Akkadian kings) atop a platform that may represent her temple Eulmash in Agade. A male figure, no doubt intended to be Naram-Sin, sits opposite her, wearing the horned cap of divinity and a tasseled kilt. He is bare-chested, signifying that he is Ishtar's lover, as Naram-Sin claimed to be. The goddess passes the lead ropes of four personified, conquered peoples into a ring Naram-Sin is holding, a well-known metaphor for leadership in the inscriptions and iconography of Naram-Sin and others throughout Mesopotamian history. Two of the leashed beings are mountain deities, who proffer bowls; two appear to be foreign rulers, one of whom (Marhashi?) wears shoes with turned-up toes, as seen in an Akkadian seal of "the king's brother" (Figure 1.9; Chapter 7 part 4), while the second stands on a square structure with a modeled brick façade, surrounded by a wall and an arched gate, perhaps the citadel of Armanum or Apishal (Chapter 11 part 4) or a place in Elam. The complete mold may have had a series of vignettes symbolizing the "four quarters" of the Akkadian world, set off from each other by double rulings.[52]

## 3.  Glyptic

Engraved stone cylinder seals form the largest corpus of art from the Akkadian period. More than 1700 of these have been published and their iconography studied in detail.[53] Although they develop from pre-Akkadian glyptic, they differ in five significant ways: the choice of stone; the importance and placement of the inscription; the artistic style of the engraving; the choice of subject matter; and the social contexts in which they were used.

The stones from which Akkadian seals were manufactured have not been so systematically examined as their imagery, but it appears that serpentine was preferred, especially for the finest seals in the possession of the elite. In a sample of 243 Akkadian seals, 46 percent were of serpentine, whereas in a sample of similar size from post-Akkadian and Ur III times serpentine drops to 5 percent or less, comparable to the 8 percent serpentine in a pre-Akkadian sample of ninety-nine seals. Serpentine was more valuable and challenging to work than softer local stones used earlier and later in the third millennium, so a good serpentine seal represented an output of labor and a high level of skill that were likely to be found in only a few specialized workshops. While the origins of the serpentine used in Akkadian Mesopotamia have not been pinpointed, it seems reasonable to associate the sharp increase in its availability and use with the campaigns in Iran, beginning already in Sargon's reign. Greenstone facies (17 percent of the sample), the next most popular stone, came into general use somewhat later than serpentine, especially for contest and battle scenes among gods. The remaining stones are more or less evenly divided among aragonite (shell), 9 percent; lapis lazuli, 7 percent; and calcite, 8 percent. A few seals were made of rock crystal, the hardest and most difficult to carve of any stone used for seals.[54]

About one-tenth of Akkadian seals are inscribed, not with reference to their imagery, as in large-scale sculpture, but with the name and titles of the owner of the seal (Figures 1.9, 9.9, 9.10). Although some pre-Akkadian seals were inscribed with the name of the owner, there the inscription was secondary to the imagery and had to be fitted around it. During the Akkadian period, especially in the reigns of Naram-Sin and Sharkalisharri, the inscription grew in length and complexity and planning for it became part of the design process. In some cases a space was left blank for insertion of an inscription later.[55] Certain fine Akkadian seals even give the inscription pride of place, arranging the imagery around it in a heraldic manner, sometimes deploying unusual animals such as water buffalo, beautifully rendered but in contorted positions. These may be the work of a single engraver or workshop active in the reign of Sharkalisharri.[56] For some Akkadian governors and other notables, the inscription had evidently evolved from a tag of ownership to a proclamation of identity.

The majority of the inscribed seals belonged to scribes and high-level administrators, and it was precisely this class that favored the new "Akkadian" style, rich in mythological motifs that may have had special, personal resonance not apparent to outsiders.[57] Figurative glyptic developed rapidly from linear rendering to naturalistic modeling. No longer the essentially decorative elements set in running bands of action seen in pre-Akkadian seals, humans and creatures became the principal subjects. The engraver's goal was to achieve corporeal verisimilitude and credibly organic forms, even for composite beings and monsters and even if there was an overall air of the fantastic about the tableau. Accordingly, fewer figures were placed in one or two individual scenes, with ample negative space to concentrate the viewer's attention on the imagery.[58]

A major shift in aesthetic priorities had taken place. The changes point to a rising Akkadian interest in depicting dramatic moments of intense, ultimately victorious struggle against seemingly overwhelming odds in believable settings, not unlike the narrative strategies of the Akkadian royal inscriptions and reliefs. Their growing concern with such specifics as the precise numbers killed, names of individual foes, apparel, hair styles, and weaponry, parallels the glyptic focus on features of anatomy, gesture, dress, vessels, furniture, and other objects in the scene. Both texts and images present dynamic, convincing milieus, in the case of texts backed up by sworn statements of truthfulness, in the case of images by attention to detail and skill in modeling.

The Akkadian seal engraver had a considerable inventory of traditional imagery to draw on, much of which is beyond the ken of the modern viewer. By and large, efforts to explain the scenes by referring to later rituals and mythological narratives carry little conviction. Certain broad statements, nevertheless, can be made. In his study of about 1700 Akkadian seals, Boehmer proposed twenty-nine categories of imagery, of which the most often presented included scenes of combat between heroes and animals or monsters (Figure 9.9, 45 percent of the group), the sun-god Shamash (Figure 6.2a, 10 percent), combat among gods (9 percent), and presentation to and worship of the god Ea (Figure 6.2b, 5 percent), vegetation deities (3 percent), or unidentified deities (9 percent).[59]

The hero, the most frequently depicted figure, may be naked, clothed, or lightly clad in a kind of girdle; he may wear shoes with upturned toes. He may be shown as a protective figure guarding a doorpost (as in Figure 6.2b), or he may be killing

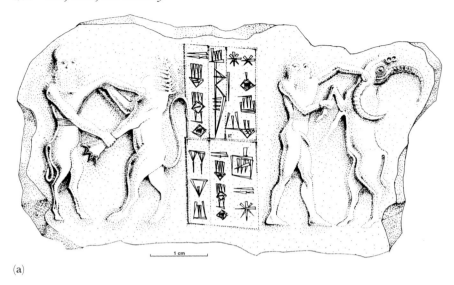

(a)

(b)

*Figure 9.9* Combat scenes: (a) sealing of Taram-Agade, daughter of Naram-Sin, showing
heroes subduing a lion and a water buffalo; (b) seal of Sakullum the scribe, with
grappling heroes and lions.

wild beasts. Sometimes he contends with another of his own kind. While it is
unlikely that a single mythological figure lies behind all of these images, the one
that fits best is the being the Akkadians called *lahmum* (borrowed already into old
Sumerian as *lahama*). This "hairy hero-man" was a mostly benevolent creature
who resided in the watery depths of Ea (Figure 6.2b).[60] Since *lahmu*-statues were
set up protectively beside doorways in the Akkadian period, it seems reasonable to
suppose that the glyptic figures signified protection of the owner of the seal, just
as Akkadian personal names often invoked protection of the name-bearer by his
family, clan, or deities (Chapter 6 part 1). Indeed, protection and patronage were

fundamental values of Akkadian society, and it would not be surprising to see this reflected in a client's choice of motif for his personal seal.

The pictorial hallmarks of these beings are their muscular strength and abundant curly hair, two of the salient traits of Akkadian royalty as shown in statues and reliefs. The image of the victorious Naram-Sin may have been modeled on these heroic figures, and it seems more than likely that the hairy, muscular hero on the seals favored by administrators evoked or implied the king himself, the first protector of his followers and subjects, not only powerful but endowed with special knowledge by Ea, god of wisdom (Chapter 6 part 1). Thus an Akkadian notable, adept in the flattery and adulation typical of the court, may have chosen the hero beside a subdued water buffalo (Figure 4.2a, 9.9a) as an adroit metonym for his king's mastery of the distant land of Magan, whence this exotic animal came; every time he rolled his seal, he was praising his lord's valor. So too the wild ox or bison may have suggested to the Akkadian seal owner the royal triumphs over Iran, where, in later Sumerian poetry, it would be sung that Lugalbanda, father of Gilgamesh, wrestled with just such a beast, high in the mountains, whereas the lion may have stood for Syria (Figures 4.2a, 9.9a).[61] Some of these images even depict, with sovereign disdain, the contorted brutes urinating in fear as they succumb to the hero's terrible hold.[62]

The second most popular imagery in Akkadian seals, the sun-god Shamash, probably served a comparable purpose, because by then the sun and kingship were closely associated. Shamash rises over the mountains (Figure 6.2a) or radiates from his throne, just as the poet of *The Curse of Agade* imagined Naram-Sin.[63] There was also ample scope in glyptic for the rich solar mythology of the Semitic peoples, who saw Shamash as the god of justice, the intrepid hero racing across the heavens or traversing the netherworld's waters of death on his regal barge (Chapter 6 part 1).[64]

The other deities identifiable in Akkadian glyptic – Ea, Ishtar, and gods of fertility – likewise had connections with royalty in the Akkadian world view: Ea gave the king wisdom; Ishtar gave him her love and victory in battle; the empire depended upon fertile flocks and fields, whose produce Sumer hauled upstream to Ishtar's city, Agade.

In short, the quickening and reorientation of Akkadian glyptic iconography endowed venerable motifs with royalist meanings peculiar to the era. Akkadian imperial ideology had infused all the visual arts, from sculpture to seals, with new purpose and intensity.

## 4. Architecture

As one would expect, the growing magnificence of the Age of Agade had its effect on architecture, especially monumental buildings. Archaeological evidence and floor plans drawn on tablets suggest that the basic modular house unit of rooms arranged around a courtyard remained the fundamental element of Akkadian design (Chapter 10 part 6). But there were several new developments. First, during the early Akkadian period, builders changed from using the traditional plano-convex brick to laying rectangular bricks in various sizes. Though this in and of itself did not affect the design of structures, it was a radical development in construction technique.[65] Second was greater scale and symmetry, of which the Akkadian fortified administrative building at Nagar is the outstanding example (Figure 3.3; Chapter 3 part 5), and, third, a marked preference for very thick walls, as at Tell el-Wilayah (Figure 3.2; Chapter 3 part 3), perhaps inspired by the enormous walls the Akkadian armies encountered in Syria. Akkadian renovations of existing structures tended to make them larger and more imposing, and with massive walls, as was the case with the Single-Shrine Temple at Eshnunna (Figure 6.1; Chapter 6 part 4). The Akkadian palace at Agade, yet to be discovered, was no doubt a grandiose, imperial version of the Old Palace at Assur (Chapter 3 part 2) or the building at Nagar. So substantial were its ruins that they were still to be found in the sixth century BCE, when the Babylonian king Nabonidus carried out excavations there (Chapter 11 part 7).

No certain depiction of an Akkadian building has survived, though the disk of Enheduanna (Figure 9.6) and the mold fragment (part 2 and Figure 9.8) may show temple towers or stepped platforms. *The Curse of Agade* mentions decorative spouts on the outside of the temple of Enlil at Nippur, as well as statues of protective spirits at its entrance, which evidently had elaborate doors with fittings in precious metal, as well as a courtyard paved in colored bricks laid in a pattern, as known at Nagar (Chapter 1 part 5, Chapter 3 part 5).[66]

Owing to the limited excavation and disputed dating of Akkadian levels in cities and towns, it is difficult to know what the Akkadian urban experience was like. On the one hand, the cases of Eshnunna and Nagar (Chapter 3 parts 2 and 5) suggest that in some neighborhoods, Akkadian official buildings and the mansions of notables, which could also serve as secondary administrative centers, encroached on residential areas, either by purchase or appropriation. At Eshnunna and Awal, houses frequently had party walls, so must have presented a uniform appearance to the street, making it difficult for the passerby to perceive differences in scale and wealth (Chapter 10 part 6). On the other hand, the case of Adab (Chapter 3 part 3) suggests that there may also have been wealthy quarters, rather than individual structures of the elite impinging on their poorer neighbors. Yet even modest temples, such as the Single-Shrine Temple at Eshnunna, must have stood out in their setting (Figure 6.1), and the great building at Nagar (Figure 3.3) surely towered over the city and was visible from far off on the surrounding plain.

## 5.  Poetry

The extant poetry of the Akkadian period is by Enheduanna, daughter of Sargon and high priestess of the moon-god, Nanna-Suen, at Ur (for translations, Appendix II). In addition to the limestone disk (Figure 9.6) discussed in part 2, two cylinder seals of her servants and the impression of a third afford contemporaneous witness to her importance, the last showing that she had a *shaperum* of her own.[67] Two major works of Sumerian literature containing autobiographical allusions are attributed to her because she self-identifies in them (Appendix IIa, b), through the literary device now termed "signature"; a third (IIc) does not but seems closely related (IIb line 109).[68] Various other Sumerian compositions not included here, some fragmentary, have been ascribed to her by ancient and modern scholars.

Since no manuscripts of Enheduanna's work are known from the Akkadian period, and those that survive, all dating centuries after her death, appear to have been modernized in spelling and grammar, some suggest that these poems were written by later authors who used her name, though why they would have done this is by no means clear.[69] Given, however, that Enheduanna was a historical personage, the best-attested member of her family outside of the kings themselves, and given the highly personal, singular style of this poetry, there is every good reason to accept the attributions as genuine and to recognize Enheduanna as the first author in world literature to whom specific writings can reliably be attributed.[70]

Her most important autobiographical references are found in the poem *Queen of All Cosmic Powers* (Appendix IIa), in which she laments that a usurper, Lugal-anne, tried to remove her from her office as high priestess, evidently hoping that she would commit suicide. There was, in fact, a Lugal-anne who was king of Ur, according to a school text of the Akkadian period, which appears to be a student's effort to copy an inscription of Naram-Sin.[71] Lugal-anne, along with Amar-girid of Uruk and Iphur-Kish of Kish, took a leading part in the Great Revolt against Naram-Sin (Chapter 1 part 4), but he defeated them and their allies. Enheduanna says that she regained her position as high priestess, crediting her reinstatement to the intervention of the goddess Inanna (Akkadian Ishtar), who came to her aid when Nanna-Suen, whom she had served her whole life, did nothing to help her in her hour of need. Although Enheduanna makes no mention of Naram-Sin, Inanna's triumph over Lugal-anne may allude to Naram-Sin's victory over the rebels, as well as to his self-proclaimed intimacy with the goddess.

Enheduanna refers to herself in *Passionate Inanna* (Appendix IIb), but the passage is heavily damaged so nothing can be gleaned from it. What remains of this poem depicts the contrasts of Inanna's violent and warlike character.

*Inanna and Ebih* (Appendix IIc), ascribed to Enheduanna on the basis of its content and style, celebrates Inanna's conquest, along with an unnamed king, of Mount Ebih, the Jebel Himrin, with the support of Enlil, no doubt alluding to some historical moment of Akkadian expansion there (Chapter 3 part 2).[72]

Enheduanna may also have composed a set of short hymns in praise of various sanctuaries, especially between Uruk and Ur, arranged in rough geographical order from southwest to northeast, ending in Akkad. According to Wilcke, Enheduanna wrote them when the gods returned to the sanctuaries that they had abandoned during Sargon's campaign against Lugalzagesi; later, other sanctuaries that did not exist in the Akkadian period were added to the composition. Other scholars, however, argue that because the collection praises these post-Akkadian sanctuaries and that nothing in its language suggests such an early date, none of the hymns could have been written by Enheduanna.[73] However this may be, their often opaque diction calls to mind Enheduanna's style and a postscript to the last hymn (line 543) specifically attributes it to her. The praise of Eulmash, for example, reads as follows:

> Ulmash is the uppermost pinnacle? of the land,
> Terrifying lion that can attack even a wild bull.
> Battle net spread over foes,
> Forcing? the silence of death upon a rebellious land,
> Spewing fell venom upon it till it yields!
> House of Inanna, of silver and lapis, treasurehouse built of gold,
> Your princess is a bird of ill omen (for the enemy),
>     the consecrated woman of its sacred space,
> In uniform of battle so beautiful they shout for joy
>     while she wields the seven-lobed mace,
> Her gear awash in battle-bath,
> The portal of war she flings wide open, . . .
> Inanna, strategist of heaven,
> Has placed (her) dwelling within your precinct, O Eulmash,
> Has taken her place upon your dais (for her throne).[74]

The dramatic events of the Great Revolt against Naram-Sin were never forgotten in Mesopotamian historical and literary memory (Chapter 11 parts 4–6). They were told and retold in many different ways, in some cases even twisting Naram-Sin's victory into defeat.[75] The intense immediacy of Enheduanna's poetry is unmatched, however, in the third millennium, for it stems from her having lived through the period and suffered at the hands of one of the leading rebels against her family's dynasty.

Two lines of an otherwise lost Sumerian hymn of praise to Manishtusu show that royal hymns, many examples of which are known for the kings of Ur, were composed in honor of the Akkadian kings:

> The king reached the mountain,
> Naram-Sin, the king's eldest son,
> Spread the great battle net over it.[76]

No poetry in the Akkadian language has been discovered from the Akkadian period. The longest composition with any poetic features is the love charm discussed in Chapter 10 part 5. While it is tempting to ascribe some of the extreme difficulty of Enheduanna's personal poetry to Akkadian being her first language, Sumerian her second, one should not underestimate an author's ability to compose in the learned language of the day. If Erasmus could write brilliantly in scholastic Latin, there is no reason why Enheduanna could not have done the same with Sumerian, the cultural language of her time and milieu.

Diakonoff has argued that the Babylonian *Epic of Gilgamesh*, the best-known work of Mesopotamian literature, dates back to the Akkadian period, in the reign of Naram-Sin or shortly thereafter.[77] Most scholars, however, believe that the *Epic* originated much later, during the early second millennium, that it incorporated episodes from Sumerian narrative poems, and that no Akkadian-language version existed in the third millennium.[78] The Sumerian poems are set in Uruk (in one case, evidently, Ur), both centers of resistance to the Akkadian dynasty, so at first glance there seems little reason to associate the Sumerian hero Gilgamesh with Akkadian rule.[79]

But in an Old Assyrian parody on Akkadian royal inscriptions and the Babylonian literary works derived from or inspired by them (Chapter 11 part 6), Sargon appears in situations otherwise known only from the *Epic*: he runs through the wilderness, loses his clothes, encounters a snake, meets a gazelle (*sabitum*, Figure 4.2a), and takes a brick out of water; in the *Epic*, Gilgamesh runs through the wilderness, wears out his clothes, puts on animal skins, meets a tavern keeper (*sabitum*), dives into water for a plant, loses it to a snake, and concludes by admiring the brickwork of his city walls. Since none of these incidents occurs in the Sumerian poems about Gilgamesh and the parody is older than any surviving Babylonian version of the *Epic*, this supports Diakonoff's idea that there was an Akkadian-era epic poem, but about Sargon, from which the author of the Babylonian *Epic of Gilgamesh* borrowed and reworked episodes. Already in the early second millennium, Sargon, like Gilgamesh, was thought to have traveled so far that he met the survivor of the Flood, whom the gods had removed from the rest of the human race. In any case, Sargon and Gilgamesh were the two great heroes of Mesopotamian tradition and there appear to be close connections among their deeds.[80]

## 6. Prose, record keeping, and letter writing

The only substantial prose documents originating in the Akkadian period are the commemorative inscriptions of its rulers, which show the same impressive stylistic development that one finds in sculpture, glyptic, calligraphy, and other arts. The earliest are short declarative sentences in the third person: "Sargon, king of Kish, was victorious in thirty-four battles. He destroyed city walls all the way to the shore of the sea."[81] His sons' statements are already more elaborated, notably with first-person declarations attesting to the veracity of the third-person narration: "By Shamash and Ilaba I swear no lies, but indeed truthfully!"[82]

Naram-Sin's sentences are longer and more complex in their syntax, using such techniques as introducing the narrative with a temporal clause: "Whereas, for all time, since the creation of the human race, no king among all kings whatsoever destroyed Armanum and Ebla, by the weapon of Nergal, Naram-Sin the mighty opened the only way and he gave him Armanum and Ebla . . ."[83] In addition, Naram-Sin's inscriptions refer to the actions of hostile rulers and enemy cities, unlike Sargon's, which state only what he did: "Between the cities of Tiwa and Urum, in the field of Sin, he (the enemy king) drew up and awaited battle."[84] They also provide inclusive geographical summaries, rather than simply listing the places captured in chronological order. Battle accounts expand from bald statements of victory to specifics as to the site of a battle: "Between Awan and Susa, at the river in the middle . . ."[85] and its aftermath: "He heaped up a burial mound over them."[86] The theological content of the narrative is enhanced by stressing divine agency: "It was Enlil who . . . gave him the scepter of kingship . . . "[87]or "(As) Enlil

disclosed . . ."[88] Both Naram-Sin and Sharkalisharri stress their personal relationship with gods, especially Ishtar and Enlil: "Through the love Ishtar bore him . . ."[89]
or "Beloved son of Enlil."[90]

The absence of figurative language is striking. No Akkadian inscription includes
a simile, though they occur in a pre-Akkadian letter from Ebla ("Ebla is false as
ever a woman")[91] and in a post-Akkadian inscription from Simurrum ("May it be
as catastrophic for his army as rainfall at harvest").[92] Simile is abundant, however,
in Akkadian magic:

"You broke (your?) forehead like a clay pot"[93] and "Seek for me among the
boxwood, as the shepherd seeks the sheep, the goat her kid, the ewe the lamb, the
jenny her foal."[94]

The most significant innovation of Akkadian commemorative prose was the
triumphal inscription on a monument occasioned by a military victory.[95] Whereas
earlier accounts of victories had formed part of narratives that included other
activities, such as setting a boundary, constructing a building, or dedicating an
object in a temple, the Akkadian kings commissioned texts that were solely motivated by triumph in battle. This type of monumental inscription was later imitated in the kingdoms of Mari and Upper Mesopotamia, and, to a lesser extent
among later Babylonian kingdoms. In the early second millennium (Chapter 11
part 8), the long sentences of the Classical Akkadian prose style were imitated.
The special respect accorded the formal written Babylonian of Eshnunna in the
nineteenth and eighteenth centuries BCE may have arisen from a belief that its
style and usage were descended from the Akkadian of Agade.[96]

As shown in Chapters 11 and 12, the bombast of royal self-presentation dominated Mesopotamian historical memory of the Akkadian period, as well as modern
understanding of it, but other types of literature were certainly in circulation. One
prose work that was probably well known to anyone who went to school at the time
was a collection of sayings by a Sumerian sage of the remote past, *The Instructions
of Shuruppak*.[97] It is known from pre-Akkadian sources and, in the early second millennium, was popular in Sumerian-language education at Nippur, Larsa, and other
centers. Translated into Akkadian and Hurrian thereafter, it was widely known, and
was still being copied in the later first millennium. Thus it was among the longest-
lived of all Mesopotamian literary works and preserves the oldest maxims about
human conduct known. Like other pieces of its kind from throughout the ancient
Near East, *The Instructions of Shuruppak* offers advice for success in everyday life, cast
in homely guise but ponderable on a broad practical and moral basis as "subtle
words," to use the composition's self-characterization.[98] For example, the saying
"Don't buy an ass that brays a lot, it will split your yoke" was probably understood
to mean that a loud speaker of empty words will impede an important project.[99]

Some of the sayings were arranged in groups linked by parallelism and internal development, such as this set concerned with protecting personal material
resources:

> Don't cultivate a field by a roadway, hard usage of it will be a loss.
> Don't plow a field where a path comes out, the boundary marker will be moved.

Don't dig a well in your field, people will do damage there.
Don't connect your house to a main street, that will be an
   entanglement.[100]

The advice then moves to how to shield oneself from awkward contractual
connections with people, especially on an unequal basis, and keeping clear of
disputes, even provocations, that can bring involvement with one side or the other
or entail a formal procedure:

Don't accept a person as pledge for a debt, that person will have a
   hold over you,
Nor should you yourself act as pledge, he who does so loses dignity.
Don't give evidence for anyone, you will be drawn in over your head.
Don't stand by where there is a dispute,
Don't let yourself be drawn into a dispute as a witness in court,
Don't let yourself be identified as a party to a dispute,
Don't start a dispute yourself! You will [end up] standing by the
   palace gate (awaiting resolution).
Give disputes a wide berth, at an insult, go some other way.[101]

Gross crimes bring harsh consequences:

Don't steal anything lest you do yourself in,
Don't break into a house, don't demand the money box,
The robber's a lion till he's caught, then he's a slave.[102]

One should avoid overly close relationships with men or women who are not
family:

Don't act as best man in a wedding lest you . . . yourself,
Don't flirt with a girl who is married,
My son, don't sit in a chamber with another man's wife,
   they will say bad things about you.[103]

The advice then moves to personal qualities that define good relationships with
others:

Don't be a quarrelsome person lest you disgrace yourself,
Don't invent dishonest schemes lest you come to a fall.
Don't offer advice all the time, your word abides,
Don't ask advice all the time, you will not have to bear long faces.[104]

Taking chances is risky:

When you draw bones for lots, an ox will make you nervous, a sheep will
   make you nervous.[105]

Look before you leap:

> Don't remove your sheep to an unfrequented pasture,
> Don't hire a man's ox for a field with no limit,
> A good boundary is a good road.[106]

Spend money wisely:

> Hire a donkey, buy an ox.[107]

The use of written documents (Figure 1.8) in legal and contractual matters was mentioned in Chapter 2 part 3. Management and administration also depended on the use of writing. In the Sumerian cities, record keeping under Akkadian rule continued their pre-Akkadian practices that varied from place to place. At Girsu, for example, three tablet sizes were used: small for individual vouchers; medium-sized in two columns for combined summary records of several vouchers; and very large ledger tablets in many columns recording scores of transactions in small, neat script. At Umma, there were no large ledger tablets, but only medium-sized four-column summaries. Umma tablets were dated by the year of appointment of the governor, whereas Girsu and Adab tablets were generally not dated at all. At Nippur and Isin, records of the Akkadian administration were written on rectangular tablets in the elegant Akkadian hand, whereas legal documents and contracts were often written on tablets with rounded corners in a less formal hand. In contrast, contracts and letters from Girsu and the estate of Mesag were usually written in the finest Akkadian script, sometimes by the governor himself. Sumerian language was used regularly for record keeping at Girsu, Adab, and Umma, but Akkadian or a mixture of Sumerian and Akkadian on Mesag's estate. Letters from Akkadian notables were often in Akkadian, sometimes in Sumerian. The basic principles of Sumerian accounting, such as responsibility and accountability for individual items, positive and negative, with a final total, were maintained.[108]

Akkadian record-keeping techniques in Akkad, especially at settlements like Mugdan or Gasur, were more schematic than in Sumer, using large, often rounded figures that suggest a preconceived scheme. This kind of accounting was exported to Mesag's estate in Sumer. The preferred language of record was Akkadian, in the case of Mesag's estate with what may be occasional grammatical mistakes, suggesting that Sumerian was his first language and that he used Akkadian as a matter of prestige. At Eshnunna, large multi-column ledger tablets were drawn up comparable to those from Girsu; one example of such a tablet survives from Mesag's estate as well.[109]

Records were retained for one or more years in labeled baskets, perhaps stored on clay benches in magazines or archive rooms. Transactions over periods of two or three years occur occasionally, so administrative records may have been kept at least that long. Since no large group of Akkadian administrative records has been excavated in its original context, the existence of archives, that is, long-term accumulations of documents in a place other than their office of origin or receipt, is uncertain. The purpose of these administrative records was presumably to provide evidence for accountability and responsibility for property that did not belong to the person of record, but, as in many bureaucracies, may have already developed a momentum of their own to justify the task of the record-keeper.[110]

The crisp, businesslike style of much Akkadian-period letter writing was noted in Chapter 7 part 4. Letters composed in Akkadian show a tendency to be more florid than those in Sumerian, introducing oaths, exclamations, and rhetorical questions to an extent unusual in Sumerian epistolography. The recurrence of distinctive idioms even in the small remaining corpus of Akkadian-language letters suggests a certain linguistic trendiness or signature jargon among the elite, who picked up and reused among themselves expressions then in fashion.[111]

## 7.   Translation and bilingualism

The early adaptations of Sumerian writing to Akkadian show that translation was part of the very process of reading in Mesopotamia. Words in Akkadian were written using Sumerian word signs that the reader was expected to translate into Akkadian as he read, presupposing his mastery of both languages.[112] Naram-Sin's reforms reduced the Sumerian content of written Akkadian; Akkadian words were spelled out, instead of being written with Sumerian word signs (Chapter 1 part 6). But, at the same time, there was growing interest in composing Sumerian and Akkadian texts that said the same thing. One may well wonder why, when the writing system was being purged of the necessity for automatic translation, that bilingualism began to be cultivated as a literary art.[113]

Some scholars see a political and cultural agenda during the Akkadian period to elevate the Akkadian language to the same high status as Sumerian; others suggest that Akkadian was imposed on the land.[114] Still others have argued that Sumero-Akkadian bilingualism of the Akkadian Empire was not a signifier of individual identity within a larger cultural matrix, as it tends to be seen today, but rather an effort to fuse two independent traditions, Sumerian and Semitic, into one. By recognizing two languages, along with two pantheons, two traditions of government, two quite different social and economic patterns of life, the Akkadians created a sense of equivalence – the northern and southern faces of the same land.[115]

In any case, the elite used both Akkadian and Sumerian. Rather than making distinctions on the basis of spoken or native language, they often wrote to each other in Akkadian, but when they wrote to the king they preferred Sumerian, as the cultural language of the realm. Notables like Lugal-ushumgal and Mesag were among those who probably spoke Sumerian as their mother tongue and regularly wrote in Akkadian as a matter of prestige. In day-to-day activity, Akkadian record-keepers wrote both languages, sometimes in the same document. Although bilingualism is not the same as translation, it suggests that in the Akkadian period there was a growth of language consciousness and that conscious or unconscious decisions were made about which language to use in a given context. There is no indication of a requirement or even an expectation to communicate in Akkadian for people who did not speak it as their first language.

For example, of Sargon's commemorative inscriptions, in both Sumerian and Akkadian, which was the original and which the translation? Or was there even such a concept at that time? Sumerian and Akkadian were the only two languages of Mesopotamian cultural tradition and the only ones for which ability to translate between them was deemed a significant personal accomplishment. Others were barbarian tongues, such as those of Gutium or Meluhha, for which mere dragomans were needed.[116]

While Sargon left unilingual and bilingual inscriptions in Sumerian and Akkadian, his daughter wrote her powerful poetry exclusively in Sumerian. Rimush and Manishtusu used Akkadian and Sumerian. Sargon's grandson, Naram-Sin, preferred his inscriptions to be in Akkadian, and his great-grandson, Sharkalisharri, left us no inscriptions in Sumerian at all, only in Akkadian. So disturbed was a much later Babylonian scholar by this that when he copied an ancient inscription of Sharkalisharri, he made up a Sumerian version, perhaps because he thought such a long-ago king should have written in Sumerian.[117]

In the decades following the fall of Agade, the Gutians and the kings of Ur had two different responses to the Akkadian dynasty's political and cultural agendas. For the Gutians, Akkadian was the prestige language. They left inscriptions only in Akkadian. The kings of Ur, on the other hand, used Akkadian mostly in peripheral areas and promoted Sumerian in the Sumerian heartland, normally without an Akkadian version, even if, as seems possible, they actually spoke Akkadian as their mother tongue. Both may have ruled out translation as no longer desirable except as a school exercise. In the wake of the Akkadian Empire, it may have looked too much like a discredited political program.

## 8.   Music

References to performers, instruments, and music in texts, as well as representations of instruments and performers in art, show that music was important in all aspects of private, religious, court, and military life, for celebration, praise, aesthetic experience, entertainment, relaxation, and mood enhancement. According to a Sumerian narrative poem, music was one of the basic arts that defined civilization.[118] *The Curse of Agade* uses music as a trope to emphasize the happiness and prosperity of the city at the height of its glory: "There was drumbeat in the city, winds and strings without."[119]

As a Sumerian proverb puts it, "The songs of a city are its own best omens."[120]

The general term for musician, *narum*, is amply attested in Akkadian records, especially ration distributions, but only rarely qualified as to specialty.[121] The most fully documented musicians of any period are court musicians. Their training, organization, and social conditions are best known from early second-millennium Mari, where it seems there was an orchestra, choir, and royal academy for training musicians, presided over by a chief musician. His purview was what might be called "secular music"; the *gala* presided over what might be called "religious music."[122]

Accomplished performers could expect a good living and enjoyed high social status. Their access to the king and important officials sometimes led to positions of responsibility and trust at court, but also meant that musicians could be taken as war booty or exchanged between courts.[123] As a result, musical culture tended to be international, with foreign instruments or styles, such as "from Marhashi," esteemed as far away as Syria.[124] At pre-Akkadian Mari, a significant proportion of the musicians had Sumerian names, as opposed to the rest of the palace population. Perhaps these were professional or stage names, rather than an indication that Sumerian musicians were particularly favored there.[125] To judge from the ivory figurine from Akkadian Tell el-Wilayah, court singers may have been chosen for their comeliness as well as their talent and their repertory probably included love songs, perhaps the erotic type later termed "bosom songs."[126]

To appease the anger of the gods, laments were sung in a special Sumerian dialect by men called *gala/kalûm*, variously referred to in modern scholarship as castrati, effeminate men, or a "third gender."[127] Their performance may have involved chanting during a circumambulation of the city or its sanctuaries, accompanied by people playing an instrument called *balag*, variously understood to be drum, lyre, or harp.[128] A letter from the Himrin Basin orders officials to remove the local singer from office and to appoint another, though without stating the reason. This suggests that the post of musician was important enough to warrant high-level administrative intervention.[129] A fine inscribed Akkadian cylinder seal shows a female lyre-player, perhaps the owner of the seal, performing before a seated woman, Tutanabšum, a daughter of Naram-Sin, who listens with rapt attention (Figure 9.10).[130] A smaller lyre and the lute appear for the first time in Akkadian seal imagery and may be innovations of this period.[131]

Two documents from Akkadian Eshnunna record a ceremony in which girls were turned over to the temple of Tishpak to become professional singers (Figure 1.8d).

*Figure 9.10* Seal of Aman-Ishtar the musician, servant of Tutanabshum, daughter of Naram-Sin.

This was clearly a solemn occasion, witnessed by numerous dignitaries and the singing teachers. The temple even had a "scribe of the singers."[132]

## 9.  Mathematics, quantification, and cartography

Akkadian mathematics is best known not from any major urban centers but from a group of problem texts that may have come from E-igi-il, a provincial town near Lagash, perhaps the seat of an Akkadian notable who kept his math tablets from school.[133] These involve finding the areas of squares and rectangles, as well as the length of the short sides of rectangles. Other Akkadian-period records of calculations concern finding the areas of irregularly shaped figures. Many of these appear to be training exercises for calculating the size of parcels of land, but in some instances the dimensions of the plots are absurdly long and narrow, as if to test the student by presenting unrealistic figures. Only one of them explains how to solve the problem:

> The long side (of a piece of land) is two rods. (What is the) short side (if the area is 1 ¾ iku? You put a double hand-span in it, a sixth (of a seed-cubit), you put a quarter (of a seed-cubit). The solution: its short side is 5 seed cubits, 1 double-hand-span, [5] fingers.[134]

Not surprisingly, Akkadian scribes often resorted to an approximative method in which they multiplied the average of the long and short sides of a quadrilateral:

> The average of the two long sides is 180 rods, what is the short side (if the area is 1 iku? Its short side is 3 seed cubits, 1 cubit, 1 half-cubit.[135]

The computational techniques are sometimes obscure to us. Metrological units were used to write sexagesimal fractions, but during the calculations sexagesimal place notation was employed. In this complex process of conversion between different modes of reckoning, it was easy to make errors, and many of the problem texts give wrong answers.

All the known examples of mathematical texts come from Sumer. Differences are to be expected for mathematics in the Akkadian-speaking north, if only because somewhat different systems of numeration were used. Akkadian-language texts used a 600-sign and a 6000-sign, but not a 3600 sign, as used in Sumerian texts. This suggests that the Akkadian-speaking part of Mesopotamia leaned toward decimal counting, whereas in Sumer, the sexagesimal system was more firmly rooted.[136]

The quantitative labor norms abundantly attested in the late third millennium were undoubtedly known or being developed earlier, but there is as yet only limited evidence for their use in the Akkadian period. A keen interest in quantification is shown by the detailed casualty figures in royal inscriptions, a forerunner for which is a pre-Akkadian stone monument from Kish that lists 36,000 prisoners.[137]

In the assignment of parcels of land, fixed ratios, at least for record-keeping purposes, were the norm in Akkad and spread from there to Akkadian Sumer (part 6).
Along with this was a growing interest in symmetry in architecture and in naturalistic canons for the human body (parts 1 and 2).

The earliest maps date to the Akkadian period: one shows a rural parcel near
Gasur, the other an area near Lagash (Figure 9.11).[138] Various building plans,

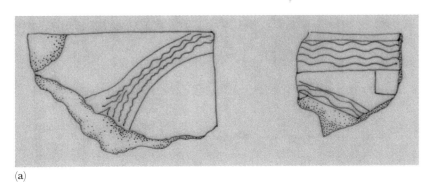

(a)

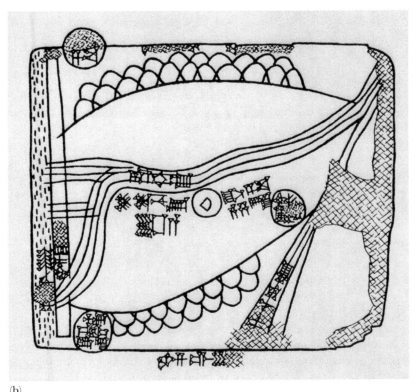

(b)

*Figure 9.11* Cartography: (a) two maps from Girsu showing watercourses; (b) map showing
fields and watercourses near Gasur.

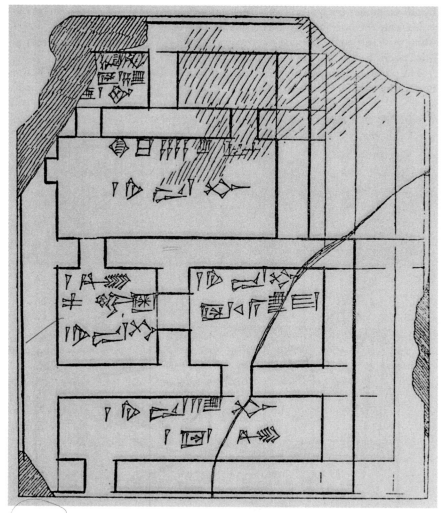

*Figure 9.12* Measured plan of an Akkadian building at Girsu.

some quite elaborate, are also known but their purpose is unclear (Figure 9.12).[139] A clay tablet lists what seem to be the boundaries of the province of Lagash, but its purpose is likewise unclear.[140] The earliest itinerary, referring to a route in the Khabur region, also dates to the Akkadian period. Unlike most later itineraries, it is carved in stone, so must have been part of a commemorative monument. Since an inscription of Naram-Sin gives the route of a lengthy march (Appendix Ib 28), this itinerary may be a fragment of a record of a military campaign in which the distance marched and places reached were deemed worthy of permanent record, like Naram-Sin's exploration of the sources of the Tigris and Euphrates rivers.[141] This evidence suggests that the Akkadian period saw the beginning of Mesopotamian efforts to explore, measure, and quantify the physical world as a consequence of conquest and expression of authority, a process that continued well into the first millennium.[142] In this spirit, Enheduanna refers to exploration and measurement of the newly defeated Mount Ebih, or Jebel Himrin:

> O An the king, I will roll out your name to the ends of the land,
> like a surveyor's line . . .
> May he [the Akkadian king] take control in the mountain,
> may he explore it, learning its dimensions,
> May he go forth on the holy campaign of heaven,
> may he learn how far it goes.[143]

## 10. The Akkadian style

Every close student of Akkadian arts and letters develops a sense that the period has a distinctive style or aesthetic, but translating this sense into modern terms presents conceptual challenges that go to the heart of how to define the Age of Agade. The Akkadian style expressed the universal, idealized Akkadian identity that was superimposed by force over quite different, often restive and resistant, local cultures.[144] After removing the monuments of previous rulers, the victors substituted images of the Akkadian king, powerful and serene as a god seated in his dwelling, or heroic and violent as a warrior killing enemies and wrecking their cities. The king's strength and magnificence were conveyed by his enviable body, his virility by his flowing beard, his superior station by his fine garments, the immanence and reality of his presence by his scrupulously detailed face, hair, and hands. Yet for all of the heightened naturalism of his depiction, he was not to be seen as other men. The king towered over trees and foes; he dwarfed mountains; he single-handedly won battles and captured enemy kings. He had an otherworldly quality that partook of divinity. His weaponry and mission were divine and he reported to the gods, worshipped and embraced them.

Nor was this left to the imagination of the viewer. Royal statues and reliefs were provided with inscriptions explaining who the king was, why he was important, in what action he was engaged. Text and image worked together to perpetuate and legitimate the centralized authority of the Akkadian order, whose ruler dominated the material realm and linked kingship to heaven.[145]

The two counterpoised dynamics of the Akkadian world view were violence and tranquility. When members of the Akkadian ruling establishment chose imagery for their seals, they preferred scenes of heroic conflict or mythological events so that their inscribed names, and by extension themselves, were removed from the everyday. The seals' theatricality was enhanced by the Akkadian artists' skillful use of negative space, focusing attention on individual episodes, rather than presenting the uninterrupted narrative of earlier glyptic. Akkadian sculpture, especially the pieces in cast copper, similarly demanded that the viewer look, react, and engage; small wonder that future enemies beheaded or mutilated every Akkadian statue and relief they could find.

If aggression and use of force created the Akkadian Empire and awaited anyone who resisted, serenity was the hallmark of its success. No other medium conveys the calm self-assurance of the period so well as its elegant, elaborate, carefully laid out script. Akkadian scribes might use twenty wedges to make a sign when half that number would do. When writing letters, they spaced the words so that each line contained only one stress unit, unlike in later periods, when the words were crowded together. Later ages recognized this and imitated Akkadian writing when trying to be calligraphic, as someone today might use neo-Gothic or Roman script to convey gravitas or beauty. While the simpler, more cursive signs of contemporaneous non-Akkadian writing have a certain flow and grace of their own, nothing in the history of cuneiform writing matches Akkadian ductus at its finest.[116] As they did with so many other aspects of Mesopotamian civilization, the Akkadian ruling class took a venerable inheritance and gave it a new form in which a love of beauty and harmony for their own sake was paramount, the first instance of a culture in which the art of calligraphy proclaimed its values and pride.

It was this very serenity that later Mesopotamian writers sought to deny Akkadian kings. For them, Sargon was cursed with a restless spirit, Naram-Sin with frightful trials, deep depression, and regrets. For outsiders, the Akkadian aesthetic aroused envy, fear, wonder, and grudging respect. For the Akkadian elite, however, it proclaimed their pride and self-confidence in having reshaped the four quarters of their world and crushed all resistance. This may be why even the closest student of Akkadian arts and letters feels at once near and far from the spirit they convey.

## Notes

1 Studies of pre-Akkadian and Akkadian stone sculpture in the round include Frankfort 1939b and 1943; Barrelet 1959; Strommenger 1960; Braun-Holzinger 1977; 2007; Spycket 1981; Invernizzi 1992 1: 336–44; Evans 2007; Marchesi and Marchetti 2011; for metal, Braun-Holzinger 1984. Major pieces discussed here have been reproduced and discussed in most books on Mesopotamian art; citations here are restricted where possible to these comprehensive works. For the specifically Akkadian character of Akkadian art, Nissen 1986; for possible Egyptian influences on Akkadian art, Langdon 1921; Börker-Klähn 1982a; for Syrian influences, Matthiae 1976: 214–15; 2009: 790; 2010: 152, 169, 172, 177–78.
2 Strommenger 1960: 376–78.
3 Braun-Holzinger 1977: 10.
4 Strommenger 1960: 31–35; Braun-Holzinger 1977: 16–28; Cooper 1990; for comparison with inscribed objects of earlier periods, which in some cases were dedicated by professional people, such as a blacksmith, gardener, or merchant, Heinz 1989; in general Radner 2005.
5 Spycket 1968; Barrelet 1970; Hallo 1983; Collon 2007.
6 Braun-Holzinger 1977: 10.
7 Strommenger 1960: 88–89; Braun-Holzinger 1977: 10; 2007: 68–70; B. Foster 2010a: 124–25.
8 Strommenger 1960: 9–31; for the question of portraiture, 92; Schlossman 1978/9; Winter 2009.

9 Strommenger 1960: 8–9; Braun-Holzinger 1977: 11.

10 Strommenger 1960: 7–45; Braun-Holzinger 1977.

11 Braun-Holzinger 1977: 66.

12 Strommenger 1960: 43–44; Cluzan and Lecompte 2011: 10; for the name and parallels, Stamm 1939: 185.

13 Brandes 1980; J. Westenholz 2012. The statue SK 4 in the Temple of Ishtar at Assur still bears the mark on its neck of an effort to behead it (Bär 2003b: 103–4). A statue of the Akkadian notable or ruler, perhaps Manishtusu or Ititi, was not only beheaded, so the head was found at some distance from its body, but the nose, left ear, eyes, and mouth had evidently been deliberately mutilated (Reade 2011: 248–49, and note 19), as was the copper head of an Akkadian ruler found at Nineveh, in which the nose, beard, both ears, and an eye had also been deliberately mutilated (Mallowan 1936), though when and by whom is unknown; further below, note 31.

14 Amiet 1976; Braun-Holzinger 2007: 82–88.

15 Winter 1996a; B. Foster 2010a.

16 Cooper 1990; J. Westenholz 1998: 52–56; Braun-Holzinger 2007.

17 Amiet 1972; Eppihimer 2010. Two show the king seated on a distinctive stool sometimes associated with banqueting, as noted by Eppihimer 2010: 376, differently Braun-Holzinger 2007: 82 (divine status); for the possibility of two workshops, Eppihimer 2010: 369; for the second, uninscribed, seated figure, Boehmer 1996: tafel 17.

18 Eppihimer 2010.

19 Body: Moortgat 1967: 138–40; Strommenger 1962, pl. 116; Klengel-Brandt 1995; head: Abu Soof 1983: 305; join: Klengel-Brandt 1993. For a dating to the Old Assyrian period, Ehrenberg 1997.

20 Frayne 1993: 310–11; compare Appendix Ib 9; Akkadian curses call for the opposite, Chapter 6 part 6 and note 107.

21 The Boston head (Amiet 1976 fig. 8), the Louvre alabaster head AO 2111 (Amiet 1976 no. 7); the De Clercq head AO 2219, of yellow limestone, said to be from Girsu (Amiet 1976 no. 8); and a small alabaster head AO 10922, said to be from Adab (Amiet 1976 no. 9).

22 *Muses*, 109 lines 52–53'.

23 AO 4754 (Amiet 1976 no. 10); various dates for this piece have been proposed, from the pre-Akkadian period to the early second millennium, but an Akkadian date has been preferred here.

24 VA 6980 (= Bär 2003b: 114 [SK 24] and plate 31); Spycket 1981: 166, fig. 51, pl. 113.

25 *Muses*, 85 lines 9–10.

26 Moortgat 1969: 48.

27 Sb 52 (Amiet 1976 No. 29).

28 Mallowan 1936. This piece is reproduced and discussed in every modern book on early Mesopotamian art.

29 Mallowan 1936: 110; J. Westenholz 2004: 14.

30 Mallowan 1936: 109–10, consultation with a London hairdresser; Börker-Klähn 1972/5: 3–4.

31 See note 13, this chapter; Nylander 1980 proposes that this was done by the Medes in the seventh century BCE, but this does not take the mutilation of other Akkadian statuary sufficiently into account.

32 AO 14 (Aruz and Wallenfels 2003 No. 137).

33 Al-Fouadi 1976; Aruz and Wallenfels 2003: 195 fig. 58; Hansen 2003: 195.

34 Barrelet 1970: 228–30; for the inscription on this piece, Appendix Ia 18 and Chapter 1 note 39.

35 For surveys of Akkadian relief work, Börker-Klähn 1972/5; Invernizzi 1992 1: 324–36.

36 Sb 1 (Amiet 1976 No. 1); Strommenger 1962, pl. 115; Börker-Klähn 1982b, 18b, c; Eppihimer 2009: 21–33. For discussions of the garment, which usually take it to be military apparel, Spycket 1981: 146–47; Braun-Holzinger 2007: 88–89; B. Foster 2010a: 121.

37 This interpretation is based on repeated study of the original monument in both natural and artificial light (similarly Strommenger 1960: 55); other interpretations, such as that Sargon is holding a weapon (Braun-Holzinger 1991: 30 note 144 (uncertain), 2007: 88–89) are excluded, if only because Sargon would strangely be holding the alleged weapon just below its head, not by the end of the handle, as he is in Sb 3, below, note 38. The shape and diagonal patterns of the net are still visible on the stone and in good photographs (Amiet 1976 plate 72, but not shown in his drawing, Fig. 1 p. 8); further Liverani 1966a: 24; Nigro 1998a: 86–87; Eppihimer 2009: 32, below, note 74, and Fig. 2. For discussion of Akkadian mace heads, a weapon of the gods but assigned to Akkadian kings in art, J. Westenholz 1998: 50–52. Naram-Sin wields a battle net in a poem, below, part 5; further below, note 74.

38 Sb 2, Sb 11388, 10482, Sb 3 (Amiet 1976 Nos. 2–6). For a detailed study and reconstruction of Sb 2, Nigro 1997; 1998a.

39 CBS 16665 (Aruz and Wallenfels 2003: No. 128, with description by Hansen (who proposes that the attendant immediately behind Enheduanna carries a fly whisk). For the foreign origin of the vessel one of Enheduanna's attendants holds, Müller-Karpe 1993/97: 143.

40 Appendix Ib 10. Winter 1987: 192–96 and note 16 suggests that the tablet copy may not be the same inscription as on the disk; for Inanna at Mari, W. Lambert 1985, 1990. Further Eppihimer 2009: 37 note 71. For the idea that the disk was preserved as a relic of a former high priestess, McHale-Moore 2000.

41 AO 2678, AO 2679, YBC 2409 (Aruz and Wallenfels 2003: No. 129a, b); B. Foster 1985 for the association of the fragments and interpretation of the inscription, with reference to earlier literature, to which should be added Heuzey 1893; Meyer 1906: 115–17; Nigro 2001/3; further Chapter 1 note 21.

42 Aruz and Wallenfels 2003: no. 131; Mellink 1963; Müller-Karpe 1993/97: 143.

43 Istanbul Archaeological Museum 1027 (Aruz and Wallenfels 2003: 203–4). King (1910: 245 note 1) located the find spot of the stele in the remains of a structure at the foot of the citadel. Although this site has been damaged by looters, it has never been explored scientifically.

44 Sb 4 (Amiet 1976 No. 27); Börker-Klähn 1982b, 26d–j. The most detailed study of this piece, with drawings that correspond most closely to my own observation of it, is Bänder 1995; despite the many merits of this ambitious and comprehensive work, a full presentation of this important object, with clear photos and professional drawings of all its details, is still lacking (Meyer 1906: 10–11 note 3, "dringend").

45 Strommenger 1963; Boese 1973.

46 Hansen 2003: 204; Braun-Holzinger 2007: 92–93; Appendix Ia 21.

47 K. Foster forthcoming.

48 Winter 2004 (three suns/stars suggests a heroic three-day campaign; Bänder 1995: plate 63 reconstructs five, however). For a proposal that the specific shape of the horns on his cap was suggested by a wild bull Naram-Sin himself slew, Barnett 1974: 441–42 and above, Chapter 4 note 56. For the different perspective of the horns from the orientation of the head and the horns emerging not from the side of the helmet but from behind, Bänder 1995: 177–78.

49 De Morgan 1900: 148, who also draws particular attention to artistry in the depiction of the dying man just in front of the king. He acutely observes that the artist had a little trouble with legs, as Naram-Sin's left leg, like those of his soldiers, is not quite proportional to his right, and the dying warrior's legs are not quite organically rendered (147, 149), but this problem was overcome in the Bassetki statue (above, note 33). Meyer 1906: 11 observes that the placement of the ear is "incorrect" and that the depiction

of the eye is not truly in profile but influenced by an older practice of showing the eye from a front view even when the face is in profile; for the perspective of the horns, above, note 48. Bänder 1995 pl. 63 reconstructs eleven Akkadian soldiers instead of nine. In general Nigro 1998b.

50 Rutten 1941; Kantor 1966; Moortgat 1969: 51–52; Hansen 2003: 195–97; Winter 1996a, 1999a; Collon 2000; Braun-Holzinger 2007: 93–94; for the inscription, Appendix Ia 15.

51 Kraus 1948; B. Foster 1982g, with discussion of the possible perspectives of the relief; Frayne 1993: 132–35.

52 Hansen 2002. For the lion throne in an Akkadian administrative text, B. Foster 1980: 33; for Naram-Sin receiving a lead rope (from Enlil), Appendix Ib 28; Frayne 1993: 97; for turned-up shoes, B. Foster 2010a: 131 note 101. Braun-Holzinger 2007: 93 note 59 considers the mold "sicherlich eine Fälschung" and adduces a variety of possible sources for its iconography, suggesting a remarkably well-read and up-to-date forger, not to mention one of consummate skill and considerable daring and originality. Each discovery of Akkadian art brings surprises. Therefore her arguments have been carefully considered here, but rejected, so also Steinkeller 2014: 695 note 13.

53 Boehmer 1965; Collon 1982; Rohn 2011. The specific uses of Akkadian seals have been less studied than their iconography; they included sealing documents, packages of goods, and door closure devices, Zettler 1987.

54 Collon 1982: 14, 26; in general Sax 1993.

55 Frankfort 1939a: 85; Collon 1982: 22–23. Somewhat less than half of her sample had inscriptions or space for them. She notes that "the seals representing mythological scenes very rarely bear an inscription or even provide a space for one. The less distinctive the seal, the more necessary the inscription as a method of identification . . ." (Collon 1982: 22); further Rohn 2011.

56 Collon 1982: 23–25.

57 Barrelet 1970: 244–51; Matthaie 1998, who notes a comparable palace style and subject matter in seals from Ebla.

58 Frankfort 1939a: 81–82; Barrelet 1970: 213–14. Frankfort writes that Akkadian glyptic depicts "men and animals with all the splendor of physical power, combats with all the grimness of merciless struggle, stories with all the richness of incidental symbolic detail," in contrast to pre-Akkadian glyptic, which the scenes of which he found "charming but unreal" and lacking "the bitterness and the grandeur of the world which the Akkadians experienced" (Frankfort 1943: 17).

59 Frankfort 1934b; Boehmer 1965; for remarks on the scepter held by deities in Akkadian glyptic, Van Buren 1956: 103.

60 Wiggermann 1981/2; Guichard 1993; Durand 1993; Edzard 1994; Ellis 1995; Heimpel 1998.

61 Vanstiphout 2003: 124–25 line 365: "Like a man of muscle he advanced against the tawny bison, the bison of the highlands, like a wrestler he bent it down."

62 Boehmer 1965: 33.

63 "Its king, the shepherd, Naram-Sin, Shone forth like sunrise on the holy throne of Agade" (Cooper 1983a: 52–53 [Appendix IIIb] lines 40–41); for the simile, Chapter 6 note 6.

64 Boehmer 1965: 171–75.

65 Salonen 1972: 25–27, with discussion of Akkadian brick sizes, 28–29. For a survey of Akkadian buildings, Invernizzi 1992 1: 322–24.

66 Cooper 1983a: 56 (Appendix IIIb) lines 120, 132; further Chapter 1 part 5.

67 Boehmer 1965 nos. 194, 204, 458.

68 B. Foster 1991.

69 Civil 1980: 229; Michalowski 1998: 65; Black 2002; Black et al. 1998: 315–16; Rubio 2009: 27–28.

70 Falkenstein 1958; Zgoll 1997; Glassner 2009a; in general, J. Westenholz 1992a.

71 Jacobsen 1978; Haul 2009: 38–57.

72  Attinger 1993; Jaques 2004.
73  Sjöberg in Sjöberg and Bergmann 1969: 1; Wilcke 1972; Black 2002.
74  Sjöberg and Bergmann 1969: 47, 143–46; ETCSL 4.80.1, both with stricter renderings than given here. Consonant with this figure, Sargon, on his victory stela, carries a net in his right hand (above, note 37) and possibly a mace in his left (above, note 37). Like the mace, the battle net may have been an obsolete weapon by this time, wielded only in art and poetry, above, note 37.
75  Haul 2009.
76  CUSAS 26 270.
77  Diakonoff 1961: 113–16.
78  Tigay 1982.
79  George 2003, 2007b.
80  Chen 2013: 170; the impact of the deeds of Sargon on the *Epic of Gilgamesh* was also suggested by Bottéro 1965: 104.
81  Appendix Ib 6; Frayne 1993: 28. For the literary development of Akkadian royal inscriptions, Franke 1995; in general J. Westenholz 1998; further below, note 95.
82  Appendix Ib 14, 16, 19; Frayne 1993: 49.
83  Appendix Ib 26; with B. Foster 1982g, followed by Gelb and Kienast 1990: 255; differently Frayne 1993: 132–33; for similar phrasing, Appendix IIb 18.
84  Appendix Ib 28; Frayne 1993: 104.
85  Appendix Ib 16; Frayne 1993: 53.
86  Appendix Ib 16; for burial mounds, A. Westenholz 1970.
87  Appendix Ib 21; Gelb and Kienast 1990: 211.
88  Appendix Ib 16 etc.; Gelb and Kienast 1990: 208, 187; the precise meaning of this expression is disputed, but since the expression occurs in an Akkadian administrative document (BIN 8 144) in which a person "shows" certain accountable goods to a royal inspector, the translation "revealed" has been chosen here.
89  Appendix Ia 18; Frayne 1993: 113; Naram-Sin was also Ishtar's "husband" (Appendix Ib 23; Frayne 1993: 88–90).
90  Appendix Ia 28; Frayne 1993: 188.
91  Fronzaroli 2003: 194–95, 19 [29]; B. Foster 2006: 110–11.
92  Gelb and Kienast 1990: 381.
93  OSP 1 7.
94  *Muses,* 67 and Chapter 10 part 5.
95  Kupper 1971; Van Driel 1973; in general on war and monuments, Nadali 2007.
96  For the prestige of the Eshnunna dialect at Mari, Charpin 1993, 2012.
97  Alster 2005: 31–220. The translations offered here are sometimes quite different from Alster's, so a few comments have been included here to justify them.
98  Alster 2005: 56 line 5. "Subtle" for GALAM is based on the passage nam-dub-sar-ra níg-galam-galam-ma-bi mu-ni-in-pàd-pàd-dè-en "You show him all the subtleties of the scribal art" (Kramer 1949: 203 line 60, who renders "fine points").
99  Alster 2005: 58 line 14.
100 Alster 2005: 59–60 lines 15–18. In line 15, the Akkadian translation lays stress on disrespect rather than damage: passers-by will heedlessly trample the cultivated land and deem its proprietor a fool. The same thought is found in line 17: people will go to the well to get water and damage the cultivated ground in the process. As for 18, the saying implies that if one's front door is on a main street, the public will find themselves engaged with what goes on inside, the same idea offered in the preceding lines.
101 Alster 2005: 60–61 lines 19–27.
102 Alster 2005: 62 lines 28–30.
103 Alster 2005: 63 lines 32–34.
104 Alster 2005: 63–64 lines 35–38. Line 38 may mean that people become annoyed by those who constantly ask their advice.

105 Alster 2005: 64 line 41. This may mean that no matter what bone you draw as a lot, large or small, you are nervous because you are taking a chance and don't know the outcome.

106 Alster 2005: lines 44–46; these mean that it is always best to know precisely what something entails before you try it.

107 Alster 2005: 64 line 41 (variant).

108 B. Foster 1982h; in general Civil 1980; Steinkeller 2004b; for the use of Sumerian and Akkadian in the same administrative document, Keetman 2014.

109 B. Foster 1983b, 1986a, b; for possible cases of grammatical mistakes in Akkadian in the Mesag archive, Salgues 2011: 265 (with different explanation; in general on the Akkadian of this archive Markina 2012).

110 B. Foster 1982h; Steinkeller 2003b, 2004b; Van De Mieroop 2004. Steinkeller's contention (2004b: 68) that administrative documents were generally drafted after the fact, sometimes much later, may in general be true but is occasionally contradicted by such texts as MVN 3 56, which were clearly being written while some activity, such as apportioning or delivery of grain, was taking place in the scribe's presence. Such drafts may have been soon discarded. Unpublished examples of this type of text are in the Yale Babylonian Collection; they likely originated at Akkadian Isin. Against his contention that clay was not readily portable (2004b: 75), B. Foster 2011c. For discussion of the concept "archive" in Mesopotamia, contending that most groups of administrative documents should not be referred to as "archives," Charpin 2010: 101–12.

111 Michalowski 1993: 2–5; Kienast and Volk 1995: 1–20. A possible example of a trendy expression or class signature jargon is (*danniš dannišme*) *asihamma* "I am (very) upset)," discussed by Veenhof 1978/9; Kienast and Volk 1995: 153–54; Edzard 1996, with reference to other proposals; he suggests it means, "As the saying goes, I can only laugh." The basic meaning of the verb is to make a loud noise with the voice, such as a cry or burst of laughter.

112 Civil 1984; Cooper 1995; for the possibility that some pre-Akkadian texts could be read in either Sumerian or a Semitic language, Civil and Rubio 1999.

113 Civil 1984; Hallo 1996a.

114 Nissen 1988: 165. For the question of whether or not Sumerian was still a living, spoken language in the Akkadian period, Foster 1982i; Sallaberger 2004b; Woods 2006; differently Michalowski 2006b: 168–69. The letter translated in Chapter 10 part 6, dealing with everyday household matters, is proof that Sumerian was still a living language in the post-Akkadian period.

115 Van Dijk 1969a; Woods 2006: 97 thinks that Akkadian was "imposed" as the "official written language," although texts in Akkadian are rare in Sumer and administrators felt free to write even to the king himself in Sumerian, Kienast and Volk 1995: 102–4, so this proposal has to be rejected.

116 For the concept of translatable versus barbarian languages, Brock 1978; Galter 1995 proposes that Sumerian and Akkadian inscriptions were not in fact bilinguals but the Sumerian column was added in the Old Babylonian copies, but if such were the case, one would expect Sumerian versions of other inscriptions as well; the only clear instance of a Sumerian column added to an authentic inscription is a Neo-Babylonian copy of an inscription of Sharkalisharri, Appendix Ib 33; below, note 117.

117 Chapter 11 note 17.

118 In general, Michalowski 2006a; Gadotti 2010, Pruzsinszky 2010, Tonietti 2010.

119 Cooper 1983a: 52 (Appendix IIIb) lines 36–39.

120 Alster 1997: 1, 18 (1.70).

121 Below, note 132; ITT I 1412.

122 Ziegler 2010; Michalowski 2010a.

123 A. Westenholz 1999: 72; Shehata 2009, Ziegler 2010; Michalowski 2010b.

124 Steinkeller 2006; Ziegler 2007, 2010.

125  Tonietti 1998.
126  Groneberg 1999.
127  Gabbai 2008; Shehata 2009.
128  Heimpel 1998b. For lyres, Kilmer 1980/3; for harps, Stauder 1972/5 (who assumes that balag = harp); for arguments that balag was a drum, Black 1991: 28; further, Krispijn 2010. It is possible that the word changed meaning or that it was onomatopoetic, referring to any instrument that made a certain range or type of sound by vibration and a box.
129  Al-Rawi 1992.
130  Collon 1987 fig. 530; the inscription on the seal states that the player, Aman-Ishtar, was a servant of Tutanabshum; J. Westenholz 2011 argues that she is not a musician but holding some sort of cultic object.
131  Collon and Kilmer 1980; Krispijn 2010: 129.
132  M. Cohen 1976a; Martos 1991 No. 5 and the references cited there, 143–44; for female singers as witnesses and principals in contracts, Steinkeller 1982b: 366–68. For musical training in the Ur III period, Michalowski 2010a.
133  Important group in Limet 1973, with mention of E-igi-íl (PUL 2.20) in the Lagash region; further B. Foster 1989a: 158 note 11; A. Westenholz 2014: 148; in general Friberg 1987/90: 540–41; Robson 1999: 168–70; B. Foster and Robson 2004: 2.
134  B. Foster and Robson 2004: 3.
135  B. Foster and Robson 2004: 4; Whiting 1984; B. Foster and Robson 2004: 5.
136  B. Foster 1997b; Edzard 2004: 106.
137  Steinkeller 2013c.
138  In general Hurowitz 1998; Rochberg 2012.
139  Thureau-Dangin 1897a; Van Buren 1930: 273–76.
140  B. Foster 1981/2; this may be a forerunner to a record from the time of Ur-Namma of Ur listing provinces in terms of points on their peripheries, Kraus 1955.
141  B. Foster 1992. For a proposal that an itinerary could be based on a "forced march," Hallo 1964: 85.
142  Rochberg 2012.
143  Appendix IIc lines 82, 85–86.
144  A. Westenholz 1993; Nadali and Verderame 2008.
145  Michalowski 1993: 87.
146  M. Lambert 1956: 95, "On sent à les lire, à suivre la rectitude calme, la finesse et le nombre serré des traits, que ces scribes appartiennent – et se savent appartenir, à une époque de maîtrise de soi et de sûreté dans l'avenir."

# 10 Akkadian human values

## 1. Identity

Self-definition, reflection, and reminiscence are not to be found in the extant Akkadian written tradition. The Akkadian sense of self, that is, an awareness of unique identity, and the Akkadian individual, as a self-sufficient organism, are thus difficult to apprehend. It is possible, nevertheless, to gain some understanding of the Akkadian person as a legal, social, and moral being from surviving documents, as well as from later literature. [1]

There were several modes of expressing identity (Chapter 2 part 2). Inferiors identified themselves by their personal dependency on someone else, such as "he of . . .,"[2] whereas great dignitaries, including Sargon, were identified only by their given name, with no other qualifier, not even parentage.[3] To convey legal and social status, a document might note a person's citizenship in a given community, or use general terms, *dumu-gir* "free citizen"[4] or *mar Akkade* "Akkadian." The latter, originally a linguistic or ethnic term, in the Akkadian period came to refer to a dependent on the royal family, without regard to native language, place of birth, or family background.[5]

The proliferation during the Akkadian period of sculpture intended to preserve an individuated image of a notable or ruler, often inscribed with his name, is good evidence for a sense of personhood and a yearning to perpetuate it in some form even after death (Chapter 9 part 1).[6] Likewise, the presence, in mostly single burials, of non-standardized grave goods, notably professional tools and personal objects of the deceased, points to a feeling for individual identity, as does the increase in the number of cylinder seals and other effects inscribed with the names of the owners (Chapter 9 part 3).

The Akkadian idea of what defined a human being can be gleaned from later sources. People, unlike animals, cut and groomed their hair, anointed and decorated their bodies, wore woven garments rather than natural fur or animal skins, drank fermented beverages rather than water, and acted as social beings by upholding and defending the interests of the group to which they belonged.[7] The last is invoked in Akkadian names that refer to the family or clan as protection and support (Chapter 6 part 1).

The Akkadian elite cultivated traits of their class and individuality in their self-presentation and way of life. Unlike the majority of the population, they were expensively dressed, used cosmetics, and wore jewelry on the head, neck, chest, arms, wrists, fingers, and toes.[8] Their cosmetics included kohl, henna, and a paste made from hematite.[9] They ate a varied diet and drank several kinds of good beer and wine. As a sign of their high status, they feasted to enjoy the conviviality and pleasures of the table and to reward their subordinates, while reminding them of their dependency.[10] They attended school, where they received sufficient education to read and write in both Sumerian and Akkadian.[11] Their personal names invoked wealth and, in later times, Naram-Sin was proverbial for his riches.[12] They expected to be obeyed by their inferiors; the rhetoric of men in authority was forceful and assertive. When dealing with their equals or superiors, they were fain to speak and write with eloquence, even a touch of hyperbole, often expressing themselves in oaths, exclamations, and flowery speech.[13]

Indeed, of the senses and faculties, the Akkadians deemed speech the most important, as shown by the numerous names built on "word" and "mouth," and they thought it should be true and effective, for these were divine attributes.[14] Sight was less frequently invoked in personal names; hearing occurs in them most often in the context of a deity hearing the parents' prayer for a child.[15] Akkadian names also refer to knowledge and wisdom, or "knowing much," as these too were divine and royal attributes.[16]

Male physical strength, athleticism, and force of character were admired.[17] The successful man was the center of a large family and a prosperous household. By contrast, the hapless man, as described in Akkadian curses, was sickly, weak, tongue-tied, and lacked both authority and patronage. He had no children to keep his name alive and was steward of a paltry patrimony.[18]

A woman, to judge from personal names and from Enheduanna's poetry, was expected to be fiercely protective of her family and to devote herself to its interests. Her privacy was to be respected; when a notable gave gifts of clothing to the royal family, for instance, he presented them to the king and princes, but not to the royal women.[19] The names of most Akkadian queens are unrecorded, though they possessed estates and staff of their own.[20] The notable Mesag, when reckoning the personnel of his estate, listed himself but not his wife and children, nor the wives and children of his principal retainers.[21] Although non-royal women owned and inherited property and carried out transactions in their own names, Akkadian female success was counted in the private sphere, no matter what a woman's public influence might have been.[22] Priestesses may have been the exception to this pattern, perhaps because of their close, even conjugal, relationship with a deity.[23] Women maintained their separate identity even in death, as no clear instance of a wife buried with her husband has been found among the burials of the period. Occasionally, women were buried with infants, perhaps instances of death in childbirth.[24]

## 2.  Childhood and education

Some glyptic of the Akkadian period shows women delivering their babies in a seated position; women depicted lying on a bed may be giving birth or incubating dreams.[25] Infancy is attested in seals that depict women of elite status, perhaps princesses, holding a child on their knees, attended by servants and a nurse.[26] On the basis of their intimacy with the royal family, nurses probably enjoyed privileged positions at court.[27]

The experiences of Akkadian children may best be approached through their toys. Infants played with rattles, a toy mentioned in *The Curse of Agade* as emblematic of the small child at play. A fine metal example was found at Akkadian Adab, perhaps the plaything of a child of the elite.[28] Excavations at Nagar produced wheeled sheep, some of which had been broken and repaired, so they had been important to their young owners.[29] A few whistles were also found, especially in the shape of birds. If the sheep were toys to nurture and the whistles toys for the child to express himself, the numerous equids and model wheeled vehicles discovered were no doubt toys representing an admired status, as fire engines or aircraft are for modern children, an interpretation borne out by the prestige of equids and wheeled vehicles in Akkadian society. At Nagar and Gawra, favorite toys were model covered wagons, perhaps the farming and transport vehicles referred to in Akkadian administrative documents, drawn by clay equids that might be donkeys or hybrids.[30] The absence of toy pigs or cattle suggests that they were neither prestigious nor creatures to be nurtured. A winsome terracotta hare from Taya may have been a child's possession.[31] No toy weapons, household utensils, or furniture have been identified, though Akkadian Gawra yielded a clay model of a bed that could have been a doll's. No doll has been recognized as such; they were probably made of cloth or other perishable materials.[32] To judge from later sources, girls played rhythmic or circle games in the street, including jump rope; for boys, wrestling and ball-and-stick games may be supposed. Well-to-do families could afford slaves or nursemaids to look after their children.[33]

Children of the elite were sent to school or taught at home by their fathers. Literacy was presumably more widespread among men than women.[34] A great deal is known about education in later times, but for the Akkadian period little information is available beyond a scattering of learner's tablets from various sites. These consist of words, phrases, and metrological expressions. Students undoubtedly first learned writing by practicing signs in traditional sequences, such as tu ta ti, and learning sign names and pronunciations, then moved on to copying short texts, such as proverbs, sayings, or fables, and legal and epistolary phrases. In due course, they also had to master mathematics, metrology, drawing, and geometry and to memorize long lists of words and the correct spellings of personal names.[35] Although no major work of literature copied out by an Akkadian student has survived, some learner's tablets contain proverbs and literary excerpts. This example is from a collection of racy sayings: "If a girl is attractive, a man must have slept with her."[36] One student quoted a riddle, without the answer: "Having no corner, having no side, he was made for water."[37]

The core of the curriculum was Sumerian, even if many of the students probably spoke another language at home. The sign and word lists they studied were in some cases very ancient, such as a list of professions, including administrators, craftsmen, and cultic personnel (in one tradition proudly headed by the scribe himself). There were also lists of plants, birds, fish, and other animals; objects of wood, metal, fabric, and clay; types of food; the names of cities and gods; and geographical and topographical features, such as fields and threshing floors. A puzzling document mainly enumerates valuable materials. Despite the political fragmentation of pre-Akkadian Sumer, the content of these lists seems to have been strikingly uniform from city to city. Already in the pre-Akkadian period, a column might be added with an explanation in the local Semitic language, but so far no substantial examples of bilingual Sumero-Akkadian lists have turned up from the Akkadian period itself. An Akkadian-period god list is illegible.[38]

Copies of these lists were written and in one instance even signed by an advanced student, who kept it, perhaps as a kind of diploma, even after he had moved up through the ranks and become governor of Lagash.[39] Akkadian notables like Mesag were proud to sign themselves "dub-sar," meaning graduate of a scribal school.[40] For the ambitious, the ability to write well the elegant new script of the reign of Naram-Sin was essential for bureaucratic preferment.[41]

Akkadian education prepared young members of the elite for positions of management and responsibility in the empire and perhaps, by the time of Naram-Sin, also indoctrinated them in the fundamental values and worldview of their class.[42]

## 3.   Happiness and sorrow

Insofar as life emerged from and ended in darkness, as later Mesopotamian traditions held, light and vitality were interconnected: the healthy person's face beamed and the gods shone brilliantly.[43] The Akkadian word for "light" or "radiance" was often used in names, such as "He-Came-Out-Radiant" (comparing birth to dawn?), "Light-Came-Out," and "Father-Is-Radiant(ly-Happy)." The Akkadian word for happiness or rejoicing occurs in personal names, such as "Joy," "Happiness," "She-Was-Happy-for-Me" and "My-Lord-Rejoiced." In this instance, "my lord" might be a god, or a term of endearment, as seems to be the case in later Babylonian love poetry, referring to a man who commanded a woman's affections.[44]

Both joy and sorrow were associated with loud vocalization, such as cheering, ululation, or wailing. In contrast, anger left Enheduanna speechless and unable to perform her duties. The savage joy that surged over her at her reinstatement led her to exult over the death and destruction of her enemies. Gentler expressions of happiness are found in *The Curse of Agade*'s description of the new capital, alive with promise and plenty:

> Like a youth building a house for the first time,
> Like a girl arranging her private chamber,
> That she provision its larders,

That lots and houses be available in that city,
That its populace dine on the best of food,
That its populace draw the best of drink,
That a person fresh washed make merry in the courtyard,
That people throng the festival grounds,
That people who knew each other feast together, . . .
Holy Inanna did not stop to rest.[15]

Moments of private sorrow may be detected in burials: a man's bag of tools laid on his chest, just before his grave was filled; a ribbon wrapped tenderly around a lock of hair; a bowl placed carefully in the deceased's hand, instead of with the other goods in his tomb.[16]

## 4. Competition and coercion

The new social order that emerged in the Akkadian period created a class of royal dependents who relied on their connections, energies, and wits for advancement. The successful Akkadian earned his place by commitment to the royal house and its ways, hoping thereby to reap benefits far beyond the expectations of ordinary people, who lived out their lives tilling the soil their ancestors had, following their father's profession, and raising their families.[17] In consequence, rivalries among the elite were perhaps more intense than in other walks of life. It was they, after all, who favored the cylinder seals showing scenes of introduction and favor at court, fierce combats, and warfare even among the gods (Chapter 9 part 3; Figures 6.2a, 9.9). We sense competition among a notable's subordinates, for example, in a letter in which one of them asks for a status-enhancing wagon, but wants the order to surrender it to come directly from the notable, in preference to transmitting it himself (Chapter 4 part 3). The word for conquering or overcoming rivals occurs in Akkadian personal names, mostly said of gods, but in one case of a newborn, meaning perhaps that a boy took precedence over his sisters.[18]

Competition carried over into athletics and games, of which various forms of combat sports may have enjoyed special prestige.[49] In *The Curse of Agade*, the poet compares Naram-Sin to an aggressive boxer and wrestler, when he took on the Ekur project in Nippur:

Like a boxer striding into the great courtyard,
He clenched his fist at Ekur.
Like a wrestler crouching to start a match,
He acted as if the god's dwelling was a lightweight.[50]

Foot-races, ball games, and other sports remain unattested as such for the period. The same is true for board games, though they undoubtedly existed. Earlier and later Mesopotamian game boards suggest that a popular game involved moving pieces through a set of squares by throwing die, with the possibility of sending the other player's piece home by landing on the square it occupied.[51]

Identifying playing pieces or astragals in the archaeological record is often problematic. There may have been public animal combats but the idea has not found wide acceptance among scholars.[52]

Coercion may be seen in cases involving someone acceding to pleas or threats: "See here, if Gutians do take any livestock, you yourself will have to pay!"[53] On the whole, Akkadian notables saw themselves as dominating local populations, rather than working pacifically with them. In a letter sent by one notable to another, the writer addresses his compeer, perhaps playfully, as "The Yoke of Ishtar."[54]

## 5.   Love and sexuality

The Akkadian royal family was the first dynasty to suggest sexual intimacy with the divine. In the case of Naram-Sin, he states that he prevailed over the rebels "on account of the love that Ishtar bore him." On his Victory Stele (Figure 1.6), the king's body is deliberately vigorous and alluring and on the stone mold, it is no doubt he who sits bare-chested in the presence of the goddess, who hands him the lead ropes of defeated peoples (Figure 9.8).[55] In other works of Akkadian sculpture (Figure 9.7), the royal body is visible through thin garments, heroically powerful but also enticing to the goddess of love and war.[56] Ivory carvers achieved similar sensuous effects in statuettes of lightly clad women, presumably singers or dancing girls (Chapter 5 part 10). The notion that gods could love mortals is found in personal names, not with Ishtar but with such deities as Malik, Dagan, Sin and Ilu(m).[57]

Although the later language of love is richly documented, that of the Akkadian period is largely restricted to a magic spell, intended to make a woman submit to a man's desire. The charm on the beloved's thighs may be a small figure, like the Greek Eros, or perhaps a love bead. Many interpretations of the passage about the young women going to a garden to collect aromatics are possible, but it likely refers to the well-known magical procedure in which some trace is gathered of the person on whom the spell is to be cast. The would-be lover addresses the beloved directly, claiming that her body and senses are already in his grasp and imagining her erotic thoughts about him. The magician concludes by granting her no release until she finds and embraces the man who desires her:

> Ea loves the love charm,
> The love charm, son of Ishtar,
> It sits on her thighs.
> I am guided by the sapflow of the incense tree.
> Two beautiful maidens were blossoming,
> They went down to the garden,
> To the garden they went down,
> They cut from the sapflow of the incense tree.
> I have seized your mouth full of saliva,
> I have seized your lustrous eyes,
> I have seized your vagina full of wetness.
> I climbed into the garden of the moon,

I cut down poplar to light her (way).
Seek for me among the boxwood,
As the shepherd seeks the sheep,
The goat her kid,
The ewe her lamb,
The jenny her foal.
"His arms are two round bundles of fruit,
"His lips are oil and harpsong.
"A cruse of cedar oil is in his hand,
"A cruse of cedar oil is on his shoulder,"
(So) the love charms have bespoken her,
Then driven her to ecstasy!
I have seized your mouth for love-making!
By Ishtar and Ishara I conjure you:
May you find no release from me
Till your neck and his neck lie close beside![58]

A miniature golden phallus found in an Akkadian-period grave at Ur suggests that sexuality was important to its owner. Since phallic symbolism was not common in Mesopotamian art, one wonders if the deceased was a prostitute or some other professional in the arts of love.[59]

An unusual erotic image is found on a seal dating to the early post-Akkadian period at Mari. It shows two men(?), apparently naked, one of whom strikes a tambourine, while the other approaches what may be a nude, somewhat steatopagous woman leaning over a kind of table before an altar-like structure. Two figures in the background seem to be piling up and measuring grain near a plant. This tableau may represent a rite of fertility, involving intercourse with a cult woman.[60]

A Babylonian text composed long after the Akkadian period opines that the man who falls in love "forgets sorrow and care."[61] A hint of the same sentiment may be found in an Akkadian student text, which apparently quotes a love poem addressed to a woman: "Prevail over misery with the delight of your loins . . ."[62]

## 6.   Home life and family

The average Akkadian urban house was modestly planned and appointed.[63] The simplest consisted of two or three rooms around an open courtyard or a roofed larger room. The walls were built of different sizes of brick, some salvaged, and were 60–80 cm. thick and covered with a thick layer of mud plaster. The floors were packed earth or debris, though bath or toilet rooms could have baked-brick floors coated with bitumen or dirt floors coated by gypsum. Windows were small (a well-preserved window in a large house is only 25 cm across) and sometimes fitted with clay grilles.[64] Doorways were narrow by modern standards, spanned by timbers or mud brick arches, and could be closed with a wooden leaf that pivoted on a stone socket.[65] Roofs were flat or slightly pitched, made of wooden rafters supporting matting covered with mud.

Larger houses expanded on the basic module, surrounding the central space with rooms on all four sides, secondary rooms adjoining them, some for such specific purposes as a family shrine, and service areas beyond. Plans for elaborate houses were sometimes drawn on clay tablets (Chapter 9 part 9; Figure 9.12).[66] An example from Nippur shows a main entrance opening into a vestibule, from which a staircase leads to a second story, while a doorway opens to a courtyard surrounded on three sides by rooms, with perhaps service rooms beyond.[67]

In the rural Akkadian-period settlement at Tell Taya, in the Tell Afar plain in northwestern Mesopotamia, the majority of the simple houses belonged to farmers who enjoyed a modest, even a good, standard of living for several generations. Their household goods included locally made and imported pottery, flint tools, small objects of faience, and imported copper implements. In some cases, people were buried in vaults beneath their houses.[68]

The principal furnishings of Akkadian houses were made of clay or mud brick (benches, ovens, and stoves); wood (roof ladder, doors, beds, chairs, stools, tables or tray-tables); textiles (bedding, hangings, rugs, clothing); reed (baskets, trunks, matting); leather (sacks, boxes). Most of these have left little or no trace in the archaeological record. Surviving items include plates and bowls, buckets, tools, weapons, garment pins (Figure 5.3a, e), cosmetic implements, and knives. There were ivory or bone combs, needles, and other small objects, as well as stone querns, grinding and polishing tools, and door-pivots.

A late pre-Akkadian inventory, consisting perhaps of the inherited contents of a typical simple house, includes one poplar bed, two wooden breadboards, two wooden hand mills, two long wooden boxes and two tall boxes, ten ox hides, and four cups, among other objects, plus small quantities of barley, emmer, and tallow.[69] Beds were probably the major piece of furniture in most houses. A list of fine beds includes one for a high priestess made of poplar with claw feet of another wood; a second made of another variety of poplar, also with claw feet; a third made of poplar with thin olive-wood feet; and another made of boxwood with oak feet. These were presumably luxury pieces seldom encountered in ordinary homes.[70]

What appear to be inventories and valuations of an inheritance portion from a family home at Nippur consisted of two lots of arable land totaling about 3.24 hectares, seventy-two square meters of living space, five pieces of lapis weighing 41.5 grams, a bowl, a chair, a piece of linen, and a cloak. A second portion of the same estate consisted of 4.32 hectares of arable land and forty-eight square meters of living space, on which the tax was forty shekels of silver. If the two areas in the inheritance document refer to the same house, then its total living space falls well within the 80–144 square meters range of the late Akkadian private houses at Eshnunna.[71]

As for household metal items, excavations of the Akkadian quarter at Adab yielded a considerable number of metal bowls, spear and arrow points, knives, long hair pins with lapis or carnelian heads, needles, rings, bracelets, tweezers and nail cutters, picks and adzes, as well as children's toys.[72] Copper implements (axe, toggle pin, measuring cups and rod) are found in a list of household effects (or a bride gift) along with festival garments, cloaks, an Akkadian toga-garment, under-shirts, headbands, a lapis cylinder seal, beads and other jewelry, sixteen shekels of silver, small quantities of flour, and a leather bucket.[73] Another list of personal effects from a wealthy Umma household includes an imposing array of metal kettles, small pots, cups, ladles, cutlery, adzes, and axes.[74]

For warmth and cooking, Akkadian houses had fire pits hollowed in the ground or brick structures. Bread was baked in ovens, with a bin next to them to hold ashes. Larger houses might have round ovens for raised or flat bread and even clay cooking ranges. The Arch House at Eshnunna, for example, had a range in the form of a clay box 1.75 m long, 1.40 m wide, and .50 m high, with burner holes on the top, divided into three parts by partitions with openings to serve as flues to the central firebox.[75]

Household valuables were sometimes hidden in jars beneath the floor. One at Eshnunna (compare Figure 5.3b) had a lapis cylinder seal with silver caps, twelve wrought silver ornaments, four cast silver ornaments, two silver ingots, one silver frog amulet, a silver ring, and eight beads, including one of gold and six of carne-lian.[76] Another such jar contained two silver rings, two silver earrings, a necklace of about forty small silver beads, various lapis and glazed quartz beads, a stone weight, and a chisel, vanity set, and ring of copper.[77]

The nuclear family was the basic unit of Akkadian society (Chapter 2 part 2). According to personal names based on kinship terms, the ideal father was kind, god-like, a mountain, radiant like the sun, worthy of praise, an object of love, while the ideal mother was loving and supportive. Names reveal ambivalence about siblings. A brother could be fair and a source of pride, but he could also be a bully, as suggested by two personal names that may mean "He-Spited-Them (his sisters)" and "He-Conquered-Them" (his sisters or, perhaps, "He-Reached-Them," meaning that he was the last in a sequence). Sisters were less clearly defined in names, being just "sister" or "my sister." A paternal uncle could also be honored in names as a protector or master.[78]

A girl learned at home the arts of cooking, brewing, and managing the house-hold. Once she was married, it was the duty of her husband to see that sufficient foods, or funds to buy them, were available to her. A housewife took pride in her domestic skills, even if they were undervalued or taken for granted. Despite its obscurities, a unique Sumerian letter from a woman, evidently to her husband, dating to a few generations later than the Akkadian period, shows the roles of the resourceful, conscientious housewife and mother, extending in this case, to her arranging to lease a field so the family could have grain:

> Say this to Ki'ag: Why is this? Concerning the children, he speaks ill of me (but) he is the one who has tied up for the larder sack (just) one left-over² loaf of bread and two measures of flour! Did he not lock up from the woman whatever grain there was in the house as well? I did not go into his strong room unless Atu was present. Would I be one to squander the goods that are his? I did take out the eleven brewing loaves that were there in his house, I used them up to sustain the household! As for the field-lease grain, it was the

workers who took that away. There isn't any grain in the house at all! I spoke to Lu-Nanna about a field, he said to me, "I'll give you this one." If he does not give the field he has, I will have to take up a field-lease somewhere else. As for oxen, he has to send me back an ox driver. This is why I have no grain in the house! He must provide me with grain! It is urgent! He must bring me some! Igidu told me that the messenger of (the god) Shara has already gone off to him. He must not detain him, he must come here![79]

## 7.   Death and burial

In Mesopotamian thought, death obliterated everything that was attractive or enjoyable about a human being, leaving only a cold, unresponsive spirit dwelling in a cheerless afterlife of hunger, thirst, and envy of the living.[80] Proper burial and remembrance of the dead were hallmarks of civilization. In late pre-Akkadian Lagash, black stone statues of rulers, made during their lifetimes, may have served after their deaths as both memorials of their appearance and objects of offerings.[81] This practice might explain the proliferation in the Akkadian period of black stone statues of Manisthusu and other rulers, and of statues in less exotic stones of such notables as Naram-Sin's majordomo, Su'ash-takal (Figure 5.4b), as well as priestesses and other elite women (Chapter 9 part 1; Figure 9.2). For people in less exalted ranks of society, remembrance of ancestors may have taken the form of a regular ceremony, presided over by the head of the family, in which their names were mentioned and food served (Chapter 11 part 1). As in later periods, fear of the ghosts of the dead motivated prayers and rituals to ward them off or appease them.[82] In some larger private houses, space was dedicated to the worship of family or household gods or remembrance of the deceased. As in later periods, there may have been family relics, such as old documents, which preserved the names of ancestors.[83]

After the body had been washed, the deceased was dressed and adorned with the dead person's best garment pins and jewelry, while the living went unwashed and unkempt, ripped their clothes or wore inferior ones, scratched themselves, and tore out their hair.[84] Wealthier families often hired professional mourners to weep or sing laments. A procession carried the deceased to the interment, where the grave goods were displayed. Favorite possessions of the deceased were brought, or gifts given of items similar to those he or she may have enjoyed in life. The deceased was also provided with toiletries, such as a comb and razor, as well as vessels and, on occasion, food.[85] Akkadian graves at Ur, for example, included dates, burned grain, a sheep's head, and the bones of animals, fish, and birds.[86] To judge from contemporaneous Ebla, the Akkadian burial ritual may have included a funeral ceremony at the place of interment (cemetery, monument, or hypogeum). A public display of grief and a rite of purification or release for the family of the deceased were performed.[87]

An Akkadian tablet of unknown provenance lists grave goods for several people, corresponding well to the typical contents of Akkadian burials at Ur. One person had 2 ½ shekels of silver (probably in the form of jewelry), a lapis brooch weighing 2 ½ shekels, and a cloak; another had ½ shekel of silver and a cylinder seal; a third had a wooden stand or stool.[88]

Akkadian graves and cemeteries are best known from those of non-elite people; no Akkadian royal tombs have been discovered. Dating burials to the Akkadian period mainly relies on the presence of diagnostic cylinder seals and ceramics. For some burials lacking these, dating depends on their stratigraphic association with securely Akkadian graves, but this can be problematic. While the dead, especially children, could be buried beneath house floors, most adults were interred individually in cemeteries, often, but not always, with a small number of objects. Graves were generally not marked with monuments, mounds, or other external indicators, so expenditures were limited to the funeral and burial.[89] At Kish it appears that there may have been a preference for interment near important religious buildings.[90] The greenish clay prevalent in many Diyala burials and the unidentified green ash that was used for the "interment" of the sanctuaries at Nagar raise the possibility that some specific, but as yet unknown, funerary practice was in use in the Akkadian north.[91]

Grave goods, from items of personal adornment and sets of implements to pottery and cylinder seals, reveal the economic and social status of the deceased, as well as the material culture of the person's daily life. In the Akkadian period, the great diversity of grave goods suggests that most probably belonged to the deceased, rather than being gifts offered after death. It is not clear if the dead were thought to need personal items in the next world, or whether survivors avoided using them, so interred them with their owners. In addition, because of the high value Akkadian society placed on individual display of wealth, especially in the form of jewelry, coiffure, and clothing (Chapter 5 parts 5 and 9), the items of personal adornment in graves are likely those worn by the deceased in his lifetime. The sets of tools and raw materials likewise suggest that they too had been the property of the deceased. Ritual objects, such as vessels or shells for libations, may sometimes have been included.[92]

The ceramic inventory of Akkadian burials also varies widely. Some burials have storage vessels rather than plates or cups, but others have clay or metal drinking sets.[93] Some burials have numerous pots in different sizes and shapes, others none at all. In certain cases, the ceramics may reflect the deceased's profession, such as a cook, potter, perfumer, or brewer.[94]

One of the most elaborate Akkadian-period graves was found at Tell Razuk in the Himrin Basin. Burial 12 consisted of a 4 × 2.5 m chamber, connected by a tunnel to a smaller one, where the body was placed. In the larger were two equids, perhaps donkeys, and a remarkable set of pottery vessels evidently for brewing or the manufacture of perfumes and aromatics. The ensemble included a vat with a strainer with exceptionally large holes in the sides set upright inside it, a spouted jar lying inside the strainer, and several large jars nearby. There was also a trough-shaped, spouted stand, with three wide supports intended to hold a jar pierced with a drain hole. The excavators suggested that some of the jars were for raw ingredients, others for finished products. Since there were no vessels for the consumption of food, these may have been made of wood. Chisels, arrowheads, and fragments of weapons were also present in this burial.[95] In Burial 11, the deceased was interred with a copper pin, and a stone bowl was set in his left hand, held up to his mouth.[96]

Of three modest burials dated by the excavators to the early Akkadian period at Tutub (Graves 159–161), one contained two adults, unlike the single burials elsewhere. Redating of the Diyala material has added additional tombs to this corpus, including one with an Akkadian cylinder seal. At Tutub, the graves seem poorer than those in Sumer, with not a piece of gold or silver jewelry.[97]

At Assur, seven of the eight burials dated to the Akkadian period are simple pits with a small space to one side for the grave goods; the eighth is a unique case of a subterranean chamber vaulted in stone.[98]

A cemetery of 367 Akkadian burials at Ur comprised mostly inhumations directly in the ground, with a few instances of wickerwork coffins.[99] Grave 503 is of particular interest, as it was for a servant of "the daughter of Sargon of Akkad" (surely Enheduanna). It contained no pottery but four copper vessels, as well as an axe, razors, a cutting tool (possibly for trimming hair?), bracelets, and earrings.[100]

People of comparable status did not have standard assemblages of grave goods. Near the royal servant's burial, Grave 577 held silver earrings, beads, a copper pin, an assortment of cockle shells, plus seven clay pots: a wide-mouthed jar, two large and one small ring-base jars, a small cup, an open cooking pot, and a stand, perhaps intended to hold the cooking pot when it was hot. This was very likely a woman's kitchenware. Grave 575 had beads, a cylinder seal, a long copper garment pin, a possible hair cutting tool, and a reticule, but its five clay vessels, all jars, were different from those in neighboring 577. Two of the jars had ring and two rounded bases, and there was one finer piece with lugs at the sides, for suspension or attaching a cover. These may have been the possessions of someone who had fine oils and unguents. The deceased in Grave 574, next to it, also had a long pin, but in addition earrings, a copper ring, and, unlike the others, considerable household crockery, including a small bowl, a tall jar for liquid, a wide-mouth jar, a large storage jar, a second storage jar with a ring base, and a jar mounted on a tall base. None of the jars in these four tombs was similar to any jar in another.

In Grave 435, one of the wealthiest Akkadian burials at Ur, the body was enclosed in a wickerwork coffin framed by natural tree branches, the head resting on a row of three bricks. The deceased wore a pair of silver earrings, four strings of beads of gold, lapis, carnelian, silver, and copper covered with gold foil, a silver bracelet on each arm, and a heavy copper toe ring. A long copper pin with a lapis and gold head lay on the arm, along with two cylinder seals, one or both of which may have been fastened to it. This person could well have been a notable, interred in an Akkadian toga-garment secured with the pin (Figures 5.4b, 5.3a, e). A copper bowl was set between the hands. Behind the body were two cockleshells containing red cosmetic pigments and fragments of a bone or ivory comb. The only ceramic vessel, a squat jar made of fine red clay covered with a thin hematite wash, was perhaps for libations, as it resembles those held by gods in cylinder seals.[101] Comparable jars in clay and copper were found in Grave 659, also inside the coffin.

As in Burial 11 at Tell Razuk, the decedent in Grave 671 held a copper bowl in the left hand, with a squat clay jar nearby. This individual, likely a woman of means, wore a gold band across the forehead, large lunate gold earrings, a necklace of gold, silver, carnelian, lapis, and agate, perhaps with a cylinder seal attached to it, two copper bracelets, a gold finger-ring, and two copper garment pins.

In several instances at Ur, it appears that craftsmen or professionals were buried with the tools of their trade, like the brewer or perfumer at Tell Razuk. The person in Grave 958 had a bag of materials for manufacturing beads, including a palette, a stone grinding or pounding tool, a flint blade attached to a long strip of thin copper, a cube of steatite, assorted chips of flint, carnelian, lapis, and other stones, an unfinished lapis bead, a small copper drill, and lumps of red hematite pigment. Surrounded by several clay vessels, including a squat jar, he had been laid in a mat-lined trough. Grave 121 was surely a woodworker's, as he was buried with an axe, cutting tool, razor, saw, chisel, and awl. A midwife may have been interred in Grave 138, for it contained a knife, a whetstone, and a single plano-convex brick, perhaps a ritual "brick of birth," as known from later evidence.[102]

A fair number of Akkadian burials at Ur included model boats of the bellum type (used in pre-modern times for short-range navigation in the Gulf), often with pots and other grave goods placed in or near them. The model boat in Grave 627, for example, was made of bitumen, .88 m long and .30 m wide, and had two pots inside and two beside it. Although some would see these as symbolic boats for crossing the river of death to the netherworld, this may be reading too much into the evidence. Instead, burial with a model boat was perhaps instead a local custom at Ur, conceivably related to Ur's role in sea trade.[103] Among the miscellaneous objects in the Ur graves were a shell lamp in the shape of a bird's head, ostrich eggs, gaming pieces, a quern, an inlaid wooden box, counting tokens, and baskets.[104]

Burials in the Akkadian quarter at Adab probably contained pottery similar to that found elsewhere, but the excavator ignored the ceramic material. One grave had jewelry consisting of a gold rosette brooch (Figure 5.3c) with a red stone carnelian encircled by nine red and blue lapis stones, eighty-six gold beads, a pair of gold earrings, and sixty-five carnelian, four lapis, and three agate beads.[105]

## 8.   The good life and respect for the past

What the well-lived life of the Akkadian period meant may be deduced from both textual and material evidence. For most people, the good life united their group identity as members of an extended family, clan, or community with their individual identity as productive members of a nuclear family (Chapter 2 part 2). The harshness, violence, and fluctuations of fortune that marked the establishment and preservation of the Akkadian state no doubt intensified personal anxiety and insecurity. Yet it was these same factors that enticed the ambitious man with new opportunities. He could forsake both his community and his parental domain to enter the king's service, hoping to attract preferment and to meet successfully the competitive challenges that would scarcely have faced him if he had tilled an inherited field or followed his father's profession. For a woman, the most likely path for advancement was to marry someone on that career trajectory, bear his children, and run his household. Careers open to the single woman were few: midwife, nurse to other people's children, dream interpreter, tavern keeper, singer.

For those who became part of the new order, the Akkadian ideal meant wealth displayed in the form of fine clothes in the latest fashion, jewelry, a large, well-furnished household, and slaves or servants. Prosperity was a sign of favor and success, good health a sign of moral rectitude, respect and obedience signs of high social status. A bright, alert face, a strong sense of personal dignity, vigor of mind and body, and serene self-confidence speak to later ages through Akkadian art and literature.

For many at the time, the Akkadian way must have felt like a rude break with a core Mesopotamian value of honoring the past. The Akkadian kings vaunted their achievements as unexampled in human experience. Akkadian notables lived as none but the gods had lived before, their opulent manors and fortified administrative centers towering over ordinary people's houses and their estates dwarfing previous holdings. As for the gods themselves, their sanctuaries were cleared of prior monuments, so that Akkadian works, as well as exotic objects brought thence by Akkadian valor, could dominate their halls and chambers. Their priests and priestesses were now drawn from the most privileged ranks of Akkadian society.

The ordinary person sometimes found it possible to meld the traditional way of life within the community and family with the high-stakes struggle for status and wealth in the new order. At Umma, for example, Ur-Shara and his wife Ama-e actively availed themselves of opportunities, but stayed in their native city, and, in a quarter century of business success, never seem to have dealt directly with an Akkadian notable.

Yet others dreamed like some anonymous Akkadian apprentice scribe at Eshnunna, stylus in hand, of the good life awaiting him in Agade, with his own donkey, house, and garden.[106]

## Notes

1 For these categories, B. Foster 2011b; Steinert 2012.
2 Gelb 1957: 249–50 suggests that this was more characteristic of the Akkadian – speaking north than of Sumer.
3 BdI 63, 3–4: gìr-gin Sar-rúm-GI-kam "journey of Sargon." By the time of Naram-Sin such entries were usually just "the king"; B. Foster 1980; BIN 8 291 (Mesag); B. Foster 1982a: 48 and CUSAS 26 174 (Yetib-Mer).
4 In administrative documents, such as BIN 8 314 and CUSAS 13 15, dumu-gi$_7$ meant "citizen" as opposed to "dependent worker"; it is not necessary to imagine a special category of workers so called (Steinkeller 2003b: 44–45; Dahl 2010: 289). This confuses legal or social status with a work obligation. In literature, the term may have meant something like "of pure Sumerian lineage," as opposed to a foreigner; Wilcke 1974: 224–30. In legal contexts, it apparently meant someone who was born free and had to perform certain service or someone who was born a slave and had been freed; Civil 2011: 254 (mostly referring to women).

5 B. Foster 2000, noting that "sons of Akkade" could be of Sumerian birth and lineage; for the concept "men of the king," Diakonoff 1959: 220–27; 1982: 69–70 and 97–98. For example, one of the "sons of Akkade," a certain Uru'inimgina, to be distinguished from the pre-Akkadian ruler of that name, came from the Sumerian ruling elite of Lagash; Hrozny 1909: 219; Sharashenidze 1973; Milone 1998; B. Foster 2000.

6 Radner 2005; Suter 2008.

7 Foster 2011b.

8 Cassin 1980/83; B. Foster 2010a; the use of jewelry is discussed below, part 6.

9 So Banks 1912: 312, but doubtful; hematite, kept in seashells, was found in various burials at Ur, e.g., Woolley 1934: 204, 245; in general Bimson 1980; Cassin 1980/3.

10 In general, Milano 1994b, 2012; Chapter 4 part 7; for banqueting and social status, Bottéro 1994.

11 Below, note 35. For schooling, A. Westenholz 1974/77; for on-the-job training, B. Foster 1982d. The high social and economic rewards awaiting the person who goes to school are promised in a programmatic post-Akkadian school text, *In Praise of the Scribal Art* (*Muses*, 1023–24). Little is known of the social context of Akkadian schooling; in general, George 2005; Veldhuis 2006a, 2010.

12 Alster 1997: 4.9. For wealth in names, Gelb 1957: 200–201 ("Ishtar-is-my-Wealth"; "My-God-is-my-Wealth"); the possibility that the word *šara'u* "to be/become rich" occurs in Akkadian names (Gelb 1957: 283) is not accepted by the dictionaries. As for wealth in general, a Sumerian proverb held that wealth makes a person important (Alster 1997: 1.17). Naram-Sin is mentioned in a saying "The east wind is the wind of prosperity, the friend of Naram-Sin" (Alster 1997: 4.9). Assuming east wind here means a wind blowing from the east, this suggests that Naram-Sin's wealth may have been seen as based on his eastern campaigns, an interesting historical retrospection.

13 References in Kienast and Volk 1995: 90, 132, 251 (s.v. *anni* "now then, see here!"); note the unique passage CUSAS 13 169 rev. 2: "*a'e a'e!*" (= "help, help!"?) Who is like my father?" (Please arrange that I be given food in the form of ducklings, dates, and fish).

14 Gelb 1957: 210–11.

15 Gelb 1957: 46, 274–75.

16 Gelb 1957: 17–18.

17 For "strong" or "mighty" as a common element in names, Gelb 1957: 112–14; "mighty" was even a royal title first used in the Akkadian period, Seux 1965; Hallo 1980; for athletics, Boese 1968/9; Rollinger 2011/x.

18 For the power of speech, post-Akkadian Sumerian proverbs say, "The wife of a man who speaks humbly is a slave woman" (Alster 1997: 7.44) and, for a woman, "My power of speech makes me the equal of a man" (Alster 1997: 7:45; Alster's interpretation takes no account of the emesal form). For curses, Pomponio 1990; further Chapter 6 part 6.

19 CT 50 52 = B. Foster 1982b: 133–34.

20 For Tashlultum, wife of Sargon, Frayne 1993: 36–37. For land held by the queen (of Naram-Sin), MAD 5 67; for Tuda-shar-libbish, the queen of Sharkalisharri, Frayne 1993: 198–200; for the evidence from Ebla of the special status of queens, Matthiae 2009.

21 Winter 1987.

22 Edzard 1968 no. 51 (BIN 8 175); MDP 14 19 = Steinkeller and Postgate 1992: 99.

23 B. Foster 1987a: 57–59.

24 Delougaz, Hill, and Lloyd 1967: 89 no. 79; 85–86 no. 72 (both pre-Akkadian).

25 Asher-Greve 1987; Parayre 1997; Battini 2006.

26 Parayre 1997.

27 Biga 1997.

28 For birth of a child, Stol 2000; Polonsky 2006. For girlhood, mostly from a legal standpoint of virginity and marriage, Landsberger 1968. For the copper rattle, Banks 1912:

310. For playing with a rattle as characteristic of a happy child in the *Curse of Agade*, Cooper 1983a: 52–53 (Appendix IIIb) lines 34–35.

29 McDonald in Oates, Oates, and McDonald 2001: 271–74.

30 Speiser 1935: pl. XXXVa; Chapter 4 part 3 and note 28.

31 McDonald in Oates, Oates, and McDonald 2001: 274; Reade 1973: pl. 68–69.

32 Speiser 1935: pl. XXXVb; for dolls, gaming pieces, and other figural toys, Landsberger 1960: 117–29.

33 Above, note 27 and in general Stol 2012: 240.

34 For literacy in general, Wilcke 2000, who suggests that more people could read than write (2000: 48). The Akkadian notable Mesag wrote some of his records in the first person, a good sign that he wrote them himself (Wilcke 2000: 23). For literacy among women, Lion 2011; Stol 2012: 234–36.

35 For the Akkadian period, A. Westenholz 1974/77; B. Foster 1982d; B. Foster and Robson 2004; Veldhuis 2014b: 139–42. For sign and word lists, A. Westenholz 1985; Veldhuis 2004, 2006a, 2010, 2014a, 2014b; Chapter 5 note 48 and below, note 39. For later periods, Robson 2001; Tanret 2002; George 2005; Rubio 2009: 39–41. For context and examples of Akkadian learner's exercises, De Lillis Forest, Milano, and Mori 2007; CUSAS 23 203–12.

36 CUSAS 23 200 ii 5–6.

37 CUSAS 23 201 rev. 6–8. Perhaps the solution was "water skin," "eel," or "fish," but why these would be referred to as "he" is unclear; for riddles, Cavigneaux 2006/8.

38 A. Westenholz 1974/7: 101; Cavigneaux 1980/83: 612–16.

39 Schileiko 1914; Bauer 1987/90. Schileiko (78 note 1) knew of a possible companion piece in the hands of a dealer; this may be the item published by W. Lambert 1988. Further Chapter 5 note 48. The prism was an Akkadian-period innovation, Chapter 1 note 57.

40 B. Foster 1987a: 57 line 1.

41 B. Foster 1986b: 49.

42 A. Westenholz 1974/7: 107–10.

43 In general, Jaques 2006; for brightness of color and divinity, Cassin 1968: 103–19.

44 *Muses,* 156 note 1.

45 Cooper 1983a: 50–55 (Appendix IIIb) lines 10–18, 24.

46 Woolley 1934: 206 grave 958; 205 Grave 205; an infant in Grave 6 at Tutub (Akkadian period?) was laid to rest with two fly amulets and numerous beads. A small stone bowl was placed tenderly in the child's hands, with other small vessels, including a cosmetic jar placed nearby, Delougaz, Hill, and Lloyd 1967: 62.

47 B. Foster 2000; Chapter 2 part 2.

48 Gelb 1957: 304: Izer-kullasin, perhaps, "He-Spited-All-of-Them."

49 Offner 1962; Boese 1968/9; Rollinger 2011/x; Barrelet 1970: 223–24 (specifically Akkadian imagery).

50 Cooper 1983a: 54–55 (Appendix IIIb) lines 102–5.

51 Rollinger 2011/x.

52 Barrelet 1970: 224.

53 *Muses.* 70.

54 Kienast and Volk 1995: 59, 106.

55 Hansen 2002; Chapter 9 note 52.

56 Winter 1996a; Chapter 9 part 1.

57 Gelb 1957: 230–31.

58 *Muses,* 66–68. For Sumerian love poetry of the third millennium, Alster 1993; Sefati 1998. For Babylonian and Assyrian love poetry, Nissinen 2001.

59 Woolley 1934: 494 grave 692, which contained as well gold and silver earrings, a cylinder seal, dagger, and pin.

60 Beyer 1985.

61 *Muses*, 924.
62 A. Westenholz 1974/7: 96, with a different interpretation of the text. I suggest a sandhi-writing in line 1: *in laluriki [lali uriki] lamanam kubbisi*. A less romantic reading would be, "Tread down evil in Laluri" (a place near Mugdan, MAD 5 91:6).
63 In general, Delougaz, Hill, and Lloyd 1967; Krafeld-Daugherty 1994, with discussion of fire pits and ovens, benches, bathrooms and toilets, storerooms, shrines, animal pens and shelters, particular consideration of Akkadian evidence from Eshnunna, Mugdan, and other sites, 97–108, 123, 190–93.
64 Delougaz, Hill, and Lloyd 1967: 153–54.
65 Delougaz, Hill, and Lloyd 1967: 153; Salonen 1961: 68–70.
66 Delougaz, Hill, and Lloyd 1967: 145–51; for domestic cult, Scurlock 2003.
67 Delougaz, Hill, and Lloyd 1967: pl. 65.
68 Reade 1973; in Curtis 1982.
69 BIN 8 110.
70 BIN 8 260.
71 OSP 2 51–52, treated in Edzard 1968 no. 68 and 101; further Wilcke 2007: 70–71 note 216. For the Eshnunna houses, Delougaz, Hill, and Lloyd 1967: pl. 28 (XI and XXIV).
72 Banks 1912: 308–12 (Adab); Delougaz, Hill, and Lloyd 1967: 218–33 (Eshnunna).
73 CUSAS 13 208.
74 CUSAS 23 158.
75 Delougaz, Hill, and Lloyd 1967: 155.
76 Delougaz, Hill, and Lloyd 1967: 223.
77 Delougaz, Hill, and Lloyd 1967: 226. For other hordes, Reade 1973: 165 and McDonald, Curtis, and Maxwell-Hyslop in Oates, Oates, and McDonald 2001: 233–36.
78 Examples drawn from Gelb 1957: 9–12 (father); 21–23 (brother and sister); 42–43 (mother, paternal uncle).
79 Owen 1980; "left-over" is a guess for a word (šu-ùr) that could mean a hand has already been "passed over" the bread; in later periods, however, this word could also refer in some way to a dry measure, but remains obscure (differently Owen). For apinlá and dab$_5$ in connection with leased land, B. Foster 1982a: 95, 99; 51–52 (differently Owen). Letters from Assyrian women to their husbands often treat of the same subjects, sometimes in the same tone: Michel 2001 nos. 307, 344, 364, 375, 380, 384.
80 Bottéro 1980, 1983; Steiner 1982; Groneberg 1990; Jonker 1995; Scurlock 2002; Lundström 2003; Selz 2004, 2205; Archi 2012.
81 For consideration of the dead, Bauer 1969; A. Cohen 2005; Ge. Selz 2005a.
82 Bayliss 1973; Bottéro 1980, 1983 (rituals from later periods); for examples of such prayers, though from later periods, *Muses*, 649–50, 658–59.
83 Van Koppen 2011: 152.
84 Alster 1983.
85 Foxvog 1980; Scurlock 1991; Sallaberger 1995; Barrett 2007.
86 Woolley 1934: 486–509.
87 Archi 2012: 19–28.
88 BdI Adab 102.
89 Woolley 1934: 146; Strommenger 1957/71; Novák 2003; Lundström 2000; De Cesari 2002.
90 Moorey 1970, 1978: 71; Gibson 1972a: 79–80.
91 Delougaz, Hill, and Lloyd 1967: 59 (Grave 1) and 67 (Grave 22) and others; Matthews, French, Lawrence, Cutler, and Jones in Oates, Oates, and McDonald 2001: 354–56 (greenish ash).
92 Pollock 1991; Müller-Karpe 1993/97: 142; Winter 1999b: 229.
93 Oates, Oates, and McDonald 2001: 241.
94 Hockmann 2010 (Ass. 20573=64); in general Mühl 2013: 131–33.

95  Gibson 1981: 73–75.
96  Gibson 1981: 75.
97  Delougaz, Hill, and Lloyd 1967: 129–30; Gibson 1981: 79; scattered Akkadian burials occur elsewhere, for example at Uruk, Boehmer, Pedde, and Salje 1995: 3–4 (dated by the presence of a Classical Akkadian seal and containing a weight and various metal objects, including a cup, pin, and awl).
98  Hockmann 2010 (Ass. 20573–64).
99  Woolley 1934; Nissen 1966: 164–91; Pollock 1983.
100  Woolley 1934: 490–91; all the Ur graves mentioned hereafter are cited from this chart, dating checked with Nissen 1966; further and in general Pollock 1983, 1991; Marchesi 2004; for orientation of objects, Chapter 3 note 15.
101  Woolley 1934: 204.
102  Kilmer 1987; Stol 2000: 118–22.
103  Woolley 1934: 205, who suggests that the boats were funerary in character.
104  Woolley 1934: 486–509.
105  Banks 1912: 312–13; Wilson 2012: 58, 62, plate 108; I thank Karen Wilson for positive identification of the stones in this piece.
106  OAIC 31.

# 11 The Akkadian period in retrospect

In terms of breadth, depth, variety, and longevity, memory of the Akkadian period is unique in Mesopotamian culture.[1] The Akkadian kings were remembered in funerary rites centuries after their deaths and honored in name-giving as gods. Their inscriptions were copied by students and scholars and imitated by later rulers, some of whom took their names. Their monuments were preserved as relics and transported as booty or museum pieces. Akkadian iconography often inspired that of later kings. Independent sovereigns proudly bore the titles they had bestowed on their officials, long after the demise of the dynasty. The names of Akkadian rulers and certain events of their reigns were cited in divination for more than 1200 years. First-millennium historical chronicles purported to include their deeds, while poetry and prose in Sumerian and Akkadian took them as their subjects. Some of these works drew on authentic sources; others were entirely fictitious. Later rulers carried out excavations in the ruins of Agade, whose location was still known, and scribes copied the texts that turned up in this activity. In the later second and first millennia, the name "Agade" was used as a learned writing for Babylon, implying that the Akkadian capital was its forerunner as the center of universal dominion.

To what extent this memory was based in reality is open to debate. A more significant question is why were the deeds of the Akkadian kings so important? Was it only the rhetoric of their inscriptions and the iconography of their monuments that succeeded in persuading later generations of their stature and achievements? Or was there historical basis for their fame? Whatever the response to these questions, it is clear that ancient Mesopotamian memory is interwoven with, even dominates, modern assessments of the Age of Agade, more than for any other period of Mesopotamian history (Chapter 12 part 2).

## 1. Honoring dead Akkadian kings

The Babylonians who inherited the kingdoms of Akkad and Ur believed that it was the duty of the heads of families to remember their ancestors in a ceremony called "the food portion" (*kispu*), in which the deceased were invited by name to partake of food and drink.[2] This ceremony connected the living with the dead, confirming the past and blessing the present. It also perpetuated a chain of memory, in commoner families stretching back several generations, in royal ones providing a basis for claiming origins in the remote past. For most people, the *kispu* was a simple ceremony in the home, but for kings, it could take place in a room lined with statues of royal predecessors, who might aid the living in such ways as ensuring an abundant harvest. Some of the images of the Akkadian kings, seated or standing in elaborate ceremonial garments, may have been invoked in these posthumous rites of remembrance.[3]

There is ample evidence in the Ur III period for the veneration of the Akkadian kings. Funerary offerings were made in shrines dedicated to Sargon, Manishtusu, and Naram-Sin, the last at Nippur, ironically the very city where *The Curse of Agade* was written and studied. People were named after Sargon and Manishtusu, and localities were named after Manishtusu and Naram-Sin, the latter including a city gate at Nippur and an agricultural district near Apishal in Umma province. It appears that Ur III Umma was one of the main centers for the worship of the Akkadian kings, and that rulers at Umma, both Gutians and Ur III governors, sought to maintain and appropriate the legacy of the Akkadian dynasty. Recent salvage excavations there may have uncovered the remains of a sanctuary with a diorite statue of an Akkadian king, perhaps Manishtusu or Naram-Sin (Chapter 3 part 3).

Remembrance of the Akkadian kings was also upheld in twice-a-month ceremonies at early second-millennium Mari under the dynasty of Shamshi-Adad I, who was himself assiduous in asserting an Akkadian connection, however indirect.[1] The statues of Akkadian and other deceased rulers were housed in a room in the palace called the "Chamber of Thrones." The ritual instructions read:

> One sheep shall be sacrificed in the Chamber of Thrones to the protective spirits of Sargon and Naram-Sin. One sheep shall be sacrificed to the various others. Before the king arrives, the sacrifice of the chamber of thrones shall be performed and the meat shall be cooked. The best meat shall be offered to Shamash; until it has been offered to Shamash, the *kispu*-rite shall not be performed. After the offering to Shamash, the food portion shall be [. . . distributed?] to Sargon and Naram-Sin, the Hanaeans, and the people of Numhi . . .[5]

Incidental references to the Chamber of Thrones suggest that it may also have contained seated statues of the *shakkanakku*'s, first military governors, then independent rulers of Mari in the Akkadian, post-Akkadian, and Ur III periods.[6]

The ritual instructions are clear that Sargon and Naram-Sin were to be honored first after the sun-god, followed by "the various others." They are the only individuals named in the ceremony, the rest being tribal or geographical terms. The Hanaeans were the northern Amorites of the Khabur triangle, who had replaced the line of *shakkanakku*'s and built the great palace over that of the Akkadian governors, transferring the funerary statues, including those of the Akkadian kings, from the old palace to the new one.[7]

The Amorite rulers of Mari, therefore, especially Shamshi-Adad and his family, regarded the Akkadian kings as the earliest identifiable rulers in their history. This is borne out by the Mari liver models (Figure 11.1a), in which they are the oldest historical figures mentioned. Although this might have been part of a move to bring more Babylonian culture to Mari under the Lim dynasty,[8] if one of the rulers of Mari had in fact married a daughter of Naram-Sin (Chapter 3 part 5), they could legitimately claim descent from the Akkadian kings and honor them as true ancestors.

That recourse to Akkadian ancestry was not universal among those of Amorite descent is shown by a document listing the ritual food portions offered by Ammi-saduga, great-great-grandson of Hammurabi of Babylon. The record traces his lineage for fourteen generations, through "the age of the Amorites, the age of the Hanaeans, the age of Gutium, the age of anyone not written in this tablet, and of the soldier who fell in the trials of his lord, be it prince or princess, (or) any sort of person, from west to east . . . "[9] According to this understanding of the

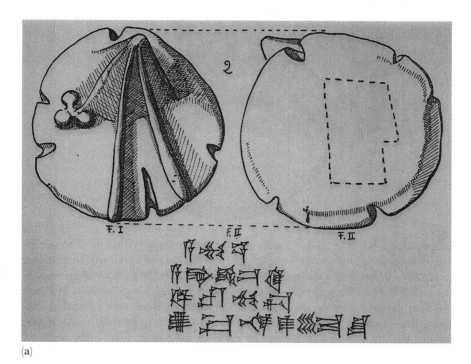

(a)

*Figure 11.1*  Liver models: (a) sheep liver from Mari, inscribed "Omen of Agade pertaining to Rimush and Manishtusu"; (b) abstract omen model from Mari inscribed "Destruction of Agade," with notches perhaps symbolizing seven enemies.

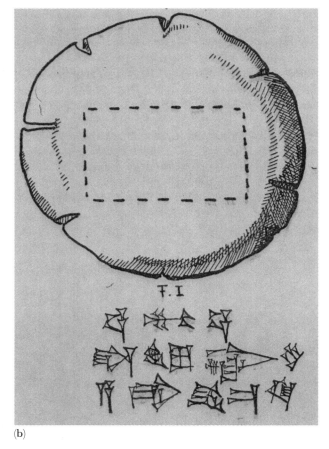

(b)

*Figure 11.1* (Continued)

history of the Amorites, they originated in the far west, moved into the Khabur triangle (Hanaeans), then passed east of the Tigris (Gutium) and south to Babylon,
a narrative in which the Akkadian kings played no role.[10] Agade itself lay outside
the heartland of Hammurabi's empire. To him and the other kings of Babylon
claiming Amorite ancestry, the Akkadian dynasty may have been associated with
Eshnunna, Assur, or other northern territories that the Amorites had only traversed in their eastward migration en route to Babylonia. Unlike the kings of
Mari, who were proud to claim a connection with the Akkadians, the Babylonian
kings preferred to look further back and further west.

## 2. Dishonoring dead Akkadian kings

As public proclamations of royal ideology, Akkadian monuments were mutilated and broken after the fall of the dynasty. To judge from the absence of scholarly copies of pre-Akkadian inscriptions, as well as the absence of pre-Akkadian works in the capitals of later conquerors, not to mention elaborate curse formulae against anyone removing their monuments, the Akkadian kings themselves had destroyed the monuments of their predecessors or removed them from important sanctuaries, such as Nippur. Furthermore, they had taken the radical step of introducing their own images into the ritual space of temples, not as worshippers before the altar, but as symbols of their authority over the human race and of their special relationship to the gods. This too invited retaliation, as in the smashing of the Akkadian statue in the temple of Ishtar at Assur.

Since Akkadian royal and elite sculpture was increasingly individuated, its mutilation or destruction obliterated both person and memory.[11] Such acts included erasing the name and inscription on the image, gouging out its eyes, cutting off its ears, nose, or lips, and beheading it (Figures 5.5, 9.3a, 9.4). The curses appended to Akkadian commemorative inscriptions threatened like punishment for any future perpetrator or his agents who did this to an Akkadian work (Chapter 6 part 6), so they must have recognized this might occur.

A survey of the shattered remains of Akkadian art (Chapter 9 part 1) reveals the ferocity of their destruction in both Sumer and the north. Those in Sumer were mostly defaced and smashed into many pieces, whereas those in Akkad and Assyria were usually mutilated.[12] The Victory Stele of Rimush from Girsu, for example, was broken into fragments, some of the Akkadian figures defaced, and the name of the king evidently hammered out where he describes his rise to power (Figure 1.4). By contrast, and presuming the damage was done in the north, the copper head found at Nineveh had an eye gouged out, the nose and ears mutilated, and perhaps it was severed from its body (Figure 9.3).

Not all kings and conquerors approved of such practices. Shulgi, a king of the Ur III dynasty, declared that he had honored both his Sumerian and Akkadian predecessors.[13] Likewise, Shutruk-Nahhunte, the Elamite king who conquered much of Mesopotamia in the twelfth century BCE, did not erase the inscriptions on the Akkadian royal monuments he carried off to Susa. On the Victory Stele of Naram-Sin, for example, he had his name and text carved in a blank space on the mountainside, claiming that he had brought it to Susa to preserve it (Figure 1.6).[11]

## 3. Copying Akkadian royal inscriptions

Beginning already in the Akkadian period, scribes copied Akkadian royal and other inscriptions, in some cases directly from the originals, in others perhaps from dictation or previous copies. Rough notes for the preparation of more definitive editions have also been found. This practice, best attested at Nippur in the late Old Babylonian period (seventeenth century BCE), is known from other sites as well, so may have become an aspect of early second-millennium scribal education or research. Akkadian inscriptions were likely the only non-Sumerian texts regularly studied in Babylonian schools of the period. Most of the copies reproduce, with admirable success, the spelling and word arrangement of the originals, using an archaizing, cursive script inspired by the lapidary Akkadian signs, though, as in any text edition, there were mistakes and misreadings. The copies from Ur, for example, are not of the same high quality as those from Nippur and Larsa.[15]

Two types of copies survive: tablets with one inscription and tablets with more than one. Sixteen single-inscription and eleven multiple-inscription tablets are known from Nippur, Ur, Larsa(?), Babylon(?), Mari, and unknown sites. Originals exist for six, including one of Sargon, one of Rimush, two of Manishtusu, and one each of Naram-Sin and Sharkalisharri. Owing to the fragmentary state of the material, it is difficult to estimate the total number of lines of authentic Akkadian commemorative prose preserved in these later copies. On the single-inscription tablets alone are many more than 1000 lines of narrative, in addition to curse formulae.[16]

The multiple-inscription tablets are remarkable achievements. The finest of them, a twenty-eight column tablet from Nippur, originally contained eight inscriptions of Sargon in Sumerian and Akkadian (thirteen if bilinguals are not considered a unit), nine of Rimush in Sumerian and Akkadian, and three of Manishtusu in Akkadian, for a total of 984 lines (not counting curse formulae and parallel texts). It is not known if any of the other multiple-inscription tablets from Nippur were drawn up by the scribe who wrote this extraordinary piece.

The practice of copying Akkadian royal inscriptions continued in the first millennium, though not on the same scale as at early second-millennium Nippur. Some seem to be close copies of originals, while one has a spurious Sumerian version, composed in an antiquarian spirit.[17] Examples come from Nippur and perhaps Babylon. One of the most intriguing is a squeeze made in clay of an inscription on a circular stone slab, found during the Neo-Babylonian period in the ruins of Naram-Sin's palace at Agade (Figure 11.2).[18]

The extant copies from all periods (Appendix Ib) include eight inscriptions of Sargon, one of Enheduanna, nine of Rimush, three of Manishtusu, ten of Naram-Sin (some of considerable length), three of Sharkalisharri, and one of Dudu.[19] This unparalleled corpus, carefully copied over many centuries, attests to the deep interest that scribes of different times and places took in this material.[20] In terms of sheer volume, it dwarfs what was copied of later Mesopotamian royal inscriptions. Since no copies of earlier Sumerian commemorative texts are known, the monuments of the Akkadian kings stand at the beginning of what scribes chose to study.

No other culture of antiquity was so assiduous in copying ancient inscriptions, together with notes explaining where they were on the monument and captions describing the imagery.[21] There is little evidence that the copies were consulted as historical sources (part 3, this chapter), so they were apparently treasured for their own sake. The modern historian's debt to the scribes who made these copies is incalculable.

*Figure 11.2* Both sides of a clay squeeze of an inscription of Sharkalisharri, with a label by a Babylonian scholar of the mid-first millennium BCE stating that he made it at Agade.

## 4.   Omens about Akkadian kings

Divination, or the systematic interpretation of signs and portents, was the queen of the Mesopotamian sciences.[22] Two types of divination are particularly relevant for the Akkadian period: celestial divination and extispicy.

Although works of celestial divination, or astrology, are known only from the second and first millennia, they may contain earlier material. In the omen series *Enuma Anu Enlil* ("When Anu and Enlil"), three total lunar eclipses portend the death of the king of Akkad. These may be correlated using modern astronomical tables with the death of Manishtusu, the death of Naram-Sin, and the death or removal of Dudu's predecessor.[23] According to Huber, the absolute chronology of the Akkadian kings can be linked to these eclipses, with the result, for example, that −2301 (= 2302 BCE) is the accession year of Naram-Sin. Even given that determining the order and lengths of reign of the Akkadian kings always requires choosing among contradictory ancient sources, the statistical data in favor of these correlations are so strong as to render mere coincidence, in Huber's words, "almost unbelievable." Furthermore, Huber suggests, if lunar eclipses had been observed at the deaths of both Manishtusu and Naram-Sin, that may well have inspired the development of celestial divination, though there is as yet no evidence that its origins go back that far.[24]

A second branch of divination, extispicy, was a Babylonian discipline built on examining the liver, gall bladder, and entrails of a sacrificed sheep (or goat) and evaluating the portentous significance of certain marks, abnormalities, or configurations.[25] Among the thousands of these omens recorded during the second millennium BCE, some are considered historical because they allude to rulers or events of the past. The earliest personages referred to are such mythical or legendary pre-Akkadian rulers as Etana, Ku-Baba, and Gilgamesh,[26] who were probably included to make divination seem more ancient than it really was. The earliest actual historical figures in the omens are the first five Akkadian kings. The omens also mention the fall of the Akkadian dynasty, the ensuing period of anarchy, and the post-Akkadian kings of Ur and Isin. Although Babylonian scholars knew of these rulers from *The Sumerian King List* (part 5, this chapter) and copies of royal inscriptions (part 2, this chapter), the historical omens often contain information not found elsewhere, especially concerning how kings died.

The surviving written records of extispicy fall into three main phases. In phase I, in the early second millennium, diviners wrote down individual omens, of which the earliest appear on a group of thirty-two clay liver models from Mari, dating perhaps to the nineteenth century BCE (Figure 11.1). Linguistic evidence suggests that they had been compiled from sources from different places and periods.[27] Most of the models are marked "omen of" on some part of the liver. Eleven of them refer to historical events or people; the remainder give only general outcomes.[28]

One of the Mari liver models preserves the strangest evocation of the Akkadian period in divination (Figure 11.1b).[29] This is not a conventional model with features of the organ, but a simple disk with seven notches at more or less even intervals around its perimeter. It is tempting to read them as symbolic of seven enemies surrounding Naram-Sin, anticipating the later legend in which "seven kings . . ., allies, glorious in form . . .," attack his kingdom with 360,000 soldiers.[30]

Phase II, possibly two or three centuries later, saw the collection of many omens on large tablets, including those few with historical references. This suggests that there must have been various dossiers of material, like the Mari liver models, available to diviners as they put together their own compilations, though new material was surely composed and added.[31] In this phase, the proportion of historical references was much lower than in the Mari models, fewer than fifty among thousands of omens, so historical events were by no means a major impetus for extispicy. Furthermore, no new historical omens applying to famous kings, such as Shamshi-Adad, Rim-Sin, or Hammurabi, were added to the early corpus, giving the impression that, in the early second millennium, the historical omens, whatever their nature, were deemed a closed group not subject to expansion, only to elaboration of the existing material.[32]

In the third and final phase, the earlier collections of omens were compiled, expanded, and rearranged into extensive series of up to 100 tablets, as represented in the mid-first millennium scholarly collections of Nineveh and Assur. Toward the end of this phase, historical omens were excerpted from the larger series and ordered chronologically; a few new ones, such as a group pertaining to Assurbanipal, were added, no doubt in an antiquarian spirit.[33]

The reliability of these historical omens, especially whether or not they should be used in writing an account of the Akkadian period, has been the subject of debate since the early years of Assyriology (Chapter 12 part 2), inspiring several studies of their content and relationship to other sources. Some have argued, on the basis of the antiquity of Mesopotamian divination, that omens with historical content preserve authentic information. If, for example, past diviners paired such important events as royal deaths with specific omens, then the death of the current king could be predicted when similar omens were observed. Accordingly, divination may be viewed as a form of history writing, with an empirical foundation.[34] Along these lines, others have suggested that certain omens have a kernel of fact and thus are of historical value if weighed individually and compared with what else is known of the period.[35] As Goetze, a proponent of the historicity of omens, noted, "The events to which reference is made are not always of great historical import . . . in other cases however, . . . the information we receive is of historical significance. . . . There is every reason to assume that it goes back to good tradition that was first drawn up contemporaneously with the respective event. Hence the historian can safely utilize the omen texts as a historical source."[36]

On the other hand, many have argued that the historical references in omens are of little or no independent value and were not empirically based, but in some cases even excogitated from the outcomes themselves, in any event of more interest for reconstructing the processes of divinatory thought than for the history of the Akkadian period. As Oppenheim wrote, "I consider the so-called 'historical omens' in no respect the empirical base for extispicy, but rather as the creation of scholars eager to 'prove' objectively that the formation of entrails predicted future events accurately."[37] As Cooper expressed it, "Only a belief in extispicy would lead one to accept their historicity."[38] Whatever one's position on these omens, their allusions to the Akkadian kings are relics of Mesopotamian historical memory, showing that learned men over a period of nearly 1500 years referred to the dynasty of Agade. At the very least, these artifacts of memory, along with other evidence, attest to how the Akkadian period was understood or used by later scholars and give an idea of what sources they may have consulted for their work.[39]

The following table summarizes the three phases of historical extispicy omens referring to the first five Akkadian kings and the fall of the dynasty. Duplicate items (e.g., 3–7) include those in which different protases (if-clauses) have the same apodosis (then-clause).[40]

### Omens about Akkadian kings

*Sargon*

PHASE I: EARLY SECOND MILLENNIUM

1. Omen of Kish, referring to Sargon.

PHASE II: MID-SECOND MILLENNIUM

  2. Omen of Sargon.
3–7.The weaponry of Sargon.
  8. Omen of Sargon, who had no equal.
  9. Omen of Sargon, who ruled the world.
10–11. Omen of Sargon, who marched in darkness and light came out for him.
  12. Omen of Sargon, who wandered in darkness but saw light.

PHASE III: FIRST MILLENNIUM

13. Omen of Sargon.
14. Omen of Sargon, who ruled the land.
15. Omen of Sargon, who had no rival.
16. Omen of Sargon, who, under this omen, [   ] Ishtar desired him
    [   ], Ishtar let him conquer, at the pointing of his finger, she [   ].
17. Omen of Sargon, who, under this omen, arose [in the age of Ishtar] and had no equal nor rival, who [spread] his awe-inspiring glory over [all lands], who crossed the western sea and in his third year conquered the west [to its remotest extent] and placed it under his sole authority and had statues of himself set up in the West, who had rafts bring their booty across the sea.
18. Omen of Sargon, who marched through darkness and light came out for him.
19. Omen of Sargon, who went to the land of Marhashi and Ishtar came out with her luminous rising.
20. Omen of Sargon, whose soldiers, enveloped by a storm, exchanged their weapons with each other.
21. [Omen of] Sargon, who extended his court 10 hours march in every direction, and the courtiers stood before him and said, "Where shall we go?"

22. Omen of Sargon, who was away on campaign and the land of Kazalla rebelled and who marched to the land of Kazalla and defeated and annihilated them, who slew their great army, who turned the land of Kazalla into dust and ruins, who left not even a place a bird could light.

23. Omen of Sargon, who, under this omen, marched against the land of Elam and slew the Elamites. He cut off from their elders the headgear² that he had set on them.

24. Omen of Sargon, who marched against the [land of Amur]ru and slew the Amorites. He conquered the four quarters of the earth.

25. [Omen of Sargon who, under this omen], marched against [the land of Amurru and a second time [ ] his warriors [ ] brought him out [from?] battle.

26. Omen of Sargon, against whom, under this omen, the people of Subartu arose in force and assembled for battle². Sargon set a trap for them and defeated and annihilated them. He [slew²] their great army. He . . . his [ ]and auxiliary troops and brought them into Agade.

27. Omen of Sargon, to whom, under this omen, the dominion of Babylon came, he took earth from the courtyard² of the . . .-gate [ ] and built a city [op]posite Agade and called its name [Babylon] and settled [ ] within it.

28. Omen of Sargon, against whom, under this omen, the elders of [or: in his old age] the entire land rebelled and besieged him in Agade and Sargon came out and defeated and annihilated them, he slew their numerous army. He tied their belongings upon them, he cried "It is yours, O Ishtar!"

## Rimush

PHASE I: EARLY SECOND MILLENNIUM

29. Omen of Akkad, referring to Rimush and Manishtusu (Figure 11.1a).

PHASE II: MID-SECOND MILLENNIUM

30. Omen of Rimush, whom his servitors killed with their cylinder seals (or: their sealed documents).

PHASE III: FIRST MILLENNIUM

31. Omen of Rimush, whom his courtiers killed with their cylinder seals (or: their sealed documents).

## Manishtusu

PHASE I: EARLY SECOND MILLENNIUM

29. Omen of Akkad, referring to Rimush and Manishtusu.

PHASE II: MID-SECOND MILLENNIUM

32. Omen of Manishtusu, whom his palace (or: ministers?) killed.

## Naram-Sin

PHASE I: EARLY SECOND MILLENNIUM

33. Omen of Naram-Sin, who took Apishal.

PHASE II: MID-SECOND MILLENNIUM

34. Omen of Naram-Sin, who ruled the world.
35. Omen of [the Apishalian] whom Naram-Sin captured.
36. Omen of Naram-Sin, who captured the Apishalian by a breach (in the wall of his city).
37. Omen of the Apishalian whom Naram-Sin captured by breaching (the wall of his city).
38. The Akkadian land will be besieged and will perish. Naram-Sin committed an act of negligence(?). The diviner will go to the grave(?).

PHASE III: FIRST MILLENNIUM

39. Omen of Naram-Sin.
40. Omen of Naram-Sin, who took the city Apishal by a breach (in the city wall).
41. Omen of Naram-Sin, who, under this omen, marched to Apishal, took it by a breach (in the city wall), and prevailed over Rish-Adad, king of the city of Apishal, and over the minister of Apishal.
42. Omen of Naram-Sin, who, under this omen, marched to [the land of Mag]an and seized the land of Magan and prevailed over [Maniu]m, king of the land of Magan.

## Sharkalisharri

PHASE II: MID-SECOND MILLENNIUM

43. Omen of 'Sharkashshari.'
44. Omen of Sharkalisharri, whom his servitors killed with their cylinder seals (or: sealed documents).

PHASE III: FIRST MILLENNIUM

45. Omen of Sharkalisharri [of the] destruction of Agade. (It means): An enemy will take advantage of your peace. For a campaign (it means): The advance man of your army will not return.

## End of the Dynasty

PHASE I: EARLY SECOND MILLENNIUM

46. Omen of the destruction of Agade (Figure 11.1b).

47. Destruction of Agade.
48. The Age of Agade came to an end.

49. Revolt of the lower orders, destruction of Agade.
50. Omen of "Who was king, who was not king?"

Given the richness of the copies based on authentic sources from the Akkadian period (part 2, this chapter), which were being made at the same time the Phase II omen collections were being compiled, the generalities, confusions, and omissions of the historical omens are striking.[11] For the reign of Sargon, the copied inscriptions could have informed a scholar five centuries or more after Sargon's death that he had defeated Ur and Uruk in a series of three battles, captured the king, Lugalzagesi, and fifty city rulers; that he had campaigned to Elam and Marhashi and the Upper Lands via Tuttul; that he had claimed to rule Mari, Armanum, and Ebla as far as the Cedar Forest and the "Shining" or "Silver" Mountains and from the Upper to the Lower Seas; that he had defeated rebellious cities; that he was victor in 34 battles; that 5400 men ate daily before him; that ships from Meluhha, Magan, and Dilmun docked at Agade; that Enlil had given him no rival; and that his daughter, Enheduanna, was priestess at Ur.

The second-millennium historical omens, however, mention only Sargon's association with Kish, his "weaponry," and his march through darkness into light. The first-millennium omens add that he defeated Elam, Kazallu, Marhashi, Subartu, Amurru and the West; that he crossed the western sea and set up statues of himself there; that he brought booty across the sea; that his soldiers were caught up in a storm; that his army perhaps rescued him in the course of a battle (no. 25); that he founded a city opposite Agade, using earth from Babylon after he conquered that city; and that he faced a widespread revolt that laid siege to Agade, but he crushed it and offered the spoils to Ishtar.

For Rimush, the copied inscriptions could have informed a later scholar that he had campaigned in Sumer against Ur, Umma, and Lagash; that he had destroyed Kazallu; that he had campaigned in Marhashi, Elam, and Zahara; that he had annexed Elam, and that he claimed to rule from the Upper to the Lower Sea. The first- and second- millennium omens, however, mention only that he was assassinated by his courtiers.

For Manishtusu, the copied inscriptions could have informed a later scholar that he had campaigned against Anshan and Shirihum and that he had shipped stone from Magan across the Lower Sea. The second-millennium omens, however, pair him with Rimush and know specifically only that he was killed by "his palace." The first- millennium omens do not mention him at all.

For Naram-Sin, the copied inscriptions could have informed a later scholar that he campaigned to Subartu and the Cedar Forest; that he had ruled Elam as far as the border with Marhashi; that he had conquered Ebla and Armanum, the latter by successfully overcoming a triple series of massive walls and capturing the king; and that he faced a Great Revolt, led by Uruk and Kish, during which he fought nine battles in one year from Jebel Bishri to the Gulf. The detailed narrative of the Great Revolt is, in fact, the longest text surviving from the third millennium.

Yet the second-millennium omens know only of Naram-Sin's successful siege of a city called Apishal, which he took by breaching the walls and where he captured the king and his minister. One omen (38) refers to him cryptically as being negligent. The first-millennium omens add that the name of the king of Apishal was Rish-Adad. They also say that he marched to the land of Magan, captured it, and defeated its king, Manium (or Mannum-dannum).

For Sharkalisharri, the copied inscriptions could have informed a later scholar that he had gone to the sources of the Tigris and Euphrates and that he had faced a revolt. The second-millennium omens state only that he was killed by his servitors and that his reign marked the destruction of Agade; the first-millennium omens only the latter.

But what sources did later scholars actually consult for their historical omens?

While it is true that Mesopotamian scholars concerned themselves with many different branches of the literate arts, one must consider the possibility that copying inscriptions was a local scribal specialty and that copies did not circulate widely outside of individual scholarly households in the cities where the original monuments had been set up. Furthermore, Nippur and Ur, where many of the copies of royal inscriptions originated, were centers of Sumerian learning, whereas compiling extispicy omens was an Akkadian-language phenomenon, at home mainly in northern Babylonia at cities such as Larsa, Sippar, Babylon, and Kish. Although fragments of early second millennium extispicy are also known from Nippur, the two activities may not have overlapped for the most part.[12]

If one leaves out of account the exceptionally detailed, authentic information available in a few learned houses at Nippur, a closer correspondence emerges between the information known from the surviving Akkadian sources and that found in the historical omens. Without the eight copied inscriptions of Sargon from Nippur, only a local copy, found at Ur, of the brief inscription of Enheduanna remains.[13] This suggests that, outside of Nippur, no original monuments of Sargon or later copies of his inscriptions were to be found. In their absence, small Akkadian objects, like the fragmentary mace head found at Ur in Kassite levels, could have been the basis for such omens as "the weaponry of Sargon." Such pieces as the calcite vase found at Ur dedicated to "Sargon, king of Kish" might have inspired the pairing of Kish and the "totality of the world" in the omens.[14] The vagueness of the early historical omens about Sargon may therefore stem from a paucity of sources.

As for Rimush, copies and originals of his authentic inscriptions were better known outside of Nippur than Sargon's. A Rimush inscription about his invasion of Iran (Appendix Ib 16) was evidently available at Larsa?; booty inscribed by Rimush was perhaps to be seen at Ur in the Kassite and Neo-Babylonian periods, as well as at Sippar, Tutub, Nagar, Girsu, Kish, and other sites. Another Rimush inscription (Appendix Ib 18), from a monument set up at Nippur and copied there, was apparently also available at Larsa?, in direct or indirect copy.[15] Yet the Rimush omens are scanty and focused on his death.

No copies of authentic inscriptions of Manishtusu are known outside of Nippur, though originals with a standard text are known from Susa, Sippar, Isin, Ur, and other sites, as well as Nippur. So prized were original Akkadian inscriptions in later ages that fragments of his inscriptions, found at Nippur late in the first millennium, were transported to the temple of Nabu at Nineveh.[16] Yet no omens refer to his campaigns and other accomplishments, but only to his assassination.

Copies of authentic Naram-Sin inscriptions are known outside of Nippur from Larsa? (one of which is duplicated in a Nippur copy), Ur, Eshnunna, Mari, and Babylon, while originals are known throughout Mesopotamia and in northern Syria and southern Anatolia.[17] The interesting case of three fragmentary inscriptions, one in the name of Naram-Sin and two in the name of Sharkalisharri, but otherwise apparently identical, which commemorate the rebuilding of the Temple of Inanna at Zabala, may be another instance of the discovery and dissemination of Akkadian originals at a later date. They were probably found in antiquity at Zabala and dispersed, one going to Borsippa, another to Babylon, and the third to an unknown site, presumably as museum specimens of authentic Akkadian inscriptions.[18]

The following six examples show the complex relationship between historical omens and authentic inscriptions of the Akkadian period.

(1) Omens 8 and 15 of Sargon state that he had no equal or rival, language reminiscent of his own repeated assertion that "Enlil gave him no rival."[19] This was the first appearance of a heroic motif in the self-presentation of the Akkadian kings, wherein they triumph over numerous challenges (Chapter 2 part 5). Despite the omen's possible derivation from an authentic Akkadian inscription, the expression was often used in post-Akkadian times,[50] so belonged to a common fund of royal epithets. There is thus little basis for arguing that it was a specific allusion to the Akkadian period.

(2) The revolt of Kazallu (or Kazalla) is known from an inscription of Rimush, but is assigned to his father in Sargon 22.[51] Kazallu, located somewhere near Marad and Kish, probably lay in ruins by the late Old Babylonian period, when the omen was written down, so it would have been easy enough to associate its destruction with Sargon, rather than with his less famous son.[52]

(3) The best-attested event in the original and copied inscriptions of Naram-Sin is the Great Revolt led by Kish and Uruk, which inspired an impressive body of Babylonian literature that clearly drew on these sources (part 6, this chapter). In a commemorative inscription, Naram-Sin claims to have saved his city, Agade, in its time of crisis. Centuries later, Hammurabi echoes the phraseology, so the event and Naram-Sin's language were probably well known to the educated (part 8, this chapter). The rebellion, however, is not referred to as such in the historical omens. On the other hand, they do attest to a revolt against Sargon (28), saying that Sargon was besieged in Agade. This is no doubt a doublet of the uprising against

Naram-Sin. Since later literary tradition transformed Naram-Sin's triumph into a series of disasters, the omens transferred to Sargon the memory of an Akkadian king successfully suppressing a widespread revolt.[53]

(4) The reference to "Rimush and Manishtusu" in the phase I omen 29 (Figure 11.1a) may mean that both were in fact killed in court conspiracies; the more explicit Phase II omens (30 and 32) specify cylinder seals (or sealed documents) as the murder weapons or courtiers as the perpetrators. It seems possible, however, that Rimush's reign ended in civil war between the brothers, otherwise unattested in royal inscriptions, and that Manishtusu's death was confused or conflated with Rimush's assassination.[54] Since revolts, usurpation, disloyalty, and other challenges to kings were important in divination, Akkadian reigns provided especially good material for these themes. The historical basis for these particular omens remains unknown.[55]

(5) No authentic source is known for the most common early omen about Sargon, that he passed through darkness and light came out for him (10–12, 18), though this event is also alluded to in an Old Assyrian parody and a Babylonian epic poem (part 6, this chapter). While there is nothing inherently improbable about Sargon and his army having experienced a total eclipse of the sun, this is not the usual way of referring to it. The archaeologically attested and regionally important "Early Akkadian Air Blast Event," an explosion in the atmosphere above northern Syria, could be the phenomenon referred to in the omens, which might further be associated with the Phase III omen 20 about the soldiery of Sargon being caught up in a blinding storm, as well as a line of Enheduanna, "To rise over this king [Sargon] like moonlight in the dust of the sky."[56]

(6) The event of the Akkadian period best attested in omen literature, Naram-Sin's victorious siege of Apishal, is not mentioned as such in any of the surviving original or copied inscriptions. Like the Great Revolt against Naram-Sin and Sargon's passage through darkness, the siege of Apishal figures in a Babylonian epic poem (part 6, this chapter), so was remembered independently of the omen tradition. Close study of the Apishal omens (33, 36, 37, 40, 41), attested in all three phases of Mesopotamian divination, reveals a complex situation. Depending on the prognosis the diviner was looking for, they refer either to Naram-Sin (favorable) or to Apishal (unfavorable). There were two versions of the omen, one making a triple wordplay on "breach" in a city wall, a "breach" in the liver (*pilšu*), and the name of Apishal, and a second with no wordplay.[57]

The only authentic inscription of Naram-Sin commemorating a siege of a city concerns his successful siege of Armanum, attested in copies from Ur that contain mistakes.[58] In that victory, as at Apishal, the enemy king was captured alive. Furthermore, the name of the king of Armanum, copied variously as Ri-id-Adad and Ri-da-Adad, is comparable to Ri-ish-Adad, the name of the king of Apishal in the omens (all three cuneiform signs resemble each other).

No easy explanation presents itself for the putative substitution of Apishal in the omens for Armanum in the inscription.[59] There were two places called Apishal, one in the region of Carchemish, the other near Umma.[60] Nothing is known of the former. The Sumerian Apishal, a small provincial town, was certainly not the site of the heroic siege described in the inscription or the omens, but it did have several connections with Naram-Sin. An agricultural district nearby was called "the field of Naram-Sin," and some irrigation installations and a canal were named after him.[61] Perhaps Naram-Sin had developed the area and held land there, or an Akkadian governor of Umma, such as Mesag, had honored his sovereign by naming a newly created agricultural district after him. The association of Naram-Sin with the southern Apishal may have caused it to be confused with the northern Apishal, which is more likely to have had massive walls.

In sum, with regard to the Great Revolt and the Apishal/Armanum episodes, one finds a certain overlap among inscriptions, historical omens, and narrative poetry. Yet the event most richly developed in literature (part 6, this chapter), the Great Revolt against Naram-Sin, is not present in historical omens, except perhaps in phantom form as a revolt against Sargon. And the event most important in historical omens, the siege of Apishal, is present in literature, but not in copied inscriptions, unless it is a doublet of the siege of Armanum.

To describe events in historical omens as doublets or phantoms does not mean that they had no basis in historical reality. Their transferences and reshapings arose because historical omens were primarily engaged with providing instances of such key themes of extispicy as a reign's success or failure, stability or instability, the untimely death of a king, and resistance and insurrection, rather than with preserving factually accurate information derived from authentic inscriptions.

With respect to the assassinations of Rimush, Manishtusu, and Sharkalisharri, which were of interest to diviners and chroniclers (part 4, this chapter), one would not expect royal deaths to be referred to in commemorative writing, nor in literature. Instead, they may have occurred in independent historical tradition, examples of which are provided by the occasional notes incorporated in *The Sumerian King List*.[62] As for the unparalleled detail that Rimush and Sharkalisharri were killed by cylinder seals, various interpretations have been offered.[63] Comparing this to the omens' treatment of the Great Revolt and the sieges, it seems reasonable to suppose that the specific method used to kill one king became a phantom in extispicy, freely transferable to another ill-omened Akkadian king. Otherwise one must accept the implausibilities that such an *outré* episode was completely invented or happened twice in one dynasty.

To dismiss even the possibility of genuine historical cores of fact in omens and other later Mesopotamian retrospection on the Akkadian period, as well as the methodological validity of looking for them, sweeps too many interesting problems under the rug and avoids the question as to why the Akkadian period stood first and foremost in Mesopotamian thinking about the past. Furthermore, the thesis that the ancient and modern perception of the importance of the Akkadian period derives from the self-presentation of its kings (Chapter 12 part 5) cannot be sustained. Most Akkadian royal monuments were broken and defaced not long after the fall of the dynasty, nor is there any literature from the period known to have been in circulation even under the kings of Ur. The Babylonian scholarly copies of the Akkadian royal inscriptions were the property of a few scribal families and, to judge from the references to the Akkadian kings in later divination and chronicles (part 5, this chapter), their contents were not generally known among educated people. No original inscription of Sargon, for example, was known in any Mesopotamian center of learning from the middle of the second millennium on. Therefore the historian is justified to consider the later Mesopotamian memory of the Akkadian period, for all its vagueness, contradictions, exaggeration, and fiction, a response to authentic achievements and specific personalities of the age.[64]

A last point is that the Phase III omens specifying Sargon's eastern, western, and northern campaigns, together with the obscure reference to Babylon (27), suggest that the deeds of the Assyrian kings Sargon II and Sennacherib served as inspiration for their expansion from the Phase II omens. Sargon II campaigned in the west and claims to have crossed the sea, meaning the Mediterranean (17). Sennacherib attacked Babylon (27) and took soil from the destroyed city to Assur, where he built a structure for the New Year festival, evidently intended to replace its counterpart in Babylon (part 5, this chapter). Thus the accretions in the Phase III omens about Sargon of Akkad may have been motivated by events well known in the late eighth and early seventh centuries, when the Babylonian chronicles (part 5, this chapter) and excerpt tablets restricted to historical omens were copied and possibly compiled for the first time. Both of these Assyrian kings died violent deaths, one by assassination, one in battle. Sargon of Assyria built a new city. Thus Babylonian diviners may have seen parallels between the Assyrian Empire at its height and the Age of Agade.[65]

## 5.    Historical chronicles

Chronicles, that is, brief prose records of past events arranged in the order in which they occurred, were drawn up in Mesopotamia from the late third millennium, perhaps as early as the time of the Akkadian kings, until well into the Hellenistic period. About fifty are known today, of differing types and purposes.[66]

The earliest chronicle, known as *The Sumerian King List* or the *Chronicle of the Single Monarchy*, is a list of Mesopotamian rulers and their dynasties, in its fullest form beginning before the Flood and ending with the First Dynasty of Isin.[67] The earliest known manuscript (still without the antediluvian section) dates to the reign of Shulgi, king of Ur (2094–2047 BCE), the latest to approximately the seventeenth century BCE. Copies exist from Nippur, Isin, Kish, Susa, Shubat-Enlil, and unknown provenances, including, possibly, Larsa. In one group of manuscripts, the Akkadian period is presented as follows:

> In Agade, Sargon – his father was a gardener – the cupbearer of Ur-Zababa, the king of Agade, the one who built Agade, became king. He ruled 56 years. Rimush, son of Sargon, ruled 9 years. Manishtusu, elder brother of Rimush, ruled 15 years. Naram-Sin, son of Manishtusu, ruled [37?] years. Sharkalisharri, son of Naram-Sin, ruled 25 years. Who was king? Who was not king? Irgigi became king, Nanum was king, [Imi] was king, Elulu was king: these four kings ruled 3 years. Dudu ruled 21 years, Shu-Durul, son of Dudu, ruled 15 years. (Total:) Eleven kings ruled 181 years. Agade was defeated, its kingship was taken away to Uruk.[68]

Not all manuscripts agree on the order of the kings or the lengths of their reigns. The earliest lists Manishtusu ahead of Rimush as successor to Sargon, but this is at variance with all other evidence, including the Mari liver models and the sequence of the Nippur copies, and fits poorly the sequence of events recorded in royal inscriptions (Chapter 1 part 3), so has not been adopted in this study. Its reordering may have been motivated by conditions in Shulgi's reign, when there were rival princes, in the hope of avoiding a prominent historical allusion to the irregular Akkadian succession.[69] Some damaged manuscripts apparently add another king in the period of anarchy after Sharkalisharri.[70]

As for the reigns, one manuscript gives Sargon 55 years, a second 54, while the oldest manuscript gives him 40. Rimush is given 15 years in three manuscripts, 7 years in two others, and 8 in the earliest. Manishtusu is given 7 years in one manuscript, 15 in others. Naram-Sin is given 56 years in one manuscript, and 54 years and 6 months in the earliest. Sharkalisharri is given 24 years in one manuscript, 25 in others. The totals for the dynasty also vary: one gives 177 years, another 197 years. From these variants it seems that there was a tendency to interchange the lengths of reign of Rimush and Manishtusu, and those of Sargon and Naram-Sin.[71]

There are several proposals for when and why *The Sumerian King List* was composed. According to one thesis, it dates to the Akkadian period because it extols divinely ordained over elective kingship, reflecting Naram-Sin's victory over two elected kings and his subsequent deification.[72] According to another, the *King List* was intended to legitimate and project into the remote past the Akkadian ideology of a single, universal kingship, so it is an essentially Akkadian reading of history, fleshed out by creating imaginary pre-Akkadian dynasties with often improbable names. Its Akkadian origins became obscured with the addition in post-Akkadian times of legendary dynasties before the Flood and, in due course, of the Ur III and Isin dynasties.[73] According to a third, the notion of one universal kingship was pre-Akkadian and the list was based on "painstaking historical investigation that drew upon all pertinent sources."[74]

Another chronicle is part of a pseudonymous royal letter, purporting to have been sent by a king of Isin to a king of Larsa, but probably composed much later. Its narrative illustrates how kings like Sargon prospered when they observed the cult of Marduk in his temple, Esagila, at Babylon, but lost their thrones when they neglected it:

Ur-Zababa [ordered] Sargon, his cupbearer, "Make a change to the wine of the libation cups of Esagila!" Sargon did not change the wine. He was careful to bring it promptly to Esagila. Marduk, king of all heaven and earth, son of the Prince of the Depths, looked upon him with pleasure and gave him the kingship of the four quarters of the earth. He took care of the provisioning of Esagila. All crowned heads [brought] their tribute to Babylon. But he for his part forgot the word that the Lord had spoken to him. He took up earth from his pit and, opposite Agade, built a city and named it Babylon. Enlil changed what he had commanded and, from east to west, they rebelled against him, and he inflicted restlessness upon him.

Naram-Sin destroyed the inhabited areas of Babylon so twice the Lord raised up against him the horde of Gutium, he harried his people like a donkey driver, he gave his kingship to the horde of Gutium.

The lamentable Gutians had not been taught how to revere the gods nor how to carry out divine rites and ceremonies correctly. Utuhegal, a fisherman, would catch fish at the seashore for an offering and, at that time, such fish, until it had been presented before the great lord Marduk, would not be presented to any other god. The Gutians snatched the fish, cooked but not presented, from his hands, so, by his exalted command, he removed the Gutian horde from kingship of the land and gave it to Utuhegal.[75]

This text draws on *The Sumerian Sargon Legend* (part 6, this chapter). Its allusion to Sargon's building a city echoes the confused account of this deed in the omens: was the city Babylon, Agade, or a replica of one or the other? In this connection, it is worth mentioning that Sargon himself claims that he combined two parts of Kish into one. While this is a possible basis for the omens, it is more likely they refer to Babylon replacing Agade as the center of universal kingship (part 7, this chapter).[76]

A mid-first-millennium chronicle includes kings of Agade, Ur, and Isin, and reads like a conflation of Phase III historical omens:

Sargon, king of Agade, arose during the age of Ishtar. He had no equal nor rival. His awe-inspiring glory spread over all lands. He crossed the sea in the East. In the eleventh year, he conquered the land of the West up to its farthest boundary. He placed it under his sole authority. He had statues of himself set up in the West. He had their booty brought over on rafts. He had his courtiers stationed every ten hours of march and ruled all lands as one. He marched to Kazalla, he turned Kazalla into ruin heaps where not even a bird could light. Afterwards, in his old age, all lands rebelled against him and besieged him in Agade. Sargon went out for battle, defeated and annihilated his enemies, and slew their numerous army. Later Subartu rose in all its power and forced him to take up arms. Sargon took them by surprise, defeated, and annihilated them. He slew their numerous army. He brought their belongings into Agade. He took earth up from the clay pit of Babylon and built near Agade a replica of Babylon. Because of the sacrilege he committed, the great lord Marduk became angry and decimated his people by famine. From west to east they revolted against him and he (Marduk) inflicted restlessness upon him.[77]

Naram-Sin, son of Sargon, [marched] to Apishal. He made a breach (in the wall) and took prisoner Rish-Adad, king of Apishal, and his minister. He marched on Magan and [took prisoner] Mannu-dannu, king of Magan.[78]

This account implies that Babylon antedated Agade, so Sargon's sin was to build a rival Babylon from the earth of the original one. A first-millennium belief that Babylon was the oldest city in the world may have motivated this chronicler to privilege it over Agade, reversing the story that Sargon had built Babylon after he had built Agade, as recounted in the pseudonymous royal letter quoted earlier.

What was the relationship between the historical omens, especially those of Phase III, and the chronicles that allude to the same events? Some scholars conclude that the entries for the Akkadian kings used omen collections as a source and quoted them directly; others prefer to restrict the borrowing or quotation to a few instances.[79]

## 6. The Age of Agade in Sumerian and Akkadian literature

Sumerian literature about the Akkadian period falls into three groups: (1) the poems attributed to Enheduanna, treated in Chapter 9 part 5 and translated in Appendix II; (2) narrative poems about Inanna/Ishtar, which, according to some modern readings, refer metonymically to the Akkadian period, discussed in Chapter 1, part 5; and (3) two narrative poems, *The Sumerian Sargon Legend* and *The Curse of Agade*, translated in Appendix III.

*The Sumerian Sargon Legend* (Chapter 1 part 2) is set in Kish in the reign of Ur-Zababa, whom Sargon serves as cupbearer (Chapter 4 part 7), and tells how Sargon escaped several plots to murder him.[80] The poet may have drawn the association of Sargon with the king of Kish from *The Sumerian King List*. The surviving poem consists of about sixty-two lines in whole or in part and is known from two manuscripts, one from Nippur, the other possibly from Larsa, dating perhaps to the late eighteenth century BCE. A three-line excerpt with Akkadian translation, found on a school tablet from Babylon, may also belong to this work. The paucity of manuscripts suggests that the *Sargon Legend* was not nearly so well known or popular as *The Curse of Agade*, one of the best-attested pieces of Sumerian literature.

The poems share a number of features. *The Sumerian Sargon Legend* opens with the glory of Ur-Zababa:

> Its king, the shepherd Ur-Zababa.
> Shone forth like the sun over the houses of Kish.[81]

In like manner, *The Curse of Agade* describes Naram-Sin reigning over a city that had triumphed over Kish and Uruk:

> Its king, the shepherd, Naram-Sin,
> Shone forth like sunrise on the holy throne of Agade.[82]

So too, when each monarch learns that something is amiss with his reign, "He knew what it meant, he found no words for it, nor could he talk of it with anyone."[83] In both poems, the gods turn against the cities and their rulers without a clear reason being given, and the rest of the narratives relate the hapless king's fruitless actions to avoid their destiny. The now-missing end of *The Sumerian Sargon*

*Legend* may have treated the destruction of Kish and Uruk, or at least the transfer of their kingships to Agade, just as *The Curse of Agade* ends with the destruction of Agade. If *The Sumerian Sargon Legend* were better preserved, it might be known today as *The Curse of Kish and Uruk*. Enough remains, however, to say that the main theme of both works was that kingship never abides in one place forever; Kish, Uruk, and Agade had their turns at glory.[84]

To a modern reader, *The Sumerian Sargon Legend* appears fantastic, overblown, and obscure in style compared to *The Curse of Agade*, as in the hyperbolic similes used for the terrified Ur-Zababa:

> Like a (wounded) lion, dribbling urine, filled with blood and pus,
> down his crotch,
> Struggling like a choking sea fish, he gasped for breath.[85]

*The Curse of Agade*, by contrast, soberly describes Naram-Sin's acts of renunciation and mourning, with no overt references to his emotions:

> He put on mourning clothes for Ekur,
> He shrouded his kingly car with a reed mat,
> He took down the canopy from his royal barge,
> He put away from himself the trappings of his reign.[86]

*The Sumerian Sargon Legend* also gives the impression that its author was well familiar with other works of Sumerian literature. There may, for instance, be a witty allusion to the story of *Enmerkar and the Lord of Aratta*, in which Enmerkar invents writing: "At that time, setting words on clay did not exist."[87] Ur-Zababa, for his part, invents the envelope for a tablet: "At that time, writing on tablets certainly existed, wrapping tablets in clay certainly did not exist!"[88] In short, the *Legend* is of exceptional interest as historical fiction, composed for an audience that could be expected to have some knowledge of the Akkadian period and other literature about it.[89]

The same is true of *The Curse of Agade*. This poem is second only to *Ninurta and the Stones*, the classic text of Sumerian literature in the second and first millennia BCE, in the number of surviving manuscripts.[90] Most come from Nippur, with a few from Ur, Isin, Kish, Susa, and unknown sites, including probably Larsa. Clearly a popular, standard work, it is fully preserved in about 280 lines. Its date of composition is unknown, but it may be as early as the Ur III period. Like *The Sumerian Sargon Legend*, it is historical fiction. For the modern scholar, it reads like the work of someone with a wealth of factual information about the period, as well as superior discernment.

The central episode is based on Naram-Sin's reconstruction of the temple of Enlil in Nippur, an event documented in Akkadian commemorative and administrative texts, but not otherwise part of Mesopotamian literary heritage about Naram-Sin. While the main theme, the reasons for the fall of the Akkadian Empire and the destruction of Agade, was well known and variously expounded in literate circles of the late third and early second millennia BCE, the poet ingeniously turned the reconstruction of Enlil's temple into an impious act.[91] This suggests an author at home in Nippur, who saw the lavish reconstruction of the temple in the imperial Akkadian style as an affront that set in motion the collapse of the empire. Unlike other Mesopotamian texts that condemn the priesthood for improper innovations or laxity, *The Curse of Agade* makes no mention of local citizenry or the clergy, many of whom no doubt prospered from Naram-Sin's largesse. Here, rather, the sole protagonist is Naram-Sin.

The poem is a tour-de-force of a wide-ranging, thoughtful mind, with deeply held convictions about the importance of Sumer and its traditional cult center at Nippur. The other provinces of the empire count for little in the author's estimation, and he stresses that the Gutian occupation of Sumer is the consequence of divine anger at Agade, not at Nippur or any other Sumerian city. The theological issue of the relationship between Enlil of Nippur and Ishtar of Agade is resolved in the opening lines by emphasizing Enlil's primacy and his role in the defeat of both Uruk and Kish, to the benefit of Agade. Naram-Sin is depicted in more tragic terms than Ur-Zababa: he strives mightily for divine approval for his project, but when denied he yields to headlong passion and plunges into his enterprise as if he were attacking the sanctuary, not rebuilding it.

The social and economic historian finds that the poet anticipated in a few lines his hard-won understanding of Akkadian agrarian policy and the economic strength of the Akkadian state. The historian of ideology finds that the basic signifiers of royal prestige in later periods, such as stockpiling specie, exacting grain and livestock from conquered areas, and collecting exotica, are adroitly worked into the story.

In sum, *The Curse of Agade* is a much more sophisticated piece of historical fiction than *The Sumerian Sargon Legend*. Its canvas was broader, its historical vision more profound, and its use of past events and personalities more skillful, daring, and original. Small wonder, then, that this poem was so popular at Nippur and elsewhere. Furthermore, the collapse of the Akkadian Empire was the first great event of its kind in Mesopotamian historical memory, and especially at Nippur were relics of its pride and vainglory still to be seen. The Age of Agade thus enjoyed a kind of immediacy and awful fascination that nothing in the more remote past could rival, save the exploits of Gilgamesh.

Like their Sumerian forerunners, the Babylonian and Assyrian literary works about the Akkadian period focus on Sargon and Naram-Sin, but reflect the contradictory judgments of Babylonian thought, according to which striving against impossible odds made either the hero or the fool.[92]

The compositions about Sargon include seven narrative poems and two pseudonymous letters.[93] The earliest of these is a satire from the Old Assyrian period (nineteenth century BCE), which has Sargon speaking in the first person.[94] He defeats seventy cities in one day, takes their rulers prisoner, and, in the spirit of the authentic inscriptions of Rimush and Manishtusu, swears to the truth of what he says. Next he sees a gazelle, runs, tears his trousers, throws a brick into the water and retrieves it. Then he gives a disastrous feast, accompanied by 1000 cupbearers, during which the cook burns some of the meat and is heavily fined. Finally, he drives an image of himself into the Amanus Mountains, like a peg. The absurdity of this composition suggests the handiwork of a witty mind amused by certain banalities of Akkadian commemorative prose. Since satire is effective only if its target is recognizable, this text affords a fascinating insight into how later literate people could perceive the Akkadian royal style.

Two other compositions are also in the first person. One of these, *I am Sargon*, from the early second millennium, consists only of six lines and some broken signs; it is composed in the style of a royal inscription, but is clearly not a copy of one. The other, *The Birth Legend of Sargon*, from the first millennium, consists of about thirty-three lines; an additional twenty lines found on two of the manuscripts may well belong to this same composition. Sargon states that his mother was a high priestess and that he did not know his father (in *The Sumerian Sargon Legend*, his father is La'ipum), that he was born in a place called Azupiranu (otherwise unattested, perhaps a wordplay on *per'um*, "scion," is intended), that his mother bore him in secret, and that he was set adrift in a basket and rescued by a gardener who raised him as his son. Ishtar fell in love with him, he says, and he eventually became king, roaming throughout the world. Nothing about this composition suggests any real knowledge of the Akkadian period; rather, it reads like a purely imaginative work. *The Birth Legend* has the distinction of being the earliest known instance of a story in which a child is exposed at birth and raised as a foundling, to emerge later in greatness or his true identity. Some would consider it inspired by the biblical story of Moses through Judaean presence at the Assyrian court; others consider it the source for the biblical story.[95]

Four Babylonian narrative poems celebrate the exploits of Sargon.[96] In *Sargon the Conquering Hero*, dating to the late eighteenth century BCE and perhaps from Larsa, Sargon harangues his troops on courage, hears two responses, then sets out to attack the distant land of Uta-rapashtim. On the way, he passes through darkness, an episode referred to in several omens (part 4, this chapter). He conquers Simurrum, an event known from an authentic year name of Sargon, and concludes by challenging future kings to do as he has done.[97] The contemporaneous *Sargon in Foreign Lands*, from Shaduppum/Tell Harmal, a site in Akkad, is similar to the preceding, though very fragmentary.[98] Sargon is impatient to show his valor and proposes to attack the land of Mardaman, on the upper Tigris.[99] His troops are less eager, but Sargon prevails, captures the enemy city, passes through a dark forest, and returns safely. In the third poem, *The King of Battle*, the manuscripts of which date to the fifteenth or fourteenth century BCE and later, Sargon attacks the city of Purushhanda in Anatolia, in response to an appeal from Mesopotamian merchants there. The king of Purushhanda, at first confident that Sargon cannot come so far, is humiliated. Sargon stays for three years, then returns safely. The fourth, *Sargon the Lion*, is apparently set in the east, unlike the two preceding poems, and includes a first-person speech by Sargon, but little else can be gleaned from it.[100]

These poems have in common with the satire and the *Birth Legend* that they are historical fiction, insofar as the anticipated audience was expected to recognize that Sargon was a famous warrior-king.[101] Although his campaign to Elam was known from actual inscriptions and copies, the other places mentioned are either unattested in Akkadian sources or fabulous. The first person is not used in any authentic inscriptions of Sargon, so may be considered a sign of pseudonymous composition. The poems' emphasis on valor and heroic exploits, while not out of keeping with Akkadian commemorative discourse, is more fully developed, even fulsome, and the dialogues with officers and troops unexampled.

There is little basis for proposing that these works were directly descended from or related to comparable literature, now lost, of the Akkadian period, rather than being original compositions of the early second millennium or later, as their language suggests, though a Sumerian epic narrative written not long after the fall of Agade contains passages of heroic praise that give an idea of what such lost compositions might have been like. Here the sky turns to earth and the day turns to night from the dust of the oncoming army, as when Sargon marched from light into darkness, and, like Naram-Sin in his Victory Stele, the hero, at the head of his army, carries more weapons than an ordinary soldier could wield:

(The hero) marched off in the enemy land like a forward scout,
He gave orders for his lance, wrapped it in terror for a binding,
The lord shouted for his weapons, marched off in full panoply of war,
The hero rushed off headlong to battle, earth was joined to sky!
Bow and sling he aimed well, the mountain crumbled and collapsed,
By the flanks of Ninurta's army,
While the hero called to his weapon "Quickly now!"
The sun no longer stood, the moon came out,
The peaks were obscured in the highland, the day turned black as pitch![102]

In any case, the compositions to hand reflect what later writers believed was characteristic of the Akkadian period. Of the group, the Old Assyrian parody seems most closely grounded in authentic inscriptions, which were perhaps studied in school, as they were in second-millennium Babylonia.

Two letters putatively by Sargon, one from Nippur, the other from Ur, include lists of people and professions of the type apprentice scribes memorized when they were learning to write.[103] In the letter from Ur, Sargon summons more than 170 professional people, ostensibly for an expedition to Purushhanda, but no troops. These compositions seem to be school-day whimsy, in which an assignment was packaged as a letter from a king of old, humorously combining epistolary style with heroic tradition and lists of words. A similarly fantastic letter is ascribed to Gilgamesh, and there are other satirical and humorous practice letters to and from scribes.[104]

A composition dating to the mid-first millennium, *The Sargon Geography*, lists numerous cities and lands supposedly ruled by Sargon of Akkad and the distances between them, as if to measure the extent of the entire world. There is nothing in this document to suggest any significant relationship to the Akkadian period. Instead, it more likely reflects the imperial reach of the first king in a thousand years to revive the name of Sargon in some form, for the list of conquests strongly resembles those of Sargon II of Assyria.[105]

The literature involving Naram-Sin tends to differ in character from that centering on Sargon, largely because some of it is inspired by authentic inscriptions. The poems focus on two episodes: the siege of Apishal, otherwise known only in the omen tradition (part 4, this chapter), and the Great Revolt, known both in the omen tradition but assigned to Sargon (part 4, this chapter), and in Naram-Sin's inscriptions.

*The Siege of Apishal* is an epic fragment, whose seventy-three remaining lines include no description of the siege itself.[106] In the extant sections, Naram-Sin, despite his fury at the king of Apishal, spares him and reinstates him on his throne, a denouement not recounted in Naram-Sin's own commemoration of his siege of Armanum (part 4, this chapter), but paralleled in *The King of Battle*, where Sargon too reinstates the defeated king. The style, narrative pace, and content of this piece are comparable to those of the later royal epics about Assyrian and Babylonian kings.[107] Given that those are grounded in real events, *The Siege of Apishal* may likewise describe an actual campaign of Naram-Sin, for which there is as yet no contemporaneous evidence.

The largest group of texts about Naram-Sin consists of eight compositions in which he is the target of a revolt by a coalition of Mesopotamian cities or is attacked by outlandish hordes of enemies.[108] In some versions of the story, Naram-Sin fights nine battles, losing all of them, a travesty of his genuine inscriptions in which he claims he was victor in nine battles in a single year. His authentic lists of defeated rulers were the model for the names of the human and supernatural opponents of the fictionalized Naram-Sin. The casualty figures known from real inscriptions were turned into gigantic losses for the Akkadian army.

There can be little doubt that the origins of these texts lie in the considerable historical documentation for the rebellion against Naram-Sin. In treatments of the theme in the late second and first millennia BCE, the story became ever more fantastic and Naram-Sin ever more chastened and humble, to the extent that he counsels prudence and pacifism rather than military derring-do. Unlike the Sargon legends, which give every appearance of being made up from such secondary sources as *The Sumerian King List*, the cycle of compositions about Naram-Sin and his enemies seems based on authentic Akkadian materials, freely and creatively manipulated.

## 7.   Akkadian artifacts

In later periods, Akkadian objects, such as mace heads and stone vases, were to be found throughout Mesopotamia, retained as interesting relics of the past. Some found their way to small collections of antiquities of various eras. The temple of Shamash at Sippar, for example, housed a collection of Mesopotamian and foreign objects and inscriptions.[109] When foundation documents of Naram-Sin and Sharkalisharri were discovered at Zabala sometime in the first millennium BCE, they were sent to Babylon, Borsippa, and other repositories of old inscriptions, presumably for preservation and study.[110] Scholars collected and copied old tablets from abandoned sites like Shuruppak/Fara; the Assyrian king Assurbanipal claims to have read very ancient texts in the course of his education, though no such documents were found in the excavations of his library and related collections.[111] The systematic copying of Akkadian royal inscriptions in the third, second, and first millennia BCE has been discussed in part 3, this chapter. Scribes copied other old writings too, including some found at Agade, and compiled manuals of largely fanciful paleography.[112]

When the sixth century BCE Babylonian king Nabonidus undertook repair work on the temple of Shamash at Sippar, he says that he built it "anew on the foundation of Naram-Sin, a king of former times," following the Akkadian plan exactly. He set his foundation inscription alongside those of Naram-Sin, which he discovered on tablets of gold, lapis, and carnelian. He believed that 3200 years had elapsed since the Akkadian deposit had been made and that Naram-Sin was a son of Sargon. At Sippar, he also found a statue of Sargon, half of whose head was broken away so the features were no longer discernible. Out of reverence for kingship and the gods, he had the head repaired, set up the statue in the new temple, and ordained offerings for it.[113]

Digging at Agade, Nabonidus describes his own successful discovery of the original remains of Eulmash, the sanctuary of Ishtar, as follows:

> The foundation of Eulmash in Agade, which had been invisible since the time of Sargon, king of Babylon, and Naram-Sin, his son, kings of former times, until the reign of Nabonidus, king of Babylon, Kurigalzu, king of Babylon, a king of former times, looked for it, but he did not find the foundation of Eulmash. He wrote in commemoration as follows: "I looked tirelessly for this foundation of Eulmash, but I did not find it." Esarhaddon, king of Assyria, and Assurbanipal, his son, upon whom Sin, king of the gods, bestowed all lands, looked for the foundation of Eulmash, but did not find it. He wrote in commemoration as follows: "I looked for this foundation of Eulmash but did not find it. I felled poplar and hardwood trees and built a replacement for Eulmash, I dedicated it to Ishtar of Agade, the great lady, my lady." Nebuchadnezzar, king of Babylon, son of Nabonasser, a king of former times, sent his numerous workmen there and looked tirelessly for this foundation of Eulmash, digging deep, but did not find the foundation of Eulmash.
>
> I, Nabonidus, king of Babylon, the provider for Esagila and Ezida, during my just reign, for reverence of Ishtar of Agade, my lady, took omens, and Shamash and Adad responded with a firm yes with respect to finding the foundation of Eulmash, and gave me a favorable prognosis in the omen. I dispatched my numerous workers, looking for this foundation of Eulmash. Three years I dug in the trench of Nebuchadnezzar, king of Babylon, looking right, left, in front, and behind, but did not find it. They said to me, "We have looked for this foundation but did not find it. We see that a downpour has caused a collapse." I said to them, "Dig a trench in this collapse until you have seen the foundation in this collapse." They dug in that collapse and found the

foundation of Eulmash laid by Naram-Sin, a king of former times, the dwelling of Ishtar of Agade, of Nanay, Anunitum, and the gods of Eulmash and informed me. I was overjoyed, my face shone, and, neither expanding nor reducing the foundation of this Eulmash even one finger's breadth, I relaid the foundation, the altar and dais, along with two ziggurats, and made firm its brickwork. I built them up to ground level so that the foundation of Eulmash shall never again be forgotten. I built Eulmash to perfection.[114]

It seems most unlikely that the four earlier kings left the inscriptions allegedly quoted here, so the historical part of this account may be fanciful. Whatever the truth of that, Nabonidus decided to appoint his daughter, named in Sumerian Ennigaldi-Nanna, as high priestess of the moon-god Sin at Ur. In two inscriptions referring to this action he explains that because he was disturbed by the portent of a lunar eclipse, he had astrological tablets brought to him which only he could understand. He also examined a stele of Nebuchadnezzar I (1125–1104) showing the high priestess performing her rites, as well as records from Ur. This research convinced him that Sin was demanding a high priestess, so he moved swiftly to revive the office vacant for centuries and to rebuild her residence at Ur. Although no preserved text indicates for certain that he knew that Sargon and Naram-Sin's daughters had served in the same capacity, he may well have been aware of this, since he does mention refurbishing the cemetery of previous high priestesses.[115]

In addition, it was during his reign that an antiquarian scribe found an inscription in the remains of the palace of Naram-Sin at Agade and made a clay squeeze of it, adding a note about the circumstances of his discovery (Figure 11.2). The scribe also discovered an inscribed bead, whose text he copied.[116]

All this activity makes clear that Nabonidus was fascinated by the Akkadian past of his realm and took it seriously as a guide for the present. For him, the Akkadian kings were kings of Babylon, thus his direct predecessors, further confirmation that Babylon had replaced Agade as the capital of the four quarters of the earth. He proudly set his own statue in the same sanctuary at Sippar as Sargon had and saw himself as giving new life and form to the traditions of Babylonia's great past.[117] As Beaulieu puts it,

> His interest in the Sargonic dynasty, which had always been remembered in the literary and historical tradition as the climax of Mesopotamian power, and which undoubtedly inspired the late Sargonid kings, can also be explained in the light of his own imperial ambitions. In short, Nabonidus considered his own reign a resurrection of the universal empire on the Assyrian and Akkadian model, but centered in Babylon, a project which his predecessors never seem to have contemplated.[118]

As late as the end of the sixth century BCE, during the reign of Cambyses, the statue of Sargon was still to be seen in the temple of Shamash at Sippar, where it continued to receive offerings. It is possible that other works of Akkadian art were similarly displayed in the Persian period, such as the looted pieces in the temple of Inshushinak at Susa.[119] At Agade, the cult of Ishtar was maintained into the Persian period; there were still people living in the city during the reign of Darius II (Chapter 3 part 2).

A lament known from a tablet of the Hellenistic period refers to the destruction of Agade and other cities by "Gutians," perhaps now a coded reference to some much later Mesopotamian power. The speaker is very likely Ishtar:

"O grieving women of Uruk,
   O grieving women of Agade, I am prostrate!"
The goddess of Uruk wept, whose attendant was gone,
The goddess of Uruk wept, whose loincloth was snatched away.
The daughter of Uruk wept, the daughter of Agade was crying aloud . . .
The goddess of Agade wept, whose sandals were mangled,
   whose lord, in whom she delighted, was killed . . .
The daughter of Nippur wept,
   "Finishing the task was for Gutians!"[120]

## 8.   Responses to the Akkadian legacy

The polities that emerged immediately after the collapse of the Akkadian Empire faced the challenge of its legacy in two principal ways. One approach was to imitate its style and rhetoric, even if replicating its geographical extent was impossible. This was evidently the strategy of the Gutians, who occupied portions of the Akkadian heartland, and the Lullubi, who had faced the army of Naram-Sin. The second approach was to accept only selected aspects of Akkadian culture and ignore the rest, which was the path followed by the dynasties at Susa, Lagash, Uruk, and Ur.

As for the Gutians, Mesopotamian historical memory credited them with the destruction of the Akkadian Empire (Chapter 1 part 8). They were a people at home in the Zagros (Chapter 2 part 1) and the Iranian plateau and were mentioned occasionally in Akkadian sources, with disparagement (Chapter 1 part 8). Beginning with *The Curse of Agade*, they became the very type of the foreign barbarian horde in Mesopotamian literature.[121]

About 2190 BCE, one or more Gutian kingdoms were established in Mesopotamia, the extent and duration of which remain unknown. The impact of Akkadian culture on the Gutians may best be judged from a copy made at Nippur of three inscriptions on statues, now missing, of Erridu-pizir, a Gutian king. They were composed in faulty Akkadian in imitation of the style of Naram-Sin. The Gutian ruler invokes Ishtar-Anunitum and Ilaba and appropriates Naram-Sin's titles of "the mighty" and "king of the four world regions."[122] He also attempts dramatic narrative and direct speech, ending with characteristic Akkadian-period curse formulae. Erridu-pizir may have ruled at Nippur, but in any case he dedicated his statues there to Enlil. The composition and technique of a copper head said to be from Iran, possibly a Gutian ruler, are comparable to those of the Akkadian head from Nineveh (Chapter 9 part 1), but stylistically it is quite different.[123]

When Anu-banini, king of the Lullubi, another people of the Zagros (Chapter 2 part 1), commemorated his deeds, he too drew up an inscription in the Akkadian style. This was carved on the cliffs at Sar-i-Pul-i-Zohab, in the region of Iranian Hulwan. Anu-banini titles himself *šarrum dannum*, "mighty king," which was also used in the Ur III period as an expansion of Naram-Sin's title of *dannum*, "mighty."[121] He patterned his rock relief on Akkadian monuments such as the cliff carving at Darband-i-Gaur attributed to Naram-Sin (Chapter 9 part 2).[125]

At Susa and elsewhere in Elam, former Akkadian notables, such as Ili-ishmani, were initially able to maintain authority, but leadership soon passed to men with local roots. Prominent among them was Kutik-Inshushinak, also known by an Akkadian form of his name as Puzur-Inshushinak. This may be an early case of a ruler using a double name for different contexts: here, the Elamite one for a regional audience and the Akkadian one for formal, external self-presentation.[126] Puzur-Inshushinak, considered in Babylonia the last dynast of Awan, a land perhaps in the central Zagros, called himself "governor of Susa" and "general of Elam," presumably Akkadian titles, but "king" in one inscription, possibly for his Elamite subjects. He used both Akkadian and Elamite in his commemorations, and the statuary associated with him shows Mesopotamian features, suggesting that he balanced Akkadian, post-Akkadian, and Elamite traditions in ways that enhanced his position both in his kingdom and abroad.[127] If he ruled as far as the Diyala watershed and Agade itself, as seems likely, he was a direct successor to the Akkadian kings.[128]

Although Girsu in the state of Lagash had prospered under Akkadian rule as a provincial capital, Gudea and the other rulers of Lagash in the post-Akkadian period presented themselves as pious, strong, and wise, far from the military adventurers that their Akkadian predecessors had been. If Naram-Sin had expected to be worshipped as a god throughout Mesopotamia, Gudea was a devoted servant of the local deities of Lagash and Girsu, whom the Akkadians had never mentioned, at least in their surviving inscriptions, and their chosen intermediary to his people. At the same time, Gudea commissioned numerous statues of himself in diorite, as had the Akkadian kings, with the serene, confident presence the Akkadian sculptors had sought to convey. Their proportions and Sumerian inscriptions, however, were of an entirely different tenor, stressing the prayerful ruler as a builder of temples, rather than a warrior of unprecedented conquests. Yet even there, Gudea takes advantage of the expanded Akkadian geographical horizon, claiming that he brought materials for his temple from Magan, Meluhha, and the Cedar Forest. The Sumerian literature of this period, as suggested in part 6, this chapter, may show greater Akkadian influence, but this possibility has not so far been explored in detail.[129]

The influence of the Akkadian Empire on its principal successor states, the kingdoms of Uruk and Ur, is a subject that awaits detailed study.[130] The kings of Ur presided over a flowering of Sumerian literary culture, countering the Akkadian period's rapid development of Akkadian as a language of commemoration, law, and possibly literature.[131] They claimed descent from the legendary rulers of Uruk, a city so ancient that it had no myth of origins. Their family tree included the hero-king Gilgamesh, the Sumerian counterpart to Sargon in later Mesopotamian tradition.[132] This is the first instance of royalty asserting a

Sumerian lineage far older than that of the preceding dynasty.[133] But the prologue to the law collection of Ur-Namma, founder of the dynasty, called for offerings to his funerary statue, an Akkadian practice, and his cadaster measured provinces in the same way the Akkadian kings had.[134] Furthermore, the personality cult of Ur's longest-lived ruler, Shulgi, is strongly reminiscent of that of Naram-Sin. In addition, Shulgi and the others were proud to bear titles first used by the Akkadian kings.[135] A century or so later, a king bearing the name Naram-Sin ruled at Uruk and gave himself the title "god of his land," reminiscent of the divine honors claimed by his Akkadian namesake, as well as by Shulgi.[136]

At Ur, one of the clearest signs of Akkadian influence may be seen in the "Reforms of Shulgi." These include deification of the king, change of his title from "King of Sumer and Akkad" to "king of the four world regions," construction of temples in honor of himself, worship of his statues, and celebration of an annual festival in his honor. Among the administrative and military reforms attributed to Shulgi by some scholars are adoption of the bow and arrow, creation of a standing army, strengthening of political connections between Nippur and Ur, standardization of weights and measures with new "royal" or "Shulgi" units, calendar reform, reorganization of temple households into the state apparatus, growth of a royal domain, expansion of industrial complexes, centralization of bureaucracy, promulgation of collected laws, founding of scribal schools, reform of the writing system, and development of new accounting methods, as well as taxation and redistribution procedures.[137] Nearly all of these were characteristic of the Akkadian period, especially the administrative reforms enacted during the reign of Naram-Sin. Whether or not Shulgi purposely patterned himself after Naram-Sin remains an open question.

By the turn of the second millennium, the era of the Akkadian Empire was receding into the past. In both Sumer and Iran, its invasive and oppressive aspects spurred the kingdoms of Ur and Awan to change direction toward a new, post-Akkadian model.[138] In contemporaneous Babylonia, the legacy of the Akkadian Empire was stylistic and cultural, rather than political or strategic. But in northern Mesopotamia it remained the ideal of successful statecraft. Thus the early second millennium kingdoms of Eshnunna, Assyria, and Upper Mesopotamia kept the Akkadian legacy immediate and vital, so much so that rulers took the names of Sargon and Naram-Sin, honored the Akkadian kings as ancestors, and made direct allusions to them.

Of the various northern Mesopotamian polities, Eshnunna was closest to the geographical heart of the former Akkadian Empire.[139] Perhaps for this reason the Akkadian used at Eshnunna enjoyed a special prestige further west at Mari, where it was preferred for formal communication under Yahdun-Lim and his successors.[140] When Eshnunna broke away from the Kingdom of Ur about 2010 BCE, the first independent ruler, Shu-iliya, was called "king" by his courtiers. He himself acknowledged the city god, Tishpak, as king of the city, even as he assumed divine honors, like Naram-Sin, Shulgi, and Shu-Sin.[141] The rulers who followed him were content to call themselves "governor" of the city, implying that they continued to regard the city god as king, as at Assur.[142]

Ipiq-Adad of Eshnunna (ca. 1862–1818 BCE) began a period of aggressive expansion, securing most of the Diyala region and the Himrin Valley, venturing into Iran, and pushing north and west to the Euphrates. On the basis of this, he took the title of king, deified himself, and was addressed by his courtiers as "king of the world," the new version of the old title "king of Kish." That he had the Sargonic dynasty in mind is shown by his naming his son and successor Naram-Sin, no doubt meaning that he had founded a northern state on the Akkadian model.[143] There was a rival Naram-Sin at Assur, whose ambitions were presumably similar, though little is known of his career, so it would seem that the Assyrians were pressing a claim to the Akkadian legacy as well.[144]

In any event, Naram-Sin of Eshnunna's program of conquests took him to the Khabur and allowed him to dominate Mari. His temple-like audience hall at Eshnunna suggests that he too emulated the deified Akkadian Naram-Sin.[145] An interesting example of the Akkadian influence on his reign is a commemorative inscription known as *Erra and Naram-Sin*. This was drawn up on a circular tablet that resembles the later commemorative inscriptions of the Babylonian kings of the eighteenth and seventeenth centuries BCE, which were often written on the heads of large clay cones. Although the opening lines are fragmentary, it seems that Naram-Sin is conversing with three deities: Erra, Sin, and Anunitum. After Ishtar promises Naram-Sin triumph in battle and gives him weapons, Erra asks for Naram-Sin's help in defeating Enlil. Naram-Sin agrees, vowing to build Erra a temple if he wins:

> I will build you a house to be your heart's delight.
> Do you reside within it, take your place on the kingly dais,
> I will make it wide and broad above you,
> I will adorn your inner chambers with green.[146]

In thanks, Erra's spouse, Laz, asks a blessing for Naram-Sin.

The text shows the capabilities of an Eshnunna court writer, who composed it in a high poetic style, intended to associate the Eshnunna king with his great namesake. The conclusion suggests that Naram-Sin carried out a campaign to the south and ruled at Cutha, not improbable, given his other successes.[147] Upon his demise, an elaborate *Elegy on the Death of Naram-Sin* was composed, describing his obsequies and entry into the netherworld.[148]

The sculptures from the reigns of the Eshnunna rulers of the nineteenth and early eighteenth centuries BCE likewise exhibit some awareness of Akkadian forerunners. The limestone statue of Ur-Ningizzida (ca. 1900 BCE), for example, depicts him in a tasseled garment of the type worn by Manishtusu, but without the folds and body-revealing drapery typical of much Akkadian art. These the sculptors may not have been able to achieve, or they were not part of Eshnunna's royal iconography.[149]

A similarly complex engagement with the Akkadian past is manifest at Assur, which may have owed its initial development as a commercial center to incorporation in the Akkadian Empire (Chapter 3 part 2). Two rulers of Assur reigned in the same order as their Akkadian namesakes: Sargon I (ca. 1920–1881 BCE) and Naram-Sin (ca. 1872–1828? BCE). Almost nothing is known of them or of the importance of Assur in this period, but they clearly associated themselves with Akkadian political tradition. Both seem to be deified in official writings, though the divinity sign may refer instead to the Akkadian Sargon and Naram-Sin as theophoric elements in their names.[150] Both bore the title "governor of Assur," which had Akkadian precedent. A cylinder seal with the name of Naram-Sin of Agade was even used to seal an Old Assyrian legal document.[151]

The Kingdom of Upper Mesopotamia was put together by Shamshi-Adad (ca. 1833–1773 BCE), whose domains at their height may have stretched from the upper Tigris to Rapiqum, Mari, and the great bend of the Euphrates or beyond. His soldiers fought in Lebanon; his diplomats traveled to Dilmun in the Gulf. After he conquered Nineveh, he swore in his building inscription there that he had incorporated and honored an earlier one of Manishtusu, and there is no good reason to doubt him. At Mari under his rule, the funerary cult of the Akkadian kings was maintained (part 1, this chapter) and the cult of the "Lady of Agade" (Ishtar) was introduced to the city during his son's reign there. Although Shamshi-Adad's origins are obscure, he seems to have personally identified with the Akkadian dynasts and did not object if people believed that he was ultimately of Akkadian royal lineage. When he took the title "king of the four world regions," he was surely mindful of its historical meaning, especially since he also called himself "king of Agade" and even visited the site, apparently for sentimental reasons. On his victory stele, the pose and clothing of the smiting figure on it (a god or Shamshi-Adad himself) are strongly reminiscent of the triumphal Naram-Sin, whatever the direct model may have been.[152]

Hammurabi of Babylon mentioned Agade in his stele of laws ("who sustained Ishtar in the Eulmash in Agade, city of broad streets and squares"), may have used phraseology taken from Naram-Sin's account of the Great Revolt ("I opened the way out of numerous pressing crises"), called himself "god among kings," and may have invoked Akkadian royal titles. Like Naram-Sin in Sumerian literature (part 6, this chapter), he "rose like the sun over the people of this land."[153]

Interest in the Akkadian period can next be documented in Middle Babylonian literature and in the possibility that one of the Kassite kings named Kurigalzu ordered building at Agade (part 7, this chapter). Imagery first seen in Akkadian art reappears in Kassite glyptic, such as a double-faced god, a nude hero kneeling while making a libation, a figure with a skirt in the form of a mountain, and a bird-and-tree motif.[154] In Middle Assyrian glyptic, a figure with the horned cap of divinity, if a king rather than a god, may be inspired by Akkadian art as well.[155]

In contemporaneous Hatti, the Hittite kings looked to Sargon and cited him as the standard of success.[156] Hattushili I (seventeenth century BCE), for instance, claimed that he had surpassed Sargon when he boasted of crossing the Euphrates and destroying two major cities:

No one had crossed the Euphrates, but I, the Great King Tabarna, crossed it [on foot], and my army crossed it [after me?] on foot. Sarg[on crossed it too], he defeated the troops of Hahha [but] did nothing to [the city of Hahha] and [did not] burn it down, nor did he show² the smoke to the Storm God of Heaven. I, the great king Tabarna, destroyed H[asshuwa] and Hahha and [burned²] them (both) down with fire and [showed] the smoke to the . . .-god in heaven.¹⁵⁷

By this time, Naram-Sin's alleged excesses and impious behavior may have served as the example of the ill-fated ruler, not to be invoked.¹⁵⁸

Sargon II of Assyria (721–705 BCE) was the first king in more than a thousand years to revive the name of Sargon, though in a somewhat different form (Sharru-ukin, rather than Sharru-kin). This was undoubtedly programmatic, as selecting a name, especially a throne name, was an important way of setting the tone for a reign.¹⁵⁹ Although it is often said he chose it for legitimation because he had usurped his throne, this seems a less likely reason than his dreams of empire, which he proceeded to pursue with extraordinary vigor. In this context, *The Empire of Sargon of Akkad*, purporting to describe the Akkadian Empire, has been read as an ideal he sought to emulate. As noted in part 4, this chapter, the Phase III omens about Sargon of Akkad may have been expanded with the campaigns of Sargon II in mind. Since during his reign, his military deeds were implicitly compared to the epic quest of Gilgamesh, it is easy to suppose that the feats of Sargon of Akkad, the other great hero of the past, also interested this king.¹⁶⁰

Yet by the eighth century little was known of the historical Sargon, whereas the exploits of the legendary Gilgamesh had been set forth in an epic masterpiece. If some writers moved to fill the gap by creating for Sargon of Akkad a birth legend, an account of his empire, and reports of his campaigns to distant lands, or by adding Assyrian elements to his omens, or even by comparing Sargon's founding of Agade with Sargon II's construction of Dur-Sharrukin, then one is justified in positing an efflorescence of interest in the Akkadian period, at least at court, resulting in the production of imaginative works about the ancient namesake. The shocking death of Sargon II in battle and the shameful failure to recover his body for burial cast gloom over the Assyrian ruling class at the height of its power, perhaps leading the learned elite to reconsider the two ideological heroes of the time: Sargon of Akkad and Gilgamesh of Uruk. If Sargon II had taken, in his own words, "the long-ago" Sargon as his imperial ideal, that now seemed ill-omened, for like Sargon he had come to power in an irregular manner, had reached the limits of the known world and had built a new city. But now, like Sargon according to the pseudonymous royal letter (part 5, this chapter), he was doomed to restlessness because he had not been properly buried.¹⁶¹

The fascination of Nabonidus with the Akkadian period, shown especially by his excavations at Agade and his restoration and honoring of a statue of Sargon, has been discussed in part 7, this chapter. The inscriptions of other Neo-Babylonian kings were drafted using archaizing spellings that scribes may have thought were Old Akkadian, and Akkadian elements have been detected in Neo-Babylonian seals.¹⁶² Thus the last Babylonian Empire harked back to the first.

For his part, Cyrus the Great, founder of the Achaemenid Empire, mentioned Agade, along with Nineveh and Assur, in his cylinder inscription commemorating the Persian conquest of Babylon in 539 BCE, intending to emphasize his role as successor to the great states of the Mesopotamian past. The Babylonian scribe who composed this work no doubt knew of Nabonidus's interest in the Akkadian kings but made no mention of it, meaning to place Cyrus in the same historical role that Nabonidus had chosen for himself.[163]

In conclusion, one may consider a persistent theme in Mesopotamian royal inscriptions, from Sargon through the end of cuneiform culture and beyond: marching to the sea and performing sacrifices or carrying out rituals on the seashore. This has sometimes been viewed as a case of long-lived Akkadian influence.[164] Manishtusu and Naram-Sin enlarged on the trope by claiming that they had gone further than the very seashore where Sargon had halted. But with them it might end, although a fragmentary second-millennium ritual tablet may prescribe cleansing of weapons in the sea,[165] since Sargon and his successors' washing of weapons in the sea was known only from authentic inscriptions but not from other Mesopotamian historical works. It therefore seems doubtful that later Mesopotamian rulers, with the possible exception of Yahdun-Lim, king of Mari (ca. 1800 BCE), where memory of the Age of Agade lingered on, could have known of or consciously followed Sargon's example.

Finally, sometime in the first millennium a clever forger used the Akkadian period as a putative source for a stone monument, purporting to be a record of certain benefactions and exemptions bestowed on the Temple of Shamash at Sippar by Manishtusu. This object was displayed in the temple collection of antiquities and several copies of it were made on clay tablets by antiquarian scribes. The descendants of Sargon of Akkad could still bestow the cachet of a glorious past.[166]

## Notes

1  For Mesopotamian approaches to its own past, Güterbock 1934/38; Finkelstein 1963; Grayson 1980; Wilcke 1982, 2001; Edzard 1989a; Charpin 1990b: 24; Hallo 1991; Renger 1996b; Glassner 1996b; Van de Mieroop 2012. Edzard 2004: 106 suggests that the Akkadian kings were better remembered than Sumerian kings in the second millennium because they used the Akkadian language, but there was surely more to the Akkadian achievement than that.

2  Tsukimoto 1985: 36, 38, 39–73; 2010; A. Cohen 1998: 107; further Chapter 10 part 7.

3  Bayliss 1973; Tsukimoto 1985: 228–41; for royalty in particular, Winter 1992; A. Cohen 1998; for the funerary use of statues, Selz 1997: 200 note 201.

4  Durand 1985: 159; 2003a: 4–5; further below, part 8.

5  Birot 1980, collation Charpin and Durand 1986: 165 note 115; re-edition Durand and Guichard 1997: 63–70 (no. 4) i 18–22; Jacquet 2002; for the Chamber of Thrones, Durand 1987: 108–9.

6  Durand 1985, 1987: 108–9; in general, Novák 2000; Michalowski 2013: 319–20.

7  Charpin and Durand 1986: 166; Durand 2003a: 2–3.

8  Charpin 2004a: 140.

9  Finkelstein 1966; for "trials" or "reverses," Durand 2003a: 6.

10  Charpin and Durand 1986; Glassner 1986: 58. Even if Hammurabi did not identify genealogically with the Akkadian kings, the prologue of his laws may show the influence of Naram-Sin's account of the Great Revolt, below, part 8 and note 153.

11  J. Westenholz 2012.

12 J. Westenholz 2012: 103.
13 Below, note 135.
14 For a list of Akkadian objects taken to Susa as booty, D. Potts 1999: 235–36.
15 Survey by Kraus 1963 and detailed analysis by Gelb and Kienast 1990: 129–56; for orthography and linguistic authenticity, Keetman 2008; Kogan 2011; for rough notes and abbreviations that the scribe might have written out in full in a final copy, Civil 1985: 42; B. Foster 1990: 39. For Akkadian-period copies of Akkadian royal inscriptions, A. Westenholz 1974/77; Marchesi 2011. For the scribes' descriptions of the monuments, Buccellati 1993. Attribution of copies to Larsa is based on the approximate date the relevant tablets appeared on the antiquities market, when the looting of Larsa was at its height.
16 The copies are treated separately in Gelb and Kienast 1990; in Frayne 1993 they are integrated with originals in a hypothetical chronological order.
17 Oelsner 1989: 404–7; Frayne 1993: 191–92. The Sumerian portion gives the appearance of being a late fabrication or pastiche, including a reinterpretation of the Akkadian title *dannum* and an unusually full Sumerian verbal chain (in-na-an-sum). Perhaps LAGAB-ta in line x is a misunderstanding of Old Akkadian SIG-ta; further, Kienast and Sommerfeld 1994: 388–90.
18 Frayne 1993: 197–98 (obscure). Perhaps it means "Squeeze from a diorite slab of the display inscriptions (*ša* MU$_x$.SA.RU [pseudo-logogram] *pa-li-su-tim* [*palisu* = "something seen"] that Nabu-zera-lishir the scribe saw in the hall of inscriptions of Naram-Sin the king in "Agade." For the reading MU$_x$ for A, Beaulieu 1989a: 141–42; further below, note 116.
19 For this and other attributions to Larsa, above, note 15.
20 Michalowski 2011: 22 suggests that only a few scribes were interested in this material, but this does not take the number and distribution of manuscripts sufficiently into account.
21 For a survey of the practice of copying earlier texts in the post-Akkadian periods, Hallo 2006; for possible Akkadian-period examples of copying or excerpting inscriptions on clay tablets, A. Westenholz 1974/77: 96, 103. For the possibility that a similar practice existed in Egypt, though only one possible instance is known, Piccato 1997 (reference courtesy Colleen Manassa).
22 For the history and practice of divination, Bottéro 1974; Rochberg 2004: 44–97; Maul 2007, 2013; Annus 2010.
23 For the reigns of the Akkadian kings, Glassner 1986: 65. The correlation depends on what chronology is used but works for all three kings using only one of the chronological possibilities, Huber 1987.
24 Huber 1987; further Boese 1982; for the omen, Cornelius 1966.
25 Above, note 22, and Jeyes 1980, 1989; Koch 2005; Maul 2013.
26 Weidner 1928/9: 227–30; I. Starr 1977: 157–60; 1986. For the text of *The Sumerian King List*, Glassner 2004: 117–26.
27 J. Rutten 1938; Snell 1974; Larsen 1987: 212–13; Meyer 1987: 190–217; Glassner 1996b: 182–83; Richardson 2010: 233–35 (who suggests that they were deliberately archaizing so orthography is not significant); differently Gelb 1992: 169–71; Durand 1983.
28 Rutten 1938.
29 J. Meyer 1987:193 and plate 14: 6–7.
30 *Muses*, 350; note that 3600 is represented in cuneiform by a large circle.
31 Glassner 1984a: 21, 2009b.
32 Richardson 2010: 234. A liver model from ME-Turan with an omen referring to the accession of Dadusha, king of Eshnunna in the first half of the eighteenth century BCE, suggests that the practice of recording historical omens may have continued or been revived in the Eshnunna region as another way of associating the Eshnunna kings with the kings of Agade, I. Starr 1985. An omen of Hammurabi, reminiscent of the

early ones of Sargon ("who ruled everything'), appears in a Neo-Babylonian extispicy text, and may have been fabricated at that date; most of that tablet is dedicated to omens pertaining to Assurbanipal, I. Starr 1985.

33 Koch 2005: 226–32.

34 Finkelstein 1963: 464–65.

35 Nougayrol 1945: 30; Glassner 2004: 47.

36 Goetze 1947: 265.

37 Oppenheim, quoted by Bottéro 1974: 149 note 3; for his later view, that historical omens were "intrusions," Oppenheim 1977: 216.

38 Cooper 1980: 102 (this logic requires that only a committed Christian or Jew could use the Bible as a historical source); modified in Cooper 1993: 13; Liverani 1993: 43–44; Reiner 1974. Although most modern students of Mesopotamian thought today are unwilling to accord divination a significant empirical basis, as that term is understood today, they do not necessarily take a position on the historicity of the omens relating to the Akkadian period; Koch-Westenholz 1995: 15–19; Lehoux 2003; Rochberg 1999; 2004: 237–86. 2009, 2010; Brown 2000: 109–13, 2006; Maul 2013: 212.

39 Weidner 1928/9: 240. Modern proponents of the empirical basis for historical omens or divination in general include Bottéro 1974: 144–52; I. Starr 1983: 7–8; Larsen 1987: 212–13. Further, Chapter 12 part 2.

40 Using the numeration of the following studies, where G = Goetze 1947; N = Nougayrol 1945; R = Rutten 1938; W = Weidner 1928/9, and the pagination of K = King 1907: Sources: Sargon 1=R1; 2=G2; 3=G3; 4=G4; G7; 5=G5; 6=G6; 7=Nougayrol 1969: 155 lines 9–10; 8=G8, Riemschneider 1965: 128 line 4; 9=G9, compare G10; 10=G11; 11=Riemschneider 1965: 130 lines 16–17; 12=G12, Koch 2005: 225–26; 13=N 3, 57, 106, WVC; 14=N12; 15=N58; 16=K30, N83; Koch 2005: 227; 17=K30–32, N61; Koch 2005: 228; 18=N55, 62, 66; 19=WVA, N54, compare N47 (with Old Akkadian spelling); 20=WVB, N20; 21=K32, N67; Koch 2005: 228; 22=K33–34, N67; Koch 2005: 228, improved reading in A. Westenholz 1999: 23 note 34; 23=K25–26, N71; Koch 2005: 226; 24=K26–27, N 72, 74; Koch 2005: 226; 25=K28–29, N75; Koch 2005: 227; 26=N36–37, N77; Koch 2005: 230; 27=K27–28, N73; Koch 2005: 227; 28=K34–35, N68; Koch 2005: 229; Rimush 29=G13, 30=N29, 42, 58; Manishtusu 32=R2; Naram-Sin 33=R3, 34=G15=Leichty 1970: 206; 35=G16, compare N53; 36=Jeyes 1989: 159; 37=G17; 38=Jeyes 1989: 183–84; 39= N8–10; 40=N53, 76b; 41=N76a, 42=N79; Sharkalisharri 43=G20, 44=G21, 45=N21; End 46=R 4, photo J. Meyer 1987: 192–93; 47=Nougayrol 1973: 48 line 16'; 48=G22; 49=N6; 50=N56.

41 Glassner 1984a: 21.

42 Kraus 1987: 194–96.

43 The original inscriptions known from Mesopotamia itself are listed together in Gelb and Kienast 1990: 63–65.

44 For "ruled the world," possibly an Akkadian or post-Akkadian explanation of "Kish," Chapter 1 note 6.

45 The original inscriptions are listed together in Gelb and Kienast 1990: 66–74.

46 The original inscriptions are listed together in Gelb and Kienast 1990: 75–80; for Nineveh, J. Westenholz 2004.

47 The original inscriptions are listed together in Gelb and Kienast 1990: 81–101.

48 A. Westenholz 2000; Steinkeller in CUSAS 17: 12–13.

49 Appendix Ib 1, 2; Frayne 1993: 11 and passim (Enlil gave him no rival).

50 The formulation of the Mari model, however, anticipates later Babylonian expression of this concept, to "have" or "acquire" a rival; so also Finkelstein 1963: 465 note 17.

51 Sargon omen 22; Appendix Ib 14; Frayne 1993: 48; A. Westenholz 2000.

52 Edzard 1976/80b; A. Westenholz 1999: 42. For the theme of destroyed cities in divination, Glassner 1986: 63.

53 A. Westenholz 1999: 53 note 189.

54 Glassner 1986: 68.
55 Bottéro 1974.
56 Courty in Oates, Oates, and McDonald 2001: 367–72; for an analysis of the omen episode as a "marvel," Haul 2009: 214–20; for eclipse terminology, Hunger 2009/11; for the Enheduanna passage, Appendix IIc Inanna and Ebih, line 75.
57 Glassner 1983.
58 Frayne 1993: 132–35.
59 There are puzzling variations in authentic inscriptions and in administrative documents from Ebla for the spelling of Armanum (Armi, Yarmuti), Archi 2011a.
60 Charpin and Ziegler 1997.
61 J. Westenholz 2008: 255.
62 Jacobsen 1939: 142–7; Hallo 1991.
63 Pelting with tablets or seals, Langdon 1923a: 409; Finkelstein 1963: 468 note 30; stabbing with pins, Hallo 1991: 155–6; whisper campaign, A. Westenholz 1999: 41 and note 127; another interpretation of this episode by D. O. Edzard, according to which the king was condemned to death using sealed documents, was never published (courtesy J.-J. Glassner).
64 Differently Liverani 1993: 43; for discovery of authentic inscriptions, below, note 113.
65 For the reigns of Sargon II and Sennacherib, Grayson 1991. For Sargon II and Sargon of Akkad, Van De Mieroop 1999; Galter 2006 and, for older literature, Chapter 12 part 2.
66 Glassner 2004.
67 Glassner 2004: 117–26; Wilcke 2001.
68 Glassner 2004: 122–5.
69 Compare Becker 1985: 300.
70 Glassner 2004: 153.
71 Glassner 2004: 153.
72 Glassner 2004: 4–5, 2005a.
73 Marchesi 2010; in general Wilcke 1988, 1989; Chen 2013.
74 A. Westenholz 1974; so also Kuhrt 1995 1:17 (based on collecting year names).
75 Glassner 2004: 266–69.
76 Edzard 1991.
77 Glassner 2004: 268–71.
78 Glassner 2004: 270–71.
79 King 1907: 1:27–55, with parallel texts; Güterbock 1934/38: 17; Grayson 1966: 72–73. An older view held that some Phase III omens were in fact drawn from chronicles, but this was before extensive Phase I and Phase II omens became available. These showed that the omen tradition antedated the Chronicles and the Phase III sources, Güterbock 1934: 17.
80 Cooper and Heimpel 1983; Alster 1987; J. Westenholz 1997: 52–55.
81 Cooper and Heimpel 1983: 74 lines 6'-7'; for the solar aspects of royalty, Charpin 2013a.
82 Cooper 1983a: 52 (Appendix IIIb) lines 40–41; Wilcke 2001: 109.
83 Cooper and Heimpel 1983: 76 line 52 = Cooper 1983a: 54 line 87.
84 Similarly Cooper and Heimpel 1983: 74.
85 Cooper and Heimpel 1983: 75 lines 10–11.
86 Cooper 1983a: 54 (Appendix IIIb) lines 88–91.
87 Vanstiphout 2003: 84 line 504.
88 Cooper and Heimpel 1983: 76 line 53.
89 Manassa 2010.
90 Cooper 1983a (Appendix IIIb); ECTSL 2.1.5, as well as the comments of Durand 1975 and Attinger 1984; further Appendix III.

91 Glassner 1986: 55–93.

92 Kraus 1973: 327–29.

93 The Akkadian material has been closely studied by J. Westenholz 1997 and Haul 2009; summary in J. Westenholz 1983a; in general, Van de Mieroop 1999: 59–76; 2012: 48–53.

94 For interpretation of the text as a parody, B. Foster 2002; for editions and other interpretations, Cavigneaux 2005; Dercksen 2005; Alster and Oshima 2007; J. Westenholz 2007; Haul 2009: 339–54. Further on Gilgamesh and Sargon, Chapter 9 part 5.

95 Lewis 1980; Glassner 1988; J. Westenholz 1997: 36–49; *Muses*, 912–13.

96 This count varies depending upon chronological criteria and whether or not certain manuscripts belong together; for a broader list, Haul 2009: 15–31. This writer does not accept the inclusion of the so-called "Old Akkadian Legend" (Haul 2009: 12) in this group, on the grounds that it is more likely a student copy of an authentic inscription of Naram-Sin; and "Erra and Naram-Sin" (Haul 2009: 27) and the "Elegy on the Death of Naram-Sin" (J. Westenholz 1997: 203–20), both on the grounds that they refer to Naram-Sin of Eshnunna, of the early second millennium; further below, note 147.

97 Haul 2009: 190–235.

98 J. Westenholz 1997: 78–93; Haul 2009: 237–51; for Mardaman, on the Tigris near the present Iraqi-Turkish border, Charpin 1994: 180 with notes 29 and 30.

99 Haul 2009: 253–310.

100 J. Westenholz 1997: 94–101.

101 Manassa 2010; for a discussion of "fictionality" in Akkadian literature, Haul 2009: 133–59.

102 Van Dijk 1983: 72–73 lines 159–67; for line 165, Geller 1985: 217. For the likelihood of such heroic poetry in the Akkadian period, J. Westenholz 1992b: 144.

103 J. Westenholz 1997: 141–69.

104 *Muses*, 1017–19.

105 Grayson 1974/7; Hurowitz 1998: 67–95 (dates to the first millennium, possibly reign of Sargon II or Sennacherib, p. 93); Liverani 1999/2000. The text refers to Sargon using the language of omen 9, above, part 4. For comments on this piece, its first-millennium context, and whether or not it contains older materials, Finkelstein 1963: 466 note 20; Seux 1965: 9–10; Liverani 1993: 64–67; Van De Mieroop 1999: 330–34 (dates to reign of Sargon II); Galter 2006: 289.

106 J. Westenholz 1997: 173–87.

107 B. Foster 2007a: 19–21.

108 Tinney 1995; Charpin 1997; T. Potts 2001; Haul 2009: 62–94, who demonstrates in detail the close dependence of some of these texts on authentic commemoration of Naram-Sin. Further above, note 10.

109 Walker 1980; Calmeyer 1993/7.

110 Steinkeller and George in CUSAS 17: 13.

111 *Muses*, 831; for pre-Akkadian tablets picked up at Shuruppak at other sites, A. Westenholz and Visicato 2000: 1123.

112 Sollberger 1967; Jursa 1997; Michel 2011.

113 Frame 1993: 24–29; Schaudig 2001: 359–61 (2.4.1); 441–44 (2.13); 422–34, 438–39 (2.12); 593–94 (P.4); W. Lambert 1969; Beaulieu 1989a: 132–37. Kennedy 1969 identified eight administrative texts from the reigns of Nabonidus, Cyrus, and Cambyses recording offerings to this statue over a period of 26 years; further on these Beaulieu 1989a: 135; Bongenaar 1997: 230 and note 205, in general Winter 1992; Schaudig 2003. There is no reason to doubt the authenticity of Nabonidus's attribution of the statue to Sargon, because most Akkadian royal sculpture was inscribed, Strommenger 1959.

114  Schaudig 2001: 454–55, 463–64 (2.14). For Ishtar of Agade in the Neo-Babylonian period, Beaulieu 1989b; Frame 1993.
115  W. Lambert 1969; Schaudig 2001: 593–94 (P.4); this event was commemorated in a special inscription, Schaudig 2001: 372–77 (2.7); incidental reference to it in a summary inscription, Schaudig 2001: 366–67, 369 (2.5). For the historical circumstances, Beaulieu 1989a: 122, 128–32 (total eclipse at Babylon, September 26, 554 BCE), although I have followed Schaudig's interpretation of the chronicle-style text P.4 as depicting Nabonidus in a positive light.
116  For the squeeze, above, note 18; for the activity of the scribe Nabu-zer-lishir, who liked to use an archaizing style in his professional work, Joannès 1988. For the bead, Jursa 1997.
117  Goosens 1948; Beaulieu 1989a: 140–43, 1994; Ehrenberg 1999; Winter 2000; Schaudig 2003.
118  Beaulieu 1989a: 143.
119  Feldman 2007: 277.
120  *Muses*, 952–53.
121  For the Gutians, Chapter 2 note 18.
122  Frayne 1993: 220–28.
123  Diakonoff 1947; Spycket 1981: 250; de Lapérouse 2003: 210–12, drawing attention to the treatment of the face, ears, and hair.
124  For Lullubum, Chapter 2 note 19; A. Westenholz 1999: 94; for Naram-Sin's presence there, Appendix Ib 15; Frayne 1993: 143–44; for Anu-banini, Edzard 1973; for the title, Chapter 10 note 17. Its occurrence in an inscription of Sharkalisharri may not be authentic, above, note 17.
125  For Darband-i-Gaur, Strommenger 1963 (Naram-Sin); Boese 1973 (post-Akkadian); for the Zagros rock reliefs in general and their Akkadian background, Eppihimer 2009: 246–79; Mühl 2013: 145–50.
126  For a comparable situation in first-millennium Syria, in which local rulers may use different names and titles in Assyrian and Aramaic, Durand and Lemaire 1984.
127  André and Salvini 1989; Potts 1999: 122–25; Eppihimer 2009: 149–61; Steinkeller 2013a.
128  Steinkeller 1988b: 52–53 and note 20.
129  Eppihimer 2009: 113–19; Edzard 2004: 98.
130  Kienast 1973: 499; Cooper 1993; J. Westenholz 2008; Becker 1985 studies the Sumerian emphasis of the dynasty, especially as portrayed in modern historiography; Eppihimer 2009: 130–48 discusses influences and responses to Akkadian art in the art of the Ur dynasty; Michalowski 2004 surveys the ideology of the dynasty in general, which may have distanced itself from the past in the interests of avoiding the errors of previous rulers, while building on their accomplishments.
131  For the dynasty of Ur, Sallaberger 1999b, with extensive bibliographies.
132  J. Klein 1976; Wilcke 2001: 100.
133  For use of this strategy by Nebuchadnezzar I, *Muses*, 376–77.
134  Edzard 2004: 106.
135  Inscriptions of Shulgi collected in Frayne 1997a; for his attitude towards past kings, A. Westenholz 1999: 26 note 45. Shulgi is paired with Naram-Sin as a universal ruler in historical omens, Leichty 1970: 206.
136  Von Dassow 2009: 73; Sanati-Müller 2011: 82–86.
137  Thureau-Dangin 1898: 71–77. King 1910: 288; Gadd 1929: 121–23; Steinkeller 1987; Waetzoldt 1991; Sallaberger 1999: 147. I thank T. Eby for bibliography on the reforms of Shulgi. For deification of Shulgi, Michalowski 2008; for deification of Shulgi's son and successor and his temple at Eshnunna, Frankfort and Lloyd 1940; Steinkeller 1987: 22; Reichel 2008.
138  Frayne 1990: 484.

139 Saporetti 2002: 34–35, though he does not stress the Akkadian background of the early second-millennium rulers of Eshnunna.
140 Durand 1985: 161–64; 1992: 121–22; Charpin 1993, 2004a: 140, who writes of the cultural "Akkadianization" of Mari at this time.
141 Whiting 1977; Yuhong 1992, 1994; Eppihimer 2009: 193.
142 Frayne 1990: 484.
143 Charpin 2004a: 129–31; Streck 1998/2001a.
144 Streck 1998/2001b.
145 Frankfort, Lloyd, and Jacobsen 1940: 110–12.
146 J. Westenholz 1997: 194–96 lines 26–30.
147 W. Lambert 1973; Frayne 1991: 380 note 5; J. Westenholz 1997: 189–201, who consider it to refer to Naram-Sin of Agade; Lambert himself noted the formal and linguistic problems of associating this text with the Akkadian king, and the numerous parallels with Babylonian inscriptions, such as those of Shamshi-Adad, Hammurabi, and Samsuiluna. These problems disappear if this composition is dated to the reign of Naram-Sin of Eshnunna and taken to be genuine, which it no doubt would have been if any other royal name were in it. Lambert, however, maintained his interpretation (W. Lambert 1986). The insistence on the wrong Naram-Sin recalls the long debate over the Naram-Sin seal found in Cyprus, which started with the assumption that it had to refer to the Akkadian Naram-Sin and eventually gravitated towards its true date in the early second millennium, Chapter 12 part 1 and note 26.
148 J. Westenholz 1997: 203–20, who considers this as well to refer to Naram-Sin of Agade, despite its later date.
149 Eppihimer 2009: 209–26.
150 Galter 1996: 121–23; Michel 2009/11.
151 Gelb and Sollberger 1957, though they did not discuss the sealing.
152 Durand and Guichard 1997: 28; Durand 1998: 108–9; Charpin 2004b: 372–76; Ziegler 2004; Eppihimer 2009: 226–40, with discussion of the stele, 231–38; differently J. Westenholz 2004.
153 For the titles, J. Oates 1979: 65–66; for "broad streets and squares," Charpin 1991; quotations from *Muses*, 128, 131 (xiii 16, xlvii 19–20, Roth 1997: 78, 133, 140); compare the Bassetki inscription of Naram-Sin (Appendix Ia 18; Frayne 1993: 113–14) "because he defended his city in crisis," the citizens of Agade asked that he be "god of their city" (Chapter 1 part 4 and note 39); further below, part 8; Chapter 3 note 56; Chapter 6 note 16.
154 Porada 1952; Trokay 1990.
155 Fischer 2000 (counterarguments in Eppihimmer 2009: 10 note 25).
156 *The King of Battle*, in which Sargon invades Asia Minor, was brought, possibly from Hattusha, to El-Amarna in Egypt, perhaps in the fourteenth century BCE (Haul 2009: 417–50); in general Glassner 1985b; Van de Mieroop 2000; Beckman 2001.
157 Güterbock 1964: 2.
158 Güterbock 1964; Beckman 2001.
159 Radner 2005: 33–35; for the possibility that Sargon II's name was actually Sharru-ukin rather than Sharru-kin, Frahm 2005; Fuchs 2009/11: 51–53.
160 *Muses*, 63–64; Foster 2005b: 63–64.
161 Rogers 1901: 365, "In warlike prowess he was the model for an Assyrian king who bore his name centuries later"; Lewis 1980; Stronach 1997: 310; Van De Mieroop 1999b; Frahm 1999; Van De Mieroop 1999b sees, on the other hand, a critique of Sargon II, though not necessarily *post mortem*, in the city-building accounts of late sources for Sargon of Agade. For further comments on Sargon II and the Akkadian tradition in general, Frahm 2005; Dalley 2008: 27–28; Galter 2006, 2014.

162  Schaudig 2001: 99–104; Ehrenberg 1999. For Akkadian and Achaemenid art, Feldman 2007, who argues for influence of the stele of Naram-Sin on Achaemenid royal
art, versus Porada 1986: 21–2, who is skeptical.
163  So Beaulieu 1989b.
164  Malamat 1965; Rollinger 2012.
165  Van Dijk 1972
166  Gelb 1949; Sollberger 1967/8; Al-Rawi and George 1994: 138–48; in general, Radner
2005: 266–70.

# 12  The Akkadian period in modern historiography

## 1.  Discovering and using the sources

Modern interpretations and responses to the Akkadian period are no less rich and varied than those of antiquity. The first phase, from 1861 to 1914, was dominated by four complementary agendas: first, the initial publications and studies of the references to the Akkadian kings in divination, Neo-Babylonian chronicles, and other late works of a historical nature; second, the discovery of the Akkadian monuments at Susa and the Akkadian-period administrative documents at Girsu; third, the appearance of some Old Babylonian copies of Akkadian royal inscriptions on the antiquities market; and fourth, the first publications of fragments of Sumerian and Akkadian literary works about the Akkadian kings and the discovery of *The Sumerian King List*. Everyone active in cuneiform research at that time commented on some aspect of the Akkadian period, from its broad historical importance to details of its history and art. Because, unlike any other phase of Mesopotamian history, the Akkadian period was first known from much later cuneiform scholarship and literary works rather than from contemporaneous sources, questions of believability arose from the outset, which continue until the present.

In the second phase (1914–1947), the Nippur copies of the Akkadian royal inscriptions enormously enlarged the corpus of contemporaneous evidence, especially for Sargon, Rimush, and Manishtusu. These, together with *The Sumerian King List*, established the existence of the Akkadian, or Sargonic, dynasty and provided a set of data to which the later omens and literary works were compared and contrasted. Substantial publications of Akkadian-period administrative documents from Adab, Nippur, Umma, Gasur, and the Diyala region added much day-to-day source material, but, in general, did not attract the same level of scholarly interest as had the documents from Girsu, even though a grammatical and lexical study of Old Akkadian language (1915) provided a useful collection of material for understanding their non-Sumerian content. The significance of the Akkadian-period archaeological evidence from the University of Chicago expeditions to the Diyala region was obscured by dating problems, whereas the importance of the discoveries at Nagar, especially the great building of Naram-Sin, was more readily grasped. The Akkadian copper head from Nineveh, first published in 1936, became an icon for the dynasty and,

along with the Victory Stele of Naram-Sin, one of the most frequently reproduced works of Mesopotamian art.

The third phase (1947–1971) saw five major historical syntheses of the Akkadian period (1956, 1959, 1965, 1966, and 1971), as well as several shorter ones.
A comprehensive edition of the commemorative inscriptions appeared in 1963,
a grammar of Old Akkadian in 1952, and a glossary in 1957. The publication of
administrative documents continued, most notably with materials from various
sources in the Yale Babylonian Collection (1958), which spurred new interest in
Akkadian legal and business practices.

The fourth phase (1971–1993) was characterized by increasing interest in Akkadian social and economic history, with detailed studies of administrative documents
from Nippur, Umma, Adab, the Himrin Basin, and other sites. At the same time,
archaeological research shifted to northern Syria, and particular attention was paid
to the fall or collapse of the Akkadian Empire. New evidence for settlement patterns
and historical processes was provided by surface surveys in Iraq and Syria. The cul-
mination of this phase was a 1993 symposium in Rome dealing with the ideological,
literary, archaeological, and documentary aspects of the Akkadian period.

The fifth phase, from 1993 to the present, has been dominated by a flood of
new sources from the looting of archaeological sites in Iraq, beginning with the
Gulf War (1991). Four major collections of illegally excavated material, held by
the Banca d'Italia, Cornell University, the Real Academia della Historia, Madrid,
and a private collector in Norway, were promptly published by teams of scholars in exemplary, even lavish, editions with photographs, copies, translations, and
indices, making available hundreds of Akkadian-period documents, especially
from Adab and Umma. Ironically, scientifically excavated sites, such as Nagar,
Mari, Tell el-Wilayah, Mugdan, and Tell Leilan, had not yielded substantial accumulations of Akkadian records.

Throughout this century and a half, the presentation and discussion of Akkadian art, especially sculpture and cylinder seals, continued as a largely autono-
mous subject, with its own internal development as a sub-field of the history of
art, rather than of the political and social history of Mesopotamia.

## 2.   A time for optimism: 1861–1914

Modern historiography of the Akkadian period began in 1861 with Norris's publication of a cylinder of Nabonidus found at Ur. This mentions Naram-Sin in a
broken passage, which Norris definitively restored to add "son of Sargon, king of
Babylon" when he published the Sippar cylinder of Nabonidus in 1882. In that
same volume, he included a vase fragment originally from Magan, taken as booty
and inscribed by Naram-Sin, "king of the four world regions."[1] In 1866, Norris
published a fragmentary tablet of lunar omens from Assurbanipal's library, which
contained historical omens about "Sargon, king of Agade," as well as two other
first-millennium tablets mentioning both Sargon and Agade.[2]

Thus from the beginning, late sources about the Akkadian period outnumbered contemporaneous ones and presented a contradiction: was Sargon a king

of Babylon or Agade? Since no inscriptions of Sargon were yet known, scholars wondered if he existed or was purely legendary. Perhaps the omens were actually about Sargon II of Assyria, or another Sargon, and were confused or even deliberately projected backwards into history.[3] The fundamental issue was whether or not the omens could be considered historically reliable, a debate that continues to the present (Chapter 11 parts 4 and 5).[4]

Far more spectacular than the omens was *The Birth Legend of Sargon*, discovered in 1867 and first published by George Smith as an authentic account in 1870 and again in 1872, together with more omens about the Akkadian kings and other sources for third-millennium history.[5] Thereafter, the *Birth Legend* was translated, in whole or in part, in every anthology of Mesopotamian literature, and was quoted, in whole or in part, in most works about Mesopotamian history and culture, though with considerable disagreement over the meaning of key passages. This bothered non-Assyriologists and led them to question the reliability of the discipline as a whole.[6] There was also much dispute over the text's authenticity, with the most creative suggestion coming from Talbot, who proposed in 1872 that it was a late copy of an epigraph for a statue of Sargon.[7] There were also numerous comparative studies of the "exposure story" in the ancient Near East and elsewhere.[8]

The Naram-Sin of the Magan vase fragment was naturally identified with the Naram-Sin of the Nabonidus cylinders. From them, it was apparent that Nabonidus thought Naram-Sin was Sargon's son and successor and had lived 3200 years prior to his own time.[9] This was one of the first chronological datum points for the Akkadian period (though it would prove to be off by some 1400 years); numerological explanations of the time span were offered instead.[10] A cylinder seal of a servant of Sharkalisharri surfaced in 1877, and this began a protracted discussion of whether or not Sargon and Sharkalisharri were the same person, intensified after 1883, when a mace head inscribed with the name Sharkalisharri was found at Sippar and acquired by the British Museum.[11] Improved reading and understanding of this name, hitherto often read Sharganisharali, was achieved by Poebel in 1908, though this took time to find its way into general histories, being still unknown to Jastrow, for example, in his 1915 book.[12]

*Th. Dangin 1912*

Already in Smith's 1875 study, *The Chaldaean Genesis* (revised by Sayce in 1880), from which the following excerpt comes, Sargon of Akkad was depicted as an exceptionally important king. The unstated evidence for this was presumably the Nabonidus cylinders, for only a ruler of extraordinary achievement would have been remembered so much later.[13] On the basis of the omen tablet published by Norris in 1866, Smith and Sayce thought Sargon was the royal patron of the astrological series *Enuma Anu Enlil*, but this misunderstanding was short-lived. Smith and Sayce also believed that the dynasty of Hammurabi succeeded that of Sargon. As was standard in the 1870s and 1880s, "Accadian" and "Turanian" mean "Sumerian."

> Khammuragas [Hammurabi] . . . had conquered the rulers of the two kingdoms into which Babylonia was at this time divided. One of these was a queen, with whom ended a dynasty, famous in the annals of early Babylonia,

whose seat was at Agané or Agadé, near Sepharvaim. She had been the successor of Naram-Sin, the son of Sargon, who, like his father, had extended his power far and wide, and had even penetrated as far as the shores of the Mediterranean. Sargon had been a great patron of learning as well as a conqueror; he had established a famous library at Agané and had caused a work on astronomy and astrology to be compiled, which remained the standard authority on the subject up to the end of the Assyrian Empire. It was entitled, "The Illumination of Bel," and was in seventy-two books . . . Like the Babylonian and Assyrians of a later day, Sargon and his subjects belonged to the Semitic stock, and were related to the Hebrews and the Arabians. But they were really intruders in Chaldea. The primitive inhabitants of the country, the builders of its cities, the inventors of the cuneiform system of writing, and the founders of the culture and civilization which was afterwards borrowed by the Semites, were of a wholly different race. They spoke an agglutinative language of the same character as that of the modern Turks or Finns; and were originally divided into two sections – the inhabitants of Sumir or Shinar, the plain country, and the Accadians or "Highlanders," who had descended from the mountains of Elam subsequently to the first settlement of their kinfolk in Shinar. At some date between B.C. 3000 and 2000, the Semitic population which bordered upon Babylonia on the west, and had long been settled in some of its western cities, such as Ur (now Mugheir), conquered Shinar or Sumir. The Accadians, however, maintained their independence for a considerable time after this conquest, until, finally, Accad also was reduced under the sway of the Semitic kings. The population of the country was gradually absorbed, and its language became extinct. The extinction of the Accadian or Sumerian language had already taken place – at all events among the educated classes – at the time that Sargon founded his library at Agané, and one of the chief reasons which led to the compilation of the great work on astronomy, was the necessity of preserving the astronomical and astrological observations recorded in a language which was beginning to be forgotten. At the same time Semitic translations of other portions of the old Accadian literature were made.[14]

In this passage, the Sumerians are considered the original inhabitants of Mesopotamia and the Semitic Babylonian and Assyrians the invaders. Many subsequent narratives about the Akkadian dynasty were likewise set in a pre-existing conceptual framework of nineteenth-century notions about the Semitic peoples, including their allegedly nomadic ways, contempt for agriculture and urban life, strongly felt but primitive religious beliefs, inability to think abstractly or systematically, lack of art, and the simplistic grammar of their languages. A thesis commonly expounded held that the Semitic peoples were hostile to the Sumerians, so that the relations between Akkad and Sumer were necessarily dynamics of conquest and resistance.[15]

Not all scholars agreed. Some argued that the original inhabitants of Mesopotamia were in fact Semites rather than Sumerians. So important was this issue in late-nineteenth-century scholarship that the universal historian of antiquity, Meyer, devoted an entire monograph to it (1906). Meyer's carefully documented analysis touched on many points, taking up such matters as skull shape, leading him to conclude that the Semites lived in Mesopotamia prior to the coming of the Sumerians, who were therefore the invaders. They came from the mountains, conquered what became the land of Sumer, and brought with them and developed in Sumer a distinctive culture, including writing, sculpture in stone, and the temple tower. In the course of time, Sumerian and Semitic blended to form something larger and richer than either of its components. Meyer's views found few adherents, despite the enormous authority of their author.[16]

Some historians of the period were keenly aware of the methodological problems with using cuneiform sources, exacerbated by the rapidity with which Assyriologists proposed new readings and new chronologies. Nothing seemed fixed enough to rely on. In response, the historian Tiele began his masterful *Babylonisch-Assyrische Geschichte* (1886) with an essay on the historical value and uses of cuneiform records, from business documents to king lists. While acknowledging that royal inscriptions could be tendentious and selective in what they conveyed, he thought them unlikely to contain outright falsehoods.[17] Tiele defended Assyriologists from the criticism of historians, asserting that it was as absurd to deny the astonishing progress that had been made, even if many mistakes were committed along the way, as it would be to deny the importance of Columbus's discovery of the New World, even if he did not realize at first what he had found. The prime task of Assyriologists, he wrote, was to edit and translate their material as carefully and accurately as possible, and perhaps to restrain their enthusiasm for finding biblical and other personalities in cuneiform sources.[18] So far as their historical method went, he felt that German and French scholarship were ahead of England's and that the only major Italian study he knew of was erudite but lacking in rigor. Tiele concluded this fascinating essay with a detailed review of the work of every leading Assyriologist of his time.[19]

For Tiele's discussion of the Akkadian period, there were no new sources. *The Birth Legend of Sargon*, still the only literary text about the dynasty then known, he viewed as a myth attached to a historical figure; because the story was mythical was no reason to deny the existence of Sargon of Akkad.[20] He considered references by later kings to earlier ones, such as Nabonidus to Naram-Sin, historical data, since the Magan vase inscription had proved that Naram-Sin, at least, was a real person. As for the omens, he saw no justification not to use them as historical sources. Although he thought it hardly credible that Semites could have created a dominion so extensive at such an early date, Tiele felt that this had to be accepted, if only because the sources contained many names of people and places unknown in later periods and because Assyria was not mentioned in them. He rejected the possibility that the omens for Sargon of Akkad were projected backwards from the reign of Sargon II, which on the surface seemed an attractive hypothesis, because some of them, such as the destruction of Kazallu, did not fit the known deeds of Sargon II.[21] For sobriety of judgment and consummate mastery of the issues, cuneiform sources, and secondary literature of the time, Tiele's book had no rival.

A major new datum appeared in 1876, when a cylinder seal di Cesnola found at Curium, Cyprus, whose inscription honored a deified Naram-Sin, was first edited by Sayce and discussed repeatedly thereafter, with various proposals for its iconography and historical and artistic significance. This inspired a new idea that the Akkadian kings had ruled in the Mediterranean and even Egypt.[22] The possibility that this Naram-Sin was not the Akkadian king but another of the same name was not then considered; similar confusion about different kings named Naram-Sin would arise much later, with the discovery of certain literary texts (Chapter 11 part 6).

Hommel, a leading Assyriologist of the day and a contemporary of Tiele, also discussed the principal evidence for the Akkadian period,[23] that is, the *Birth Legend* and the omens, concluding that the *Birth Legend* was essentially authentic but the omens were first composed in the time of Sargon II or even Assurbanipal and applied to Sargon II rather than to Sargon of Akkad.[24] The destruction of Kazallu, which had led Tiele to believe that the omens could apply only to Sargon of Akkad, Hommel explained away by equating Kazallu with Karalla, a place taken by Sargon II in his campaigns. Hommel disposed of the revolt in Sargon's old age by reference to a fragmentary passage in Sargon II's inscriptions. For him, dispensing with the omens made the *Birth Legend* seem more genuine.[25] In his discussion of Naram-Sin, Hommel noted that the cuneiform writing on the seal from Cyprus did not resemble that on the Magan vase, so he questioned its authenticity.[26]

In the last two decades of the nineteenth century, various Assyriologists and general historians produced histories of ancient Mesopotamia, which, for the Akkadian period, had to make do with essentially the same sources, so there is no gain in mentioning them all. Most repeated the view that the Akkadians or Semites invaded Mesopotamia. Some, like Menant and Schmidt, were ignorant or highly selective of the technical literature of Assyriology then available; Menant placed Sargon of Akkad after the First Dynasty of Isin, while Schmidt did not mention the Akkadian kings at all in the 1300 pages of his Mesopotamian history.[27]

Winckler was, on the other hand, a well-informed Assyriologist of the late nineteenth and early twentieth centuries, but showed little precision and interest in detail in his influential but rambling 1899 survey of Mesopotamian history, translated into English and revised by the American Assyriologist Craig (1907). In the German edition of his work and elsewhere, Winckler suggested that Sargon was purely a legendary figure because he was known only from late and unreliable omens, but this idea was dropped from the English edition. Winckler was, like others of his time, preoccupied by racial questions and the putative Semitic invasion:

> The numerous monuments of this period evince technical skill of the highest order. The earliest inscriptions and monuments of the kings of Lagash are naturally very crude, so markedly so that we are tempted to attribute lack of skill to a decline consequent upon the Semitic invasion. But there quickly followed a new stage comparable to that of the Old Empire in Egypt. The inscriptions of Sargon and Naram-Sin are distinguished by a beautiful script,

and so excellent is the technical execution of Gudea's statues that archaeologists once thought it necessary to assume a Greek influence.[28]

Rogers' two-volume history, published in 1901, was on a different plane from Winckler's. Beginning with a comprehensive narrative of the decipherment of cuneiform writing and the exploration of Mesopotamia, followed by a description of ancient sites drawn from early travel accounts, his study got to the Akkadian period, calling it the Dynasty of Kish, only after 358 pages. Rogers ordered the "Kishite" kings as follows: Rimush (under the name of Alusharshid), "Lasirab" (a Gutian), Manishtusu, and Anu-banini.[29]

For Rogers, the Akkadian period proper, as it is understood today, began with Sharkalisharri, "also called Shargina," anticipating King's argument that the two were different names for the same person, and following Hommel and others, who believed this too. "Most of that which is told of him comes to us in a legendary text [*The Birth Legend of Sargon*] – hardly the place to which one would commonly go for sober history. But a little sifting of this source speedily reveals its historic basis . . ."[30] The story of Sargon moved Rogers: "A lonesome figure he is, in the dull gray dawn of human history, stalking across the scene, bringing other men to reverence the name of Ishtar, and making his own personality dreaded."[31] Like Gadd seventy years later, Rogers was willing to accept information from omens if it seemed inherently believable: "The fact that these details occur in an astrological text makes one wary of placing much reliance upon them. On the other hand, they are perfectly reasonable in themselves, and we should accept them at once from any other inscription." When they can be compared with other texts, omens "prove to be worthy of credence."[32]

In his account of Naram-Sin, Rogers referred to the known evidence, but followed Hilprecht in attributing the outer wall of Nippur to Naram-Sin, an idea that dropped from later literature.[33] The furthest reach of that king was suggested to him, as it was to Tiele and others, by the seal from Cyprus. There was as yet no sense of the fall of Agade: "The kingdom of Sargon and his son vanishes from our view as rapidly as it came, leaving not a trace of its effects."[34] Rogers stressed that Sargon was "of Semitic stock," and relayed the usual information that the Semites had invaded Mesopotamia from Arabia and their "distinctive Semitic type" had prevailed over the Sumerian.[31]

Other Assyriologists and ancient Near Eastern historians of the period produced histories in the same vein, continuing with variations on the theme of racial struggle. Radau, for example, argued that the Semites came originally through southern Mesopotamia and pushed north, no doubt having in mind the Arabian peninsula as the original home of the Semites. Some of these Semites, he wrote, remained in the south and adopted Sumerian language and ways, so the early rulers of Lagash, for example, were Semites who wrote in Sumerian. In due course, the northern branch of the Semites returned to take over the south.[35]

In 1902, Goodspeed, a biblical scholar, produced a general history of Mesopotamia for Bible students, based on his wide reading in Assyriology. He inclined toward another view. Searching for a broad interpretive theme for the events now placed in the third millennium (in his time the early fourth), he saw a "movement toward expansion, incorporation, and unification."[36] His paradigm was north versus south, in which the earlier and higher culture of the south "had pressed upon the northern communities and attempted to absorb them in the process of giving them civilization."[37] The hardier peoples of the north, having mastered these arts and coveting the riches of the south, thereupon overran the south, which had fallen into decay. He preferred not to follow the trend by making the northern peoples Semites and the southern ones Sumerians, but used neutral regional designations for them.[38]

Although Goodspeed considered authentic inscriptions of Sargon of no importance, and focused instead on the omens and *The Birth Legend of Sargon*, his assessment of the significance of the Akkadian period is not dissimilar to that of scholars a century later:

> The achievement of these kings [Sargon and Naram-Sin] were both a culmination of the activities of the earlier city-kings, and a model for those who followed. The former had from time to time gathered parts of the larger world under their own sway, as Lugalzaggisi the west, and Alusharshid [Rimush, placing him at Kish and earlier than Sargon] the east. But the incorporation of the whole into a single empire was the work of the Sargonids, and no dynasty followed which did not strive after this ideal.[39]

Thus the idea that the Akkadian period was a turning point in Mesopotamian history was well established by the beginning of the twentieth century.

Goodspeed's opinion of early Mesopotamian sculpture and glyptic was unfavorable. He did not know of the Akkadian monuments found in 1898 at Susa and the aesthetic judgments of the day were largely based on Classical Greek canons:

> The artist has little sense of the ideal or the general. To present the fact as it is, with simplicity verging on bareness, and with a directness that is almost too abrupt, – this was at the same time the weakness and the strength of the Babylonian sculptor or engraver . . . his anthropomorphism is rude and crude. The divine beings are not greater or grander than the men who worship them . . . it was reserved for the Greeks to improve upon it by glorifying and idealizing the human forms under which they represented Apollo and their Zeus. Another peculiarity which worked to the disadvantage of Babylonian art was the convention which demanded drapery in the representation of the human form . . . Hence the study of the nude body and the sense of beauty and grace which it develops were absent . . ."[40]

King's *History of Sumer and Akkad*, published barely a decade later (1910), was more definite on the relationship between Akkadians and Sumerians: "The early history of Sumer and Akkad is dominated by the racial conflict between Semites and Sumerians, in the course of which the latter were gradually worsted."[41] In his 35-page study of the Akkadian period (with an earlier section on Rimush and Manisuhtusu as kings of Kish), King wrote authoritatively on chronology, art, administration, society, royal deification and the place of the Akkadian rulers in Mesopotamian memory. He was convinced that the omens and chronicles contained authentic information and argued his reasons in detail.[42] King, like many Assyriologists, considered the course of discovery part of "Mesopotamian" history, so there is a constant counterpoint in his writing between ancient events and personalities and their unearthing and publication in modern times.

In his 1913 book, Hall called his Chapter on the Akkadian period, which closely resembles King's, "Semites and Sumerians." His presentation of the Akkadian kings was evenly divided among the monuments found at Susa, the Neo-Babylonian chronicles, and the omens. Echoing Smith and Sayce, he wrote "Few monarchs of the ancient world are so well known to us moderns as 'Sargon of Agade,' and we may say that to the Babylonians he was their hero of heroes, their Menes, Charlemagne, or Alfred the Great. . . . He . . . typified the first triumphant establishment of the Semites as the dominant race in Babylonia . . ."[43] Like Winckler, Hall preferred sweeping statements and comparisons to specifics.

Two years later, Jastrow gave this theme an interesting slant, arguing that "the struggle between the non-Semites or the Sumerians, and the Semites or Akkadians for supremacy" was the catalyst for Mesopotamian civilization:

This struggle represents the natural process in the assimilation of two apparently incompatible elements. Civilization may be described as the spark that ensues when opposing ethnic elements come into contact. Culture up to a certain grade may develop in any centre spontaneously, but a high order of civilization is always produced through the combination of heterogeneous ethnic elements . . . There is no more foolish boast than that of purity of race. A pure race . . . if it exists at all, is also a sterile race.[44]

Breasted, writing *Ancient Times* in 1916, vigorously upheld nineteenth-century stereotypes. The Akkadians were "Semitic wanderers of the desert" who had never learned discipline and drill in war, though they knew the use of the bow and arrow, which the Sumerians did not. Sargon's conquests may have forced the Akkadian nomadic tribesmen to stop living in tents, but they could not write and had no industry or experience with administration. All this they appropriated from the Sumerians, taking over their calendar, metrology, use of metal, and sculptural arts, but soon surpassing their Sumerian teachers. They were swarthy, heavily bearded, and had a distinctive skull. For Breasted, the rise of Sargon was the "first Semitic triumph." In the many reprintings of his work over the years, no significant modifications of his views were made.[45]

As these books show, there was considerable uncertainty about the order of the Akkadian kings, to what extent they were a dynasty, if they ruled from Kish or Agade, and whether or not Sargon and Sharkalisharri were the same person. On this last, Oppert, for example, dismissed the idea as a "joke," whereas King solved the problem by arguing that they were different people but that Sharkalisharri had taken Sargon's name.[46] Confusion was compounded by the general view that Sharkalisharri's father was named Itti-Bel or Dati-Enlil, a misunderstanding of a passage in an inscription from Nippur published in 1893, which referred to Sharkalisharri as *mar dadi Enlil* "beloved son of Enlil."[47] Unlike later Mesopotamian rulers, in fact the Akkadian kings gave no genealogical information in their inscriptions, so there was no way to know from their own accounts of their deeds in what order they ruled. A fragmentary letter mentioning an action by Sargon and a later one by Naram-Sin was evidence that Naram-Sin came after Sargon, confirming the cylinders of Nabonidus.[48]

The three later sources from the Akkadian period then known – the Neo-Babylonian chronicle, the *Cuthaean Legend of Naram-Sin*, and the cylinders of Nabonidus – called Naram-Sin the son of Sargon, so that seemed a reasonable point of departure, the problem then being where to place Rimush and Manishtusu. King and Rogers, for example, thought they belonged to an earlier dynasty ruling at Kish, especially since they both called themselves "king of Kish." The discovery of more sources, such as the Akkadian statues and stelae from Susa, the Cruciform Monument of Manishtusu, an assortment of original inscriptions from Nippur, as well as the Akkadian-period tablets from Telloh, added much new data but did not clarify whether or not the kings of Kish and Agade were the same dynasty and in what order they ruled.

For most scholars, after Scheil published in 1911 an early second-millennium manuscript of *The Sumerian King List*, the existence of the Akkadian dynasty was established. Even historians who criticized the use of later sources for the Akkadian period, such as the chronicles and omens, accepted the evidence of *The Sumerian King List* as inherently more reliable, and this situation has continued until the present. The possibility that *The Sumerian King List* originated in the Akkadian period was not then considered, though this idea has found adherents more recently (Chapter 11 part 4). As it happened, Scheil's manuscript was damaged after it listed Sargon and someone in modern times had glued a fragment of another tablet over the break, so the order of his successor kings remained uncertain.[49]

Thureau-Dangin, the leading master of Assyriology of the early twentieth century, did not write a comprehensive study of the Akkadian period, but in brief, incisive notes he commented on aspects of it. In a youthful essay of 1897, based on administrative documents from Girsu, he pioneered the use of exclusively contemporaneous material and was the first to observe the following key traits of the Age of Agade: the development of calligraphy and the change in writing habits (Chapter 1 part 6); the presence of Semitic words in ostensibly Sumerian documents; the spread of Akkadian names in Sumer; the documentary evidence for the distribution of food and luxury goods to Akkadian notables; the inscribed fragment of the Victory Stele from Telloh, which he suggested showed extensive redistribution of land in Sumer (Chapter 1 part 3); the significance of Akkadian year names; and the frequent mention of Agade in the Girsu tablets, as well as their broad geographical horizon (Chapter 3 part 6). Without reference to Nabonidus, omens, chronicles, or even the claims of commemorative inscriptions, his assessment of the Akkadian period is striking in its prescience:

> Everything pertaining to the reigns of Sargon and Naram-Sin is of special interest. The importance of this period can scarcely be overestimated. Because it saw a large, unified empire replace a patchwork of small rival kingdoms, a remarkable stimulus to all branches of activity, and the full flowering and diffusion in all directions of an art, culture, and civilization that had been slowly developing in the centuries and millennia preceding, the epoch of Sargon and Naram-Sin was beyond doubt a climactic moment in the history of the ancient Near East.[50]

No modern reader of the work of these years can miss its sense of excitement from the rapid emergence of new information. The horizons of history seemed vastly expanded and the possibilities unlimited. The task of the cuneiformist who wished to write a history of the Akkadian period was to weave the latest discoveries into a coherent narrative, working in each detail in its place, with only occasional misgivings about their reliability. There were then, as in every generation, skeptics. As Winckler cautioned,

> The more or less isolated facts known to us of these times do not furnish sufficient material for the framing of an adequate picture of them . . . It is still impossible to bring the majority of the events recorded in their inscriptions into sure and satisfactory relation chronologically or geographically. At present they are of importance only to the specialist.[51]

Yet he too was fascinated by the conquests of Sargon and Naram-Sin over large expanses of Western Asia at such an early date and accepted them as sure facts of early Babylonian history. In contrast, the often blasé, dismissive essays of a century later, with their discourses on method, tend to leave the general reader disengaged, discouraged, and with a sense that Mesopotamian history is founded in naive illusion.

## 3. New sources and approaches: 1914–1947

The major scholarly contribution of this period was Poebel's 1914 publication of the Old Babylonian collections of copies of Akkadian royal inscriptions from Nippur in the University Museum of the University of Pennsylvania, especially the 28-column tablet of the inscriptions of Sargon, Rimush, and Manishtusu (Chapter 11 part 3). Poebel's work was brilliantly executed; it would be impossible to overstate the importance of his volume for subsequent study of the Akkadian period. The First World War and its aftermath meant, however, a protracted delay before these texts became generally known in Assyriology.[52] In 1926, Legrain published more Nippur sources, including a fragment joining Poebel's 28-column tablet.[53] The reigns and succession order of the first three Akkadian kings were finally documented by authentic sources. A duplicate tablet in the Istanbul Archaeological Museums remains unpublished; detailed information about it became known only in 1963, collations in 1990.[54]

As for Naram-Sin, another large tablet in the same Nippur collection was a copy of his commemoration of his victory in the Great Revolt. While awaiting study, the tablet was stolen from the University Museum. It turned up seventy-five years later in a collection in Haifa, Israel, and was not published until 1989.[55] This meant that, for much of the twentieth century, a key event of Naram-Sin's reign was known primarily from later literary texts. Thus the many discussions of these later compositions took for granted that the Great Revolt was a fiction, proceeding unaware that a long and detailed authentic inscription describing it existed. As luck would have it, a second tablet with a copy of Naram-Sin's account of the Great Revolt was included in Hilprecht's bequest to the University of Jena, but it was not published until 1997.[56]

Olmstead produced the first historical essay making use of the new sources Poebel had published, but as this appeared in 1917, its accessibility to European scholars was delayed. He wrote of Sargon, "We now need no more depend on these legends for our general view of the reign, than do we on other later accounts, whether in the form of chronicles or connected with the omens, for we now have a large collection of his own inscriptions."[57]

Among the many historical studies that came out in the interwar years, the two most important for the Akkadian period were Langdon's chapter in the 1923 *Cambridge Ancient History* and Güterbock's dissertation on Mesopotamian historical tradition, printed in two parts in 1934 and 1938. Langdon had available to him the published Nippur copies of the royal inscriptions, as well as the order of the kings as given in *The Sumerian King List*, a superb manuscript of which he had discovered in the Ashmolean Museum and published in 1923. He sought to synthesize all the sources, earlier and later, so in content and coverage, his chapter more closely resembles the historical essays of the 1950s and 1960s than it does those of the previous half-century. Writing of Sargon, for example, he used *The Sumerian King List*, *The Birth Legend of Sargon*, *The Sumerian Sargon Legend*, and juxtaposed the historical omens and chronicles with authentic inscriptions known from the Nippur copies. He mentioned Armanum and Ebla (which he identified with the Classical Piera, north of Antioch), the foundation of Agade, the revolt in Sargon's old age, the Susa stele, as well as Sargon's claim that foreign ships docked at Agade. He also considered *The King of Battle* to be a Hittite text translated into Akkadian, so a non-Mesopotamian source for the reign.[58]

Langdon's account of the reign of Rimush was mostly based on the Nippur copies of the royal inscriptions, ending with the omen that he was killed by his courtiers with cylinder seals, which he found "entirely credible, as the seals of the period are noted for their extraordinary size and beauty."[59] For the reign of Manishtusu, he used not only the Nippur copies and omens, but also the obelisk (to which he devoted two pages), as well the Cruciform Monument and the statues found at Susa.

A new feature of Langdon's approach was the prominence he gave to Naram-Sin, whose was "the most glorious reign of the period."[60] He narrated the Great

Revolt at length and stressed Naram-Sin's deification (which he considered a practice borrowed from Sumerian religion), engagement with Elam (citing the treaty) and with Magan (which he located at el-Hasa, its name compounded from Sumerian *ma*, "ship" because the inhabitants were a seagoing people), and conquests, with particular attention to the Pir Hussein relief and the Victory Stele ("It seems unmistakably to reveal the influence of Egyptian art of the IInd and IIIrd Dynasties").[61] Langdon also discussed the importance of Nippur and especially Lagash, with reference to the inscribed part of the Victory Stele from Telloh. He described Naram-Sin's role as a builder and the extent of his empire, noting the seal found on Cyprus. His was by far the most comprehensive narrative of this reign to date.

Langdon's presentation of the reign of Sharkalisharri, still believed to be a son of "Dati-Enlil," alluded to the references in his texts to Amorites and the "warlike and cruel nomads of Gutium." He thought the relief portion of the Victory Stele from Telloh belonged to this reign, and he mentioned some cylinder seals of Sharkalisharri's royal servants.[62] Thanks to *The Sumerian King List*, Langdon was able to include the period of anarchy and the later kings of Agade in his account. It is noteworthy that, compared to earlier histories, such as those of King and Hall, Langdon placed far less emphasis on race or racial conflict in his presentation. For him, Sargon and his successors were warrior kings first and of "Semitic character" second.[63]

Langdon's essay synthesized everything that was known of the Akkadian period at the time, together with asides on a wide range of topics which show at once his enormous learning and his penchant for what would now be considered free association, not to mention erroneous and inconsistent citation. It is instructive to compare his chapter with the 1915 survey by Jastrow, for they show how different a narrative was possible in less than a decade.

Written ten years later, Güterbock's dissertation focused on Mesopotamian historiography, rather than on historical events.[64] He distinguished two types of Mesopotamian historical writing: royal inscriptions commemorating the deeds of kings, and tradition, which embodied what was remembered about them and became the source of poetic narratives. Since the dynasty of Sargon and his successors early on entered the realm of saga, historical tradition about them lay near the heart of Güterbock's inquiry. As he saw it, epic poetry about these and other long-ago kings framed their history in terms of good periods of unified native rule and bad periods of foreign domination. Taking up the perennial question of the relationship between Mesopotamian chronicles and omens, Güterbock suggested that the omens were derived from the chronicles and that the anecdotal chronicles were older than the drily annalistic ones of the mid-first millennium. Rutten's 1938 publication of the early liver models from Mari appeared too late for him to take them into account, as he would certainly have modified this view. The models proved that the memory of the Akkadian kings and the fall of Agade were part of the earliest attested divinatory tradition in Mesopotamia (Chapter 11 part 4).[65]

Güterbock introduced a new term, "*narû*-literature" (historical fiction composed in the style of a commemorative stele), to refer to putative royal or tomb inscriptions that narrated some historical event with a positive or negative lesson, showing that the ruler's character determined whether he was successful as an empire builder or unsuccessful as an empire loser. Memory of the Akkadian kings was the source of important examples of *narû*-literature, such as *The Birth Legend of Sargon* and *The Cuthaean Legend of Naram-Sin*. Other literary works about the Akkadian kings, such as *The King of Battle*, were clearly based on historical events, but, he felt, should not be used to write history, for they were intended to be tales of marvels and adventures.[66]

Güterbock's dissertation became the point of departure for all subsequent discussion of Mesopotamian historiography, and, because of his extensive analysis of the sources for the Akkadian period, every essay on that topic for the next half-century was obliged to consider his theses and conclusions.

## 4.   A time for synthesis: 1947–1971

Between 1947 and 1971, six major historical studies of the Akkadian period appeared, by Van der Meer (1947), Tyumenev (1956), Diakonoff (1959), Bottéro (1965), Liverani (1966), and Gadd (1971). The last three, since they were written at approximately the same time, were not only independent of each other but were also unfamiliar with the two preceding them, so the historian has the singular advantage of separate presentations of essentially the same issues and evidence. Only Gadd's and Bottéro's became widely known, because Tyumenev's and Diakonoff's were in Russian, while Liverani's, in Italian for a popular audience, did not reach many readers outside Italy, and Van der Meer's, in Dutch, was intended primarily for a readership in Holland. Shorter studies included ones by Garelli, originally written in 1969 (second edition 1982) for a French popular historical handbook, and by Schmökel (1955), for a German one, which nonetheless offer more than passing summaries of the usual information. Worthy of mention is Nikolski's discussion of land ownership in the Akkadian period, mostly written while he was active duty with the Red Army in the Second World War and printed at Minsk in 1948, so unknown in Assyriology. In view of their relative inaccessibility, the Dutch and Russian books are discussed here in more detail than the others.

Because Van der Meer believed that the transition from the late pre-Akkadian to the Akkadian period was smooth and initially more a change of regime than a cultural watershed, his essay gave considerable attention to pre-Akkadian Lagash, including a detailed summary of its economic activity. To him, the "Akkadian period" was a broader concept than specifically "Akkadian" culture, so he brought many topics into his discussion that other writers did not. In his summary of the political history, he used all sources on an equal basis, including the later omens and chronicles and *The Sargon Geography*. His discussion of archaeology was the first to make use of the University of Chicago's excavations in the Diyala region, along with materials from Adab, Lagash, and Susa.[67]

Nikolski focused on land tenure, suggesting that plots of royal land were distributed in the Akkadian period in direct continuation of pre-Akkadian practice but in smaller parcels, possibly because less cultivable land was available. In his view, the reason for Manishtusu's purchase was that he did not have sufficient royal land to sustain his retainers so had to buy fields from community owners, who formed clans or tribes ruled by elders. The sellers were parting with ancestral lands at a low price and were not rich families or local nobility selling their estates, as had been argued in earlier Soviet scholarship.[68]

Tyumenev's large volume is a social and economic history of Mesopotamia in the third millennium BCE, but despite its scale and massive documentation, it had no impact outside the former Soviet Union. Tyumenev was particularly interested in the question of chattel slavery in Mesopotamia. Although the prevailing view in the Soviet Union, as put forward by Struve, then a dominating figure in Soviet historiography of the ancient Near East, was that Mesopotamia was an example of a slave-holding society and that its production was based on slavery, Tyumenev argued that this was not correct and sought to show, through close study of administrative records, that chattel slavery was of marginal importance and not at all significant in production.[69]

Tymenev devoted forty pages to the Akkadian period, which he considered a time of "transition" from the Old Sumerian temple-based economy to the Neo-Sumerian crown-dominated one. Although he referred in passing to royal inscriptions and to the Neo-Babylonian chronicle of Sargon, nearly all of Tyumenev's documentation was derived from administrative records. He considered centralization the key feature of Akkadian rule, as seen especially in the royal purchases of family-owned land and in increased attention to the registry of land, as evidenced by the first appearance of field plans. The *ensi*, or city ruler, had now become a governor and the arable land previously reserved for him was absorbed into a larger regional economy. Administrators were maintained by land allotments exploited directly rather than through leasing, the main crop being grain intended for rations. From his study of herding and animal husbandry he concluded that all of that production was sent to central storehouses. Along with a rise in references to the textile industry, the records of central storehouses show a remarkable variety of products and manufactured goods on hand. There was also considerable circulation of goods among different centers. He thought that the appearance of dated texts implied a central government repository, rather than dispersed archives.[70]

In addition, the Akkadians simplified the elaborate grades of workers typical of pre-Akkadian Lagash into a more streamlined system. Staff not specifically subordinate to the governor were drawn into a new "royal" household, which increasingly relied on an internal workforce rather than levies of citizens, as was also true of the military. From a study of personnel records, he estimated that the ratio of skilled to unskilled workers was about 1:5. The principal workforce was referred to as *guruš* and *dumu* "men and boys." Blind people did gardening and orchard work. Chattel slaves were mentioned only in private ownership, which showed that they were of no economic significance. Extensive building activities suggested to him that prisoners of war, attested now in large numbers for the first time, were used for forced labor.[71]

Tyumenev then turned his attention to individual archives or groups of administrative records, such as the early and Classical Akkadian records from Umma and the Classical Akkadian records from Lagash (Girsu), a place that he thought gained in status during the Akkadian period. Nearby Adab he considered unimportant, because the documents known to him were mostly small, undated transactions and there were no large rosters of workers. At all these cities, there was evidence for direct exploitation of land, from tiny parcels to extensive areas. He noted records of animal husbandry, lists of "greeting gifts," and accounts of food, beverages, dairy products, wood, and silver and other metals, mostly issued by administrative personnel.[72]

Tyumenev's study of the Akkadian administrative documents from the Diyala region suggested to him that a strong temple economy flourished there, though less developed than in Sumer, because there was extensive private ownership of land. Lists of personnel, ration distributions, and skilled workers, plus records of very large herds, and substantial arrears of grain gave a strong impression of the centralized management of extensive resources. He noted only a dozen chattel slaves in the records, as opposed to instances of up to 900 rationed workers. Tutub seemed to Tyumenev a less economically developed place, though he noted some reference to workers and fugitives.[73]

The records from Gasur showed royal land being worked by large teams using royal plows and draught animals, with the produce stored there. Slave labor was unknown; rather, workers were recruited from the local population, with people of various statuses assigned to the same project and receiving rations. Finished products, from prepared foods to industrial goods, were stored centrally and distributed by the royal establishment.[74]

The archival documents that formed the basis for Tyumenev's work were largely ignored by all other scholars who wrote on the period for the next thirty years. Even when studies of the individual text groups finally began to appear, these tended to ignore his prior work on them. Thus his book stands as an isolated and nearly forgotten monument to his enormous research capacity and vision for the possibilities that Akkadian administrative documents presented to the economic historian.

Diakonoff took a broader historical approach, though he too referred to specific administrative documents in support of his arguments. His was the most analytical history of the period so far attempted. Addressing a readership conversant with Marxist discourse, Diakonoff began with discussion of the problems of Sargon's name, parentage, relationship to Lugalzagesi, and rise to power. While Sargon may have started out as a "man of the people" and of "common origin," relying on popular support against traditional community rulers, who controlled much of the arable land and water resources of the community, his rise to power was not a "revolution" of exploited people but of free landholders; true democratic conditions could not exist in Sumer because the necessary social preconditions were not present.[75]

Diakonoff saw Sumerian society as consisting of a hereditary nobility and a strong priesthood on the one side and, on the other, non-noble members of the community, such as non-royal artisans and important land owners; clients dependent on nobility; free members of the temple staff with allotments of temple land; and domestic slaves. Councils of elders (Chapter 2 part 5) were the main basis for popular influence on the nobility. Sargon's objective was to create a new royal or bureaucratic "nobility" to exercise that same influence and thereby to weaken the old lineage-based nobility.[76]

The Akkadian conquest therefore tended to replace community-based government and kinship-based oligarchy with centralized exploitation of resources, despotism, and bureaucracy. To achieve this, Sargon adopted a "double-edged" policy of both promoting change and selectively linking with the past. He used ancient titles and restored Kish as a long-time center of political power, but founded a new capital at Agade. Some members of the old notable class were incorporated into the new power structure; Rimush went so far as to liquidate those who were unwilling to take part. The world of traditional Mesopotamian society based on kinship relations, as shown, for example, by the transactions recorded on the Obelisk of Manishtusu, was fast coming to an end.[77]

Priests, for their part, often belonged to the nobility and were closely bound up in the economic importance of temples in Sumer. The Akkadian kings' development of a royal theology and wooing of the priesthood with privileges and concessions helped separate their interests from those of the city rulers and local nobility. Appointing a princess as high priestess was another tactic to cement relations with the priesthood and ensure their cooperation. Thus during the Akkadian period, the temples and their hierarchy were gradually fully subsumed under royal control and integrated into the royal bureaucracy, completing a process Diakonoff and Tyumenev argued had begun already in the pre-Akkadian period. Royal and temple personnel were classed together in administrative documents, with royal officials now receiving income from temple estates. An estate needed no longer to be attached to a specific temple, but might serve several temples that were not even in the same district. The Akkadian kings had become the most powerful landholders and managers of dependent labor.[78]

Key to Sargon's success was his formation of a standing army, in whose ranks were egalitarian opportunities for advancement, rather than using traditional militias. The army and the new bureaucratic elite living off royal allotments of land were the main supports of the Empire. Under the new order, the small merchant class also prospered from royal patronage and crown participation in the market.[79]

There were, however, large sectors of the population that gained nothing more than new masters in the transition from oligarchy to bureaucratic government. The land-owning notable class, which had lost control of local government to the crown, was further undermined by a new tendency toward private rather than hereditary ownership of real property and social status based on individual wealth and preferment rather than birth. Workers and functionaries who had depended on rations rather than allotments of temple land found themselves part of a growing dependent class without direct access to means of production.[80]

As a result, the revolts against Sargon were fomented among those whose power he had usurped, such as *ensi*'s and elders, and were marked by the killing of royal functionaries rather than members of the hereditary ruling class. A major rebellion was that of the "elders" (according to Diakonoff, misunderstood in some later sources as a revolt in his "old age," Chapter 11 part 4), because Sargon posed a greater threat to their way of life than had Lugalzagesi. For Diakonoff, the weakness of the Akkadian Empire was that it had neither the support of the old aristocracy nor a popular base. He concluded that all the class antagonisms of early Mesopotamia came to a climax in the Akkadian period, and this was a crucial factor in its downfall.[81]

Bottéro's 1965 essay, "The First Semitic Empire," is noteworthy for its breadth of view, inclusiveness, and originality. He began by summarizing the diversity of sources for the Akkadian period, as well as the hazards of making use of the later ones, such as chronicles, omens, and literary works. Exceptionally, he considered *The Sumerian King List* near enough in date to the Akkadian kings to be reliable for their order and length of reign. He argued that the empire depended on royal control of the flow of foreign and prestige goods, such as wood and metal, through both tribute and monopoly of foreign trade. Akkadian administration of conquered territories was largely geared toward extracting tribute, so often entailed leaving existing governmental structures and even rulers in place, though members of the royal family and royal dependents were assigned supervisory posts throughout Mesopotamia. This dual source of revenue provided the royal house with enormous riches with which the king rewarded and supported his followers and carried out large public works. The impressive Akkadian building at Nagar, for example, was a central place for stockpiling resources and regulating commerce.[82]

Bottéro also discussed Akkadian cultural changes. In religion, these included the emergence of new gods in the pantheon and the deification of the king. Akkadian art he saw as the "classical" art of Mesopotamia, stressing its vitality, naturalism, and imagination compared to the stiff, formal norms of pre-Akkadian Sumer. He considered the diversification of the Akkadian language and writing and their spread throughout Western Asia, for example among the Hurrians and Elamites, as the specifically "Semitic" aspect of the new order, using that term in its linguistic sense.[83]

Bottéro's essay was the first to stress the Akkadian impact on the Zagros, Elam and Susiana, the Indus Valley, the eastern coast of Arabia, and Syria. He suggested that the "Akkadianization" of Kurdistan and especially Assyria at this time were turning points in their history. He concluded that the empire of Agade not only transformed Babylonian civilization, it created a widespread commonality or "koine" that was a decisive factor for centuries thereafter in the cultural development of the whole of Western Asia.[84]

The following year saw publication of Liverani's study, which focused on Sargon, rather than the period as a whole, contending that his achievement was to lay the foundations for the earliest universal empire by realizing a new ideology of kingship. This transcended a city or group of cities to assert dominion over the known world, at least from the perspective of Mesopotamia. Lugazagesi led the way by claiming hegemony from sea to sea, but Sargon brought this to pass and became the model for the successful conqueror-king, even a "national hero." Although Sargon originated in Semitic-speaking northern Mesopotamia, his repeated campaigns against the Sumerian cities were territorial rather than ethnic in nature. The geographical sweep of Sargon's conquests made the new ideology possible, culminating in the deification of his grandson, Naram-Sin.[85]

Along with the scant contemporaneous records, Liverani took up the later legends and historical omens about Sargon. Whereas Sargon's surviving inscriptions deal with Sumer and Iran, the legends, historical omens, and *The Empire of Sargon* (Chapter 12 part 6) broadened their scope to a world stretching from eastern Mediterranean to the Indus Valley. Liverani suggested that the agents and mechanisms of control over the new territories included creating an extensive "royal house" with numerous dependents. In his view, the frequent revolts against Sargon and his successors arose because a significant portion of the population reaped no share of the prosperity and glory of the Akkadian conquests; only the ruling elite and the commercial class benefited. Unlike Diakonoff, Liverani saw no great change in the relationship between the monarchy and the ancient Sumerian temples, beyond Sargon's and Naram-Sin's appointment of their daughters as high priestesses of the moon-god at Ur and the intrusion of the royal house into the cult by placing the images and monuments of kings in Sumerian temples.[86]

The heroic ideal created for Sargon, "king without rival," may have originated in his lifetime, but in any case the concept remained thereafter deeply rooted in Mesopotamian culture. Much of Liverani's essay was devoted to sorting out the different strands of later tradition that led back to the pivotal figure of Sargon, especially the parallel divinatory and historical-fictional memory. Liverani returned to many of these issues in 1993 (part 5), taking a position that had evolved considerably over thirty years.[87]

Gadd's narrative of the Akkadian period (1971) eloquently combined the content of the Akkadian royal inscriptions and other contemporaneous monuments with all of the later sources. Although he held no brief for divination ("very curious medium," "absurd but widely accepted belief"), he suggested that the historical omens stood apart from the outcomes or apodoses typical of most extispicy, deemed them worthy of consideration, quoted them at length, and compared them to other sources. In general, Gadd used a criterion of believability. There was to him "nothing incredible" even in the latest sources, such as *The Birth Legend of Sargon*, though he hesitated over *The King of Battle* ("it is hard to decide," "applying romantic colour to the facts"). Unlike Tyumenev and Diakonoff, he did not address society and economy and made only brief reference to the existence of administrative and business documents, which did not interest him. Apart from that, Gadd's chapter in the *Cambridge Ancient History* showed a superb mastery of the sources then known and a consistent, openly stated approach to them, even if some later critics considered his account methodologically naive and rooted in the tradition of King and Rogers.[88]

For Garelli, writing in 1982, Sargon was the most important single figure in Mesopotamian history, even if his conquests were less global than later historical tradition would have it. Like Liverani, he saw Sargon's invasion of Sumer as a territorial rather than an ethnic struggle. Although he cited examples of migrations of Semitic-speaking peoples, he did not frame the Akkadian period in such terms. In his view, there was a sedentary, culturally integrated Semitic-speaking population in northern Mesopotamia before the rise of Agade. What Sargon did was to create a forerunner of an imperial system of heartland and provinces by subsuming Akkadian-speaking areas into the sphere of the capital, while allowing non–Akkadian-speaking territories, such as Sumer and Susiana, to maintain their own institutions of rule. According to Garelli, this policy inevitably led to revolts; Naram-Sin's triumph over a broad coalition of rebels meant that a much larger Akkadian state was passed on to his son, Sharkalisharri.[89]

Garelli also discussed other aspects of the Age of Agade. He too regarded the major Akkadian innovation to be the enlargement of the idea of kingship from rule over a city and its territory to one claiming dominion over the entire world, an ideology sustained by a superior military force and deification of the ruler. Sumerian religion, far from being suppressed, was integrated with the gods of the Akkadians, and the Sumerian god Enlil thereby gained in status. At the same time, though, he saw "secularization," with temples losing their economic primacy, while private ownership of land expanded, largely thanks to the forced purchase and redistribution of extensive lands by the royal household. This led to the formation of individual estates supporting both agricultural and industrial activities. Urban centers prospered under royal governors. Akkadian Mesopotamia experienced considerable growth in trade and commerce. There was, however, a concomitant decline in the availability of both lapis and tin, the latter resulting in inferior bronze compared to that of pre-Akkadian times.[90]

Overall, Garelli felt that a new spirit infused the realm, manifest most clearly in art (however much that had developed from Sumerian subjects and styles). In his final judgment, "the period was not lacking in either talents or resources, but the undertaking was too vast, the internal rivalries too recent, the external enemies too numerous, to keep watch over territories that extended too far. Human error is less to be blamed for its collapse than the force of circumstances."[91]

Schmökel's brief essay (1955) on the Akkadian period for a popular handbook found wide circulation. His narrative combined omens, literary sources, and original inscriptions, without discrimination. Among other points, he suggested that the Akkadian military advantage was their use of hunting weaponry (bow, short spear), which they used without shields in the open-rank style of Bedouins, giving them a great advantage over the Sumerian battle phalanx. He saw Sargon as ordering that Akkadian be written for the first time. He revived a notion, popular in the nineteenth and early twentieth centuries, that the advent of the Akkadians meant promotion of the sun-god in Mesopotamia. His work concluded with a discussion of art and archaeology.[92]

A technical publication of primary importance was Hirsch's comprehensive edition (1963) of all the inscriptions of the Akkadian period then known, with an extensive commentary that included reference to later tradition. This formed the basis for every historical study of the Age of Agade for the next thirty years.[93] Gelb's grammar (1952) and glossary (1957) of Old Akkadian put study of the language on a sound basis, while Hackman and Stephens' volume of legal and administrative texts made available much new source material, including the first documents published from the Mesag archive (Chapter 3 part 3).[94]

## 5. New theses: 1971–1993

The 1975 discovery of the archives of Ebla forced a rethinking of the early history of the Semitic peoples in northern Mesopotamia. In response, a radical new proposal for the historical background and origins of the Akkadian Empire was offered by Gelb, beginning in 1977, and developed by Steinkeller in 1993. This posited the formation of a long-lasting state or political confederation in northern Babylonia during the Early Dynastic II and III periods, under the hegemony of Kish, whose dominion may have extended into the Diyala and Trans-Tigris regions. Expanding up the Euphrates, Kish encountered (or perhaps founded) Mari, which eventually became a rival.[95] The Sumerian city-states tried to counter the threat of the northern polity by developing stronger kingship and building political alliances, but these were to prove inadequate in the face of first Kishite, then Akkadian power.

In Gelb's hypothesis, Kishite kingship was secular, authoritarian, and centralized, with universalist pretensions, but without the theocratic component of the Sumerian south. As opposed to the temple-dominated southern landscape, the northern plains were dominated by royal lands and privately owned manors. Northern society, more stratified than Sumerian society, was further characterized by chattel slavery and a more extensive patronage system. The structure of Akkadian society and state had therefore their closest analogues in northern Syria, as known from Ebla, and, perhaps, at pre-Akkadian Mari.[96]

Gelb stressed the economic importance of sheep husbandry in the north, since the flocks of Ebla were vastly larger than those of southern Mesopotamia and, compared to agriculture, sheepherding was a high-yield, low-risk way of generating wealth. Although Gelb did not suggest it, a corollary to his proposal is that, aware of its potential returns, the Akkadian and especially the Ur III states may have encouraged and expanded animal husbandry in the south.[97]

In the Gelb-Steinkeller reconstruction, in sum, the Akkadian Empire was a northern entity's successful expansion from its heartland in all directions, imposing royal domains and manors onto Sumer and elsewhere.

A quite different theory of both the origin and collapse of the Akkadian Empire was advanced in 1993 by Weiss and Courty. Weiss had already written on the historical ramifications of the northern versus the southern economic regimes; he and Courty now suggested that the urban centers of Sumer in the pre-Akkadian period may have been approaching the limits of the irrigation agriculture sustainable by the Euphrates, given the technology of the time. Continued economic and population growth that demanded increased agricultural production in the face of local constraints may have motivated imperial expansion elsewhere, notably up the Euphrates into the Jezirah region, and, as a consequence, the establishment of a permanent Akkadian presence there, which sought to reorganize and exploit its agriculture for the benefit of the Akkadian state. The abrupt abandonment of Akkadian installations in that region may correlate with a period of prolonged drought, resulting in significant dislocation of peoples, and, ultimately, in the collapse of the Akkadian Empire.[98] Weiss's subsequent work on this theory continues to provoke lively debate and reconsideration of the archaeology of northern Syria in the late third millennium.[99]

Glassner offered a monographic study of the fall of Agade in 1986, addressed to a specialist readership. This began with a concise survey of the Empire's social and historical background, then defined essential characteristics of the Akkadian state, which he grouped around concepts of centralization and compulsion, together with consideration of its agricultural regime and reliance on patronage. Unlike many other writers on this period, he saw trade as of little importance in comparison to booty-taking. Separating the contemporaneous evidence from Mesopotamian historical memory, Glassner analyzed both in detail. Since fascination with the Akkadian period lasted until the end of Mesopotamian civilization, this opened a wide range of subjects: the fall of Agade as an ominous event in extispicy and astrology, specific related themes such as the destruction of cities in divination, the external versus the internal enemy, divine anger as a historiographical theme, Naram-Sin as the archetype of the bad king, the literary "casualty figures," and the problem of the historical kernel in later Mesopotamian writing previously discussed by Güterbock. This study was noteworthy both for its analytic approach and its careful grounding in all the ancient source material.[100]

In 1988, Liverani returned to the Akkadian period, with a survey of social and economic history, richly illustrated with maps and figures. He discussed the extent of the empire and its administration, agreeing with Garelli that this comprised a core management zone and a more indirectly ruled, colonized outlying zone, opening the way to frequent revolts. Other topics included religion, royal purchase of land, record-keeping strategies, commerce on the fringes of the empire, art, literature, the development of the royal titulary, the Akkadian memory in later Mesopotamian literature and scholarship, and the Empire's foreign neighbors. His systematic evaluation of the sources set his survey apart from many of its predecessors, but, despite its importance, it was seldom cited outside of Italy. A revised English translation appeared in 2011.[101]

Neumann's 1989 treatment of the Akkadian period drew attention for the first time to its role in the development of Mesopotamian law and mathematics. He commented as well on political history, literature, art, and architecture. Calling the Akkadian Dynasty and the Kingdom of Ur the "First Territorial States," Neumann also discussed land management, administration, the military, concepts of monarchy, and the expansion of the royal household. Unlike his predecessors, Neumann chose not to consider the later omens, chronicles, and literary works.[102]

Even as historians were still making difficult decisions about using the original versus the later sources for the Akkadian period, Liverani fired a shot across the bow of the whole enterprise. Although in 1966 and again in 1971 he had criticized historians of the ancient Near East for their lack of theoretical bases, his 1973 polemic was the first to attract wide interest outside of Italy, largely because it was in English and published in an international journal.[103] With respect to the reading of Mesopotamian texts, he argued that neither inscriptions nor later literary and scholarly writings should be seen as sources for historical facts, explicit or implied, to be selected and redeployed in a modern narrative, as Assyriologists had been doing for the past century. Instead, an ancient document was itself an historical fact "which must no more be forced, dissected, plagiarized for our aims. Rather, its literary structure, terminology, and implications must be tactfully analyzed toward an understanding as complete and conscious as possible."[104]

While Liverani's approach had its roots in centuries-long debate over how to read the Christian Bible, in which questions of authorship, intent, audience, and cultural context had long been at issue, he preferred to draw his arguments and analogies from then-current cultural anthropology and literary theory, thereby taking aim at the positivist, historicist attitude to ancient languages and texts characteristic of late-nineteenth-century German universities. This, he thought, tended to substitute myth and paraphrase of ancient texts for substance and generally ignored social and economic factors. Throughout the twentieth century, the values of German philological and historical scholarship stood firm as the dominating presence and widely accepted standard in ancient Near Eastern studies in general and Assyriology in particular, owing to the sheer number of academic posts and publications and to its high standards of philological rigor.[105] As a result, Liverani's manifesto came to many Assyriologists as an entirely new approach, even reproach.

In 1993, Liverani renewed his interest in the Akkadian period, first in a trenchant essay summarizing in a few broad strokes modern historiographic approaches to the era, then in a study of the Akkadian rulers as later models for kingship, suggesting that this happened not necessarily because they were really so important but because they had left an imposing mass of commemorative material that remained available in later times for copying, imitation, and interpretation. With respect to the omens, chronicles and literary works about the Akkadian kings, he called for abandonment of the longtime search for any "historical kernel," dismissing their apparent echoes of the commemorative inscriptions as "phraseological repertory," and suggesting that "all the rest must have been made up."[106] For him, literature about the Akkadian period, such as *The King of Battle*, *The Curse of Agade*, and the compositions about the revolt against Naram-Sin, was politically motivated by circumstances, agendas, or controversies of the times and places in which they were written. It is the task of the historian, he contended, to reconstruct what those were, focusing on the author rather than the putative subject. Well aware of the potential criticism that he was merely exchanging a new, imagined "historical kernel" for an older one that had some basis, at least, in the text at hand, Liverani nonetheless insisted that his "logical procedure is the right one," even if the specific results of such an inquiry might be open to challenge and correction.[107]

In the same mode, a 1993 essay by Michalowski questioned the evidence for the extent, duration, and legacy of alleged Akkadian rule in Western Asia, including the Khabur region, Mari, Nineveh, the Gulf, and Susiana, but concluded:

> ... the memory of these overlords remained vivid in the minds of local dynasts. One cannot deny that later kings of these regions benefited from the general memories of Agade that survived in cuneiform traditions periodically imported from the south, but there is evidence that local weavers of history had their own view on the matter, and their own sources of information that could be molded and recast for their own purposes.[108]

Michalowski further proposed that the "images of glory" left by the Akkadian kings for later generations were their greatest accomplishment, in that they persuaded two millennia of Babylonians and Assyrians of their importance, and, once rediscovered, persuaded modern scholarship likewise.[109]

## 6.    The Age of Agade on its own terms: 1993 to the present

In 1999, A. Westenholz, the first Assyriologist to make the Akkadian period his professional specialty, produced by far the most comprehensive and authoritative assessment of it, with extensive documentation and bibliography. His essay was frankly personal in its rhetoric, in wry acknowledgment that most people who wrote about the Age of Agade believed, and tended to cite, only themselves. He began with the pre-Akkadian background, the problem of the location of Agade, and the reigns of the first five kings, then turned to selected topics: the religious center at Nippur, the city and army, slavery, and the status of women. Five further chapters explored literature, religion, art, neighboring lands and peoples, and foreign relations (war, trade, and diplomacy). Although prepared for a series intended to introduce phases of third-millennium history to scholars not expert in them, Westenholz's study assumed considerable familiarity with the issues and evidence, so in fact found its most appreciative audience among Assyriologists specializing in the third millennium.[110]

Harsh in his assessment of Liverani's position and generally positivist in his approach, Westenholz thought the Akkadian period a "heroic age," but, unlike the imagined heroic ages of history, one for which extensive evidence, contemporaneous and later, is available for studying it. In company with Meyer, Jastrow, and Olmstead, he saw in the fusion of the two cultures of Sumer and Akkad the distinctive genius of the age, especially since they merged as equals rather than one being absorbed by the other.[111] For future research agendas, Westenholz urged more work on the primary data, on which he thought only a beginning had been made, and less theorizing and literary criticism.[112] The reader of Westenholz's chapter will have a sense of the vast accumulation of new detail, even if the corpus of commemorative inscriptions and literary works, the backbone of all historical writing on the period, has remained essentially the same, and however wide apart the theoretical starting points may be.

The production of historical essays on the Akkadian period shows no signs of abating in the 21st century. Edzard, for example, began his concise 2004 account of Sargon with *The Birth Legend of Sargon* and referred, positively and programmatically, to the "historical kernel" in later traditions about the period. Among his interesting new suggestions about various aspects of Akkadian history and culture is that Naram-Sin looted the temple of Enlil at Nippur to pay for his foreign wars.[113] Such an imaginative proposal, with no basis in any ancient evidence, from an otherwise very cautious scholar, illustrates once again that every historian of Mesopotamia must think about and come to terms with the Age of Agade in a manner somehow different from his engagement with any other period of Mesopotamian history.

## Notes

1  I R pl. 69, ii, line 30; Pinches 1882: 8–9, 1883/4. The fragment of the vase, brought by Naram-Sin as booty from Magan, was found at Babylon but said to have been lost in the Tigris River (I R pl. 3 no. VII); further Muscarella 1981: 81. For the Nabonidus inscription, Chapter 11 part 7.

2  II R pl. 39 No. 5, line 41 = (K 4336, *Enuma Anu Enlil* Tablet 5). Sargon's name was explained in a Sumero-Akkadian tablet (K 4386) published in the same volume (II R pl. 48 ii 40), as "True King" [literally: "King of Truth"], "Who Speaks the Truth," and "Who Speaks Good [Words]" (republished as CT 19 pl. 19 ii 41). Agade was mentioned in a Sumero-Akkadian geographical list also published in this volume (II R pl. 50 ii 9). Further omens of Sargon and Naram-Sin appeared in IV R$^2$ pl. 34 No. 1 (K 2130).

3  Hommel 1885: 307 note 3 (confusion with Sargon I rather than Sargon II of Assyria); Winckler 1892a: 38, 1895: 238, 1906: 47.

4  Hilprecht 1893: 18 note 2; Thureau-Dangin 1896: 357 (the Akkadian-period tablets from Girsu "confirm and complement the data of the omens, so often in dispute"); King 1908: 242: ". . . grounds for refusing to accept blindly the late traditions of Assyrian and Neo-Babylonian scribes with regard to the earlier history of their country"; Schott 1934: 307 note 2 ("apokryph"), further, of omen apodoses in general, "völlig grundlose Entsprechungen, Kinder der freisten Willkür oder eines gewaltätigen Scharfsinns" (312); Weidner 1941/4: 175 note 19 ("übertreibene Skepsis").

5  III R pl. IV no. 7; Smith 1872: 46–7

6  On the reliability of Assyriology, below, note 18. For example, the identification of Sargon's mother was much discussed (noble? poor? changeling? priestess? – an old manuscript note in the Yale copy of Radau 1900: 155 suggests "virgin").

7  Talbot 1872: 271: "It seems probable that there was an ancient statue of Sargina in the city of Agani, where he was worshiped as a hero. These lines may have been inscribed on the pedestal and may have been copied by one of the Assyrian *literati.*" Talbot later contributed his translation to the series *Records of the Past*, an early anthology of ancient Near Eastern texts in translation (Birch 1876: v no. 1).

8  Winckler 1906: 47–50, 61, who compared a text of Assurnasirpal II.

9  I R pl. 3 no. VII.

10  Winckler 1906: 46, 40 days times 80 sun years; Craig *apud* Winckler 1907: 33, 40 = vernal constellation of the Pleiades times 80 (the Muslim *khuqub*, or cycle of 80).

11  King 1910: 219–22.

12  Dhorme 1907: 208 (last part of the name); Poebel 1908: 228 note 1; Jastrow 1915: 133, 137; earlier etymologies cited by Hilprecht 1893: 16. As for the middle word of his name, then read "gani," Dhorme and Thureau-Dangin suggested that it was a

theophoric element (Dhorme's proposal for the meaning of the name: "Sois juste, ô Gani, mon rois"), Thureau-Dangin 1908: 313 note 2; further below, note 46.

13 This argument was taken up by Hilprecht in 1893: 18 note 2.

14 Smith and Sayce 1880: 19–20.

15 For authoritative summaries of the historical perception of Semites at this time, Cook 1924; Levi della Vida 1938.

16 E. Meyer 1906; further Christian 1919/20.

17 Tiele 1886: 24.

18 Tiele 1886: 40–41.

19 One may cite his comment on George Smith, "Von der Meisterhand Geo. Smiths, der, wie mangelhaft seine philologische Schulung auch sein mochte, mit unerreichter Gabe der Entzifferung auch wohl kritischen Blick verband . . ." Tiele 1886: 49.

20 Tiele 1886: 25.

21 Tiele 1886: 112–15.

22 Sayce 1876; Tiele 1886: 115; Hilprecht 1893: 22 note 9. The seal was said to have been part of the so-called "Treasure of Curium," for which the date and circumstances of discovery are obscure (Myres 1914: xvi and p. 429 No. 4300 = Cesnola 1876 pl. XXXI No. 1). For more recent studies of this seal, which dates to the reign of Naram-Sin of Eshnunna, Frayne 1990: 554–55. Curiously, a small stone object with a dedicatory inscription of Naram-Sin of Eshnunna, giving his filiation as son of Ipiq-Adad, was found on the island of Cythera in the Aegean and published in 1853, but this piece escaped the attention of everyone who wrote about the Akkadian period in the nineteenth century, Frayne 1990: 554.

23 Hommel 1885: 299–311.

24 Hommel 1885: 306.

25 Hommel 1885: 308.

26 Hommel 1885: 309; Olmstead (1916/17: 310) suggested that it "imitated" an Akkadian seal of the deified Naram-Sin, so the seal no longer showed the extension of Akkadian rule into the Mediterranean; according to Langdon (1923a: 406), the seal was "Syro-Hittite" and the appearance of Naram-Sin on it was because he had become "a mythical hero in the Syro-Hittite region and his cult survived there for at least five centuries." On the other hand, omens suggested that Sargon had campaigned in the Mediterranean and some scholars associated the Mannum-dannum or Manium whom Naram-Sin defeated with Menes, an early ruler of Egypt: Albright 1920 (who suggested that Magan = Ma'ân, Iarmuti [Chapter 1 note 36] = Iarmut, south of Joppa (Joshua XV: 33), and that Ebla was a "Sumerian corruption of Byblos").

27 Menant 1875: 98–103 (with magnificent engravings); Schmidt 1872/77: 233–35 and 347 (I thank Ulla Kasten for assistance with Danish).

28 Winckler 1907: 49; King 1910: 219.

29 Rogers 1901: 360; the first to suggest the correct reading of the name Rimush was King 1908: 239, further Sommerfeld 2003a.

30 Rogers 1901: 361.

31 Rogers 1901: 365.

32 Rogers 1901: 363, 365.

33 Rogers 1901: 367.

34 Rogers 1901: 361, 305–7.

35 Radau 1900: 176–80.

36 Goodspeed 1902: 60.

37 Goodspeed 1902: 60; by coincidence this idea was revived in a thesis that Sumerians colonized northern Babylonia at an early date, Steinkeller 1993.

38 Goodspeed 1902: 61.

39 Goodspeed 1902: 63.

40 Goodspeed 1902: 97.

41 King 1910: ix.
42 King 1910: 219–27.
43 Hall 1913: 185–86.
44 Jastrow 1915: 45; his contemporary, Olmstead, had similar thoughts, writing of the Akkadian period, "Most of all, from political and cultural standpoint alike, the Semite had made his appearance in Babylonian history, and soon the mixed culture which resulted from the fusion of the two elements was to enrich all Western Asia" (Olmstead 1916/17: 321); likewise A. Westenholz (1999), below, part 6 and note 111.
45 Breasted 1916: 159–62; 1938: 137–39.
46 Oppert 1888: 124: "Il est temps d'en finir avec cette inadmissible plaisanterie, de lire le nom de Sargon – *Sargani* . . . il n'est pas plus Sargon, que les empéreurs Louis et Lothaire ne sont un même personnage." The problems of the order of the kings and who belonged to the dynasty were not cleared up even with Hilprecht's publication of the authentic Akkadian inscriptions from Nippur in 1893. These included numerous Rimush vase fragments and inscriptions of Naram-Sin and Sharkalisharri, but none of Sargon, so this reinforced the conviction of those who still believed that Sargon and Sharkalisharri were the same person. For this debate, Winckler 1892b; Scheil 1908: 4 (different people); 1912 (proof that they were different people); Thureau-Dangin 1908 (different people); Ungnad 1908; Hrozny 1909; King 1908 (different people confused in later Mesopotamian sources); 1910: 216–25 (different people but Sharkalisharri took Sargon's name); Jastrow 1915: 133, 137.
47 Appendix Ia 28; Gelb and Kienast 1990: 114; Frayne 1993: 188.
48 Volk 1992: 22–29; Kienast and Volk 1995: 102–4.
49 Scheil 1911. Later Scheil was able to decipher traces of Sharkalisharri's name as its fifth king and published a photo without the glued fragment, Scheil 1912; Thureau-Dangin 1918: 58–63, re-editing this manuscript, discussed Akkadian chronology and noted inscriptions of Dudu and Shu-Durul; then the manuscript published by Scheil was acquired by the British Museum and republished by Gadd 1921: 3–7 and plates 1–2, with discussion of Akkadian chronology, 42–43. For modern concern about *The Sumerian King List* as a basis for chronology, Marchesi 2010; Nissen 2012: 80.
50 Thureau-Dangin 1897b: 79: "Tout ce qui touche aux règnes de Sargon et de Naram-Sin présente un haut intérêt. On ne saurait en effet attribuer trop d'importance à cette époque: par la substitution d'un grand Empire compact au morcellement des petites principautés rivales, par la remarquable impulsion donnée à toutes les branches de l'activité, par la plein épanouissement et le rayonnement dans toutes les directions d'un art, d'une culture, d'une civilisation dont le lent développement avait rempli les siècles et les millénaires precedents, l'époque de Sargon et de Naram-Sin marque certainement un point culminant dans l'histoire de l'ancien Orient." At that time, Thureau-Dangin (1896) believed that Sharkalisharri and Sargon were the same person, so understood that the administrative documents from Girsu dated to these two reigns; further Heuzey 1897.
51 Winckler 1907: 33–34.
52 Poebel 1914.
53 Legrain 1926; Gelb and Kienast 1990: 139–47.
54 Gelb and Kienast 1990: 150–55.
55 Kutscher 1989; I am indebted to him for an account of the modern history of the tablet.
56 Wilcke 1997; further, Sommerfeld 2000; there is as yet no complete edition of this inscription, which has to be pieced together from various tablets and fragments, Appendix Ib 28.
57 Olmstead 1916/17: 310.
58 Langdon 1923a: 403–8.
59 Langdon 1923a: 409.

60 Langdon 1923a: 409.
61 Langdon 1923a: 417.
62 Langdon 1923a: 420–22.
63 Langdon 1923a: 409.
64 Güterbock 1934/38.
65 Rutten 1938; Snell 1974; J. Meyer 1987; further, Chapter 11 note 1.
66 Güterbock 1934: 21.
67 Van der Meer 1947: 180, 239. I thank Riets De Boer and Nelleke Van Deusen-Scholl for help with Dutch.
68 Nikolski 1948: 22–31.
69 Tyumenev 1956: 14–25, 209; for an appreciation of Tyumenev's place in early Soviet historical scholarship, Krikh 2012: 73–83.
70 Tyumenev 1956: 204, 206, 209, 213.
71 Tyumenev 1956: 207–8, 212.
72 Tyumenev 1956: 214–32; the only Adab tablets published at the time he wrote were Luckenbill 1930; further Chapter 3 note 102.
73 Tyumenev 1956: 232–38.
74 Tyumenev 1956: 239–40.
75 Diakonoff 1959: 69–79, 196–248; an English summary of his views on the Akkadian period, with some updates, is Diakonoff and Kohl 1991: 84–99. For Sargon's rise to power, Diakonoff 1959: 217–220.
76 Diakonoff 1959: 218–19.
77 Diakonoff 1959: 213, 221, 227.
78 Diakonoff 1959: 219–21, 226.
79 Diakonoff 1959: 221–23.
80 Diakonoff 1959: 224–25.
81 Diakonoff 1959: 212–16, 219, 227, 240.
82 Bottéro 1965: 92–113. The English version was not used here because it deviated too far from the German, which was clearly closer to the unpublished French original.
83 Bottéro 1965: 112–14.
84 Bottéro 1965: 123–28.
85 Liverani 1966a: 3–5.
86 Liverani 1966a: 8–17.
87 Liverani 1966a: 25–28.
88 Gadd 1971; Liverani 1993: 53, "complete lack of historical methodology."
89 Garelli 1982: 82–94.
90 Garelli 1982: 90–92.
91 Garelli 1982: 93: "L'époque n'a manqué ni de talents, ni de ressources. Mais la tentative était trop vaste, les rivalités intestines trop récentes, les ennemis du dehors trop nombreux, aux aguets de territoires trop étendus. L'échec paraît moins imputable aux erreurs humaines qu'à la pression des circonstances."
92 Schmökel 1955: 41–50.
93 Hirsch 1963; replaced by Gelb and Kienast 1990 and Frayne 1993.
94 Gelb 1952b, 1957; Hackman, G. and F. Stephens 1958.
95 Gelb 1977, 1981, 1986, 1992 (with primary attention to language and writing); Steinkeller 1993a.
96 Steinkeller 1993a: 120–23.
97 Gelb 1986.
98 Weiss and Courty 1993.
99 Weiss 2012b; further Chapter 1 note 78.
100 Glassner 1986; comments on trade on p. 24.
101 Liverani 1988b; for example, this work was not cited in B. Foster 1993b; A. Westenholz 1999; Edzard 2004.

102 Neumann in Klengel 1989: 86–43; revised in Neumann 2014.
103 Liverani 1966b: 73 ("in una situazione di notevole arretratezza metodologica," largely because Mesopotamian history was written by philologists, who tended to collect and paraphrase ancient sources without critical analysis, rather than historians); 1971.
104 Liverani 1973: 179.
105 Liverani 1993a: 42.
106 Liverani 1993a: 51.
107 Liverani 1993a: 56; for a critique of Liverani's approach, Hallo 1998; in general, A. Westenholz 1999: 20–28.
108 Michalowski 1993: 85.
109 Michalowski 1993: 90.
110 A. Westenholz 1999.
111 A. Westenholz 1999: 22.
112 A. Westenholz 1999: 20.
113 Edzard 2004: 90–91; for another brief survey, Selz 2005b: 63–74, unusual for its extended section on Enheduanna; for the 2013 study of the Akkadian period by Buccellati, Chapter 3 part 6.

# Appendix I
## Akkadian royal inscriptions

For scientific editions of these inscriptions, the reader is referred in the first instance to those of Gelb and Kienast (1990) and Frayne (1993); additional philological information will be found in Kienast and Sommerfeld (1994). This appendix includes for ready reference a selection of them, with a concordance to those two collections. For the inscriptions known from originals, where possible indication is also given of the nature of the objects bearing the inscriptions and where they were found in modern times, though this may not always have been their original location. Those purchased on the antiquities market are indicated by "elsewhere" or omission of provenance. For the inscriptions known from copies, the place of origin of the copy is given; in some instances the copy may refer to an original elsewhere.

For the expression translated here as "king of the world," Chapter 1 note 6. The verb regularly translated here as "conquered" means literally "smote on the head," as illustrated in Figure 9.5b.

### (a) Original inscriptions

#### Sargon

(1) [To the god . . . ] (by) Sargon, king of the world. (*stone vase at Ur*)
(2) [To the god . . . Sargon, king of Agade], conqueror of Uruk and Ur, dedicated (this). (*mace head at Ur*)
(3) . . . who smote [ ] in battle (*large gap*) . . . may they tear out [his foundations] and take away his seed. (*Caption to image*): Sargon the king. (*stela at Susa*)

#### Rimush

(4) Rimush, king of the world. (*mace heads at Ur and Assur, stone vases and plates, seashell, at Nagar, Tutub, Sippar, Girsu, Nippur, Girsu, Ur, Uruk*)
(5) Rimush, king of the world, conqueror of Elam and Marhashum. (*stone vases at Ur and elsewhere*)
(6) Rimush, king of the world, when he conquered Elam and Marhashum, dedicated (this), from the booty of Elam, to Enlil (*or*: to Sin, Dagan). (*stone vases, mace head at Nagar, Tutub, Sippar, Nippur, Ur, Tuttul and elsewhere*)

### Manishtusu

(7) Manishtusu, king of the world, dedicated this to Enlil (*or:* to Beltaya, Ninisina, Shamash). (*mace heads at Sippar and Isin, stone vase at Nippur*)

(8) Manishtusu, king of the world, when he conquered Anshan and Sherihum, had war? ships cross the Lower Sea. The cities beyond the sea, 32 of them, assembled for battle and he was victorious then smote their cities and slew their rulers. Then he took away (the people/territory?) from the [ ] River all the way to the silver mines. He quarried and loaded on boats the black stones of the mountains beyond the Lower Sea and moored them at the wharf of Agade. He made a statue of himself (from it) and dedicated it to Enlil. By Shamash and Ilaba I swear no lies but truthfully! Anyone who shall make away with this monument, may Enlil and Shamash (*or:* Shamash and Ishtar) tear out his foundation and take away his seed. (*statues and stelae at Susa, Sippar, Nippur*)

### Naram-Sin

(9) Naram-Sin. (*bricks at Nagar*)

(10) Naram-Sin (*variant inserts:* the mighty), king of the four quarters of the earth. (*stone vases and stone and metal plates at Drehem, Girsu, Ur and elsewhere*)

(11) Naram-Sin, builder of the Temple of Enlil (or: Temple of Ishtar, Sin). (*bricks and brick stamps from Nippur, Adab, Girsu*)

(12) Naram-Sin the mighty, king of the four quarters of the earth, conqueror of Armanum and Ebla. (*stone lamp and plaque at Girsu, metal bowl*)

(13) Naram-Sin, king of the four quarters of the earth, [dedicated] this vase, booty of Magan (*stone vases at Babylon, Susa and elsewhere*)

(14) Naram-Sin the mighty, king of the four quarters of the earth, dedicated this to Enlil in Nippur (*or:* to Ishtar in Nippur, Nisaba in Eresh, to Ishtaran). (*mace heads at Nippur and Ur, stone vase at Nippur*)

(15) Naram-Sin the mighty (*large gap*) . . .they assembled (in?) the mountains of Lullubum and . . . battle . . . (large gap). He dedicated it to [          ]. (*stela at Susa*)

(16) To Erra?, for the well-being of his comrade Naram-Sin the mighty, king of the four quarters of the earth, Suashtakal the scribe, supervisor of his household (*shaperum*), dedicated this statue of himself. (*statue at Susa*)

(17) [Naram-Sin, king of Agade, king of the four quarters of the earth], laid the [foundations of Ekur], the temple of Enlil. At that time, Suashtakal, supervisor of the king's household, was in charge of it, Urunabadbi was the temple administrator of Enlil. (*stamped brick at Nippur*)

(18) Naram-Sin the mighty, king of Agade, when the four quarters of the earth attacked him together, through the love Ishtar bore him was victorious in nine battles in a single year and captured the kings whom they had raised up against him. Because he defended his city in crisis, the people of his city asked

of him that he be god of their city Agade, with Ishtar in Eanna, with Enlil in Nippur, with Dagan in Tuttul, with Ninhursag in Kesh, with Enki in Eridu, with Sin in Ur, with Shamash in Sippar, with Nergal in Cutha, and they built his temple in Agade. Whoever shall make away with this monument, may Shamash and Ishtar and Nergal, the king's bailiff, and all these very gods tear out his foundations and take away his seed. (*copper statue at Bassetki, between Mosul and Zakho*)

*For discussion of this translation,* Chapter 1 *note 39.*

(19) Naram-Sin the mighty, king of Agade, builder of Kubara[ ], the temple of Ishtar in Zabala, when the four quarters of the earth attacked him together, then did he conquer all of the peoples and mountains from beyond the Lower Sea all the way to the Upper Sea for Enlil, and brought their kings in fetters before Enlil. Naram-Sin the mighty, in Enlil's fray, showed mercy to no one in those battles . . . He reached Hashlahash, the source of Tigris, and . . . the source of the Euphrates, and they cut cedars in the Amanus for the enhancement of the temple of Ishtar. Whoever shall make away with this monument, may Enlil and Shamash tear out his foundations and take away his seed. (*stone tablets at Nineveh and elsewhere, some with same inscription in the name of Sharkalisharri*)

(20) Naram-Sin the mighty, king of the four quarters of the earth, victor in nine battles in a single year, after he was victorious in these battles, then did he [capture] their three [kings and bring them before Enlil] (*large gap*) [When . . .] and Magan he smote, then captured Manium, lord of Magan, he cut diorite stones in their mountains and brought them to Agade and made a statue of himself (from it). He dedicated it to [     Whoever shall make away with this monument], may [     ] and the God of Agade tear out his foundations and take away his seed. (*statue at Susa*)

(21) Naram-Sin the [might]y (*large gap*) Enki gave him to rival in the four quarters of the earth (*large gap*) . . . he set and heaped up a burial mound. Whoever shall make away with this monument, may Ishtar (*large gap*) tear out his foundations and take away his seed, [may they give him] no heir, no descendants. (*stone stela at Pir Huseyin, near Diyarbekir in Anatolia*)

(22) (*large gap*) [when the four quarters of the earth attacked] him [together]. . . (*large gap*) they confronted him (*large gap*) he was victorious over them and the kings (of those cities) whom he had captured . . ., [he brought] in neck stocks before Enlil, his father (*large gap*). (*stone tablets*)

(23) Naram-Sin the mighty, king of the four quarters of the earth, victor in nine battles in a single year, after he was victorious in those battles, then did he capture their three kings and brought them before Enlil. At that time, Lipit-ili, his son, governor of Marad, built the temple of Lugal-Marad in Marad. Whoever shall make away with this monument, may Shamash and Lugal-marad tear out his foundations and take away his seed. (*pivot stones for doors, at Marad, near Kish?*)

**Sharkalisharri** *(versions of Naram-Sin 12 in his name as well)*

(24) Sharkalisharri, king of Agade. (*stamped brick from Nippur?, brick stamp, stone vase, bowl*)

(25) Sharkalisharri, king of Agade, builder of the temple of Enlil. (*brick stamps at Nippur and elsewhere*)

(26) Sharkalisharri the mighty, king of the subjects of Enlil. (*Neo-Babylonian squeeze of inscription said to have been made at Agade*)

(27) Sharkalisharri, king of Agade, dedicated this to Shamash in Sippar. (*mace head at Sippar*)

(28) Sharkalisharri, beloved son of Enlil, the mighty, king of Agade and the subjects of Enlil, builder of the Ekur, temple of Enlil, in Nippur. Whoever shall make away with this monument, may Enlil and Shamash tear out his foundations and take away his seed. (*pivot stones for door, Nippur; gold leaf*)

(29) As Enlil revealed: Sharkalisharri the mighty, king of Agade, builder of the Ekur, temple of Enlil, in Nippur. Whosoever shall make away with this monument, may Enlil and Shamash and Ishtar tear out his foundations and take away his seed. (*pivot stones for door, Nippur*)

### *Dudu*

(30) Dudu the mighty, king of Agade. (*stone vases at Nippur and elsewhere*)

### *Shu-Durul*

(31) Shu-Durul the mighty, king of Agade. (*axehead*)

### *Sources*

Sargon 1: Gelb and Kienast 1990: 64; Frayne 1993: 37 (differently). Sargon 2: Gelb and Kienast 1990: 63–4; Frayne 1993: 17–18. Sargon 3: Gelb and Kienast 1990: 62–3; Frayne 1993: 26–7.

Rimush 4: Gelb and Kienast 1990: 70–2; Frayne 1993: 70–2. Rimush 5: Gelb and Kienast 1990: 70; Frayne 1993: 66–7. Rimush 6: Gelb and Kienast 1990: 67–9; Frayne 1993: 60–7.

Manishtusu 7: Gelb and Kienast 1990: 78–9; Frayne 1993: 78–80, with different arrangements of the material. Manishtusu 8: Gelb and Kienast 1990: 75–7; Frayne 1993: 74–7.

Naram-Sin 9: Gelb and Kienast 1990: 101; Frayne 1993: 125–6. Naram-Sin 10: Gelb and Kienast 1990: 99; Frayne 1993: 150–2. Naram-Sin 11: Gelb and Kienast 1990: 100–101; Frayne 1993: 119–22. Naram-Sin 12: Gelb and Kienast 1990: 97; Frayne 1993: 136. Naram-Sin 13: Gelb and Kienast 1990: 98; Frayne 1993: 99–100, with different arrangement of the material. Naram-Sin 14: Gelb and Kienast 1990: 96–7; Frayne 1993: 146–9. Naram-Sin 15: Gelb and Kienast 1990: 90–2; Frayne 1993: 143–4. Naram-Sin 16: Gelb and

Kienast 1990: 106–7; Frayne 1993: 164–5. Naram-Sin 17: Gelb and Kienast 1990: 107–8; Frayne 1993: 118. Naram-Sin 18: Gelb and Kienast 1990: 81–3; Frayne 1993: 113–14. Naram-Sin 19: Gelb and Kienast 1990: 84–8; Frayne 1993: 137–8; Steinkeller CUSAS 17: 12–14. Naram-Sin 20: Gelb and Kienast 1990: 89–90; Frayne 1993: 116–18. Naram-Sin 21: Gelb and Kienast 1990: 92–3; Frayne 1993: 128–9. Naram-Sin 22: Gelb and Kienast 1990: 95–6; Frayne 1993: 109–11. Naram-Sin 23: Gelb and Kienast 1990: 102–3; Frayne 1993: 111–12.

Sharkalisharri 24: Gelb and Kienast 1990: 117; Frayne 1993: 195–7. Sharkalisharri 25: Gelb and Kienast 1990: 115–16; Frayne 1993: 189–90. Sharkalisharri 26: Gelb and Kienast 1990: 116–17; Frayne 1993: 197–8. Sharkalisharri 27: Gelb and Kienast 1990: 115; Frayne 1993: 196–7. Sharkalisharri 28: Gelb and Kienast 1990: 114–15; Frayne 1993: 188–9. Sharkalisharri 29: Gelb and Kienast 1990: 113–14; Frayne 1993: 186–7.

Dudu 30: Gelb and Kienast 1990: 121; Frayne 1993: 210–11.

Shu-Durul 31: Gelb and Kienast 1990: 122; Frayne 1993: 214–15.

## (b)　Ancient copies of inscriptions

### Sargon

(1) Sargon, king of Agade, emissary for Ishtar, king of the world, attendant of Anu, lord of the land, chief governor for Enlil, conquered the city of Uruk and destroyed its walls. He was victorious over Uruk in battle, [conquered the city], captured Lugalzagesi, king of Uruk, in battle, brought him to the gate of Enlil in a neck stock. Sargon, king of Agade, was victorious over Ur in battle, conquered the city, and destroyed its walls. He conquered Eninmar, and destroyed its walls, and conquered its land and Lagash all the way to the sea. He washed his weapons in the sea. He was victorious over Umma in battle and [conquered the city, and destroyed its walls]. Enlil [indeed gave no] rival [to Sargon], king of the land, Enlil indeed gave him [the Upper Sea and] the Lower Sea. Men of Agade hold governorships all the way from the Lower Sea <to the Upper Sea?>. Mari and Elam stand before Sargon, king of the land. Sargon, king of the land, changed the two locations of Kish, he caused the city to be inhabited. Whoever shall make away with this inscription, may Shamash tear out his foundation and take away his seed. (*Nippur*)

(2) Sargon, king of Agade, emissary for Ishtar, king of the world, attendant of Anu, king of the land, governor for Enlil, was victorious over Uruk in battle and conquered fifty governors with the mace of Ilaba and the city and destroyed its walls and captured Lugalzagesi, king of Uruk, and brought him to the gate of Enlil in a neck stock. Sargon, king of Agade, was victorious in over Ur in battle and conquered the city and destroyed its walls. He [conquered Eninmar] and destroyed its walls and conquered its land and Lagash all the way to the sea. He washed his weapons in the sea. He was victorious over Umma in battle and conquered the city and destroyed its walls. Sargon,

king of the land, Enlil indeed gave him no rival, he indeed gave him the Upper and Lower Sea. Mari and Elam stand (in service) before Sargon, king of the land. Sargon, king of the land, changed the two locations of Kish and caused the city to be inhabited. Whoever shall make away with this inscription, may Enlil and Shamash tear out his foundations and take away his seed. Whoever shall remove this statue, may Enlil remove his name, may he break his weapon, may he not stand before Enlil. (*Nippur*)

(3) Sargon, king of Agade, [conquered Uruk and was victorious in battle and he himself took prisoner fifty governors] and the king. Whoever shall make away with this inscription, may Enlil and Shamash tear out his foundations and take away his seed. (*Nippur*)

(4) Ilaba is his god! Sargon, king of Kish, with nine contingents from Agade, conquered Uruk and was victorious in battle, and he himself captured fifty governors and the king. Then in Nagurzam he fought a second battle and was victorious and a third time in Ur they fought each other and he was victorious. Further, he was victorious over Umma in battle and conquered the city. Further, he was [victorious] over Lagash in battle and [washed] his weapons in [the sea]. (*Caption*): Ilaba, the mightiest of the gods, Enlil gave him his weapon. (*Nippur*)

(5) Sargon, king of Agade, emissary for Ishtar, [king of] the world, attendant of Anu, chief governor for Enlil. When Enlil rendered a verdict for him and he conquered Uruk, . . . he dedicated this to Enlil and purified Nippur for Enlil. Whoever shall make away with this inscription, may Enlil and Shamash tear out his foundation and take away his seed. Whoever shall remove this statue, may Enlil remove his name, may he break his weapon, may he not stand before Enlil. (*Caption*): Sargon, king of the land, to whom Enlil gave no rival. (*Nippur*)

(6) To Enlil: Sargon, king of the world, conqueror of Elam and Marhashum, dedicated this to Enlil. He who shall make away with this inscription, may Enlil and Shamash tear out his foundations and take away his seed. (*Nippur*)

(7) Sargon, king of the world, was victorious in thirty-four battles. He destroyed city walls all the way to the shore of the sea. He moored boats of Meluhha, Magan, and Dilmun at the wharf of Agade. Sargon the king bowed down and prayed to Dagan in Tuttul. He gave him the Upper Land, Mari, Iarmuti, and Ebla, all the way to the cedar forest and the shining (or: silver) mountains. Sargon, king of the world, he to whom Enlil gave no rival, 5,400 men eat daily before him. Whoever shall make away with this inscription, may Anu make away with his name, may Enlil take away his seed, may Ishtar cut off his descendants. (*Nippur*)

(8) Sargon, (*large gap*), as Enlil revealed, Sargon showed mercy to no one. He gave him the Upper Sea and the Lower Sea. Sargon, king of the world, Ra[  ] is his general. (*Nippur*)

(9) Sargon, king [of the world] (*gap*) before Enlil. Sargon, king of the world, when Enlil gave him the scepter, he made his intelligence surpassing. He set up [  ] of Sargon. Sargon, as Enlil revealed, showed mercy to no one. . . .the great mountain of the gods (Enlil) is his . . . [  ]. (*Nippur*)

(10) Enheduanna, lady bird of Nanna, wife of Nanna, daughter of Sargon, [king] of the world, made an altar in the temple of Inanna in Ur and named it "Altar that is the Table of Heaven." (*Ur*)

## *Rimush*

(11) Rimush, king of the world, was victorious over Adab and Zabala in battle and slew 15,718 men. He took 14,576 captives. Further, he captured Meski-gal, governor of Adab, and Lugal-galzu, governor of Zabala. He conquered their cities [and destroyed their walls]. Further, he expelled [men from their cities] and put them in a camp. Whoever shall make away with this inscription, may Enlil and Shamash tear out his foundations and take away his seed. (*Nippur*)

(12) Rimush, king of the world, was victorious over Umma and Kidingir in battle and slew 8,960 men. He took 3,540 captives [   ] Further, he captured En[nalum], governor of Umma, and Lugal-KA, governor of Kidingir. and conquered their cities and destroyed their walls. Further, he expelled 3,600 men from their cities and put them in a camp. Whoever shall make away with this inscription, may Enlil and Shamash tear out [his foundations and take away his name]. (*Nippur*)

(13) Rimush, king of the world, was victorious over Ur and [Lagash] in battle and slew 8,040 men. He took 5,460 captives. Further, he captured KA-ku, king of Ur, and Kitush-id, governor of Lagash and conquered their cities and destroyed their walls. Further, he expelled 5,985 men from their cities and put them in a camp. Whoever shall make away with this inscription, may Enlil and Shamash tear out his foundations and take away his seed. (*Nippur*)

(14) Rimush, king of the world – Enlil verily gave kingship to him – was as many as three times victorious over Sumer in battle! He slew 11,322 men. He took 2520 captives. Further, he captured KA-ku, king of Ur, and captured his governors. Further, he took their tribute all the way to the Lower Sea. Further, he expelled 14,100 men from the cities of Sumer and put them in camps. Further, he conquered their cities and destroyed their walls. Then, during his return, Kazallu was in rebellion. He conquered it and slew 12,052 men inside Kazallu. He took 5,862 prisoners. Further, he captured Ashared, governor of Kazallu, and destroyed its walls. Total: 54,016 men, including the slain, including the captives, including the men whom he put in camps, the campaign is not lies!' By Shamash and Ilaba I swear no lies but truthfully! On the occasion of this battle he made a statue of himself and dedicated it to Enlil for his well-being. Whoever shall make away with this inscription, may Enlil and Shamash tear out his foundations and take away his seed. Whoever shall remove the name of Rimush, king of the world, and set his own name there, saying "My statue!" – may Enlil, owner of this statue, and Shamash tear out his foundations and take away his seed. May he [not] go before his god. (*Nippur*)

(15) Rimush, king of the world, when he conquered Kazallu, he slew 12,052 men in the battle of Kazallu. He took 5,864 prisoners. Further, he captured

Ashared, governor of Kazallu, and destroyed its walls. Whoever shall make away with this inscription, may Enlil and Shamash tear out his foundations and take away his seed. (*Nippur*)

(16) Rimush, king of the world, was victorious in battle over Abalgamash, king of Marhashum. Both Zahara and Elam [*variant*: Zahar, Elam, Gupin, and Meluhha] assembled in Marhashum for battle but he was victorious and slew 16,212 men, he took 4,216 captives. Further, he captured Emahsini, king of Elam, and all the [     ] of Elam. Further, he captured Sidga'u, general of Marhashum, and Shargapi, general of Zahara. Between Awan and Susa, at the river in the middle, further, he heaped up a burial mound over them in the place of a city. Further, he conquered the cities of Elam and destroyed their walls and tore out the foundations [= power] of Marhashum [from the land of Elam]. Rimush, king of the world, became ruler of Elam, as Enlil revealed. In but the third year of Enlil's having given kingship to him, a total of 74,444? (*figure uncertain*) men, including the slain and the captives! By Shamash and Ilaba I swear no lies but truthfully! On the occasion of this battle he made a statue of himself, he dedicated it to Enlil for his well-being. Whoever shall make away with this inscription, may Enlil and Shamash tear out his foundations and take away his seed. Whoever shall make away with the name of Rimush, king of the world, and set his own name on the statue of Rimush and say, "My statue!" may Enlil, owner of this statue, and Shamash tear out his foundations and take away his seed. May they give him no heir, may he not stand before his god. When he conquered Elam and Marhashum, he brought 30 minas of gold, 3,600 minas of copper, and 360 male and female slaves and dedicated them to Enlil. (*variant*: Diorite, yellow and other gemstones that I took, choice booty of Marhashum).

Rimush, king of the world, he to whom Enlil gave no rival. (*Nippur, Larsa?*)

(17) Rimush, king of the world. [Enlil] gave him the entire [land]. He holds the Upper Sea and the Lower Sea and all the mountains for Enlil. Whoever shall make away with this inscription, may Enlil and Shamash tear out his foundations and take away his seed.

Rimush, king of the world, conqueror of Elam and Marhashum. (*Nippur*)

(18) [Rimush, king of world. From earliest times] no one had made a statue of tin [for Enlil?]. Rimush, king of world, made a statue of himself of tin and it stands before Enlil. He accounted himself among the gods. Whoever shall make away with this inscription, may Enlil and Shamash tear out his foundations and take away his seed. (*Nippur, Larsa?*)

## Manishtusu

(19) Manishtusu, king of the world, when he conquered Anshan and Shirihum, had war? ships cross the Lower Sea. The cities beyond the sea, thirty-two of them, assembled for battle but he was victorious. Further, he conquered their cities, he slew their rulers. Further, he took away . . . all the way to the silver mines. He quarried and loaded on boats the black stone of the mountains beyond

the Lower Sea and moored them at the wharf of Agade. He made a statue of himself, he dedicated (it) to Enlil. By Shamash and Ilaba I swear no falsehoods but truthfully! Whoever shall make away with this inscription, may Enlil and Shamash tear out his foundations and take away his name. (*Nippur*)

(20) Manishtusu, king of the world, dedicated this to Enlil. (*Nippur*)

(21) Enlil! It was Enlil who made Manishtusu, king of the world, the greatest, called his name, and gave him the scepter of kingship. Whoever shall make away with this inscription, may Enlil and Shamash tear out his foundations and take away his name. (*Nippur*)

### Naram-Sin

(22) [Naram-Sin the mighty, king] of Agade, conqueror of . . ., who smashed the weapons of all of Subartu, who made firm the foundations of Ummanum, *(large gap)* revolted and raised an army. All the way from Tutusshe and its land, Urke[sh and its land] . . . all the way to [ ] and its land (*there follows a long list of what appear to be Hurrian cities and their territories*) After he smote it . . . fourteen fortresses for [ ] (*there follow more cities and their territories*) . . . all the way to [ ] and the cities beyond the Tigris River . . . (*Nippur*)

(23) Naram-Sin the mighty, king of Agade and the four quarters of the earth, husband of Ishtar-Annunitum, leader of the troops of the city of Ilaba, when Ishtar [ ] him (*large gap*) Pususu, his brother; Dudu, elder of the city, Surush-kin, the major domo; Ur-Nisaba, the chief scribe; Sin-KAR, overseer of scribes, Shumshu-paluh, Mumu, Puzrum, Ilish-takal, Ishtar-alshu (*gap*) Talmus, merchants of the land of Subartu, those whom he . . . and led off before the mace of Ilaba and Ishtar to the land of (*gap*) (*Nippur*)

(24) [Naram]-Sin, king of the four [quarters of the earth], when he defeated HAR-shamat and he himself slew a wild bull at Mount Tibar, he made an image of it (*or*: himself) and dedicated it to Enlil, his father. Whoever shall make away with this inscription, may Enlil and Shamash tear out his foundation and take away his seed. (*Nippur*)

(25) Naram-Sin, king of Agade, commander of the Mesopotamians?*, all the land of Elam as far as Marhashi, and the land of Subartu as far as the Cedar Forest, further, when he went to Talhadum – no king among all kings went on that campaign – Naram-Sin, king of Agade indeed went! Ishtar gave him no rival. The city rulers of Subartu and the lords of the Upper Lands brought their offerings before him . . . Naram-Sin, king of Agade, dedicated this to Ningublaga. Whoever shall make away with this inscription, may Ningublaga, owner of this statue, and Shamash tear out his foundations and take away his seed. May they give him no [heir] or descent. May he not stand before his god. (*Ur, Nippur*)

(26) Whereas, for all time since the establishment of the human race, no king among all kings whatsoever destroyed Armanum and Ebla, by the weapon of Nergal, Naram-Sin the mighty opened the only way and he gave him Armanum and Ebla. Further, he gave him the Amanus, the Cedar Mountains, and

the Upper Sea. By the weapon of Dagan, who makes his kingship great, Naram-Sin the mighty conquered Armanum and Ebla. Further, all the way from the head of the Euphrates (at Sippar) to Ulishum, he smote the people whom Dagan had given to him for the first time, and they perform service for Ilaba, his god. Further, he went to the end of the Amanus, the Cedar Mountain. When Dagan rendered the verdict of Naram-Sin, and gave Rid-Adad, king of Armanum, into his power and he himself captured him inside his entryway, he made a statue of himself of diorite and dedicated it to Sin.

Thus says Naram-Sin the mighty, king of the four quarters of the earth, "Dagan gave me Armanum and Ebla and I captured Rid-Adad, king of Armanum! Then did I make a likeness of myself and dedicated it to Sin. May no one remove my inscription, may my statue stand before Sin. Further, whatever his god will give him, may he take it (to the end). The deed I performed is too great to surpass." Whoever shall make away with the inscription of Naram-Sin, king of the four quarters of the earth, and shall set on the statue of Naram-Sin the mighty his own name and shall say "My statue," or show it to an outsider and say, "Erase his name, set my name on it," may Sin, owner of this statue, and Ishtar-Annunitum, Anu, Enlil, Ilaba, Sin, Shamash, Nergal, Umu, Ninkarrak, all of the great gods, lay upon him a horrible curse. May he hold no scepter for Enlil, no kingship for Ishtar, may he not stand before his god. May Ninhursag and Nintu give him no heir nor descent, may Adad and Nisaba make no furrow of his straight. May Enki measure out only mud$^?$ to his watercourses, may he not increase his understanding . . .

(*Captions to relief depicting the city*): From the fortification wall to the great walls, 130 cubits is the height of the mound, 44 cubits is the height of the wall. From the quay wall to the fortification wall: 180 cubits is the height of the mound, 30 cubits is the height of the wall. Total: 404 cubits height, from ground level to the top of (that) wall. He undermined Armanum. From the river to the quay wall: 196 cubits is the height of the mound, 20 cubits is the height of the wall. From the quay wall to the fortification wall: 156 cubits is the height of the mound, 30 cubits is the height of the wall. (*Ur*)

(27) *Is a tablet copy of the original inscription Naram-Sin 19. (Zabala?) (Same inscription for Sharkalisharri, below, 34)*

(28) *The inscription Naram-Sin placed at Nippur narrating his suppression of the Great Revolt is one of the longest known from the third millennium. It is preserved in several copies but large gaps remain and the remaining text is not always fully understandable. From what remains it is clear that it was a masterpiece of its kind.*

Enlil is his god, Ilaba, mightiest of the gods, is his cohort. Naram-Sin the mighty, king of the four quarters of the earth [. . . in Kish] they raised up [Iphur]-Kish to kingship and in Uruk they raised up Amar-Girid to kingship as well. Iphur-Kish, king of Kish, raised an army against me and <mobilized> Kish, Cutha, Tiwa, Sippar, Kazallu, Kiritab, Apiak [  ] and the Amorite highlanders. Between Tiwa and Urum, in the field of Sin, he drew up and awaited battle. Naram-Sin the mighty seized his men and held Agade and prayed(?) to Shamash, saying, "O Shamash, the Kishite *(large gap)* (Sargon?) . . . their . . . and he shaved their heads. See now, he has turned hostile . . ."

In the field of Sin they made battle and fought each other. By the verdict of Ishtar-Annunitum, Naram-Sin the mighty [was victorious over] the Kishite in the battle at Tiwa. Further, he [slew] Ili-resi, the general; Ilum-muda, Ibbi-Zababa, Imtalik, Puzur-Asar, captains of Kish, and Puzur-Ningal, governor of Tiwa; Ili-re'a, his captain; Kulizum, captain of Eresh; Edam'u, captain of Cutha, *(large gap)* Further, he captured in battle [ ], Ilum-dan, governor of Borsippa; Dada, governor of Apiak, total: 5 officers and 4,932 soldiers he captured in battle.

Further, he pursued him all the way to Kish, and, beside Kish, at the gate of Ninkarrak, they made battle and fought each other a second time. By the verdict of <Ishtar>-Annunitum and Anu, Naram-Sin the mighty was victorious over the Kishite in the battle of Kish. Further, [he slew] Puzur-Numushda, governor of Kazallu; Dannum, captain of Borsippa; Pu-palim, captain of Apiak *(large gap)* Iddin-[ ], governor of Cutha, Ilish-takal, governor of Sippar; Shalim-beli, governor of Kiritab; Qishum, governor of Eresh; Ita-Ilum, governor of Dilbat; Imtalik, captain of Tiwa, total: 9 officers and 2,015 he captured in battle.

Further, he filled the Euphrates River with them and conquered the city of Kish and destroyed its walls. Further, he made the river run over inside it and slew 2,525 men in the city. *(large gap)* Further, he [ ] the Kishite?.

[Amar-girid, king] of Uruk, raised an army against me and mobilized Uruk, Ur, Lagash, Umma, Adab, Shuruppak, Isin, Nippur, all the way from the Lower Sea. Between Uru'a and Ashnak he drew up and awaited battle. Naram-Sin the mighty heard about him and hastened against him from Kish and they made battle and fought with each other. By the verdict of Ishtar-[Annunitum and Anu, Naram-Sin the mighty was victorious over the Urukite in the battle . . . ] *(large gap)* and he made the river run over inside it [ ]. *(large gap)* Further, Lugal-[ ], governor of Nippur [ ] *(large gap)*

He kept sending messages to the lords of the Upper Lands and the city rulers of Subartu, beseeching, "Let us be allies . . ." The lords of the Upper Lands and the city rulers of Subartu, since they feared Ilaba, none of them . . . followed him. Amar-girid, king of Uruk, trembled in fear, "I must march, [he having been vic]torious, so be it that he die, I live, or otherwise!" He went from Asimanum to Shishil to the head of the Euphrates. He crossed the Euphrates and went up to Basar, the mountain of the Amorites. Naram-Sin the mighty heard about him and released nine captains of Agade he held against him and he hurried to Habshat. Naram-Sin the mighty himself went up the Euphrates to Mount Basar. They fought a seventh battle and, by the verdict of Annunitum and Enlil, Naram-Sin the mighty was victorious over the Urukian in battle in Basar, the mountain of the Amorites. Further, he slew [ ], captain of Umma; Aba-Enlil, captain of Adab, total: 9 officers and 4325(?) men in the battle. Naram-Sin the mighty took prisoner in the battle Amar-girid, king of Uruk, E'e the general, Enlil-galzu, city elder of Uruk *(there follows a long list of notables from Uruk, Ur,*

*Lagash, Umma, Adab, Nippur, and two Amorite leaders*).Total: 31 officers and 4980(?) soldiers he captured in battle; [Grand Total: 2] kings, 1210(?) notables and 4980(?) captive soldiers. [Grand total: 2] kings; Grand total: 13(?) generals; Grand total: 23(?) governors; Grand total: 1210(?) officers; Grand total: 80,940(?) men, as Enlil revealed, did Naram-Sin slay or take captive in battle.

Then Naram-Sin the mighty broke(?) their standards at the gates of his gods. I swear by [Ishtar-Annunitum and] En[lil] no lies but truthfully, this many kings, by Ishtar-Annunitum and Enlil! Naram-Sin the mighty did indeed capture them, did indeed bring them in, with the weapon of Ilaba his lord, in truth! Naram-Sin the mighty, emissary of Ishtar his goddess, king of Agade and king [of the four quarters of the earth, attendant of Anu], governor for Enlil, general for Ilaba, who reached(?) the sources of the Irnina River, who defended Agade, who showed forth might to all kings, what no king has experienced since the creation of the human race, an attack by all four quarters of the earth together, when Naram-Sin the mighty was emissary of Ishtar, all four quarters of the earth attacked him together and challenged him. [ . . . By the verdict of . . . Naram-Sin the mighty], emissary of Ishtar, was victorious over them in the battle of [. . .] [by] verdict of Enlil, father of the gods, with the weapon of Ilaba his lord, and restored their freedom. Further . . ., he he[ard of it], he crossed and conquered Magan, in the midst of the sea, and washed his weapons in the Lower Sea. Naram-Sin the mighty, emissary of Ishtar, when Enlil had rendered his verdict and given to him the lead rope of the people and gave him no rival, he dedicated to [Enlil] . . . a great flagon for oil [ ] Whoever shall make away with the inscription of Naram-Sin, shall set his own name on it and say, "My great flagon for oil," or shall show it to another man as agent and say, "Erase his name," may Ishtar-Annunitum, Anu, Enlil, Ilaba, Sin, Shamash, [Nergal], [Umu, Ninkar, the great gods, all of them, lay upon him a horrible cur]se. May he hold no scepter for Enlil, may he take up no kingship for Ishtar. May Ninursag and Nintu give him no heir or descent . . . his kingship. May [Adad] and Nisaba make no furrow? of his straight. May Enki measure out only mud for his water courses. (*Nippur*)

(29) Naram-Sin the [mighty, king] of the four quarters of the earth, victor in nine battles in one year, [dedi]cated this to Enlil. Whoever shall make away with this inscription, may [Enlil and Shamash tear out his foundations and take away his seed]. (*Nippur*)

(30) [Naram-Sin the mighty, king of Agade and the four quarters of the earth, [Ishtar?] gave him no rival. He made a likeness of himself, a gold statue for all time to commemorate his might and the battles in which he was victorious and [dedicated it to Enlil. Whoever shall make away with this inscription, may Enlil and Shamash tear out his foundations and take away his seed].

(31) . . . Ebla, Mari, Tuttul, . . ., Urkesh, Mukish . . . Abarnium, and the mountain where cedars are cut, and all their lands; the land of Subartu, the shores of the Upper Sea and . . . and Magan and all its lands beyond the [sea . . .] (*Nippur*)

(32) [Naram-Sin, king of] the four quarters of the earth, Enmenanna, lady bird of Nanna, wife of Nanna, high priestess of Sin at Ur, is his daughter. (*Ur*)

## Sharkalisharri

(33) As Enlil [revealed]: Sharkalisharri the mighty, cupbearer to Enlil, king of Agade and of Enlil's subjects, he gave him . . . in its entirety. When he reached the sources of the Tigris and Euphrates rivers, he dedicated (this) to Enlil. (*Nippur*)

(34) *Is a tablet copy of the original inscription Naram-Sin 19, but in the name of Sharkalisharri. (Zabala?) (Same inscription for Naram-Sin, above, 27)*

(35) For Enlil, king of the gods, Sharkalisharri, his beloved son, [   ] of his father, he will come to Nippur, he will stand over him. Whoever shall make away with the inscription of the temple of [Enlil, shall put is own] name (there) or say [to a stranger "Remove the name of [Sharkali]sharri, write my name" or who puts it away⁷ in his storeroom, may Enlil, king of the gods, [and judge] his [case], may they take away his seed. (*Nippur*)

## Dudu

(36) To Ishtar, Dudu, king of Agade, when he conquered Girsu, dedicated (this) from the booty of Girsu. (*Nippur*)

## Sources

Sargon 1: Gelb and Kienast 1990: 157–63; Frayne 1993: 9–12. Sargon 2: Gelb and Kienast 1990: 170–4; Frayne 1993: 13–15. Sargon 3: Gelb and Kienast 1990: 177–8; Frayne 1993: 21. Sargon 4: Gelb and Kienast 1990: 167–70; Frayne 1993: 16–17. Sargon 5: Gelb and Kienast 1990: 174–6; Frayne 1993: 19–20. Sargon 6: Gelb and Kienast 1990: 187–9; Frayne 1993: 24–5. Sargon 7: Gelb and Kienast 1990: 163–7; Frayne 1993: 27–9. Sargon 8: Gelb and Kienast 1990: 182–3; Frayne 1990: 32. Sargon 9: Gelb and Kienast 1990: 186–7; Frayne 1993: 33–4. Sargon 10: Gelb and Kienast 1990: 64–5; Frayne 1993: 35–6.

Rimush 11: Gelb and Kienast 1990: 200–201; Frayne 1993: 41–2. Rimush 12: Gelb and Kienast 1990: 202–5; Frayne 1993: 43–5. Rimush 13: Gelb and Kienast 1990: 196–8; Frayne 1993: 45–6. Rimush 14: Gelb and Kienast 1990: 191–6; Frayne 1993: 47–50. Rimush 15: Gelb and Kienast 1990: 198–9; Frayne 1993: 50–1. Rimush 16: Gelb and Kienast 1990: 205–11; Frayne 1993: 51–7. Rimush 17: Gelb and Kienast 1990: 211–12; Frayne 1993: 59–60. Rimush 18: Gelb and Kienast 1990: 215–17; Frayne 1993: 67–9.

Manishtusu 19: Gelb and Kienast 1990: 75–7; Frayne 1993: 74–6. Manishtusu 20: Frayne 1993: 77 (top, taken to be part of the preceding); Gelb and Kienast 1990: 223 (treated separately). Manishtusu 21: Gelb and Kienast 1990: 223–5; Frayne 1993: 77–8.

Naram-Sin 22: Gelb and Kienast 1990: 284–91; Frayne 1993: 141–3. Naram-Sin 23: Gelb and Kienast 1990: 251–3; Frayne 1993: 88–90. Naram-Sin 24: Gelb and Kienast 1990: 265–6; Frayne 1993: 126–7. Naram-Sin 25: Gelb and Kienast 1990: 249–51; Frayne 1993: 129–31; *reading sag$^i$-gi$_6$-kam "black-headed folk," a general term for Sumerians and Akkadians, but this is hypothetical. Naram-Sin 26: Gelb and Kienast 1990: 253–64; Frayne 1993: 132–5. Naram-Sin 27: Frayne 1993: 139–40; above, Appendix Ia 19 and below, Sharkalisharri 34. Naram-Sin 28: Gelb and Kienast 1990: 226–48; Frayne 1993: 90–99, 103–8. Naram-Sin 29: Gelb and Kienast 1990: 267–8; Frayne 1993: 115–16. Naram-Sin 30: Gelb and Kienast 1990: 266–7; Frayne 1993: 160. Naram-Sin 31: Frayne 1993: 163. Naram-Sin 32: Gelb and Kienast 1990: 273; Frayne 1993: 145–6.

Sharkalisharri 33: Frayne 1993: 191–2; Sharkalisharri 34: Gelb and Kienast 1990: 276–9; Frayne 1993: 192–4; Sharkalisharri 35: Gelb and Kienast 1990: 279–81; Frayne 1993: 194–5.

Dudu 36: Gelb and Kienast 1990: 283; Frayne 1993: 211.

# Appendix II
## Works attributed to Enheduanna

Enheduanna was appointed by her father, Sargon, to be high priestess of the moon-god, Nanna-Suen, at Ur. Three major compositions attributed to her are translated here; for others, Sjöberg and Bergmann 1969 (ECTSL C.4.8.0) and J. Westenholz 1992a: 550–6 (ECTSL C.4.13.03). For the debate as to whether or not she really wrote all these works, Chapter 9 part 5. These poems are very difficult to understand, so significant differences in translation will be found in other treatments of them, cited at the end of each poem as "Sources," to which the reader is referred for detailed discussion and further bibliography. Explanatory material in parentheses has been added by the translator.

### (a)  Queen of all cosmic powers

According to this extraordinary autobiographical Sumerian poem, a usurper, Lugalanne, expelled Enheduanna from office. When she prayed to the moon-god, he did nothing. When she prayed to Inanna-Ishtar, the goddess destroyed her enemies and Enheduanna was triumphantly reinstated.

*(The limitless power of the goddess Inanna)*

Queen of all cosmic powers, bright light shining from above, (1)
Steadfast woman, arrayed in splendor, beloved of earth and sky,
Consort of Heaven, whose gem of rank is greatest of them all,
Favored for the noblest diadem, meet for highest sacral rank,
Who has taken up in hand cosmic powers sevenfold, (5)
My lady! You are warden of the greatest cosmic powers,
You bore them off on high, you took them firm in hand,
You gathered them together, you pressed them to your breast.

You spew venom on a country, like a dragon.
Wherever you raise your voice, like a tempest, no crop is left standing. (10)
You are a deluge, bearing that country away.
You are the sovereign of heaven and earth, you are their warrior goddess!

*(Inanna harshly punished Sumer for rebelling)*

You are the raging fire that rained down upon this land,
Given power by heaven, the queen who stands on lions' backs,
Whose command, once spoken, is the command of holy heaven,    (15)
The greatest duties fall to you, who else could understand them?
You brought havoc on the country, it was you who gave the storm
    its strength,
With Enlil's favor, you taught this land respect,
An himself assigned you this mission.

My lady! The country bows down at your battle cry!    (20)
When the trembling human race has found its place before you,
Midst your awe-inspiring, overwhelming splendor,
For of all cosmic powers you hold those most terrible,
And at your behest the storage house of tears is opened wide,
They walk the pathway to the house of deepest mourning,    (25)
Defeated, ere the battle had begun.

*(Inanna's terrible anger)*

My lady! With your force, a tooth could chip a stone.
You charge forward with the onrush of a tempest,
You raise your battle cry, like a raging storm,
Your voice resounds, like a thunderclap.    (30)
Though one contrary wind after another may tire at last,
Your footfalls never tire,
They sound the drumbeat of a funeral dirge.
My lady! The great, the ruling gods seek refuge from you
Like fluttering bats in ruin heaps,    (35)
Not one can stand up to your furious glare,
Not one can face your furious brow.
Who can calm your angry heart?
Calming your angry heart is far too much to do.

O Queen, might your feelings be mild? O Queen, might your
    heart be kind?    (40)
Will you not calm from your anger, O Child of the Moon?

*(The frightful consequences of her anger on the rebellious land)*

O Queen, supreme over the country, who could take
    from you your place?
Even mountains you parcel out as your terrain, where grain is unnatural,

While flames flicker in their passage paths.
You made their watercourses run in blood, their people drink it,                   (45)
Their forces fled before you, of their own accord,
Their ranks parted before you, of their own accord,
Their fighting men ran before you, of their own accord.
The storm broke upon their cities, where people had celebrated,
They rounded up their finest fighting men for captives.                             (50)
The city that did not say, "This country is yours!"
Which did not say, "It is your father's!"
Speaks now your blessing, lies once more beneath your feet.
No one, indeed, had set foot in its sheepfolds,
No woman there spoke tenderly to her husband,                                       (55)
No converse would she have with him at night,
Nothing of her inmost treasures would she reveal.

*(Enheduanna wants to write this poem, but feels inadequate to the task)*

Great daughter of the Moon, charging like a bison,
Queen supreme in heaven, who could take from you your place?
Great queen among queens, worthy of your cosmic power,                              (60)
Born of a holy womb, surpassing your mother,
Omniscient queen who oversees all countries,
Who makes their swarming populations thrive,
    I will sing a song consecrated to you!
Steadfast Goddess, worthy of your cosmic powers, what you
    have so mightily commanded, is something too great for me to do,
Steadfast, brilliant woman, deep of heart,
    I must sing to you of your cosmic powers!                               (65)

*(She hints at the abuse by the rebel Lugalanne, which left her speechless)*

Yes, I took up my place in the sanctuary dwelling,
I was high priestess, I, Enheduanna.
Though I bore the offering basket, though I chanted the hymns,
A death offering was ready, was I no longer living?
I went towards light, it felt scorching to me,                                      (70)
I went towards shade, it shrouded me in swirling dust.
A slobbered hand was laid across my honeyed mouth,
What was fairest in my nature was turned to dirt.
O Moon-god Suen, is this Lugalanne my destiny?
Tell heaven to set me free of it!                                                   (75)
Just say it to heaven! Heaven will set me free!
The Woman will take Lugalanne's destiny from him,
For high- and flood-land lie beneath her feet.

Yes, that Woman is indeed all-powerful, she will make the city tremble,
She stands paramount, let her heart take pity on me!                    (80)

*(Enheudanna's desperate prayer to Inanna when the moon-god, whom*
*she serves, does nothing to help her)*

I am Enheduanna, let me speak to you my prayer,
My tears flowing like some sweet intoxicant:
"O Holy Inanna, may I let you have your way?
    I would have you judge the case.
"I cannot make him, the silver nighttime orb, exert himself for me.
"That man has defiled the rites decreed by holy heaven,                 (85)
"He has robbed An of his very temple!
"He honors not the greatest god of all,
"The abode that An himself could not exhaust its charms, its beauty infinite,
"He has turned that temple into a house of ill repute,
"Forcing his way in as if he were an equal,
    he dared approach me in his lust!                                   (90)

"O wild bison, steadfast to me, do you be the one to hunt him down,
    do you be the one to catch him!
"What is to become of me in this place I had my living,
"This unruly place that spurns your night-sky father?
    May Heaven bring it to heel!
"May An slash it, through and through!
"May Enlil cut short its destiny!                                       (95)
"May no mother comfort any baby crying there.
"O Queen, any mourning for this place,
"Your mourning-vessel should jettison it off some foreign shore!
"Am I to die for my sacral song?
"Me? My moonlight has no care for me!                                   (100)
"He destroys me in this place of hopes deceived.
"He, the silver nighttime orb, has spoken no judgment for me.
"If he spoke it, what then? If he spoke it not, what then?

*(Lugalanne has forced her out of office and suggests that she kill herself)*

"When Lugalanne stood paramount, he expelled me from the temple,
"He made me fly out the window like a swallow, I had had
    my taste of life,                                                   (105)
"He made me walk a land of thorns.
"He took away the noble diadem of my holy office,
"He gave me a dagger: "This is just right for you," he said.

*(Her climactic plea to Inanna)*

"O precious, precious Queen, beloved of heaven,
"Your sublime will prevails, let it be for my restoration!             (110)

"O beloved spouse of Amaushumgalanna,

"You are the great queen of horizon and vault of heaven,

"The ruling gods submit to you,

"Even at birth, when you were an infant queen,

"You surpassed all the great gods who ruled,                    (115)

"The ruling gods pressed their lips to the ground before you.

"My case has not been closed, an unfavorable
    verdict looms up as mine.

"My hands are no longer clasped together on
    the god's bed, richly dight,

"Nothing did I reveal to anyone of what his lady confided to him.

"I am the glorious high priestess to the Moon-god, Nanna.        (120)


"O Queen beloved of Heaven, may your heart feel pity for me!

"Show it, Oh show it: If Nanna said nothing, he meant, 'Do as you will.'

"Show that you stand high as heaven

"Show that you reach wide as the world

"Show that you destroy all unruly lands                          (125)

"Show that you raise your voice to foreign countries

"Show that you smash head after head,

"Show that you feed on kill, like a lion,

"Show that your eyes are furious,

"Show that your stare is full of rage,

"Show that your eyes gleam and glitter                           (130)

"Show that you are unyielding, that you persevere,

"Show that you stand paramount,

"For if Nanna said nothing, he meant, 'Do as you will.'

"My Queen! This made you greater, this made you greatest,

"O Queen beloved of Heaven, I would tell of your furious deeds!  (135)

"I banked the coals, I prepared myself for the rite.

"Your chapel is ready for you, will your heart feel no pity for me?


*(Enheduanna produces this poem, once private inside her, now born in agony and there for all to sing)*

"This filled me, this overflowed from me, Exalted Lady,
    as I gave birth for you.

"What I confided to you in the dark of night, a singer shall
    perform for you in the bright of day!                     (140)

"Because of your assaulted wife, because of your assaulted child,

"Great was your fury, remorseless your heart."


*(Inanna heeds her entreaties, Enheduanna is restored to office)*


The almighty queen, who presides over the priestly congregation,
She accepted her prayer.

Inanna's sublime will was for her restoration.                                    (145)
It was a sweet moment for her, she was arrayed in her finest,
    she was beautiful beyond compare,
She was lovely as a moonbeam streaming down.
Nanna stepped forward to admire her.
Her divine mother, Ningal, joined him with her blessing,
The very doorway gave its greeting too.                                           (150)

*(Concluding praise to the goddess)*

What she commanded for her consecrated woman prevailed.
To you, who can destroy countries, whose cosmic powers are bestowed
    by Heaven,
To my queen arrayed in beauty, to Inanna be praise!

## Sources

Hallo and Van Dijk 1968; Zgoll 1997; ECTSL C.4.07.02; Attinger 2014 4.7.2.

## (b)   Passionate Inanna

Like the preceding, this poem contains a self-referential passage by Enheduanna (line 219), but most of it is lost. `This poem celebrates the contrasts of Inanna's nature and her contradictory roles in human life: goddess of tenderness and violence, falling in love, creating a household and family, and massacre and destruction; bliss and grief.

*(Inanna as Queen among the Gods)*

O Inanna, passionate, impetuous lady, proudest among the ruling gods,    (1)
Unsurpassed in the land, great daughter of the Moon,
    exalted among the leading gods,
Lady of mighty deeds, who has gathered to herself the cosmic powers of
    heaven and earth, to rival great An himself,
She is the sublime leader of the great gods,
    it is she who renders their final verdicts.
The ruling gods bow low at her exalted command,                                   (5)
An himself cannot fathom her behavior,
    nor would he go against her instructions,
She changes her own actions, no one knows how that will happen.
She exercises to the fullest her cosmic powers,
    she holds the lead rope in her hand, as she goes before them,
She is a massive neck stock holding firm the gods of this land.
Her splendor shrouds the highest crag, it hushes the thoroughfare.               (10)
The gods of this land are terrified by her loud battle cry,

At her clamor the ruling gods quake like solitary reeds,
At her hubbub they run off and hide together.
Without Inanna great An makes no decision,
    Enlil has determined no destiny,
Inanna, who holds her head high, taller than a mountain,
    who can oppose her? (15)
At her command, cities fall to ruins, houses lie desolate,
    sanctuaries become barren land,
The trembling her fury brings on is like a fever,
    torture such as a demon inflicts on a man,
Those who disobey her she throws into panic and confusion.

*(Inanna as Warrior)*

When she moves into battle, she is an onrushing flood,
    her uniform an angry glow,
The fray is her celebration, while she dances, untiring, in battle,
    with her combat footgear on, (20)
A raging storm, whirling in battle, her queenly robe glinting,
Where she strikes is a rout, a scorching? south wind blasting against
    the brow.
Inanna stands on leashed lions, she slashes to pieces anyone who does not
    respect her,
She is mountain lion preying on the roadway . . .
Inanna, like a mighty wild bull, is self-confident in her strength,
    no one can resist her, (25)
. . . Foremost among the greatest nobles, she is a pitfall for the unruly,
A trap for the wicked man, a [snare] for the foe,
Her venom is a pelting storm, wherever it falls is awash,
Her anger is an irresistible flood, . . .
A rising swell, crumpling the man she despises. (30)
Inanna is an eagle, her pinions [soaring over] the rebellious land,
    she lets no one go,
Inanna is the hawk of the gods, slashing to death the teeming paddock.

*( fragmentary lines)*

*(Inanna exults in killing)*

This song describes . . . weeping, the sustenance of death, (40)
Inanna [administers] the sustenance of death,
    the one who partakes will die before his time,
The one whom she forcefeeds it, gall will wrack him with pain, . . .
She performs the death-song in the steppe for her enjoyment,
While she performs her favorite song,
She bathes these weapons in blood and gore . . . (45)

*(fragmentary lines)*

She drenches their first fruits with blood, engorging them with gore.
In the steppe, vast and empty, she darkens the glow of day,
    turns high noon to gloom,
People confront each other in anger, they go looking for a fight,    (50)
Their challenges disrupt the steppe, engulfing field and empty plain.
Her battle cry is like thunder, it makes flesh creep throughout the land.
No one can stand before her murderous assault, who could rival her?
She is a rising flood sweeping over the land, leaving nothing behind.    (55)

*(fragmentary lines)*

*(Inanna brings destruction wherever she wishes)*

Her haughty heart bids her act as she does, only Inanna acts this way.
In command of the assembled forces, occupying the place of authority,
    dignitaries at her right and left.
She brings down a huge mountain like a heap of rubble, . . .    (60)
She wrecks the mountain land in every direction.
Inanna, triumphant, demolishes fortifications with sledgehammers,
The hardest rock she shatters like a dish, rendering it like tallow.
That proud lady holds a dagger in her hand, its terrible gleam
    reaches over this land,
Her net ensnares the deepest fish, . . .    (65)
She is like the skillful fowler leaving no bird escape through the skeins of his
    outstretched mesh,

*(fragmentary lines, large gap)*

*(Inanna empowers women, making men lament her fickleness)*

She cuts open the tie of the sealed portal of the house of knowledge,
    she makes known what is inside,
But the ones who feared not her net have no escape from the web
    she spreads before them.    (85)
Having no regard for a man whose name she once invoked, she approaches
    a woman, she has her cut a weapon, gives her the spear,
The reed players, the masked man, the raving lunatic, she makes
    them bear the burden, she makes them do the wailing,
The visionary, the female impersonator who has been altered, the cross-
    dresser, the he-man's boy,
Lament for a song [she makes them sing],
They wear themselves out weeping and wailing, they
    perform lamentations,    (90)
Though they weep all the time, they do not [calm] your heart,
"Woe is me!" is their cry, but you are not about to lament.

*(fragmentary lines)*

*( The victorious goddess takes control of Eanna, "House of Heaven," sanctuary of An, her father, to rule the other gods in his stead)*

Inanna, your triumph is a terrible thing, . . .
The ruling gods prostrate themselves, flinging themselves to the ground.
You come down from heaven riding on seven great lions,                (105)
Great An himself feared your countenance,
    An was frightened at your stance.
He let you take up your dwelling in Great Heaven's own sanctuary,
    An felt no fear of you after that:
"I hand over to you sublime sovereignty and the scepter
    of the gods!"
The great gods did obeisance, they undertook to serve you.
The uplands submit, but Mount Ebih did not.
The far-off mountain land, the land of carnelian and lapis,
    prostrated itself before you,                                 (110)
But Mount Ebih did not prostrate itself before you,
    it did not send submissive greetings.

*(Inanna's wonderful contrasting powers)*

When you raise your furious battle cry, like thunder,
    you are a beating storm,
Queen, exalted by An and Enlil, . . .
Without your consent, no destiny at all is determined,
    The most ingenious solution finds no favor.
To run fast, to slip away, to calm, to pacify are yours, Inanna,      (115)
To dart aimlessly, to go too fast, to fall, to get up,
    to [sustain] a comrade are yours, Inanna,
To open high road and byroad, safe lodging on the way,
    helping the worn-out along are yours, Inanna,
To make footpath and trail go the right direction,
    to make the going good are yours, Inanna,
To destroy, to create, to tear out, to establish are yours, Inanna,
To turn man into woman and woman into man are
    yours, Inanna,                                               (120)
Attraction, arousal, getting goods and chattels are yours, Inanna,
Gain, income, windfall, growing rich are yours, Inanna,
Business, profit, loss, and insolvency are yours, Inanna,
Revealing, instructing, inspecting, scrutinizing, approval
    are yours, Inanna,
Apportioning virility, vigor, vitality, good fortune and protection,
    a place to worship are yours, Inanna,                        (125)

*(large gap)*

Neglect, preparedness, triumph, submission are yours, Inanna,
Making a home, living quarters, getting utensils, kissing a baby's lips
    are yours, Inanna,
Taking strides, running, winning the race are yours, Inanna,
To change the brawny and the strong for the weak and powerless
    are yours, Inanna,                                                    (140)
To change the height for the low place, the peak for the plain
    are yours, Inanna,
To bestow the royal crown, throne, and scepter are yours, Inanna,

*(large gap)*

To make small, great, skimpy, ample, all in lavish measure,
    are yours, Inanna.                                                    (155)
To bestow the royal office, its powers and authority,
    are yours, Inanna,
Slander, falsehood, to bring charges and reinforce them with perjury
    are yours, Inanna,
Recanting what is false and true, acts of force are yours, Inanna,
Starting a quarrel, making jokes, laughing, to be vile, to be important
    are yours, Inanna,
Misery, suffering, grief, happiness, bringing light are yours, Inanna,   (160)
Agitation, terror, fear, awe-inspiring glow and radiance are yours, Inanna,
Victory, soldiery, shivering, anxiety, and sleeplessness are yours, Inanna,
    . . . .
Dispute, insurrection, confrontation, battle, massacre are yours, Inanna,

*(fragmentary lines and large gaps follow)*

*(Enheduanna introduces herself.)*

You are great, your name is praised, you alone are great!                (218)
I am Enheduanna, the lady-bird of Nanna,

*(large gap)*

I am yours, it will always be that way! May your heart be soothed for my
    sake!
    . . . .

*(She entreats the goddess to calm her fury.)*

Your divinity has shown itself in this land.
I have undergone your great punishment,                                  (250)
    . . .

Pity, compassion, watchfulness, mercy, blessing are yours, <Inanna>,
To soak with water, to develop wasteland, to turn darkness into light
    <are yours, Inanna>,
My queen! I will proclaim your dominion and glory in all lands,
Your ways, your great deeds I will praise everywhere.      (255)
You! Who could rival your divinity?
Who could equal your divine office?
May great An whom you love ask pity from you,
May the great gods calm your mood.
May that gem-like dais worthy of a queen
    [say to you], "Come hither,"?      (260)
May your chair of supreme power say to you, "Sit down."
May your holy bed say to you, "Take your ease."
. . .
They show forth your supremacy, you are their queen.
An and Enlil have decreed your greatness throughout heaven,      (265)
They have granted that, in the throne room, you be queen,
You who are most worthy to be queen, to decree the destinies
    of queens.
Mistress, you are supreme, you are first in precedence,
Inanna, you are supreme, you are first in precedence!
My queen, your supremacy is manifest!      (270)
May your heart, for my sake, be as it once was,
Your great deeds have nothing to compare!
May your supremacy everywhere be praised!
Maiden Inanna, your praise is sweet!

### Sources

Sjöberg 1975; ECTSL C.4.07.03.

## (c)  **Inanna and Ebih**

*(Inanna as a fierce warrior who does not hide behind her shield
but unleashes frightful weapons)*

O goddess astride sublime powers terrible, arrayed in splendor,      (1)
O Inanna, full-armed with your uncanny weaponry, awash in blood,
Prancing in the worst of combats, holding your shield low
    to the ground,
Keeping storm and flood as your reserve,
Great Queen, Inanna, who knows forming strategy in battle,      (5)
You take down mountains with the force of your arrows,
    against very mountains you can bring your power!

Filling earth and sky with your roaring, like a lion,
   you make its people tremble,
Like a huge wild bull, you stand poised to charge an enemy land,
Like a raging lion, you snuff out restive and disobedient
   with your slaver.

*(Inanna as the Morning Star, ready for war)*

My Lady! When you wax tall as heaven,                         (10)
Maiden Inanna! When you grow great as earth,
When you rise like the kingly Sun, stretching out your arms afar,
When you take your place in heaven, arraying yourself in
   terrifying splendor,
When you rise over the mountain ranges, a gleaming jewel,     (15)
When you bathe among the mountain flowers,
When you, maiden, produce the mountain gems high in the hills,
When you sit yourself among them as the brightest jewel of all,
When you take up your battle mace, with a householder's
   anticipation (of a harvest) from his verdant fertile field,
When you slash off heads in battle, as if reaping with a blade, (20)
The people of this land make song to you,
Foreign folk sing their sweet hymns of praise to you!
O mistress of battle, great daughter of the Moon,
I too would praise you, maiden Inanna.

*(Inanna speaks her own praises. When she campaigned*
*throughout the world, only Ebih showed her no respect)*

"I, the goddess, as I made my rounds in heaven,
"I, Inanna, as I made my rounds on earth,                     (25)
"As I made my rounds in Elam and Subir,
"As I made my rounds in Lullubum,
"As I pushed deep into the mountains,
"I, the goddess, as I approached the mountain,
   it showed me no respect,                                   (30)
"I, Inanna, as I approached the mountain,
   it showed me no respect,
"As I approached Mount Ebih, it showed me no respect!
"Because it did not act as it should of its own free will,
"Because it did not bring its nose close to the ground,
"Because it did not press its lips into the dirt,             (35)
"I will take that lofty mountain peak in hand,
"I will teach it to respect me!
"Against its greatest strength, I will set a greater bull,
"Against its lesser strength, I will set a lesser bull!
"I will prance there, I will play the rope game of holy Inanna,
"I will bring warfare to the mountain,

"I will start a battle there,                                    (40)
"I will aim a quivered shaft,
"I will pour forth sling stones in a stream,
"I will put some polish to my spear,
"I will have my shield and throw-stick ready.
"I will set fire to its dense forests,                           (45)
"I will take an axe to its malefactors,
"I will let purifying Fire do his task in the basins,
"I will cast fear of this as far as the unreachable peaks
    of Aratta!
"Like a city An has cursed, may it never be restored,
"Like a city Enlil glared at balefully, may it never stand up proud.   (50)
"May the mountain mark well what I do,
"Ebih must honor me, it must sing my praises!"

*(Inanna dresses in her finest and mounts to her place
in the evening sky)*

Inanna, daughter of the Moon, put on her regal garment,
    hung a ravishing sash around her neck,
With fearsome, terrifying radiance she bedizened her brow,          (55)
She drew a carnelian necklace with rosettes around her
    divine throat,
She made a hero's gesture with the seven-lobed mace
    in her right hand.
She set her foot on the deep blue step.
As night fell, she ascended nobly,
She took her place in the path of the Wondrous Gate.                (60)

*(Inanna presents herself before An, god of heaven.
She asks his consent to attack Mount Ebih)*

To Heaven she made an offering, to him she said a prayer,
An was delighted with Inanna,
He motioned her, she sat,
He took the celestial seat of precedence.
"O An, my father, I hail you, may you listen to my words,          (65)
"It was An who brought me respect throughout heaven,
"Thanks to you, my command has no rival in heaven
    or earth.
"It is the battle axe at the perimeter of heaven,
"The insignia, the royal standard of war.
"To keep the dais in position, to hold the throne's
    foundations firm,                                            (70)
"To wield the power of the battle mace,
    bending it like a withe,
"To close with six and hold my ground,

"To close with four and push forward,

"To destroy campaigns, to follow the march to its end,

"To rise over this king like moonlight in the dust of
    the sky,                                                    (75)

"To let my arm launch arrows, to fall on field, garden,
    and grove like biting locusts,

"To pass like a harrow over the unruly land,

"To take away the bolts from city gates, leaving their
    doors open wide,

"This is what you, An the king, have put in my power . . .

"You stationed me at the king's right hand
    to destroy unruly lands,                                    (80)

"May he, with me, smash heads like a falcon on the breast
    of the mountain.

"O An the king, I will roll out your name to the ends of the land,
    like a surveyor's line,

"May he destroy the mountains with me like snakes
    in a crevice,

"May he, with me, make them slither off like
    serpents coming down a slope,

"May he take control in the mountain, may he explore it,
    learning its dimensions,                                    (85)

"May he go forth on the holy campaign of Heaven,
    may he learn how far it goes.

"I will surpass the other gods,

"I, Inanna, will overtake the great gods as I go!

"How could it be that, on heaven and earth, for me
    the mountain had no respect, for me?

"I, Inanna, in heaven and earth, the mountain
    had no respect for me!                                      (90)

"Mount Ebih, in heaven and earth, the mountain had no respect
    for me!

"Because it did not act as it should of its own free will,

"Because it did not bring its nose close to the ground,

"Because it did not press its lips into the dirt,

"I will take that lofty mountain peak in hand,
    I will teach it to respect me.                              (95)

"Against its greatest strength I will set a greater bull,

"Against its lesser strength I will set a lesser bull,

"I will prance there, I will play the rope game of holy Inanna,

"I will bring warfare to the mountain,
    I will start a battle there,

"I will aim a quivered shaft,                                   (100)

"I will pour forth sling stones in a stream,

"I will put some polish to my spear,

"I will have my shield and throw-stick ready.
"I will set fire to its dense forests,
"I will take an axe to its malefactors,                                    (105)
"I will let purifying Fire do his work in the basins,
"I will cast fear of this as far as the unreachable peaks
      of Aratta!
"Like a city An has cursed, may it never be restored,
"Like a city Enlil glared at balefully, may it never stand up proud.
"May the mountain mark well what I do,                                      (110)
"Ebih must honor me, it must sing my praises!"

*(An objects that Ebih is too much of a challenge)*

An, king of the gods, answered her,
"My little one demands the mountain, what to do
      with its consequence?
"Inanna demands the mountain, what to do
      with its consequence?
"She demands Mount Ebih, what to do with its consequence?                   (115)
"As a dwelling of the gods it gives off fearsome splendor,
"As a sacred dwelling of the great gods it is endowed with eerie glory,
"It gives off its terrible fearsomeness in the land,
"The mountain gives off its terrible radiance in all lands,
"Its height rises nobly in the center of the sky,                          (120)
"Its lush gardens are hung about with fruit, each
      replete with beauty,
"Its huge trees chuck the chin of heaven,
      they stand a wonder to behold.
"In Ebih, under the trees' canopy of crisscross branches,
      lion pairs are abundant,
"Wild sheep and deer are abundant there,
"Wild bulls stand in the verdant grass,                                    (125)
"Gazelles couple among the evergreens on the mountain,
"Its fearsomeness is terrible, you cannot go therein.
"The mountain's radiance is something terrible,
"Maiden Inanna, you cannot go against it."
Thus he dealt with her.                                                    (130)

*(Inanna, in a passion, proceeds without An's consent)*

The consecrated goddess, in rage and fury,
Flung open the arsenal room,
Thrust aside its deep blue doors.
She brought out biggest battle, she set huge storm
      upon the ground.
Holy Inanna took up the quiver,                                            (135)

She raised a towering flood of harmful debris,
She stirred up a high harmful wind of rubble.
My queen moved against the mountain,
With double strides she made her way,
Both edges of her dagger she honed,                                              (140)
She took Ebih's neck as if to pull a weed,
She thrust the dagger's point far down deep inside,
She roared loud as a clap of thunder.
On Ebih, the rocks that were its body
Rumbled down its flanks,                                                         (145)
From its sides, from its crevices, she cut off the venom
      of gigantic serpents,
She cursed its forest, she damned its trees,
She set fire to its flanks, she made its smoke billow up.
The goddess took control of the mountain,                                        (150)
Holy Inanna did as she wanted.

*(Inanna denounces the defeated mountain)*

She went up on the mountain, she raised a cry,
"O Mountain! Because you rose so high,
"Because you were so green and fair to look upon,
"Because you garbed yourself in a holy garment,                                  (155)
"Because you reached up to heaven,
"Because you did not bring your nose close to the ground,
"Because you did not press your lips into the dirt,
"I killed you, I brought you down!
"I seized your tusks, as if you were an elephant,                               (160)
"I took you to the ground by your massive horns,
      as if you were a wild bull,
"I forced your great shoulders to the ground,
      I pinned you cruelly, as if you were an ox,
"I brought steady tears into your eyes,
"I made grief the feeling of your heart,
"Birds of sorrow have nested on those flanks."                                  (165)

*(Inanna assigns Enlil, not An, credit for her victory)*

A second speech in furious, terrible triumph, she addressed it rightfully,
"My father Enlil has let terror of me reign among the mountains,
"He let the weaponry go at my right,
"He let the army? march at my left,
"He let me gouge it in my fury, a harrow with gigantic teeth.                    (170)
"I have built a temple there, I have made of it a work surpassing,
"I have set a throne therein, I have made its foundations firm,
"I have given the cult-players their daggers and goads?,

"I have given the singers of laments their drums and tambours,
"I have changed the sex of the cult impersonators.                    (175)
"Victorious, I have attacked the mountains,
"Victorious, I have attacked Mount Ebih!
"When I set off there, it was like the rising of a flood,
"I flowed off towards it like surging water past a weir!
"I was victorious over the mountain,                                  (180)
"I was victorious over Mount Ebih!
Ebih is destroyed! The great daughter of the Moon,
The maiden Inanna be praised!"

## Sources

ECTSL 1.3.2; Attinger 2014 1.3.2.

# Appendix III

## Two Sumerian poems about the Akkadian period

For discussion of these post-Akkadian narrative poems about Sargon and Naram-Sin, Chapter 11 part 6. Like the works of Enheduanna, these poems present numerous challenges to the translator, for which reference is made to the "Sources" at the end of each.

### (a)   The Sumerian Sargon legend

*(Kish enjoys her time of good fortune)*

| | |
|---|---:|
| That its canals [run] once more with pleasing waters, | (3) |
| That hoe once more work its farmlands and fields . . ., | |
| That the houses of Kish, once a ghost town, turn once more | |
|     into a settlement, | |
| Ur-Zababa, its king and shepherd, | |
| Shone forth like the sun over the houses of Kish. | |
| But An and Enlil, by their holy command, | |
|    [decreed] firmly that his kingdom would be handed to another, | |
| The glory of his palace rule would soon forsake him. | |
| Thereupon Sargon, whose city was [ ], | (10) |
| Whose father was La'ibum, whose mother was [ ], | |
| Sargon it was, with happy hearts, they [chose], | |
| Because he was born to it [ ]! | |

*(gap)*

*(Sargon is favored of Inanna)*

| | |
|---|---:|
| One day, when darkness had fallen, | (1') |
| When Sargon had brought the appointed viands to the palace, | |
| He laid himself down to sleep in his august bed chamber in his august | |
|     dwelling, | |
|  – He knew it in his heart, he could not speak it loud, | |
| He could say naught of it to any man – | |
| When he, Sargon, had received the appointed viands for the palace, | |

And he, the cupbearer, had served them, holding the wooden caddy,
Holy Inanna was there, all the time beside him!

Five days passed by, or maybe ten,
She frightened' King Zababa, made him shake with fear
    in that dwelling,
Like a (wounded) lion, dribbling urine, full of blood and pus,
    down his crotch,           (10')
Struggling like a beached sea fish, he gasped for breath.
For then the "cupbearer, in the wine room where the grain
    goddess dwells,
Sargon laid himself down, not to sleep, but to dream,
Holy Inanna, in his dream, was drowning him in a river of blood!
Sargon, moaning, chewed at the floor.        (15')

King Ur-Zababa heard about his moaning,
He had them bring him to his august presence.
When they had brought Sargon before Ur-Zababa,
"Cupbearer, did you have a dream in the night?"
Sargon answered his king,       (20')
"Your majesty, in my dream, what I can tell is,
"There was an extraordinary young woman, high as the sky, wide as
    the world,
"Standing strong as a fortress wall.
"To me it seemed as if she drowned me in a great flood,
    a river of blood!"
Then king Ur-Zababa bit his lips, fear overcame him.
He [summoned] his courier and said to him,
"[  ], my royal sister, holy Inanna,
"[  ] she will turn my fingers towards bloodshed.
"[  ] Sargon, the cupbearer, she will drown him in a great river."
"You, who can write out what I have in mind,    (30')
"I will give you an order for Belish-tikal, the master smith,
    a man after my own heart,
"He must carry out my instructions to the letter:
"'See here, so soon as the cupbearer brings to you to the
    drinking vessels,
"'In the pure house, the house of doom decided, cast him into the mold,
    like a statue.'
Belish-tikal heeded his king's command,    (35')

He readied the molds in the pure house, the house of doom decided.
The king said to Sargon,
"Go, take my drinking vessels to the master smith."
Sargon left Ur-Zababa's palace,

Holy Inanna was always there, at his right hand!
When he was no further than ten cubits, maybe five, from the
    pure house, the house of doom decided,               (40')
Holy Inanna confronted him, she blocked his path.
"Is the pure house not a holy temple? No man with blood
    may go therein!"
He met the king's master smith outside the door of the house of doom
    decided,
When he delivered the king's drinking vessels to the master smith,
Belish-tikal, the master smith, was afraid' to cast him into the mold,
    like a statue.
Sargon, after five days had passed, maybe ten,
Came in before Ur-Zababa, his king,
Came right in before him in his own palace, built solid as a mountain,
King Ur-Zababa was afraid, shook with fear in his own dwelling,
He knew what it meant, he found no words for it, nor could he talk
    of it with anyone.                      (50')


In those days, writing on tablets certainly existed, wrapping tablets in
    clay envelopes certainly did not exist.
King Ur-Zababa had a tablet made for Sargon, who was created
    among the gods,
That would bring about his own death!
He sent him off with it to Lugalzagesi

*( The remainder of the text is fragmentary and obscure. It seems that when Sargon arrived in Uruk, Inanna directed him to her own temple, Eanna, rather than to Lugalzagesi's palace. By her intervention she saves him from the plot. Sargon thereafter defeated both Kish and Uruk to become king of the land.)*


### Sources

Cooper and Heimpel 1983; ECTSL 2.1.4; Attinger 2014 2.1.4.


### (b)  The curse of Agade

*(The triumph of Agade over Kish and Uruk. Inanna makes her dwelling there)*

After Enlil's baleful glare
Had slain Kish like the Bull of Heaven,
Had slaughtered house and land of Uruk in the dust,
    like that monster bull,
And Enlil had then and there given Sargon, king of Agade,
Lordship of Uruk, kingship of Kish,              (5)
From the lowlands to the upper regions,

Then did holy Inanna busy herself to build
Agade, the temple city, as her sublime dwelling,
In Ulmash let her throne be set.

*(Agade's people live well as citizens of an imperial capital)*

Like a youth building a house for the first time,                    (10)
Like a girl arranging her private chamber,
That she provision its larders,
That lots and houses be available in that city,
That its populace dine on the best of food,
That its populace draw the best of drink,                            (15)
That a person fresh washed make merry in the courtyard,
That people throng the festival grounds,
That people who know each other feast together,
That outsiders circle like outlandish birds of prey aloft,
That even farthest Marhashi be writ once more on tribute lists,      (20)
That monkey, monstrous elephant, buffalo, beasts of
    exotic climes,
Rub shoulders in the broad streets with dogs and lions,
Mountain ibex, and shaggy sheep,
Holy Inanna never stopped to rest.

Then did she pack Agade's very granaries with gold,                  (25)
Its gleaming granaries did she pack with silver,
She delivered copper, tin, and blocks of lapis even to
    its barns,
Sealed them up in clay like heaps of grain.
She endowed its old women with sound advice,
She endowed its old men with weighty words,                          (30)
She endowed its young women with play and dance,
She endowed its young men with fighting strength,
She endowed its toddlers with joyous hearts,
Even the infants of military men on duty
Played with rattles in their nursemaid's arms.                       (35)
There was drumbeat in the city, winds and strings without.
Its harbor, where ships tied up, hummed cheerfully,
Foreign lands rested peaceably,
Their peoples looked upon it as a favored place.

*(Naram-Sin, king of Agade, rules over a great empire)*

Its king, the shepherd, Naram-Sin,                                   (40)
Shone forth like sunrise on the holy throne of Agade.
Its walls, like a mountain range, reached up to graze the sky.
Holy Inanna opened in them spacious gates,

Big enough to let the Tigris flow out through them to the sea,
She made Sumer haul boats upstream with its own goods,                    (45)
The upland Amorites, men who know not grain,
Brought before her gamboling bulls and prancing goats,
Meluhha, people of the black-stone mountains,
Brought up to her strange things they made,
Elam and Subir bore goods to her like laden donkeys,                      (50)
The governors of cities, the managers of temples,
The scribes who parceled out the farmland in the steppe,
Brought in steadily their monthly and New Year offerings of food,
Such a care it was at the city gate of Agade,
Holy Inanna hardly knew how to take it all in,                           (55)
No more than any citizen could she build houses and structures
     fast enough to hold them!


*(Enlil withdraws his favor)*

He set down his verdict in Ekur like a ghastly hush,
In Agade she felt a shudder on his account,
In Ulmash fear crept over her,
She moved her dwelling from the city.                                    (60)
Like a young woman forsaking her childhood home,
Holy Inanna forsook the sanctuary, Agade.
Like a warrior advancing to arms,
She came forth from the city in battle,
Drawing up herself as its enemy!                                         (65)


Not five days, not ten days had gone by,
Ninurta brought into his own dwelling, Eshumesha,
     the sash of Uruk's lordship, the crown of Kish's kingship,
Standard and royal throne, erstwhile bestowed.
Utu took away the city's weighty words,                                  (70)
Enki took away its wisdom.
Its brilliance that had rayed to heaven,
An took up from it, into the sky.
Its gleaming moorings, set firmly in the ground,
Enki pulled down from it, into the watery depths.                        (75)
Inanna took away its defenses.
The sanctuary Agade drowned in deep water, like a puny fish,
While other cities were looking on.
Like a mighty elephant, it crumpled to the ground,
While they, like mighty bulls, tossed their horns.                       (80)
Like a dragon in its death throes, it writhed its head,
While they sought to strip it of its finery.

*(Naram-Sin has a dream portending evil for Agade)*

That the kingship of Agade would no longer abide and prosper,
That its outlook held nothing positive to view,
That its household would quake, that its stores be scattered, (85)
Naram-Sin saw it in a dream.
He knew what it meant, he found no words for it, nor could he
 talk of it with anyone.
He put on mourning clothes for Ekur,
He shrouded his kingly car with a reed mat,
He took down the canopy from his royal barge, (90)
He put away from himself the trappings of his reign.
For seven years Naram-Sin persevered,
Who has ever seen a king abase himself so, for seven years?
When he took omens concerning the temple,
There was no omen present for building the temple. (95)
When he took omens again concerning the temple,
There was no omen present for building the temple.
Seeking to change what had been vouchsafed him,
He tried to change what Enlil had commanded, ?, *what*
He threw out the findings compiled for him. (100)

Like a boxer striding into the great courtyard,
He clenched his fist at Ekur.
Like a wrestler crouching to start a match,
He acted as if the god's dwelling was a lightweight. (105)
Like a sieger storming a city,
He laid tall ladders against the temple.
To stave in Ekur like a mighty ship,
To open its fabric, like mining a silver mountain,
To quarry it, like a peak of lapis, (110)
To make it collapse, like a city in a floodstorm,
For that temple, though it was no mountain where cedar trees are cut,
He cast large hatchets,
He whetted double-bladed axes.
He laid spades to its roots, (115)
The foundation of the land was laid low.
He laid hatchets to its branches,
The temple, like a dying soldier, fell to the ground,
All foreign lands fell to the ground with it.
He tore out its ornamental spouts, (120)
The rains of heaven disappeared.
He pulled out its door frames, the land's vigor was weakened.
He caused grain to be cut off at the gate where grain is not cut off,

Grain was thereby cut off from the reach of the land.
He struck its Gate of Peace with a mattock,                               (125)
Peace turned to enmity in all foreign lands.
In Ekur's cella, as if in broad farmland full of fish,
He turned over huge spades, like casting from a mould.
People (of Sumer) saw the inner chamber, a room that
    never sees the light,
Akkad saw the sacred vessels of the gods.                                 (130)
Its guardian figures that stood by the ceremonial entryway,
Though they had done no forbidden thing,
Naram-Sin threw them into the fire.
Cedar, cypress, juniper, boxwood,
The woodwork of the god's dwelling he made ooze out in flames.           (135)
He put its gold in coffers,
He put its silver in sacks,
He heaped up its copper at the harborside, like a massive
    yield of grain.
The metal worker was to rework its precious metal,
The jeweler was to rework its precious stone,                            (140)
The smith was to rehammer its copper.
Though these were no goods of a conquered city,
Great ships were docked at the temple,
Great ships were docked at Enlil's temple,
The goods were taken from the city.                                      (145)
As he took the goods from the city,
So too was the reason of Agade taken away,
As the ships tossed at the docks, Agade's good sense
    became unbalanced.

*(Enlil summons the Gutians)* —

That storm that drowns out all others, that besets the entire land,
That rising flood that nothing can withstand,                            (150)
Enlil, because his beloved Ekur had been destroyed,
What should he destroy in turn for it?
He cast his eye towards the Gubin mountains,
He brought them down from the sprawling foothills,
Beings not considered people, not counted as a land,
Gutium, a race who know no order,                                        (155)
Made like humans but with the brains of dogs, the shapes of apes,
These Enlil brought down from the mountains!
Like a plague of locusts they scoured the land,
He let them stretch out their arms over it, as if corralling livestock,
Nothing escaped their reach,

No one was beyond their power.                                        (160)
No messenger went on the highroad,
No courier's boat would set out on the channel.
They drive the goats, rightfully Enlil's, from the fold
    and the herdsman with them,
They drive the cows from the paddock
    and the cowherd with them.                      (165)
The watchman was put in the stock,
The cutthroat occupied the main road,
The doors of the land's city gates lodged in dirt,
Foreign lands cried out bitterly on the walls of their cities,
In the downtown, rather than in the broad outlying plain,
    they planted truck patches.                     (170)

*(Famine and disorder in Agade)*

As when cities were first being built and founded,
The great farming tracts brought forth no grain,
The irrigated farming tracts brought forth no fish,
The well-watered orchard brought forth neither
    syrup nor wine,
The gathering clouds brought no rain, not
    even weeds would grow.                            (175)
At that time, one shekel's worth of oil was only half a quart,
One shekel's worth of wool was only half a mina,
One shekel's worth of fish was only ten quarts,
That is what they sold for in the city's market!                     (180)
He who slept on the roof, died on the roof,
He who slept in the house had no burial.
People fought among themselves for hunger,
In the built-up area, Enlil's great place,
Dogs formed packs in the silent streets.
Two men would go there and both be eaten,
Three men would go there and all be eaten,
Teeth crushed, heads strewn about,
Each crushed tooth or head dropped down like a seed,
The heads of honest men, the heads of scoundrels in alternation.     (190)
Young men lay atop young men,
The blood of the scoundrel running over the blood of the honest man.

*(The inhabitants try to appease the gods with mourning rites.)*

Then did Enlil make from his many great buildings
A group of tiny huts of reed,
From one side of the world to the other, the storehouses diminished. (195)

The old women who still survived those days,
The old men who still survived those days,
The chief singer of laments who still survived those years,
Set out seven tambours for mourning, as if marking the horizon,          (200)
Sounded kettle, snare, and hand drums among them, like
   (a rising cloud of) thunder, for seven days and nights.
The old women did not hold back their cries, "Alas for my city!"
The old men did not hold back their cries, "Alas for its people!"
The singers of laments did not hold back their cries, "Alas for Ekur!"
Its young women did not hold back from tearing out their hair,          (205)
Its young men did not hold back their sharpened knives
   (from slashing themselves).
They wept as much Enlil's ancestors wept
As they made their own supplications in Holy Hill, the awe-inspiring
   Holy Hall of Enlil.
From all of this, Enlil retired to his holy chamber, fasting, he fell asleep.

### (The gods curse Agade)

Then did Sin, Enki, Inanna, Ninurta, Ishkur, Utu, Nusku, Nisaba,
   the great gods,          (210)
Soothe Enlil's heart with cool libations, say this prayer to him:
"O Enlil! May any city that destroyed your city be done to as your city,
"Which defiled your sacred dwelling be done to as Nippur!
"May the man who knew that city peer down into the clay
   pit where it was,
"May the man who knew a man there find no trace of him at all.          (215)
"May brother see no sign of brother,
"May its young woman be cruelly beaten in her chamber,
"May its old man bitterly lament his murdered wife,
"May its pigeons moan in their crannies,
"May its swallows be pelted in their nooks,          (220)
"May it, like a terrified pigeon, find nowhere to go."

Once again, Sin, Enki, Inanna, Ninurta, Ishkur,
   Utu, Nusku, Nisaba,
all the gods whoever they may be,
Cast their eyes upon the city,
Laid a horrible curse on Agade.
"O City that attacked Ekur, O Enlil, let this be,          (225)
"O Agade that attacked Ekur, O Enlil, let this be:
"May the sound of mourning rise as high as your august wall,
   however lofty it may be,
"May your sacred dwelling crumble in a heap, like dirt,

"May the guardian figures towering on the stairway,
"Tumble to the ground, like giants drunk with wine.                    (230)
"May your clay go back to its watery depth,
"May it be clay that Enki has cursed.
"May your grain go back to its furrow,
"May it be grain the grain-goddess has cursed.
"May your timber return to its forest,                                 (235)
"May it be timber the carpenter-god has cursed.
"May the slaughterer of cattle slaughter his wife,
"May the butcher of sheep butcher his child.
"May your pauper drown the child who begged for money for him,
"May your harlot hang herself at the door of her brothel,              (240)
"May your cult women who are mothers kill their children,
"May your gold be bought for the price of silver,
"May your silver be bought for a bit of fool's gold,
"May your copper be bought for alloy.

"Agade, may your strong man lose his strength,                         (245)
"May he be unable to lift his sack of provisions to the saddle.
"May your riding donkey no longer rejoice in his strength,
      but lie motionless till nightfall.
"May that city die of hunger,
"May your citizens who dined on the finest foods lie down in the
      grass (like cattle),
"May your man who rose from a meal of first fruits                     (250)
"Eat the binding from his roof,
"As for the grand door of his family home,
"May he gnaw its leather hinges.
"May gloom befall your palace, built up in joy,
"May the evil creature of the silent steppe howl, howl, and howl again.  (255)
"In the pens for special livestock, fattened for the rites,
"May the fox who lurks in ruin-mounds drag its brush.
"In your city gate, set up in the land,
"May the slumber bird, harbinger of gloom, build its nest.
"O city that could not sleep for drumbeat,                             (260)
"May the moon-kine that filled its pens
"Moan, moan, and moan again, like wandering waifs in the steppe,
      silent as the grave.
"May rank grass grow tall where boats used to haul,
"May sad weeds curl where cartwheels would whirl.                      (265)
"Once again: on the canal bank, where boat is hauled and landed,
"May the splay-horned monster and darting snake let no one pass.
"On your steppe land, where grass grew lush, may canes of woe thrust up,
"O Agade, may your flowing fresh water run with salt.

"Whoever says, 'I will dwell in this city', may he find not
  good place to dwell,                                                          (270)
"Whoever says, 'I will sleep in Agade', may he find
  no good place to sleep!"

That very day, so it was:
The rank grass grew tall, where boats used to haul,
The sad weeds curled where cartwheels had whirled,
Once again: on the canal bank where boat was hauled and landed,            (275)
The splay-horned monster and the darting snake let no one pass.
On its steppe land, where grass grew lush, canes of woe thrust up,
Agade's flowing fresh water ran with salt.
Whoever said, "I will live in this city" found no good place to dwell,
Whoever said, "I will sleep in Agade," found no good place to sleep.       (280)

Agade was destroyed, to Inanna be praise!

by?,

### Sources

Cooper 1983a; ETCSL 2.1.5; Attinger 2014 2.1.5.

# Sources for figures

1.1    Louvre Sb 20, photo Karen Polinger Foster.

1.2    Louvre Sb 1, photo Karen Polinger Foster.

1.3    Louvre Sb 3, photo Karen Polinger Foster.

1.4    Louvre AO 2678, Strommenger 1962, fig. 117.

1.5    Louvre Sb 49, 50, photo Karen Polinger Foster

1.6    Louvre Sb 4, Zervos 1935, 165.

1.7    Bible Lands Museum 2784, courtesy of the Bible Lands Museum Jerusalem, photo D. Widmer.

1.8    Yale Babylonian Collection, (a) YBC 3135; (b) YBC 3114; (c) NBC 5868; (d) NBC 10920, photos Carl Kaufman.

1.9    BM 89137, © Trustees of the British Museum.

3.1    Delougaz and Lloyd 1942, pl. 37, courtesy of the University of Chicago Press.

3.2    Madhloom 1960 pl. 2a, courtesy of The Ministry of Tourism and Antiquities, Republic of Iraq.

3.3    Mallowan 1947, pl. 60, courtesy of The British Institute for the Study of Iraq.

4.1    (a) Yale Babylonian Collection NBC 5990, photo Carl Kaufman; (b) Iraq Museum IM 3849 (U 8385), courtesy of the Penn Museum; (c) BM 125793, © Trustees of the British Museum.

4.2    (a) Hommel 1885, 299; (b) Iraq Museum IM 14674, drawing © Karen Polinger Foster after Rashid and Ali-Huri 1983, 53.

5.1    Drawings © Karen Polinger Foster, after (a) Delougaz 1952, pl. 177 C.504.370; (b) Delougaz 1952, pl. 169 C.053.312; (c) Delougaz 1952, pl. 164 B.664.540a; (d) Delougaz 1952, pl. 191 D466.360; (e) Delougaz 1952, pl. 150 B.151.210; (f) Delougaz 1952, pl. 171 C216.210.

5.2    Müller-Karpe 1993/97, 140 © Walter de Gruyter GmbH.

5.3    Drawings © Karen Polinger Foster, after (a) Maxwell-Hyslop 1971, fig. 24a; (b) Frankfort 1933, fig. 31; (c) Wilson 2012, pl. 108a; (d) Maxwell-Hyslop 1971, fig. 15a; (e) Maxwell-Hyslop 1971, fig. 24c.

5.4    (a) Louvre Sb 47, photo Karen Polinger Foster; (b) Louvre Sb 53, drawing © Karen Polinger Foster after Moortgat 1969, fig. 150.

5.5    Vorderasiatisches Museum VA 2147, drawings © Karen Polinger Foster after Moortgat 1969, figs. 139, 140.

6.1    Delougaz and Lloyd 1942, 205, courtesy of the University of Chicago Press.

6.2    (a) Iraq Museum IM 14577 [U 9750], courtesy of the Penn Museum; (b) Morgan Library 202, courtesy of Sydney Babcock, Curator and Department Head, The Morgan Library & Museum.

9.1     (a) Louvre AO 21367, A. Parrot, *Sumer: The Dawn of Art.* New York: Golden Press, 1961 pl. 219; (b) Oriental Institute A 173, courtesy of The Oriental Institute of the University of Chicago.

9.2     (a) Vorderasiatisches Museum VA 6980, photo Olaf M.Tessmer, courtesy of Lutz Martin; (b) AO 4754, Zervos 1935, 153.

9.3     Iraq Museum IM 11331, Moortgat 1969, fig. 154.

9.4     Iraq Museum IM 77823, courtesy of The Ministry of Tourism and Antiquities, Republic of Iraq.

9.5     (a) Louvre Sb 2, photo Karen Polinger Foster; (b) Louvre Sb 2, drawing © Karen Polinger Foster after Amiet 1976, pl. 6d.

9.6     Penn Museum B16665, courtesy of the Penn Museum, image # 150424.

9.7     Eski Şark Museum, Istanbul 1027, Zervos 1935, 164.

9.8     Courtesy of Sidney Babcock and Jonathan Rosen.

9.9     (a) Buccellati, G. and M. Kelly-Buccellati 2002, fig. 2d, drawing by Pietro Pozzi © The International Institute for Mesopotamian Area Studies, courtesy of Giorgio Buccellati; (b) British Museum 89147, © Trustees of the British Museum.

9.10    Drawing © Karen Polinger Foster after C.J. Ball, *Light from the East,* London: Ayre and Spottiswoode, 1899, 153. Text copy courtesy of Aage Westenholz.

9.11    (a) Drawings © Karen Polinger Foster after Thureau- Dangin 1898, 25; (b) Harvard Semitic Museum SMN 4172, Meek 1935, pl. 1:1, courtesy of the Harvard Semitic Museum.

9.12    Thureau-Dangin 1903, pl. 66 b 356.

11.1    (a) Rutten 1938, pl. 1: 2, courtesy of Dominique Charpin; (b) Rutten 1938, pl. 2: 4, courtesy of Dominique Charpin.

11.2    Penn Museum B16106, courtesy of the Penn Museum, images #152612, 152613.

# Bibliography

Abrahami, P. 2008 "L'Armée d'Akkad," in P. Abrahami and L. Battini, eds., *Les armées du Proche-Orient ancien (III<sup>e</sup> – I<sup>er</sup> mill. av. J.-C.)*, 1–22. *BAR International Series* 1855. Oxford: Archaeopress.

Abu Al-Soof, B. N. 1983 "Iktišāfu ra'si timthālin min al-hajari li-ahadi mulūki al-'asri al-ašuri al-qadīmi fi ašur," *Sumer* 39: 304–5 (Arabic portion).

Adams, R. M. 1965 *Land behind Baghdad: A History of Settlement on the Diyala Plains*. Chicago: University of Chicago Press.

————1972 "Settlement and Irrigation Patterns in Ancient Akkad," in M. Gibson, *The City and Area of Kish*, 182–208. Coconut Grove, Fla.: Field Research Projects.

————1974 "The Mesopotamian Social Landscape: A View from the Frontier," in C. B. Moore, ed., *Reconstructing Complex Societies: An Archaeological Colloquium*, 1–20. Missoula, Mt.: American Schools of Oriental Research.

————1978 "Strategies of Maximization, Stability, and Resilience in Mesopotamian Society, Settlement and Agriculture," *Proceedings of the American Philosophical Society* 122: 329–35.

————1981 *Heartland of Cities: Surveys of Ancient Settlement and Land Use on the Central Floodplain of the Euphrates*. Chicago: University of Chicago Press.

————1982 "Die Rolle der Bewässerungsbodenbaus bei der Entwicklung von Institutionen in der altmesopotamischer Gesellschaft," in J. Herrmann and I. Sellnow, eds., *Produktivkräfte und Gesellschaftsformationen in vorkapitalistischer Zeit*, 119–40. Berlin: Akademie-Verlag.

————2006 "Shepherds at Umma in the Third Dynasty of Ur," *Journal of the Economic and Social History of the Orient* 49: 133–69.

————2011 "Slavery and Freedom in the Third Dynasty of Ur: Implications of the Garšana Archives," in D. Owen, ed., *Garšana Studies*, 1–9. *Cornell University Studies in Assyriology and Sumerology* 6. Bethesda, Md.: CDL Press.

Adams, R. and H. Nissen 1972 *The Uruk Countryside: The Natural Setting of Urban Societies*. Chicago: University of Chicago Press.

Alberti, A. 1987 "šu-nígin: Ein neuer Anhaltspunkt zu Datierung der Texte der Akkade-Zeit," *Die Welt des Orients* 18: 20–25.

Albright, W. 1920 "Menes and Narâm-Sin," *Journal of Egyptian Archaeology* 6: 89–98.

Al-Fouadi, A. 1976 "Bassetki Statue with an Old Akkadian Royal Inscription of Naram-Sin of Agade (2291–2255 B.C.)," *Sumer* 32: 122–29.

Almamori, H. 2014 "Gišša (Umm al-Aqarib), Umma (Jokha), and Lagaš in the Early Dynastic III Period," *Al-Rafidan* 35: 1–37.

Al-Rawi, F. 1992 "Two Old Akkadian Letters Concerning the Offices of kala'um and narum," *Zeitschrift für Assyriologie* 82: 180–85.

————1994 "Texts from Tell Haddad and Elsewhere," *Iraq* 56: 35–43.

Al-Rawi, F. and A. George 1994 "Tablets from the Sippar Library III. Two Royal Counterfeits," *Iraq* 56: 135–48.

Alster, B., ed., 1980 *Death in Mesopotamia. XXVI<sup>e</sup> Rencontre Assyriologique Internationale. Mesopotamia* 8. *Copenhagen Studies in Assyriology*. Copenhagen: Akademisk Forlag.

————1983 "The Mythology of Mourning," *Acta Sumerologica* 5: 1–16.

————1985 Review of Cooper 1983c, *Die Welt des Orients* 16: 159–62.

————1987 "A Note on the Uriah Letter in the Sumerian Sargon Legend," *Zeitschrift für Assyriologie* 77: 169–73.

————1993 "Marriage and Love in the Sumerian Love Song," in M. Cohen, D. Snell, and D. Weisberg, eds., *The Tablet and the Scroll, Near Eastern Studies in Honor of William W. Hallo*, 15–27. Bethesda, Md.: CDL Press.

————1997 *Proverbs of Ancient Sumer: The World's Earliest Proverb Collections*. Bethesda, Md.: CDL Press.

————2005 *Wisdom of Ancient Sumer*. Bethesda, MD: CDL Press.

Alster, B. and T. Oshima 2007 "Sargonic Dinner at Kaneš: The Old Assyrian Sargon Legend," *Iraq* 69: 1–20.

Amiet, P. 1952 "L'homme-oiseau dans l'art mésopotamien," *Orientalia* NS 21: 149–67.

————1972 "Les statues de Manishtusu, roi d'Agadé," *Revue d'Assyriologie* 66: 97–109.

————1976 *L'art d'Agadé au Musée du Louvre*. Paris: Edition des Musées Nationaux.

————1977 "Pour une interprétation nouvelle de la répertoire iconographique de la glyptique d'Agadé," *Revue d'Assyriologie* 71: 107–16.

————1980 "The Mythological Repertory in Cylinder Seals of the Agade Period," in E. Porada, ed., *Ancient Art in Seals*, 35–59. Princeton, N.J.: Princeton University Press.

Andersson, J. 2012 *Kingship in the Early Mesopotamian Onomasticon 2800–2200 BCE. Studia Semitica Upsaliensia* 28. Uppsala: Uppsala Universitet.

Andrae, W. 1922 *Die archaischen Ischtar-Tempel in Assur. Wissenschaftliche Veröffentlichungen der Deutschen Orient-Gesellschaft* 39. Leipzig: Hinrichs.

André, B. and M. Salvini 1989 "Réflexions sur Puzur-Inšušinak," *Iranica Antiqua* 24: 53–78.

Annus, A. 2010 *Divination and Interpretation of Signs in the Ancient World. Oriental Institute Seminars* 6. Chicago: Oriental Institute of the University of Chicago Press.

Archi, A. 1981 "Kiš nei testi di Ebla," *Studi Eblaiti* 4: 77–87.

————1985a "Les rapports politiques et économiques entre Ebla et Mari," *MARI* 4: 63–83.

————1985b "Le synchronisme entre les rois de Mari et les rois d'Ebla au III<sup>e</sup> millénaire," *MARI* 4: 47–51.

————1985c "Mardu in the Ebla Texts," *Orientalia* NS 54: 7–13.

————1987a "More on Ebla and Kish," *Eblaitica* 1: 125–40.

————1987b "Les titres de en et lugal à Ebla et des cadeaux pour le roi de Kish," *MARI* 5: 37–52.

————1987c "Gifts for a Princess," in C. Gordon, ed., *Eblaitica: Essays on the Ebla Archives and Eblaite Language*, 115–24. Winona Lake, Ind.: Eisenbrauns.

————1996a "*Il* in the Personal Names," *Orientalistische Literaturzeitung* 91: 133–51.

————1996b "Eblaita: *pāšīšu* colui che è addetto all'unizione; sacerdote purificatore; cameriere al servizio di una persona," *Vicino Oriente* 10: 37–71.

————1996c "Les comptes rendus annuels de métaux (CAM)," *Amurru* 1: 73–99.

————1998 "The Regional State of Nagar According to the Texts of Ebla," in M. Lebeau, ed., *About Subartu, Studies Devoted to Upper Mesopotamia*, 1–15. *Subartu* 4/2. Turnhout: Brepols.

————1999 "The Steward and His Jar," *Iraq* 61: 147–58.

————2002 "Jewels for the Ladies of Ebla," *Zeitschrift für Assyriologie* 92: 161–99.

————2010 "The God Ḥay(y)a (Ea/Enki) at Ebla," in S. Melville and A. Slotsky, eds., *Opening the Tablet Box: Near Eastern Studies in Honor of Benjamin R. Foster*, 15–36. Leiden: E.J. Brill.

————2011a "In Search of Armi," *Journal of Cuneiform Studies* 63: 5–34.

————2011b "Gifts at Ebla," in E. Ascalone and L. Peyronel, eds., *Studi Italiani di Metrologia ed Economia del Vicino Oriente Antico dedicati a Nicola Parise in Occasione del Suo Settantesimo Compleanno*, 43–56. Rome: Herder.

————2012 "Cult of the Ancestors and Funerary Practices at Ebla," in P. Pfälzner, H. Niehr, E. Pernicka, and A. Wissing, eds., *(Re-)Constructing Funerary Rituals in the Ancient Near East, Proceedings of the First International Symposium of the Tübingen Post-Graduate School "Symbols of the Dead" in May 2009*, 5–31. Wiesbaden: Harrassowitz.

————2014a "Who Led the Army of Ebla? Administrative Documents vs. Commemorative Texts," in H. Neumnn, R. Dittmann, S. Paulus, G. Neumann, and A. Schuster-Brandis, eds., *Krieg und Frieden im Alten Vorderasien, 52e Rencontre Assyriologique Internationale International Congress of Assyriology and Near Eastern Archaeology Münster, 17.–21. Juli 2006*, 19–25. *Alter Orient und Altes Testament* 401. Münster: Ugarit Verlag.

————2014b "La situation géopolitique de la Syrie avant l'expansion d'Akkad," *Syria* supplement 2: 161–71.

Archi, A. and M. Biga 2003 "A Victory over Mari and the Fall of Ebla," *Journal of Cuneiform Studies* 55: 1–44.

Aruz, J. and R. Wallenfels, eds. 2003 *Art of the First Cities: The Third Millennium B.C. from the Mediterranean to the Indus*. New York: Metropolitan Museum of Art.

Asher-Greve, J.M. 1987 "The Oldest Female Oneiromancer," in J.-M. Durand, ed., *La Femme dans le Proche-Orient antique, XXXIIIᵉ rencontre assyriologique internationale (Paris, 7–10 juillet 1986)*, 27–32. Paris: Editions Recherche sur les Civilisations.

————1989 "Observations on the Historical Relevance of Visual Imagery in Mesopotamia," in *Conscience Historique dans les civilisations du Proche-Orient Ancien*, 175–95. *Cahiers du Centre d'Etude du Proche-Orient Ancien* 5. Leuven: Peeters.

————1995 "A Seal-cutter's Trial-piece in Berlin and a New Look at the Diqdiqqeh Lapidary Workshops," *Iraq* 57: 49–60.

Astour, M. 1992 "An Outline of the History of Ebla (Part 1)," in C. Gordon and G. Rendsburg, eds., *Eblaitica, Essays on the Ebla Archives and Eblaite Language*, 3–82. Winona Lake, Ind.: Eisenbrauns.

————2002 "A Reconstruction of the History of Ebla (Part 2)," in C. Gordon and G. Rendsburg, eds., *Eblaitica, Essays on the Ebla Archives and Eblaite Language*, 57–195. Winona Lake, Ind.: Eisenbrauns.

Attinger, P. 1984 "Remarques à propos de la 'Malédiction d'Akkad,'" *Revue d'Assyriologie* 78: 99–121.

————1993 "Inana et Ebiḫ," *Zeitschrift für Assyriologie* 88: 164–95.

————2014 [Editions and translations of Sumerian literature], ancientworldonline. blogspot.com

Bänder, D. 1995 *Die Siegesstele des Naramsîn und ihre Stellung in Kunst-und Kulturgeschichte*. Idstein: Schulz-Kirchner.

Bär, Jürgen 2003a "Sumerians, Gutians and Hurrians at Ashur? A Re-examination of Ishtar Temples G and F," *Iraq* 65: 143–60.

————2003b *Die älteren Ischtar-Tempel in Assur, Stratigraphie, Architektur und Funde eines altorientalischen Heiligtums von der zweiten Hälfte des 3. Jahrtausends bis zur Mitte des 2. Jahrtausends v. Chr, Wissenschaftliche Veröffentlichung der Deutschen Orient-Gesellschaft* 105. Saarbrücken: Saarbrücker Druckerei und Verlag.

Banks, E. J. 1912 *Bismya, or the Lost City of Adab.* New York: Putnam's.

Barnett, R. D. 1974 "Lions and Bulls in Assyrian Palaces," in P. Garelli, ed., *Le palais et la royauté, archéologie et civilisation, XIXᵉ Rencontre Assyriologique Internationale organisée par le groupe François Thureau-Dangin, Paris, 29 juin–2 juillet 1971,* 441–46. Paris: Geuthner.

Barrelet, M.-T. 1959 "Notes sur quelques sculptures mésopotamiennes de l'époque d'Akkad," *Syria* 36: 20–37, pl. IV–VI.

——1968 *Figurines et reliefs en terre cuite de la Mésopotamie ancienne.* Paris: Geuthner.

——1970 "Etude de glyptique akkadienne: L'imagination figurative et le cycle d'Ea," *Orientalia* NS 39: 213–51.

——1974 "Dispositifs à feu et cuisson des aliments à Ur, Nippur, Uruk," *Paléorient* 2/2: 243–300.

——, ed. 1977 *Méthodologie et critiques I: Problèmes concernant les hurrites, Centre de Recherches Archéologiques, Publications de l'U. R.A.* 8. Paris: Centre National de la Recherche Scientifique.

——1984 *Problèmes concernant les hurrites* 2. Paris: Editions Recherche sur les Civilisations.

Barrett, C. E. 2007 "Was Dust Their Food and Clay Their Bread? Grave Goods, the Mesopotamian Afterlife, and the Liminal Role of Inana/Ishtar," *Journal of Ancient Near Eastern Religions* 7: 7–65.

Bartash, V. 2013 *Miscellaneous Early Dynastic and Sargonic Texts in the Cornell University Collections, Cornell University Studies in Assyriology and Sumerology* 23. Bethesda, Md.: CDL Press.

Battini, L. 2006 "Les images de la naissance en Mésopotamie," in L. Battini and P. Villard, eds., *Médecine et médecins au Proche-Orient ancien, Actes du Colloque International organisé à Lyon les 8 et 9 novembre 2002, Maison de l'Orient et de la Méditerrannée,* 1–37. BAR International Series 1528. Oxford: Archaeopress.

Bauer, J. 1969 "Zum Totenkult im altsumerischen Lagasch," *Zeitschrift der Deutschen Morgenländischen Gesellschaft Supplement* 1(1): 107–14.

——1987/90 "Lugal-ušumgal." *Reallexikon der Assyriologie* 7: 155. Berlin: De Gruyter.

Bayliss, M. 1973 "The Cult of Dead Kin in Assyria and Babylonia," *Iraq* 35: 115–25.

Beaulieu, P.-A. 1989a *The Reign of Nabonidus, King of Babylon 556–539 B.C. Yale Near Eastern Researches* 10. New Haven, Conn.: Yale University Press.

——1989b "Agade in the Late Babylonian Period," NABU 1989/66.

——1994 "Antiquarianism and Concern for the Past in the Neo-Babylonian Period," *Bulletin of the Canadian Society for Mesopotamian Studies* 28: 37–42.

——2002 "Eanna = *Ayakkum* in the Basetki Inscription of Narām-Sîn," NABU 2002/36.

Becker, A. 1985 "Neusumerische Renaissance? Wissenschaftsgeschichtliche Untersuchungen zur Philologie und Archäologie," *Baghdader Mitteilungen* 16: 229–316.

Beckman, G. 2001 "Sargon and Naram-Sin in Hatti: Reflections of Mesopotamian Antiquity among the Hittites," in D. Kuhn and H. Stahl, eds., *Die Gegenwart des Altertums: Formen und Funktionen des Altertumsbezugs in den Hochkulturen der Alten Welt,* 85–91. Heidelberg: Edition Forum.

Bernbeck, R. 1996 "Siegel, Mythen, Riten: Etana und die Ideologie der Akkad-Zeit," *Baghdader Mitteilungen* 27: 159–213.

Beyer, Dominique 1985 "Documents iconographiques de l'époque des Shakkanakku," MARI 4: 173–89.

Biga, M. 1987 "Femmes de la famille royale d'Ebla," in J.-M. Durand, ed., *La Femme dans le Proche-Orient antique, XXXIIIᵉ rencontre assyriologique internationale (Paris, 7–10 juillet 1986),* 41–47. Paris: Editions Recherche sur les Civilisations.

——1997 "Les nourrices et les enfants à Ebla," *Ktema* 22: 35–44.

————1998 "The Marriage of Eblaite Princess Tagriš-Damu with a Son of Nagar's King," *Subartu* 4: 17–22.

————2005 "A Sargonic Foundation Cone," in Y. Sefati, P. Artzi, C. Cohen, B. Eichler, and V. Hurowitz, eds, *"An Experienced Scribe Who Neglects Nothing": Ancient Near Eastern Studies in Honor of Jacob Klein*, 29–38. Bethesda, Md.: CDL Press.

Biggs, R. 1973 "On Regional Cuneiform Handwritings in Third Millennium Mesopotamia," *Orientalia* NS 42: 39–46.

————1981 "Ebla and Abu-Ṣalābīkh: The Linguistic and Literary Aspects," in L. Cagni, ed., *La Lingua di Ebla, Atti del Convegno Internazionale (Napoli, 21–23 aprile 1980)*, 9–73. Seminario di Studi Asiatici, *Series Minor* 14. Naples: Istituto Universitario Orientale.

Bimson, M. 1980 "Cosmetic Pigments from the 'Royal Cemetery' at Ur," *Iraq* 41: 75–77.

Birch, S., ed. 1876 "The Legend of the Infancy of Sargina the First, King of Agani," *Records of the Past, Being English Translations of the Assyrian and Egyptian Monuments*, vol. 5 No. 1: 1–14. London: Samuel Bagster.

Birot, M. 1980 "Fragment de rituel de Mari relatif au *kispum*," in B. Alster, ed. *Death in Mesopotamia, XXVIᵉ Rencontre Assyriologique Internationale*, 139–50. *Mesopotamia* 8. *Copenhagen Studies in Assyriology*. Copenhagen: Akademisk Forlag.

Bjorkman, J. 1973 "Meteors and Meteorites in the Ancient Near East," *Meteoritics* 8: 91–132.

Black, J. 1991 "Eme-sal Cult Songs and Laments," *Aula Orientalis* 9: 23–36.

————2002 "En-hedu-ana not the Composer of the Temple Hymns," NABU 2002/4.

Black, J., G. Cunningham, E. Robson, and G. Zólyomi, eds. 1998 *The Literature of Ancient Sumer*. Oxford: Oxford University Press.

Boehmer, R. 1964 "Datierte Glyptik der Akkade-Zeit," in K. Bittel, E. Heinrich, B. Hrouda, and W. Nagel, eds., *Vorderasiatische Archäologie, Studien und Aufsätze, Anton Moortgat zum 65. Geburtstage gewidmet von Kollegen, Freunden und Schülern*, 42–56. Berlin: Mann.

————1965 *Die Entwicklung der Glyptik während der Akkad-Zeit. Untersuchungen zur Assyriologie und Vorderasiatischen Archäologie* 4. Berlin: De Gruyter.

————1966 "Die Datierung des Puzur/Kutik-Inšušinak, und einige sich daraus ergebende Konsequenzen," *Orientalia* NS 35: 345–76.

————1967 "Zur Datierung des Epirmupi," *Zeitschrift für Assyriologie* 58: 302–10.

————1974 "Das Auftreten des Waserbüffels in Mesopotamien in historischer Zeit und seine sumerische Bezeichnung," *Zeitschrift für Assyriologie* 64: 1–19.

————1996 "Uruk und Madain: Glyptik der Akkad-Zeit," *Baghdader Mitteilungen* 27: 145–57.

Boehmer, R., F. Pedde, and B. Salje 1995 *Uruk, die Gräber. Ausgrabungen in Uruk-Warka. Endberichte*. Mainz: von Zabern.

Börker-Klähn, J. 1972/5 "Haartrachten, Archäologisch," *Reallexikon der Assyriologie* 4, 1–12. Berlin: De Gruyter.

————1982a "Die Reichsakkadische Kunst und Ägypten," *Wiener Zeitschrift für die Kunde des Morgenlandes* 74, 57–94.

————1982b *Altvorderasiatische Bildstelen und vergleichbare Felsreliefs. Baghdader Forschungen* 4. Mainz am Rhein: von Zabern.

Boese, J. 1968/69 "Ringkampf-Darstellungen in frühdynastischer Zeit," *Archiv für Orientforschung* 22: 30–38.

————1973 "Zur stilistischen und historischen Einordnung des Felsreliefs von Darband-i-Gaur," *Studia Iranica* 2: 3–48.

————1982 "Zur absoluten Chronologie der Akkad-Zeit," *Die Welt des Orients* 74: 33–55.

Boese, J. and W. Sallaberger 1996 "Apil-kin und die Könige der III. Dynastie von Ur," *Altorientalische Forschungen* 23: 4–39.

Bonechi, M. and J.-M. Durand 1992 "Oniromancie et magie à Mari à l'époque d'Ebla," *Quaderni di Semitistica* 18: 151–61.

Bongenaar, A. 1997 *The Neo-Babylonian Ebabbar Temple at Sippar. Publications de l'Institut historique-archéologique néerlandais de Stamboul* 80. Leiden: Nederlands Instituut voor het Nabije Oosten.

Borger, R. 1957/71 "Gottesbrief," *Reallexikon der Assyriologie* 3: 575–76.

Bottéro, J. 1965 "Das erste semitische Großreich," in E. Cassin, J. Bottéro, and J. Vercoutter, eds., *Die altorientalischen Reiche* I, 91–128. *Fischer Weltgeschichte* 2. Frankfurt-am-Main: Fischer Taschenbuch Verlag = "The First Semitic Empire," translated by R. F. Tannenbaum, in E. Cassin, J. Bottéro, and J. Vercoutter, eds., *The Near East: The Early Civilizations*, 19–32. Delacorte World History. New York: Delacorte.

————1970/71 "Antiquités assyro-babyloniennes," *Annuaire de l'Ecole Pratique des Hautes Etudes, IV^e Section, Sciences Historiques et Philologiques*, 87–116. Paris: La Sorbonne.

————1971/72 "Antiquités assyro-babyloniennes," *Annuaire de l'Ecole Pratique des Hautes Etudes, IV^e Section, Sciences Historiques et Philologiques*, 110–16. Paris: La Sorbonne.

————1974 "Symptômes, signes, écritures," in R. Guideri, ed., *Divination et Rationalité*, 70–197. Paris: Editions du Seuil.

————1980 "La Mythologie de la mort en Mésopotamie ancienne," in B. Alster, ed., *Death in Mesopotamia, XXVI^e Rencontre Assyriologique Internationale*, 25–52. *Mesopotamia* 8. Copenhagen: Akademisk Forlag.

————1980/83 "Küche," *Reallexikon der Assyriologie* 6: 277–98. Berlin: De Gruyter.

————1981 "L'ordalie en Mésopotamie ancienne," *Annali della scuola normale superiore di Pisa*, Classe di Lettere e Filosofia, serie III, vol. XI, 3, 1005–67.

————1983 "Les Morts et l'au-delà dans les rituals en akkadien contre l'action des 'revenants,'" *Zeitschrift für Assyriologie* 73: 153–203.

————1994 "Boisson, banquet et vie sociale en Mésopotamie," in L. Milano, ed., *Drinking in Ancient Societies, History and Culture of Drinks in the Ancient Near East, Papers of a Symposium held in Rome, May 17–19, 1990*, 3–13. History of the Ancient Near East/Studies 6. Padua: Sargon.

————2001 *Religion in Ancient Mesopotamia*, Teresa Lavender Fagan, trans. Chicago: University of Chicago Press.

Brandes, M. 1980 "Destruction et mutilation de statues en Mésopotamie," *Akkadica* 16: 28–41.

Braun-Holzinger, E. 1977 *Frühdynastische Beterstatuetten, Abhandlungen der Deutschen Orient-Gesellschaft* 19. Berlin: Mann.

————1984 *Figürliche Bronzen aus Mesopotamien*. Munich: Beck.

————1987/90 "Löwe B, Archäologisch," *Reallexikon der Assyriologie* 7: 88–97.

————1991 *Mesopotamische Weihgaben der Frühdynastischen bis altbabylonischen Zeit, Heidelberger Studien zum Alten Orient* 3. Heidelberg: Heidelberger Verlag.

————1993 "Die Ikonographie des Mondgottes in der Glyptik des III. Jahrtausends v. Chr.," *Zeitschrift für Assyriologie* 83: 119–35.

————1999 "Apotropaic Figures at Mesopotamian Temples in the Third and Second Millennium," in T. Abusch and K. Van der Toorn, ed., *Mesopotamian Magic: Textual, Historical, and Interpretive Perspectives*, 149–72. Studies in Ancient Magic and Divination 1. Groningen: Styx.

————2007 *Das Herrscherbild im Mesopotamien und Elam, Alter Orient und Altes Testament* 342. Münster: Ugarit-Verlag.

Breasted, J. 1916 *Ancient Times: A History of the Early World*. Boston: Ginn, second edition 1935.

————1938 *The Conquest of Civilization*, edited by Edith Williams Ware, new edition. New York: Literary Guild of America.

Breniquet, C. 2008 *Essai sur le tissage en Mésopotamie des premières communautés au milieu du III<sup>e</sup> millénaire avant J.-C.* Paris: De Boccard.

Breniquet, C. and C. Michel, eds., 2014 *Wool Economy in the Ancient Near East and the Aegean: From the Beginnings of Sheep Husbandry to Institutional Textile Industry.* Oxford: Oxbow Books.

Brentjes, B. 1961 "Der Elefant im Alten Orient," *Klio* 39: 8–31.

Bridges, S. J. 1981 *The Mesag Archive: A Study of Sargonic Society and Economy.* Dissertation: Yale University.

Brisch, N. 2010 "Rebellions and Peripheries in Sumerian Royal Literature," in S. Richardson, ed., *Rebellions and Peripheries in the Cuneiform World*, 29–45. *American Oriental Series* 91. New Haven, Conn.: American Oriental Society.

Brock, S. 1978 "Aspects of Translation Technique in Late Antiquity," in *Syriac Perspectives on Late Antiquity*, 69–87. London: Variorum Reprints [1984].

Brown, D. 2000. *Mesopotamian Planetary Astronomy-Astrology. Cuneiform Monographs* 18. Groningen: Styx.

Brumanti, A. 2012 *Testi Amministrativi da Zabalam del Regno di Lugalzagesi.* Dissertation: Università di Roma La Sapienza, Facoltà di Lettere e Filosofia.

Brunke, H. 2011a *Essen in Sumer: Metrologie, Herstellung und Terminologie nach Zeugnis der Ur III-zeitlichen Wirtschaftsurkunden.* Munich: Herbert Utz Verlag.

———2011b "Feasts for the Living, the Dead, and the Gods," in K. Radner and E. Robson, eds., *The Oxford Handbook of Cuneiform Culture*, 167–83. Oxford: Oxford University Press.

Buccellati, G. 1966 *The Amorites of the Ur III Period.* Naples: Istituto Orientale di Napoli.

———1992 "Ebla and the Amorites," in C. Gordon and G. Rendsburg, eds., *Eblaitica: Essays on the Ebla Archives and Eblaite Language*, 3: 83–104. Winona Lake, Ind.: Eisenbrauns.

———1993 "Through a Tablet Darkly: A Reconstruction of Old Akkadian Monuments Described in Old Babylonian Copies," in M. Cohen, D. Snell, and D. Weisberg, eds., *The Tablet and the Scroll: Near Eastern Studies in Honor of William W. Hallo*, 58–71. Bethesda, Md.: CDL Press.

———1999 "Urkesh and the Question of Early Hurrian Urbanism," in M. Hudson and B. Levine, eds., *Urbanization and Land Ownership in the Ancient Near East*, 229–50. *Peabody Museum Bulletin* 7. Cambridge, Mass.: Peabody Museum of Archaeology and Ethnology.

———2013 *Alle origini della politica: La formazione e la crescita dello stato in Siro-Mesopotamia.* Milan: Jaca Book.

Buccellati, G. and M. Kelly-Buccellati 2000 "The Royal Palace at Urkesh, Report on the 12th Season at Tell Mozan/Urkesh: Excavations in Area AA, June-October 1999," *Mitteilungen der Deutschen Orient-Gesellschaft* 132: 133–83.

———2002 "Tar'am-Agade, Daughter of Naram-Sin, at Urkesh," in L. Al-Gailani Werr, J. Curtis, H. Martin, A. McMahon, J. Oates, and J. Reade, eds., *Of Pots and Plans: Papers on the Archaeology and History of Mesopotamia and Syria Presented to David Oates in Honour of His 75th Birthday*, 11–31. London: NABU.

Calmeyer, P. 1970 "Federkränze und Musik," in A. Finet, ed., *Actes de la XVII<sup>e</sup> Rencontre Assyriologique Internationale, Université Libre de Bruxelles, 30 juin–4 juillet 1969*, 184–95. Ham-sur-Heure: Comité Belge de Recherches en Mésopotamie.

———1993/7 "Museum," *Reallexikon der Assyriologie* 8: 453–5.

Campbell Thompson, R. 1904 *Cuneiform Texts from Babylonian Tablets in the British Museum* 19. London: British Museum.

Carena, O. 1989 *History of the Near Eastern Historiography and Its Problems: 1852–1985. Part One: 1852–1945. Alter Orient und Altes Testament* 218/1. Neukirchen-Vluyn: Neukirchener Verlag.

Cassin, E. 1968 *La Splendeur divine, introduction à l'étude de la mentalité mésopotamienne*. The Hague: Mouton.

——1980/3 "Kosmetik," *Reallexikon der Assyriologie* 6: 214–18.

Catagnoti, A. 2003a "Ebla," in R. Westbrook, ed., *A History of Ancient Near Eastern Law*, 1: 227–39. Leiden: Brill.

——2003b "Two Sargonic Tablets Mentioning Mesag, Ensi of Umma," in P. Marrassini, ed., *Semitic and Assyriological Studies Presented to Pelio Fronzaroli by Pupils and Colleagues*, 105–15. Wiesbaden: Harrassowitz.

Catagnoti, A. and M. Bonechi 1998 "Magic and Divination at IIIrd Millennium Ebla, 1: Textual Typologies and Preliminary Lexical Approach," *Studi Epigrafici e Linguistici* 15: 17–39.

Caubet, A. 1983 "Les Oeufs d'autruche au Proche Orient ancien," *Report of the Department of Antiquities, Cyprus*, 193–98.

Cavigneaux, A. 1980/3 "Lexikalische Listen," *Reallexikon der Assyriologie* 6: 609–41.

——2005 "Les soirées sargoniques des marchands assyriens," in A. Kolde, A. Lukinovich, and A.-L. Rey, eds., κορυφαιω ανδρι, *Mélanges offerts à André Hurst*, 595–602. Geneva: Droz.

——2006/8 "Rätsel (Enigme)," *Reallexikon der Assyriologie* 11: 224.

Cesnola, L. P. 1876 *Cyprus: Its Cities, Tombs, and Temples. A Narrative of Ten Years' Residence as American Consul in That Island*. London: John Murray.

Charpin, D. 1984 "Inscriptions votives d'époque assyrienne," MARI 3: 41–82.

——1990a "Les divinités des babyloniens d'après les légendes de leurs sceaux-cylindres," in Ö. Tunca, ed., *De la babylonie à la Syrie en passant par Mari, Mélanges offerts à Monsieur J.-R. Kupper à l'occasion de son 70ᵉ anniversaire*, 59–78. Liège: Université de Liège.

——1990b "Les édits de 'restauration' des rois babyloniens et leur application," in C. Nicolet, ed., *Du Pouvoir dans l'Antiquité; mots et réalités*, 13–24. *Cahiers du Centre Glotz* I, Ecole Pratique des Hautes Etudes IV Section, Sciences historiques et philologiques. Geneva: Droz.

——1991 "*Rebîtum* 'centre,'" NABU 1991/112.

——1992 "De la vallée du Tigre au 'triangle du Habur': un engrenage géopolitique?" in J.-M. Durand, ed., *Recherches en Haut Mésopotamie, Mémoires de N.A.B.U.* 2, 98–103. Paris: SEPOA.

——1993 "Usages épistolaires des chancelleries d'Ešnunna, d'Ekallâtum et de Mari," NABU 1993/110.

——1994 "Une Campagne de Yahdun-Lim en Haute-Mésopotamie (textes nᵒ 90 à 115)," *Mémoires de N.A.B.U.* 3, *Florilegium Marianum* 2, 177–200. Paris: SEPOA.

——1997 "La version mariote de l'insurrection générale contre Narâm-Sin," *Mémoires de N.A.B.U.* 4, *Florilegium Marianum* 3: 9–18. Paris: SEPOA.

——2004a "Histoire politique du Proche-Orient Amorrite (2002–1595)," in P. Attinger, W. Sallaberger, and M. Wäfler, eds., *Mesopotamien: Die altbabylonische Zeit*, 23–480. *Orbis Biblicus et Orientalis* 160/4. Fribourg: Academic Press.

——2004b "Mari und die Assyrer," in J.-W. Meyer and W. Sommerfeld, eds., *2000 v. Chr.: politische, wirtschaftliche und kulturelle Entwicklung im Zeichen einer Jahrtausendwende*, 371–82. Saarbrücken: Saarbrücker Druckerei und Verlag.

——2004c "La dot-*nidittum* de l'*ênum* de Sîn à Tuttub," NABU 2004/78.

——2007 "Chroniques bibliographiques 10. Économie, société et institutions paléo-babyloniennes: nouvelles sources, nouvelles approches," *Revue d'Assyriologie* 101: 147–82.

——2008 "La dot de la princesse mariote Inbatum," in T. Tarhan, T. Tarhan, and E. Konyar, eds., *Muhibbe Darga Armagani*, 159–72. Istanbul: Sadberg Hanim Müzesi.

————2010 *Reading and Writing in Babylon*, J. M. Todd, trans. Cambridge, Mass.: Harvard University Press.

————2011 "Zur Funktion mesopotamischer Tempel," in G. Selz and K. Wagensonner, eds., *The Empirical Dimension of Ancient Near Eastern Studies*, 403–22. *Wiener Offene Orientalistik* 6. Vienna: Lit.

————2012 "Mari à l'école d'Ešnunna: écriture, langue, formulaires," in C. Mittermayer and S. Ecklin, eds., *Altorientalische Studien zu Ehren von Pascal Attinger*, *Orbis Biblicus et Orientalis* 256, 119–38. Göttingen: Vandenhoeck & Ruprecht.

————2013a "'I am the Sun of Babylon': Solar Aspects of Royal Power in Old Babylonian Mesopotamia," in J. Hill, P. Jones, and A.J. Morales, eds., *Experiencing Power, Generating Authority: Cosmos, Politics, and the Ideology of Kingship in Ancient Egypt and Mesopotamia*, 65–96. Penn Museum International Research Conferences 6. Philadelphia: Penn Museum.

————2013b "'To Write or Not to Write': le devoir d'informations envers le roi dans le Proche-Orient amorrite (XVIIIe siècle av. J.-C.)," *Journal Asiatique* 301: 1–18.

————2013c "Les usages politiques des banquets d'après les archives mésopotamiennes du début du deuxième millénaire av. J.-C.," in C. Grandjean, C. Hugoniot, and B. Lion, eds., *Le banquet du monarque dans le monde antique*, 31–52. Tours: Presses Universitaires François-Rabelais.

Charpin, D. and J.-M. Durand 1986 "'Fils de Sim'al': Les origines tribales des rois de Mari," *Revue d'Assyriologie* 80: 141–83.

Charpin, D. and N. Ziegler 1997 "Mekum, roi d'Apišal," MARI 8: 243–47.

Chen, Y. S. 2013 *The Primeval Flood Catastrophe: Origins and Early Development in Mesopotamian Tradition*. Oxford: Oxford University Press.

Christian, V. 1919/20 "Akkader und Südaraber als ältere Semitenschichte," *Anthropos* 14/15: 729–39.

————1940 *Altertumskunde des Zweistromlandes von der Vorzeit bis zum Ende der Achämeniden-herrschaft*. Leipzig: Verlag Karl W. Hiersemann.

Civil, M. 1964 "A Hymn to the Beer Goddess and a Drinking Song," in *From the Workshop of the Chicago Assyrian Dictionary, Studies Presented to A. Leo Oppenheim, June 7, 1964*, 67–89. Chicago: Oriental Institute of the University of Chicago.

————1973 "The Sumerian Writing System: Some Problems," *Orientalia* NS 42: 21–34.

————1980 "Les limites de l'information textuelle," in *L'archéologie de l'Iraq du debut de l'époque néolithique à 333 avant notre ère: Perspectives et limites de l'interprétation anthropologique des documents*, 225–32. Paris: Centre National de la Recherche Scientifique.

————1984 "Bilingualism in Logographically Written Languages: Sumerian in Ebla," in L. Cagni, ed., *La Lingua di Ebla, Atti del Convegno Internazionale (Napoli, 21–23 aprile 1980)*, 75–97. Seminario di Studi Asiatici, *Series Minor* 14. Naples: Istituto Universitario Orientale.

————1985 "On Some Texts Mentioning Ur-Namma," *Orientalia* NS 54: 27–45.

————1993 "On Mesopotamian Jails and Their Lady Wardens," in M. Cohen, D. Snell, and D. Weisberg, eds., *The Tablet and the Scroll, Near Eastern Studies in Honor of William W. Hallo*, 72–78. Bethesda, Md.: CDL Press.

————1994 *The Farmer's Instructions, A Sumerian Agricultural Manual. Aula Orientalis Supplementa* 5. Barcelona: Editorial AUSA.

————2003 "Of Bows and Arrows," *Journal of Cuneiform Studies* 55: 49–54.

————2008 *The Early Dynastic Practical Vocabulary A (Archaic HAR-ra A), Archivi Reali di Ebla, Studi* 4. Rome: Missione Archeologica Italiana in Siria.

————2011 "The Law Collection of Ur-Namma," in A. George, ed., *Cuneiform Royal Inscriptions and Related Texts in the Schøyen Collection*, 221–86. Cornell University Studies in Assyriology and Sumerology 17. Bethesda, Md.: CDL Press.

————2013 "Remarks on AD-GI₄ (a.k.a. 'Archaic Word List C' or 'Tribute')," *Journal of Cuneiform Studies* 65: 13–68.

Civil, M. and G. Rubio 1999 "An Ebla Incantation against Insomnia and the Semiticization of Sumerian: Notes on ARET 5 8b and 9," *Orientalia* NS 68: 254–66.

Clutton-Brock, J. and S. Davies 1993 "More Donkeys from Tell Brak," *Iraq* 55: 209–21.

Cluzan, S. and C. Lecompte 2011 *Ebih-Il*. Paris: Editions du Louvre.

Cohen, A. 1998 "De-historicizing Strategies in Third-Millennium B.C.E. Royal Inscriptions and Rituals," in T. Abusch, P.-A. Beaulieu, J. Huehnergard, P. Machinist, and P. Steinkeller, eds., *Historiography in the Cuneiform World, Proceedings of the XLVᵉ Rencontre Assyriologique Internationale* 1: 99–111. Bethesda, Md.: CDL Press.

————2005 *Death Rituals, Ideology, and the Development of Early Mesopotamian Kingship. Ancient Magic and Divination* 7. Leiden: Brill.

Cohen, M. 1976a "A New Naram-Sin Date Formula," *Journal of Cuneiform Studies* 28: 227–32.

————1976b "The 'Monkey-Letter': A Different Perspective," *Orientalia* NS 45: 270–74.

————1993 *The Cultic Calendars of the Ancient Near East*. Bethesda, Md.: CDL Press.

Colbow, G. 1997 "More Insights into Representations of the Moon God in the Third and Second Millennium B.C.," in I. Finkel and M. Geller, eds., *Sumerian Gods and Their Representations*, 19–31. *Cuneiform Monographs* 7. Groningen: Styx.

Collon, D. 1977 "Ivory," *Iraq* 39: 219–22.

————1982 *Catalogue of the Western Asiatic Seals in the British Museum, Cylinder Seals II, Akkadian-Post Akkadian Ur III-Periods*. London: British Museum.

————1983 "Hunting and Shooting," *Anatolian Studies* 33: 51–56.

————1987 *First Impressions*. Chicago: University of Chicago Press.

————1992 "The Near Eastern Moon God," in J. Meijer, ed., *Natural Phenomena, Their Meaning, Depiction and Description in the Ancient Near East*, 19–37, Koninklijke Nederlandse Akademie van Wetenschappen, *Verhandelingen*, Afd. Letterkunde Nieuwe Reeks, deel 152. Amsterdam: North-Holland.

————1993/7a "Mondgott, B," *Reallexikon der Assyriologie* 8: 371–76.

————1993/7b "Musik I.B," *Reallexikon der Assyriologie* 8: 488–91.

————1997 "Moons, Boats, and Battle," in I. Finkel and M. Geller, eds., *Sumerian Gods and Their Representations*, 11–17. *Cuneiform Monographs* 7. Groningen: Styx.

————2000 "Early Landscapes," in L. Milano, S. de Marino, F. Fales, and G. Lanfranchi, eds., *Landscape: Territories, Frontiers and Horizons in the Ancient Near East, Papers Presented to the XLIV Rencontre Assyriologique Internationale Venezia, 7–11 July 1997* 3: 15–22. Padua: Sargon.

————2001 "How Seals Were Worn and Carried: The Archaeological and Iconograpic Evidence," in W. Hallo and I. Winter, eds., *Seals and Seal Impressions, Proceedings of the XLVᵉ Rencontre Assyriologique Internationale* 2: 15–30. Bethesda, Md.: CDL Press.

————2007 "Iconographic Evidence for Some Mesopotamian Cult Statues," in B. Groneberg and H. Spieckerman, eds., *Die Welt der Götterbilder*, 57–84. Berlin: De Gruyter.

Collon, D. and A. Kilmer 1980 "The Lute in Ancient Mesopotamia," in *Music and Civilisation*, 13–23. *British Museum Yearbook* 4. London: British Museum.

Cook, S. 1924 "The Semites," *The Cambridge Ancient History*, second edition 1: 181–237. Cambridge: Cambridge University Press.

Cooper, J. 1973 "Sumerian and Akkadian in Sumer and Akkad," *Orientalia* NS 42: 239–46.

————1980 "Apodictic Death and the Historicity of 'Historical' Omens," in B. Alster, ed., *Death in Mesopotamia, XXVIᵉ Rencontre assyriologique internationale*, 99–105. Copenhagen: Akademisk Forlag.

————1983a *The Curse of Agade*. Baltimore, Md.: Johns Hopkins University Press.

————1983b *Reconstructing History through Boundary Inscriptions, Sources from the Ancient Near East* 2/1. Malibu: Undena.

————1985 "Sargon and Joseph: Dreams Come True," in A. Kort and S. Morschauser, eds., *Biblical and Related Studies Presented to Samuel Iwry*, 33–9. Winona Lake, Ind.: Eisenbrauns.

————1990 "Mesopotamian Historical Consciousness and the Production of Monumental Art in the Third Millennium B.C.," in A. Gunter, ed. *Investigating Artistic Environments in the Ancient Near East*, 39–51. Washington, D.C.: Smithsonian Institution.

————1993 "Paradigm and Propaganda: The Dynasty of Agade in the 21st Century," in M. Liverani, ed., *Akkad, The First Universal Empire: Structure, Ideology, Traditions*, 11–23. *History of the Ancient Near East/Studies* 5. Padua: Sargon.

————1995 "Sumerian and Semitic Writing in Most Ancient Syro-Mesopotamia," in K. Van Lerberghe and G. Voet, eds., *Languages and Cultures in Contact: At the Crossroads of Civilizations in the Syro-Mesopotamian Realm, Proceedings of the 42th* [sic] *RAI*, 61–77. *Orientalia Lovaniensia Analecta* 96, 61–77. Leuven: Peeters.

————2001 "Literature and History: The Historical and Literary Referents of Sumerian Literary Texts," in T. Abusch, P.-A. Beaulieu, J. Huehnergard, P. Machinist, and P. Steinkeller, eds., *Historiography in the Cuneiform World, Proceedings of the XLVᵉ Rencontre Assyriologique Internationale* 1: 131–47. Bethesda, Md.: CDL Press.

Cooper, J. and W. Heimpel 1983 "The Sumerian Sargon Legend," in J. Sasson, ed., *Studies in Literature from the Ancient Near East by Members of the American Oriental Society*, 67–82. *American Oriental Series* 65 = *Journal of the American Oriental Society* 103.

Cornelius, F. 1966 "Die Mondfinsternis von Akkad," in *La divination en Mésopotamie ancienne et dans les régions voisines, XIVᵉ Rencontre Assyriologique Internationale (Strasbourg, 2–6 juillet 1965)*, 125–29. Paris: Presses Universitaires de France.

Crawford, H. 1973 "Mesopotamia's Invisible Exports in the Third Millennium B.C.," *World Archaeology* 1973: 232–41.

————2013a "Trade in the Sumerian World," in H. Crawford, ed., *The Sumerian World*, 447–61. London: Routledge.

————2013b *The Sumerian World*. London: Routledge.

Cripps, E. 2007 *Land Tenure and Social Stratification in Ancient Mesopotamia: Third Millennium Sumer before the Ur III Dynasty. BAR International Series* 1676. Oxford: Archaeopress.

————2010 *Sargonic and Presargonic Texts in The World Museum Liverpool. BAR International Series* 2135. Oxford: Archaeopress.

Culbertson, L., ed. 2011 *Slaves and Households in the Near East. Oriental Institute Seminars* 7. Chicago: Oriental Institute of the University of Chicago.

Curtis, J., ed., 1982 *Fifty Years of Mesopotamian Discovery*. London: British School of Archaeology in Iraq.

Dahl, J. 2007 *The Ruling Family of Ur III Umma: A Prosopographical Analysis of an Elite Family in Southern Iraq 4000 Years Ago. Publications de l'Institut historique-archéologique néerlandais de Stamboul* 108. Leiden: Nederlands Instituut voor het nabije Oosten.

————2010 "A Babylonian Gang of Potters: Reconstructing the Social Organization of Crafts Production in the Late Third Millennium BC Southern Mesopotamia," in L. Kogan, N. Koslova, S. Loesov, and S. Tishchenko, eds., *City Administration in the Ancient Near East, Proceedings of the 53ᵉ Rencontre Assyriologique Internationale* 2: 275–305. *Orientalia et Classica* 31, *Babel und Bibel* 5. Winona Lake, Ind.: Eisenbrauns.

Dalley, S. 1980 "Old Babylonian Dowries," *Iraq* 42: 53–74.

————2008 "Babylon as a Name for Other Cities Including Nineveh," in R. Biggs, J. Myers, and M. Roth, eds., *Proceedings of the 51st Rencontre Assyriologique Internationale Held at the Oriental Institute of the University of Chicago July 18–22, 2005*, 25–33. *Studies in Ancient Oriental Civilization* 62. Chicago: Oriental Institute of the University of Chicago.

Dandamayev, M. A. 1984 *Slavery in Babylonia: From Nabopolassar to Alexander the Great (626–333 BC)*, revised edition, Victoria A. Powell, trans. DeKalb: Northern Illinois University Press.

Danmanville, J. 1955 "La libation en Mésopotamie," *Revue d'Assyriologie* 49: 57–68.

De Cesari, C. 2002 "Graves and Public Space: Some Questions about Possible 'Public' Aspects of Graves and Cemeteries in Mesopotamia," *Altorientalische Forschungen* 29: 355–66.

De Graef, K. and J. Tavernier 2013 *Susa and Elam. Archaeological, Philological, Historical and Geographical Perspectives. Proceedings of the International Congress held at Ghent University, December 14–17, 2009. Mémoires de la Délégation en Perse* 58. Leiden: Brill.

De Graeve, M.-C. 1982 "A Drinking Scene on a Late Akkadian Seal," in J. Quaegebeur, ed., *Studia Paulo Naster Oblata II. Orientalia Antiqua*, 17–24. *Orientalia Lovaniensia Analecta* 13. Louvain: Peeters.

De Lapérouse, J. 2003 "Lost-Wax Casting," in J. Aruz and R. Wallenfels, ed. *Art of the First Cities: The Third Millennium* B.C. *from the Mediterranean to the Indus*, 210–23. New York: Metropolitan Museum of Art.

De Lillis-Forrest, F., L. Milano, and L. Mori 2007 "The Akkadian Occupation in the Northwest Area of the Tell Leilan Acropolis (with an Appendix on the Epigraphic Finds from the 'Tablet Room' of the Leilan IIb3 Akkadian Building and from Later Akkadian Layers)," *Kaskal* 4: 43–64.

Delougaz, P. 1952 *Pottery from the Diyala Region. Oriental Institute Publications* 63. Chicago: University of Chicago Press.

Delougaz, P., H. Hill, and S. Lloyd 1967 *Private Houses and Graves in the Diyala Region. Oriental Institute Publications* 88. Chicago: University of Chicago Press.

Delougaz, P. and S. Lloyd 1942 *Pre-Sargonid Temples in the Diyala Region. Oriental Institute Publications* 58. Chicago: University of Chicago Press.

De Maigret, A. 1976 *Le lance nell'Asia anteriore nell'eta dell bronzo: Studio Tipologico. Studi Semitici* 47. Rome: Istituto di Studi del Vicino Oriente, Università di Roma.

De Maaijer, R. 2001 "Late Third Millennium Identifying Marks," in W. van Soldt, ed., *Veenhof Anniversary Volume: Studies Presented to Klaas R. Veenhof on the Occasion of his Sixty-fifth Birthday*, 301–24. *Publications de l'Institut historique-archéologique néerlandais de Stamboul* 89. Leiden: Nederlands Instituut voor het nabije Oosten.

Démare-Lafont, S. 2006/8 "Prozeß A," *Reallexikon der Assyriologie* 11: 72–91.

De Morgan, J. 1900 "Stèle triomphale de Naram-Sin," *Mémoires de la délégation en Perse* 2, 144–58.

Dercksen, J., ed. 1999 *Trade and Finance in Ancient Mesopotamia, MOS Studies* 1. Istanbul: Nederlands Instituut voor het Nabije Oosten.

———2005 "Adad Is King! The Sargon Text from Kültepe," *Jaarbericht van het Voor-Aziatisch Egyptisch Genootschap. Ex Oriente Lux* 39: 107–29.

Dhorme, E. 1907 "Valeurs archaïques des signes . . . ," *Orientalistische Literaturzeitung* 1907: 229–31.

Diakonoff, I. 1947 "Ob odnoj drevne-vostočnoj skul'pture," *Trudy Ermitaža* 4: 107–18.

———1956 *Istorija Midii ot drevnejših vremen do konca IV veka do n.e.* Moscow: Akademia Nauk.

———1959 *Obščestvennyj i gosudarstvennyj stroj drevnego Dvureč'ja: Šumer.* Moscow: Izdatel'stvo Vostočnoj Literatury.

———1961 *Epos o Gil'gameshe ("o bce vidavshem").* Moscow: Akademia Nauk SSSR.

———1976 "Slaves, Helots and Serfs in Early Antiquity," in J. Harmatta and G. Komoróczy, eds., *Wirtschaft und Gesellschaft im alten Vorderasien*, 49–78. Budapest: Académiae Kiadó.

————1982 "The Structure of Near Eastern Society before the Middle of the 2nd Millennium B.C.," *Oikumene* 3: 7–100.

Diakonoff, I. and P. Kohl, eds. 1991 *Early Antiquity*, A. Kirjanov, trans. Chicago: University of Chicago Press.

Dick, M. 2005 "The Mesopotamian Cult Statue: A Sacramental Encounter with Divinity," in N. Walls, ed., *Cult Image and Divine Representation in the Ancient Near East*, 43–67. Boston: American Schools of Oriental Research.

Dittmann, R. 1994 "Glyptikgruppen am Übergang von der Akkad-zur Ur III-Zeit," *Baghdader Mitteilungen* 25: 75–117.

DiVito, R. 1993 *Studies in Third Millennium Sumerian and Akkadian Personal Names: The Designation and Conception of the Personal God*. Studia Pohl Series Maior 16. Rome: Pontificio Istituto Biblico.

Dobbs-Allsopp, F. 1993 *Weep, O Daughter of Zion: A Study of the City-Lament Genre in the Hebrew Bible*, Bublica et Orientalia 44. Rome: Pontificio Istituto Biblico.

Doyle, M. 1996 *Empires*. Ithaca, N.Y.: Cornell University Press.

Dunham, S. 1985 "The Monkey in the Middle," *Zeitschrift für Assyriologie* 75: 234–64.

Durand, J.-M. 1975 "Rapport sur les conférences de sumérien," *Annuaire de l'Ecole Pratique des Hautes Etudes* IV, 149–81. Paris: La Sorbonne.

————1983 "A propos des foies de Mari," MARI 2: 218.

————1985 "La situation historique des šakkanakku: nouvelle approche," MARI 4: 147–72.

————1987 "L'Organisation de l'espace dans le palais de Mari: Le témoinage des textes," in E. Lévy, ed., *Le Système palatial en Orient, en Grèce et à Rome, Actes du Colloque de Strasbourg 19–22 juin 1985*, 39–110. Leiden: Brill.

————1989 "L'Assemblée en Syrie à l'époque pré-amorite," *Quaderni di Semitistica* 16: 27–44.

————1991a "Précurseurs syriens aux protocols néo-assyriens: considérations sur la vie politique aux Bords-de-l'Euphrate," in D. Charpin and F. Joannès, eds., *Marchands, diplomats et empereurs. Études sur la civilisation mésopotamienne offertes à Paul Garelli*, 13–72. Paris: Editions Recherche sur les Civilisations.

————1991b "Agade *rebîtum*," NABU 1991/31.

————1992 "Unité et diversités au Proche-Orient à l'époque amorrite," in D. Charpin and F. Joannès, eds., *La Circulation des biens, des personnes et des idées dans le Proche-Orient ancien, Actes de la XXXVIII Rencontre Assyriologique Internationale (Paris, 8–10 juillet 1991)*, 97–128. Paris: Editions Recherche sur les Civilisations.

————1993 "Notes de lecture: *Old Sumerian and Old Akkadian Texts in Philadelphia*," MARI 7: 377–82.

————ed. 1996 *Mari, Ebla, et les Hurrites, dix ans de travaux: Actes du colloque international mai 1993*. Paris: Editions Recherche sur les Civilisations.

————1997 *Documents épistolaires du Palais de Mari, Tome I. Littératures anciennes du Proche-Orient* 16. Paris: Les Editions Du Cerf.

————1998 *Documents épistolaires du Palais de Mari, Tome II. Littératures anciennes du Proche-Orient* 17. Paris: Les Editions Du Cerf.

————2003a "La conscience du temps et sa commemoration en Mésopotamie: l'exemple de la documentation mariote," *Akkadica* 124: 1–11.

————2003b "La vengeance à l'époque amorrite," *Florilegium Marianum* 6: 39–50.

————2006/8 "Šakkanakku," *Reallexikon der Assyriologie* 11: 560–63.

————2010 "Être chef d'un état amorrite," in L. Kogan, N. Koslova, S. Loesov, and S. Tishchenko, eds., *City Administration in the Ancient Near East, Proceedings of the 53ᵉ Rencontre*

*Assyriologique Internationale*, 2: 31–58. *Orientalia et Classica* 31, *Babel und Bibel* 5. Winona Lake, Ind.: Eisenbrauns.

———2012 "Sargon a-t-il détruit la ville de Mari?" *Revue d'Assyriologie* 106: 117–32.

Durand, J.-M. and M. Guichard 1997 "Les rituels de Mari," in D. Charpin and J.-M. Durand, eds., *Florilegium Marianum 3: Recueil d'études à la mémoire de Marie-Thérèse Barrelet*, 19–78. Paris: SEPOA.

Durand, J.-M. and F. Joannès 1998 "Contrat néo-babylonien d'Agadé," NABU 1988/74.

Durand, J.-M. and A. Lemaire 1984 *Inscriptions araméennes de Sfiré et l'Assyrie de Shamshi-ilu*. Geneva: Droz.

During Caspers, E. 1973 "De handeslbetrekkingen van de Indus-beschaving in de 'Perzische Golf' in het IIIe mill. v. Chr.," *Phoenix* 19: 241–66.

Edzard, D. 1957 *Die "Zweite Zwischenzeit" Babyloniens*. Wiesbaden: Harrassowitz.

———1960a "Sumerer und Semiten in der frühen Geschichte Mesopotamiens," in E. Sollberger, ed., *Aspects du contact suméro-akkadien, IX^e Rencontre Assyriologique Internationale, Genève, 20–23 juin 1960*, 241–58. *Genava* NS 8. Geneva: Musée d'Art et d'Histoire.

———1960b "Die Beziehungen Babyloniens und Assyriens in der mittelbabylonischen Zeit und das Gold," *Journal of the Economic and Social History of the Orient* 3: 38–55.

———1962 "Mesopotamien," in H. Haussig, ed., *Wörterbuch der Mythologie 1: Götter und Mythen im vorderen Orient*, 19–139. Stuttgart: Ernst Klett Verlag.

———1968 *Sumerische Rechtsurkunden des III. Jahrtausends aus der Zeit vor der III. Dynastie von Ur, Abhandlungen der Bayerischen Akademie der Wissenschaften, Philosophisch-historische Klasse*, Neue Folge 67. Munich: Beck.

———1968/9 "Die Inschriften der altakkadischen Rollsiegel," *Archiv für Orientforschung* 22: 12–20.

———1970 "Die *bukānum*-Formel der altbabylonischen Kaufverträge und ihrer sumerische Entsprechungen," *Zeitschrift für Assyriologie* 60: 8–53.

———1973 "Zwei Inschriften am Felsen von Sar-i-Pūl-i-Zohâb: Anubanini 1 und 2," *Archiv für Orientforschung* 24: 73–77.

———1974 "Problèmes de la royauté dans la période présargonique," in P. Garelli, ed., *Le Palais et la royauté, archéologie et civilisation, XIX^e rencontre assyriologique internationale, Paris, 29 juin–2 juillet 1971*, 141–49. Paris: Geuthner.

———1976 "Zum sumerischen Eid," in S. Lieberman, ed., *Sumerological Studies in Honor of Thorkild Jacobsen on His Seventieth Birthday June 7, 1974*, 63–98. *Assyriological Studies* 20. Chicago: Oriental Institute of the University of Chicago.

———1976/80a "Il," *Reallexikon der Assyriologie* 5: 46–48.

———1976/80b "Kazallu," *Reallexikon der Assyriologie* 5: 542–43.

———1976/80c "Kiš A. Philologisch," *Reallexikon der Assyriologie* 5: 607–13.

———1989a "La vision du passée et de l'avenir en Mésopotamie," in *Conscience Historique dans les civilisations du Proche-Orient Ancien*, 157–66. *Cahiers du Centre d'Etude du Proche-Orient Ancien* 5. Leuven: Peeters.

———1989b "Das 'Wort im Ekur' oder die peripatie in 'Fluch über Agade,'" in H. Behrens, D. Loding, and M. Roth, eds., *DUMU-E₂-DUB-BA-A, Studies in Honor of Åke W. Sjöberg*, 99–105. *Occasional Publications of the Samuel Noah Kramer Fund* 11. Philadelphia: University Museum of Anthropology and Archaeology.

———1991 "Sargon's Report on Kish: A Problem in Akkadian Philology," in M. Cogan and I. Eph'al, eds., *Ah, Assyria . . . Studies in Assyrian History and Ancient Near Eastern Historiography Presented to Hayim Tadmor*, 258–63. *Scripta Hierosolymitana* 38. Jerusalem: Magnes Press.

———1993/97 "Mesikigala," *Reallexikon der Assyriologie* 8: 93.

————1994 "Encore sur le *laḫmu*," NABU 1994/7.

————1996 "Das ist ja zum lachen," NABU 1996/52.

————2004 *Geschichte Mesopotamiens, von den Sumerern bis zu Alexander dem Großen.* Munich: Beck.

Edzard, D. and A. Kammenhuber 1972/5 "Hurriter," *Reallexikon der Assyriologie* 4: 507–14.

Ehrenberg, E. 1997 "An Old Assyrian Precursor of the Neo-Assyrian Royal Image," in H. Waetzoldt and H. Hauptmann, eds., *Assyrien im Wandel der Zeiten: XXXIX<sup>e</sup> Rencontre Assyriologique Internationale, Heidelberg, 6.–10. Juli, 1992*, 259–64. Heidelberg: Heidelberger Orientverlag.

————1999 "Archaism and Individualism in the Late Babylonian Period," in Jiří Prosecký, ed., *Intellectual Life of the Ancient Near East, Papers Presented at the 43rd Rencontre Assyriologique Internationale Prague, July 1–5, 1996*, 125–40. Prague: Academy of Sciences of the Czech Republic.

Elayi, J. 2013 *Histoire de la Phénicie.* Paris: Perrin.

Ellis, R. 1968 *Foundation Deposits in the Ancient Near East. Yale Near Eastern Researches* 2. New Haven, Conn.: Yale University Press.

————1995 "The Trouble with 'Hairies,'" *Iraq* 57: 159–65.

Ellison, R. 1984 "Methods of Food Preparation in Mesopotamia (c. 3000–600 BC)," *Journal of the Economic and Social History of the Orient* 27: 89–98.

El-Samarraie, H. 1972 *Agriculture in Iraq during the 3rd Century A.H.* Beirut: Librarie du Liban.

Emberling, G. and McDonald, H. 2003 "Excavations at Tell Brak 2001–2002: Preliminary Report," *Iraq* 65: 1–75.

Emberling, G. and Yoffee, N. 1999 "Thinking about Ethnicity in Mesopotamian Archaeology and History," in H. Kühne, R. Bernbeck, and K. Bartl, eds., *Fluchtpunkt Uruk. Archäologische Einheit aus methodischer Vielfalt: Schriften für Hans Jörg Nissen*, 272–81. Rahden: Marie Leidorf.

Englund, R. 1990 *Organisation und Verwaltung der Ur III-Fischerei. Berliner Beiträge zum Vorderen Orient* 10. Berlin: Dietrich Reimer.

————1991 "Hard Work, Where Will It Get You? Labor Management in Ur III Mesopotamia," *Journal of Near Eastern Studies* 50: 255–80.

Eppihimer, M. 2009 *The Visual Legacy of Akkadian Kingship.* Dissertation: Harvard University.

————2010 "Assembling King and State: The Statues of Manishtushu and the Consolidation of Akkadian Kingship," *American Journal of Archaeology* 114: 365–80.

Evans, J. 2007 "The Square Temple at Tell Asmar and the Construction of Early Dynastic Mesopotamia, ca. 2900–2350 B.C.E." *American Journal of Archaeology* 111: 509–632.

Faivre, X. 2009 "Pots et plats," in X. Faivre, B. Lion, and C. Michel, eds., *Et il y eut un esprit dans l'Homme: Jean Bottéro et Mésopotamie*, 157–82. Paris: De Boccard.

Falkenstein, A. 1958 "Enhedu'anna, die Tochter Sargons von Akkade," *Revue d'Assyriologie* 52: 129–31.

————1959a "*akiti*-Fest und *akiti*-Festhaus," in R. Kienle, A. Moortgat, H. Otten, E. von Schuler, and W. Zaumseil, eds., *Festschrift Johannes Friedrich zum 65. Geburtstag am 27. August 1958 gewidmet*, 147–82. Heidelberg: C. Winter.

————1959b *Sumerische Götterlieder I. Teil. Abhandlungen der Heidelberger Akademie der Wissenschaften, Philosophisch-historische Klasse* 1959/1. Heidelberg: Carl Winter Universitätsverlag.

Farber, W. 1974 "Von Ba und anderen Wassertiere," *Journal of Cuneiform Studies* 29: 195–207.

————1983 "Die Vergöttlichung Narām-Sîns," *Orientalia* NS 52: 67–72.

Feldman, M. 2007 "Darius I and the Heroes of Akkad: Affect and Agency in the Bisitun Relief," in J. Cheng and M. Feldman, eds., *Ancient Near Eastern Art in Context, Studies in Honor of Irene J. Winter by Her Students*, 265–93. Leiden: Brill.

Figulla, H. 1953 "Accounts concerning Allocations of Provisions for Offerings in the nin-gal-Temple at Ur," *Iraq* 15: 88–122; 171–92.

Finet, A. 1982 "L'oeuf d'autruche," in J. Quaegebeur, ed., *Studia Paul Naster Oblata II. Orientalia Antiqua*, 69–77. *Orientalia Lovaniensia Analecta* 13. Leuven: Peeters.

Finkel, I. 2011 "Drawings on Tablets," *Scienze dell'Antichità* 17: 337–44.

Finkelstein, J. 1963 "Mesopotamian Historiography," in *Cuneiform Studies and the History of Civilization, Proceedings of the American Philosophical Society* 107/6: 461–72.

———1966 "The Genealogy of the Hammurapi Dynasty," *Journal of Cuneiform Studies* 20: 95–118.

Firth, R. 2011 "A Discussion of the Use of im-babbar$_2$ by the Craft Workers of Ancient Mesopotamia," Cuneiform Digital Library Journal [internet resource] 2011:2: 1–9.

Firth, R. and M.-L. Nosch 2012 "Spinning and Weaving Wool in Ur III Administrative Texts," *Journal of Cuneiform Studies* 64: 65–82.

Fischer, C. 2000 "Die Bildsymbolik der Assyrer in der akkadischen Tradition," *Altorientalische Forschungen* 27: 157–94.

Foster, B. 1977 "Commercial Activity in Sargonic Mesopotamia," *Iraq* 39: 31–43.

———1979a "Murder in Mesopotamia?" *Revue d'Assyriologie* 73: 179.

———1979b "New Light on the *mu-iti* Texts," *Orientalia* NS 48: 153–62.

———1980 "Notes on Sargonic Royal Progress," *Journal of the Ancient Near Eastern Society of Columbia University* 12: 29–42.

———1981 "ni-is-ku," *Revue d'Assyriologie* 75: 190.

———1981/2 "The Circuit of Lagash," *Archiv für Orientforschung* 28: 141.

———1982a *Administration and Use of Institutional Land in Sargonic Sumer. Mesopotamia* 9. Copenhagen: Akademisk Forlag.

———1982b *Umma in the Sargonic Period. Memoirs of the Connecticut Academy of Arts & Sciences* 20. Hamden, Conn.: Shoestring Press.

———1982c "An Agricultural Archive from Sargonic Akkad," *Acta Sumerologica* 4: 7–51.

———1982d "Education of a Bureaucrat in Sargonic Sumer," *Archiv Orientální* 50: 239–41.

———1982e "Notes on Sargonic Legal and Juridical Procedures," *Die Welt des Orients* 13: 15–24.

———1982f "Administration of State Land at Sargonic Gasur," *Oriens Antiquus* 20: 39–48.

———1982g "The Siege of Armanum," *Journal of the Ancient Near Eastern Society of Columbia University* 14: 27–36.

———1982h "Archives and Record-keeping in Sargonic Mesopotamia," *Zeitschrift für Assyriologie* 72: 1–27.

———1982i "Ethnicity and Onomastics in Sargonic Mesopotamia," *Orientalia* NS 51: 297–354.

———1983a "Selected Business Documents from Sargonic Mesopotamia," *Journal of Cuneiform Studies* 35: 147–75.

———1983b "Ebla and the Origins of Akkadian Accountability," *Bibliotheca Orientalis* 40: 298–305.

———1985 "The Sargonic Victory Stele from Telloh," *Iraq* 47: 15–30.

———1986a "Agriculture and Accountability in Ancient Mesopotamia," in H. Weiss, ed., *The Origins of Cities in Dry-Farming Syria and Mesopotamia in the Third Millennium B.C.*, 109–28. Guilford, Conn.: Four Quarters.

———1986b "Archives and Empire in Sargonic Mesopotamia," in K. Veenhof, ed., *Cuneiform Archives and Libraries, Papers Read at the 30ᵉ Rencontre Assyriologique Internationale, Leiden, 4–8 July 1983*, 46–52. Publications de l'Institut historique-archéologique néerlandais de Stamboul 57. Leiden: Nederlands Historisch-Archaeologisch Instituut te Istanbul.

————1987a "Notes on Women in Sargonic Society," in J.-M. Durand, ed., *La Femme dans le Proche-Orient antique, XXXIII^e rencontre assyriologique internationale (Paris, 7–10 juillet 1986),* 53–61. Paris: Editions Recherche sur les Civilisations.

————1987b "People, Land, and Produce at Sargonic Gasur," in D. Owen and M. Morrison, eds., *Studies on the Civilization and Culture of Nuzi and the Hurrians* 2, 89–107. Winona Lake, Ind.: Eisenbrauns.

————1989a "A Sargonic Archive from the Lagash Region," in H. Behrens, D. Loding, and M. Roth, eds., *DUMU-E₂-DUB-BA-A, Studies in Honor of Åke W. Sjöberg,* 155–65. *Occasional Publications of the Samuel Noah Kramer Fund* 11. Philadelphia: University Museum of Anthropology and Archaeology.

————1989b "Another Sargonic Water Ordeal?" NABU 1989/82.

————1990 "Naram-Sin in Martu and Magan," *Annual of the Royal Inscriptions of Mesopotamia Project* 8: 25–44.

————1991 "On Authorship in Cuneiform Literature," *Annali dell'Istituto Orientale di Napoli* 51: 17–32.

————1992 "A Sargonic Itinerary," in D. Charpin and F. Joannès, eds., *La Circulation des biens, des personnes et des idées dans le Proche-Orient ancien, Actes de la XXXVIII^e Rencontre Assyriologique Internationale (Paris, 8–10 juillet 1991),* 73–76. Paris: Editions Recherche sur les Civilisations.

————1993a "Management and Administration in the Sargonic Period," in M. Liverani, ed., *Akkad, the First Universal Empire: Structure, Ideology, Traditions,* 25–38. *History of the Ancient Near East Studies* 5. Padua: Sargon.

————1993b "'International' Trade at Sargonic Susa," *Altorientalische Forschungen* 20: 98–102.

————1997a "Akkadians," in E. Meyers, ed., *The Oxford Encyclopedia of Archaeology in the Near East* 1: 49–54. Oxford: Oxford University Press.

————1997b "A Sumerian Merchant's Account of the Dilmun Trade," *Acta Sumerologica* 19: 53–62.

————1997c "Sargonic Numeration Revisited," NABU 1997/123.

————1999 "A Century of Mesopotamian Agriculture," in H. Klengel and J. Renger, eds., *Landwirtschaft im Alten Orient, Ausgewählte Vorträge der XLI. Rencontre Assyriologique Internationale Berlin, 4.-8.7.1994,* 1–10, *Berliner Beiträge zum Vorderen Orient* 18. Berlin: Dietrich Reimer.

————2000 "The Forty-nine Sons of Agade," in S. Graziani, ed., *Studi sul Vicino Oriente Antico dedicati alla memoria di Luigi Cagni,* 309–18. Naples: Istituto Universitario Orientale, Dipartimento di Studi Asiatici, *Series Minor* 61.

————2002 "The Sargon Parody," NABU 2002/82.

————2005a *Before the Muses: An Anthology of Akkadian Literature,* third edition. Bethesda, Md.: CDL Press.

————2005b "A New Edition of the Epic of Gilgamesh," *Journal of the American Oriental Society* 125: 59–65.

————2006 Review of Fronzaroli 2003, *Bibliotheca Orientalis* 63: 108–12.

————2007a *Akkadian Literature of the Late Period. Guides to the Mesopotamian Textual Record* 2. Münster: Ugarit-Verlag.

————2007b "Mesopotamia," in J. Hinnells, ed., *Penguin Handbook of Ancient Religions,* 161–213. London: Penguin Books.

————2010a "Clothing in Sargonic Mesopotamia: Visual and Written Evidence," in C. Michel and M.-L. Nosch, eds., *Textile Terminologies in the Ancient Near East and Mediterranean from the Third to the First Millennia BC. Ancient Textile Series* 8, 110–45. Oxford: Oxbow Books.

————2010b "On Personnel in Sargonic Girsu," in S. Dönmez, ed., *DUB.SAR É.DUB. BA.A, Studies Presented in Honour of Veysel Donbaz*, 143–51. Ankara: Ege Yayınları.

————2011a "The Sargonic Period: Two Historiographical Problems," in G. Barjamovic, J. Dahl, U. Koch, W. Sommerfeld, and J. Westenholz, eds., *Akkade Is King, a Collection of Papers by Friends and Colleagues Presented to Aage Westenholz on the Occasion of His 70th Birthday 15th of May 2009*, 127–37. *Publications de l'Institut historique-archéologique néerlandais de Stamboul* 118. Leiden: Nederlands Instituut voor het Nabije Oosten.

————2011b "The Person in Mesopotamian Thought," in K. Radner and E. Robson, eds., *The Oxford Handbook of Cuneiform Culture*, 117–39. Oxford: Oxford University Press.

————2011c "An Old Babylonian Tablet Blank," *Scienze dell'Antichità* 17: 279–80.

————2014a "Diorite and Limestone: A Sumerian Perspective," in L. Sassmanshausen and G. Neumann, eds., *He Has Opened Nisaba's House of Learning: Studies in Honor of Åke Waldemar Sjöberg on the Occasion of His 89th Birthday on August 1st 2013*, 51–56. *Cuneiform Monographs* 46. Leiden: Brill.

————2014b "Wool in the Economy of Sargonic Mesopotamia," in C. Breniquet and C. Michel, eds., *Wool Economy in the Ancient Near East and the Aegean: From the Beginnings of Sheep Husbandry to Institutional Textile Industry*, 115–23. Oxford: Oxbow Books.

————2015 "Akkadian Economics," *Rivista di Storia Economica* 31: 7–23.

Foster, B. and V. Donbaz 1982 *Sargonic Texts from Telloh in the Istanbul Archaeological Museums, with the assistance of Mustafa Eren. Occasional Publications of the Babylonian Fund, 5 and American Research Institute in Turkey Monographs* 2. Philadelphia: University Museum of the University of Pennsylvania.

Foster, B. and E. Robson 2004 "A New Look at the Sargonic Mathematical Corpus," *Zeitschrift für Assyriologie* 94: 1–15.

Foster, B. and E. Salgues 2011 "Everything Except the Squeal: Pigs in Early Mesopotamia," in B. Lion and C. Michel, eds., *De la domestication au tabou: Le cas des suidés au Proche-Orient ancien*, 283–91. Paris: De Boccard.

Foster, K. forthcoming "The Lion King in the Aegean and Ancient Near East".

Foxvog, D. 1980 "Funerary Furnishings," in B. Alster, ed., *Death in Mesopotamia. XXVI^e Rencontre Assyriologique Internationale*. 67–75. *Mesopotamia* 8. *Copenhagen Studies in Assyriology*. Copenhagen: Akademisk Forlag.

————1994 "A New Lagaš Text Bearing on Uruinimgina's Reforms," *Journal of Cuneiform Studies* 46: 11–15.

Frahm, E. 1999 "Nabû-zuqup-kēnu, das Gilgameš Epos und der Tod Sargons II." *Journal of Cuneiform Studies* 51: 73–90.

————2005 "Observations on the Name and Age of Sargon II., and on Some Patterns of Assyrian Royal Onomastics," NABU 2005/44.

Frahm, E. and E. Payne 2003/4 "Šuruppak under Rimuš: A Rediscovered Inscription," *Archiv für Orientforschung* 50: 50–55.

Frame, G. 1993 "Nabonidus and the History of the Eulmaš Temple at Akkad," *Mesopotamia* 28: 21–50.

Frangipane, M. 1996 *La nascita dello Stato nel Vicino Oriente, dai lignaggi all burocrazia nella Grande Mesopotamia*. Bari: Laterza.

Franke, S. 1995 *Königsinschriften und Königsideologie: Die Könige von Akkade zwischen Tradition und Neuerung*. Münster and Hamburg: Lit.

Frankfort, H. 1927 *Studies in Early Pottery of the Near East II. Asia, Europe and the Aegean, and their Earliest Interrelations*. Royal Anthropological Institute, *Occasional Papers* 3.8. London: Royal Anthropological Institute of Great Britain and Ireland.

————1933 *Tell Asmar, Khafaje and Khorsabad, Second Preliminary Report of the Iraq Expedition*, *Oriental Institute Communications* 16. Chicago: University of Chicago Press.

————1934a *Iraq Excavations of the Oriental Institute 1932/33, Third Preliminary Report of the Iraq Expedition, Oriental Institute Communications* 17. Chicago: University of Chicago Press.

————1934b "Gods and Myths on Sargonic Seals," *Iraq* 1: 2–29.

————1939a *Cylinder Seals: A Documentary Essay on the Art and Religion of the Ancient Near East*. London: Macmillan.

————1939b *Sculpture of the Third Millennium from Tell Asmar and Khafaje. Oriental Institute Publications* 44. Chicago: University of Chicago Press.

————1943 *More Sculpture from the Diyala Region. Oriental Institute Publications* 60. Chicago: University of Chicago Press.

————1970 *The Art and Architecture of the Ancient Orient.* Penguin Books: Baltimore.

Frankfort, H., S. Lloyd, and T. Jacobsen 1940 *The Gimilsin Temple and the Palace of the Rulers at Tell Asmar. Oriental Institute Publications* 43. Chicago: University of Chicago Press.

Frayne, D. 1990 *The Old Babylonian Period (2003–1595 B.C.), Royal Inscriptions of Mesopotamia, Early Periods* Volume 4. Toronto: University of Toronto Press.

————1991 "Historical Texts in Haifa: Notes on R. Kutscher's 'Brockmon Tablets,'" *Bibliotheca Orientalis* 48: 378–410.

————1993 *Sargonic and Gutian Periods (2334–2113 BC). The Royal Inscriptions of Mesopotamia, Early Periods* 2. Toronto: University of Toronto Press.

————1997a *Ur III Period (2112–2004 BC), The Royal Inscriptions of Mesopotamia, Early Periods* 3/2. Toronto: University of Toronto Press.

————1997b "On the Location of Simurrum," in G. Young, M. Chavalas, and R. Averbeck, eds., *Crossing Boundaries and Linking Horizons: Studies in Honor of Michael C. Astour on His 80th Birthday*, 243–69. Bethesda, Md.: CDL Press.

————1998/2001 "Narām-Sîn. König von Akkade. A," *Reallexikon der Assyriologie* 9: 169–74.

————1999 "The Zagros Campaigns of Šulgi and Amar-Suena," in D. Owen and G. Wilhelm, eds., *Nuzi at Seventy-five*, 141–201. *Studies on the Civilization and Culture of Nuzi and the Hurrians* 10. Bethesda, Md.: CDL Press.

————2004 "Geographical Notes on the Land of Akkad," in G. Frame, ed., *From the Upper Sea to the Lower Sea, Studies on the History of Assyria and Babylonia in Honour of A. K. Grayson*, 103–16. *Publications de l'Institut historique-archéologique néerlandais de Stamboul* 101. Leiden: Nederlands Instituut voor het Nabije Oosten.

Friberg, J. 1987/90 "Mathematik," *Reallexikon der Assyriologie* 7: 531–85.

Fronzaroli, P. 2003 *Testi di cancelleria: I rapporti con le città (Archivo L. 2769), Archivi Reali di Ebla, Testi* XIII. Rome: Missione Archeologica Italiana in Siria.

Fuchs, A. 2009/11 "Sargon II.," *Reallexikon der Assyriologie* 12: 51–61.

Gabbay, U. 2008 "The Akkadian Word for 'Third Gender': The *kalû* Once Again," in R. Biggs, J. Myers, and M. Roth, eds., *Proceedings of the 51st Rencontre Assyriologique Internationale Held at the Oriental Institute of the University of Chicago July 18–22, 2005*, 49–56. *Studies in Ancient Oriental Civilization* 62. Chicago: Oriental Institute of the University of Chicago.

Gadd, C. 1921 *The Early Dynasties of Sumer and Akkad.* London: Luzac.

————1929 *History and Monuments of Ur.* London: Chatto and Windus.

————1940 "Tablets from Chagar Bazar and Tall Brak, 1937–38," *Iraq* 7: 22–66.

————1971 "The Dynasty of Agade and the Gutian Invasion," in *The Cambridge Ancient History*, third edition I/2, 417–63. Cambridge: Cambridge University Press.

Gadotti, A. 2010 "The Nar and Gala in Sumerian Literary Texts," in R. Pruzsinszky and D. Shehata, eds., *Musiker und Tradierung. Studien zur Rolle von Musikern bei der Verschriftlichung und Tradierung von literarischen Werken*, 51–65. *Wiener Offene Orientalisk* 8. Vienna: Lit.

Galter, H. 1983 *Gott Ea/Enki in der akkadischen Überlieferung: eine Bestandaufnahme des vorhandenen Materials*. Graz: Verlag der Technische Universität Graz.

——1995 "Cuneiform Bilingual Royal Inscriptions," *Israel Oriental Studies* 15: 25–50.

——1996 "Gott, König, Vaterland. Orthographisches zu Aššur in altassyrischer Zeit," *Wiener Zeitschrift für die Kunde des Morgenlandes* 86: 127–41.

——2006 "Sargon der Zweite: Über die Wiedereinsetzung von Geschichte," in R. Rollinger, ed., *Altertum und Mittelmeerraum: die Antike Welt diesseits und jenseits der Levante, Festschrift für Peter W. Haider zum 60. Geburtstag*, 279–302. *Oriens et Occidens* 12. Stuttgart: Steiner.

——2014 "Sargon II. und die Eroberung der Welt," in H. Neumnn, R. Dittmann, S. Paulus, G. Neumann, and A. Schuster-Brandis, eds., *Krieg und Frieden im Alten Vorderasien, 52e Rencontre Assyriologique Internationale International Congress of Assyriology and Near Eastern Archaeology Münster, 17–21. Juli 2006*, 329–43. *Alter Orient und Altes Testament* 401. Münster: Ugarit-Verlag.

Garelli, P. 1982 "Akkad," in *Le Proche-Orient Antique des origines aux invasions des peuples de la mer*, 82–96. *Nouvelle Clio* 2, second edition. Paris: Presses Universitaires de France.

Garfinkle, S. 2010 "Merchants and State Formation in Early Mesopotamia," in S. Melville and A. Slotsky, eds., *Opening the Tablet Box, Near Eastern Studies in Honor of Benjamin R. Foster*, 185–202. Leiden: Brill.

——2013 "Ancient Near Eastern City-States," in P. Bang and W. Scheidel, eds., *The Oxford Handbook of the State in the Ancient Near East and Mediterranean*, 94–119. Oxford: Oxford University Press.

Gehler, M. and R. Rollinger, eds. 2014 *Imperien und Reiche in der Weltgeschichte, Epochenübergreifende und globalhistorische Vergleiche*. Wiesbaden: Harrassowitz.

Gelb, I. 1944 *Hurrians and Subarians. Studies in Ancient Oriental Civilizations* 22. Chicago: Oriental Institute of the University of Chicago.

——1949 "The Date of the Cruciform Monument of Maništušu," *Journal of Near Eastern Studies* 8: 346–48.

——1952a *Sargonic Texts from the Diyala Region. Materials for the Assyrian Dictionary* 1. Chicago: University of Chicago Press.

——1952b *Old Akkadian Writing and Grammar. Materials for the Assyrian Dictionary* 2. Chicago: University of Chicago Press.

——1955 *Old Akkadian Inscriptions in the Chicago Natural History Museum, Texts of Legal and Business Interest. Fieldiana: Anthropology* 44/2. Chicago: Natural History Museum.

——1957 *Glossary of Old Akkadian, Materials for the Assyrian Dictionary* 3. Chicago: University of Chicago Press.

——1959 "Hurrians at Nippur in the Sargonic Period," in R. Kienle, A. Moortgat, H. Otten, E. von Schuler, and W. Zaumseil, eds., *Festschrift Johannes Friedrich zum 65. Geburtstag am 27. August 1958 gewidmet*, 183–94. Heidelberg: C. Winter.

——1960 "Sumerians and Akkadians in Their Ethno-linguistic Relationship," in E. Sollberger, ed., *Aspects du contact suméro-akkadien*, 258–71. *IXᵉ Rencontre Assyriologique Internationale, Genève, 20–23 juin 1960, Genava NS 8*, 241–58. Geneva: Musée d'Art et d'Histoire.

——1961 *Old Akkadian Writing and Grammar*, second edition. *Materials for the Assyrian Dictionary* 2. Chicago: University of Chicago Press.

——1964 "Social Stratification in the Old Akkadian Period," *Proceedings of the 25th International Congress of Orientalists*, 1: 225–26. Moscow: Izdavitelstvo Vostočnoi Literatury.

————1965 "The Ancient Mesopotamian Ration System," *Journal of Near Eastern Studies* 24: 230–43.

————1970a *Sargonic Texts in the Louvre Museum. Materials for the Akkadian Dictionary* 4. Chicago: University of Chicago Press.

————1970b *Sargonic Texts in the Ashmolean Museum, Oxford. Materials for the Assyrian Dictionary* 5. Chicago: University of Chicago Press.

————1970c "From Freedom to Slavery," in D. O. Edzard, ed., *Gesellschaftsklassen im Alten Zweistromland und in den angrenzenden Gebieten–XVIII. Rencontre assyriologique internationale, München, 29. Juni bis 3. Juli 1970*, 81–92. *Abhandlungen der Bayerischen Akademie der Wissenschaften, Philosophisch-historische Klasse* NF 75. Munich: Beck.

————1973 "Prisoners of War in Early Mesopotamia," *Journal of Near Eastern Studies* 32: 70–98.

————1975 "Homo ludens in Early Mesopotamia," *Studia Orientalia* 41: 43–76.

————1976 "Quantitative Evaluation of Slavery and Serfdom," in B. Eichler, ed., *Kramer Anniversary Volume*, 195–208. *Alter Orient und Altes Testament* 25. Neukirchen-Vluyn: Neukirchener Verlag.

————1977 *Thoughts about Ibla. Syro-Mesopotamian Studies* 1/1. Malibu: Undena Publications.

————1979 "Household and Family in Early Mesopotamia," in E. Lipinski, ed., *State and Temple Economy in the Ancient Near East* 1, 1–97. *Orientalia Lovaniensia Analecta* 5. Leuven: Peeters.

————1981 "Ebla and the Kish Civilization," in L. Cagni, ed., *La Lingua di Ebla, Atti del Convegno Internazionale (Napoli, 21–23 aprile 1980)*, 9–73. Seminario di Studi Asiatici, Series Minor 14. Naples: Istituto Universitario Orientale.

————1982 "Terms for Slaves in Ancient Meopotamia," in M. Dandamayev, I. Gershevitch, H. Klengel, G. Komoróczy, M. Larsen, and N. Postgate, eds., *Societies and Languages of the Ancient Near East: Studies in Honour of I. M. Diakonoff*, 81–98. Warminster: Aris & Phillips.

————1986 "Ebla and Lagash," in H. Weiss, ed., *The Origins of Cities in Dry-Farming Syria and Mesopotamia in the Third Millennium B.C.*, 157–67. Guilford, Conn.: Four Quarters.

————1992 "Mari and the Kish Civilization," in G. Young, ed., *Mari in Retrospect: Fifty Years of Mari and Mari Studies*, 121–202. Winona Lake, Ind.: Eisenbrauns.

Gelb, I. and B. Kienast 1990 *Die altakkadischen Königsinschriften des dritten Jahrtausends v. Chr. Freiburger Altorientalische Studien* 7. Stuttgart: Steiner.

Gelb, I. and E. Sollberger 1957 "The First Legal Document from the Later Old Assyrian Period," *Journal of Near Eastern Studies* 16: 163–75.

Gelb, I., P. Steinkeller, and R. Whiting, 1991 *Earliest Land Tenure Systems in the Near East: Ancient Kudurrus. Oriental Institute Publications* 104. Chicago: Oriental Institute of the University of Chicago.

Geller, M. 1980 "A Middle Assyrian Tablet of *utukkū lemnūtu*, Tablet 12," *Iraq* 42: 23–51.

————1985 "Notes on Lugale," *Bulletin of the School of Oriental and African Studies* 48: 215–23.

George, A. 1997 "Sumerian tiru = 'eunuch,'" *NABU* 1997/97.

————2003 *The Babylonian Gilgamesh Epic: Introduction, Critical Edition and Cuneiform Texts.* Oxford: Oxford University Press.

————2005 "In Search of the é.dub.ba.a: The Ancient Mesopotamian School in Literature and Reality," in Y. Sefati, P. Artzi, C. Cohen, B. Eichler, and V. Hurowitz, eds., *"An Experienced Scribe Who Neglects Nothing": Ancient Near Eastern Studies in Honor of Jacob Klein*, 127–37. Bethesda, Md.: CDL Press.

————2007a "Babylonian and Assyrian: A History of Akkadian," in J. N. Postgate, ed., *Languages of Iraq, Ancient and Modern*, 31–71. London: British School of Archaeology in Iraq.

————2007b "The Civilizing of Ea-Enkidu: An Unusual Tablet of the Babylonian Gilgameš Epic," *Revue d'Assyriologie* 101: 59–80.

————, ed. 2011 *Cuneiform Royal Inscriptions and Related Texts in the Schøyen Collection, Cornell University Studies in Assyriology and Sumerology* 17. Bethesda, Md.: CDL Press.

Gibson, M. 1972a *The City and Area of Kish.* Coconut Grove, Fla.: Field Research Projects.

————1972b "Umm el-Jir, A Town in Akkad," *Journal of Near Eastern Studies* 31: 237–94.

————1976/80 "Kiš B," *Reallexikon der Assyriologie* 5: 613–20.

————, ed., 1981a *Uch Tepe I, Tell Razuk, Tell Ahmed al-Mughir, Tell Ajamat.* Chicago and Copenhagen: Oriental Institute, Institute of Assyriology, Institute of Classical and Near Eastern Archaeology.

————1981b "Pottery of the Himrin and Diyala," *Sumer* 40: 93–94.

————1982 "A Re-evaluation of the Akkad Period in the Diyala Region on the Basis of Recent Excavations at Nippur and in the Hamrin," *American Journal of Archaeology* 86: 531–38.

————2011 "The Diyala Sequence: Flawed at Birth," in P. Miglus and S. Mühl, eds., *Between the Cultures: The Central Tigris Region from the 3rd to the 1st Millennium* BC, Conference at *Heidelberg January 22nd–24th, 2009*, 59–84. Heidelberger Studien zum Alten Orient 14. Heidelberg: Heidelberger Orientverlag.

Gibson, M. and A. McMahon 1995 "Investigation of the Early Dynastic-Akkadian Transition: Report of the 18th and 19th Seasons of Excavation in Area WF, Nippur," *Iraq* 57: 1–39.

————1997 "The Early Dynastic-Akkadian Transition, Part 2," *Iraq* 59: 9–14.

Glassner, J.-J. 1983 "Narām-Sîn poliorcète, Les avatars d'une sentence divinatoire," *Revue d'Assyriologie* 77: 3–10.

————1984a "Pour un lexique des termes et figures analogiques en usage dans la divination mésopotamienne," *Journal Asiatique* 272: 15–43.

————1984b "La division quinaire de la terre," *Akkadica* 40: 17–34.

————1985a "Aspects du don, de l'échange et formes d'appropriation du sol dans la Mésopotamie du III<sup>e</sup> millénaire, avant la fondation de l'empire d'Ur," *Journal Asiatique* 273: 11–59.

————1985b "Sargon 'roi du combat,'" *Revue d'Assyriologie* 79: 115–26.

————1986 *La Chute d'Akkadé, l'événement et sa mémoire.* Berliner Beiträge zum Vorderen Orient 5. Berlin: Reimer.

————1988 "Le récit autobiographique de Sargon," *Revue d'Assyriologie* 82: 1–11.

————1989 "Mesopotamian Textual Evidence on Magan/Makan in the Late 3rd Millennium B.C.," in P. Costa and M. Tosi, eds., *Oman Studies, Papers on the Archaeology and History of Oman*, 181–91. Serie Orientale Roma 63. Rome: Istituto Italiano per il Medio ed Extremo Oriente.

————1993/7 "Mundschenk," *Reallexikon der Assyriologie* 8: 420–22.

————1994a "La fin d'Akkadé: approche chronologique," NABU 1994/9.

————1994b "La chute de l'Empire d'Akkadé, les volcans d'Anatolie et la desertification de la vallée du Habur," *Les Nouvelles de l'Archéologie* 56: 49–51.

————1995 "La gestion de la terre en Mésopotamie selon le témoinage des kudurrus anciens," *Journal Asiatique* 52: 5–24.

————1996a "From Sumer to Babylon: Families as Landowners and Families as Rulers," in A. Burguière, ed., *A History of the Family. Volume One: Distant Worlds, Ancient Worlds*, 92–127. Cambridge: Polity Press.

————1996b "Les temps de l'histoire en Mésopotamie," in A. de Pury, T. Römer, and J.-D. Macchi, eds., *Israël construit son histoire, l'historiographie deutéronomiste à la lumière des recherches récentes*, 167–89. Geneva: Droz.

————2000 "Questions mésopotamiennes à propos de l'esclavage," *Revue Droit et Cultures* 39: 39–57.

————2001 "Peut-on parler de monnaie en Mésopotamie au IIIe millénaire avant notre ère?" in A. Testart, ed., *Aux origines de la monnaie*, 61–71. Paris: Errance.

————2004 *Mesopotamian Chronicles. Writings from the Ancient World* 19. Atlanta, Ga.: Society of Biblical Literature.

————2005a "La date de la composition de la chronique de la monarchie une," in Y. Sefati, P. Artzi, C. Cohen, B. Eichler, and V. Hurowitz, eds., *"An Experienced Scribe Who Neglects Nothing": Ancient Near Eastern Studies in Honor of Jacob Klein*, 138–41. Bethesda, Md.: CDL Press.

————2005b "L'onomastique de Marhashi," NABU 2005/13.

————2009a "En-hedu-Ana, une femme auteur en pays de Sumer, au 3e millénaire," *Topoi* Supplément 10: 219–31.

————2009b "Ecrire des livres à l'époque paléo-babylonienne: le traité d'extispicine," *Zeitschrift für Assyriologie* 99: 1–81.

Godecken, K. 1973 "Bemerkungen zur Göttin Annunitum," *Ugarit-Forschungen* 5: 141–62.

Goetze, A. 1947 "Historical Allusions in Old Babylonian Omen Texts," *Journal of Cuneiform Studies* 1: 253–65.

————1948 "Umma Texts Concerning Reed Mats," *Journal of Cuneiform Studies* 2: 165–202.

————1965 "Tavern Keepers and the Like in Ancient Babylonia," in H. Güterbock and T. Jacobsen, eds., *Studies in Honor of Benno Landsberger on His Seventy-fifth Birthday April 21, 1965*, 211–15. Assyriological Studies 16. Chicago: University of Chicago Press.

Goodspeed, G. 1902 *A History of the Babylonians and Assyrians.* New York: Charles Scribner's Sons.

Goosens, G. 1948 "Les recherches historiques à l'époque néo-babylonienne," *Revue d'Assyriologie* 42: 149–59.

Grandjean, C., C. Hugoniot, and B. Lion, eds., 2013 *Le banquet du monarque dans le monde antique.* Tours: Presses Universitaires François-Rabelais.

Grayson, A. 1966 "Divination and the Babylonian Chronicles: A Study of the Role which Divination Plays in Ancient Mesopotamian Chronography," in *La Divination en Mésopotamie ancienne et dans les regions voisines, XIV$^e$ Rencontre Assyriologique Internationale (Strasbourg, 2–6 juillet 1965)*, 69–76. Paris: Presses Universitaires de France.

————1972 *Assyrian Royal Inscriptions* 1. Wiesbaden: Harrassowitz.

————1974/7 "The Empire of Sargon of Akkad," *Archiv für Orientforschung* 25: 56–64.

————1975 *Assyrian and Babylonian Chronicles. Texts from Cuneiform Sources* 5. Locust Valley, N.Y.: J.J. Augustin.

————1980 "Assyria and Babylonia," *Orientalia* NS 49: 140–94.

————1987 *Assyrian Rulers of the Third and Second Millennia* BC *(to 1115* BC), *Royal Inscriptions of Mesopotamia, Assyrian Periods* 1. Toronto: University of Toronto Press.

————1991 "Assyria: Tiglath-Pileser III to Sargon II (744–705 B.C.)," and "Assyria: Sennacherib and Esarhaddon (704–669 B.C.)," *Cambridge Ancient History*, third edition, 71–141. Cambridge: Cambridge University Press.

Groneberg, B. 1990 "Zu den mesopotamischen Unterweltsvorstellungen: Das Jenseits als Fortsetzung des Diesseits," *Altorientalische Forschungen* 17: 224–61.

————1999 "'Brust' (*irtum*)-Gesänge," *Munuscula Mesopotamica, Festschrift für Johannes Renger. Alter Orient und Altes Testament* 267: 169–95. Münster: Ugarit-Verlag.

Guichard, M. 1993 "Les 'lahmû' de Mari," NABU 1993/118.

Guinan, A. 2002 "A Severed Head Laughed: Stories of Divinatory Interpretation," in L. Ciraolo and J. Seidel, eds., *Magic and Divination in the Ancient World*, 7–40. *Ancient Magic and Divination* 2. Leiden: Brill.

384    *Bibliography*

Gurney, O. 1969 "A List of Copper Objects," *Iraq* 31: 3–7.

———2003 "The Upper Land, *mātum elītum*," in G. Beckman, R. Beal, and G. McMahon, eds., *Studies in Honor of Harry A. Hoffner Jr. on the Occasion of His 65th Birthday*, 119–26. Winona Lake, Ind.: Eisenbrauns.

Gut, R., J. Reade, and R. Boehmer 2001 "Nineve—Das späte 3. Jahrtausend v. Chr.," in J. Meyer, M. Novák, and A. Pruss, eds., *Beiträge zur vorderasiatischen Archäologie Winfried Orthmann gewidmet*, 74–92. Frankfurt: Johann Wolfgang Goethe-Universität, Archäologisches Institut, Archäologie und Kulturgeschichte der Vorderen Orient.

Güterbock, H. 1934/38 "Die historische Tradition und ihre Gestaltung bei Babyloniern und Hethitern bis 1200," *Zeitschrift für Assyriologie* 42: 1–91; 44: 45–149.

———1954 "The Hurrian Element in the Hittite Empire," *Cahiers d'Histoire Mondiale* 2: 383–94.

———1964 "Sargon of Akkad Mentioned by Hattušili I of Hatti," *Journal of Cuneiform Studies* 18: 1–6.

Hackman, G. and F. Stephens, 1958 *Sumerian and Akkadian Administrative Texts from Predynastic Times to the End of the Akkad Dynasty. Babylonian Inscriptions in the Collection of J. B. Nies* 8. New Haven: Yale University Press.

Hall, H. 1913 *The Ancient History of the Near East from the Earliest Times to the Battle of Salamis.* London: Methuen.

Hallager, E. 1985 *Master Impression: A Clay Sealing from the Greek-Swedish Excavations at Kastelli, Khania.* Göteborg: Paul Åströms Förlag.

Hallo, W. 1957/71 "Gutium," *Reallexikon der Assyriologie* 3: 709–20.

———1959 "Money and Merchants in Ur III," *Hebrew Union College Annual* 30: 103–39. With J. B. Curtis.

———1960 "A Sumerian Amphictyony," *Journal of Cuneiform Studies* 14: 88–114.

———1963 "Lexical Notes on the Neo-Sumerian Metal Industry," *Bibliotheca Orientalis* 20: 136–42.

———1964 "The Road to Emar," *Journal of Cuneiform Studies* 18: 57–88.

———1972 "The House of Ur-Meme," *Journal of Near Eastern Studies* 31: 87–95.

———1978/80 "Simurrum and the Hurrian Frontier," *Revue Hittite et Asianique* 36: 71–83.

———1980 "Royal Titles from the Mesopotamian Periphery," *Anatolian Studies* 30: 189–95.

———1981 "Letters, Prayers, and Letter-Prayers," in *Proceedings of the Seventh World Congress of Jewish Studies, Studies in the Bible and the Ancient Near East* , 17–27. Jerusalem: Magnes Press.

———1983 "Cult Statue and Divine Image: A Preliminary Study," in W. Hallo, J. Moyer, and L. Purdue, eds., *Scripture in Context II: More Essays on the Comparative Method*, 1–17. Winona Lake, Ind.: Eisenbrauns.

———1985 "Back to the Big House: Colloquial Sumerian, Continued," *Orientalia* NS 54: 56–64.

———1991 "The Death of Kings: Traditional Historiography in Historical Perspective," in M. Cogan and I. Eph'al, eds., *Ah Assyria! ...: Studies in Assyrian History and Ancient Near Eastern Historiography Presented to Hayim Tadmor*, 148–65. *Scripta Hierosolymitana* 33. Jerusalem: Magnes Press.

———1996a "Bilingualism and the Beginnings of Translation," in M. Fox, V. Hurowitz, A. Hurvitz, M. Klein, B. Schwartz, and N. Shupak, eds., *Texts, Temples, and Traditions, A Tribute to Menahem Harran*, pp. 345–57. Winona Lake, Ind.: Eisenbrauns.

———1996b "Notes on Neo-Sumerian Animal Husbandry," in Ö. Tunca and D. Deheselle, eds., *Tablettes et images aux pays de Sumer et Akkad, Mélanges offerts à Monsieur H. Limet*, 69–78. Leuven: Peeters.

Hallo, W., ed. 1997 *The Context of Scripture 1: Canonical Compositions from the Biblical World.* Leiden: Brill.

————1998 "New Directions in Historiography (Mesopotamia and Israel)," in M. Dietrich, O. Loretz, and T. Balke, eds., *dubsar anta-men, Studien zur Altorientalistik, Festschrift für Willem H. Ph. Römer zur Vollendung seines 70. Lebensjahres mit Beiträgen von Freunden, Schülern und Kollegen,* 109–28. *Alter Orient und Altes Testament* 253. Münster: Ugarit-Verlag.

————1999 "'They Requested Him as God of Their City': A Classical Moment in the Mesopotamian Experience," in G. Holst-Warhaft and D. McCann, ed., *The Classical Moment: Views from Seven Literatures,* 23–35. Lanham, Md.: Rowan & Littlefield.

————2005 "New Light on the Gutians," in W. Van Soldt, ed., *Ethnicity in Ancient Mesopotamia, Papers Read at the 48th Rencontre Assyriologique Internationale Leiden 1–4 July 2002*: 147–61. *Publications de l'Institut historique-archéologique néerlandais de Stamboul* 102. Leiden: Nederlands Instituut voor het Nabije Oosten.

————2006 "Another Ancient Antiquary," in A. Guinan, M. de J. Ellis, S. Freedman, M. Rutz, L. Sassmannshausen, S. Tinney, and M. Waters, eds., *If a Man Builds a Joyful House: Assyriological Studies in Honor of Erle Verdun Leichty,* 187–96. *Cuneiform Monographs* 31. Leiden: Brill.

Hallo, W. and J. Van Dijk 1968 *The Exaltation of Inanna. Yale Near Eastern Researches* 3. New Haven: Yale University Press.

Hamoto, A. 1995 *Der Affe in der altorientalischen Kunst. Forschungen zur Anthropologie und Religionsgeschichte* 28. Münster: Ugarit-Verlag.

Hansen, D. 2002 "Through the Love of Ishtar," in L. Al-Gailani Werr, J. Curtis, H. Martin, A. McMahon, J. Oates, and J. Reade, eds., *Of Pots and Plans: Papers on the Archaeology and History of Mesopotamia and Syria Presented to David Oates in Honour of His 75th Birthday,* 91–112. London: NABU.

————2003 "Art of the Akkadian Dynasty," in J. Aruz and R. Wallenfels, eds. *Art of the First Cities: The Third Millennium B.C. from the Mediterranean to the Indus,* 189–98. New York: Metropolitan Museum of Art.

Harper, P., E. Klengel-Brant, J. Aruz, and K. Benzel 1995 *Discoveries at Ashur on the Tigris: Antiquities in the Vorderasiatisches Museum.* New York: Metropolitan Museum of Art.

Harrak, A. 1988 "La tête en pierre trouvée à Assur," *Akkadica* 58: 27–32.

Harris, R. 1991 "Inanna-Ishtar as Paradox and a Coincidence of Opposites." *History of Religions* 30: 261–78.

Haul, M. 2009 *Stele und Legende, Untersuchungen zu den keilschriftlichen Erzählwerken über die Könige von Akkade. Göttinger Beiträge zum Alten Orient* 4. Göttingen: Universitätsverlag Göttingen.

Hauptmann, H. and F. Pernicka, eds. 2004 *Die Metallindustrie Mesopotamiens von den Anfängen bis zum 2. Jahrtausend v. Chr., Orient-Archäologie* 3. Rahden/Westf.: Verlag Marie Leidorf.

Haussperger, M. 2003 *Die Einführungsszene, Entwicklung eines mesopotamischen Motivs von der altakkadischen bis zum Ende der altbabylonischen Zeit. Münchener Vorderasiatische Studien* 11. Munich: Profil.

Hawkins, D. 2007 "Hurrian," in J N. Postgate, ed., *Languages of Iraq, Ancient and Modern,* 72–84. London: British School of Archaeology in Iraq.

Heermann, J. and I. Sellnow, eds. 1982 *Produktivkräfte und Gesellschaftsformationen in vorkapitalistischer Zeit.* Berlin: Akademie-Verlag.

Herrmann, G. and P. Moorey 1980/83 "Lapislazuli B.," *Reallexikon der Assyriologie* 6: 489–92.

Heimpel, W. 1972/75 "Hirsch," *Reallexikon der Assyriologie* 4: 418–21.

————1974 "Sumerische und akkadische Personennamen in Sumer und Akkad," *Archiv für Orientforschung* 25: 171–4.

————1982 "A First Step in the Diorite Question," *Revue d'Assyriologie* 76: 65–7.

————1986 "The Sun at Night and the Doors of Heaven in Babylonian Texts," *Journal of Cuneiform Studies* 38: 127–51.

————1987 "Das untere Meer," *Zeitschrift für Assyriologie* 77: 22–91.

————1987/90a "Libation," *Reallexikon der Assyriologie* 7: 1–5.

————1987/90b "Magan," *Reallexikon der Assyriologie* 7: 195–9.

————1993/97 "Meluhha," *Reallexikon der Assyriologie* 8: 53–5.

————1998a "Anthropomorphic and Bovine Lahmus," in M. Dietrich, O. Loretz, and T. Balke, eds., *dubsar anta-men, Studien zur Altorientalistik, Festschrift für Willem H. Ph. Römer zur Vollendung seines 70. Lebensjahres mit Beiträgen von Freunden, Schülern und Kollegen*, 129–56. *Alter Orient und Altes Testament* 253. Münster: Ugarit-Verlag.

————1998b "A Circumambulation Rite," *Acta Sumerologica* 20: 13–16.

————2011 "Twenty-eight Trees Growing in Sumer," in D. Owen, ed., *Garšana Studies, Cornell University Studies in Assyriology and Sumerology* 6: 75–152. Bethesda, Md.: CDL Press.

Heimpel, W. and M. Liverani 1991 "Observations on Livestock Management in Babylonia," *Acta Sumerologica* 17: 127–44.

Heinrich, E. 1974 "Viertes vorläufige Bericht über die von der Deutschen Orient-Gesellschaft mit Mitteln der Stiftung Volkswagenwerk in Habuba Kabira … und in Mumbaqat … Ausgrabungen," *Mitteilungen der Deutschen Orient-Gesellschaft* 106: 5–52.

————1982 *Die Tempel und Heiligtümer im alten Mesopotamien: Typologie, Morphologie und Geschichte.* Deutsches Archäologisches Institut, *Denkmäler Antiker Architektur* 14. Berlin: De Gruyter.

————1984 *Die Paläste im alten Mesopotamien.* Deutsches Archäologisches Institut, *Denkmäler Antiker Architektur* 15. Berlin: De Gruyter.

Heinz, M. 1989 "Die Steingefäße aus Süd-und Mittelmesopotamien als Inschriftenträger der Frühdynastischen Zeit," *Baghdader Mitteilungen* 20: 197–224.

————2007 "Sargon of Akkad: Rebel and Ursurper in Kish," in M. Heinz and M. Feldman, eds., *Representations of Political Power: Case Histories from Times of Change and Dissolving Order in the Ancient Near East*, 67–86. Winona Lake, Ind.: Eisenbrauns.

Hetzron, R. 1997 *The Semitic Languages.* New York: Routledge.

Heuzey, L. 1893 "Le nom d'Agadé sur un monument de Sirpourla," *Revue d'Assyriologie* 3: 113–17.

————1897 "Sceaux inédits des rois d'Agadé," *Revue d'Assriologie* 4: 1–12.

Hilprecht, H. 1893 *Old Babylonian Inscriptions, chiefly from Nippur. The Babylonian Expedition of the University of Pennsylvania, Series A: Cuneiform Texts* 1 = *Transactions of the American Philosophical Society* NS 18 No. 1. Philadelphia: D. Anson Partridge.

Hinz, W. 1967 "Elams Vertrag mit Narām-Sîn von Akkade," *Zeitschrift für Assyriologie* 58: 66–96.

Hirsch, H. 1961 *Untersuchungen zur altassyrischen Religion. Archiv für Orientforschung Beiheft* 13/14. Graz.

————1963 "Die Inschriften der Könige von Agade," *Archiv für Orientforschung* 20: 1–82.

————1967 "Die 'Sünde' Lugalzagesis," *Festschrift für Wilhelm Eilers, Ein Dokument der internationalischen Forschung zum 27. September 1966*, 99–106. Wiesbaden: Harrassowitz.

Hockmann, D. 2010. *Gräber und Grüfte in Assur I, Von den zweiten Hälfte des 3. bis zur Mitte des 2. Jahrtausends v. Chr. Wissenschaftliche Veröffentlichungen der Deutschen Orient-Gesellschaft* 129. Wiesbaden: Harrassowitz.

Hommel, F. 1885 *Geschichte Babyloniens und Assyriens.* Berlin: G. Grote.

Hritz, C. 2004 "The Hidden Landscape of Southern Mesopotamia," *Akkadica* 125: 93–106.

Hrozny, F. 1909 "Das Problem der altbabylonischen Dynastien von Akkad und Kiš," *Wiener Zeitschrift für die Kunde des Morgenlandes* 23: 191–219.

Hruška, B. 1990 "Das Landwirtschaftliche Jahr im alten Sumer," *Bulletin on Sumerian Agriculture* 5: 105–14.

———1995 *Sumerian Agriculture: New Findings.* Preprint 26. Berlin: Max Planck-Institut für Wissenschaftsgeschichte.

Huber, P. 1987 "Dating by Lunar Eclipses with Speculations on the Birth of Omen Astrology," in J. Berggren and B. Goldstein, eds., *From Ancient Omens to Statistical Mechanics, Essays on the Exact Sciences Presented to Asger Aaboe,* 3–13. Copenhagen: University Library.

Hunger, H. 1976/80 "Kalender," *Reallexikon der Assyriologie* 5: 297–303.

———1993/7 "Mondfinsternis," *Reallexikon der Assyriologie* 8: 358–9.

———2009/11 "Sonne, Sonnenfinsternis," *Reallexikon der Assyriologie* 12: 598–9.

Hurowitz, V. 1998 *Mesopotamian Cosmic Geography.* Winona Lake, Ind.: Eisenbrauns.

Hussein, S. Y., M. Altaweel, and Z. Rejeb. 2009 "Report on Excavations at Tell al'Wilayah, Iraq. Further Information on the 1999 and 2000 Seasons," *Akkadica* 130: 3–42.

Invernizzi, A. 1992 *Dal Tigri all'Eufrate I: Sumeri i Accadi.* Florence: Le Lettere.

Jacquet, A. 2002 "Lugal-meš et *malikum*: nouvel examen du *kispum* à Mari," in D. Charpin and J.-M. Durand, eds., *Recueil d'études à la mémoire d'André Parrot,* 51–68. *Mémoires de NABU* 7, *Florilegium Marianum* 6. Paris: SEPOA.

Jacobsen, T. 1939 *The Sumerian King List. Assyriological Studies* 11. Chicago: Oriental Institute of the University of Chicago.

———1943 "Primitive Democracy in Ancient Mesopotamia," *Journal of Near Eastern Studies* 2: 159–72.

———1957 "Early Political Development in Mesopotamia," *Zeitschrift für Assyriologie* 52: 91–140.

———1978 "Iphur-Kish and His Times," *Archiv für Orientforschung* 26: 1–14.

———1991 "The Term ensí," in P. Michalowski, P. Steinkeller, E. Stone, and R. Zettler, eds., *Velles Parules, Ancient Near Eastern Studies in Honor of Miguel Civil on the Occasion of his Sixty-fifth Birthday,* 113–22, *Aula Orientalis* 9.

Jahn, B. 2007 "The Migration and Sedentarization of the Amorites from the Point of View of the Settled Babylonian Population," in M. Heinz and M. Feldman, eds., *Representations of Political Power: Case Histories from Times of Change and Dissolving Order in the Ancient Near East,* 193–209. Winona Lake, Ind.: Eisenbrauns.

Jans, G. and J. Breetschneider, with W. Sallaberger 1998 "Wagon and Chariot Representations in the Early Dynastic Glyptic. 'They Came to Tell Beydar with Wagon and Equid,'" in M. Lebeau, ed., *About Subartu, Studies Devoted to Upper Mesopotamia,* 155–94. *Subartu* 4/2. Turnhout: Brepols.

Jaques, M. 2004 "Inanna et Ebiḫ: Nouveaux texts et remarques sur le vocabulaire du combat et de la victoire," *Zeitschrift für Assyriologie* 94: 202–25.

———2006 *Le vocabulaire des sentiments dans les textes sumériens, Recherche sur le lexique sumérien et akkadien, Alter Orient und Altes Testament* 332. Münster: Ugarit-Verlag.

Jas, R., ed. 2000 *Rainfall and Agriculture in Northern Mesopotamia (MOS Studies 3), Proceedings of the Third MOS Symposium (Leiden 1999).* Leiden: Nederlands Historisch-Archaeologisch Instituut te Istanbul.

Jastrow, M. 1915 *The Civilization of Babylonia and Assyria.* Philadelphia: J. B. Lippincott.

Jeyes, U. 1980 "The Act of Extispicy in Ancient Mesopotamia: An Outline," *Assyriological Miscellanies* 1: 13–32. Copenhagen: Institute of Assyriology.

———1989 *Old Babylonian Extispicy, Omen Texts in the British Museum. Publications de l'Institut historique-archéologique néerlandais de Stamboul* 64. Leiden: Nederlands Historisch-Archaeologish Instituut te Istanbul.

Joannès, F. 1988 "Un lettré néo-babylonien," NABU 1988/55.

Joannès, F. and J.-M. Durand 1988 "Contrat néo-babylonien d'Agadé," NABU 1988/74.

Jonker, G. 1995 *The Topography of Remembrance: The Dead, Tradition, and Collective Memory in Mesopotamia.* Leiden: Brill.

Jursa, M. 1996 "Akkad, das Eulmash und Gubāru," *Wiener Zeitschrift für die Kunde des Morgenlandes* 86: 197–211.

———1997 "Nochmals Akkad," *Wiener Zeitschrift für die Kunde des Morgenlandes* 87: 101–10.

———2003/5 "Parfüm(rezepte) A.," *Reallexikon der Assyriologie* 10: 335–6.

———2006/8 "Räucherung," *Reallexikon der Assyriologie* 11: 225–9.

———2010 *Aspects of the Economic History of Babylonia in the First Millennium* BC: *Economic Geography, Economic Mentalities, Agriculture, the Use of Money and the Problem of Economic Growth, with Contributions by J. Hackl, B. Janković, K. Kleber, E. Payne, C. Waerzeggers and M. Weszeli. Alter Orient und Altes Testament* 377. Münster: Ugarit-Verlag.

Kalla, G. 2009/11 "Sippar. A.1," *Reallexikon der Assyriologie* 12: 528–33.

Kammenhuber, A. 1976 "Historisch-geographische Nachrichten aus der althurritischen Überlieferung, dem altelamischen und den Inschriften der Könige von Akkad für die Zeit vor dem Einfall der Gutäer (ca. 2200/2136)," in J. Harmatta and G. Komoróczy, eds., *Wirtschaft und Gesellschaft im alten Vorderasien*, 157–247. Budapest: Akadémiai Kiadó.

Kantor, H. 1966 "Landscape in Akkadian Art," *Journal of Near Eastern Studies* 25: 145–52.

Katz, D. 1993 *Gilgamesh and Akka.* Groningen: Styx.

———2003 *The Image of the Netherworld in the Sumerian Sources.* Bethesda, Md.: CDL Press.

Keetman, J. 2008 "Schrift und Phoneme im Reichsakkadischen," *Journal of Cuneiform Studies* 60: 101–15.

———2014 "Bilingualismus in Sumer: zum Gebrauch des Akkadischen und Sumerischen in der Verwaltungspraxis des Reiches von Akkad unter Narām-Sujēn und Šar-kali-šarrī," *Revue d'Assyriologie* 108: 1–14.

Kennedy, D. 1969 "Realia," *Revue d'Assyriologie* 63: 79–82.

Kienast, B. 1973 "Der Weg zur Einheit Babyloniens unter staatsrechtlichen Aspekten," *Orientalia* NS 42: 489–501.

———1990 "Narāmsîn mut ᵈINANNA," *Orientalia* NS 59: 196–203.

Kienast, B. and K. Volk 1995 *Die sumerischen und akkadischen Briefe des III. Jahrtausends aus der Zeit vor der III. Dynastie von Ur. Freiburger Altorientalische Studien* 7. Stuttgart: Steiner.

Kienast, B. and W. Sommerfeld 1994 *Glossar zu den altakkadischen Königsinschriften. Freiburger Altorientalische Studien* 8. Stuttgart: Steiner.

Kilmer, A. 1980/3 "Leier A.," *Reallexikon er Assyriologie* 6: 572–76.

———1987 "The Brick of Birth," *Journal of Near Eastern Studies* 46: 211–13.

———1993/7 "Musik A.I," *Reallexikon der Assyriologie* 8: 463–82.

King, L. 1896 *Cuneiform Texts from Babylonian Tablets in the British Museum* 1. London: British Museum.

———1907 *Chronicles Concerning Early Babylonian Kings, Containing Records of the Early History of the Kassites and the Country of the Sea.* London: Luzac.

———1908 "Shar-gani-sharri, King of Akkad," *Proceedings of the Society of Biblical Archaeology* 30: 238–42.

———1910 *A History of Sumer and Akkad: An Account of Early Races of Babylonia from Prehistoric Times to the Foundation of the Babylonian Monarchy.* London: Chatto and Windus, new printings 1916 and 1923.

Kitz, A. 2014 *Cursed are You! The Phenomenology of Cursing in Cuneiform and Hebrew Texts.* Winona Lake, Ind.: Eisenbrauns.

Klein, H. 1992 *Untersuchung zur Typologie bronzezeitlicher Nadel in Mesopotamien und Syrien.* *Schriften zur Vorderasiatischen Archäologie* 4. Saarbrücken: Saarbrücker Druckerei und Verlag.

Klein, J. 1976 Šulgi and Gilgameš: The Two Brother-Peers," in B. Eichler, ed., *Kramer Anniversary Volume: Cuneiform Studies in Honor of Samuel Noah Kramer,* 271–92. *Alter Orient und Altes Testament* 25. Neukirchen-Vluyn: Neukirchener Verlag.

——1997 "The God Martu in Sumerian Literature," in I. Finkel and M. Geller, eds., *Sumerian Gods and Their Representations,* 99–116. *Cuneiform Monographs* 7. Groningen: Styx.

——2014 "From Agade to Samaria: The Inflationary Price of Barley in Situations of Famine," in Z. Csabai, ed., *Studies in Economic and Social History of the Ancient Near East in Memory of Péter Vargyas,* 167–80. Budapest: Department of Ancient History, The University of Pécs l'Harmattan, 2014.

Kleinerman, A. 2011a *Education in Early 2nd Millennium* BC *Mesopotamia: The Sumerian Epistolary Miscellany. Cuneiform Monographs* 42. Leiden: Brill.

——2011b "Craft Production at Garšana: The Leather and Textile Workshops," in D. Owen, ed., *Garšana Studies, Cornell University Studies in Assyriology and Sumerology* 6: 183–207. Bethesda, Md.: CDL Press.

——2013 "The Barbers of Iri-Sagrig," in S. Garfinkle and M. Molina, eds., *From the 21st Century* B.C. *to the 21st Century* A.D., *Proceedings of the International Conference on Neo-Sumerian Studies Held in Madrid, 22–24 July 2010,* 301–11. Winona Lake, Ind.: Eisenbrauns.

Klengel, H. 1966 "Lullubum, Ein Beitrag zur Geschichte der altvorderasiatischen Gebirgsvölker," *Mitteilungen des Instituts für Orientforschung* 11: 349–71.

——1987/90 "Lullu(bum)." *Reallexikon der Assyriologie* 7: 164–8.

——, ed. 1989 *Kulturgeschichte des alten Vorderasien.* Berlin: Akademie-Verlag.

Klengel-Brandt, E. 1993 "Die Rekonstruktion einer altakkadischen Königsstatue aus Assur," *Mitteilungen der Deutschen Orient-Gesellschaft* 125: 133–41.

——1995 "Monumental Sculpture 22: Torso of a Male Statue," in P. Harper, E. Klengel-Brandt, J. Aruz, K. Benzel, eds., *Discoveries at Ashur on the Tigris: Assyrian Origins: Antiquities in the Vorderasiatisches Museum, Berlin,* 42–3. New York: The Metropolitan Museum of Art.

Koch, U. 2005 *Secrets of Extispicy; The Chapter* Multābiltu *of the Babylonian Extispicy Series Nişirti bārūti Texts Mainly from Aššurbanipal's Library, Alter Orient und Altes Testament* 326. Münster: Ugarit-Verlag.

Köcher, F. and A. Oppenheim 1957/8 "The Old-Babylonian Text VAT 7525," *Archiv für Orientforschung* 18: 62–77.

Koch-Westenholz, U. 1995 *Mesopotamian Astrology: An Introduction to Babylonian and Assyrian Celestial Divination.* Copenhagen: Museum Tusculaneum Press.

Kogan, L. 2011 "Old Babylonian Copies of Sargonic Royal Inscriptions as Linguistic Evidence," in G. Barjamovic, J. Dahl, U. Koch, W. Sommerfeld, and J. Westenholz, eds., *Akkade is King, A Collection of Papers by Friends and Colleagues Presented to Aage Westenholz on the Occasion of His 70th Birthday 15th of May 2009,* 163–88. *Publications de l'Institut historique-archéologique néerlandais de Stamboul* 118. Leiden: Nederlands Instituut voor het Nabije Oosten.

Kolinski, R. 2007 "The Upper Khabur Region in the Second Part of the Third Millennium BC," *Altorientalische Forschungen* 34: 342–69.

Krafeld-Daugherty, M. 1994 *Wohnen im Alten Orient, Eine Untersuchung zur Verwendung von Räumen in altorientalischen Wohnhäusern. Altertumskunde des Alten Orients, Archäologische Studien zur Kultur und Geschichte des Alten Orients* 3. Münster: Ugarit-Verlag.

Kramer, C. 1982 *Village Ethnoarchaeology: Rural Iran in Archaeological Perspective.* New York: Academic Press.

Kramer, S. 1949 "Schooldays: A Sumerian Composition Relating to the Education of a Scribe," *Journal of the American Oriental Society* 69: 199–215.

Kraus, F. 1948 "Ein altakkadisches Festungsbild," *Iraq* 10: 81–92.

——1953 *The Role of Temples from the Third Dynasty of Ur to the First Dynasty of Babylon*, translated by B. R. Foster, *Monographs on the Ancient Near East* 2/4. Malibu: Undena [1990].

——1955 "Provinzen des neusumerischen Reiches von Ur," *Zeitschrift für Assyriologie* 51: 45–75.

——1963 "Altbabylonische Quellensammlungen zur altmesopotamischen Geschichte," *Archiv für Orientforschung* 20: 153–5.

——1965 *Könige, die in Zelten wohnten, Betrachtungen über den Kern der assyrischen Königsliste. Mededelingen der Koninlijke Nederlandse Akademie van Wetenschappen*, Afd. Letterkunde NR 28, No. 2.

——1966 *Staatliche Viehhaltung im altbabylonischen Lande Larsa. Mededelingen der Koninlijke Nederlandse Akademie van Wetenschappen*, Afd. Letterkunde NR 29, No. 5.

——1970 *Sumerer und Akkader, ein Problem der altmesopotamischen Geschichte. Mededelingen der Koninlijke Nederlandse Akademie van Wetenschappen*, Afd. Letterkunde NR 33, No. 8.

——1973 *Vom mesopotamischen Menschen der altbabylonische Zeit und seiner Welt. Mededelingen der Koninlijke Nederlandse Akademie van Wetenschappen*, Afd. Letterkunde NR 36, No. 6.

——1984 *Königliche Verfügungen in altbabylonischer Zeit, Studia et Documenta ad Iura Antiqui Pertinentia* 11. Leiden: Brill.

——1987 "Verstreute Omentexte aus Nippur im Istanbuler Museum," *Zeitschrift für Assyriologie* 77: 194–206.

Krebernik, M. 1987/90 "Malik," *Reallexikon der Assyriologie* 7: 305–6.

——1993/7 "Mondgott, A." *Reallexikon der Assyriologie* 8: 360–9.

——2009/11 "Sonnengott A.1," *Reallexikon der Assyriologie* 12: 599–611.

Krecher, J. 1987 "/ur/ 'Mann', und /eme/ 'Frau' und die sumerische Herkunft des Wortes urdu(-d) 'Sklave.' " *Die Welt des Orients* 18: 7–19.

——1993/7 "Miete," *Reallexikon der Assyriologie* 8: 156–62.

Krikh, S. 2012 *Obraz drevnosti v sovetskoy istoriografii*. Moscow: Krasand.

Krispijn, T. 2010 "Musical Ensembles in Ancient Mesopotamia," in R. Dumbrill and I. Finkel, eds., *Iconea 2008, Proceedings of the International Conference of Near Eastern Archaeomusicology held at the British Museum December 4, 5 and 6, 2008*, 125–50. London: Iconea.

Kuhrt, A. 1995 *The Ancient Near East c. 3000–330 BC*. London: Routledge.

Kupper, J.-R. 1971 "Les inscriptions triomphales akkadiennes," *Oriens Antiquus* 10: 91–106.

Kutscher, R. 1989 *Royal Inscriptions. The Brockmon Tablets at the University of Haifa*. Wiesbaden: Harrassowitz.

Lafont, B. 1991 "Les forgerons sumériens de la ville de Girsu," in J. des Courtils, J.-Ch. Moretti, and F. Planet, ed., *De Anatolia Antiqua I. Travaux et recherches de l'Institut Français des Etudes Anatoliennes*, 119–29. Paris: Institut Français des Etudes Anatoliennes.

——1996 "L'extraction du minerai de cuivre en Iran à la fin du IIIe millénaire," in Ö. Tunca and D. Deheselle, eds., *Tablettes et images aux pays de Sumer et Akkad, Mélanges offerts à Monsieur H. Limet*, 87–93. Leuven: Peeters.

——2001 "Relations internationales, alliances et diplomatie au temps des royaumes amorrites," *Amurru* 2: 213–327.

——2008 "L'Armée des rois d'Ur: ce qu'en disent les textes," in P. Abrahami and L. Battini, eds., *Les armées du Proche-Orient ancien (IIIe – Ier mill. av. J.-C.)*, 23–48. *BAR International Series* 1855. Oxford: Archaeopress.

Lambert, M. 1953/5 "Textes commerciaux de Lagash," *Revue d'Assyriologie* 47: 57–69, 105–20; *Archiv Orientálni* 23: 557–74.

———1956 "Epigraphie présargonique (X)," *Revue d'Assyriologie* 50: 95–100.

———1965 "La vie économique à Umma à l'époque d'Agadé," *Revue d'Assyriologie* 59: 61–72, 115–126.

———1974 "Les villes du sud-mésopotamie et de l'Iran au temps de Naram-Sin," *Oriens Antiquus* 13: 1–24.

———1975 "Mesag le prince et Mesag le shabra (la vie économique à l'époque d'Agadé)," *Rivista degli Studi Orientali* 49: 159–84.

———1979 "Le prince de Suse Ilish-mani et l'Elam de Naramsin à Ibbisin," *Journal Asiatique* 267: 11–39.

Lambert, M. and J.-M. Kientz 1967 "L'Elévage du gros bétail à Lagash au temps de Lugalanda et d'Urukagina," *Rivista degli Studi Orientali* 38: 93–117, 198–218.

Lambert, W. 1969 "A New Source for the Reign of Nabonidus," *Archiv für Orientforschung* 22: 1–8.

———1972/5 "Honig," *Reallexikon der Assyriologie* 4: 469.

———1973 "Studies in Nergal," *Bibliotheca Orientalis* 30: 355–63.

———1979 "The Training of a Seal-Cutter," *Revue d'Assyriologie* 73: 89 no. 4.

———1985 "The Pantheon of Mari," MARI 4: 525–39.

———1986 "Narām-Sin of Ešnunna or Akkad?" *Journal of the American Oriental Society* 106: 793–5.

———1988 "An Old Akkadian List of Sumerian Personal Names," in E. Leichty, M. deJ. Ellis, and P. Gerardi, eds., *A Scientific Humanist: Studies in Memory of Abraham Sachs*, 251–60. *Occasional Publications of the Samuel Noah Kramer Fund* 9. Philadelphia: University Museum of Archaeology and Anthropology.

———1990a "Addenda to W. G. Lambert, 'The Pantheon of Mari' (MARI 4 (1985) pp. 525–539)," MARI 6: 644.

———1990b "The Name of Umma," *Journal of Near Eastern Studies* 49: 75–80.

———1992 "Nippur in Ancient Ideology," in M. de J. Ellis, ed., *Nippur at the Centennial, Papers Read at the 35ᵉ Rencontre Assyriologique Internationale, Philadelphia, 1988*, 119–26. *Occasional Publications of the Samuel Noah Kramer Fund* 14. Philadelphia: University Museum of Archaeology and Anthropology.

Lambert, W. and A. Millard 1969 *Atra-Ḫasīs: The Babylonian Story of the Flood*. Oxford: Oxford University Press.

Landsberger, B. 1924 "Über die Völker Vorderasiens im dritten Jahrtausend," *Zeitschrift für Assyriologie* 35: 213–38.

———1960 "Einige unerkannt gebliebene oder verkannte Nomina des Akkadischen," *Wiener Zeitschrift für die Kunde des Morgenlandes* 56: 109–29.

———1968 "Jungfräulichket: ein Beitrag zum Thema 'Beilager und Eheschliessung'," in *Symbolae Iuridicae et Historicae Martino David Dedicatae* 1: 41–103. Leiden: Brill.

Langdon, S. 1917 *Sumerian Grammatical Texts. Publications of the Babylonian Section* 12/1. Philadelphia: University Museum.

———1921 "The Early Chronology of Sumer and Egypt, and Similarities of their Culture," *Journal of Egyptian Archaeology* 7: 133–53.

———1923a "The Dynasties of Akkad and Lagash," *The Cambridge Ancient History* second edition 1: 402–34. Cambridge: Cambridge University Press.

———1923b "The Sumerian Revival: The Empire of Ur," *The Cambridge Ancient History* second edition 1: 435–463. Cambridge: Cambridge University Press.

Larsen, M. 1987 "The Babylonian Lukewarm Mind: Reflections on Science, Divination, and Literacy," in F. Rochberg-Halton, ed., *Language, Literature, and History: Philological and Historical Studies Presented to Erica Reiner*, 203–25. *American Oriental Series* 67. New Haven: American Oriental Society.

Laufer, B. 1926 *Ostrich Egg-shell Cups of Mesopotamia and the Ostrich in Ancient and Modern Times. Anthropology Leaflet* 23. Chicago: Field Museum of Natural History.

Lebeau, M. 1985 "Rapport préliminaire sur la céramique du Bronze Ancien IVa découverte au 'palais présargonique 1' de Mari," MARI 4: 127–36.

Lecompte, C. 2014 "Mari au IIIe millénaire à l'époque des cités sumériennes," in P. Butterlin and S. Cluzan, eds., *Voués à Ishtar*, 115–28. Paris: Institut Français du Proche-Orient.

Leemans, W. F. 1972/5 "Handel," *Reallexikon der Assyriologie* 4: 76–90.

Legrain, L. 1913 "Tablettes de comptabilité, etc. de la dynastie d'Agadé," *Mémoires de la Délégation en Perse* 14. Paris: Leroux.

————1926 *Royal Inscriptions and Fragments from Nippur and Babylon. Publications of the Babylonian Section* 15. Philadelphia: University of Pennsylvania, the Museum.

Lehoux, D. 2003 "The Historicity Question in Babylonian Divination," in J. Steele and A. Imhausen, eds., *Under One Sky: Astronomy and Mathematics in the Ancient Near East*, 209–22. *Alter Orient und Altes Testament* 297. Münster: Ugarit-Verlag.

Leichty, E. 1970 *The Omen Series Šumma Izbu. Texts from Cuneiform Sources* 4. Locust Valley, NY: J.J. Augustin.

Lerouxel, F. 2002 "Les échanges de présents entre souverrains amorrites au XVIIIᵉ siècle av. n. è ," in D. Charpin and J.-M. Durand, eds., *Recueil d'études à la mémoire d'André Parrot*, 413–63. *Mémoires de NABU* 7, *Florilegium Marianum* 6. Paris: SEPOA.

Levi della Vida, G. 1938 *Les Sémites et leur role dans l'histoire religieuse*. Paris: Geuthner.

Lewis, Brian 1980 *The Sargon Legend: A Study of the Akkadian Text and the Tale of the Hero Who Was Exposed at Birth. American Schools of Oriental Research Dissertation Series* 4. Cambridge, Mass.: American Schools of Oriental Research.

Lieberman, S. 1992 "Nippur: City of Decisions," in M. de J. Ellis, ed., *Nippur at the Centennial, Papers Read at the 35ᵉ Rencontre Assyriologique Internationale, Philadelphia, 1988*, 127–36. *Occasional Publications of the Samuel Noah Kramer Fund* 14. Philadelphia: University Museum of Archaeology and Anthropology.

Limet, H. 1960 *Le travail du métal au pays de Sumer au temps de la IIIᵉ dynastie d'Ur. Bibliothèque de la Faculté de Philosophie et Lettres de l'Université de Liège* 155. Paris: Les Belles Lettres.

————1968 *L'Anthroponymie sumérienne dans les documents de la 3ᵉ dynastie d'Ur. Bibliothèque de la Faculté de Philosophie et Lettres de l'Université de Liège* 180. Paris: Les Belles Lettres.

————1972 "Les métaux à l'époque d'Agadé," *Journal of the Economic and Social History of the Orient* 15: 3–34.

————1973 *Etude du documents de la période d'Agadé appartenant à l'Université de Liège, Bibliothèque de la Faculté de Philosophie et Lettres de l'Université de Liège* 206. Paris: Les Belles Lettres.

————2008 "Ethnicity," in D. Snell, ed., *A Companion to the Ancient Near East*, 392–405. Malden, Mass.: Blackwells.

Lion, B. 1992 "La Circulation des animaux exotiques au Proche-Orient antique," in D. Charpin and F. Joannès, eds., *La Circulation des biens, des personnes et des idées dans le Proche-Orient ancien, Actes de la XXXVIIIᵉ Rencontre Assyriologique Internationale (Paris, 8–10 juillet 1991)*, 357–65. Paris: Editions Recherche sur les Civilisations.

————2011 "Literacy and Gender," in K. Radner and E. Robson, eds., *The Oxford Handbook of Cuneiform Culture*, 90–112. Oxford: Oxford University Press.

Lion, B. and C. Michel, eds. 2006 *De la domestication au tabou: Le cas des suidés au Proche-Orient ancien*. Paris: De Boccard.

Lipinski, E., ed., 1979 *State and Temple Economy in the Ancient Near East* 1, 2. *Orientalia Lovaniensia Analecta* 5, 6. Leuven: Peeters.

———1982 "Sale, Transfer, and Delivery in Ancient Semitic Terminology," in H. Klengel, ed., *Gesellschaft und Kultur im alten Vorderasien,* 173–85. *Schriften zur Geschichte und Kultur des Alten Orients* 15. Berlin: Akademie Verlag.

Littauer, M. and J. Crouwel 1979 *Wheeled Vehicles and Ridden Animals in the Ancient Near East.* Leiden: Brill.

Liverani, M. 1966a *Sargon di Akkad. I Protagonisti della Storia Universale,* fasc. 57: *La Civiltà delle Origini.* Milan: C.E.I.

———1966b "Problemi e indirizzi degli studi storici sul Vicino Oriente antico," *Cultura e Scuola* 20: 72–9.

———1971 "Gli studi di storia orientale antica," in *Gli Studi sul Vicino Oriente in Italia dal 1921 al 1970, 1: L'Oriente Preislamico,* 1–9. *Pubblicazioni dell'Istituto per l'Oriente* 68. Rome: Istituto per l'Oriente.

———1973 "Memorandum on the Approach to Historiographic Texts," *Orientalia* NS 42: 178–94.

———1988a "The Growth of the Assyrian Empire in the Habur/Middle Euphrates Area: A New Paradigm." *State Archives of Assyria Bulletin* 2: 81–98.

———1988b *Antico Oriente: Storia Società Economia.* Bari: Laterza.

———1990 "The Shape of Neo-Sumerian Fields," *Bulletin on Sumerian Agriculture* 5: 147–86.

———1993a "Model and Actualization: The Kings of Akkad in the Historical Tradition," in Mario Liverani, ed., *Akkad, The First Universal Empire: Structure, Ideology, Traditions,* 41–67. *History of the Ancient Near East/Studies* 5. Padua: Sargon.

Liverani, M., ed. 1993b *Akkad, The First Universal Empire: Structure, Ideology, Traditions. History of the Ancient Near East/Studies* 5. Padua: Sargon.

———1995 "Reconstructing the Rural Landscape in the Ancient Near East," *Journal of the Economic and Social History of the Orient* 39: 1–41.

———1997 "Lower Mesopotamian Fields: South vs. North," in B. Pongratz-Leisten, ed., *Ana šadî Labnāni lū allik: Beiträge zu altorientalischen und mittelmeerischen Kulturen, Festschrift für Wolfgang Röllig,* 219–27. *Alter Orient and Altes Testament* 247. Münster: Ugarit-Verlag.

———1999 "History and Archaeology in the Ancient Near East: 150 Years of a Difficult Relationship," in H. Kühne, R. Bernbeck, and K. Bartl, eds., *Fluchtpunkt Uruk. Archäologische Einheit aus methodischer Vielfalt: Schriften für Hans Jörg Nissen,* 1–11. Rahden: Marie Leidorf.

———1999/2000 "The Sargon Geography and the Late Assyrian Mensuration of the Earth," *State Archives of Assyrian Bulletin* 13: 57–85.

———2001/2 Review of A. Westenholz 1999. *Archiv für Orientforschung* 48/9: 180–1.

———2011 *The Ancient Near East: History, Society and Economy,* translated by S. Tabatabai. London: Routledge.

Lloyd, S. 1940 "Iraq Government Soundings at Sinjar," *Iraq* 7: 13–21.

Luckenbill, D. 1930 *Inscriptions from Adab. Oriental Institute Publications* 14. Chicago: Oriental Institute of the University of Chicago.

Lundström, S. 2000 "*Kimaḫḫu* und *Qabru*. Untersuchungen zur Begrifflichkeit akkadischer Grabbezeichnungen," *Altorientalische Forschungen* 27: 6–20.

———2003 "Zur Aussagekraft schriftlicher Quellen hinsichtlich der Vorstellungen vom Leben nach dem Tod in Mesopotamien," *Altorientalische Forschungen* 30: 30–50.

Madhloom, T. 1960 "Ḥafriyyātu Tall al-Wilāyah fī liwā'i al-Kūt," *Sumer* 16: Arabic portion 62–92.

Maeda, T. 1979 "On the Agricultural Festivals in Sumer," *Acta Sumerologica* 1: 19–34.

———1981 "'King of Kish' in Pre-Sargonic Sumer," *Orient* 17: 1–17.

———2005 "Royal Inscriptions of Lugalzagesi and Sargon," *Orient* 40: 3–30.

Maekawa, K. 1981 "The Agricultural Texts of Ur III Lagash of the British Museum," *Acta Sumerologica* 3: 37–61.

———1984 "Cereal Cultivation in the Ur III Period," *Bulletin on Sumerian Agriculture* 1: 73–96.

———1987 "The Agricultural Texts of Ur III Lagash of the British Museum V," *Acta Sumerologica* 9: 89–129.

———1989 "Rations, Wages and Economic Trends in the Ur III Period," *Altorientalische Forschungen* 16: 42–50.

———1990 "Cultivation Methods in the Ur III Period," *Bulletin on Sumerian Agriculture* 5: 115–45.

Maekawa, K. and W. Mori 2011 "Dilmun, Magan, and Meluhha in Early Mesopotamian History: 2500–1600 BC," in T. Osada and M. Witzel, eds., *Cultural Relations between the Indus and the Iranian Plateau during the Third Millennium BCE, Indus Project, Research Institute for Humanities and Nature June 7–8, 2008*, 245–69. Harvard Oriental Series, Opera Minora 7. Cambridge, Mass.: Harvard University Department of South Asian Studies.

Maiocchi, M. 2009 *Classical Sargonic Tablets Chiefly from Adab in the Cornell University Collections, Cornell University Studies in Assyriology and Sumerology* 13. Bethesda, Md.: CDL Press.

———2010a "The Sargonic "Archive" of Me-$^{sá}$sag$_7$, Cupbearer of Adab," in L. Kogan, N. Koslova, S. Loesov, and S. Tishchenko, eds., *City Administration in the Ancient Near East, Proceedings of the 53$^e$ Rencontre Assyriologique Internationale* 2: 141–52. Orientalia et Classica 31, Babel und Bibel 5. Winona Lake, Ind.: Eisenbrauns.

———2010b "Decorative Parts and Precious Artifacts at Ebla," *Journal of Cuneiform Studies* 62: 1–24.

Maiocchi, M. and G. Visicato 2012 *Classical Sargonic Tablets Chiefly from Adab in the Cornell University Collections, Part II. Cornell University Studies in Assyriology and Sumerology* 19. Bethesda, Md.: CDL Press.

Malamat, A. 1965 "Campaigns to the Mediterranean by Iahdunlim and Other Early Mesopotamian Rulers," in H. Güterbock and T. Jacobsen, eds., *Studies in Honor of Benno Landsberger on His Seventy-fifth Birthday April 21, 1965*, 365–73. Assyriological Studies 16. Chicago: University of Chicago Press.

Mallowan, M. 1936 "The Bronze Head of the Akkadian Period from Nineveh," *Iraq* 3: 104–10.

———1937 "The Excavations at Tall Chagar Bazar and an Archaeological Survey of the Ḫabur Region, Second Campaign, 1936," *Iraq* 4: 91–177.

———1947 "Excavations at Tell Brak and Chagar Bazar," *Iraq* 9.

Manassa, C. 2010 "Defining Historical Fiction in New Kingdom Egypt," in S. Melville and A. Slotsky, eds., *Opening the Tablet Box: Near Eastern Studies in Honor of Benjamin R. Foster*, 245–69. Leiden: E. J. Brill.

Mann, M. 1994 *Geschichte der Macht 1: Von den Anfängen bis zur griechisichen Antike*. Frankfurt: Campus Verlag.

Marchesi, G. 2004 "Who Was Buried in the Royal Tombs of Ur? The Epigraphic and Textual Data," *Orientalia* NS 73: 153–97.

———2010 "The Sumerian King List and the Early History of Mesopotamia," in *ana turri gimilli, studi dedicati al Padre Werner R. Mayer, S.J. da amici e allievi*, 231–48. Vicino Oriente Quaderno 5. Rome: Università di Roma.

———2011 "A New Historical Synchronism Relating to Sargon of Akkade," *Studi Epigrafici e Linguistici* 28: 17–23.

————2015 "History and Philology," in U. Finkbeiner, M. Novák, F. Sakal, and P. Sconzo, eds., *Middle Euphrates*, 423–9. *Associated Regional Chronologies for the Ancient Near East and the Eastern Mediterranean*. Turnhout: Brepols.

Marchesi, G. and N. Marchetti 2011 *Royal Statuary of Early Dynastic Mesopotamia*. Winona Lake, Ind.: Eisenbrauns.

Margueron, J. 1982 *Recherches sur les palais mésopotamiens de l'Âge du Bronze*. Paris: Geuthner.

————1996 "Mari à l'époque des šakkanakku," in Ö. Tunca and D. Deheselle, eds., *Tablettes et images aux pays de Sumer: Mélanges offerts à Monsieur H. Limet*, 95–103. Liège: Université de Liège.

————2006 *Mari, Métropole de l'Euphrate*. Paris: Picard.

————2007 "Mari et la chronologie: Acquisitions récentes et problèmes," in P. Matthiae, F. Pinnock, L. Nigro, and L. Peyronel, eds., *Proceedings of the International Colloquium From Relative Chronology to Absolute Chronology: The Second Millennium* BC *in Syria-Palestine (Rome 29th November – 1st December 2001)*, 285–301. Contributi del Centro Linceo Interdisciplinare "Beniamino Segre" 117. Rome: Accademia Nazionale dei Lincei.

————2013 *Cités invisibles: La naissance de l'urbanisme au Proche-Orient ancien, approche archéologique*. Paris: Geuthner.

Markina, E. 2012 "Akkadian of the Me-ság Archive," *Annual of Ancient Near Eastern, Old Testament, and Semitic Studies*, 169–88. *Orientalia et Classica* 43, *Babel und Bibel* 6. Winona Lake: Eisenbrauns.

Marti, L. 2014 "Akkad à l'époque néo-assyrienne," in N. Ziegler and E. Cancik-Kirschbaum, eds., *Entre les fleuves – II, D'Aššur à Mari et au-delà, Berliner Beiträge zum Vorderen Orient* 24, 207–9. Berlin: PeWe-Verlag.

Martiny, G. 1932 *Die Kultrichtung in Mesopotamien, Studien zur Bauforschung* 3. Berlin: Hans Schoetz.

Martos, M. 1991 "Tablillas sargónicas del Museo de Monserrat, Barcelona" *Aula Orientalis* 9: 137–54.

Matthews, R., ed. 2003 *Excavations at Tell Brak, Vol. 4: Exploring an Upper Mesopotamian Regional Centre, 1994–1996*. London: British School of Archaeology in Iraq.

Matthiae, P. 1976 "Ebla à l'époque d'Akkad: archéologie et histoire," *Comptes Rendus de l'Académie des Inscriptions & Belles-Lettres* 1976: 190–215. Paris: Alphonse Picard.

————1998 "Figurative Themes and Literary Texts," *Quaderni di Semitistica* 18: 219–41.

————2007 "The Destruction of Old Syrian Ebla at the End of Middle Bronze II: New Historical Data," in P. Matthiae, F. Pinnock, L. Nigro, and L. Peyronel, eds., *Proceedings of the International Colloquium From Relative Chronology to Absolute Chronology: The Second Millennium* BC *in Syria-Palestine (Rome 29th November — 1st December 2001)*, 5–32. Contributi del Centro Linceo Interdisciplinare "Beniamino Segre" 117. Rome: Accademia Nazionale dei Lincei.

————2009 "Temples et reines de l'Ebla protosyrienne: Resultats des fouilles à Tell Mardikh en 2007 et 2008," *Comptes Rendus d'Académie des Inscriptions & Belle-Lettres* 2009: 747–91.

————2010 *Ebla, la città del trono*. Turin: Einundi.

Matthiae, P. and N. Marchetti, eds. 2013 *Ebla and Its Landscape: Early State Formation in the Ancient Near East*. Walnut Creek, Cal.: Left Coast Press.

Maul, S. 2007 "Divination Culture and the Handling of the Future," in G. Leick, ed., *The Babylonian World*, 361–72. London: Routledge.

————2013 *Die Wahrsagekunst im Alten Orient, Zeichen des Himmels und der Erde*. Munich: Beck.

Maxwell-Hyslop, K. 1946 "Daggers and Swords of Ancient Western Asia," *Iraq* 8: 1–65.

————1949 "Western Asiatic Shaft-hole Axes," *Iraq* 11: 90–129.

————1971 *Western Asiatic Jewellery c. 3000–612 B.C.* London: Methuen.

————1977 "Sources of Sumerian Gold," *Iraq* 39: 83–6.

McEwan, G. 1982 "Agade after the Gutian Destruction: The Afterlife of a Mesopotamian City," *Archiv für Orientforschung Beiheft* 19, 8–15.

McHale-Moore, R. 2000 "The Mystery of Enheduanna's Disk," *Journal of the Ancient Near Eastern Society of Columbia University* 27: 69–74.

McHugh, F. 1999 *Theoretical and Quantitative Approaches to the Study of Mortuary Practice, British Archaeological Reports International Series* 785. Oxford: Archaeopress.

McKerrell, H. 1978 "The Use of Tin Bronze in Britain and the Comparative Relationship with the Near East," in A. Franklin, J. Olin, and T. Wertime, eds., *The Search for Ancient Tin*, 7–24. Washington: US Government Printing Office.

McMahon, A. 2006 *Nippur V, The Early Dynastic to Akkadian Transition, The Area WF Sounding at Nippur. Oriental Institute Publications* 129. Chicago: The Oriental Institute of the University of Chicago.

————2012 "The Akkadian Period: Empire, Environment, and Imagination," in D. Potts, ed., *A Companion to the Archaeology of the Ancient Near East*, 2: 649–67. Oxford: Blackwells.

————2013 "North Mesopotamia in the Third Millennium BC," in H. Crawford, ed., *The Sumerian World*, 462–77. London: Routledge.

Mellink, M. 1963 "An Akkadian Illustration of a Campaign in Cilicia," *Anatolia* 7: 101–15.

Menant, J. 1875 *Babylone et la Chaldée.* Paris: Maisonneuve.

Meyer, E. 1906 *Sumerier und Semiten in Babylonien. Abhandlungen der Königlich Preussischen Akademie der Wissenschaften* 1906/III. Berlin: Reimer.

Meyer, J.-W. 1987 *Untersuchungen zu den Tonlebermodellen aus dem alten Orient. Alter Orient und Altes Testament* 39. Neukirchen-Vluyn: Neukirchener Verlag.

Michalowski, P. 1980 "New Sources Concerning the Reign of Naram-Sin," *Journal of Cuneiform Studies* 32: 233–46.

————1981 "Tutanapšum, Naram-Sin and Nippur," *Revue d'Assyriologie* 75: 173–6.

————1985 "Third Millennium Contacts: Observations on the Relationships between Mari and Ebla," *Journal of the American Oriental Society* 105: 293–302.

————1986 "The Earliest Hurrian Toponymy: A New Sargonic Inscription," *Zeitschrift für Assyriologie* 76: 4–11.

————1988 "Magan and Meluhha Once Again," *Journal of Cuneiform Studies* 40: 156–64.

————1989 *The Lamentation over the Destruction of Sumer and Ur. Mesopotamian Civilizations* 1. Winona Lake, Ind.: Eisenbrauns.

————1993 "Memory and Deed: The Historiography of the Political Expansion of the Akkad State," in M. Liverani, ed., *Akkad, The First Universal Empire: Structure, Ideology, Traditions*, 69–90. *History of the Ancient Near East/Studies* 5. Padua: Sargon.

————1995 "The Men from Mari," in K. van Lerberghe, ed., *Immigration and Emigration within the Ancient Near East, Festschrift E. Lipinski*, 181–8. *Orientalia Lovaniensia Analecta* 65. Leuven: Peeters.

————1998 "Literature as a Source of Lexical Inspiration: Some Notes on a Hymn to the Goddess Inana," in J. Braun, K. Lyczkowska, M. Popko, and P. Steinkeller, eds., *Written on Clay and Stone, Ancient Near Eastern Studies Presented to Krystyna Szarzynska on the Occasion of her 80th Birthday*, 65–73. Warsaw: Agade.

————1999a "Sumer Dreams of Subartu: Politics and the Geographical Imagination," in K. Van Lerberghe and G. Voet, eds., *Languages and Cultures in Contact: At the Crossroads of Civilizations in the Syro-Mesopotamian Realm, Proceedings of the 42th (sic) Rencontre Assyriologique Internationale*, 305–15, *Orientalia Lovaniensia Periodica* 96. Leuven: Peeters.

————1999b "Sumer 3. Histoire," in J. Briend and M. Quesnel, eds., *Supplément au Diction-naire de la Bible, fascicule 72, Sophonie – Sumer*, 108–23. Paris: Letouzey & Ané.

————2004 "The Ideological Foundations of the Ur III State," in J.-W. Meyer and W. Sommerfeld, eds., *2000 v. Chr., Politische, wirtschaftliche und kulturelle Entwicklung im Zeichen einer Jahrtausendwende, 3. Internationales Colloquium der Deutschen Orient-Gesellschaft*, 219–35. Saarbrücken: Saarbrücker Druckerei und Verlag.

————2006a "Love or Death? Observations on the Role of the Gala in Ur III Ceremonial Life," *Journal of Cuneiform Studies* 58: 49–61.

————2006b "The Lives of the Sumerian Language," in S. Sanders, ed., *Margins of Writing, Origins of Cultures*, 163–88. Oriental Institute Seminars 2. Chicago: Oriental Institute of the University of Chicago.

————2008 "The Mortal Kings of Ur: A Short Century of Divine Rule in Mesopotamia," in N. Brisch, ed., *Religion and Power, Divine Kingship in the Ancient World and Beyond*, Oriental Institute Seminars 4, 33–45. Chicago: Oriental Institute of the University of Chicago.

————2010a "Learning Music: Schooling, Apprenticeship and Gender in Early Mesopotamia," in R. Pruzsinszky and D. Shehata, eds., *Musiker und Tradierung. Studien zur Rolle von Musikern bei der Verschriftlichung und Tradierung von literarischen Werken*, 199–239. *Wiener Offene Orientalistik* 8. Vienna: Lit.

————2010b "A Traveler's Tales: Observations on Musical Mobility in Mesopotamia and Beyond," in R. Dumbrill and I. Finkel, eds., *Iconea 2008, Proceedings of the International Conference of Near Eastern Archaeomusicology held at the British Museum December 4, 5 and 6, 2008*, 117–24. London: Iconea.

————2011 "Early Mesopotamia," in A. Feldherr and G. Hardy, eds., *The Oxford History of Historical Writing I: Beginnings to* AD *600*, 1: 5–28. Oxford: Oxford University Press.

————2013 "Of Bears and Men: Thoughts on the End of Šu-Sin's Reign and on the Ensuing Succession," in D. Vanderhooft and A. Winitzer, eds., *Literature as Politics, Politics as Literature: Essays on the Ancient Near East in Honor of Peter Machinist*, 285–320. Winona Lake, Ind.: Eisenbrauns.

Michel, C. 2001 *Correspondance des marchands de Kanish au début du II* millénaire avant J.-C. Littératures anciennes du Proche-Orient*. Paris: Du Cerf.

————2009/11 "Sargon I.," *Reallexikon der Assyriologie* 12: 49–51.

————2011 "Une liste paléographique de signes cunéiformes: Quand les scribes assyriens s'intéressaient aux écritures anciennes ...," in F. Wateau, ed., *Profils d'objets: Approches d'anthropologues et d'archéologues*, 245–57. Colloques de la Maison René-Ginouvès 7. Paris: De Boccard.

Milano, L. 1987 "OAkk. BAN-ḫa-tum = tirḫatum 'bridal price,'" *Orientalia* NS 56, 85–86.

————1993/7a "Mehl," *Reallexikon der Assyriologie* 8: 22–31.

————1993/7b "Mühle," *Reallexikon der Assyriologie* 8: 393–400.

————1994a "Vino e birra in Oriente. Confini geografici e confini culturali," in L. Milano, ed., *Drinking in Ancient Societies, History and Culture of Drinks in the Ancient Near East, Papers of a Symposium held in Rome, May 17–19, 1990*, 421–40. *History of the Ancient Near East/Studies* 6. Padua: Sargon.

————ed. 1994b *Drinking in Ancient Societies, History and Culture of Drinks in the Ancient Near East, Papers of a Symposium held in Rome, May 17–19, 1990. History of the Ancient Near East/ Studies* 6. Padua: Sargon.

————2003 "Sistemi finanziari in Mesopotamia e Siria nel III millenio a.C.," in L. Milano and N. Parise, eds., *Il regolamento degli scambi nell'antichità*, 3–58. Bari: Laterza.

————2008 "Regine fondario e compravendite immobiliari nella Mesopotamia de III millennio," in M. Liverani and C. Mora, eds., *I diritti del mondo cuneiforme (Mesopotamia e regioni adiacenti, ca. 2500–500 a.C.)*, 91–120. Pavia: IUSS.

————2012 *Mangiare Divinamente, Pratiche e simbologie alimentari nell'antico Oriente. Eothen* 20. Florence: LoGisma.

Milano, L. and E. Rova 2000 "Ceramic Provinces and Political Borders in Upper Mesopotamia in the Late Early Dynastic Period," in S. Graziani, ed., *Studi sul Vicino Oriente Antico dedicati alla memoria di Luigi Cagni*, 709–41. Naples: Istituto Universitario Orientale, Dipartimento di Studi Asiatici, *Series Minor* 61.

Milano, L. and Tonietti, M. 2012 "Ceremonialità alimentare ad Ebla: offerte, pasti, sacrifici," in L. Milano, ed., *Mangiare Divinamente, Pratiche e simbologie alimentari nell'antico Oriente*, 33–81. *Eothen* 20. Florence: LoGisma.

Milone, M.-E. 1998 "Irikagina, figlio de Engisa, ensik di Lagash," NABU 1998/106.

————2005 "Un piccolo archivio di tavolette presargoniche provenienti da Umma-Zabala," *Sefarad* 65: 327–51.

Molina, M. 2014 *Sargonic Cuneiform Tablets in the Real Academia de la Historia, The Carl L. Lippmann Collection*. Madrid: Real Academia de la Historia.

Monaco, S. 2013 "Some New Light on Pre-Sargonic Umma," in L. Feliu, J. Llop, A. Millet Albà, and J. Sanmartín, eds., *Time and History in the Ancient Near East, Proceedings of the 56th Rencontre Assyriologique Internationale at Barcelona 26–30 July 2010*, 745–50. Winona Lake, Ind.: Eisenbrauns.

Monaco, S. and F. Pomponio 2009 "L'impiego dell'argento nei testi mesopotamici dal periodo arcaico a quello paleo-accadico," *Rivista di Storia Economica* 25: 19–50.

Moorey, P. 1970 "Cemetery A at Kish: Grave Groups and Chronology," *Iraq* 32: 86–128.

————1978 *Kish Excavations 1923–1933*. Oxford: Clarendon Press.

————1994 *Ancient Mesopotamian Materials and Industries, The Archaeological Evidence*. Oxford: Clarendon Press.

Moorey, P. and F. Schweizer 1972 "Copper and Copper Alloys in Ancient Iraq, Syria and Palestine," *Archaeometry* 14: 177–98.

Moortgat, A. 1969 *The Art of Ancient Mesopotamia, the Classical Art of the Near East*. Judith Filson, trans. London: Phaidon.

Moortgat, A. and U. Moortgat-Correns 1974 "Archäologische Bemerkungen zu einem Schatzfund im vorsargonischen Palast in Mari, mit einer Tabelle der wichtigsten Vergleichsstücke," *Iraq* 36: 155–67.

Muhamed, A. 1992 *Old Babylonian Cuneiform Texts from the Hamrin Basin, Edubba* 1. London: NABU.

Mühl, S. 2013 *Siedlungsgeschichte im mittleren Osttigrisgebiet, Vom Neolithikum bis in die neuassyrische Zeit. Abhandlungen der Deutschen Orient-Gesellschaft* 28. Wiesbaden: Harrassowitz.

Muhly, J. 1993/97 "Metalle, B," *Reallexikon der Assyriologie* 8: 119–36.

Müller-Karpe, M. 1993 *Metallgefäße im Iraq I: Von den Anfängen bis zur Akkad-Zeit*, Stuttgart: Steiner.

————1993/97 *Metallgefäße Reallexikon der Assyriologie* 8: 137–44.

Muscarella, O., ed. 1981 *Ladders to Heaven: Art Treasures from the Lands of the Bible*. Toronto: McClelland and Stewart.

Musche, B. 1992 *Vorderasiatischer Schmuck. Von den Anfängen bis zur Zeit der Achämeniden, Handbuch der Orientalistik 1,7, 1/2B, 7*. Leiden: Brill.

Myres, J. 1914 *Handbook of the Cesnola Collection of Antiquities from Cyprus*. New York: Metropolitan Museum of Art.

Nadali, D. 2007 "Monuments of War, War of Monuments: Some Considerations on War in the Third Millennium BC," *Orientalia* NS 76: 336–67.

Nadali, D. and L. Verderame 2008 "The Akkadian 'Bello Stile'," in R. Biggs, J. Myers, and M. Roth, eds., *Proceedings of the 51st Rencontre Assyriologique Internationale Held at the Oriental Institute of the University of Chicago July 18–22, 2005*, 309–20. *Studies in Ancient Oriental Civilization* 62. Chicago: Oriental Institute of the University of Chicago.

Nagel, W. and E. Strommenger 1968 "Reichsakkadische Glyptik und Plastik im Rahmen der mesopotamisch-elamischen Geschichte," *Berliner Jahrbuch für Vor-und Frühgeschichte* 8: 137–206.

Neumann, H. 1987 *Handwerk in Mesopotamien, Untersuchungen zu seiner Organisation in der Zeit der III. Dynastie von Ur*. Akademie der Wissenschaften der DDR, Zentralinstitut für Alte Geschichte und Archäologie, *Schriften zur Geschichte und Kultur des Alten Orients* 19. Berlin: Akademie Verlag.

————1989 "Mesopotamien zur Zeit der ersten Territorialstaaten (etwa 2350–2000)," in H. Klengel, ed., *Kulturgeschichte der alten Vorderasien*, 86–143. Berlin: Akademie-Verlag.

————1997 "Assur in altakkadischer Zeit: Die Texte," in H. Waetzoldt and H. Hauptmann, eds., *Assyrien im Wandel der Zeiten, XXXIXᵉ Rencontre Assyriologique Internationale Heidelberg 6.-10. Juli 1992*, 133–8. *Heidelberger Studien zum Alten Orient* 6, Heidelberg: Heidelberger Orientverlag.

————2002 "Der sogennante *Oikos*-Ökonomie und das Problem der Privatwirtschaft im ausgehenden 3. Jahrtausend v. Chr. in Mesopotamien," in A. Hausleiter, S. Kerner, and B. Müller-Neuhof, eds., *Material Culture and Mental Spheres. Rezeption archäologischer Denkrichtigungen in der Vorderasiatischen Altertumskunde. Internationales Symposium für Hans J. Nissen, Berlin, 23.-24. Juni 2000*, 273–84. *Alter Orient und Altes Testament* 293. Münster: Ugarit-Verlag.

————2003 "Recht im alten Mesopotamien," in U. Manthe, ed., *Die Rechtskulturen der Antike, vom Alten Orient bis zum Römischen Reich*, 55–122. Munich: Beck.

————2012 "Todes-und Körperstrafe versus Versklavung und Geldbuse. Überlegungen zur mesopotamischen Strafrechtspraxis im 3. und frühen 2. Jt. v. Chr.", in R. Rollinger, M. Lang, and H. Barta, eds., *Strafe und Strafrecht in den antiken Welten, Unter Berücksichtigung von Todesstrafe, Hinrichtung und peinlicher Befragung*, 163–9. *Philippika* 51. Wiesbaden: Harassowitz.

————2014 "Altorientalische 'Imperien' des 3. und frühen 2. Jahrtausends v. Chr.: Historische Voraussetzungen und sozioökonomische Grundlagen," in M. Gehler, M. and R. Rollinger, eds. *Imperien und Reiche in der Weltgeschichte, Epochenübergreifende und globalhistorische Vergleiche*, 33–64. Wiesbaden: Harrassowitz.

Newman, J. 1932 *The Agricultural Life of the Jews in Babylonia between the Years 200 C.E. and 500 C.E.* London: Oxford University Press.

Nigro, L. 1992 "Per una analisi formale dello schema compositivo della stele di Naram Sin," *Contributi e Materiali di Archeologia Orientale* 4: 61–100.

————1997 "Legittimazione e consenso: iconologia, religione e politica nelle stele di Sargon di Akkad," *Contributi e Materiali di Archeologia Orientale* 7: 351–92.

————1998a "The Two Steles of Sargon: Iconology and Visual Propaganda at the Beginning of Royal Akkadian Relief," *Iraq* 60: 85–102.

————1998b "Visual Role and Ideological Meaning of the Enemies in the Royal Akkadian Relief," in J. Prosecky, ed., *Intellectual Life of the Ancient Near East: Papers Presented at the 43rd Rencontre Assyriologique Internationale Prague, July 1–5, 1996*, 283–97. Prague: Oriental Institute.

————2001/3 "La Stele di Rimush da Tello e l'indicazione del rango dei vinti nel rilievo reale Accadico," *Scienze dell'Antichità: Storia Archeologia Anthropologia* 11: 71–93.

Nikolski, N. M. 1948 *Častnoe zemlevladenie i zemlepol'zovanie v drevnem Dvureč'e*. Minsk: Akademia Nauk BSSR.

Nissen, H. J. 1966 *Zur Datierung des Königsfriedhofes von Ur, unter besonderer Berücksichtigung der Stratigraphie der Privatgraber. Beiträge zur ur-und frühgeschichtlichen Archäologie des Mittelmeer-Kuturraumes für das Institut für Ur-und Frühgeschichte der Universität Heidelberg* 3. Heidelberg: Rudolf Habelt.

—————1980 "The Mobility between Settled and Non-Settled in Early Babylonia: Theory and Evidence," in *L'Archéologie de l'Iraq du début de l'époque néolithique à 333 avant notre ère, Perspectives et limites de l'interprétation anthropologique des documents, Colloques internationaux du Centre National de la Recherche Scientifique* 580, *Paris, 13–15 juin 1978,* 285–90. Paris: Editions du Centre National de la Recherche Scientifique.

—————1982 "Die 'Tempelstadt': Regierungsform der frühdynastischen Zeit in Babylonien," in H. Klengel, ed., *Gesellschaft und Kultur im alten Vorderasien,* 195–200. *Schriften zur Geschichte und Kultur des Alten Orients* 15. Berlin: Akademie Verlag.

—————1986 " 'Sumerian' vs. 'Akkadian' Art: Art and Politics in Babylonia of the Mid-Third Millennium BC," in M. Kelly-Buccellati, ed., *Insight through Images: Studies in Honor of Edith Porada,* 189–96. Malibu: Undena.

—————1988 *The Early History of the Ancient Near East, 9000–2000 B.C.,* E. Lutzeier and K. Northcott, trans. Chicago: University of Chicago Press.

—————1993 "Settlement Patterns and Material Culture of the Akkadian Period: Continuity and Discontinuity," in M. Liverani, ed., *Akkad, The First World Empire: Structure, Ideology, Traditions,* 91–106. *History of the Ancient Near East/Studies* 5. Padua: Sargon.

—————2012 *Geschichte Alt-Vorderasiens,* 2nd edition. Munich: Oldenbourg.

Nissinen, M. 2001 "Akkadian Rituals and Poetry of Divine Love," in R. Whiting, ed., *Mythology and Mythologies: Methodological Approaches to Intercultural Influences, Proceedings of the Second Annual Symposium of the Assyrian and Babylonian Intellectual Heritage Project Held in Paris, France October 4–7, 1999,* 93–136. *Melammu Symposia* 2. Helsinki: Neo-Assyrian Text Corpus.

Norris, E. 1861 *The Cuneiform Inscriptions of Western Asia I: A Selection from the Historical Inscriptions of Chaldaea, Assyria, and Babylonia.* London: British Museum.

—————1866 *The Cuneiform Inscriptions of Western Asia II: A Selection from the Miscellaneous Inscriptions of Assyria.* London: British Museum.

Notizia, P. and I. Schrakamp 2010 "Ein sargonischer Personenkauf aus dem British Museum, London (BM 103707)," *Altorientalische Forschungen* 37: 242–51.

Nougayrol, J. 1945 "Note sur la place des 'présages historiques' dans l'extispicine babylonienne," *Annuaire de l'Ecole Pratique des Hautes Etudes,* section des sciences religeuses, *1944–1945,* 5–41. Melun: Imprimerie Administrative.

—————1969 "Nouveaux textes sur le *zihhu* (I), *Revue d'Assyriologie* 63: 149–57.

—————1973 "Trois nouveaux recueils d'haruspicine ancienne," *Revue d'Assyriologie* 67: 41–56.

Novák, M. 2000 "Das 'Haus der Totenpflege'," *Altorientalische Forschungen* 27: 132–54.

—————2003 "Divergierende Bestattungskonzepte und ihre sozialen, kulturellen und ethnischen Hintergründe," *Altorientalische Forschungen* 30: 63–84.

Nylander, C. 1980 "Earless in Nineveh: Who Mutilated Sargon's Head?" *American Journal of Archaeology* 84: 329–33.

Oates, D. 1968 *Studies in the Ancient History of Northern Iraq.* London: British Academy.

Oates, D. and J. Oates 1989 "Akkadian Buildings at Tell Brak," *Iraq* 51: 193––211.

—————1995 "A Further Note on Administration at Tell Brak in the Akkadian Period," in U. Finkbeiner, R. Dittmann, and H. Hauptmann, eds., *Kulturgeschichte Vorderasiens, Festschrift zu Rainer Michael Boehmer,* 491–506. Mainz: von Zabern.

Oates, D., J. Oates, and H. McDonald 2001 *Excavations at Tell Brak 2: Nagar in the Third Millennium BC.* London: British School of Archaeology in Iraq.

Oates, J. 1979 *Babylon.* London: Thames and Hudson.

Ochsenschlager, E. 1992 "Ethnographic Evidence for Wood, Boats, Bitumen and Reeds in Southern Iraq," *Bulletin on Sumerian Agriculture* 6: 47–78.

Oelsner, J. 1989 "Einige Königsinschriften des 3. Jahrtausends," in H. Behrens, D. Loding, and M. Roth, eds., *DUMU-E₂-DUB-BA-A, Studies in Honor of Åke W. Sjöberg,* 403–9. *Occasional Publications of the Samuel Noah Kramer Fund* 11. Philadelphia: University Museum of Anthropology and Archaeology.

Offner, G. 1962 "Jeux corporals en Sumer. Documents relatifs à la compétition athlétique," *Revue d'Assyriologie* 56: 31–8.

Oh'e, S. 1979 "On the Distinction between Lú-inim-ma and Lú-ki-inim-ma," *Acta Sumerologica* 1: 69–84.

Olmstead, A. 1916/17 "The Political Development of Early Babylonia," *American Journal of Semitic Languages and Literatures* 33: 283–321.

Opificius, R. 1970 "Gilgamesch und Enkidu in der bildenden Kunst," in H. Pohle and G. Mahr, eds., *Festschrift zum hundertjährigen Bestehen der Berliner Gesellschaft für Anthropologie, Ethnologie und Urgeschichte, 1869–1969,* 286–92. Berlin: Berliner Institut für Anthropologie, Ethnologie und Urgeschichte.

Oppenheim, A. 1961 "The Mesopotamian Temple," in G. Wright and D. Freedman, eds., *The Biblical Archaeologist Reader,* 1: 158–69. Garden City, NY: Anchor Books.

————1965 "A Notes on the Scribes in Mesopotamia," in H. Güterbock and T. Jacobsen, eds., *Studies in Honor of Benno Landsberger on his Seventy-fifth Birthday April 21, 1965,* 253–6. *Assyriological Studies* 16. Chicago: University of Chicago Press.

————1977 *Ancient Mesopotamia, Portrait of a Dead Civilization.* Revised edition completed by Erica Reiner. Chicago: University of Chicago Press.

Oppert, J. 1888 "Bingani-sar-ali," *Zeitschrift für Assyriologie* 3: 124.

Oraibi See Almamori.

Otto, A. 2006 "Archaeological Perspectives on the Location of Naram-Sin's Armanum," *Journal of Cuneiform Studies* 58: 1–26.

Owen, D. 1975 *The John Frederick Lewis Collection, Materiali per il Vocabulario Neosumerico* 3. Rome: Multigrafica Editrice.

————1980 "A Sumerian Letter from an Angry Housewife(?)," in G. Rendsburg, R. Adler, M. Arfa, and N. Winter, eds., *The Bible World: Essays in Honor of Cyrus H. Gordon,* 189–202. New York: Ktav.

————1988 "A Unique Late Sargonic Water Ordeal in the John Frederick Lewis Collection," in E. Leichty, M. deJ. Ellis, and P. Gerardi, eds., *A Scientific Humanist: Studies in Memory of Abraham Sachs,* 305–11. *Occasional Publications of the Samuel Noah Kramer Fund* 9. Philadelphia: University Museum of Anthropology and Archaeology.

Paoletti, P. 2012 *König und sein Kreis: Das staatliche Schatzarchiv der III. Dynastie von Ur. Bibliotheca del Próximo Oriente Antiguo* 10. Madrid: Consejo Superior de Investigaciones Científicas.

Pappi, C. 2006/8 "Salbe, Salbengefäß," *Reallexikon der Assyriologie* 11: 572–4.

Parayre, D. 1997 "Les âges de la vie dans le répertoire figurative oriental," *Ktema* 22: 59–89.

Parpola, A. 1994 "Harappan Inscriptions," in F. Højlund and H. Andersen, *Qala'at al-Bahrein I: The Northern City Wall and the Islamic Fortress.* Moesgard: Jutland Archaeological Society.

Parrot, A. 1940 "Les fouilles de Mari, sixième campagne (automne 1938)," *Syria* 21: 1–28.

————1954 "Les fouilles de Mari, neuvième campagne (automne 1953)," *Syria* 31: 151–71.

————1955 "Les fouilles de Mari, dixième campagne," *Syria* 32: 185–211.

————1974 "Un cylinder agadéen trouvé à Mari," *Iraq* 36: 189–91.

Paulus, S. 2014 "Akkade in mittelbabylonischer Zeit (ca. 1500–1000 v. Chr.)," in N. Ziegler and E. Cancik-Kirschbaum, eds., *Entre les fleuves – II, D'Aššur à Mari et au-delà, Berliner Beiträge zum Vorderen Orient* 24, 199–206. Berlin: PeWe-Verlag.

Pedde, F. and S. Lundström 2008 *Der Alte Palast in Assur. Wissenschaftliche Veröffentlichungen der Deutschen Orient-Gesellschaft* 120. Wiesbaden: Harrassowitz.

Pethe, W. 2014 "Akkade in der mittelassyrischen Textdokumentation," in N. Ziegler and E. Cancik-Kirschbaum, eds., *Entre les fleuves – II, D'Aššur à Mari et au-delà, Berliner Beiträge zum Vorderen Orient* 24, 191–7. Berlin: PeWe-Verlag.

Pettinato, G. 1969 Review of Spycket 1968, *Bibliotheca Orientalis* 26: 212–16.

———1972 "Il commercio con l'estero della Mesopotamia meridionale nel 3. millennio av. Cr. alla luce delle fonti letterarie e lessicali sumeriche," *Mesopotamia* 7: 43–166.

Pettinato, G. and H. Waetzoldt 1985 "Dagan in Ebla und Mesopotamien nach den Texten des 3. Jahrtausends," *Orientalia* NS 54: 234–56.

Peyronel, L. 2010 "Ancient Near Eastern Economies: The Silver Question between Methodology and Archaeological Data," in P. Matthiae, F. Pinnock, L. Nigro, and N. Marchetti, eds., *Proceedings of the 6th International Congress of the Archaeology of the Ancient Near East, 5 May – 10 May 2009, "Sapienza" Università di Roma*, 1: 925–41. Wiesbaden: Harrassowitz.

Philip, G. 1995 "New Light on North Mesopotamia in the Earlier Second Millennium B.C.: Metalwork from the Hamrin," *Iraq* 57: 119–44.

Piccato, A. 1997 "The Berlin Leather Roll and the Egyptian Sense of History," *Lingua Aegyptia* 5: 137–59.

Pinches, T. 1882 "Some Recent Discoveries bearing on the Ancient History and Chronology of Babylonia," *Proceedings of the Society of Biblical Archaeology* 13th Session, 6–13.

———1883/4 "On Babylonian Art, Illustrated by Mr. Rassam's Latest Discoveries," *Proceedings of the Society of Biblical Archaeology* 14th Session, 11–15.

———1891 *The Cuneiform Inscriptions of Western Asia, Vol. IV: A Selection from the Miscellaneous Inscriptions of Assyria.* London: British Museum.

Pinnock, F. 1985 "About the Trade of Early Syrian Ebla," MARI 4: 85–92.

———1994 "Considerations on the 'Banquet Scene' in the Figurative Art of Mesopotamia and Syria," in L. Milano, ed., *Drinking in Ancient Societies, History and Culture of Drinks in the Ancient Near East, Papers of a Symposium held in Rome, May 17–19, 1990*, 15–26. *History of the Ancient Near East/Studies* 6. Padua: Sargon.

———2006 "The Raw Lapis Lazuli in the Royal Palace of Ebla: New Evidence from the Annexes of the Throne Room," in M. E. Alberti, E. Ascalone, and L. Peyronel, eds., *Proceedings of the International Colloquium, Rome 22nd–24th November 2004: Weights in Context: Bronze Age Weighing Systems of the Eastern Mediterranean, Chronology, Typology, Material and Archaeological Contexts*, 347–57. Rome: Istituto Italiano di Numismatica.

Pirngruber, R. 2014 "Die Stadt Akkad in den babylonischen Quellen des 1. Jahrtausends v. Chr.," in N. Ziegler and E. Cancik-Kirschbaum, eds., *Entre les fleuves – II, D'Aššur à Mari et au-delà, Berliner Beiträge zum Vorderen Orient* 24, 211–15. Berlin: PeWe-Verlag.

Pizzimenti, S. 2013 "The Other Face of the Moon: Some Hints on the Visual Representation of the Moon on Third-Millennium B.C.E. Mesopotamian Glyptic," in L. Feliu, J. Llop, A. Millet Albà, and J. Sanmartín, eds., *Time and History in the Ancient Near East, Proceedings of the 56th Rencontre Assyriologique Internationale at Barcelona 26–30 July 2010*, 265–72. Winona Lake, Ind.: Eisenbrauns.

Poebel, A. 1908 "Das Verbum im Sumerischen," *Zeitschrift für Assyriologie* 21: 162–236.

———1914 *Historical and Grammatical Texts. Publications of the Babylonian Section* 5. Philadelphia: University Museum.

Pollock, S. 1983 "Chronology of the Royal Cemetery of Ur," *Iraq* 57: 129–58.

————1991 "Of Priestesses, Princes and Poor Relations: The Dead in the Royal Cemetery of Ur," *Cambridge Archaeological Journal* 1: 171–89.

————1999 *Ancient Mesopotamia: The Eden that Never Was*. Cambridge: Cambridge University Press.

Polonsky, H. 2006 "The Mesopotamian Conceptualization of Birth and the Determination of Destiny at Sunrise," in A. Guinan, M. deJ. Ellis, A. Ferrara, S. Freedman, M. Rutz, L. Sassmannshausen, S. Tinney, and M. Waters, eds., *If a Man Builds a Joyful House, Assyriological Studies in Honor of Erle Verdun Leichty,* 297–311. *Cuneiform Monographs* 31. Leiden: Brill.

Pomponio, F. 1990 *Formule di Maledizione della Mesopotamia preclassica*. Brescia: Paideia.

————2002 "Funzionari di Ebla e di Mari," in S. de Martino and F. Pecchioli Daddi, eds., *Anatolica Antica, Studi in memoria di Fiorella Imparati,* 653–63. *Eothen* 11. Florence: LoGisma.

————2011 "Quello che Accade (forse) dopo la morte di Šar-kali-šarrī," in G. Barjamovic, J. Dahl, U. Koch, W. Sommerfeld, and J. Westenholz, eds., *Akkade is King, A Collection of Papers by Friends and Colleagues Presented to Aage Westenholz on the Occasion of His 70th Birthday 15th of May 2009,* 227–43. *Publications de l'Institut historique-archéologique néerlandais de Stamboul* 118. Leiden: Nederlands Instituut voor het Nabije Oosten.

————2013 "Some Scraps of Information and Discussion about the Economy of the Third Millennium Babylonia," in F. D'Agostino, ed., *L'economia dell'antica Mesopotamia (III – I millennio a.C), Per un dialogo interdisciplinare,* 23–39. Rome: Istituto Italiano di Studi Orientali, Università di Roma.

Pomponio, F. and G. Visicato 2011 "I Mezzi di Pagamento nei Contratti di Fara e il loro Rapporto con il Funzionario-Bala," in E. Ascalone and L. Peyronel, eds., *Studi Italiani di Metrologia ed Economia del Vicino Oriente Antico dedicati a Nicola Parise in Occasion del Suo Settantsesimo Compleanno,* 163–80. Rome: Herders.

Pomponio, F., G. Visicato, and A. Westenholz 2006 *Le Tavolette Cuneiformi di Adab delle Collezioni della Banca d'Italia*. Rome: Banca d'Italia.

Pongratz-Leisten, B. 2002 "'Lying King' and 'False Prophet': The Intercultural Transfer of a Rhetorical Device within Ancient Near Eastern Ideologies," in A. Panaino and G. Pettinato, eds., *Ideologies as Intercultural Phenomena,* 215–43. *Proceedings of the Third Annual Symposium of the Assyrian and Babylonian Intellectual Heritage Project Held in Chicago, USA, October 27–31, 2000 (Melammu Symposia III)*. Milan: University of Bologna.

Porada, E. 1952 "On the Problem of Kassite Art," in G. Miles, ed., *Archaeologica Orientalia in Memoriam Ernst Herzfeld,* 179–88. Locust Valley, NY: J.J. Augustin.

————1984 "Pottery in Scenes of the Period of Agade," in P. Rice, ed., *Pots and Potters: Current Approaches in Ceramic Archaeology,* 21–4. *Monograph* 24. Los Angeles: Institute of Archaeology.

————1986 "The Use of Art to Convey Political Meanings in the Ancient Near East," in D. Castriota, ed., *Artistic Strategy and the Rhetoric of Power, Political Uses of Art from Antiquity to the Present,* 15–26. Carbondale: Southern Illinois University Press.

————1992 "A Lapis Lazuli Disk with Relief Carving for King Rimuš," in D. Charpin and F. Joannès, eds., *La Circulation des biens, des personnes et des idées dans le Proche-Orient ancien,* 69–72. *Actes de la XXXVIII^e Rencontre Assyriologique Internationale (Paris, 8–10 juillet 1991)*. Paris: Editions Recherche sur les Civilisations.

Porada, E., D. Hansen, S. Dunham, and S. Babcock 1992 "The Chronology of Mesopotamia, ca. 7000–1600 BC," in R. Ehrich, ed., *Chronologies in Old World Archaeology,* third edition, 1: 77–121, 2: 90–124. Chicago: University of Chicago Press.

Postgate, J. 1976 "Inscriptions from Tell Al-Wilayah," *Sumer* 32: 77–100.

————1979 "The Historical Geography of the Hamrin Basin," *Sumer* 35: 594–1.

————1984 "Processing of Cereals in the Cuneiform Record," *Bulletin on Sumerian Agriculture* 1: 103–13.

————1992 *Early Mesopotamia, Society and Economy at the Dawn of History*. London: Routledge.

Postgate, J. and M. Powell, eds. 1993 *Domestic Animals of Mesopotamia*, Part I. *Bulletin on Sumerian Agriculture* 7.

————1995 *Domestic Animals of Mesopotamia*, Part II. *Bulletin on Sumerian Agriculture* 8.

Potts, D. 1984 "Salt and Salt-Gathering in Ancient Mesopotamia," *Journal of the Economic and Social History of the Orient* 27: 225–71.

————1986 "The Booty of Magan," *Oriens Antiquus* 25: 271–85.

————1997 *Mesopotamian Civilization: The Material Foundations*. Ithaca: Cornell University Press.

————1999 *The Archaeology of Elam: Formation and Transformation of an Ancient Iranian State*. Cambridge: Cambridge University Press.

————2010 "Adamšah, Kimaš and the Miners of Lagaš," in H. Baker, E. Robson, and G. Zólyomi, ed., *Your Praise is Sweet, A Memorial Volume for Jeremy Black from Students, Colleagues and Friends*, 245–54. London: British Institute for the Study of Iraq.

————2011 "The Size of the Cultivated Area of the Mesopotamian Alluvium as an Historical and Politico-Empirical Problem," in G. Selz and K. Wagensonner, eds., *The Empirical Dimension of Ancient Near Eastern Studies*, 271–91. *Wiener Offene Orientalistik* 6. Vienna: Lit.

Potts, T. 1989 "Foreign Stone Vessels of the Late Third Millennium B.C. from Southern Mesopotamia: Their Origins and Mechanisms of Exchange," *Iraq* 51: 123–64.

————1993 "Patterns of Trade in Third-Millennium BC Mesopotamia and Iran," *World Archaeology* 24/3: 379–402.

————1994 *Mesopotamia and the East: An Archaeological and Historical Study of Foreign Relations 3400–2000 B.C.* Oxford: Oxford Institute of Archaeology.

————2001 "Reading Sargonic 'Historical-Literary' Tradition: Is There a Middle Course (Thoughts on *The Great Revolt against Naram-Sin*)," in T. Abusch, P.-A. Beaulieu, J. Huehnergard, P. Michinist, and P. Steinkeller, eds., *Historiography in the Cuneiform World, Proceedings of the XLV* Rencontre Assyriologique Internationale* 1: 391–408. Bethesda, Md.: CDL Press.

Powell, M. 1977 "Sumerian Merchants and the Problem of Profit," *Iraq* 39: 23–9.

————1978a "Götter, Könige und 'Kapitalisten' im Mesopotamien des 3. Jahrtausends v. Chr. v. u. Z.," *Oikumene* 2: 127–44.

————1978b "Ukubi to Mother … The Situation is Desperate: A Plaidoyer for Methodological Rigor in Editing and Interpreting Sumerian Texts with an Excursus on the Verb taka: $da_x$-$da_x$ (TAG$_{\downarrow}$)," *Zeitschrift für Assyriologie* 68: 163–95.

————1978c "A Contribution to the History of Money in Mesopotamia prior to the Invention of Coinage," in B. Hruška and G. Komoróczy, eds., *Festschrift Lubor Matouš*, 211–43. Budapest: Eötvös Loránd Tudományegyeten.

————1978d "Texts from the Time of Lugalzagesi: Problems and Perspectives in their Interpretation," *Hebrew Union College Annual* 49: 1–58.

————1985 "Salt, Seed, and Yields in Sumerian Agriculture: A Critique of the Theory of Progressive Salinization," *Zeitschrift für Assyriologie* 75: 7–38.

————, ed. 1987 *Labor in the Ancient Near East*. American Oriental Series 68. New Haven: Amiercan Oriental Society.

————1991 "Narām-Sin, Son of Sargon: Ancient History, Famous Names, and a Famous Babylonian Forgery," *Zeitschrift für Assyriologie* 81: 20–30.

————1992 "Timber Production in Presargonic Lagaš," *Bulletin on Sumerian Agriculture* 6: 99–122.

————1994 "Metron Ariston: Measure as a Tool for Studying Beer in Ancient Mesopotamia," in L. Milano, ed., *Drinking in Ancient Societies, History and Culture of Drinks in the Ancient Near East, Papers of a Symposium held in Rome, May 17–19, 1990*, 91–119. *History of the Ancient Near East/Studies* 6. Padua: Sargon.

————1996 "Money in Mesopotamia," *Journal of the Economic and Social History of Mesopotamia* 39: 224–42.

————1999 *"Wir müssen unsere Nische nutzen*: Monies, Motives, and Methods in Babylonian Economics," in J. Dercksen, ed., *Trade and Finance in Ancient Mesopotamia, MOS Studies 1. Proceedings of the First MOS Symposium (Leiden 1997)*, 5–23. Leiden: Nederlands Historisch-Archaeologisch Instituut te Istanbul.

————2003/5 "Obst und Gemüse. A.I.," *Reallexikon der Assyriologie* 10: 13–22.

Poyck, A. P. G. 1962 *Farm Studies in Iraq (An Agro-Economic Study of the Agriculture in the Hilla-Diwaniya Area in Iraq), Mededelingen van de Landbouwhogeschool te Wageningen, Nederland* 62/1.

Prentice, R. 2010 *The Exchange of Goods and Services in Pre-Sargonic Lagash. Alter Orient und Altes Testament* 368. Münster: Ugarit-Verlag.

Pruß, A. and W. Sallaberger 2003/4 "Tierhaltung in Nabada / Tell Beydar und die Bilderwelt der Terrakotten als Spiegel von Wirtschaft und Umwelt," *Archiv für Orientforschung* 50: 293–307.

Pruzsinszky, R. 2010 "Die königlichen Sänger der Ur III-Zeit als Werkzeug politischer Propaganda," in R. Pruzsinszky and D. Shehata, eds., *Musiker und Tradierung, Studien zur Rolle von Musikern bei der Verschriftlichung und Tradierung von literarischen Werken*, 95–118. *Wiener Offene Orientalistik* 8. Vienna: Lit.

Radau, H. 1900 *Early Babylonian History down to the End of the Fourth Dynasty of Ur.* New York: Oxford University Press American Branch.

Radner, K. 2005 *Die Macht des Namens: Altorientalische Strategien zur Selbtserhaltung. Santag* 8. Wiesbaden: Harrassowitz.

Ramazzotti, M. 2010 "Anatomia di Akkad: l'ombre di una città invisibile dal suo paesaggio storiografico, etetico et storico," in R. Dolce, ed., *Quale Oriente? Omaggio a un Maestro: Studi di Arte e Archeologia del Vicino Oriente in Memoria di Anton Moortgat a 30 Anni dalla sua Scomparsa*, 341–75. Palermo: Flaccovio.

Rasheed, F. 1981 *The Ancient Inscriptions in Himrin Area, Himrin 4: Results of the Salvage Excavations at Himrin Reservoir.* Baghdad: State Organization of Antiquities and Heritage.

Rashid, S. and H. Ali-Huri 1983 *The Akkadian Seals of the Iraq Museum.* Baghdad: State Organization of Antiquities and Heritage.

Reade, J. 1968 "Tell Taya (1967): Summary Report," *Iraq* 30: 234–64.

————1971 "Tell Taya (1968–9): Summary Report," *Iraq* 33: 87–100.

————1973 "Tell Taya (1972–3): Summary Report," *Iraq* 35: 155–87.

————1982 "Tell Taya," in J. Curtis, ed., *Fifty Years of Mesopotamian Discovery*, 72–8. London: British School of Archaeology in Iraq.

————2001/2 "Unfired Clay, Models, and 'Sculptors' Models' in the British Museum," *Archiv für Orientforschung* 48/49 (2001/2), 147–64.

————2002 "Early Monuments in Gulf Stone at the British Museum, with Observations on some Gudea Statues and the Location of Agade," *Zeitschrift für Assyriologie* 92: 258–95.

————2011 "The Search for Old Akkadian Rule at Nineveh," in G. Barjamovic, J. Dahl, U. Koch, W. Sommerfeld, and J. Westenholz, eds., *Akkade is King, A Collection of Papers by Friends and Colleagues Presented to Aage Westenholz on the Occasion of His 70th Birthday 15th of May 2009*, 245–51. *Publications de l'Institut historique-archéologique néerlandais de Stamboul* 118. Leiden: Nederlands Instituut voor het Nabije Oosten.

Reichel, C. 2008 "The King is Dead, Long Live the King: The Last Days of the Šu-Sin Cult at Ešnunna and its Aftermath," in N. Brisch, ed., *Religion and Power: Divine Kingship in the Ancient World and Beyond*, 133–55. *Oriental Institute Seminars* 4. Chicago: Oriental Institute of the University of Chicago.

Reiner, E. 1963 "Mâlamir," *Revue d'Assyriologie* 57: 169–74.

————1974 "New Light on Some Historical Omens," in K. Bittel, P. Houwink Ten Cate, and E. Reiner, eds., *Anatolian Studies Presented to Hans Gustav Güterbock on the Occasion of His 65th Birthday*, 257–61. *Publications de l'Institut historique-archéologique néerlandais de Stamboul* 33. Istanbul: Nederlands Historisch-Archaeologisch Instituut.

Reisman, D. 1969 *Two Neo-Sumerian Royal Hymns*. Dissertation: University of Pennsylvania.

Renger, J. 1967/69. "Untersuchungen zum Priestertum in der altbabylonischer Zeit," *Zeitschrift für Assyriologie* 58: 110–88, 59: 104–230.

————1994 "On Economic Structures in Ancient Mesopotamia," *Orientalia* NS 63: 157–208.

————1995a "Institutional, Communal, and Individual Ownership or Possession of Arable Land in Ancient Mesopotamia from the End of the Fourth to the End of the First Millennium BC," in J. Lindgren, L. Mayali, and G. Miller, eds., *Symposium on Ancient Law, Economics, and Society*, Part II, 269–319. *Chicago-Kent Law Review* 71/1.

————1995b "Subsistenzproduktion und redistributive Palastwirtschaft: Wo bleibt die Nische für das Geld? Grenzen und Möglichkeiten für die Verwendung von Geld im alten Mesopotamien," in W. Schelke and M. Nitsch, eds., *Rätsel Geld. Annäherungen aus ökonomischer, soziologischer und historischer Sicht*, 271–324. Marburg: Metropolis-Verlag.

————1996a "Handwerk und Handwerker im alten Mesopotamien," *Altorientalische Forschungen* 23: 211–31.

————1996b "Vergangenes Geschehen in der Textüberlieferung des alten Mesopotamien," in H.-J. Gehrke and A. Müller, eds., *Vergangenheit und Lebenswelt. Soziale Kommunikation, Traditionsbildung und historische Bewußtsein*, 9–60. Tübingen: G. Narr.

————2002 Wirtschaftsgeschichte des alten Mesopotamien. Versuch einer Standortbestimmung," in A. Hausleiter, S. Kerner, and B. Müller-Neuhof, eds., *Material Culture and Mental Spheres. Rezeption archäologischer Denkrichtungen in der Vorderasiatischen Altertumskunde. Internationales Symposium für Hans J. Nissen, Berlin, 23.-24. Juni 2000*, 239–65. *Alter Orient und Altes Testament* 293. Münster: Ugarit-Verlag.

————2007 "Economy of Ancient Mesopotamia: A General Outline," in G. Leick, ed., *The Babylonian World*, 187–97. London: Routledge.

Richardson, S. 2010 "On Seeing and Believing: Liver Divination and the Era of Warring States," in A. Annus, ed., *Divination and Intepretation of Signs in the Ancient World*, 225–66. Oriental Institute Seminars 6. Chicago: Oriental Institute of the University of Chicago.

Riemschneider, K. 1965 "Ein altbabylonischer Gallenomentext," *Zeitschrift für Assyriologie* 57: 125–45.

Ristvet, L., T. Guilderson, and H. Weiss 2004 "The Dynamics of State Development and Imperialization at Third Millennium Tell Leilan, Syria," *Orient-Express* 21/2: 94–9.

Rmaidh *see* Rumaidh

Roaf, Michael 2000 "Survivals and Revivals in the Art of Ancient Mesopotamia," in P. Matthiae, ed., *Proceedings of the First International Congress of the Archaeology of the Ancient Near East, Rome, May 18th-23rd 1998*, 1447–62. Rome: La Sapienza.

Roberts, J. 1972 *The Earliest Semitic Pantheon: A Study of the Deities Attested in Mesopotamia before Ur III*. Baltimore: Johns Hopkins University Press.

Robson, E. 1999 *Mesopotamian Mathematics, 2100–1600 BC, Technical Constants in Bureaucracy and Education*. Oxford Editions of Cuneiform Texts 14. Oxford: Clarendon Press.

————2001 "The Tablet House: A Scribal School in Old Babylonian Nippur," *Revue d'Assyriologie* 95: 39–66.

Rochberg, F. 1999 "Empiricism in Babylonian Omen Texts and the Classification of Mesopotamian Divination as Science," *Journal of the American Oriental Society* 119: 559–69.

————2004 *The Heavenly Writing*. Cambridge: Cambridge University Press.

————2010 "'If P, then Q': Form and Reasoning in Babylonian Divination," in A. Annus, ed., *Divination and Interpretation of Signs in the Ancient World*, 19–27. Oriental Institute Seminars 6. Chicago: Oriental Institute of the University of Chicago.

————2012 "The Expression of Terrestrial and Celestial Order in Ancient Mesopotamia," in R. Talbert, ed., *Ancient Perspectives and Their Place in Mesopotamia, Greece, and Rome*, 9–46. Chicago: University of Chicago Press.

Rogers, R. 1901 *A History of Babylonia and Assyria*. New York: Eaton & Mains.

Rohn, K. 2011 *Beschriftete mesopotamischer Siegel der frühdynastischen und der Akkad-Zeit*, Orbis Biblicus et Orientalis, Series Archaeologica 32. Göttingen: Vandenhoeck & Ruprecht.

Rollinger, R. 2010 "Berg und Gebirge aus altorientalischer Perspecktive," in W. Kofler, M. Korenjak, and F. Schaffenrath, eds., *Gipfel der Zeit: Berge in Texten aus fünf Jahrtausenden. Karlheinz Töchterle zum 60. Geburtstag*, 11–53. Paradeigmata 12. Freiburg: Rombach Verlag.

————2011/x "Sport und Spiel," *Reallexikon der Assyriologie* 13: (in press). Berlin: De Gruyter.

————2012 "From Sargon of Agade and the Assyrian Kings to Kusrau I and Beyond: On the Persistence of Ancient Near Eastern Traditions," in G. Lanfranchi, D. Bonacossi, C. Pappi, and S. Ponchia, eds., *Leggo! Studies Presented to Frederick Mario Fales on the Occasion of His 65th Birthday*, 725–43. Leipziger Altorientalische Studien 2. Wiesbaden: Harrassowitz.

Rosengarten Y. 1960 *Le régime des offrandes*. Paris: De Boccard.

Ross, J. 2001 "Text and Symbol: Precious Metals and Politics in Old Akkadian Mesopotamia," in T. Abusch, P. Beaulieu, J. Huehnergard, P. Machinist, and P. Steinkeller, eds., *Historiography in the Cuneiform World, Proceedings of the XLV<sup>e</sup> Rencontre Assyriologique Internationale 1998* 1, 417–28. Bethesda, MD: CDL Press.

Roth, M. 1997 *Law Collections from Mesopotamia and Asia Minor*, second edition. *Writings from the Ancient World Series* 6. Atlanta: Society of Biblical Literature.

Rowton, M. 1967 "The Physical Environment and the Problem of the Nomads," in J.-R. Kupper, ed., *XV<sup>e</sup> Rencontre Assyriologique Internationale: La civilisation de Mari*, 101–121. Paris: Les Belles Lettres.

Rubio, G. 2005 "On the Linguistic Landscape of Early Mesopotamia," in W. Van Soldt, ed., *Ethnicity in Ancient Mesopotamia, Papers Read at the 48th Rencontre Assyriologique Internationale Leiden, 1–4 July 2002*, 316–32. Leiden: Nederlands Instituut voor het Nabije Oosten.

————2009 "Sumerian Literature," in C. Ehrich, ed., *From an Antique Land: An Introduction to Ancient Near Eastern Literature*, 11–75. Lanham, Md: Rowman & Littlefield.

Rumaidh, S. S. 1981 "Tanqībātu Tall Suleimeh," *Sumer* 40 (1981), Arabic portion 43–54.

Rutten, M. 1938 "Trente-deux modèles de foie en argille inscrits provenant de Tell-Hariri (Mari)," *Revue d'Assyriologie* 35: 36–70.

————1941 "Le paysage dans l'art de la Mésopotamie ancienne," *Syria* 22: 137–54.

Ryder, M. L. 1993 "Sheep and Goat Husbandry with Particular Reference to Textile Fibre and Milk Production," *Bulletin on Sumerian Agriculture* 7: 9–32.

Saadoon, A. 2014 "New Cuneiform Texts from Tell Al-Wilayah (Ancient Kesh?) Kept in the Iraqi Museum," *Sumer* 59: 42–61.

Salgues, E. 2011 "Naram-Sin's Conquests of Subartu and Armanum," in G. Barjamovic, J. Dahl, U. Koch, W. Sommerfeld, and J. Westenholz (eds.), *Akkade is King: A Collection of Papers by Friends and Colleagues Presented to Aage Westenholz on the Occasion of His 70th Birthday*

*15th of May 2009*, 253–72. *Publications de l'Institut historique-archéologique néerlandais de Stamboul* 118. Leiden: Nederlands Instituut voor het Nabije Oosten.

Sallaberger, W. 1989 "Zum Schilfrohr als Rohstoff in Babylonien," in B. Scholz, ed., *Der orientalische Mensch und seine Beziehungen zur Umwelt: Beiträge zum 2. Grazer Morgenländischen Symposion (2.-5. März 1989)*, 311–30. *Grazer Morgenländische Studien* 2. Graz: Dvb-Verlag.

———1993 *Der kultische Kalender der Ur III-Zeit.* Berlin: De Gruyter.

———1995 "Eine reiche Bestattung im neusumerischen Ur," *Journal of Cuneiform Studies* 47: 15–21.

———1996 *Der Babylonische Töpfer und seine Gefässe, nach Urkunden altsumerischer bis altbabylonsicher Zeit sowie lexikalischen und literarischen Zeugnissen. Mesopotamian History and Environment, Memoirs* III. Ghent: University of Ghent.

———1997 "Nippur als religiöses Zentrum Mesopotamiens im historischen Wandel," in G. Wilhelm, ed., *Die orientalische Stadt: Kontinuität, Wandel, Bruch*, 147–68. *1. Internationales Colloquium der Deutschen Orient-Gesellschaft*. Saarbrücken: Saarbrücker Druckerei und Verlag.

———1999a "Nagar in den frühdynastischen Texten aus Beydar," in K. van Lerberghe and G. Voet, eds., *Languages and Cultures in Contact: At the Crossroads of Civilisations in the Syro-Mesopotamian Realm, Proceedings of the 42ᵗʰ (sic) Rencontre Assyriologique Intenationale*, 393–407. *Orientalia Lovaniensia Analecta* 96. Leuven: Peeters.

———1999b "Ur III-Zeit," in P. Attinger, M. Wäfler, eds., *Mesopotamien: Akkade-Zeit und Ur III-Zeit*, 121–390. *Orbis Biblicus et Orientalis* 160/3. Göttingen: Vandenhoeck & Ruprecht.

———2004a "Relative Chronologie von der frühdynastischen bis zur altbabylonischen Zeit," in J.-W. Meyer and W. Sommerfeld, ed., *2000 v. Chr., Politische, wirtschaftliche und kulturelle Entwicklung im Zeichen einer Jahrtausendwende, 3. Internationales Colloquium der Deutschen Orient-Gesellschaft*, 15–43. Saarbrücken: Saarbrücker Druckerei.

———2004b "Das Ende des Sumerischen: Tod und Nachleben einer altmesopotamischen Sprache," in P. Schrijver and P. Mumm, eds., *Sprachtod und Sprachgeburt*, 108–40. Bremen: Hempen.

———2006/8 "Ritual," *Reallexikon der Assyriologie* 11: 421–30.

———2007 "From Urban Culture to Nomadism: A History of Upper Mesopotamia in the Late Third Millennium," in C. Marro and C. Kuzuoglu, eds., *Sociétés humaines et changement climatique à la fin du troisième millénaire: Une crise a-t-elle eu lieu en Haute Mésopotamie? Actes du Colloque de Lyon, 5–8 décembre 2005*, 417–56. *Varia Anatolica* 19. Istanbul: Institut français d'études anatoliennes Georges-Dumézil.

———2008 "Rechtsbrüche in Handel, Diplomatie und Kult, Ein Memorandum aus Ebla über Verfehlungen Maris (ARET 13, 15)," *Kaskal* 5: 93–110.

———2011 "Sumerian Language Use at Garšana: On Orthography, Grammar, and Akkado-Sumerian Bilingualism," in D. Owen, ed., *Garšana Studies*, 335–72. *Cornell University Studies in Assyriology and Sumerology* 6. Bethesda, Md.: CDL Press.

———2012 "Bierbrauen in Versen: Eine neue Edition und Interpretation der Ninkasi-Hymne," in C. Mittermayer and S. Ecklin, ed., *Altorientalische Studien zu Ehren von Pascal Attinger*, 291–328. *Orbis Biblicus et Orientalis* 256. Göttingen: Vandenhoeck & Ruprecht.

———2013 "The Management of Royal Treasure: Palace Archives and Palatial Economy in the Ancient Near East," in J. Hill, P. Jones, and A. Morales, eds., *Experiencing Power, Generating Authority: Cosmos, Politics, and the Ideology of Kingship in Ancient Egypt and Mesopotamia*, 219–55. Philadelphia: University of Pennsylvania Museum of Archaeology and Anthropology.

Sallaberger, W. and Huber Vulliet, F. 2003/5 "Priester," *Reallexikon der Assyriologie* 10: 617–40.

Sallaberger, W. and I. Schrakamp, eds. 2010 *Historical and Epigraphic Data for a Chronology of Mesopotamia in the Third Millennium BC. Associated Regional Chronologies for the Ancient Near East and the Eastern Mediterranean* 1. Turnhout: Brepols.

————2015 *History and Philology. Associated Regional Chronologies for the Ancient Near East and the Eastern Mediterranean* 3. Turnhout: Brepols.

Salman *see* Rumaidh

Salonen, A. 1939 *Die Wasserfahrzeuge in Babylonien. Studia Orientalia* 8/4. Helsinki: Societas Orientalis Fennica.

————1951 *Die Landfahrzeuge des alten Mesopotamien, Annales Academiae Scientiarum Fennicae* ser. B tom. 72,3. Helsinki: Academia Scientiarum Fennica.

————1961 *Die Türen des alten Mesopotamien, Annales Academiae Scientiarum Fennicae* ser. B tom. 124. Helsinki: Academia Scientiarum Fennica.

————1963 *Die Möbel des alten Mesopotamien nach sumerisch-akkadischen Quellen: Eine lexikalische und kulturgeschichtliche Untersuchung, Annales Academiae Scientiarum Fennicae* ser. B tom. 127. Helsinki: Academia Scientiarum Fennica.

————1964 "Die Öfen der alten Mesopotamier," *Baghdader Mitteilungen* 3: 100–124.

————1966 *Die Hausgeräte der alten Mesopotamier nach sumerisch-akkadischen Quellen: Eine lexikalische und kulturgeschichtliche Untersuchung, Teil II: Gefässe. Annales Academiae Scientiarum Fennicae* ser. B tom. 144. Helsinki: Academia Scientiarum Fennica.

————1970 *Die Fischerei im alten Mesopotamien nach sumerisch-akkadischen Quellen. Annales Academiae Scientiarum Fennicae* ser. B tom. 166. Helsinki: Academia Scientiarum Fennica.

————1972 *Die Ziegeleien im alten Mesopotamien. Annales Academiae Scientiarum Fennicae* ser. B tom. 171. Helsinki: Academia Scientiarum Fennica.

Sanati-Müller, S. 2011 "Zwei altbabylonische Tonkegelfragmente aus der Heidelberger Uruk-Warka Tontafelsammlung," *Zeitschrift für Orient-Archäologie* 4: 82–91.

Saporetti, C. 2002 *La rivale di Babylonia: Storia di Ešnunna, un potente regno che sfidò Ḫammurapi.* Rome: Newton & Compton.

Sax, M. 1993 "The Availability of Raw Materials for Near Eastern Cylinder Seals during the Akkadian, Post-Akkadian, and Ur III Periods," *Iraq* 55: 77–90.

Sayce, A. 1872 "The Origin of Semitic Civilisation, Chiefly upon Philological Evidence," *Transactions of the Society of Biblical Archaeology* 1: 294–302.

————1876 "The Babylonian Cylinders found by General di Cesnola in the Treasury of the Temple at Kurium," *Proceedings of the Society of Biblical Archaeology* 5: 441–4.

Sazonov, V. 2007 "Vergöttlichung der Könige von Akkade," in T. Kämmerer, ed., *Studien zur Ritual and Sozialgeschichte im Alten Orient. Tartuer Symposien 1998–2004*, 325–43. *Beiheft zur Zeitschrift für die Alttestamentliche Wissenschaft* 374. Berlin: De Gruyter.

Schaudig, H. 2001 *Die Inschriften Nabonids von Babylon und Kyros' des Großen samt den in ihrem Umfeld entstandenen Tendenzschriften, Textausgabe und Grammatik. Alter Orient und Altes Testament* 256. Münster: Ugarit-Verlag.

————2003 "Nabonid, der 'Archäolog auf der Königsthron'. Zur Geschichtsbild des ausgehenden neubabylonischen Reiches," in G. Selz, ed., *Festschrift für Burkhart Kienast zu seinem 70. Geburtstage dargebracht von Freunden, Schülern und Kollegen*, 447–97. *Alter Orient und Altes Testament* 274. Münster: Ugarit-Verlag.

Scheil, V. 1908 "Inscription de Šarru-ukîn," *Mémoires de la Délégation en Perse* 10: 4–8. Paris: Ernest Leroux.

————1911 "Les plus anciennes dynasties connues de Sumer-Accad," *Comptes Rendus de l'Académie des Inscriptions et Belles-Lettres* 1911: 606–20. Paris: Alphonse Picard.

————1912 "Narâm-Sin – Šargani šarri," *Revue d'Assyriologie* 9: 70.

————1913 "L'armure au temps de Narâm-Sin, *Recueil de Travaux* 35: 26–35.

## 410    Bibliography

——— 1918 "Gilgameš et la chaussure à pointe recourbée," *Revue d'Assyriologie* 15: 84–5.

——— 1925 "Fourniture d'ailes," *Revue d'Assyriologie* 22: 156–7.

Schileico, W. 1914 "Das sechseitige Tonprisma Lugal-ušumgal's aus der Sammlung Lichatschew," *Zeitschrift für Assyriologie* 29: 78–84.

Schlossman, B. 1978/9 "Portraiture in Mesopotamia in the Late Third and Early Second Millennium B.C., Part I: The Late Third Millennium," *Archiv für Orientforschung* 26: 56–77.

Schmidt, V. 1872/77 *Assyriens og Ægyptens Gamle Historie eller Historisk-Geographiske Undersøgelser om det Gamle Testamentes Lande og Folk.* Copenhagen: Fr. Wøldikes Forlag.

Schmökel, H. 1955 *Ur, Assur und Babylon, Drei Jahrtausende im Zweistromland, Grosse Kulturen der Frühzeit.* Stuttart: Gustav Klipper Verlag.

Schott, A. 1934 "Das Werden der babylonisch-assyrischen Positions-Astronomie und einige seiner Bedeutungen," *Zeitschrift der Deutschen Morgenländischen Gesellschaft* 88: 302–37.

Schrakamp, I. 2006 "Kommentar zu der altakkadischen 'Rüstkammerurkunde' Erm. 14380," *Annual of Ancient Near Eastern, Old Testament, and Semitic Studies*, 161–77. *Orientalia et Classica 14, Babel und Bibel* 3. Winona Lake, Ind.: Eisenbrauns.

——— 2009/11 "Schleuder A," *Reallexikon der Assyriologie* 12: 222–5.

——— 2010 *Krieger und Waffen im frühen Mesopotamien, Organisation und Bewaffnung des Militärs in frühdynastischen und sargonischer Zeit.* Dissertation: Philipps-Universität Marburg.

——— 2015 "Geographical Horizons of the Presargonic and Sargonic Archives," in W. Sallaberger and I. Schrakamp, eds., *History and Philology. Associated Regional Chronologies for the Ancient Near East and the Eastern Mediterranean* 3, 197–270. Turnhout: Brepols.

Schretter, M. 1990 *Emesal-Studien: Sprach-und literaturgeschichtliche Untersuchungen zum sogennanten Frauensprache des Sumerischen. Innsbrucker Beiträge zur Kulturwissenschaft, Sonderheft* 69. Innsbruck: Institut für Sprachwissenschaft.

Schuster-Brands, A. 2008 *Steine als Schutz-und Heilmittel: Untersuchungen zu ihrer Verwendung in der Beschwörungskunst Mesopotamiens im 1. Jt. V. Chr., Alter Orient und Altes Testament* 46. Münster: Ugarit-Verlag.

Schwemer, D. 2001 *Die Wettergottgestalten Mesopotamiens und Nordsyriens im Zeitalter der Keilschrifturkunden.* Wiesbaden: Harrassowitz.

——— 2010 "Magic Rituals: Conceptualization and Performance," in K. Radner and E. Robson, eds., *The Oxford Handbook of Cuneiform Culture*, 418–42. Oxford: Oxford University Press.

Scurlock, J. 1991 "Taklimtu: A Display of Grave Goods?" NABU 1991/3.

——— 2002 "Soul Emplacements in Ancient Mesopotamian Funerary Rituals," in L. Ciraolo and J. Seidl, eds., *Magic and Divination in the Ancient World*, 1–6. *Ancient Magic and Divination* 2. Leiden: Brill.

——— 2003 "Ancient Mesopotamian House Gods," *Journal of Ancient Near Eastern Religions* 3: 99–106.

——— 2008 "On Some Terms for Leatherworking in Ancient Mesopotamia," in R. Biggs, J. Myers, and M. Roth, eds., *Proceedings of the 51st Rencontre Assyriologique Internationale Held at the Oriental Institute of the University of Chicago July 18–22, 2005*, 171–6. *Studies in Ancient Oriental Civilization* 62. Chicago: Oriental Institute of the University of Chicago.

Sefati, Y. 1998 *Love Songs in Sumerian Literature.* Ramat-Gan: Bar Ilan University Press.

Selz, Ge. 1991 "'Elam' und 'Sumer'" – Skizze einer Nachbarschaft nach inschriftlichen Quellen der vorsargonischen Zeit," in L. De Meyer and H. Gasche, eds., *Mésopotamie et Elam, Actes de la XXXVIème Rencontre assyriologique internationale, Gand, 10–14 juillet 1989*, 27–43. *Mesopotamian History and Environment, Occasional Publications* 1. Ghent: University of Ghent.

——— 1995a "Den Fährmann bezahlen! Eine lexikalisch-kulturhistorische Skizze zu den Bedeutungen von addir," AoF 22: 197–209.

————1995b "Maš-da-ri-a und Verwandtes: Ein Versuch über da-ri 'an der Seite führen': ein zusammengesetztes Verbum und einige nominale Ableitungen," *Acta Sumerologica* 17:251–74.

————1997 "The Holy Drum, the Spear, and the Harp: Towards an Understanding of the Problems of Deification in the Third Millennium Mesopotamia," in I. Finkel and M. Geller, eds., *Sumerian Gods and Their Representations*, 167–213, *Cuneiform Monographs* 7. Groningen: Styx.

————1998a "Die Etana-Erzählung, Ursprung und Tradition einer der ältesten epischen Texte in einer semitischen Sprache," *Acta Sumerologica* 20: 135–79.

————1998b "Über Mesopotamische Herrschaftskonzepte: Zu den Ursprüngen mesopotamischer Herrschaftsideologie im 3. Jahrtausend," in M. Dietrich, O. Loretz, and T. Balke, eds., *dubsar anta-men, Studien zur Altorientalistik, Festschrift für Willem H. Ph. Römer zur Vollendung seines 70. Lebensjahres mit Beiträgen von Freunden, Schülern und Kollegen*, 281–344. *Alter Orient und Altes Testament* 253. Münster: Ugarit-Verlag.

————1999 "Vom 'vergangenen Geschehen' zur 'Zukunftsbewältigung': Überlegungen zur Rolle der Schrift in Ökonomie und Geschichte," in B. Böck, E. Cancik-Kirschbaum, and T. Richter, eds., *Munuscula Mesopotamica, Festchrift für Johannes Renger*, 465–512. *Alter Orient und Altes Testament* 267. Münster: Ugarit-Verlag.

————2000a "Wirtschaftskrise – Legitimationskrise – Staatskrise. Zur Genese mesopotamischer Rechtsvorstellungen zwischen Planwirtschaft und Eigentumsverfassung," *Archiv für Orientforschung* 47: 1–44.

————2000b "Five Divine Ladies," *NIN* 1: 29–62.

————2002 "'Streit herrscht, Gewalt droht' – Zu Konfliktregelung und Recht in der frühdynastischen und altakkadischen Zeit," *Wiener Zeitschrift für die Kunde des Morgenlandes* 92: 155–203.

————2004 "'Tief ist der Brunnen der Vergangenheit,' Zu 'Leben' und 'Tod' nach Quellen der mesopotamischen Frühzeit – Interaktion zwischen Diesseits und Jenseits," in F. Schipper, ed., *Zwischen Euphrat und Tigris*, 39–59. *Österreichische Forschungen zum Alten Orient, Wiener Offene Orientalistik* 3. Vienna: Lit.

————2005a "Was bleibt? I. Ein Versuch zu Tod und Identität im Alten Orient," in R. Rollinger, ed., *Von Sumer bis Homer, Festschrift für Manfred Schretter zum 60. Geburtstag am 25. Februar 2004*, 577–94. *Alter Orient und Altes Testament* 325. Münster: Ugarit-Verlag.

————2005b *Sumerer und Akkader.* Munich: Beck.

————2011 "Zu einer frühdynastischen Bezeichnung von 'Unfreien': Ur(a)du(-d), eine Bemerkung zum 'Hausgeborenen Sklaven'," NABU 2011/70.

————2014 "Feeding the Travellers: On Early Dynastic Travel, Travel Networks and Travel Provisions in the Frame of Third Millennium Mesopotamia," in L. Milano, ed., *Palaeonutrition and Food Practices in the Ancient Near East: Towards an Interdisciplinary Approach, Proceedings of the International Meeting* Methods and Perspectives Applied to the Study of Food Practices in the Ancient Near East *Venezia, June 15th–17th, 2006*, 261–79. Padua: Sargon.

Selz, Gu. 1983 *Die Bankettszene: Entwicklung eines "überzeitlichen" Bildmotiv in Mesopotamien. Von der frühdynastischen bis zur Akkad-Zeit, Freiburger Orientalische Studien* 11. Stuttgart: Steiner.

————1992 "Enlil und Nippur nach präsargonischen Quellen," in M. de J. Ellis, ed., *Nippur at the Centennial, Papers Read at the 38e Rencontre Assyriologique Internationale, Philadelphia, 1988*, 189–225. Occasional Publications of the Samuel Noah Kramer Fund 14. Philadelphia: University Museum of Archaeology and Anthropology.

Senior, L. and H. Weiss 1992 "Tell Leilan 'sila bowls' and the Akkadian Reorganization of Subarian Agricultural Production," *Orient-Express* 1992/2: 16–23.

Seri, A. 2006 *Local Power in Old Babylonian Mesopotamia*. Sheffield: Equinox.

Seux, M. 1965 "Les titres royaux *"šar kiššati"* et *šar kibrāt arba'i*," Revue d'Assyriologie 59: 1–18.

Shaheed, I. 1979 *Muhammad and Alexander, The Andrew W. Mellon Lecture Delivered at Georgetown University, May 2, 1978*. Georgetown: Georgetown University Press.

Sharashenidze, D. 1973 "K perevody obeliska Maništušu," *Voprosy Drevney Istorii, Kavkazski Bliznevostočnyj Sbornik* 4, 49–60. Tiflis: Izdatelstvo Metzniereba.

Sharlach, T. 2001 "Beyond Chronology: The Šakkanakkus of Mari and the Kings of Ur," in W. Hallo and I. Winter, eds., *Seals and Seal Impressions, Proceedings of the XLV^e Rencontre Assyriologique Internationale Part II*, 59–70. Bethesda, CDL Press.

————2004 *Provinicial Taxation and the Ur III State. Cuneiform Monographs* 27. Leiden: Brill.

Shehata, D. 2009 *Musiker und ihr vokales Repertoire, Untersuchungen zu Inhalt und Organisation von Musikerberufen und Liedgattungen in altbabylonsicher Zeit. Göttinger Beiträge zum Alten Orient* 3. Göttingen: Universitätsverlag Göttingen.

Sjöberg, Å. 1967 "Zu einigen Verwandtschaftsbezeichnungen im Sumerischen," in *Heidelberger Studien zum Alten Orient: Adam Falkenstein zum 17. September 1966*, 201–31. Wiesbaden: Harrassowitz.

Sjöberg, Å. and E. Bergmann 1969 *The Collection of Sumerian Temple Hymns. Texts from Cuneiform Sources* 3 Locust Valley, NY: J.J. Augustin.

————1975 "in-nin-šà-gur₄-ra, A Hymn to the Goddess Inanna by the en-Priestess Enh) eduanna," *Zeitschrift für Assyriologie* 65: 161–253.

Smith, G. 1872 "Early History of Babylonia," *Transactions of the Society of Biblical Archaeology* 1: 28–92.

Smith, G. and A. Sayce 1880 *The Chaldaean Account of Genesis*, new edition revised by A. H. Sayce. London: Sampson Low, Marston, Serle, and Rivington: 1880.

Snell, D. 1974 "The Mari Livers and the Omen Tradition," *Journal of the Ancient Near Eastern Society of Columbia University* 6: 117–23.

————1982 *Ledgers and Prices: Early Mesopotamian Merchant Accounts. Yale Near Eastern Researches* 8. New Haven: Yale University Press.

Sollberger, E. 1954/6 "Sur la chronologie des rois d'Ur et quelques problèmes connexes," *Archiv für Orientforschung* 17: 10–48.

————1965 *Royal Inscriptions, Part II. Ur Excavations, Texts* 8. London: British Museum.

————1967 "Lost Inscriptions from Mari," in J.-R. Kupper, ed., *La civilisation de Mari, XV^e Rencontre Assyriologique Internationale organisée par le Groupe François Thureau-Dangin (Liège, 4–8 juillet 1966)*, 103–7. Paris: Les Belles Lettres.

————1967/8 "The Cruciform Monument," *Jaarbericht van het Voor-Aziatisch Egyptisch Genootschap. Ex Oriente Lux* 20: 50–70.

————1982 "Les pouvoirs publics sous l'empire d'Ur: Les pouvoirs locaux," in A. Finet, ed., *Les pouvoirs locaux en Mésopotamie et dans les regions adjacentes*, 69–75. *Actes du Colloque organisé par l'Institut des Hautes Etudes de Belgique, 28 et 29 janvier 1980*. Bruxelles: Institut des Hautes Etudes de Belgique.

————1988 "Old Akkadian Texts," in I. Spar, ed., *Tablets, Cones, and Bricks of the Third Millennium B.C.*, 6–9. *Cuneiform Texts in the Metropolitan Museum of Art* 1. New York: Metropolitan Museum of Art.

Sommerfeld, W. 1999 *Die Texte der Akkade-Zeit, 1. Das Dijala-Gebiet: Tutub. Imgula* 3.1 Münster: Rhema.

————2000 "Narām-Sîn, de 'Große Revolte' und MAR.TU^ki," in J. Marzahn and H. Neumann, eds., *Assyriologica et Semitica: Festschrift für Joachim Oelsner anlässlich seines 65.*

*Geburtstages am 18. Februar 1997*, 419–36. *Alter Orient und Altes Testament* 252. Münster: Ugarit Verlag.

————2003a "Der Name Rimuš," in L. Kogan, ed., *Studia Semitica*, 407–23. *Orientalia* 3. Moscow: Russian State University for the Humanities.

————2003b "Bemerkungen zur Dialektgliederung, Altakkadisch, Assyrisch und Babylonisch," in G. Selz, ed., *Festschrift für Burkhart Kienast zu seinem 70. Geburtstage dargebracht von Freunden, Schülern und Kollegen*, 569–86. *Alter Orient und Altes Testament* 274. Münster: Ugarit-Verlag.

————2004 "Die inschriftliche Überlieferung des 3. Jahrtausends aus Tutub," in H. Waetzoldt, ed., *Von Sumer nach Ebla und zurück: Festschrift Giovanni Pettinato zum 27. September 1999 gewidmet von Freunde, Kollegen und Schülern*, 285–92. *Heidelberger Studien zum Alten Orient* 9. Heidelberg: Heidelberger Orientverlag.

————2006a "Eine Sammeltafel der Akkad-Zeit aus der St. Petersburger Eremitage über die Ausgabe von Waffen," *Annual of Ancient Near Eastern, Old Testament, and Semitic Studies*, 149–59. *Orientalia et Classica 14, Babel und Bibel* 3. Winona Lake, Ind.: Eisenbrauns.

————2006b "Der Beginn des offiziellen Richteramts in Alten Orient," in J. Hengstl and U. Sick, eds., *Recht gestern und heute, Festschrift zum 85. Geburtstag von Richard Haase*, 3–30. Wiesbaden: Harrassowitz.

————2006/8 "Rīmuš (*Rí-mu-uš*). 2. oder 3. König der Dynastie von Akkade," *Reallexikon der Assyriologie* 11: 372–5.

————2009/11 "Sargon (*Šar-ru-GI* usw.). Begründer der Dynastie von Akkade," *Reallexikon der Assyriologie* 12: 44–9.

————2010 "Prä-Akkadisch: Die Vorläufer der 'Sprache der Akkade' in der frühdynastischen Zeit," in L. Kogan, N. Koslova, S. Loesov, and S. Tishenko, ed., *Orientalia et Classica, Papers of the Institute of Oriental and Classical Studies* 30/1, 77–163. *Babel und Bibel* 4/1. Winona Lake, Ind.: Eisenbrauns.

————2011a "Geschichte des Dijala-Gebietes in der Akkade-Zeit," in P. A. Miglus and S. Mühl, eds., *Between the Cultures: The Central Tigris Region from the 3rd to the 1st Millennium* BC, *Conference at Heidelberg January 22nd–24th, 2009*, 85–96. *Heidelberger Studien zum Alten Orient* 14. Heidelberg: Heidelberger Orientverlag.

————2011b "Altakkadische Duelle," in G. Barjamovic, J. Dahl, U. Koch, W. Sommerfeld and J. Westenholz, eds., *Akkade is King: A Collection of Papers by Friends and Colleagues Presented to Aage Westenholz on the Occasion of His 70th Birthday 15th of May 2009*, 287–99. *Publications de l'Institut historique-archéologique néerlandais de Stamboul* 118. Leiden: Nederlands Instituut voor het Nabije Oosten.

————2013 "Untersuchungen zur prä-akkadischen Überlieferung der frühdynastischen Zeit," *Babel und Bibel* 7: 231–76.

————2014 "Die Lage von Akkade und die Dokumentation des 3. Jahrtausends," in N. Ziegler and E. Cancik-Kirschbaum, eds., *Entre les fleuves – II, D'Aššur à Mari et au-delà*, *Berliner Beiträge zum Vorderen Orient* 24, 151–75. Berlin: PeWe-Verlag.

Sommerfeld, W., K. Martina, and N. Roudik 2005 "Altakkadische Texte der St. Petersburger Eremitage," in L. Kogan, N. Koslova, S. Loesov, and S. Tishenko, ed., *Orientalia et Classica, Papers of the Institute of Oriental and Classical Studies* 8, *Memoriae Igor M. Diakonoff*, 185–231. *Babel und Bibel* 2. Winona Lake, Ind.: Eisenbrauns.

Speiser, E. 1935 *Excavations at Tepe Gawra I, Levels I-VIII*. Philadelphia: University of Pennsylvania Press.

————1952 "Some Factors in the Collapse of Akkad," *Journal of the American Oriental Society* 72: 97–101.

————1967 "Religion and Government in the Ancient Near East," in J. Finkelstein and M. Greenberg, eds., *Oriental and Biblical Studies, Collected Writings of E. A. Speiser*, 556–72. Philadelphia: University of Pennsylvania Press.

Spycket, A. 1968 *Les statues de culte dans les texts mésopotamiens: des origines à la I$^{re}$ dynastie de Babylone*. Paris: J. Gabalda.

————1981 *La statuaire du Proche-Orient ancien*. Leiden: Brill.

————1998 "'Le carnival des animaux': On Some Musical Monkeys from the Ancient Near East," *Iraq* 60: 1–10.

Stamm, J. 1939 *Die akkadische Namengebung, Mitteilungen der Vorderasiatisch-Aegyptischen Gesellschaft* 44. Leipzig: Hinrichs.

Starr, I. 1977 "Notes on Some Published and Unpublished Historical Omens," *Journal of Cuneiform Studies* 29: 157–66.

————1983 *The Rituals of the Diviner, Bibliotheca Mesopotamica* 12. Malibu: Undena.

————1985 "Historical Omens Concerning Ashurbanipal's War against Elam," *Archiv für Orientforschung* 32: 60–7.

————1986 "The Place of the Historical Omens in the System of Apodoses," *Bibliotheca Orientalis* 43: 628–42.

Starr, R. 1939 *Nuzi*. Cambridge: Harvard University Press.

Stauder, W. 1972/5 "Harfe," *Reallexikon der Assyriologie* 4: 114–20.

Steele, C., H. McDonald, R. Matthews, and J. Black 2003 "Impact of Empire, Later Third-millennium Investigations: the Late Early Dynastic and Akkadian Periods," in R. Matthews, ed., *Excavations at Tell Brak, Vol. 4: Exploring an Upper Mesopotamian Regional Centre, 1994–1996*, 193–269. London: British School of Archaeology in Iraq.

Steele, J. and A. Imhausen, eds., 2002 *Under One Sky, Astronomy and Mathematics in the Ancient Near East. Alter Orient und Altes Testament* 297. Münster: Ugarit-Verlag.

Stein G. and M. Blackman 1993 "The Organizational Context of Specialized Craft Production in Early Mesopotamian States," *Research in Economic Anthropology* 14: 29–59.

Steiner, G. 1982 "Das Bedeutungsfeld 'TOD' in den Sprachen des Alten Orients," *Orientalia* 51: 239–48.

————1992 "Nippur und die sumerische Königsliste," in M. de J. Ellis, ed., *Nippur at the Centennial, Papers Read at the 35$^e$ Rencontre Assyriologique Internationale, Philadelphia, 1988*, 261–79. *Occasional Publications of the Samuel Noah Kramer Fund* 14. Philadelphia: University Museum of Archaeology and Anthropology.

Steinert, U. 2012 *Aspekte des Menschseins im Alten Mesopotamien, Cuneiform Monographs* 44. Leiden: Brill.

Steinkeller, P. 1981a "The Renting of Fields in Early Mesopotamia and the Development of the Concept of 'Interest' in Sumerian," *Journal of the Economic and Social History of the Orient* 24: 113–45.

————1981b "Early History of the Hamrin Basin in the Light of Textual Evidence," in M. Gibson, ed., *Uch Tepe I, Tell Razuk, Tell Ahmed al-Mughir, Tell Ajamat*, 163–8. Chicago and Copenhagen: The Oriental Institute, The Institute of Assyriology, Institute of Classical and Near Eastern Archaeology.

————1982a "The Question of Marḫaši: A Contribution to the Historical Geography of Iran in the Third Millennium B.C.," *Zeitschrift für Assyriologie* 72: 237–265.

————1982b "Two Sargonic Sale Documents Concerning Women," *Orientalia* 51: 355–368.

————1984 "The Old Akkadian Term for 'Easterner'," *Revue d'Assyriologie* 74: 1–9.

————1987a review of Foster 1982b, *Wiener Zeitschrift für die Kunde des Morgenlandes* 77: 182–95.

———1987b "On the Meaning of zabar-šu," *Acta Sumerologica* 9: 347–9.

———1987c "The Foresters of Umma: Toward a Definition of Ur III Labor," in M. Powell, ed., *Labor in the Ancient Near East*, 73–116. *American Oriental Series* 68. New Haven: American Oriental Society.

———1987d "The Administrative and Economic Organization of the Ur III State: The Core and the Periphery," in M. Gibson and R. Biggs, eds., *The Organization of Power: Aspects of Bureaucracy in the Ancient Near East*, 19–41. *Studies in Ancient Oriental Civilizations* 46. Chicago: The Oriental Institute of the University of Chicago.

———1987/90 "Man-ištūšu. A," *Reallexikon der Assyriologie* 7: 334–5.

———1988a "Notes on the Irrigation System in Third-Millennium South Babylonia," *Bulletin on Sumerian Agriculture* 4: 73–92.

———1988b "The Date of Gudea and His Dynasty," *Journal of Cuneiform Studies* 40: 47–53.

———1988c "Grundeigentum in Babylonien von Uruk IV bis zur frühdynastischen Periode II," in *Das Grundeigentum in Mesopotamien, Jahrbuch für Wirtschaftsgeschichte, Sonderband*, 11–27.

———1989 *Sale Documents of the Ur III Period. Freiburger Altorientalische Studien* 17. Stuttgart: Steiner.

———1991 "The Sumerian Word for Prison," *Aula Orientalis* 9: 227–33.

———1992 "Mesopotamia in the Third Millennium BC," in D. Freedman, ed., *The Anchor Bible Dictionary* 4: 724–32. New York: Doubleday.

———1993a "Early Political Development in Mesopotamia and the Origins of the Sargonic Empire," in M. Liverani, ed., *Akkad, The First World Empire, Structure, Ideology, Traditions. History of the Ancient Near East, Studies* 5 107–29. Padua: Sargon.

———1993b "Early Semitic Literature and Third Millennium Seals with Mythological Motifs," *Quaderni di Semitistica* 18: 243–83.

———1995a "Sheep and Goat Terminology in Ur III Sources from Drehem," *Bulletin of Sumerian Agriculture* 8: 49–70.

———1995b "A Rediscovered Akkadian City?" *Acta Sumerologica* 17: 275–81.

———1996 "The Organization of Crafts in Third Millennium Babylonia: The Case of Potters," *Altorientalische Forschungen* 23: 232–53.

———1997 "City and Countryside in Southern Babylonia," in E. Stone, ed., *Settlement and Society: Essays Dedicated to Robert McCormick Adams*, 185–211. Los Angeles: Cotsen Institute of Archaeology.

———1998 "The Historical Background of Urkesh and the Hurrian Beginnings in Northern Mesopotamia," in G. and M. Buccellati, ed., *Urkesh and the Hurrians: Studies in Honor of Lloyd Cotsen*, 75–98. *Bibliotheca Mesopotamica* 26. Malibu: Undena.

———1999a "On Rulers, Priests and Sacred Marriage: Tracing the Evolution of Early Sumerian Kingship," in K. Watanabe, ed., *Priests and Officials in the Ancient Near East*, 103–36. Heidelberg: Winter.

———1999b "Land-tenure Conditions in Southern Babylonia under the Sargonic Dynasty," in B. Böck, E. Cancik-Kirschbaum, and T. Richter, eds., *Munuscula Mesopotamica: Festschrift für Johannes Renger*, 553–71. *Alter Orient und Altes Testament* 267. Münster: Ugarit-Verlag.

———1999c "Land-tenure Conditions in Early Mesopotamia: The Problem of Regional Variation," in M. Hudson and B. Levine, eds., *Urbanization and Land Ownership in the Ancient Near East*, 289–329. *Peabody Museum Bulletin* 7. Cambridge, Mass.: Peabody Museum of Archaeology and Ethnology.

———2001 "New Light on the Hydrology and Topography of Southern Babylonia in the Third Millennium," *Zeitschrift für Assyriologie* 91: 22–84.

————2002a "Money-Lending Practice in Ur III Babylonia: The Issue of Economic Motivations," in M. Hudson and M.Van De Mieroop, eds., *Debt and Economic Renewal in the Ancient Near East*, 109–37. *International Scholars Conference on Ancient Near Eastern Economies* 3. Bethesda, Md.: CDL Press.

————2002b "Archaic City Seals and the Question of Mesopotamian Unity," in T. Abusch, ed., *Riches Hidden in Secret Places, Ancient Near Eastern Studies in Memory of Thorkild Jacobsen*, pp. 249–57. Winona Lake, Ind: Eisenbrauns.

————2002c "More on the Archaic City Seals," NABU 2002/30.

————2003a "The Question of Lugalzagesi's Origin," in G. Selz, ed., *Festschrift für Burkhart Kienast zu seinem 70. Geburtstage dargebracht von Freunden, Schülern und Kollegen*, 621–37. *Alter Orient und Altes Testament* 274. Münster: Ugarit-Verlag.

————2003b "Archival Practices at Babylonia in the Third Millennium," in M. Brosius, ed., *Ancient Archives and Archival Traditions: Concepts of Record-Keeping in the Ancient World*, 37–58. Oxford: Oxford University Press.

————2004a "Towards a Definition of Private Economic Activity in Third Millennium Babylonia," in R. Rollinger and C. Ulf, eds., *Commerce and Monetary Systems in the Ancient World: Means of Transmission and Cultural Interaaction, Proceedings of the Fifth Annual Symposium of the Assyrian and Babylonian Intellectual Heritage Project, Held in Innsbruck, Austria, October 3rd–8th 2002*, 91–111. *Oriens et Occidens* 6. Stuttgart: Steiner.

————2004b "The Function of Written Documentation in the Administrative Praxis of Early Babylonia," in M. Hudson and C. Wunsch, eds., *Creating Economic Order: Record-keeping, Standarization, and the Development of Accounting in the Ancient Near East* 65–88. *International Scholars Conference on Ancient Near Eastern Economies* 4. Bethesda, Md.: CDL Press.

————2006 "New Light on Marhaši and Its Contact with Makkan and Babylonia," *Journal of Magan Studies* 1: 1–17.

————2007 "City and Countryside in Third Millennium Babylonia," in E. Stone, ed., *Settlement and Society: Essays Dedicated to Robert McCormick Adams*, 185–211. Chicago: Oriental Institute of the University of Chicago.

————2008 "Joys of Cooking in Ur III Babylonia," in P. Michalowski, ed., *On the Third Dynasty of Ur: Studies in Honor of Marcel Sigrist*, 185–92. *The Journal of Cuneiform Studies Supplemental Series* 1.

————2013a "Puzur-Inšušinak at Susa: A Pivotal Episode of Early Elamite History Revisited," in K. De Graef and J. Tavernier, eds., *Susa and Elam. Archaeological, Philological, Historical and Geographical Perspectives. Proceedings of the International Congress held at Ghent University, December 14–17, 2009*, 293–317. *Mémoires de la Délégation en Perse* 58. Leiden: Brill.

————2013b "Trade Routes and Connected Networks in the Persian Gulf during the Third Millennium BCE," in C. Faizee, ed., *Collection of Papers Presented at the Third International Biennial Conference of the Persian Gulf (History, Culture, and Civilization), Compiled by Scientific Board of the Third International Conference of the Persian Gulf in Department of History, University of Tehran*, 413–28. Teheran: University of Tehran Press.

————2013c "An Archaic 'Prisoner Plaque' from Kiš," *Revue d'Assyriologie* 107: 131–57.

————2014 "Marhaši and Beyond: The Jiroft Civilization in a Historical Perspective," in C. C. Lamberg-Karlovsky, B. Genito, and B. Cerasetti, eds., *'My Life is like the Summer Rose', Maurizio Tosi e l'Archeologia come modo di vivere: Papers in Honour of Maurizio Tosi for his 70th Birthday*, 691–707. *BAR International Series* 2690. Oxford: Archaeopress.

Steinkeller, P. and J. Postgate 1992 *Third-Millennium Legal and Administrative Texts in the Iraq Museum, Baghdad. Mesopotamian Civilizations* 4. Winona Lake, Ind.: Eisenbrauns.

Stève, M. and H. Gasche 1971 *L'Acropole de Suse, nouvelles fouilles. Mémoires de la Délégation Archéologique en Iran* 46, *Mission de Susiane*. Paris: Geuthner.

Stol, M. 1971 "Zur altmesopotamischen Bierbereitung," *Bibliotheca Orientalis* 28: 167–71.
———1976 *Studies in Old Babylonian History.* Leiden: Nederlands Historisch-Archaeologisch Instituut te Istanbul.
———1979 *On Trees, Mountains, and Millstones in the Ancient Near East.* Leiden: Ex Oriente Lux.
———1980/83 "Leder(industrie)," *Reallexikon der Assyriologie* 6: 527–43.
———1987/90a "Lugal-Marada," *Reallexikon der Assyriologie* 7: 148–9.
———1987/90b "Malz," *Reallexikon der Assyriologie* 7: 322–9.
———1992 "The Moon as Seen by the Babylonians," in J. Meijer, ed., *Natural Phenomena, Their Meaning, Depiction and Description in the Ancient Near East*, 245–77, Koninklijke Nederlandse Akademie van Wetenschappen, *Verhandelingen*, Afd. Letterkunde Nieuwe Reeks, deel 152. Amsterdam: North Holland Publishing Company.
———1993/7 "Milch(produkte), A," *Reallexikon der Assyriologie* 8: 189–201.
———2000 *Birth in Babylonia and the Bible: Its Mediterranean Setting, with a Chapter by F. A.M. Wiggermann. Cuneiform Monographs* 14. Groningen: Styx.
———2004 "Wirtschaft und Gesellschaft in altbabylonischer Zeit," in D. Charpin, D. Edzard, and M. Stol, eds., *Mesopotamien: Die Altbabylonische Zeit*, 643–975. *Orbis Biblicus et Orientalis* 160/4. Göttingen: Vandenhoeck & Ruprecht.
———2012 *Vrouwen van Babylon: Prisessen, Priesteressen, Prostitutees in de Bakermat van de Cultuur.* Utrecht: Kok.
Stone, E. 1997 "City-States and Their Centers: The Mesopotamian Example," in D. Nichols and T. Charlton, eds., *The Archaeology of City-States: Cross-Cultural Approaches*, 15–26. Washington, D.C.: Smithsonian.
———2003 "Remote Sensing and the Location of the Ancient Tigris," in M. Forte and P. Williams, eds., *The Reconstruction of Archaeological Landscapes through Digital Technologies: Proceedings of the 1st Italy-United States Workshop, Boston, Massachusetts, USA, November 1–3, 2001*, 157–62. *BAR International Series* 1151. Oxford: Archaeopress.
Streck, M. 1998/2001a "Naram-Sin von Aššur," *Reallexikon der Assyriologie* 9: 177.
———1998/2001b "Naram-Sin von Ešnunna," *Reallexikon der Assyriologie* 9: 177–8.
———2004 "Dattelpalme und Tamariske in Mesopotamien nach dem akkadischen Streitgespräch," *Zeitschrift für Assyriologie* 94: 250–90.
———2006/8 "Salz, Versalzung, A," *Reallexikon der Assyriologie* 11: 593–9.
Strommenger, E. 1957/71 "Grab I.," *Reallexikon der Assyriologie* 3: 581–93.
———1959 "Statueinschriften und ihre Datierungswert," *Zeitschrift für Assyriologie* 53, 27–50.
———1960 "Das Menschenbild in der altmesopotamischen Rundplastik von Mesilim bis Hammurapi," *Baghdader Mitteilungen* 1: 1–103.
———1962 *Fünf Jahrtausende Mesopotamien.* Munich: Hirmer.
———1963 "Das Felsrelief von Darband-i-Gaur," *Baghdader Mitteilungen* 2: 83–8.
———1971 "Mesopotamische Gewandtypen von der frühsumerischen bis zur Larsa-Zeit," *Acta Praehistorica et Archaeologica* 2: 37–55.
———1980/83 "Kleidung B. Archaeologisch," *Reallexikon der Assyriologie* 6: 31–33.
———1998/2001 "Naram-Sin, König von Agade B," *Reallexikon der Assyriologie* 9: 174–177.
Stronach, D. 1997 "Notes on the Fall of Nineveh," in S. Parpola and R. Whiting, eds., *Assyria 1995, Proceedings of the 10th Anniversary Symposium of the Neo-Assyrian Text Corpus Project Helsinki, September 7–11, 1995*, 307–24. Helsinki: Neo-Assyrian Text Corpus Project.
Struve, V. 1963 "Obščina, hram i dvoretz," *Vestnik Drevnej Istorii* 1963 No. 3: 11–55.

Studevent-Hickman, B. 2007 "The Ninety-Degree Rotation of the Cuneiform Script," in J. Cheng and M. Feldman, eds., *Ancient Near Eastern Art in Context, Studies in Honor of Irene J. Winter by Her Students*, 485–513. Leiden: E.J. Brill.

————2009 "Tablets and Other Inscriptions," *Akkadica* 130: 136–43.

Such-Gutiérrez, M. 2005/6 "Untersuchungen zum Pantheon von Adab im 3. Jdt.," *Archiv für Orientforschung* 51: 1–44.

————2013 "Der Kalendar von Adab im 3. Jahrtausend," in L. Feliu, J. Llop, A. Millet Albà, and J. Sanmartín, eds., *Time and History in the Ancient Near East, Proceedings of the 56th Rencontre Assyriologique Internationale at Barcelona 26–30 July 2010*, 325–40. Winona Lake, Ind.: Eisenbrauns.

Suter, C. 2007 "Between Human and Divine: High Priestesses in Images from the Akkad to the Isin-Larsa Period," in J. Cheng and M. Feldman, eds., *Ancient Near Eastern Art in Context, Studies in Honor of Irene J. Winter by Her Students*, 315–60. Leiden: Brill.

————2008 "Who are the Women in Mesopotamian Art from ca. 2334–1763 BCE?" *Kaskal* 5: 1–55.

Szuchman, J., ed. 2009 *Nomads, Tribes, and the State in the Ancient Near East, Cross-disciplinary Perspectives. Oriental Institute Seminars* 5. Chicago: Oriental Institute of the University of Chicago.

Talbot, F. 1872 "A Fragment of Ancient Mythology," *Transactions of the Society of Biblical Archaeology* 1: 271–80.

Tallon, F., ed. 1995 *Les pierres précieuses de l'Orient ancien des Sumériens aux Sassanides*. Paris: Réunion des Musées Nationaux.

Tanret, M. 2002 *Per aspera ad astra: L'apprentissage du cunéiforme à Sippar-Amnānum pendant la période paléobabylonienne tardive, Mesopotamian History and Environment*. Texts 1/2. Ghent: The University of Ghent.

Taylor, J. 2010 "Ḫazannum: The Forgotten Mayor," in L. Kogan, N. Koslova, S. Loesov, and S. Tischenko, eds., *City Administration in the Ancient Near East, Proceedings of the 53ᵉ Rencontre Assyriologique Internationale* 2: 207–22. *Babel and Bibel* 5. Winona Lake, Ind.: Eisenbrauns.

Thornton, C. 2013 "Mesopotamia, Meluhha, and Those in Between," in H. Crawford, ed., *The Sumerian World*, 600–19. London: Routledge.

Thureau-Dangin, F. 1896 "Les tablettes de Sargon l'Ancien et de Naram-Sin," *Comptes Rendus de l'Académie des Inscriptions et Belles-Lettres* 1896, 355–61. Paris: Alphonse Picard.

————1897a "Plans de l'époque de Sargon l'Ancien et de Naram-Sin," *Revue d'Assyriologie* 4: 20–25.

————1897b "Tablettes chaldéennes inédites I–V," *Revue d'Assyriologie* 4: 69–84.

————1897c ""Un fragment de stèle de victoire d'un roi d'Agadé," *Revue Sémitique* 1897: 166–73.

————1898 "Notice sur la troisième collection de tablettes découverte par M. de Sarzec à Tello," *Revue d'Assyriologie* 5: 67–77.

————1903 *Recueil de tablettes chaldéennnes*. Paris: Leroux.

————1908 "Sargon l'Ancien," *Orientalistische Literaturzeitung* 11: 312–15.

————1910 *Inventaire des Tablettes de Telloh conservées au Musée Impérial Ottoman I. Textes de l'époque d'Agadé*. Paris: Académie des Inscriptions et Belles-Lettres.

————1912 "Rois de Kish et rois d'Agadé," *Revue d'Assyriologie* 9: 33–7.

————1918 *La Chronologie des dynasties de Sumer et d'Accad*. Paris: Ernest Leroux.

Tiele, C. 1886 *Babylonisch-Assyrische Geschichte, 1. Teil: von den ältesten Zeiten bis sum Tode Sargons II*. Gotha: Friedrich Andreas Perthes.

Tigay, J. 1982 *The Evolution of the Gilgamesh Epic*. Philadelphia: University of Pennsylvania Press.

Tinney, S. 1995 "A New Look at Naram-Sin and the 'Great Rebellion,'" *Journal of Cuneiform Studies* 47: 1–14.

Tolini, G. 2009 "Le repas du Grand Roi en Babylonie: Cambyse et le palais d'Abanu," in X. Faivre, B. Lion, and C. Michel, eds., *Et il y eut un esprit dans l'Homme: Jean Bottéro et Mésopotamie*, 237–54. Paris: De Boccard.

Tonietti, M. 1998 "The Mobility of the NAR and the Sumerian Personal Names in the Pre-Sargonic Mari Onomasticon," in M. Lebeau, ed., *About Subartu, Studies Devoted to Upper Mesopotamia*, 83–101. *Subartu* 4/2. Turnhout: Brepols.

————2010 "Musicians in the Ebla Texts: A Third-Millennium Local Source for Northern Syria," in R. Pruzsinszky and D. Shehata, eds., *Musiker und Tradierung. Studien zur Rolle von Musikern bei der Verschriftlichung und Tradierung von literarischen Werken*, 67–93. *Wiener Offene Orientalistik* 8. Vienna: Lit.

Tosi, M. 1976/80 "Karneol," *Reallexikon der Assyriologie* 5: 448–52.

Tricoli, S. 2005 "Sargon the Semite: Preliminary Reflections to a Comparative Study of Sargon and His Dynasty," in W. Van Soldt, ed., *Ethnicity in Ancient Mesopotamia, Papers Read at the 48th Rencontre Assyriologique Internationale Leiden 1–4 July 2002*: 372–92. *Publications de l'Institut historique-archéologique néerlandais de Stamboul* 102. Leiden: Nederlands Instituut voor het Nabije Oosten.

Trokay, M. 1990 "Renaissance thématique accadienne dans la glyptique kassite," in Ö. Tunca, ed., *De la Babylonie à la Syrie, en passant par Mari: mélanges offers à monsieur J.-R. Kupper à l'occasion de son 70° anniversaire*, 87–97. Liège: Université de Liège.

Tsukimoto, A. 1985 *Untersuchungen zur Totenpflege (kispum) im alten Mesopotamien. Alter Orient und Altes Testament* 216. Neukirchen-Vluyn: Neukirchener Verlag.

Tunca, Ö. 1984 *L'Architecture religieuse protodynastique en Mésopotamie, Akkadica Supplementum* II. Leuven: Peeters.

Tymenev, A. 1956 *Gosudarstvennoe stroj drevnego Šumera*. Moscow: Akademia Nauk.

Ungnad, A. 1908 "Sumerer und Akkader," *Orientalistische Literaturzeitung* 11: 62–67.

Ur, J. 2010 "Cycles of Civilization in Northern Mesopotamia," *Journal of Archaeological Research* 18: 387–431.

————2013 "Patterns of Settlement in Sumer and Akkad," in H. Crawford, ed., *The Sumerian World*, 131–55. London: Routledge.

Van Buren, E. 1930 *Clay Figurines of Babylonia and Assyria. Yale Oriental Series* 16. New Haven: Yale University Press.

————1941 "The Ṣalmê in Mesopotamian Art and Religion," *Orientalia* 10: 65–92.

————1947 "The Guardians of the Gate in the Akkadian Period," *Orientalia* NS 16: 312–32.

————1953 "An Investigation of a New Theory concerning the Bird-Man," *Orientalia* NS 22: 47–58.

————1955 "The Sun-God Rising," *Revue d'Assyriologie* 49: 1–14.

————1956 "The Scepter, its Origin and Significance," *Revue d'Assyriologie* 50: 101–3.

Van de Mieroop, M. 1997 "On Writing a History of the Ancient Near East," *Bibliotheca Orientalis* 54: 286–305.

————1999a *Cuneiform Texts and the Writing of History*. London: Routledge.

————1999b "Literature and Political Discourse in Ancient Mesopotamia: Sargon II of Assyria and Sargon of Agade," in B. Böck, E. Cancik-Kirschbaum, and T. Richter, eds., *Munuscula Mesopotamica: Festschrift für Johannes Renger*, 327–39. *Alter Orient und Altes Testament* 267. Münster: Ugarit-Verlag.

————2000 "Sargon of Agade and His Successors in Anatolia," *Studi Micenei et Egeo-Anatolici* 42: 133–59.

————2004 "Accounting in Early Mesopotamia: Some Remarks," in M. Hudson and C. Wunsch, eds., *Creating Economic Order: Record-keeping, Standardization, and the Development of Accounting in the Ancient Near East*, 47–64. *International Scholars Conference on Ancient Near Eastern Economics* 4. Bethesda, Md.: CDL Press.

————2012 "The Mesopotamians and their Past," in J. Wiesehöfer and T. Krüger, eds., *Periodisierung und Epochenbewusstsein im Alten Testament und in seinem Umfeld*, 37–56. *Oriens et Occidens* 20. Stuttgart: Steiner.

————2013 "Recent Trends in the Study of Ancient Near Eastern History: Some Reflections," *Journal of Ancient History* 1: 83–98.

Van der Meer, P. 1947 *De Agadeperiode, haar geschiedenis en cultuur*, in *Kernmomenten: Die Antieke Beschaving in Haar Moderne Beleving*, 179–241. Leiden: Brill.

Van Dijk, J. 1969a "Les contacts ethniques dans la Mésopotamie et les syncrétismes de la religion sumérienne," in S. Hartman, ed., *Syncretism*, 171–206. Stockholm: Almqvist & Wiksell.

————1969b "Vert comme Tishpak," *Orientalia* NS 38: 539–47.

————1970 "Le site de Guti'um et d'Ak-š[a?-a]k$^{ki}$," *Archiv für Orientforschung* 23: 71–2.

————1971 "Sumerische Religion," in J. Asmussen and J. Laessøe, eds., *Handbuch der Religionsgeschichte* 1, 431–96. Göttingen: Vandenhoeck & Ruprecht.

————1972 "Un rituel de purification des armes et de l'armée, Essai de traduction de YBC 4184," in M. Beek, A. Kampman, C. Nijland, and J. Ryckmans, ed., *Symbolae biblicae et mesopotamicae Francisco Mario Theodoro Böhl dedicatae*, 107–17. Leiden: Brill.

————1983 *LUGAL UD ME-LÁM-bi NIR-GÁL, Texte, Traduction et Introduction.* Leiden: Brill.

Van Driel, G. 1973 "On 'Standard' and 'Triumphal' Inscriptions," in M. Beek, A. Kampman, C. Nijland, and J. Ryckmans, ed., *Symbolae biblicae et mesopotamicae Francisco Mario Theodoro Böhl dedicatae*, 99–106. Leiden: Brill.

————2000 "The Mesopotamian North: Land Use, An Attempt," in R. M. Jas, ed., *Rainfall and Agriculture in Northern Mesopotamia (MOS Studies 3), Proceedings of the Third MOS Symposium (Leiden 1999)*, 265–99. Leiden: Nederlands Historisch-Archaeologisch Instituut te Istanbul.

————2002 *Elusive Silver: In Search of a Role for a Market in an Agrarian Environment, Aspects of Mesopotamian Society. Publications de l'Institut historique-archéologique néerlandais de Stamboul* 95. Leiden: Nederlands Instituut voor het Nabije Oosten.

Van Ess, M. 1988 "Keramik von der Akkad- bis zum Ende der altbabylonischen Zeit aus den Planquadraten N XV und XVI und aus dem Sinkašid-Palast in Uruk-Warka," *Baghdader Mitteilungen* 19: 321–442.

————1991 "Die Keramik, die Typen und ihre Verbreitung nach Zeitstufen. Akkad- bis altbabylonische Zeit," in U. Finkbeiner, ed., *Uruk, Kampagne 35–37, 1982–1984, Die archäologische Oberflächnuntersuchung (Survey), Ausgrabungen in Uruk-Warka, Endbrichte.* Mainz: Von Zabern.

Van Koppen, F. 2011 "The Scribe of the Flood Story and His Circle," in K. Radner and E. Robson, eds., *The Oxford Handbook of Cuneiform Culture*, 140–66. Oxford: Oxford University Press.

Van Soldt, W. 2003/5 "Ordal A," *Reallexikon der Assyriologie* 10: 124–9.

Vanstiphout, H. 2003 *Epics of Sumerian Kings: The Matter of Aratta. Writings from the Ancient World* 20. Atlanta: Society for Biblical Literature.

Veenhof, K. 1978/9 "An Old Akkadian Private Letter, with a note on *ṣiāḫum-ṣīḫtum*," *Jaarbericht "Ex Oriente Lux"* 24: 105–10.

Veldhuis, N. 2003 "Entering the Netherworld," *Cuneiform Digital Library Bulletin* [internet resource] 2003/6.

————2004 *Religion, Literature, and Scholarship: The Sumerian Composition 'Nanše and the Birds' with a Catalogue of Sumerian Bird Names. Cuneiform Monographs* 22. Leiden: Brill.

————2006a "How did They Learn Cuneiform? 'Tribute List C' as an Elementary Exercise," in P. Michalowski and N. Veldhuis, ed., *Approaches to Sumerian Literature: Studies in Honour of Stip (H. L. J. Vanstiphout)*, 181–200. *Cuneiform Monographs* 35. Leiden: Brill.

————2006b "Divination: Theory and Use," in A. Guinan, M. deJ. Ellis, A. Ferrara, S. Freedman, M. Rutz, L. Sassmannshausen, S. Tinney, and M. Waters, eds., *If a Man Builds a Joyful House, Assyriological Studies in Honor of Erle Verdun Leichty*, 487–97. *Cuneiform Monographs* 31. Leiden: Brill.

————2010 "Guardians of Tradition: Early Dynastic Lexical Texts in Old Babylonian Copies," in H. Baker, E. Robson, and G. Zólyomi, ed., *Your Praise is Sweet, A Memorial Volume for Jeremy Black from Students, Colleagues and Friends*, 379–400. London: British Institute for the Study of Iraq.

————2014a "The Early Dynastic Kiš Tradition," in L. Sassmannshausen with G. Neumann, eds., *He Has Opened Nisaba's House of Learning: Studies in Honor of Åke Waldemar Sjöberg on the Occasion of His 89th Birthday on August 1st 2013*, 241–59. *Cuneiform Monographs* 46. Leiden: Brill.

————2014b *History of the Cuneiform Lexical Tradition. Guides to the Mesopotamian Textual Record* 6. Münster: Ugarit-Verlag.

Verderame, L. 2009 "Mar-tu nel III millennio: fonti e interpretazioni," *Rivista degli Studi Orientali* 82: 229–60.

Visicato, G. 1997 "A Temple Institution in the Barley Records from Sargonic Eshnunna," *Acta Sumerologica* 19: 235–59.

————1999 "The Sargonic Archive of Tell el-Suleimah," *Journal of Cuneiform Studies* 51: 17–30.

————2000 *The Power and the Writing: The Early Scribes of Mesopoamia.* Bethesda, Md.: CDL Press.

————2001 "The Journey of the Sargonic King to Assur and Gasur," in T. Abusch, P.-A. Beaulieu, J. Huehnergard, P. Machinist, and P. Steinkeller, eds., *Historiography in the Cuneiform World, Proceedings of the XLV^e Rencontre Assyriologique Internationale* 1: 467–72. Bethesda, Md.: CDL Press.

————2010 "New Light from an Unpublished Archive of Meskigalla, ensi of Adab, housed in the Cornell University Collection," in L. Kogan, N. Koslova, S. Loesov, and S. Tischenko, eds., *City Administration in the Ancient Near East, Proceedings of the 53^e Rencontre Assyriologique Internationale* 2: 263–71. *Babel and Bibel* 5. Winona Lake, Ind.: Eisenbrauns.

Volk, K. 1992 "Puzur-Mama und die Reise des Königs," *Zeitschrift für Assyriologie* 82: 22–29.

Von Dassow, E. 2009 "Narām-Sîn of Uruk: A New King in an Old Shoebox," *Journal of Cuneiform Studies* 61: 63–91.

Von der Osten-Sacken, E. 2014 "Federn für Pfeile," in H. Neumnn, R. Dittmann, S. Paulus, G. Neumann, and A. Schuster-Brandis, eds., *Krieg und Frieden im Alten Vorderasien, 52e Rencontre Assyriologique Internationale International Congress of Assyriology and Near Eastern Archaeology Münster, 17.— 21. Juli 2006*, 609–28. *Alter Orient und Altes Testament* 401. Münster: Ugarit-Verlag.

Waetzoldt, H. 1971 "Zwei unveröffentliche Ur-III-Texte über die Herstellung von Tongefässen," *Die Welt des Orients* 6: 7–41.

————1972 *Untersuchungen zur neusumerischen Textilindustrie, Studi Economici e Tecnologici*, 1. Rome: Centro per le Antichità e la Storia dell'Arte del Vicino Oriente.

————1984 "'Diplomaten,' Boten, Kaufleute und Verwandtes in Ebla," in L. Cagni, ed., *La Lingua di Ebla, Atti del Convegno Internazionale (Napoli, 21–23 aprile 1980)*, 405–37. Seminario di Studi Asiatici, *Series Minor* 14. Naples: Istituto Universitario Orientale.

————1990a "Zur Bewaffnung des Heeres von Ebla," *Oriens Antiquus* 29: 1–38.

————1990b "Zur Lesung und Aussprache ᵈEN.ZU am Ende des 3. Jahrtausends," NABU 1990/95.

————1991 Review of Steinkeller 1987d, *Journal of the American Oriental Society* 111: 637–41.

————1991/2 "'Rohr' und dessen Verwendungsweisen anhand der neusumerischen Texte aus Umma," *Bulletin on Sumerian Agriculture* 6: 125–46.

————1998 "Die Göttin Nanše und die Traumdeutung," NABU 1998/60.

————2011 "Die Textilproduktion von Garšana," in D. Owen, ed., *Garšana Studies*, 405–54. *Cornell University Studies in Assyriology and Sumerology* 6. Bethesda, Md.: CDL Press.

Waetzoldt, H. and H. Bachmann 1984 "Zinn-und Arsenbronzen in den Texten aus Ebla und aus Mesopotamien des 3. Jahrtausends," *Oriens Antiquus* 23: 1–18.

Walker, C. 1980 "Hormuzd Rassam's Excavations for the British Museum at Sippar in 1881–1882," in L. De Meyer, ed., *Tell ed-Der* I, 13–114. Leuven: Peeters.

Wall-Romana, C. 1990 "An Areal Location of Agade," *Journal of Near Eastern Studies* 49: 205–45.

Wartke, R.-B. 1995 "The Copper Hoard from the Ashur Temple," in P. Harper, E. Klengel-Brandt, J. Aruz, K. Benzel, eds., *Discoveries at Ashur on the Tigris: Assyrian Origins: Antiquities in the Vorderasiatisches Museum, Berlin*, 37–41. New York: The Metropolitan Museum of Art.

Weadock, P. 1975 "The Giparu at Ur," *Iraq* 37: 101–28.

Weidner, E. 1922 *Der Zug Sargons von Akkad nach Kleinasien, Boghazköy Studien* 6. Leipzig: Hinrichs.

————1928/9 "Historisches Material in der babylonischen Omina-Literatur," in *Altorientalische Studien Bruno Meissner zum sechzigsten Geburtstag am 25. April 1928 gewidmet von Freunden, Kollegen und Schülern*, 226–40. *Mitteilungen der Altorientalischen Gesellschaft* 4. Leipzig: Harrassowitz.

————1941/4 "Alter und Geschichte der Serie Enûma Anu Enlil," *Archiv für Orientforschung* 14: 175–95.

————1952/3 "Das Reich Sargons von Akkad," *Archiv für Orientforschung* 16: 1–24.

Weiss, H. 1975 "Kish, Akkad and Agade," *Journal of the American Oriental Society* 95: 434–53.

————1986 "The Origins of Tell Leilan and the Conquest of Space in Third Millennium Mesopotamia," in H. Weiss, ed., *The Origins of Cities in Dry-Farming Syria and Mesopotamia in the Third Millennium* B.C., 71–108. Guilford, Ct.: Four Quarters.

————2012a "Quantifying Collapse: The Late Third Millennium Khabur Plains," in H. Weiss, ed., *Seven Generations Since the Fall of Akkad*, 1–24. *Studia Chaburensia* 3. Wiesbaden: Harrassowitz.

————, ed. 2012b *Seven Generations Since the Fall of Akkad, Studia Chaburensia* 3. Wiesbaden: Harrassowitz.

Weiss, H. and M. Courty 1993 "The Genesis and Collapse of the Akkadian Empire: The Accidental Refraction of Historical Law," in M. Liverani, ed., *Akkad, the First World Empire: Structure, Ideology, Traditions*, 131–155. *History of the Ancient Near East/Studies* 5. Padua: Sargon.

Weiss, H., S. Manning, L. Ristvet, L. Mori, M. Besonen, A. McCarthy, P. Quenet, A. Smith, and Z. Bahrani 2012 "Tell Leilan Akkadian Imperialization, Collapse and Short-Lived Reoccupation Defined by High-Resolution Radiocarbon Dating," in H. Weiss, ed., *Seven Generations Since the Fall of Akkad*, 163–92. *Studia Chaburensia* 3. Wiesbaden: Harrassowitz.

Westbrook, R. 1995 "Slave and Master in Ancient Near Eastern Law," *Chicago-Kent Law Review* 70: 1631–76.

————2005 "Patronage in the Ancient Near East," *Journal of the Economic and Social History of the Orient* 48: 210–33.

Westenholz, A. 1970 "*berūtum, damtum*, and Old Akkadian KI.GAL: Burial of Dead Enemies in Ancient Mesopotamia," *Archiv für Orientforschung* 23: 27–31.

————1974 "Early Nippur Year Dates and the Sumerian King List," *Journal of Cuneiform Studies* 26: 154–6.

————1974/77 "Old Akkadian School Texts: Some Goals of Sargonic Scribal Education," *Archiv für Orientforschung* 25: 95–110.

————1975a *Literary and Lexical Texts and the Earliest Administrative Documents from Nippur. Old Sumerian and Old Akkadian Texts in Philadelphia Chiefly from Nippur, Bibliotheca Mesopotamica* 1. Malibu: Undena.

————1975b *Early Cuneiform Texts in Jena, Pre-Sargonic and Sargonic Documents from Nippur and Fara in the Himprecht-Sammlung vorderasiatischer Altertümler Institut für Altertumswissenschaften der Friedrich-Schiller-Universität. Jena. Det Kongelige Danske Videnskabernes Selskab, Historisk-Filosofiske Skrifter* 7,3. Copenhagen: Munksgaard.

————1976 "The Earliest Akkadian Religion," *Orientalia* NS 45: 154–6.

————1979 "The Old Akkadian Empire in Contemporary Opinion," in M. Larsen, ed., *Power and Propaganda: A Symposium on Ancient Empires*, 107–24. Copenhagen: Akademisk Vorlag.

————1984 "The Sargonic Period," in A. Archi, ed., *Circulation of Goods in Non-Palatial Context in the Ancient Near East*, 17–30. Incunabula Graeca 82. Rome: Edizioni dell'Ateneo.

————1985 "An Essay on the Sumerian 'Lexical' Texts of the Third Millennium," *Orientalia* NS 54: 294–8.

————1987 *Old Sumerian and Old Akkadian Texts in Philadelphia, Part Two: The 'Akkadian' Texts, the Enlilemaba Texts, and the Onion Archive. CNI Publications* 3. Copenhagen: University of Copenhagen.

————1987/90 "Lugalzaggesi," *Reallexikon der Assyriologie* 7: 155–7.

————1988 "Personal Names in Ebla and Pre-Sargonic Babylonia," in A. Archi, ed., *Eblaite Personal Names and Semitic Name-Giving, Papers of a Symposium Held in Rome July 15–17, 1985*, 99–117. Archivi Reali di Ebla, Studi 1. Rome: Missione Archeologica Italiana in Siria.

————1993 "The World View of Sargonic Officials, Differences in Mentality between the Sumerian and Akkadian," in M. Liverani, ed., *Akkad, The First World Empire: Structure, Ideology, Traditions*, 157–69. History of the Ancient Near East/Studies 5. Padua: Sargon.

————1999 "The Old Akkadian Period: History and Culture," in P. Attinger and M. Wäfler, eds., *Mesopotamien, Akkade-Zeit und Ur III-Zeit*, 17–117. Orbis Biblicus et Orientalis 160/3. Göttingen: Vandenhoeck & Ruprecht.

————2000 "Assyriologists, Ancient and Modern, on Naramsin and Sharkalisharri," in J. Marzahn and H. Neumann, eds., *Assyriologica et Semitica: Festschrift für Joachim Oelsner anlässlich seines 65. Geburtstages am 18. Februar 1997*, 545–56. Alter Orient und Altes Testament 252. Münster: Ugarit Verlag.

————2002 "The Sumerian City-State," in M. Hansen, ed., *A Comparative Study of Six City-State Cultures, An Investigation Conducted by the Copenhagen Polis Center*, 23–42. Det Kongelige Danske Videnskabernes Selskab. Copenhagen: Reitzels Forlag.

————2004 "'Have You Been Near Prof. Larsen too Long?'" in J. Dercksen, ed., *Assyria and Beyond: Studies Presented to Mogens Trolle Larsen*, 599–606. Publications de l'Institut historique-archéologique néerlandais de Stamboul 100. Leiden: Nederlands Instituut voor het Nabije Oosten.

————2014 *A Third-Millennium Miscellany of Cuneiform Texts, Cornell University Studies in Assyriology and Sumerology* 26. Bethesda, MD: CDL Press.

Westenholz, A. and G. Visicato 2000 "Some Unpublished Sale Contracts from Fara," in S. Graziani, ed., *Studi sul Vicino Oriente Antico dedicati alla memoria di Luigi Cagni*, 1107–33. Naples: Istituto Universitario Orientale, Dipartimento di Studi Asiatici, *Series Minor* 61.

Westenholz, J. 1983a "Heroes of Akkad," in J. Sasson, ed., *Studies in Literature from the Ancient Near East by Members of the American Oriental Society, American Oriental Series* 65 = *Journal of the American Oriental Society* 103: 327–36.

————1983b "Die Prinzessin Tutanapšum," *Altorientalische Forschungen* 10: 212–16.

————1991 "The Clergy of Nippur: The Priestess of Enlil," in M. de J. Ellis, ed., *Nippur at the Centennial, Papers Read at the 35ᶜ Rencontre Assyriologique Internationale, Philadelphia, 1988*, 297–310. *Occasional Publications of the Samuel Noah Kramer Fund* 14. Philadelphia: University Museum of Archaeology and Anthropology.

————1992a "Enheduanna, En-Priestess, Hen of Nanna, Spouse of Nanna," in H. Behrens, D. Loding, M. Roth, eds., *DUMU-E₂-DUB-BA-A, Studies in Honor of Åke W. Sjöberg, Occasional Publications of the Samuel Noah Kramer Fund* 11, 539–56. Philadelphia: University Museum of Archaeology and Anthropology.

————1992b "Oral Traditions and Written Texts in the Cycle of Akkade," in M. Vogelzang and H. Vanstiphout, eds., *Mesopotamian Epic Literature: Oral or Aural?* 123–54. Lewiston, NY: Edwin Mellon.

————1997 *Legends of the Kings of Akkade. Mesopotamian Civilizations* 7. Winona Lake, Ind.: Eisenbrauns.

————1998 "Objects with Messages: Reading Old Akkadian Royal Inscriptions," *Bibliotheca Orientalis* 55: 44–59.

————2004 "The Old Akkadian Presence at Nineveh: Fact or Fiction?" *Iraq* 66: 7–18.

————2007 "Notes on the Old Assyrian Sargon Legend," *Iraq* 59: 21–7.

————2008 "The Memory of the Sargonic Kings under the Third Dynasty of Ur," in P. Michalowski, ed., *On the Third Dynasty of Ur: Studies in Honor of R. Marcel Sigrist*, 251–60. *The Journal of Cuneiform Studies Supplemental Series* 1.

————2010 "Drink to Me Only with Thine Eyes," in S. Melville and A. Slotsky, eds., *Opening the Tablet Box: Near Eastern Studies in Honor of Benjamin R. Foster*, 463–84. Leiden: E. J. Brill.

————2011 "Who Was Aman-Aštar?" in G. Barjamovic, J. Dahl, U. Koch, W. Sommerfeld and J. Westenholz, eds., *Akkade is King: A Collection of Papers by Friends and Colleagues Presented to Aage Westenholz on the Occasion of His 70th Birthday 15th of May 2009*, 315–32. Publications de l'Institut historique-archéologique néerlandais de Stamboul 118. Leiden: Nederlands Instituut voor het Nabije Oosten.

————2012 "*Damnatio memoriae*: The Old Akkadian Evidence for the Destruction of Name and Destruction of Person," in N. May, ed., *Iconoclasm and Text Destruction in the Ancient Near East and Beyond*, 89–122. *Oriental Institute Seminars* 8. Chicago: Oriental Institute of the University of Chicago.

Whiting, R. 1977 "The Reading of the Name DINGIR-*šu-i-lí-a*," *Journal of the American Oriental Society* 97: 171–7.

————1984 "More Evidence for Sexagesimal Calculations in the Third Millennium B.C.," *Zeitschrift für Assyriologie* 74: 59–66.

Wicke, D. 2010 *Kleinfunde aus Elfenbein und Knochen aus Assur. Wissenschaftliche Veröffentlichungen der Deutschen Orient-Gesellschaft* 131. Wiesbaden: Harrassowitz.

Wiener, M. 2009a "The State of the Debate about the Date of the Thera Eruption," in D. Warburton, ed., *Time's Up! Dating the Minoan Eruption of Santorini, Acts of the Minoan Eruption*

*Chronology Workshop, Sandbjerg November 2007*, 197–206. *Monographs of the Danish Institute at Athens* 10. Aarhus: Aarhus University Press.

————2009b "Cold Fusion: The Uneasy Alliance of History and Science," in S. Manning and M. Bruce, eds., *Tree-Rings, Kings, and Old World Archaeology and Environment: Papers Presented in Honor of Peter Ian Kuniholm*, 277–92. Oxford: Oxbow Books.

Wiesehöfer, J. 2001 *Ancient Persia from 550 BC to 650 A.D.*, translated by Azizeh Azodi. London: I. B. Tauris.

Wiggermann, F. 1981/2 "Exit TALIM! Studies in Babylonian Demonology," *Jaarbericht Ex Oriente Lux* 27: 90–105.

Wilcke, C. 1972 "Der aktuelle Bezug der Sammlung der sumerischen Tempelhymnen und ein Fragment eines Klageliedes," *Zeitschrift für Assyriologie* 62: 35–62.

————1973 "Politische Opposition nach sumerischen Quellen: Der Konflikt zwischen Königtum und Ratversammlung: Literaturwerke als politische Tendenzschriften," in A. Finet, ed., *La voix de l'opposition en Mésopotamie, Colloque organisé par l'Institut des Hautes Etudes de Belgique 19 et 20 mars 1973*, 37–65. Brussels: Institut des Hautes Etudes de Belgique.

————1974 "Zum Königtum in der Ur III-Zeit," in P. Garelli, ed., *Le palais et la royauté, archéologie et civilisation. XIX^e Rencontre Assyriologique Internationale organisée par le groupe François Thureau-Dangin, Paris, 29 juin – 2 juillet 1971*, 177–232. Paris: Geuthner.

————1976/80a "Kauf A," *Reallexikon der Assyriologie* 5: 490–512.

————1976/80b "Inanna/Ištar," *Reallexikon der Assyriologie* 5: 74–87.

————1978 "Philologische Bemerkungen zum *Rat des šuruppag* und Versuch einer neuen Übersetzung," *Zeitschrift für Assyriologie* 68: 196–232.

————1982 "Zum Geschichtsbewusstsein im Alten Mesopotamien," in H. Müller-Karpe, ed., *Archäologie und Geschichtsbewusstsein* 31–52. Munich: Beck.

————1985 "Familiengründung im Alten Orient," in E. Müller, ed., *Geschlechtsreife und Legitimation zur Zeugung*, 213–317. *Veröffentlichungen des Instituts für historische Anthropologie* 3. Freiburg: Alber.

————1988 "Die Sumerische Königsliste und erzählte Vergangenheit," in J. von Ungern-Sternberg and H. Reinau, eds., *Vergangenheit in mündlicher Überlieferung*, 113–40. *Colloquium Rauricum* 1. Stuttgart: Teubner.

————1989 "Genealogical and Geographical Thought in the Sumerian King List," in H. Behrens, D. Loding, and M. Roth, eds., *DUMU-E₂-DUB-BA-A, Studies in Honor of Åke W. Sjöberg, Occasional Publications of the Samuel Noah Kramer Fund* 11, 557–69. Philadelphia: University Museum of Archaeology and Anthropology.

————1992 "Diebe, Räuber, Mörder," in V. Haas, ed., *Aussenseiter und Randgruppen: Beiträge zu einer Sozialgeschichte des Alten Orients*, 53–78. *Xenia* 32. *Konstanzer Althistorische Vorträge und Forschungen* 32. Konstanz: Universitätsverlag.

————1993 "Politik im Spiegel der Literatur, Literatur as Mittel der Politik im älteren Babylonien," in. K. Raaflaub, ed., *Anfänge politischen Denken in der Antike, Die nahöstlichen Kulturne und die Griechen*, 29–75. *Schriften des Historischen Kollegs*, Kolloquien 24. Munich: Oldenbourg.

————1997 "Amar-girids Revolte gegen Narām-Su'en," *Zeitschrift für Assyriologie* 87: 11–32.

————2000 *Wer las und schrieb in Babylonien und Assyrien: Überlegungen zur Literalität im Alten Zweistromland. Sitzungsberichte der Bayerischen Akademie der Wissenschaften, Philosophisch-Historische Klasse* 2000/6. Munich: Beck.

————2001 "Gestaltetes Altertum in antiker Gegenwart: Königslisten und Historiographie des älteren Mesopotamien," in D. Kuhn and H. Stahl, eds., *Die Gegenwart des Altertums: Formen und Kunktionen des Altertumsbezugs in den Hochkulturen der Alten Welt*, 93–116. Heidelberg: Edition Forum.

————2007 *Early Ancient Near Eastern Law, A History of Its Beginnings: The Early Dynastic and Sargonic Periods*, revised edition. Winona Lake, Ind.: Eisenbrauns.

Wilhelm, G. 1989 *The Hurrians*, Jennifer Barnes, trans. Warminster: Aris & Phillips.

Wilkinson, T. 1994 "The Structure and Dynamics of Dry-Farming States in Upper Mesopotamia," *Current Anthropology* 35: 483–520.

————2000 "Settlement and Land Use in the Zone of Uncertainty in Upper Mesopotamia," in R. Jas, ed., *Rainfall and Agriculture in Northern Mesopotamia (MOS Studies 3), Proceedings of the Third MOS Symposium (Leiden 1999)*, 3–35. Leiden: Nederlands Historisch-Archaeologisch Instituut te Istanbul.

Wilson, K. 2012 *Bismaya: Recovering the Lost City of Adab. Oriental Institute Publications* 138. Chicago: Oriental Institute of the University of Chicago.

Winckler, H. 1892a *Geschichte Babyloniens und Assyriens*. Leipzig: Eduard Pfeiffer.

————1892b "Ueber einige alt-babylonische Inschriften," *Revue d'Assyriologie* 2: 61–5.

————1895 *Altorientalische Forschungen* III. Leipzig: Eduard Pfeiffer.

————1906 *Altorientalische Geschichtsaufassung, Ex Oriente Lux* II/2. Leipzig: Eduard Pfeiffer.

————1907 *The History of Babylonia and Assyria*, translated and edited by James Alexander Craig, revised by the Author. New York: Charles Scribner's Sons.

Winter, I. 1987 "Women in Public: the Disk of Enheduanna, the Beginning of the Office of *EN*-Priestess and the Weight of Visual Evidence," in J.-M. Durand, ed., *La Femme dans le Proche-Orient antique, Compte Rendu de la XXXIII^e Rencontre Assyriologique Internationale (Paris, 7–10 juillet 1986)*, 189–201. Paris: Editions Recherche sur les Civilisations.

————1992 "Idols of the King: Royal Images as Recipients of Ritual Action in Ancient Mesopotamia," *Journal of Ritual Studies* 6: 13–42.

————1996a "Sex, Rhetoric, and the Public Monument: The Alluring Body of Naram-Sin of Agade," in N. Kampen, ed., *Sexuality in Ancient Art*, 11–26. Cambridge: Cambridge University Press.

————1996b "Artists' Trial Pieces from Susa?" in *Collectanea Orientalia: Histoire, arts de l'espace et industrie de la terre. Etudes offertes en homage à Agnès Spycket*, 397–406. Paris: Recherches et Publications.

————1999a "Tree(s) on the Mountain: Landscape and Territory on the Victory Stele of Naram-Sin of Agade," in L. Milano, S. de Martino, F. Fales, and G. Lanfranchi, ed., *Landscapes: Territories, Frontiers, and Horizons in the Ancient Near East, Papers Presented to the XLIV^e Rencontre Assyriologique Internationale, Venezia, 7–11 July 1997*, 1: 63–72. Padua: Sargon.

————1999b "Reading Ritual in the Archaeological Record: Deposition Pattern and Function of Two Artifact Types from the Royal Cemetery of Ur," in H. Kühne, R. Bernbeck, and K. Bartl, eds., *Fluchtpunkt Uruk: Archäologische Einheit aus methodischer Vielfalt. Schriften für Hans Jörg Nissen*, 229–56. Rahden: Verlag Marie Leidorf.

————2000 "Babylonian Archaeologists of the(ir) Mesopotamian Past," in P. Matthiae, ed., *Proceedings of the First International Congress of the Archaeology of the Ancient Near East, Rome, May 18th–23rd 1998*, 1787–98. Rome: La Sapienza.

————2004 "The Conquest of Space in Time: Three Suns on the Victory Stele of Naram-Sin," in J. Dercksen, ed., *Assyria and Beyond: Studies Presnted to Mogens Trolle Larsen*, 607–28. *Publications de l'Institut historique-archéologique néerlandais de Stamboul* 100. Leiden: Nederlands Instituut voor het Nabije Oosten.

————2008 "Touched by the Gods: Visual Evidence for the Deification of Rulers in the Ancient Near East," in N. Brisch, ed., *Religion and Power: Divine Kingship in the Ancient World and Beyond*, 75–101. *Oriental Institute Seminars* 4. Chicago: Oriental Institute of the University of Chicago.

————2009 "What/When Is a Portrait? Royal Images of the Ancient Near East," *Proceedings of the American Philosophical Society* 153: 254–70.

Woolley, C. L. 1934 *Ur Excavations, the Royal Cemetery*. Oxford: Oxford University Press.

Woods, C. 2006 "Bilingualism, Scribal Learning, and the Death of Sumerian," in S. Sanders, ed., *Margins of Writing, Origins of Culture*, 95–124. *Oriental Institute Seminars* 2. Chicago: Oriental Institute of the University of Chicago.

Worthington, M. 2006/8 "Salbung," *Reallexikon der Assyriologie* 11: 574–5.

————2009/11 "Schankwirt(in)," *Reallexikon der Assyriologie* 12: 132–4.

Yamada, K. 2005 "'From the Upper Sea to the Lower Sea' – The Development of the Names of Seas in the Assyrian Inscriptions," *Orient* 40: 31–55.

Yıldız, F. and T. Ozaki 2001 *Die Umma Texte aus den Archäologischen Museen zu Istanbul* 6. Bethesda, Md.: CDL Press.

Yoffee, N. 1995 "Political Economy in Early Mesopotamian States," *Annual Review of Anthropology* 24: 281–311.

————2004 *Myths of the Archaic State: Evolution of the Earliest Cities, States, and Civilizations*. Cambridge: Cambridge University Press.

Yoffee, N. and G. Cowgill, eds. 1988 *The Collapse of Ancient States and Civilizations*. Tucson: University of Arizona Press.

Yoshikawa, M. 1989 "The Sumerian Verbal Aspect," in H. Behrens, D. Loding, M. Roth, eds., *DUMU-E₂-DUB-BA-A, Studies in Honor of Åke W. Sjöberg*. 585–90. *Occasional Publications of the Samuel Noah Kramer Fund* 11. Philadelphia: University Museum of Archaeology and Anthropology.

Yuhong, W. 1992 "The Deification of Šu-iliya of Eshnunna While Being a 'Scribe'," NABU 1992/102.

————1994 *A Political History of Eshnunna, Mari and Assyria during the Early Old Babylonian Period (from the End of Ur III to the Death of Šamši-Adad), Supplement to the Journal of Ancient Civilizations* 1. Changchun: Institute for the History of Ancient Civilizations.

Zaccagnini, C. 1973 *Lo Scambio dei doni nel Vicino Oriente durante i secoli XV-XIII. Orientis Antiqui Collectio* 11. Rome: Centro per le Antichità e la Storia dell'Arte del Vicino Oriente.

Zadok, R. 1994 "Elamites and Other Peoples from Iran and the Persian Gulf Region in Early Mesopotamian Sources," *Iran* 32: 31–51.

————1995 "Foreigners and Foreign Linguistic Material in Mesopotamia and Egypt," in K. Van Lerberghe and A. Schoors, eds., *Immigration and Emigration in the Ancient Near East, Festschrift E. Lipiński*, 431–47. *Orientalia Lovaniensia Analecta* 65. Leuven: Peeters.

Zajdowski, K. 2013 "Transformation of the Mesopotamian Banquet Scene into the Presentation Scene in the Early Dynastic, Akkadian and Ur III Periods," *Akkadica* 134: 1–16.

Zarins, J. 1986 "Equids Associated with Human Burials in Third Millennium B.C. Mesopotamia: Two Complementary Facets," in R. Meadow and H.-P. Uerpmann, eds., *Equids in the Ancient World*, 164–93. Wiesbaden: Reichert.

————1990 "Early Pastoral Nomadism and the Settlement of Lower Mesopotamia," *Bulletin of the American Schools of Oriental Research* 280: 31–65.

————2014 *The Domestication of Equidae in Third-Millennium BCE Mesopotamia. Cornell University Studies in Assyriology and Sumerology* 24. Bethesda, Md.: CDL Press.

Zeder, M. 1998 "Pigs and Emergent Complexity in the Near East," *MASCA Papers in Science and Archaeology* 15: 109–22.

Zettler, R. 1977 "The Sargonic Royal Seal: A Consideration of Sealing in Ancient Mesopotamia," in M. Gibson and R. Biggs, eds., *Seals and Sealing in the Ancient World*, 33–9. *Bibliotheca Mesopotamica* 6. Malibu: Undena.

————1984 "The Genealogy of the House of Ur-Me-me: A Second Look," *Archiv für Orientforschung* 31, 1–9.

————1987 "Sealings as Artifacts of Institutional Administration in Ancient Mesopotamia," *Journal of Cuneiform Studies* 39: 210–14.

————2003 "Reconstructing the World of Ancient Mesopotamia: Divided Beginnings and Holistic History," *Journal of the Economic and Social History of the Orient* 46: 3–45.

————2006 "Tišatal and Nineveh at the End of the 3rd Millennium BCE," in A. Guinan, M. deJ. Ellis, A. Ferrara, S. Freedman, M. Rutz, L. Sassmannshausen, S. Tinney, and M. Waters, eds., *If a Man Builds a Joyful House: Assyriological Studies in Honor of Erle Verdun Leichty*, 503–14. Cuneiform Monographs 31. Leiden: Brill.

Zgoll, A. 1997 *Der Rechtsfall der En-hedu-Ana im Lied nin-me-šara. Alter Orient und Altes Testament* 246. Münster: Ugarit-Verlag.

Zhi, Yang 1989 *Sargonic Inscriptions from Adab. Periodic Publications on Ancient Civilizations* 1. Changchun, China: Institute for the History of Ancient Civilizations.

Ziegler, N. 2004 "The Conquest of the Holy City of Nineveh and the Kingdom of Nurrugûm by Samsi-Addu," *Iraq* 66: 19–26.

————2007 *Les Musiciens et la musique d'après les archives de Mari. Mémoires de NABU* 10, *Florilegium marianum* 9. Paris: SEPOA.

————2010 "Teachers and Students: Conveying Musical Knowledge in the Kingdom of Mari," in R. Pruzsinszky and D. Shehata, eds., *Musiker und Tradierung. Studien zur Rolle von Musikern bei der Verschriftlichung und Tradierung von literarischen Werken*, 119–33. *Wiener Offene Orientalistik* 8. Vienna: Lit.

————2014 "Akkade à l'époque paléo-babylonienne," in N. Ziegler and E. Cancik-Kirschbaum, eds., *Entre les fleuves – II, D'Aššur à Mari et au-delà, Berliner Beiträge zum Vorderen Orient* 24, 177–90. Berlin: PeWe-Verlag.

# Index